D0215283

The Regulatory Environment of Human Resource Management

Harcourt College Publishers

Where Learning Comes to Life

TECHNOLOGY

Technology is changing the learning experience, by increasing the power of your textbook and other learning materials; by allowing you to access more information, more quickly; and by bringing a wider array of choices in your course and content information sources.

Harcourt College Publishers has developed the most comprehensive Web sites, e-books, and electronic learning materials on the market to help you use technology to achieve your goals.

PARTNERS IN LEARNING

Harcourt partners with other companies to make technology work for you and to supply the learning resources you want and need. More importantly, Harcourt and its partners provide avenues to help you reduce your research time of numerous information sources.

Harcourt College Publishers and its partners offer increased opportunities to enhance your learning resources and address your learning style. With quick access to chapter-specific Web sites and e-books . . . from interactive study materials to quizzing, testing, and career advice . . . Harcourt and its partners bring learning to life.

Harcourt's partnership with Digital:Convergence™ brings :CRQ™ technology and the :CueCat™ reader to you and allows Harcourt to provide you with a complete and dynamic list of resources designed to help you achieve your learning goals. You can download the free :CRQ software from www.crq.com. Visit any of the 7,100 RadioShack stores nationwide to obtain a free :CueCat reader. Just swipe the cue with the :CueCat reader to view a list of Harcourt's partners and Harcourt's print and electronic learning solutions.

http://www.harcourtcollege.com/partners

The Regulatory Environment of Human Resource Management

Robert K. Robinson

University of Mississippi

Geralyn McClure Franklin

University of Texas of the Permian Basin

Robert Wayland

Eastern Illinois University

Harcourt College Publishers

Fort Worth   Philadelphia   San Diego   New York   Austin   Orlando   San Antonio
Toronto   Montreal   London Sydney   Tokyo

PUBLISHER	Michael P. Roche
ACQUISITIONS EDITOR	Tracy Morse
DEVELOPMENTAL EDITOR	CJ Jasieniecki
MARKET STRATEGIST	Beverly Dunn
PROJECT EDITOR	Rebecca Dodson
ART DIRECTOR	Burl Sloan
PRODUCTION MANAGER	Lois West

ISBN: 0-03-025867-7
Library of Congress Catalog Card Number: 2001092948

Copyright © 2002 by Harcourt, Inc.

All rights reserved. No part of this publication may be reproduced or transmitted in any form or by any means, electronic or mechanical, including photocopy, recording, or any information storage and retrieval system, without permission in writing from the publisher.

Requests for permission to make copies of any part of the work should be mailed to the following address: Permissions Department, Harcourt, Inc., 6277 Sea Harbor Drive, Orlando, FL 32887-6777.

Copyrights and Acknowledgments appear on page 472, which constitutes a continuation of the copyright page.

Address for Domestic Orders Harcourt College Publishers, 6277 Sea Harbor Drive, Orlando, FL 32887-6777 800-782-4479

Address for International Orders International Customer Service Harcourt, Inc., 6277 Sea Harbor Drive, Orlando, FL 32887-6777 407-345-3800 (fax) 407-345-4060 (e-mail) hbintl@harcourt.com

Address for Editorial Correspondence Harcourt College Publishers, 301 Commerce Street, Suite 3700, Fort Worth, TX 76102

Web Site Address http://www.harcourtcollege.com

Printed in the United States of America

1 2 3 4 5 6 7 8 9 0   039   9 8 7 6 5 4 3 2 1

Harcourt College Publishers

Dedicated to

*My parents, Lt. Col. (ret.) Robert G.
and Rosemary P. Robinson, who taught me never
to begin anything without finishing it.*

My wife, Betty, who learned to put up with me.

My daughter, Mackenzie, who is learning to put up with me.

My sister, Dr. Mary Pat Viguerie, who never put up with me.

—RKR

———————————■———————————

*My parents, Gerald C. and Marie McClure,
who made me who I am.*

My husband, Kenny, who accepts and puts up with who I am.

My son, Tanner, who is learning to accept who I am.

—GMF

———————————■———————————

*My parents, the late Robert F. Wayland, Sr.
and Laurinda S. Wayland, who helped form
my values and ideals.*

My wife, Jane, who shares my values and ideals.

*My sons, Bill, Terry, Steve, and Ryan,
who have accepted my values and ideals.*

*My daughters-in-law, Kathy, Diane, Pauline,
and Nancy, along with my grandchildren,
who have learned to accept me.*

—RFW

ABOUT THE AUTHORS

Robert K. Robinson, Ph.D., SPHR (University of North Texas), is Associate Professor of Management in the School of Business at The University of Mississippi (Ole Miss).

Dr. Robinson has published over eighty articles on human resource management, employment law, and small business management issues in various journals, including *Business Horizons, Employee Responsibilities & Rights Journal, Hospital & Health Services Administration, Human Resource Planning, Issues in Accounting Education, Journal of Business & Entrepreneurship, Journal of Psychology, Journal of Small Business Management, Journal of Small Business Strategy, Labor Law Journal, Personnel Administrator, Public Administration Quarterly, Public Personnel Management,* and many other business and government journals. His research interests involve federal regulation of the workplace, affirmative action policies, sexual harassment, business ethics, and employee recruiting and selection.

Dr. Robinson holds a certificate and an advanced certificate in employee relations law from the Institute of Applied Management and Law (IAML). Dr. Robinson is also certified as a Senior Professional in Human Resources (SPHR) by the Human Resource Certification Institute.

Geralyn McClure Franklin, Ph.D. (University of North Texas), is Dean of the School of Business and Professor of Management at The University of Texas of the Permian Basin. Dr. Franklin served as Chair of the Department of Management, Marketing, and International Business at Stephen F. Austin State University from 1994–1998 and Director of the Division of Management and Marketing at The University of Texas at San Antonio from 1998–1999 before her current appointment in July of 1999.

Dr. Franklin has published numerous articles on human resource management, employment law, and small business management issues in various journals, including *Journal of Small Business Management, Journal of Small Business Strategy, Employee Responsibilities & Rights Journal, Journal of Individual Employment Rights, Hospital & Health Services Administration, Labor Law Journal, Public Personnel Management,* and *Journal of Business & Entrepreneurship.* In addition, she has co-authored *Human Resource Management* (Dame Publications, 1995) and *Management* (Dame Publications, 1997).

Dr. Franklin has served in various leadership roles in several academic and professional organizations. Currently, she is the director of exhibitor relations for the Academy of Management, treasurer for Southern Management Association, and a board member for Sigma Beta Delta International Honor Society. Dr. Franklin is a past president of the Small Business Institute Directors' Association, the Association for Small Business & Entrepreneurship (formerly the Southwestern Small Business Institute Association), and the Southwest Academy of Management. She has been named a Fellow of the Small Business Institute Directors' Association and the Association for Small Business & Entrepreneurship.

Robert F. Wayland, Ph.D., SPHR (University of North Texas), is Director of Employee and Labor Relations and Associate Professor of Management at Eastern Illinois University. Dr. Wayland has more than twenty-five years human resource management and labor relations experience in private industry. In addition, he has more than ten years experience in teaching, labor relations, and human resources management in higher education. Dr. Wayland also serves as a human resources management/labor relations consultant for two private industry firms.

Dr. Wayland has published numerous articles on human resource management, labor and employee relations, arbitration, and management issues in various journals and periodicals. In addition, he is co-authoring a compensation management textbook.

Dr. Wayland was granted lifetime certification as a Senior Professional in Human Resources from the Society for Human Resource Management (SHRM). He has served in numerous leadership roles in several academic and professional organizations.

PREFACE

There is little doubt that the United States of America has become a very litigious society. A 1995 survey conducted by the Society for Human Resource Management revealed that 57 percent of the responding firms had experienced at least one employment litigation during the previous five years.[1] Roughly, 2.2 percent of the gross domestic product is now consumed by lawsuits.[2] Not surprisingly, this trend toward settling disputes through litigation has impacted the American workplace.

A significant factor contributing to the increase in workplace litigation is the belief held by many employees that they possess certain inalienable rights upon which their employers may not encroach. Consequently, employees are far more likely to use litigation in order to protect these rights—both real, and in many cases, perceived. The dilemma facing many organizations is that too often management does not fully understand compliance requirements. Just when does the employee have a legitimate concern, and when is the demand unreasonable and even detrimental to the organization's operation? This misunderstanding of employee rights and responsibilities may result in employers maintaining policies and practices that violate the law and expose the organization to litigation, or the initiation of unnecessary policies that hamper the efficient operation of the organization. In either case, the organization is adversely affected. To compound matters, the legal environment is dynamic and in a constant state of flux, making it difficult for human resource (HR) professionals and managers to remain abreast of compliance requirements. What was a lawful practice yesterday may be unlawful today, or yesterday's affirmative action program may have become today's reverse discrimination lawsuit.

In short, human resource compliance, or HR compliance, has become an increasingly critical component of all HR activities. Failure to execute compliance obligations properly may have material consequences for employers. Without question, federal regulation affects every function performed by the HR department. Recruiting, selection, placement, promotions, transfers, and compensation must all be done in accordance with the equal opportunity provisions mandated by Title VII of the Civil Rights Act of 1964, the Age Discrimination in Employment Act, and the Americans with Disabilities Act. Compensation and benefits administrators are responsible for ensuring that pay and benefits programs are in compliance with the Equal Pay Act, the Employee Income and Security Act, the

Consolidated Omnibus Budget and Reconciliation Act, and the Health Insurance Portability and Accountability Act, just to name a few.

Obviously, human resource management (HRM) is a highly regulated management discipline, and failure to know the compliance responsibilities can unnecessarily expose employers to employment litigation. So extensive is the scope of employment regulation that roughly 30 percent of the examination for certification as a Professional in Human Resources (PHR) deals with some form of regulatory compliance related to employment or labor law.

We do not wish to imply that it is just HR managers who have to be knowledgeable of regulatory responsibilities. *All managers* who actively engage in making decisions regarding hiring, promotions, terminations, raises, and employee performance evaluations are equally affected. Any decision made regarding personnel which impermissibly considers the employee's or applicant's race, color, religion, sex, national origin, age, or disability exposes the entire process and organization to a violation of the law. Furthermore, management decisions are not the only activities that are potentially damaging to organizations. In recent years, managers at all levels of an organization have become responsible for maintaining work environments that are free from racial and sexual harassment. Every year workplace practices and behaviors come under increasing government scrutiny and regulation, all of which affect an organization's daily operation. This book examines the impact of federal regulation of HR activities and introduces readers to the more common practices that may trigger scrutiny under the law.

PURPOSE

The purpose of this book is to acquaint readers with the major federal statutes and regulations that control management and employment practices in the American workplace. The authors are aware that the functional activities which HRM performs and the employment practices in which all organizations engage are subject to evaluation within a broad range of economic, social, legal, and institutional contexts. However, the scope of this book is confined only to the legal context. We have, therefore, focused our discussions on the effect of employment practices, and their subsequent impact on employees, in relation to existing federal statutes, regulations, and court decisions.

This textbook endeavors to present a comprehensive but practical view of the regulatory environment of human resource management. Most businesspeople are not motivated in their decision making by racial, gender, or ethnic biases because it is bad for business. Many merely blunder into noncompliance through ignorance of the law rather than through a discriminatory intent. The sin is often one of omission, rather than one of commission. Therefore, we have worked diligently to make this text legally correct rather than politically correct. Again, our concern is compliance with existing employment law which we view as an externality with which all affected organizations must deal.

The material in this textbook is presented from the perspective that the HR professional is the employer's representative and is, therefore, responsible for protecting the employer's interests and reducing the employer's exposure to litigation through monitoring activities and viable employee policies. The text is designed as a tool for today's business and management professionals. If we have a bias, that bias is pro-business or pro-management.

Our purpose is to introduce readers to the manager's legal responsibilities in the utilization of human resources. In accomplishing this goal, a discussion and examination of the growing body of legislation, federal regulation, and case law which governs personnel practices is presented. This includes examining the procedural standards that must be met in order to comply with equal employment opportunity laws and other employment regulations governing workplace behavior. Through our discussion of these compliance obligations, readers will develop a basic understanding and appreciation for the challenges confronting HR managers in formulating and implementing strategies and policies that enable organizations to attain a sustained competitive advantage.

Additionally, the text will enhance readers' abilities to interpret and understand the legal requirements that all managers must meet in order to comply with equal employment opportunity, wage and hour, safety and health, and other statutes and regulations governing workplace behavior. We have endeavored to develop a framework of analysis to enable readers to identify central issues and problems in personnel activities and then evaluate their potential for noncompliance.

ORGANIZATION

This book is organized in four parts that include twelve chapters. Part I's Chapter 1 sets the stage by introducing readers to the federal regulatory environment and discussing its evolution, the principal sources of regulatory obligations, and the judicial system and how it works.

Parts II and III examine employment law for all workplaces, subject to individual statutory definitions, both nonunion and union workplaces. Part II, Regulation of Equal Employment Opportunity, contains five chapters. Chapters 2 and 3 examine Title VII prohibitions on employment discrimination with a detailed discussion of intentional and unintentional discrimination. Issues specifically related to sex discrimination are addressed in Chapter 4. Discrimination against other protected classes (i.e., religion, national origin, age, and disability) is the focus of Chapter 5. Ultimately, Chapter 6 investigates the nuances of affirmative action programs in light of both Title VII and the Equal Protection Clause of the Fourteenth Amendment.

Part III, Regulation of Employee Relations, includes four chapters. Chapter 7 examines the employment-at-will doctrine, with particular attention devoted to both the statutory and common law exceptions. The primary legislation governing wages and benefits is the focus of Chapters 8 and 9. Finally, Chapter 10 discusses compliance issues related to health, safety, and security in the workplace.

Part IV's two remaining chapters focus on the regulation of labor relations. Chapters 11 and 12 apply only to organizations which currently have a recognized or certified bargaining agent, or are currently undergoing a union organizing campaign. These two chapters provide practical value to readers because the national labor code immediately affects an employer once a union formally begins an organizing campaign. Organizations that currently do not see a need for developing an expertise in labor relations may need such knowledge if a campaign is initiated.

Each of the twelve chapters begins with a scenario based on an actual court case or workplace occurrence which is related to the chapter's subject. These opening scenarios are intended not only to provide an example of a real problem confronting an employer, but to also provide a practice or policy to which the chapter subject matter may be applied. It is one thing to discuss what the compliance requirements are; it is yet another to understand how they are applied.

It is our intention that this textbook will provide a practical benefit to readers. We have attempted to translate the "legalese" into English as much as possible without sacrificing accuracy. Should you find any errors or other points within our book upon which you would like to comment, we would appreciate hearing from you. By incorporating your ideas, we hope to continue writing a textbook which best serves you and future readers.

We are HR professionals and have approached the subject matter in this textbook from that perspective. Our objective is strictly informative in nature, to make readers aware of their general compliance obligations. Because of the dynamic nature of regulatory issues, readers must be forewarned that though this book's contents were current as the book went to press, subsequent legislation or, even more likely, federal court decisions may have rendered some of the contents out-of-date. Readers are encouraged to periodically check our Web site for updates affecting the book's subject matter at www.harcourtcollege.com/management/robinson/.

Finally, we are not attorneys and are not offering legal advice. This book is not intended to offer legal recommendations for specific legal problems. Readers who are involved in legal disputes are advised to seek competent legal counsel.

ACKNOWLEDGMENTS

We would like to recognize and thank the following individuals for their support. Without their support, this textbook would not have been completed. First, we wish to express our sincerest appreciation to the Harcourt College Publishers support staff including CJ Jasieniecki, development editor; Rebecca Dodson, project editor; Tracy Morse, acquisitions editor; Lois West, production manager; Burl Sloan, art director; and Beverly Dunn, marketing strategist.

We would also like to thank the HRM and legal scholars who reviewed the manuscript for their very detailed and valuable suggestions. These include: Harvey Boller, *Loyola University Chicago*; Molly Bowers, *University of Baltimore*; Dalton Brannen, *Augusta State University*; James H. Brown, *University of Southern Colorado*; Debra Burke, *Western Carolina University*; Hank Findley, *Troy State University*; David S. Hamer, *University of Nevada–Las Vegas*; Beverly Little, *Western Carolina University*; Robert J. Paul, *Kansas State University*; and William Ross,

University of Wisconsin–La Crosse. We are particularly grateful for their attention to detail and efforts in bringing this textbook to fruition. We are also grateful to Thomas Lloyd, *Westmoreland Community College,* for preparing the supplementary materials for our textbook.

Additional thanks go to Bob Robinson's Employee Relations (MGMT 582) and Advanced Human Resource Management (MGMT 527) classes at The University of Mississippi for being the "guinea pigs" for early drafts of the textbook. Their insightful comments allowed us to make important changes to the textbook. Special thanks also go to John R. Beal, James E. Blackburn, Dee Dee Martz, John R. Carter, Jennifer Edmonds, Stacy Hinton, and Maria Johnson for their written critiques and editorial suggestions to make the textbook more student friendly.

Special recognition goes to our mentors from the doctoral program at the University of North Texas: J. D. Dunn, Elvis Stephens, William McKee, and Walt Sharp.

Bob Robinson would like to particularly recognize the efforts of his wife, Betty, for the many long hours of word processing, proofing, and critical contributions made to this textbook. And above all else, Bob is especially appreciative of the fact that she did not take advantage of the situation and use the countless hours in producing this textbook as grounds for divorce.

Bob would also like to recognize colleagues and co-authors who, in one way or another, aided in the creation of this book. These include Victoria Bush, *The University of Mississippi;* Steve Crow, *University of New Orleans;* Scott Douglas, *University of Montana;* Ross L. Fink, *Bradley University;* Gerald R. Ferris, *Florida State University;* Dwight D. Frink, *The University of Mississippi;* Neal Mero, *The University of Mississippi;* Dave L. Nichols, *The University of Mississippi;* Brian J. Reithel, *The University of Mississippi;* Gregory Rose, *The University of Mississippi;* Larry Tunnell, *New Mexico State University;* Scott Vitell, *The University of Mississippi;* Milam Walker, *The University of Mississippi;* and David Wyld, *Southeastern Louisiana University.*

Bob would further like to recognize the Robert M. Hearin Support Foundation of Jackson, Mississippi, for funding two faculty development grants that allowed him to attend certification programs in employment law offered by the Institute of Applied Management and Law. These programs contributed greatly to the currency of the subject matter contained in this textbook. Finally, Bob would like to extend special thanks and recognition to William H. Holley, Jr. of Auburn University for his meticulous editorial comments and invaluable suggestions which added substantially to the content of the labor relations chapters.

Geralyn Franklin would like to acknowledge her mother, Marie McClure, for continuing to proofread and edit her work even though she is a grown woman! In addition, Geralyn would like to thank her husband, Kenny, and son, Tanner, for the sacrifices they made so this book could become a reality. Geralyn also would like to acknowledge many of the same co-authors that Bob Robinson acknowledged earlier. In addition, she wishes to recognize Delaney J. Kirk, *Drake University;* Franz T. Lohrke, *University of Alabama;* and Johnny Lang, formerly of *Stephen F. Austin State University.* Without those faithful co-authors and colleagues, Bob and she would not have so much to write about. Finally, Geralyn owes special thanks to The University of Texas of the Permian Basin administration and the School of Business faculty and staff who provided support and encouragement during the writing of this book. Quite frankly, she is glad they did not kill her while this book was being written! This thanks goes to Charles Sorber, outgoing president; W. David Watts, incoming president; William Fannin, vice president for academic affairs; Paul Hodges; William Jackson; Corbett Gaulden; Cathie Tinney; John Theis; Paul Wilhelm; Barbara Scofield; Paul Haensly; Wilma Dye; Rusty Calk; Scott Carson; Linda Felts; A. M. Nunley; Joshua Levy; Susan Barron; Art Connor; LuAnn Morgan; Carolyn Jennings; Ruby Rowe; Amy Garcia; and Chelsea Whitaker.

BOB WAYLAND would like to thank his wife, Jane Wayland, and his son, Ryan, for their patience and understanding during the time devoted to working "the book" rather than doing other activities. Bob is also very appreciative to his many colleagues in academic affairs and business affairs at Eastern Illinois University who provided inspiration and enlightening comments during the undertaking of this project.

NOTES

1. Minehan, M. (1997). Employment litigation: An ongoing concern. *HRMagazine,* 42 (8): 144.

2. France, M. (January 29, 2001). The litigation machine. *Business Week,* No. 3717, p. 114+; Bowers, B. (1998). The next big risks. *Best's Review Property/Casualty Edition,* 99 (1): 36–40; Malanga, S. (April 6, 1998). It's no accident that trial lawyers are laughing all the way to the bank. *Crain's New York Business,* p. 9, c. 1.

BRIEF CONTENTS

CONTENTS

I

INTRODUCTION

1. Overview of the Regulation of Human Resource Management

OVERVIEW OF THE REGULATION OF HUMAN RESOURCE MANAGEMENT

LEARNING OBJECTIVES

- ☐ Understand the different regulatory environments for union and nonunion employees.
- ☐ Discuss the evolution of government regulation in the workplace.
- ☐ Understand the costs associated with government regulation in the workplace.
- ☐ Discuss the sources of laws and government regulations in the workplace.
- ☐ Identify the responsibilities and enforcement powers of the principal regulatory agencies overseeing the workplace.
- ☐ Describe the federal judicial system and how its decisions affect workplace practices.

OPENING SCENARIO

Manuel Ortega and his coworkers had grown weary of working long hours without being paid overtime. But each time Manuel and his friends complained, they were always told the same thing by their supervisor: "You are undocumented workers and in this country illegally. You have no right to overtime compensation if you have no right to work here. Now get back to work before you are fired or turned over to the Immigration and Naturalization Service."

Several months later, Manuel meets an organizer for the International Brotherhood of Teamsters (IBT). The organizer not only convinced Manuel that the union could improve his treatment by management but also encouraged Manuel to file a complaint with the Wage and Hour Division of the Department of Labor in order to get the overtime compensation that has been withheld from him by his employer. The following day Manuel filed a complaint and began handing out IBT organizing pamphlets in the break area during break time. He was soon approached by his supervisor who said, "I thought I told you that you 'illegals' don't have the same rights as citizens and resident aliens. I guess you're hard of hearing. Now you and the rest of your undocumented buddies can get off the company's property, and get off now! You're all fired!"

Is Manuel's supervisor correct? If Manuel and his friends are undocumented workers, what United States employment and labor laws have been violated by the employer, if any?

UNION VERSUS NONUNION WORKPLACES

This textbook examines the impact of federal regulation on two distinct types of work environments—union and nonunion. In 1999, employees who were union members represented less than 13.5 percent of all employees, public and private, in the United States.[1] Public sector workers (government employees) continue to have a substantially higher unionization rate (37.3 percent) than workers in the private sector (9.0 percent).[2]

In organized work environments, the terms, conditions, and privileges of employment are specified under a contractual arrangement called a **collective bargaining agreement (CBA).** Representatives of the employees meet with the employer to negotiate the provisions of this CBA. Thus, many employment practices and employee rights are formalized and guaranteed in this "contract." For example, most CBAs stipulate benefit packages for all employees in the bargaining unit. The bargaining unit includes all employees that the union is authorized to represent. In the CBA, the wages that employees draw are usually based on job assignments and seniority. The CBA also governs such employment practices as due process for disciplinary actions, and, in some instances, how work assignments and promotions are conducted. During the latter half of the nineteenth century through the first half of the twentieth century, workers were drawn to unions because of the protection the CBA provided. Under such contractual arrangements, workers received protection from arbitrary and capricious treatment by employers. Through the collective bargaining process (which will be discussed in greater detail in Chapter 12) employees in organized workplaces have the opportunity to negotiate for more favorable working conditions, employment practices, and treatment. In essence, the negotiation process allows employees to establish contractual rights which their employer is required to honor.

Labor relations is that part of human resource management (HRM) that addresses employment issues arising from the organized workplace, a workplace in which a union represents the interests of the employees. In such a work environment, human resource (HR) professionals and managers are not only responsible for ensuring compliance with the federal and state laws that govern all work-places but also must be especially familiar with federal and state labor laws. In addition to these laws, HR professionals must be knowledgeable of the specific CBA covering their company or facility. Labor relations deals with issues such as avoiding unfair labor practices under existing labor laws, negotiating the collective bargaining agreement, the union's duty to fair representation, resolving grievances, and contract administration. Chapter 11 of this textbook examines labor relations practices and processes.

Does this mean that employees who are not represented by labor unions have little or no protection in the workplace? Not at all. A growing body of employment law provides an increasing number of safeguards for nonunion employees. Note here that the authors make a distinction between employment law, which applies to all workplaces, and labor law which applies only to unionized workplaces. These employment laws place an increasing compliance and reporting burden on all employers. In fact, so many employment laws have been enacted that the United States currently enjoys the dubious distinction of being one of the most regulated work environments in the industrialized world. Not surprisingly, regulatory compliance has become such a concern for American companies that approximately 30 percent of the certification exam for Professional in Human Resources (PHR) covers legal and regulatory factors affecting HRM areas.[3]

The area of HRM that deals with the relationship between managers and employees in a regulated, but nonunionized, work environment is called **HR compliance.** HR compliance emphasizes employee rights and employer responsibilities in areas such as health, safety, security, and equal employment opportunity (EEO). In practice, this involves developing, communicating, and monitoring HR policies that ensure regulatory compliance. It also emphasizes the necessity for all managers to be knowledgeable of the laws, agency regulations, and court decisions that affect employment practices. Though states and, in some cases, municipalities have created laws and ordinances that regulate employment practices, the greatest source of workplace regulation is the federal government.

This textbook examines the effects of federal regulation. The first ten chapters examine employers' responsibilities in these areas and the laws affecting them. The remaining two chapters focus on labor relations.

THE HISTORY OF THE REGULATION OF EMPLOYMENT PRACTICES

Before the twentieth century, there were very few federal laws that governed employee–employer relations. The Civil Rights Act of 1866 removed annual labor contracts (discussed in greater detail in Chapter 2), and the Civil Service Reform Act of 1883 provided protection for civil servants from the spoils system. However, it was not until the 1920s and 1930s that the first major wave of federal regulation began.

THE FIRST WAVE OF FEDERAL REGULATION

The first large-scale attempt by the federal government to restrict management's actions in the workplace was the Railway Labor Act of 1926. This legislation gave employees in the railway industry the right to organize labor unions and bargain collectively for wages and working conditions. The motivation for this law was the frequent strikes that plagued the railroad industry during the post-World War I era. It is important to remember that railroads were *the* means of transportation during this period. When railroad management refused to allow workers to form unions or ignored their demands, the workers would strike. The strike would shut down the specific railroad, and all commerce dependent upon that rail line would grind to a halt. Congress eventually intervened under pressure from the businesses affected by railroad strikes. The Railway Labor Act was very narrow in scope; it only applied to workers in the railway and steamship industries. A 1936 amendment added airline employees.[4]

As the Great Depression loomed, labor agitation heightened and civil unrest became an increasing concern. In an attempt to appease the growing labor movement, Congress enacted the Labor Disputes Act of 1932, commonly known as the Norris-LaGuardia Act. Although it made "yellow-dog contracts"—contracts under which workers promised not to join unions—unenforceable in federal courts and made it more difficult to obtain federal injunctions against strikers, it had little effect on state courts. The Norris-LaGuardia Act was quickly seen as a "paper tiger." It sounded good, but it did little to change the plight of industrial workers. As a result, greater pressure was placed on the Roosevelt administration and Congress to provide genuine labor reform.

The needed reforms came with the National Labor Relations Act of 1935 (NLRA; also known as the Wagner-Connerly Act or sometimes just Wagner Act). This legislation guaranteed the right of private sector employees to organize and bargain collectively in much the same manner as the Railway Labor Act had done for railroad employees. To ensure that employees' rights to organize and bargain were not interfered with by management, the Act also established unfair labor practices by management, which are discussed in detail in Chapter 11. Additionally, the NLRA created an agency which was responsible for enforcing the Act, the National Labor Relations Board (NLRB). This federal agency was responsible for overseeing certification elections and investigating complaints of unfair labor practices. When the NLRA was enacted, its intrusions into the workplace and restrictions on employers' property rights were considered outrageous.[5] The new law was immediately challenged in court. However, in *NLRB v Jones & Laughlin Steel Corp.*,[6] the Supreme Court upheld the Act's constitutionality. A new era of "big government" was beginning.

The NLRA was a less than perfect remedy for America's growing problems. In fact, it may have made them worse. Enacted to reduce labor unrest, the NLRA may have contributed to unrest. Work stoppages (strikes) numbered 4,956 in 1944, at a time when the nation was at war (see Exhibit 1-1).[7]

■ EXHIBIT 1-1

LABOR STOPPAGES 1930–2000

Year	Work Stoppages Beginning in Year	Year	Work Stoppages Beginning in Year	Year	Work Stoppages Beginning in Year
1930	637	1954	3468	1978	4230
1931	816	1955	4320	1979	4827
1932	841	1956	3825	1980	3885
1933	1695	1957	3673	1981	*2568
1934	1856	1958	3694	1982	96
1935	2014	1959	3708	1983	81
1936	2172	1960	3333	1984	62
1937	4740	1961	3367	1985	54
1938	2772	1962	3614	1986	69
1939	2613	1963	3362	1987	46
1940	2508	1964	2655	1988	40
1941	4288	1965	3963	1989	51
1942	2968	1966	4405	1990	44
1943	3752	1967	4595	1991	40
1944	4956	1968	5045	1992	35
1945	4750	1969	5700	1993	35
1946	4985	1970	5716	1994	45
1947	3693	1971	5138	1995	31
1948	3419	1972	5010	1996	37
1949	3606	1973	5353	1997	29
1950	4843	1974	6074	1998	34
1951	4737	1975	5031	1999	17
1952	5117	1976	5648	2000	39
1953	5091	1977	5506		

SOURCES: U.S. Bureau of the Census, *Statistical Abstract of the United States 1951, 1962, 1981–82.* U.S. Bureau of Labor Statistics (February 24, 2001). Work stoppages involving 1,000 workers or more. *Work Stoppages Summary.* **http://stats.bls.gov.80/ news.release/wkstp.nro.htm**

*Beginning in 1982, the Bureau of Labor Statistics only recorded work stoppages involving 1,000 or more employees. Previously it recorded work stoppages of six or more employees (*Handbook of Labor Statistics 1983*, p. 378).

Under the NLRA, it was unlawful for management to interfere with an employee's right to organize. But labor unions were under no such restrictions. To solve these abuses, and several other shortcomings (see Chapter 11), Congress amended the NLRA in 1947 with the Labor-Management Relations Act (LMRA; also known as the Taft-Hartley Act). The LMRA curbed the power of unions by instituting unfair labor practices by unions.[8] It further permitted individual states to pass laws limiting compulsory union membership in collective bargaining agreements (the so-called "right-to-work laws").[9] The LMRA is also the statute that provided for a process to resolve labor disputes that threaten the national health or safety (national emergency strikes).[10]

Twelve years after the LMRA, another major amendment to the national labor code was passed. Due to rising concerns regarding the influence of organized crime in organized labor, Congress enacted the Labor Management Reporting and Disclosure Act of 1959 (LMRDA; commonly called the Landrum-Griffin Act). It was designed to resolve many of the problems resulting from corruption and the infiltration by organized crime into union operations uncovered by the Senate Committee on Improper Union Activities (the McClellan Committee). Of particular concern was guaranteeing union members' rights to nominate and elect union officers, attend union meetings, and have their union pension funds safeguarded.

During this first wave of federal regulation, most government efforts concentrated on establishing procedures by which employees could organize. If these efforts were successful, then the union, as the employees' representative, could create a contractual relationship with the employer to ensure higher wages, better working conditions, and greater job security. Two other statutes enacted during this period were also designed to encourage union organizing. The Davis-Bacon Act of 1931 was designed to remove the incentive for hiring nonunion labor in federal government construction contracts exceeding $2,000. Any employer with such a contract was required to pay the "prevailing wage" for the geographic area in which the construction was taking place. The *prevailing wage* was based on the average union scale in the area. Hence, the employer was required to pay nonunion employees just as much as union workers. The incentive for cheaper nonunion labor was removed. Five years later, Congress enacted the Walsh-Healy Act to accomplish the same ends in federal supply contracts exceeding $10,000.

THE SECOND WAVE OF FEDERAL REGULATION

The second wave of federal regulation of the workplace began in the early 1960s under John Kennedy's New Frontier and more notably under Lyndon Johnson's Great Society. This wave of regulation continues today and is characterized by increasing government regulation of daily operations in the workplace.

Without a doubt, the most far-reaching legislation affecting employee relations in the United States is the Civil Rights Act of 1964.[11] Many of the subsequent employment laws are actually amendments to this Act. The relevant part of this statute for managers is Title VII. This is the portion of the Civil Rights Act of 1964 that mandates equal employment opportunity (EEO) and is the central focus of Chapters 2 through 6 of this textbook. In short, Title VII makes it unlawful for any employer covered by the Act to discriminate against any individual in the conditions and privileges of employment because of that individual's race, color, religion, sex, or national origin.[12] The five categories against whom discrimination is prohibited are referred to as the **protected classes.** In the original legislation, the protected classes were based on race, color, religion, sex, and national origin. The simplest example of the type of discrimination that Title VII makes unlawful would be refusing to hire a qualified engineer because he is an African

American. The decision not to hire the engineer is not based on his qualifications but on his protected class status (in this instance, his race). Similarly, refusing to hire an applicant for a job based solely on the fact that he is a man would be an example of discrimination on the basis of sex.

Since its enactment in 1964, the protected classes of workers now include those who are over the age of forty and those workers with physical or mental disabilities who can still perform their work with reasonable accommodation. This last class, qualified individuals with a disability, was added to the growing list of protected classes by the enactment of the Americans with Disabilities Act of 1990. According to the Bureau of the Census, approximately 62 percent of the American workforce are members of at least one protected class.[13]

Perhaps the most influential statute affecting employment discrimination, aside from the Civil Rights Act of 1964, is the Civil Rights Act of 1991. Chapter 2 will point out some of the provisions of this statute that have had a dramatic effect on increasing Title VII complaints. This Act not only provided for punitive and compensatory damages in specific cases of intentional employment discrimination,[14] but also permitted employment discrimination cases to be heard by a jury. Prior to the Civil Rights Act of 1991, all Title VII suits were heard before a federal judge only. This Act also expanded the jurisdiction of Title VII to the overseas plants, offices, and facilities of American-owned companies. Previously, Title VII was enforced only within the United States and its territories.

Besides focusing its attention on employment law, the federal government also involved itself in other workplace issues. In 1970, the Occupational Safety and Health Act was passed with the expressed purpose of making American factories and businesses safer places to work (see Chapter 10). Not only does this statute attempt to curb workplace accidents and injuries, it is also concerned with workplace illnesses. The Occupational Safety and Health Administration (OSHA), the agency responsible for enforcing the Act, also publishes the *Occupational Safety and Health Standards* (all 563 pages) to provide further explanation.[15]

The federal government has not only regulated the workplace by banning certain practices, as it did with the Polygraph Protection Act of 1988, but it also requires employers to engage in certain practices. The most recent example of the increasing administrative burdens on employers (thus making managing human resources more complicated) came in the form of the Family and Medical Leave Act (FMLA). This 1993 law requires employers with fifty or more full-time employees to grant up to twelve weeks unpaid leave to qualified employees to attend to serious family or medical problems. Some of the "problems" that would justify this leave are: (1) the birth or adoption of a child, (2) serious injury or illness of a spouse, child, or parent, or (3) serious injury or illness of the employee. Unfortunately, due to vague language in the FMLA, many employees are using this Act to take unfair advantage of their employers. The FMLA, as noted in Chapter 9, has very little popular support among employers.

Since their inception, the second wave of federal regulation laws appear to be expanding (see Exhibit 1-2). Over time, more and more employee "rights" are

■ EXHIBIT 1-2

FEDERAL AND STATE LAWS AND REGULATIONS
GOVERN THESE EMPLOYMENT PRACTICES

■ Recruiting

■ Selection/hiring

■ Promotions

■ Work assignments

■ Layoffs

■ Terminations

■ Disciplinary actions

■ Wage and salary administration

■ Harassment

■ Training and development

■ Performance appraisal

■ Worker safety

■ Worker security

turned into legal requirements with which management must comply. In a constantly evolving legal environment, it becomes absolutely essential that managers and HR professionals remain abreast of these latest developments.

During the second wave, the courts were busy as well. The judicial activism of the Supreme Court was developing employment discrimination law through numerous landmark decisions. **Judicial activism** is the concept that judges must go beyond their power of merely interpreting the law to actually making law. There are liberal and conservative judicial activists. Judicial restraint is the antithesis of judicial activism.[16] The most noteworthy decision illustrating judicial activism was *Griggs v Duke Power Co.*,[17] which created a new form of unlawful discrimination, *disparate impact* (discussed in Chapter 2). Two years later, in 1973, the Supreme Court standardized the process for determining whether *disparate treatment*, the other form of unlawful discrimination, had occurred in its ruling in *McDonnell-Douglas Corp. v Green*[18] (also discussed in Chapter 2).

The concept of *sexual harassment* is judicial invention as well.[19] This "new" Title VII violation is now the fastest-growing EEO complaint. Sexual harassment has evolved from a prohibition of coercing sexual favors in exchange for tangible job benefits to creating work environments that are free of sexual innuendo and reference (see Chapter 4).

Federal courts have led the evolution and transformation of EEO laws far more than the other two branches. In the 1979 case, *Steelworkers v Weber*, the Supreme Court held that formal, voluntary affirmative action programs (AAPs) did not necessarily violate Title VII, and then it outlined the conditions under which such programs were permissible.[20] These decisions have had a profound effect on how AAPs are structured. Through the 1980s and 1990s, the Supreme Court would devote much energy to further defining both disparate impact and disparate treatment, sexual harassment, and permissible affirmative action.

THE IMPACT OF GOVERNMENT REGULATION

Despite some instances of abuse, all federal employment laws were enacted for the best of reasons. Some of these objectives include protecting workers' rights to organize, ending discriminatory practices, creating job opportunities for certain groups in society, and promoting safe work environments. However, along with these actual or intended benefits are the costs that such programs impose on both public and private sector employers. Whether in the form of a constraint on management actions or a monetary expenditure, compliance imposes definite costs on the organizations it affects. Under ideal conditions, these costs are offset by the law's intended benefits. As with any costs, the employer who is able to minimize them, relative to competitors, will usually achieve an advantage. Therefore, an important duty of both managers and HR professionals is to help reduce compliance costs.

If the costs of compliance attract the organization's attention, the costs of non-compliance are of even greater concern. The penalties for noncompliance not only result in fines, legal expenses, and damage awards but also result in bad publicity that may damage a firm's image. What follows is an overview of the compliance costs confronting organizations.

ADMINISTRATIVE COSTS OF COMPLIANCE

Most federal employment laws impose some compliance reporting requirements on employers. Employers are usually required to document their activities and maintain reports for periodic review or inspection by the specific regulatory agency. Failure to maintain such records or submit the required reports may result in the employer being fined, losing its government contracts, or being subjected to other measures that the regulatory agency may feel are appropriate. To avoid these negative consequences, HR staffs must collect, compile, and synthesize relevant employment information. They are then required to document this data on the appropriate government form in the approved format.

One example of this reporting requirement is the Employer Employment Report (EEO-1), which is required of all employers with one hundred or more employees who are subject to Title VII of the Civil Rights Act of 1964. The employers must submit an EEO-1 annually to the Equal Employment Opportunity Commission (EEOC).[21] The EEO-1 report requires employers to provide employment data of five racial/ethnic classifications, by gender, in nine job categories (see Exhibit 1-3). It is the HR staff's responsibility to compile and store this information. The HR staff is also responsible for compiling the report, assuring its accuracy, and ensuring that it is submitted in a timely manner. If the employer holds a federal contract or subcontract, an additional EEO-1 report must be sent to the Office of Federal Contract Compliance Programs (OFCCP). Failure to properly provide this information can result in fines or loss of government contracts.

An example of the importance of this reporting and documentation obligation is demonstrated in the Immigration Reform and Control Act (IRCA) of 1986. All

Joint Reporting
Committee

● Equal Employment
Opportunity Com-
mission

● Office of Federal
Contract Compli-
ance Programs (Labor)

EQUAL EMPLOYMENT OPPORTUNITY

EMPLOYER INFORMATION REPORT EEO-1

Standard Form 100
(Rev. 3/97)

O.M.B. No. 3046-0007
EXPIRES 10/31/99
100-214

Section A—TYPE OF REPORT

Refer to instructions for number and types of reports to be filed.

1. Indicate by marking in the appropriate box the type of reporting unit for which this copy of the form is submitted (MARK ONLY ONE BOX).

(1) ☐ Single-establishment Employer Report

Multi-establishment Employer:

(2) ☐ Consolidated Report (Required)

(3) ☐ Headquarters Unit Report (Required)

(4) ☐ Individual Establishment Report (submit one for each establishment with 50 or more employees)

(5) ☐ Special Report

2. Total number of reports being filed by this Company (Answer on Consolidated Report only) _____

Section B—COMPANY IDENTIFICATION (To be answered by all employers)

OFFICE USE ONLY

1. Parent Company

a. Name of parent company (owns or controls establishment in item 2) omit if same as label

a.

Address (Number and street)

b.

City or town	State	ZIP code

c.

2. Establishment for which this report is filed. (Omit if same as label)

a. Name of establishment

d.

Address (Number and street)	City or Town	County	State	ZIP code

e.

b. Employer Identification No. (IRS 9-DIGIT TAX NUMBER)

f.

c. Was an EEO–1 report filed for this establishment last year? ☐ Yes ☐ No

Section C—EMPLOYERS WHO ARE REQUIRED TO FILE (To be answered by all employers)

☐ Yes ☐ No 1. Does the entire company have at least 100 employees in the payroll period for which you are reporting?

☐ Yes ☐ No 2. Is your company affiliated through common ownership and/or centralized management with other entities in an enterprise with a total employment of 100 or more?

☐ Yes ☐ No 3. Does the company or any of its establishments (a) have 50 or more employees AND (b) is not exempt as provided by 41 CFR 60–1.5, AND either (1) is a prime government contractor or first-tier subcontractor, and has a contract, subcontract, or purchase order amounting to $50,000 or more, or (2) serves as a depository of Government funds in any amount or is a financial institution which is an issuing and paying agent for U.S. Savings Bonds and Savings Notes?

If the response to question C–3 is yes, please enter your Dun and Bradstreet identification number (if you have one):

NOTE: If the answer is yes to questions 1, 2, or 3, complete the entire form, otherwise skip to Section G.

Section D—EMPLOYMENT DATA

Employment at this establishment—Report all permanent full-time and part-time employees including apprentices and on-the-job trainees unless specifically excluded as set forth in the instructions. Enter the appropriate figures on all lines and in all columns. Blank spaces will be considered as zeros.

JOB CATEGORIES		OVERALL TOTALS (SUM OF COL. B THRU K)	MALE					FEMALE				
			WHITE (NOT OF HISPANIC ORIGIN)	BLACK (NOT OF HISPANIC ORIGIN)	HISPANIC	ASIAN OR PACIFIC ISLANDER	AMERICAN INDIAN OR ALASKAN NATIVE	WHITE (NOT OF HISPANIC ORIGIN)	BLACK (NOT OF HISPANIC ORIGIN)	HISPANIC	ASIAN OR PACIFIC ISLANDER	AMERICAN INDIAN OR ALASKAN NATIVE
		A	B	C	D	E	F	G	H	I	J	K
Officials and Managers	1											
Professionals	2											
Technicians	3											
Sales Workers	4											
Office and Clerical	5											
Craft Workers (Skilled)	6											
Operatives (Semi-Skilled)	7											
Laborers (Unskilled)	8											
Service Workers	9											
TOTAL	10											
Total employment reported in previous EEO-1 report	11											

NOTE: Omit questions 1 and 2 on the Consolidated Report.

1. Date(s) of payroll period used: 2. Does this establishment employ apprentices?

                                       1 ☐ Yes   2 ☐ No

Section E—ESTABLISHMENT INFORMATION *(Omit on the Consolidated Report)*

1. What is the major activity of this establishment? (Be specific, i.e., manufacturing steel castings, retail grocer, wholesale plumbing supplies, title insurance, etc. Include the specific type of product or type of service provided, as well as the principal business or industrial activity.)

OFFICE USE ONLY

g.

Section F—REMARKS

Use this item to give any identification data appearing on last report which differs from that given above, explain major changes in composition of reporting units and other pertinent information.

Section G—CERTIFICATION *(See Instructions G)*

Check one   1 ☐ All reports are accurate and were prepared in accordance with the instructions (check on consolidated only)

            2 ☐ This report is accurate and was prepared in accordance with the instructions.

Name of Certifying Official	Title	Signature	Date
Name of person to contact regarding this report (Type or print)	Address (Number and Street)		
Title	City and State	ZIP Code	Telephone Number (Including Area Code)	Extension

All reports and information obtained from individual reports will be kept confidential as required by Section 709(e) of Title VII.
WILLFULLY FALSE STATEMENTS ON THIS REPORT ARE PUNISHABLE BY LAW. U.S. CODE. TITLE 18. SECTION 1001.

employers are required to verify the eligibility of all employees to work in the United States with the Immigration and Naturalization Service (INS), and an Employee Eligibility Verification Form (INS Form I-9) must be maintained on file. The HR staff must collect and process the relevant personnel information required by this statute. Once collected, the information must then be protected and made readily accessible to the appropriate federal regulatory agency (in this case, the INS) upon demand.

Sometimes the requirement is more than completing and maintaining government forms. If the employer holds a federal contract or subcontract, receives federal grant and aid money, or is a depository of federal funds, there is an obligation under several statutes and regulations to develop and maintain formal AAPs.[22] Meeting the government's requirements for a permissible AAP requires complicated utilization analysis (discussed in Chapter 6) and the development of realistic goals and timetables. All of this takes time and expertise if it is to be done properly. If it is not done correctly, the employer may be exposed to unnecessary litigation. These are only a few examples of the documentation requirements placed upon employers.

Naturally, members of the HR staff are assigned the responsibility of knowing what the current regulatory requirements are and ensuring that they are properly met. In larger companies, this is often a full-time job. In very large companies, this may require the services of several staffers. In any case, data gathering, analysis, and record keeping translates into money in the form of the HR staff's payroll. Compliance requires a good deal of data retrieval and record keeping. Naturally, the greater the need for documentation, the larger the HR staff. Even by the federal government's own modest estimate, regulatory compliance costs organizations over $286 million per year in administrative expenses.[23]

FINES OR CONTRACT LOSSES

An unpleasant cost associated with regulatory compliance is the resulting fines from noncompliance. These frequently result from an employer's failure to maintain proper documentation. Remember the IRCA's requirement to maintain an INS Form I-9 and supporting documentation? This means that all employees hired after November 6, 1986, must have the required INS form in their personnel files. IRCA also requires that each employee's identity and status be appropriately verified (two forms of identification), and there must be some tangible proof of this verification. Keep in mind that the purpose of this law was to make it unlawful to hire undocumented workers (illegal aliens) and protect jobs for citizens and resident aliens. IRCA documentation requirements immediately resulted in the modification of recruiting and selection procedures for virtually all business and public sector organizations nationwide. Additionally, employers had to absorb the time and cost of preparing and communicating new policies. But these were only the initial compliance costs; noncompliance with these requirements can expose the organization to even greater costs. Under IRCA, any employer who fails to maintain the appropriate documentation could face a fine ranging from $100 to $1,000 for *each employee* without an INS Form I-9 and supporting records.[24] Furthermore, the fine for failure to maintain required documents can be imposed regardless of whether or not the organization actually hired any illegal aliens. The fine, straightforwardly, is for failing to comply with IRCA's record keeping requirements, not for having illegal aliens on the payroll. The employer may also be subject to further fines for hiring undocumented workers.

In the case of government contractors or subcontractors, the worst penalty is often the loss of the current contract and ineligibility for future contracts. The same is true for financial institutions that hold federal funds—those deposits would be removed. Further, any institution that currently receives federal grant or aid money, such as universities, risks having the aid withdrawn as a consequence of any noncompliance.

Many of the federal acts discussed in this textbook provide for direct noncompliance costs (fines or loss of contracts) and indirect noncompliance costs. The indirect noncompliance costs often result from conciliation agreements with the regulatory agency involving reinstating affected employees or applicants, paying back pay, paying front pay, or any legal expenses incurred by the employee or candidate. However, even greater costs can be incurred if the matter must be resolved through litigation.

LITIGATION COSTS

Perhaps no cost currently heightens employers' compliance concerns more than the fear of litigation. The United States is one of the most litigious societies in the world, and American businesses are painfully aware of this phenomenon. The Judicial Conference Committee on Long-Range Planning estimates that nearly thirty million lawsuits are filed each year in the American judicial system,[25] and this trend is showing no signs of slowing.

From a business perspective, employment litigation can translate into real business costs, and many of these costs affect HRM. According to a 1995 survey conducted by the law firm of Jackson, Lewis, Schmitzler and Krupman for the Society for Human Resource Management, 57 percent of the responding firms had experienced at least one employment litigation during the previous five years.[26] With average awards in employment cases exceeding $200,000,[27] it is easy to understand how such litigation can affect the organization's bottom line. Unfortunately, even when employers win a case, they still lose. In the vast majority of cases, even when the company wins, it still must pay court costs and attorney fees. This creates a very strong incentive for managers to quickly identify compliance problems and take steps to resolve them internally. In this manner, HR professionals and line managers provide a tangible return to their organizations by reducing compliance costs.

To further complicate the litigation problem, many employees believe they have certain rights in the workplace upon which their employers may not

■ EXHIBIT 1-4

TOTAL CHARGE RECEIPTS INVESTIGATED
BY THE EEOC, 1985–2000

Year	Total Charge Receipts	Percent Change	Year	Total Charge Receipts	Percent Change
1985	72,002	+4.5	1993	87,942	+21.6
1986	68,822	−4.4	1994	91,189	+3.7
1987	62,074	−9.8	1995	87,529	−4.0
1988	58,583	−5.6	1996	77,990	−10.9
1989	55,952	−4.5	1997	80,680	+3.5
1990	62,405	+11.5	1998	79,591	−1.3
1991	63,830	+2.3	1999	77,444	−2.7
1992	72,302	+13.3	2000	79,896	+3.2

SOURCE: Information drawn from the Annual Reports of the U.S. Equal Employment Opportunity Commission 1985–1994; after 1994, U.S. Equal Employment Opportunity Commission (January 18, 2001). *Enforcement Statistics and Litigation.* http://www.eeoc.gov/stats/charges.html

infringe. Consequently, employees are far more prone to use litigation in order to protect these real or perceived rights. Many employees assume that they have the right to freedom of speech in the workplace. In most private employment situations this "right" may not exist. As a private entity, a private employer may be allowed to abridge an employee's free speech rights without violating public policy.[28]

In a similar vein, many employees believe they enjoy the right to freely date whomever they please. Moreover, these employees believe that any employer's nonfraternization policy, which prohibits coworkers from dating, violates their right to free association. Though the enforceability of these policies varies from state jurisdiction to state jurisdiction, "no dating" policies have been upheld in a number of courts.[29]

Besides legally protected rights (i.e., right to health and safety, right to organize, etc.), some workers and worker advocates believe workers are entitled to an even broader range of rights, many of which are currently without legal recognition. For example, some workplace rights advocates believe workers have the right to meaningful work, the right to self-management, the right to freedom of expression (i.e., such as wearing particular clothing), and many other "rights" not recognized by federal statutes or regulations.[30] This employee concern for "rights" and the resulting belief that they are entitled to them makes some employees more prone to litigate. Not surprisingly, after over thirty-six years of EEO laws, litigation is increasing, rather than decreasing (see Exhibit 1-4).

Since the laws that regulate employment practices are in a constant state of flux, managers and HR professionals are constantly reviewing their existing policies to ensure that they remain in compliance with the ever-changing legal environment. As new laws or regulations are created and existing ones are modified or amended, HR professionals must update their policies and practices or develop new ones. The impact of litigation cannot be overstated. Consequently, both managers and HR professionals are constantly under pressure to stay familiar with an increasing number of potential legal liabilities.[31]

OPPORTUNITY COSTS

A direct result of the escalation in litigation has been what some authors call the "culture of fear."[32] In this instance, the fear is the fear of being sued. In order to avoid litigation, some argue that intimidated companies may consciously eliminate product lines that are susceptible to lawsuits along with the jobs that go with them. In some situations, employers' concerns regarding potential product liability may be so severe that they may choose not to offer a new product.[33] However, since employers do not report such decisions, it is extremely difficult to project the actual extent of this activity and its related costs.

Regretfully, this fear of litigation may also affect an organization's management of its human resources. Some employers may retain less productive and more disruptive employees through fear that terminations would result in legal action. After all, EEO complaints arising from terminations are four times greater than all other sources combined.[34] Failing to take corrective action against "problem" employees may actually increase, rather than diminish, the potential for litigation. These practices not only expose employers to potential reverse discrimination litigation (discussed in Chapter 6) but also create a dangerous precedent in allowing substandard performance or disruptive behavior to gain a degree of acceptance in the workplace. Such a course of action not only has undesirable organizational consequences for the employer but also may expose the organization to litigation if it attempts to take corrective action later.

To illustrate this point, assume that a plant superintendent has allowed certain employees, who happen to be Hispanic, to leave early for lunch and return late. The reason she has permitted this to occur is a result of these employees' negative reactions when she first attempted to correct them. When confronted, some of the tardy Hispanic employees accused her of discriminating against them because they were Hispanic. Wishing to minimize conflict in the workplace, the plant superintendent gave up on taking action against these employees and hoped the situation would correct itself. Unfortunately, other employees are now taking longer than authorized lunch breaks. What is the likely response from a non-Hispanic employee when he or she is disciplined for not obeying the work rules on lunch break? The response in today's diverse workplace would most likely be, why are you punishing me for not coming back to work on time when you allow the Hispanic employees to do it all the time? By not equitably enforcing a work rule against a group of disruptive employees, the plant superintendent has created several new problems. First, other employees do not see offenders being disciplined and may conclude that the work rule in question is no longer being enforced. Second, when "other" employees are disciplined, they think it is unfair, and rightly so. Finally, because the "other" employees are being disciplined for breaking the work rule because they are *not* Hispanic (obviously the Hispanic employees were not disciplined because they *were* Hispanic), the "other" employees have grounds for filing a Title VII complaint. And all of this resulted because the plant superintendent was afraid the Hispanic employees would file a Title VII complaint—an allegation which, by the way, was without merit.

CORPORATE LEGITIMACY

Another concern for organizations is the adverse effect noncompliance may have on their corporate legitimacy. **Corporate legitimacy** is the extent to which an organization's objectives, actions, and activities are viewed as being consistent with society's expectations. When an organization conforms to these societal expectations, it may enjoy a positive public image. When, however, an organization's actions are contrary to societal expectations, that organization loses its legitimacy—this translates into loss of public support and may place it at a competitive disadvantage.[35]

It is only natural that organizations are concerned about their public images. Poor images can have undesirable consequences for a firm's financial future. If the public, as a whole, feels that a given firm has acted in an irresponsible manner, a boycott of its products or services could easily result. This in turn could have a direct effect on the company's ability to compete in its industry. If the company's conduct is particularly outrageous, the public could call on their representatives in government to enact more restrictive laws and regulations. The old adage rings true that organizations which behave irresponsibly eventually cause laws to be enacted that affect *all* organizations, even the responsible ones.[36]

In the public arena, no organization intentionally wants to appear to be unfair, arbitrary, insensitive, or discriminatory. Negative media coverage resulting from an alleged violation of federal employment laws may be sufficient to damage the firm's reputation. Even when allegations are untrue, the firm's public image can be damaged. Such was the case when *The New York Times* reported that Texaco executives were using racial epithets when referring to African American employees.[37] Although the paper eventually admitted to gross inaccuracies in its story,[38] the damage to the company's reputation had been done.

SOURCES OF LAWS AND REGULATIONS

Since laws and government regulations have such a substantial impact on HRM, a brief description of their sources is in order. It is not surprising that each of the three traditional branches of government (legislative, executive, and judicial) is a producer of laws or regulations that affect the workplace. Each branch of government imposes some requirements to which employers are expected to comply.

STATUTORY LAW

Legislative bodies create statutes. In the strictest sense, when someone uses the term "law" they are referring to a "statute." In the federal government, enacting **statutory law** is strictly the right of the Congress of the United States. Congress receives this authority from Article I of the Constitution of the United States, which empowers it, among other things, to "regulate commerce with foreign nations and among the several States."[39] This is the Commerce Clause, which is the legal foundation for most of the labor and employment laws passed by Congress. Since this textbook focuses on federal laws, Congress is the legislative body which produces the relevant federal statutes. Exhibit 1-5 provides an overview of the federal statutes that are examined in this textbook.

In terms of employment law, most statutes tend to list employment practices in which employers are prohibited from engaging. However, these prohibitions are broadly worded and, therefore, are broad in scope. Too often, the details tend to be vague. To resolve this inherent ambiguity and the problems that arise from the day-to-day enforcement, many statutes either create or designate an enforcement agency.

KNOWING WHO IS PROTECTED. It is important for managers to determine which employees are protected by the specific law and which are not. In some instances, like the Civil Rights Act of 1964, an extremely broad range of employees is covered, with very few exceptions. In other statutes, several substantial classes of employees may be specifically excluded or exempted from the law's provisions.

To illustrate the importance of knowing who is entitled to a statute's protection, let's look at a possible complaint made by an employee that her employer is violating the Fair Labor Standards Act (FLSA), the federal statute that requires employers to pay covered employees 1½ times their hourly rate of pay for each hour worked in excess of 40 in a 168 consecutive hour work week.[40] The employee is concerned that she has not been paid overtime. The employee has proof that she has worked at least 50 hours in each of the three preceding work weeks. However, before we can conclude that the employer has violated the FLSA, we must first determine whether she is entitled to the overtime mandated in the Act. To do this, the manager must examine the employee's job classification, particularly the tasks, duties, and responsibilities of the job in question. In this illustration, let's assume the employee making the complaint was employed as an "outside salesperson" and that our review of her job description confirms this. Her job duties reveal that she is primarily engaged in making sales away from the employer's place of business. Because she is a bona fide outside salesperson, she is among those job categories specifically exempted from the FLSA's minimum wage and overtime provisions.[41] In other words, the FLSA does not require the employer to pay overtime to this employee. On the other hand, if the employee was not among the "exempted employees," she would have been entitled to overtime payments. The distinctions between exempt and nonexempt employees are discussed in greater detail in Chapter 8.

Date	Statute	Enforcement Agency	Provision(s)
1926	**Railway Labor Act**	National Railroad Adjustment Board (NRAB) National Mediation Board (NMB)	Permits employees in the railroad, airline, and steamship industries to organize and bargain collectively.
1932	**Labor Disputes Act (Norris-LaGuardia Act)**	National Labor Relations Board (NLRB)	Made "yellow dog" contracts unenforceable in federal court. Made it more difficult to secure a federal court injunction for labor disputes.
1935	**National Labor Relations Act (Wagner Act)**	NLRB	Permits most private sector employees to organize and bargain collectively. Created unfair labor practices (ULPs) for management.
1935	**Social Security Act**	Social Security Administration	Provides for unemployment compensation.
1938	**Fair Labor Standards Act**	Wage and Hour Division, Department of Labor	Regulates child labor and provides for minimum wage and overtime.
1947	**Labor-Management Relations Act (Taft-Hartley Act)**	NLRB	Balances power in labor-management relations by creating unfair labor practices (ULPs) for the union.
1959	**Labor Management Reporting and Disclosure Act (Landrum-Griffin Act)**	Employee Standards Administration, Department of Labor	Provides protection for union members against abuses by the union.
1963	**Equal Pay Act**	Equal Employment Opportunity Commission (EEOC)	Prohibits differentials in wages and benefits based on an employee's sex.
1964	**Civil Rights Act (as amended) (CRA 64)**	EEOC	Prohibits discrimination in the conditions and privileges of employment based on an individual's race, color, religion, sex, or national origin.
1970	**Occupational Safety and Health Act (OSH Act)**	Occupational Safety and Health Administration (OSHA)	Regulates worker safety and health in the workplace.
1972	**Equal Employment Opportunity Act**	EEOC	Amended CRA 64 to include private sector employers with 15 or more employees. Added state and local governments to Title VII coverage.
1973	**Vocational Rehabilitation Act (as amended)**	EEOC (§§ 501 & 505) and Office of Federal Contract Compliance Programs (OFCCP) (§ 503)	Holders of federal contracts or subcontracts in excess of $2,500 cannot discriminate against qualified individuals with physical or mental handicaps and must take affirmative action to hire such individuals.
1974	**Employee Retirement Income Security Act (ERISA)**	Pension and Welfare Benefits Administration (PWBA) and Internal Revenue Service (IRS)	Regulates employee pension programs.
1974	**Vietnam Era Veteran's Readjustment Assistance Act**	OFCCP	Holders of federal contracts or subcontracts in excess of $10,000 cannot discriminate against Vietnam era veterans and must take affirmative action to hire such individuals.

Date	Statute	Enforcement Agency	Provision(s)
1976	Age Discrimination in Employment Act (as amended) (ADEA)	EEOC	Prohibits discrimination in the conditions of employment based on an individual's age (persons 40 years or older).
1978	Pregnancy Discrimination Act	EEOC	Prohibits discrimination in the conditions of employment based on pregnancy and related medical conditions.
1978	Civil Service Reform Act (CSRA 78)	Federal Labor Relations Authority (FLRA)	Prohibits discrimination in the conditions of federal employment based on an individual's race, color, religion, sex, or national origin.
1986	Immigration Reform and Control Act (IRCA)	Immigration and Naturalization Service (INS)	Prohibits hiring of undocumented workers while prohibiting discrimination based on national origin.
1986	Consolidated Omnibus Budget Reconciliation Act (COBRA)	Internal Revenue Service (IRS)	Mandates extended health care coverage for retirees and some classes of terminated employees and dependents.
1988	Worker Adjustment and Retraining Notification Act (WARN)	Federal courts (through civil action against the employer)	Requires certain employers to provide a 60-day advanced notification of "mass" layoffs and plant closings.
1988	Drug-Free Workplace Act	All federal agencies granting contracts in excess of $100,000	Holders of federal contracts or subcontracts in excess of $100,000 must implement programs reasonably expected to reduce and eliminate employee drug use.
1988	Polygraph Protection Act	Wage and Hour Division, Department of Labor	Restricts the use of polygraph testing in hiring and other employment decisions.
1990	Americans with Disabilities Act (ADA)	EEOC	Prohibits discrimination in the conditions of employment based on an individual's physical or mental disability provided the individual is qualified for the position, or could be qualified through reasonable accommodation.
1991	Civil Rights Act (CRA 91)	EEOC	Provides for punitive and compensatory damages in some instances of disparate treatment, provides for jury trials, and extends Title VII extraterritorially.
1993	Family and Medical Leave Act (FMLA)	Wage and Hour Division, Department of Labor	Mandates up to 12 weeks unpaid leave for covered employees to care for family or medical emergencies as defined in the Act.

In most statutes, the section or part titled "definitions" usually defines both the "employees" who are entitled to the statute's protection and the "employers" who must comply. Because federal laws are designed to cover a broad range of employers and employees, it is often more effective for many of the laws discussed in this text to identify employers and employees they do not cover.

To illustrate this point, let's briefly return to this chapter's opening scenario. Remember that the supervisor informed the undocumented workers that because they were not U.S. citizens or resident aliens, they were not entitled to protection under U.S. employment laws. This assumption was false. Even though these workers were illegally working in the United States (both they and the employer were violating IRCA),[42] undocumented workers are nevertheless protected by most U.S. employment laws. That is right—undocumented workers are entitled to the minimum wage and overtime under the FLSA,[43] even though they have no legal right to be in the country. Furthermore, they are protected under the NLRA in regard to their right to organize a union free from interference from management.[44]

The rationale for this apparently paradoxical state of affairs lies squarely in the definition of "employee" in each of the affected statutes. Since the definitions do not *specifically* exclude undocumented workers (in fact, they are not mentioned at all), the courts have concluded that illegal aliens are entitled to the same protection of any other "employee".[45] Again, the lesson learned from this is simple: unless it is explicitly stated in a given statute that a specific class of employees is *not* covered, assume that class is covered.

ADMINISTRATIVE REGULATIONS

The executive branch of the government is charged with the responsibility of enforcing the laws enacted by the legislative branch. In the federal government, the executive branch draws its power from Article II of the Constitution.[46] As previously mentioned, some laws enacted by Congress create regulatory agencies to enforce the law in question. These regulatory agencies operate under the executive branch of government. Some are directly under the control of the President, such as the Office of Federal Contract Compliance Programs (OFCCP), the Immigration and Naturalization Service (INS), and the Wage and Hour Division of the Department of Labor. Other so-called independent agencies like the Equal Employment Opportunity Commission (EEOC) and the National Labor Relations Board (NLRB) operate with a greater degree of autonomy since their respective heads are appointed by the President, confirmed by the Senate, and are subject to removal only in the event of misconduct.

Some of these agencies are created by Congress and brought into existence to enforce enacted legislation. For example, the Civil Rights Act of 1964 created the EEOC to enforce its provisions.[47] Similarly, the NLRB was created by the National Labor Relations Act to enforce that statute.[48] Other regulatory agencies are not created by Congress but instead are created by executive order. That is to say, the President may create the agency to enforce either a statute or executive orders. Such was the case for the OFCCP, which was created to monitor and enforce AAPs mandated by Executive Order 11246.[49]

In accomplishing the task of the day-to-day administration of a particular statute, regulatory agencies create definitive regulations. Remembering that the statutes are broadly worded, the regulations provide the details. For example, Title VII of the Civil Rights Act of 1964 makes it an unlawful employment practice

> to fail or refuse to hire or to discharge any individual or otherwise to discriminate against any individual with respect to his compensation, terms, conditions, or privileges of employment, because of such individual's race, color, religion, sex, or national origin.[50]

However, the statute does not go into the "specifics" of just exactly what a term, condition, or privilege of employment is. Neither does it tell us how to determine whether or not unlawful discrimination has actually occurred. These details usually fall within the jurisdiction of the regulatory agency.

For example, to define what is lawful and unlawful in the a hiring or promotion of an employee, the EEOC developed the twenty-six-page *Uniform Guidelines on Employee Selection Procedures* (commonly referred to as the *Uniform Guidelines*).[51] These administrative regulations tell the employer how the EEOC determines whether or not a given employment practice is in violation of Title VII. It further provides the standards for determining whether or not a given selection criterion is job related (a process called *validation*) and tells the employer what records it is expected to maintain.

In addition to the *Uniform Guidelines*, the EEOC has also developed regulations for investigating allegations of sex discrimination,[52] religious discrimination,[53] national origin discrimination,[54] age discrimination,[55] and reverse discrimination.[56] Still, this only scratches the surface. The twenty-ninth volume of the *Code of Federal Regulations*, those federal regulations that apply to civil rights, exceeds 6,150 total pages, and these are expanded every year. The forty-second volume, which deals with labor regulations, exceeds 1,100 pages.

THE REGULATORY AGENCIES. A regulatory agency exercises a great deal of power through its specific statute. It is up to the agency to interpret its statute and create regulations. Once the regulations are in place, the agency is in a position to conduct investigations to ensure that employers are in compliance with the statute and the subsequent regulations. Many agencies exercise the power to impose penalties and remedies. For example, the NLRB may enforce the NLRA through the use of administrative law judges. These agencies can enjoin (a legal term meaning that a court orders a person to either perform or cease from performing some action) employers from carrying out certain decisions like employee terminations, promotions, and assignments; they may impose fines; or they may require employers to reinstate specific employees or eliminate certain employment practices.

Equal Employment Opportunity Commission. The Equal Employment Opportunity Commission is the primary federal agency responsible for overseeing federal EEO laws. Though initially created by Congress to enforce Title VII of the Civil Rights Act of 1964, the EEOC has since become responsible for enforcing the following statutes:

- Equal Pay Act of 1963.
- Age Discrimination in Employment Act of 1967.
- Section 501 of the Rehabilitation Act of 1973.
- Title I of the Americans with Disabilities Act of 1990.

The EEOC is headed by five commissioners. Each commissioner is appointed by the President and confirmed by the Senate to serve a five-year term. The terms are staggered. The President designates a chairman and vice chairman of the EEOC.

National Labor Relations Board. Like the EEOC, the National Labor Relations Board is an independent federal agency.[57] Similarly, its board is comprised of five members; each member serves a staggered five-year term. A member is appointed by the President of the United States and approved by the Senate. The duties of the NLRB in enforcing the national labor codes are twofold:

- To oversee employee free choice as to whether or not they will be represented by a labor union through democratic secret-ballot elections.
- To investigate violations of the national labor code by either the employer or the union (such violations are known as *unfair labor practices*).

There will be a more detailed discussion of these duties in Chapters 11–12.

Occupational Safety and Health Administration. The Occupational Safety and Health Administration is a division of the Department of Labor responsible for enforcing the provisions of the Occupational Safety and Health Act of 1970. OSHA accomplishes its duties by:

- Establishing standards for workplace safety.
- Investigating complaints of unsafe conditions or serious workplace accidents.

Workplace safety and health issues, as well as OSHA's role, will be examined in Chapter 10.

Office of Federal Contract Compliance Programs. The Office of Federal Contract Compliance Programs is also a division within the Department of Labor. As its name implies, the OFCCP's efforts are concentrated on enforcing the antidiscrimination provisions of various federal laws pertaining to government contracts and subcontracts.[58] Such laws require contractors and subcontractors

THE FEDERAL JUDICIAL SYSTEM

not to discriminate against protected groups but to establish AAPs for any groups that are *underrepresented* in the contractor's workforce. To serve this end, the OFCCP:

- Conducts compliance reviews of federal contractors' HR policies and practices.
- Monitors federal contractors' progress toward achieving affirmative action goals.
- Investigates complaints of discrimination.

The OFCCP is the agency that establishes the federal standards for AAPs. These guidelines are commonly referred to as *Revised Order No. 4.*[59] The provisions of *Revised Order No. 4* and permissible AAPs are discussed in detail in Chapter 6.

Office of Labor Management Standards. The Office of Labor Management Standards is another division of the Department of Labor. Its major functions entail ensuring that labor unions are in compliance with their obligations to provide internal union democracy and are meeting the financial integrity requirements imposed under the Labor Management Reporting and Disclosure Act of 1959.

Wage and Hour Division. The Wage and Hour Division is a division of the Department of Labor and has a broad range of federal statutes to enforce.[60] The Wage and Hour Division is responsible for administering:

- Minimum wage provisions under the Fair Labor Standards Act, Davis-Bacon Act, and Service Contract Act.
- Child labor restrictions under the Fair Labor Standards Act.
- Overtime provisions under the Fair Labor Standards Act, Davis-Bacon Act, and Service Contract Act.
- Restrictions in the use of polygraphs in employment decisions under the Polygraph Protection Act.
- Granting emergency employee leave with job security under the Family and Medical Leave Act.

THE FEDERAL JUDICIAL SYSTEM

The third source of employment law is the judiciary, which produces case law. Since 1964, the federal judiciary has been responsible for the majority of the significant changes in EEO laws and their application. Through their power of judicial review, activist courts have created many more conscientious theories of discrimination than the other two branches of government. Both disparate impact[61] and sexual harassment[62] were court creations. Additionally, the standards for

STRUCTURE OF THE FEDERAL COURTS

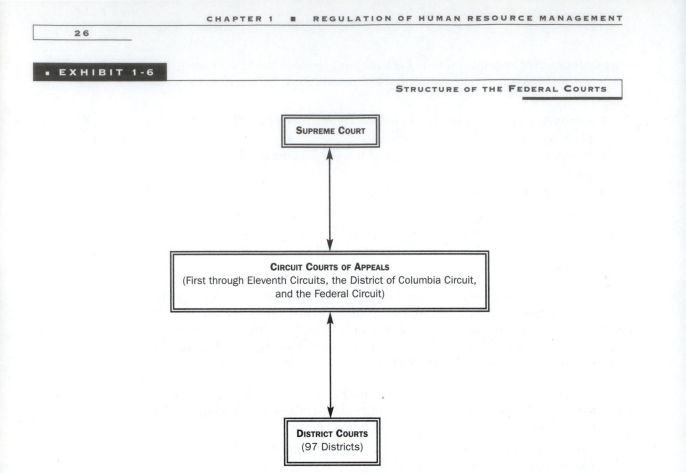

permissible affirmative action programs evolved through the judicial, rather than the legislative, branch of government.[63] Because of its impact on EEO and other workplace laws, a brief discussion of the federal court system is provided.

FEDERAL DISTRICT COURTS

The federal courts are arranged in a hierarchy of courts beginning with the Federal District Courts and culminating with the United States Supreme Court (see Exhibit 1-6). There are ninety-seven District Courts located in the fifty states as well as the District of Columbia and Puerto Rico. Three of these District Courts cover the Territories of the Virgin Islands, Guam, and the Northern Mariana Islands. There are approximately 649 District Court judges authorized to preside over cases in the ninety-seven federal districts.[64] The number of District Court judges in each district is largely determined by the caseload arising from the specific district.

Federal District Courts exercise original jurisdiction over most of the federal criminal and civil suits arising within the geographical boundaries of their

■ EXHIBIT 1-7

THE THIRTEEN FEDERAL JUDICIAL CIRCUITS

Circuit	States
First	Massachusetts, Maine, New Hampshire, Rhode Island, and Puerto Rico
Second	Connecticut, New York, and Vermont
Third	Delaware, New Jersey, Pennsylvania, and the Virgin Islands
Fourth	Maryland, North Carolina, South Carolina, Virginia, and West Virginia
Fifth	Louisiana, Mississippi, and Texas
Sixth	Kentucky, Michigan, Ohio, and Tennessee
Seventh	Illinois, Indiana, and Wisconsin
Eighth	Arkansas, Iowa, Minnesota, Missouri, Nebraska, North Dakota, and South Dakota
Ninth	Alaska, Arizona, California, Hawaii, Idaho, Montana, Nevada, Oregon, Washington, Guam, and the Northern Mariana Islands
Tenth	Colorado, Kansas, New Mexico, Oklahoma, Utah, and Wyoming
Eleventh	Alabama, Florida, and Georgia
Federal	Various Courts
District of Columbia	District of Columbia

SOURCE: Emory Law Library, U.S. Circuit Court Directories. *U.S. Federal Courts Finder*. **http://www.law.emory.edu/FEDCTS/**

districts. Original jurisdiction means that this court has the right to try a case and pass judgment based on the law and the facts of the case. This is also the court which can impose a remedy (injunction or fine). Violations of federal employment laws are civil matters, and most violations of the laws discussed in this textbook would originate in the Federal District Courts. In the event that either party to a District Court ruling feels that the Court made an error of law in their case, the party may appeal it to the appropriate Court of Appeals.

UNITED STATES COURTS OF APPEALS

The Federal Courts of Appeals are organized in thirteen circuits. Eleven of these circuits, sometimes called the geographic circuits, are identified by ordinal numbers, the First through Eleventh Circuits, and consist of three or more states (see Exhibit 1-7). As their name implies, the geographic courts hear cases on appeal from the Federal District Courts within their geographical jurisdiction. Each Court of Appeals consists of at least six judges depending on the given circuit's caseload. The smallest court, in terms of judges, is the First Circuit in Boston, Massachusetts.[65] The largest court is the Ninth Circuit in San Francisco, California, with twenty-eight judges.[66]

One Court of Appeals, the U.S. Court of Appeals for the Federal Circuit, was created primarily to hear cases appealed from the U.S. Court of Federal Claims, Court of International Trade, Court of Veterans Appeals Merit Service Protection Board, and the Patent and Trademark Office. Under certain circumstances, the Court of Appeals for the Federal Circuit will hear appeals from District Courts involving patents and minor claims against the federal government including issues arising from federal employment.

The Thirteenth Circuit is the U.S. Court of Appeals for the District of Columbia. This circuit addresses appeals originating in the District of Columbia and hears cases arising from legislation affecting the departments and agencies of the federal government. As previously mentioned, some statutes create regulatory agencies that often operate like quasi judicial bodies. For example, the NLRB is authorized by the National Labor Relations Act to resolve labor disputes. Any appeal against a NLRB decision is filed in the U.S. Court of Appeals for the District of Columbia rather than the nearest Federal District Court.

Regardless of the circuit, the Federal Courts of Appeals all have the same basic functions:

- Review District Court cases for errors of law—misinterpretation of federal law.
- In extremely rare instances, overturn District Court decisions on factual grounds.[67]

This occurs only when the appellate court has strong evidence that the lower court was wholly unreasonable in considering the facts of the case.

Most often, the Court of Appeals rules on the District Court's interpretation of the law it used in making its decision. If the Court of Appeals concludes that the District Court's interpretation and application of the law was appropriate, then the Court of Appeals will *affirm* the lower court's decision. This essentially means the District Court's decision will stand, as will the remedies it imposed.

If it is concluded that the lower court made an error in applying the law, the Court of Appeals may **vacate** or *reverse* the district court's decision. This means that the District Court's decision has been overturned or voided. Sometimes the Court of Appeals may vacate part of the decision, instruct the lower court where it erred (improperly interpreted the law), and then return the case (a process called **remand**) to the District Court for reexamination under the Courts of Appeals' previous instructions on the point of the law. If either party feels that the Court of Appeals made an error in its interpretation of the law, that party may attempt to appeal the case to the Supreme Court.

THE SUPREME COURT

At the very top of the federal judicial hierarchy is the Supreme Court of the United States. This Court hears cases on appeal from the U.S. Courts of Appeals and State Supreme Courts. Appeals to the Supreme Court are not automatic. A party requesting the appeal applies for a *writ of certiorari*. This **writ of certiorari,** if approved, would compel the Court of Appeals to provide records of a case for review by the Supreme Court. In order for a *writ of certiorari* to be granted, at least four of the nine justices of the Supreme Court must agree to hear the case in question. If the party appealing the lower court decision is unable to secure the necessary four justices, *certiorari* is denied. This means that the decision of the Court of Appeals stands.

To demonstrate how this works, let us assume that a party in Muncie, Indiana, sued his employer for reverse discrimination. The suit was first heard in the U.S. District Court for the Northern District of Indiana, the federal court exercising original jurisdiction. The District Court concluded that the employer's AAP was permissible and its actions did not violate the Civil Rights Act of 1964. Feeling that the District Court erred in its interpretation of the law, the complaining party appealed this decision to the appropriate Court of Appeals, in this case the U.S. Court of Appeals for the Seventh Circuit. On appeal, the Seventh Circuit concluded that the lower court had erred (perhaps it failed to consider whether the employer's actions created an absolute bar) and, therefore, reversed the District Court's decision. The employer now feels that the Courts of Appeals' decision is in error, and petitions the Supreme Court to hear the case in the hope that the Seventh Circuit's decision will be reversed. As an appellate court, the Supreme Court can affirm, reverse, or remand a case just like the circuit courts. In this example, let us assume that four justices did not agree to hear the case and *certiorari* is denied. This would mean that the decision rendered by the Seventh Circuit would stand, as would its standard for judging similar claims of reverse discrimination. However, the standards would only apply to federal District Courts within the jurisdiction of the Seventh Circuit (Indiana, Illinois, and Wisconsin). The Seventh Circuit's decision would not affect federal District Courts in the Eleventh Circuit (Alabama, Georgia, and Florida) or any other circuit.

If, on the other hand, a *writ of certiorari* had been granted and the case was heard by the Supreme Court, the Supreme Court's decision would apply to all Federal Courts in all thirteen circuits. Assume that the employer has argued that its affirmative action goal is to mirror the relevant external labor market and that the AAP would cease to operate. The complaining party argues that the employer must establish an identifiable numerical goal (not a vague "when it mirrors the relevant labor market") which should be the benchmark for program termination. Assume the Seventh Circuit agreed with the complaining party, but the employer still feels its standard would satisfy the requirement that its plan is temporary and, therefore, permissible under Title VII. If the Supreme Court hears the case and concludes that the employer's action is correct, this standard will now be applied to future cases addressing the issue of AAPs being temporary. This means that in all ninety-seven federal districts and thirteen circuits, affirmative action goals can be stated as achieving proportional representation with their relevant labor markets and *not* violate the temporary-in-nature requirement. On the other hand, had the *certiorari* been denied, then only stated numerical goals would be permissible, but this would only apply within the jurisdiction of the Seventh Circuit. Another Circuit could permit the "mirroring the relevant labor market" standard.

CASE LAW

The judicial branch, through court decisions, sometimes produces what is referred to as common law. These are "laws" that result from a process known as judicial review. This process is based upon the interpretation which a court applies to the Constitution, statutes, or administrative regulation. Particularly in instances when a statute is especially vague, or fails to adequately address the issue in question, the court may actually create "law" by resolving the ambiguity. "Disparate impact" was one such instance in which a court, in this case the Supreme Court, created "law." Prior to the *Griggs v Duke Power Company* decision, unlawful discrimination was limited to intentional discrimination against an individual because of that individual's race, color, religion, sex, or national origin (a form of discrimination known as disparate treatment). The Supreme Court's decision in *Griggs* created a second form of actionable discrimination by making it unlawful when a selection procedure results in a statistical imbalance of one of the protected classes and the procedure *cannot* be shown to be job related.[68] Interestingly, the EEOC defined what that statistical imbalance was in its *Uniform Guidelines,* an example of case law resulting in administrative law. The term **actionable discrimination** merely means that a person is seeking legal redress for the discrimination under a specific statute.

When creating case law, the courts are expected to follow two guiding principles: congressional intent and precedent. **Congressional intent** means that the court must view the issue in terms of what Congress was trying to accomplish *at the time the statute was enacted*. To illustrate congressional intent, let us look at the Supreme Court's decision in *EEOC v Arabian American Oil Co*. In this case, the employee sued his employer because he was being harassed at a Middle Eastern processing plant. The employee was a naturalized United States citizen born in Lebanon and was being harassed by foreign employees at the site because of his national origin (Lebanese) and his religion (Christianity). The employee claimed that the employer has a responsibility under Title VII to provide a harassment-free work environment. The employer contended that Title VII only applied within the boundaries of the United States and its territories. Since the plant is located on foreign soil, only the host country's laws and not United States law (to include Title VII) apply. Under the concept of congressional intent, the Court had to determine, based on the wording of Title VII, whether or not Congress (in 1964) intended the Civil Rights Act to be enforced beyond the territorial boundaries of the United States. When this issue appeared before the Supreme Court, it concluded that the 91st Congress (the Congress that had enacted the Civil Rights Act of 1964) had not intended for Title VII to be applied extraterritorially (beyond the boundaries of the United States or its territories).[69] As a result of this interpretation of congressional intent, United States EEO laws did not receive extraterritorial applications until the Civil Rights Act of 1991.[70]

Congressional intent is drawn from the legislative branch of government, but precedent is drawn from the judicial. **Precedent** is based on the legal principle of *stare decisis* which means to adhere to decided cases.[71] When judges are required to make a decision on a case in which statutory guidance is vague or absent, they rely on legal interpretations from previous cases on the same subject. For example, a case involving a voluntary AAP would refer to the Supreme Court decision in *Steelworkers v Weber*[72] to determine if the program was in compliance with Title VII. Consequently, all such cases refer back to this landmark ruling to determine whether or not a given AAP is permissible. The *Steelworkers v Weber* decision provides the precedent for all subsequent rulings to follow.

One school of judicial thought, judicial activism, views the judicial branch of government as a means to achieve social justice. The federal courts are used as a means to extend civil rights protections in the workplace. Proponents of judicial activism, therefore, call on the courts to make social policies, particularly in the area of protecting minority rights and the public interest at the hands of majorities motivated by folly or injustice.[73] In practice, this means that a court makes significant changes in public policy, particularly in policies made by other governmental institutions.[74]

The avoidance of judicial activism is **judicial restraint.**[75] Essentially the court refrains from law making and restricts its activities to the settlement of legal conflicts. Proponents of judicial restraint tend to see judicial activism as the courts exceeding their authority and advocate that courts should restrict their activities to enforcing existing laws, not creating new ones.

There can be little doubt that the federal court system has exercised an increasingly activist role in government policy making. Though this has resulted in national policies regarding such issues as abortion, birth control, capital punishment, and school prayer (just to name a few), the decisions involving the ethnic and gender composition of the workplace are the major concern for an organization's managers. Therefore, HR professionals and managers must remain alert to the changes imposed by the courts.

USING LEGAL CITATIONS TO ACCESS RULINGS

Since so much of compliance is concerned with legal documents (statutes, agency regulations, and court cases), it is necessary that managers understand the mysteries of legal citations. Many government and legal documents are referenced under what is called the *Uniform System of Citation*. What follows is a very cursory explanation of how this system works. Take for example the legal citation for the landmark Supreme Court decision on the constitutionality of the National Labor Relations Act, *NLRB v Jones & Laughlin Steel Corp.*, 301 U.S. 1 (1937). If you wanted to locate a copy of this decision and read it yourself, the citation provides all the information you need. First, it provides the title of the decision, *NLRB v Jones & Laughlin Steel Corp.* Next, the citation tells you

COMMON LEGAL SOURCE CITATIONS USED IN THIS TEXT

Abbreviations	Law Reporter	Material Reported
U.S.	*United States Reports*	U.S. Supreme Court decisions
S.Ct.	*Supreme Court Reporter*	U.S. Supreme Court decisions
F.3d	*Federal Reporter, 3rd Series*	Federal Appeals Court decisions
F.2d	*Federal Reporter, 2nd Series*	Federal Appeals Court decisions
F.Supp.2d.	*Federal Supplement, 2nd Series*	Federal District Court decisions
F.Supp.	*Federal Supplement*	Federal District Court decisions

Abbreviations	Government Document	Material Reported
U.S.C.	*United States Code*	Federal statutes
Stat.	*Statutes at Large*	Federal statutes
C.F.R.	*Code of Federal Regulations*	Federal agency regulations

the volume of the particular legal reporter that contains the case. In this instance, the decision is found in the 301st volume of *United States Reports* (that is what the "U.S." stands for). *United States Reports* is provided by the U.S. Supreme Court and printed by the Government Printing Office. This law reporter contains only decisions rendered by the U.S. Supreme Court. Next, the citation tells the reader on which page in volume 301 the *Jones & Laughlin Steel* decision begins. In this instance, it begins on page 1. Finally, the citation informs the researcher that this ruling occurred in 1937; the year in parentheses is the year of the decision.

Sometimes, especially in footnotes, other numbers are added to the citation. This usually is done to identify a page in the text of a decision containing an important legal point or explanation. For example, a researcher wants to reference the exact point in the decision's text where the federal government has the right to regulate industrial relations under the "commerce clause" of the Constitution of the United States. This information is found on page 29 of the legal reporter. This location would be conveyed in the following citation form: *NLRB v Jones & Laughlin Steel Corp.*, 301 U.S. 1, 29 (1937). The number "29" following the number "1" (the page on which the decision begins) tells the researcher that the specific information sought is found on page 29 of the 301st volume of *United States Reports*.

Statutes are handled in the same manner as cases, though their form changes once they are codified. The Civil Rights Act of 1964 provisions prohibiting discrimination in employment on the basis of race, color, religion, sex, or national origin were initially found, after enactment, in a legal report called *Statutes at Large* in the following format: 78 Stat. 255 (1964). Like the case format, the first number, "78" tells the researcher that the information is found in the 78th volume of *Statutes at Large* (Stat.) and is found on page 255. This same section of the 1964 act is also found in its codified form as: 42 U.S.C. § 2000-2. Again, this indicates that it can be found in the 42nd volume of the *United States Code*. However, this time, instead of referring the reader to a page, the reader is referred to a section (§), specifically § 2000e-2. Exhibit 1-8 provides the abbreviations for the most common legal sources containing information used in this textbook.

MANAGING RISK IN A LEGAL ENVIRONMENT

Due to the litigious nature of American society, it is becoming increasingly important for managers to fully understand the impact of federal regulation of HR practices in their workplaces. This includes being aware of the sources of such regulation (legislative, executive, and judicial). It further means that managers must understand their obligations in conducting investigations and how these will affect, or be affected by, the investigations of the regulatory agencies and the courts. It is equally crucial that these professionals understand the importance of their roles in reducing their organizations' exposure to employment litigation and the related costs of compliance.

How do managers and HR professionals assist their organizations in reducing compliance costs? By:

- Monitoring the legal environment for changes in compliance requirements.
- Updating existing personnel policies when necessitated by changes in the legal environment.
- Continually monitoring employment practice to ensure compliance.
- Providing training and information to management and supervisory employees.
- Providing training and information to nonsupervisory employees.

In order to reduce exposure to litigation from noncompliance, managers should consider including a risk analysis of the legal implication of major human resource decisions. This has become such a concern in human resource practices that the Society for Human Resource Management's (SHRM) Employment Practices Committee encourages the use of risk management techniques. The five basic steps of classic risk management theory are:

1. Identify and evaluate loss exposure.
2. Develop policies and procedures for minimizing and preventing loss.
3. Disseminate the policies and procedures.
4. Provide training.
5. Implement organization policies and procedures.[76]

SUMMARY

This chapter provides an overview of the federal system and its effect on HR practices. You have been introduced to the differences between union and nonunion workplaces, the different sources of "law" for these workplaces, and the impact of regulation on HR practices.

Labor relations is the part of HRM that addresses employment issues arising from the organized workplace, a workplace in which a union represents the interests of the employees. The area of HRM that deals with the relationship between managers and employees in a regulated, but nonunionized, environment is called HR compliance.

Before the twentieth century, there were very few federal laws that governed employee–employer relations. Since that time, there have been two waves of federal regulation. The first wave began with the passage of the Railway Labor Act of 1926 and included the major legislation related to unions. The second wave began in the early 1960s with the passage of the Civil Rights Act of 1964 and is still in process. This wave includes all of the EEO/AA laws. Such government regulation has impacted employers through administrative costs of compliance, fines or contract losses, litigation costs, and opportunity costs.

This chapter also introduced the federal judicial system and regulatory agencies, both of which have a direct effect on risk management for any organization and the resulting costs associated with compliance. The knowledge of the origins of federal regulations, statutes, and decisions is essential if organizations are to operate effectively in the current legal environment.

The laws that regulate the workplace come from many sources. With three branches of government (legislative, executive, and judicial), it is not surprising that each produces laws or regulations that affect the workplace.

The remaining chapters in this textbook provide the basic knowledge and understanding of federal laws and regulations necessary to meet the organization's legal obligations and still achieve organizational objectives. The legal environment of HR practices will continue to increase in complexity, and it is incumbent upon all managers and HR professionals to remain abreast of these developments.

KEY TERMS AND CONCEPTS

actionable discrimination

collective bargaining agreement (CBA)

congressional intent

corporate legitimacy

HR compliance

judicial activism

judicial restraint

labor relations

precedent

protected classes

remand

statutory law

vacate

writ of certiorari

QUESTIONS

1. How is labor relations different from HR compliance?
2. Discuss the significance of the first and second waves of federal legislation.
3. What are the protected classes covered under Title VII of the Civil Rights Act of 1964? From what are they protected?
4. What is the impact of government regulation on the workplace?
5. What are the three sources of employment law?
6. Identify and briefly describe the functions of the regulatory agencies.
7. Where would one look for the following legal information: 443 U.S.193, 91 F.3d 1547, 933 F.Supp. 1157, 42 U.S.C. § 2000e, and 29 C.F.R. §1604.11?

NOTES

1. U.S. Bureau of Labor Statistics (January 18, 2001). Union Members Summary. **http://stats.bls.gov:80/news.release/union2.nro.htm**

2. Ibid.

3. Human Resource Certification Institute (1999). *Certification Information Handbook*. Bala Cynwyd, PA: Assessment Systems, Inc., pp. 21–24.

4. 25 U.S.C. § 181.

5. Manchester, W. (1974). *The Glory and the Dream: A Narrative History of America, 1932–1972*. Boston, MA. Little Brown and Company, pp. 133–134.

6. 301 U.S. 1 (1937).

7. U.S. Bureau of the Census (1951). *Statistical Abstract of the United States: 1951 (71st ed.)*. Washington, DC.

8. 29 U.S.C. § 158(b).

9. 29 U.S.C. § 164(b).

10. 20 U.S.C. § 176-9.

11. 42 U.S.C. § 2000e *et. seq*.

12. 42 U.S.C. § 2000e-2(a)(1).

13. U.S. Bureau of the Census (1997). *Statistical Abstract of the United States (117th ed.)*. Austin, TX: The Reference Press, Table No. 628.

14. 42 U.S.C. § 1981, 9(a).

15. 29 C.F.R. Part 1910.

16. Hall, K. L. (ed.) (1992). *The Oxford Companion to the Supreme Court of the United States*. New York: Oxford University Press, p. 454.

17. 401 U.S. 424 (1971).

18. 411 U.S. 792, 802 (1973).

19. *Williams v Saxbe*, 413 F. Supp. 654 (D. D.C. 1976).

20. 411 U.S. 972 (1973).

21. 29 C.F.R. § 1602.7.

22. E.O. 11246; 42 U.S.C. § 2000e.

23. Howard, P. K. (1994). *The Death of Common Sense: How Law Is Suffocating America.* New York: Random House, p. 74.

24. 8 U.S.C. § 1324 (5).

25. Judicial Conference Committee on Long-Range Planning (1995). Conserving core values. *Report on the Judiciary.* Washington, DC: Government Printing Office, p. 11.

26. Minehan, M. (1997). Employment litigation an ongoing concern. *HRMagazine,* 42 (8): 144.

27. Ibid.

28. *Teleflex Information Systems, Inc. v Arnold,* 513 S.E.2d 85, 88 (N.C. App. 1999).

29. *Smith v Wal-Mart Stores,* 891 F.2d 1177, 1180 (5th Cir. 1990); *Wilson v Scruggs,* 1999 U.S. Dist. LEXIS 2607, (N.D. Miss. 1999).

30. Ezorsky, G. (ed.) (1977). *Moral Rights in the Workplace.* Albany, NY: State University of New York Press.

31. Edwards, R. B. (May 1998). Legal skills important part of HR professional's tool kit. *HR News* 17 (5): 26.

32. Garry, P. M. (1997). *A Nation of Adversaries: How the Litigation Explosion Is Reshaping America.* New York: Plenum Press; Howard, P. K. (1994). *The Death of Common Sense.* New York: Random House.

33. Ibid.

34. U.S. Equal Employment Opportunity Commission. *Annual Report 1985.* Washington, DC: Government Printing Office; *Combined Annual Report 1986, 1987, 1988; Annual Report 1989; Annual Report 1990; Combined Annual Report 1991 and 1992; Annual Report 1993;* and *Annual Report 1994.*

35. Parsons, T. and Perrow, C. (1979). *Complex Organizations (2d ed.).* Glenview, IL: Scott, Foresman.

36. Davis, K. (1974). The meaning and scope of social responsibility. In J. W. McGuire (ed.), *Contemporary Management: Issues and Viewpoints.* Englewood Cliffs, NJ: Prentice-Hall, p. 631.

37. Anonymous (November 4, 1996). Excerpts from tapes in discrimination lawsuit. *The New York Times,* p. D4.

38. Eichenwald, K. (November 11, 1996). Investigation finds no evidence of slur on Texaco tapes. *The New York Times,* p. A1.

39. U.S. Constitution, Article 1, § 8, clause 3.

40. 29 U.S.C. § 207.

41. 29 U.S.C. § 541.500.

42. 8 U.S.C. § 1324a(a).

43. *NLRB v Apollo Tire Co., Inc.,* 604 F.2d 1180 (9th Cir. 1979).

44. *Sure-Tan, Inc. v NLRB,* 467 U.S. 883 (1984).

45. *Sure-Tan, Inc.,* 467 U.S. at 892; *Apollo Tire Co.,* 604 F.2d at 1184; *Fuentes v INS.,* 765 F.2d 886, 888 (9th Cir. 1985); *DeCanas v Bica,* 424 U.S. 351, 356–357 (1976).

46. U.S. Constitution, Article 2, § 3.

47. 42 U.S.C. § 2000e-4.

48. 29 U.S.C. § 153.

49. 28 Fed. Reg. 11717 (1965).

50. 42 U.S.C. § 2000e-2.

51. 29 C.F.R. Part 1607.

52. 29 C.F.R. Part 1604.

53. 29 C.F.R. Part 1605.

54. 29 C.F.R. Part 1606.

55. 29 C.F.R. Part 1625.

56. 29 C.F.R. Part 1606.

57. 29 U.S.C. § 153.

58. 29 C.F.R. §§ 7 and 8.

59. 41 C.F.R. Part 60-2.

60. 29 U.S.C. § 204.

61. *Griggs v Duke Power Company*, 401 U.S. 424 (1971).

62. *Meritor Savings Bank v Vinson*, 477 U.S. 57 (1986).

63. Belz, H. (1992). *Equality Transformed: A Quarter-Century of Affirmative Action.* New Brunswick, NJ: Transaction Publishers.

64. Posner, R. A. (1996). *The Federal Courts: Challenge and Reform.* Cambridge, MA: Harvard University Press.

65. The First Circuit consists of Massachusetts, Maine, New Hampshire, Rhode Island, the Virgin Islands, and Puerto Rico.

66. The Ninth Circuit consists of Alaska, Arizona, California, Hawaii, Idaho, Montana, Nevada, Oregon, Washington, Guam, and the Northern Mariana Islands.

67. *DeJarnette v Corning, Inc.,* 133 F.3d 293, 297 (4th Cir. 1998).

68. 401 U.S. 424 (1971).

69. *EEOC v Arabian American Oil Co.,* 499 U.S. 244 (1991).

70. 42 U.S.C. § 2000e(f).

71. Black, H. C. (1990). *Black's Law Dictionary.* St. Paul, MN: West Publishing, p. 1406.

72. 443 U.S. 193 (1979).

73. Holland, K. M. (1991). *Judicia Activism in Comparative Perspective.* New York: St. Martin's Press.

74. Canon, B. C. (1982). A framework for the analysis of judicial activism. In S. C. Halpern & C. M. Lamb (eds.), *Supreme Court Activism and Restraint.* Lexington, MA: Lexington Books, pp. 385–419.

75. Baum, L. (1998). *The Supreme Court (6th ed.).* Washington, DC: CQ Press.

76. Edwards, R. B. (May 1998). Legal skills important part of HR professional's tool kit. *HR News,* 17 (5): 26; Petesch, P. J. (Summer 1998). The ADA, HIV, and risk management strategies. *Legal Report,* pp. 1–6.

REGULATION OF EQUAL EMPLOYMENT OPPORTUNITY

DISPARATE TREATMENT

| LEARNING OBJECTIVES |

☐ Explain what employment practices are unlawful under Title VII.

☐ Identify the classes of employers and types of people required to comply with Title VII.

☐ Describe how an EEO complaint is filed with the EEOC or a fair employment practice agency.

☐ Explain how "reasonable cause" is determined by an investigative agency.

☐ Describe the burdens of proof for both the complaining party and the respondent under the disparate treatment theory of discrimination.

☐ Describe the conditions under which religion, sex, or national origin could be a *bona fide* occupational qualification.

☐ Define what a tester is and how a tester can affect an organization.

☐ Explain practices that employers can pursue that would reduce the likelihood of disparate treatment claims.

OPENING SCENARIO

In May, the board of education accepted a recommendation from the superintendent of schools to reduce the teaching staff in the Business Department at Central High School by one. At that time, two of the teachers in the department were of equal seniority, both having begun their employment with the school on the same day nine years earlier. One of those teachers is white, and the other is African American. The African American teacher was the only minority teacher among the faculty in the Business Department.

Decisions regarding layoffs by school boards are highly circumscribed by state law; nontenured faculty must be laid off first, and layoffs among tenured teachers in the affected subject area or grade level must proceed in reverse order of seniority. Seniority for this purpose is calculated according to specific guidelines set by state law. Thus, local boards lack discretion to choose between employees for layoff, except in the rare *instance of a tie in seniority between the two or more employees eligible to fill the last remaining position.*

The board determined that it was facing a rare circumstance in deciding between the white and African American teachers. In prior decisions involving the layoff of employees with equal seniority, the board had broken the tie through "a random process which included drawing numbers out of a container, drawing lots, or having a lottery." In none of those instances, however, had the employees involved been of different races.

According to the school board's vice president, after the board recognized that two teachers were of equal seniority, it assessed their classroom performance, evaluations, volunteerism, and certifications and determined that they were "two teachers of equal ability" and "equal qualifications." The superintendent made the recommendation that the African American teacher be retained and the white teacher be laid off "because he believed both teachers had equal seniority, were equally qualified, and because one of the teachers was the only African American teacher in the Business Department." The board made a discretionary decision to invoke the policy to break the tie between the white and African American teachers. The white teacher was informed that she was being laid off.[1]

Upon learning this rationale, the white teacher immediately filed a charge with the Equal Employment Opportunity Commission claiming that she had been intentionally discriminated against because of her race—in direct violation of Title VII.

———————— ■ ————————

HISTORICAL BACKGROUND OF EQUAL OPPORTUNITY

The history of federal civil rights law begins with the end of the Civil War and the abolition of slavery. Following the abolition of slavery by the Thirteenth Amendment to the Constitution, many states had passed "Black Codes" to prevent freedmen—newly emancipated slaves—from enjoying the full benefits of citizenship.[2] Under these Black Codes, freedmen could not bear arms, assemble after sunset, or marry whites. Some states even limited the professions in which African Americans could engage (usually to domestic servants or agricultural laborers), and some required African Americans to sign annual employment contracts.[3] In a few states, laws restricted the rights of newly emancipated slaves to purchase, hold, or convey property.

Contrary to popular belief, these limitations on the rights of African American citizens were not confined to the southern states. At the end of the Civil War, only five northern states allowed African American citizens to vote on the same terms as whites.[4] Because of this environment of unequal treatment by state governments, the first federal civil rights act was passed, the Civil Rights Act of 1866. For the next ninety-eight years, the terms "civil rights," "equal rights," and "equal opportunity" would be synonymous with eliminating government-sanctioned racial discrimination. One residual effect of the Civil Rights Act of 1866 is that this statute has become the basis for imposing punitive and compensatory damages for intentional racial discrimination in employment contracts.

This first attempt to remove the effects of *de jure* discrimination (discrimination that is required by law) had minimal impact in practice. Other than to eliminate the oppressive annual labor contracts that were forced on African American citizens in some states, it accomplished little. The primary objectives of this statute were to guarantee that African Americans were granted the same rights to own or rent property, have access to the courts, and to make and enforce the contracts that were enjoyed by white citizens.[5] Today, this statute has been held to protect any citizen against discrimination on the basis of race.[6] However, it does not apply to religious, sex, age, or national origin discrimination.[7]

Because state governments were not complying with the Civil Rights Act of 1866, a new civil rights measure, the Fourteenth Amendment to the Constitution, was ratified on July 9, 1868. The Fourteenth Amendment compelled *all* state governments to treat *all* of their citizens equally under state laws. Specifically, a state government or agency is prohibited from denying "any person within its jurisdiction the equal protection of the laws."[8] This so-called *equal protection clause* was passed to remedy the problem of second-class citizenship. In theory, a state could not pass a law that applied to members of only one race. In practice, however, racial discrimination continued.

The Civil Rights Act of 1866 was further reinforced by the Civil Rights Act of 1875, which provided for equal access to all public accommodations for African Americans with one noted exception—schools. *Public accommodation* means that any individual has the right to enter and use facilities that are open to the public in general (libraries, government buildings, stores, parks, eating establishments, etc.).

However, by the end of the nineteenth century, "Jim Crow" laws proliferated throughout the nation. **Jim Crow laws,** named for a character in minstrel shows, were a means to get around the Civil Rights Acts of 1866, 1870, 1871, and 1875. States circumvented the federal civil rights laws by establishing a race relations system based on the concept of *separate but equal accommodations.* Under the concept of separate but equal, states passed legislation that provided for separate schools, separate railcars on trains, separate restrooms, and separate counters in eating establishments to accommodate their African American constituents. In most instances they were hardly equal. Nevertheless, the Supreme Court in 1896 ruled that this separate but equal arrangement was lawful.[9] John Marshall Harlan was the only justice of the Supreme Court to take exception to the *Plessy v Ferguson* ruling. Harlan declared that the high court was in error because the Constitution was color-blind and that no government could treat its citizens differently because of their race.[10] The concept of separate but equal continued until 1954 when the landmark case of *Brown v Topeka Board of Education* [11]overturned *Plessy v Ferguson.* However, it would be another ten years before equal treatment in the workplace would emerge as a national policy.

EXECUTIVE ORDERS

In addition to federal civil rights law, the executive branch made several attempts to ensure equal employment opportunity, at least where federal contracts were concerned. Among the first of these executive actions was President Franklin Roosevelt's Executive Order 8802, which forbade discrimination based on race in federal employment and by private companies holding federal defense contracts. This order also created the Fair Employment Practice Commission (the precursor to the Office of Federal Contract Compliance Programs) to enforce its provisions. Similarly, the Truman, Eisenhower, and Kennedy administrations would all initiate executive orders continuing and expanding this prohibition on racial discrimination by federal contractors.[12] However, none of these executive actions had any effect on employee–employer relations in the vast majority of private sector workplaces that did not hold federal contracts or subcontracts.

THE CIVIL RIGHTS ACT OF 1964

The struggle for equal treatment in the workplace reached its peak with the Civil Rights Act of 1964. Without a doubt, this is the most comprehensive federal statute to regulate employee–employer relations. This legislation was enacted to ensure that employers and managers did not take an individual's race, color, religion, sex, or national origin into account when making an employment decision. In his dissenting opinion in *Plessy v Ferguson*, Justice Harlan believed in a color-blind Constitution. In 1964, Congress *demanded* a color-blind workplace. Because the primary social concerns in 1964 focused on race relations, the remainder of this chapter will focus on racial discrimination prohibited by the Civil Rights Act of 1964's Title VII. Title VII is the portion that governs discrimination in the workplace.

THE PURPOSE OF TITLE VII

Title VII is the foundation of most of the laws and regulations that affect equal employment opportunity in the workplace. However, to understand how comprehensive Title VII's concept of equal employment opportunity is, one must first understand Section 703, which specifically prohibits certain forms of discrimination in employment. According to Section 703:

It shall be an unlawful employment practice for an employer—

1. to fail or refuse to hire or to discharge any individual or otherwise to discriminate against any individual with respect to his compensation, terms, conditions, or privileges of employment, because of such individual's race, color, religion, sex, or national origin; or

2. to limit, segregate, or classify his employees or applicants for employment in any way which would deprive or tend to deprive any individual of employment opportunities or otherwise adversely affect his status as an employee, because of such individual's race, color, religion, sex, or national origin.[13]

■ **EXHIBIT 2-1**

WORKPLACE DECISIONS THAT AFFECT COMPENSATION, TERMS, CONDITIONS, OR PRIVILEGES OF EMPLOYMENT

- Recruiting
- Selection
- Promotion
- Transfers
- Layoffs
- Training

- Wages
- Benefits
- Terminations
- Work assignments
- Apprenticeships
- Performance appraisal

Specifically, Section 703 forbids any employer from using an applicant's race, color, religion, sex, or ethnicity in making any employment-related decision. If the employer considers an applicant's ethnicity in making a decision, then Title VII is violated. If the fact that an applicant is an African American affects a promotion decision, Title VII is violated. Its main purpose is to get employers to make employment decisions based on an individual's qualifications. Exhibit 2-1 provides typical employment decisions that could result in Title VII violations.

Congress intended Title VII to create a work environment in which only an individual's qualifications and performance were the appropriate considerations for hiring, firing, or any other action.[14] In short, *different* treatment of anyone in the workplace because of race, color, religion, sex, or national origin is an unlawful activity.

This ban on different (or unequal) treatment of employees is broad and does not differentiate between unfavorable and favorable treatments. The bottom line is that an employee's protected class status cannot be used in *any* decision making. The term **protected class** will be used throughout this book to identify the classification of employees that are expressly protected by Title VII's antidiscrimination provisions. These protected classes are identified in Exhibit 2-2. The one

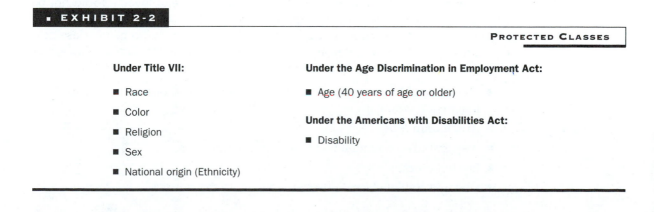

■ **EXHIBIT 2-2**

PROTECTED CLASSES

Under Title VII:

- Race
- Color
- Religion
- Sex
- National origin (Ethnicity)

Under the Age Discrimination in Employment Act:

- Age (40 years of age or older)

Under the Americans with Disabilities Act:

- Disability

notable exception to this principle is formal permissible affirmative action which will be discussed at length in Chapter 6.

Essentially, the equal employment opportunity guaranteed under Title VII ensures that all employees or applicants will be treated according to their qualifications and job performance. This point is demonstrated in *McDonald v Santa Fe Transportation Company*, in which three employees of a shipping company were caught stealing merchandise from a shipping container.[15] The company's long-standing policy had been that any employee caught pilfering company or customer property would be terminated. After an investigation, all three employees were found guilty of theft, but only two (both white) were fired. The third employee (an African American) was reprimanded but returned to his job on the grounds that the company had very few African American employees and desired to increase representation of African Americans in its workforce. Remembering Section 703, do you believe Title VII was violated? Was the employer's decision to terminate or retain employees based on an employee's protected class status? In this instance, the Supreme Court answered "yes" to both questions. All three employees were equally guilty of breaking the company's nonpilferage rule. Yet two were fired, while the other was allowed to return to work. The Supreme Court found that the employees were treated differently for the same misconduct. After further examination, it was concluded that the only factor accounting for the different treatment (who was fired and who was retained) was the individual employee's race. Even though race earned the African American employee more favorable treatment than his peers, that favorable treatment nonetheless violated Title VII.[16]

As a consequence of the *McDonald* ruling, the Supreme Court concluded that Title VII protected white employees from racial discrimination just as it protected African Americans from racial discrimination. The company had unlawfully discriminated against two whites by firing them and not firing the African American.

EMPLOYEES NOT PROTECTED BY TITLE VII

Some employees do not receive Title VII protection even if an action is based on their race, color, religion, sex, or national origin. Any person who works for an organization that does not meet the Act's definition of "employer" would not be covered. Not all employers are required to comply with Title VII because the Civil Rights Act of 1964 does not apply to them. Additionally, some job classifications are expressly excluded from the statute. According to the Civil Rights Act of 1964, the term "employer" does not include:

■ The United States government or any corporation wholly owned by the federal government.

■ Any Indian tribe.

■ Any employer having fewer than fifteen employees.[17]

■ Elected officials.

■ Personal staff of elected officials.

You probably realize that the federal government is the largest employer not covered by Title VII. Before continuing, there are two points that should be made about the federal government exclusion. First, employees of the U.S. Congress are now covered by Title VII as a result of the Civil Rights Act of 1991.[18] However, this inclusion is very limited and only applies to employees of the House of Representatives and the Senate. It does not include federal employees who do not work for Congress. This does not mean, however, that other federal employees are not protected from employment discrimination. All other federal employees receive similar employment protection under the Civil Service Reform Act of 1978.[19] This Act provides federal civil servants with essentially the same protection as their counterparts in the private sector that state governments enjoy against discrimination on the basis of race, sex, and ethnicity.

The second class of employees that do not enjoy Title VII protection is elected officials and individuals appointed to such officials' personal staff.[20] A person who qualifies as a member of an elected official's personal staff would exercise some degree of discretion or autonomy in carrying out assigned duties, serve in some advisory capacity, or have access to confidential information. For example, a governor's public relations director would not be eligible for Title VII protection as a personal staff member. However, the receptionist for the public relations director would be entitled to full Title VII protection.

Additionally, Title VII does not apply to citizens of other countries working for a U.S. firm outside the United States and its territories,[21] although the Act does protect U.S. citizens working for U.S. firms at facilities outside the United States and its territories.[22] Title VII also protects foreign nationals working *within* the United States and its territories.

The only other employee classification that is not protected under Title VII is actually a holdover from the Cold War. Members of the Communist Party or any other organization required to register as a Communist-front organization under the Subversive Activities Control Act of 1950 do not come under the Act's protection.[23]

Finally, some religious exemptions are permitted under Title VII. Under Section 702 of the Civil Rights Act of 1964, religious corporations, associations, educational institutions, and societies may give preference to members of their religion in hiring. This is not a *carte blanche* preference. The preferential treatment must be for work and activities that are connected to the religious purpose of the corporation, association, educational institution, or society. This will be examined in greater detail in Chapter 5.

FILING A CHARGE WITH THE EEOC

If an employee believes he or she has been discriminated against in employment or workplace decisions, a complaint may be filed with the Equal Employment Opportunity Commission (EEOC). Exhibit 2-3 provides an overview of the complaint process.

EEO COMPLAINT PROCESS

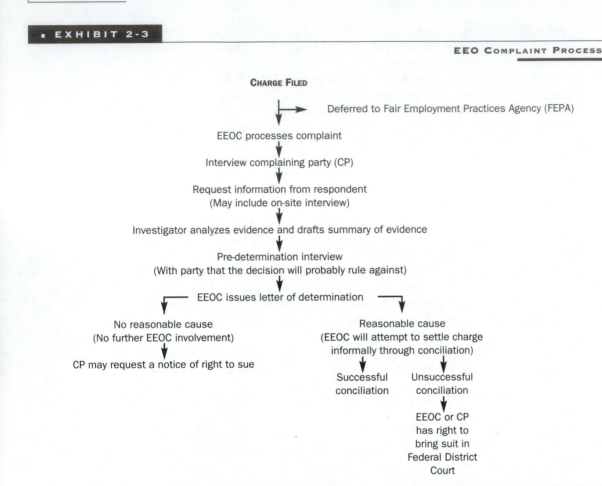

CHARGE FILED

→ Deferred to Fair Employment Practices Agency (FEPA)

EEOC processes complaint

Interview complaining party (CP)

Request information from respondent
(May include on-site interview)

Investigator analyzes evidence and drafts summary of evidence

Pre-determination interview
(With party that the decision will probably rule against)

EEOC issues letter of determination

No reasonable cause
(No further EEOC involvement)

CP may request a notice of right to sue

Reasonable cause
(EEOC will attempt to settle charge
informally through conciliation)

Successful
conciliation

Unsuccessful
conciliation

EEOC or CP
has right to
bring suit in
Federal District
Court

The party making the complaint (technically known as the complaining party)[24] may contact the EEOC by telephone, letter, or visiting a regional office. A charge sheet is then completed by the complaining party or, if necessary, an EEOC staff member may assist in the preparation of the complaint. One of the first things that the EEOC will ensure is the complaint was filed in a timely manner. For all Title VII complaints, *except* those filed under a state law covering the same violation, the complaint must be filed within one hundred eighty days from the date the discriminatory action occurred.[25]

If a state has antidiscrimination laws and a state agency (collectively referred to as **fair employment practices agencies** or **FEPAs**) to investigate racial discrimination, the charge may be filed under state antidiscrimination law with the FEPA first. In such cases, the complaining party could later file a complaint with the EEOC within three hundred days of the alleged discriminatory act, or within thirty days of the state FEPA closing the charge.[26]

■ EXHIBIT 2-4

EEOC AND FAIR EMPLOYMENT PRACTICES AGENCIES
CHARGE RECEIPTS, 1985–1999

Fiscal Year	EEOC Charge Receipts	FEPA Charge Receipts	Total Charge Receipts
1985	58,853	47,693	106,546
1986	62,074	50,645	112,719
1987	68,822	49,692	118,514
1988	70,749	54,154	124,903
1989	66,209	48,995	115,204
1990	67,415	50,493	117,908
1991	68,366	53,961	121,859
1992	72,305	54,080	126,385
1993	87,942	61,389	149,231
1994	91,189	64,423	155,612
1995	87,529	67,453	154,982
1996	77,990	66,242	144,232
1997	80,680	69,854	150,534
1998	79,591	65,678	145,269
1999	77,444	61,708	139,152

SOURCE: U.S. Equal Employment Opportunity Commission (January 12, 2000). *Enforcement Statistics & Litigation.* **http://www.eeoc.gov/stats/all.html;** Annual Reports for fiscal years 1985 to 1994; and U.S. Equal Employment Opportunity Commission (April 10, 2000). FEPA Receipts Nationwide. *National Database.* Washington, DC: EEOC Automatic Reporting Facility.

DEFERRAL TO A STATE AGENCY

A case filed with the federal EEOC can be deferred to the state FEPA that has jurisdiction over the alleged discrimination.[27] Because these deferrals are authorized under Section 706 of the Civil Rights Act of 1964,[28] state FEPAs are sometimes referred to as *Section 706 agencies.* When a complaining party files a complaint with the EEOC, the EEOC can elect to turn the complaint over to the state FEPA for investigation and resolution.

INVESTIGATION OUTCOMES

Whether the complaint is investigated by the EEOC or the FEPA, an investigator is assigned to the case and the employer is notified. Investigators may then question relevant witnesses and may even require employers to provide pertinent personnel records and documents. Once the initial investigation is completed, the complaint is assigned one of three outcomes:

■ No cause.
■ Dismissal.
■ Reasonable cause.

NO CAUSE. Under **no cause,** sufficient evidence is not found in the investigation to establish that an unlawful employment practice has occurred.[29] In the ten-year period 1989 to 1998, 465,449 of the 812,634 charges resolved by the EEOC (approximately 57.3 percent) ended in a finding of no cause (see Exhibit 2-5). Managers and human resource (HR) professionals should take note that even though the EEOC's investigation may have concluded with a finding of no cause, the complaining party may still bring suit against the employer in federal court. If

■ EXHIBIT 2-5

PERCENTAGE OF EEOC RESOLUTIONS RESULTING IN NO CAUSE DETERMINATIONS, 1985–2000

Fiscal Year	Total EEOC Resolutions	No Cause Determinations	Percentage of No Cause
1985	62,494	35,138	56.2%
1986	62,203	37,014	59.1
1987	53,482	29,578	55.3
1988	70,749	35,148	49.7
1989	66,209	35,896	54.2
1990	67,415	38,537	57.2
1991	64,342	38,369	59.6
1992	68,366	41,736	61.0
1993	71,716	40,183	56.0
1994	71,563	34,451	48.1
1995	91,774	46,700	50.9
1996	103,467	63,216	61.1
1997	106,312	64,567	60.7
1998	101,470	61,794	60.9
1999	97,846	58,174	59.5
2000	93,672	54,578	58.3

SOURCE: U.S. Equal Employment Opportunity Commission (January 18, 2001). *Enforcement Statistics & Litigation.* **http://www.eeoc.gov/stats/all.html**

the complaining party requests a **notice of right to sue** (sometimes referred to as a "right to sue letter")[30] within ninety days of being formally notified of the EEOC's no cause determination, the agency must issue the notice.[31]

DISMISSAL. When the finding is **dismissal,** the EEOC stops the investigation without a final determination. A complaint may be dismissed for a number of reasons. For one, the complaint may not have been made in a timely manner. Typically, the complaining party may have waited too long and filed the complaint more than one hundred eighty days after the alleged unlawful discrimination occurred (three hundred days after a violation occurred that affected a state-covered practice).[32] Sometimes the party filing the complaint cannot be located after the charge was filed. Without a complaining party, the investigation cannot proceed. Occasionally, the complaining party fails to provide the EEOC with requested information. And in some cases, the complaining party may refuse to appear at scheduled interviews. A dismissal will result under most circumstances when a complaining party refuses to cooperate with the investigation.[33]

REASONABLE CAUSE. Under **reasonable cause,** the EEOC's investigation has found enough evidence to believe that an unlawful employment practice has occurred.[34] In the event that the EEOC or FEPA investigator has determined that there is reasonable cause, the employer is formally notified. Even when cause was indeed found, the matter is not automatically concluded. The employer may request the EEOC to reconsider the matter. A request for reconsideration may be based on new evidence that has surfaced since the initial investigation. Failing that, the employer is left only with the options of **conciliation** (a negotiated settlement with the complaining party) or litigation.

Conciliation. If the employer chooses conciliation, the EEOC will attempt to work out a mutually agreeable settlement between the complaining party and the employer. This option is preferred by the EEOC; in fact, it is encouraged even before the determination of reasonable cause is reached.[35]

To illustrate this point, let us assume that an employee has filed a charge with the EEOC alleging that she was terminated from her position because of her race and the investigation is well under way. In the complaint, the employer allegedly keeps African American employees on the payroll only as long as it takes to find a non-African American to replace them. The EEOC investigates and discovers, according to payroll records, that no African American employee has been employed by the company for a period longer than two months. The EEOC further notes that job specifications require an applicant to have a high school diploma and a valid driver's license—both of which the complaining party possesses. No other evidence for termination is presented by either the complaining party or by her employer. Based on this evidence, the EEOC would most likely conclude that there was reasonable cause or sufficient evidence to indicate that a Title VII violation had occurred. In other words, there is sufficient evidence to establish a *prima facie* **case** of unlawful discrimination. Bringing this to the employer's attention, the EEOC would encourage the employer to initiate a remedy that is mutually acceptable to the complaining party. The intent is that the employer would meet with the complaining party and attempt to produce an agreeable solution. In this case, an attempted settlement might begin with an offer by the employer to reinstate the complaining party (essentially rehire her) and pay her estimated wages from the time she was fired to the time she was reinstated (back pay). The complaining party may offer the counterproposal that she should also be given seniority for the time period between her termination and reinstatement. If the employer accepts this counterproposal the EEOC is notified, and the matter is closed.

Litigation.   If the parties cannot agree to conciliation, or the employer refuses to even consider conciliation, the EEOC has the option of filing suit on behalf of the complaining party. When the EEOC decides to litigate a complaint, it uses the resources of its own Solicitor General's Office—essentially its own legal staff. If the EEOC chooses not to file suit, as it does in the vast majority of complaints, the EEOC may issue the complaining party a notice of right to sue. Because the EEOC has limited legal resources, it regularly issues a notice of right to sue rather than litigating the complaint itself. Only on rare occasions does the EEOC litigate. Such cases usually involve large employers, affect large numbers of complaining parties (class actions), or involve cases that substantially impact equal employment opportunity (EEO) policy or enforcement. Exhibit 2-6 lists the cases recently handled by the EEOC.

Managers are cautioned not to forget a disturbing fact about notices of right to sue—they are available upon request.[36] Even if the EEOC or FEPA investigations result in findings of no cause, the complaining party is still entitled to request a notice of right to sue, and the agency must fulfill that request.

Who Litigates?   Whether the litigation is initiated by the complaining party using a notice of right to sue, or whether it is filed by the EEOC's Solicitor General's Office, the case will be tried in a federal district court. This is the court of original jurisdiction, meaning this court has the authority to hear and decide the specific case. The federal district court exercises the authority to impose a legal remedy for the injured party, whether it is monetary relief (i.e., back pay, punitive damages, etc.) or enforcement of a right (i.e., stop harassment, reinstatement, etc.).[37]

Prior to 1991, EEO cases were heard before a judge only. Since the enactment of the Civil Rights Act of 1991, complaining parties may request jury trials under specific circumstances. Because juries may arrive at their verdicts through emotion rather than the facts of the case, some employers fear jury trials for Title VII complaints. In order to qualify for a jury trial, the complaining party must allege that the employer's discriminatory actions were done with "malice" or with "reckless indifference" to federally protected rights.[38] In the event that either party feels the ruling in the district court (either as a result of a trial by jury or a bench trial by a judge) is in error, and many do, the case may then be appealed to a federal appellate court (see Chapter 1).

■ EXHIBIT 2-6

CASES LITIGATED BY THE SOLICITOR GENERAL'S OFFICE, 1985–2000

Fiscal Year	Suits Filed	Total EEOC Charge Receipts
1985	411	58,853
1986	526	62,074
1987	527	68,822
1988	555	70,749
1989	598	66,209
1990	643	67,415
1991	593	68,366
1992	447	72,305
1993	481	87,942
1994	425	91,189
1995	373	87,529
1996	193	77,990
1997	338	80,680
1998	405	79,591
1999	465	77,444
2000	327	79,896

SOURCE: U.S. Equal Employment Opportunity Commission (January 31, 2001). *EEOC Litigation Statistics.* **http://www.eeoc.gov/stats/litigation.html**

Though appellate courts were not created to impose remedies, they may overturn the remedies imposed by the district courts. If an appellate court wants to modify a remedy, it **vacates** the lower court's remedy (this means the original damage award is annulled or canceled)[39] and then sends the case back to the district court (the court exercising original jurisdiction) with instructions on how a new remedy should be fashioned. The legal term used for this process of returning an appealed case to the court of original jurisdiction is **remand.**

Frivolous Appeals.   Though it is quite rare, federal circuit courts have held parties, and sometimes their attorneys, liable for legal cost if an appeal was frivolous. An appeal is frivolous when the challenge to the district court's decision is proven to be meritless. In a strict legal sense, this means that the result of the appeal is "obvious, or the arguments of error are wholly without merit."[40]

An appeal can only occur when one of the parties proves the lower court made an error in its interpretation or application of the law. If it can be clearly shown that a party has made an appeal that is blatantly meritless, the court may assess double legal costs to the party making the frivolous appeal and that party's attorney.[41] If the complaining party made the frivolous appeal, she would also incur her employer's legal expenses. If the employer initiated the meritless appeal, then he or she would be responsible for the complaining party's expenses.[42]

The district courts may also award attorneys' fees for respondents when a complaint is proven frivolous, unreasonable, and groundless, and the complaining party continues to litigate after this becomes clearly apparent.[43] Again, such awards are rare, but they do occur, especially when the complaint is made fraudulently or under other forms of bad faith.[44]

In the event that either party believes the appellate court's decision is in error, that party may appeal the case to the U.S. Supreme Court. Such appeals are rare.

TWO THEORIES OF DISCRIMINATION

There are two basic theories of unlawful discrimination under Title VII: *disparate treatment* and *disparate impact*. **Disparate treatment** results from treating individuals in the workplace differently because of their membership in a protected class. It is intentional and is characterized by imposing different standards on different people. **Disparate impact** is a child of the courts, born from the *Griggs v Duke Power Company* decision. Disparate impact focuses managers' and HR professionals' attention on statistical imbalances in their workforces. It is often unintentional and is characterized by imposing the same standards on all people with different outcomes for different groups. A detailed examination of disparate impact is covered in Chapter 3.

DISPARATE TREATMENT THEORY OF DISCRIMINATION

When the Civil Rights Act of 1964 was first enacted, there was essentially only one form of unlawful discrimination, disparate treatment. To engage in disparate treatment, an employer, or its agent, treats applicants or employees differently because of their protected class status. Thus, there are different standards for applicants or employees, based on an individual's race, color, religion, sex, or national origin.

The most blatant example of imposing different standards would be a company in which no women are ever promoted to management positions because the owner believes women do not make good leaders. As a consequence of this personal bias, no female that applies for a management position is ever seriously considered. Or all female candidates for promotion are automatically "deselected" because of their sex—before relevant job qualifications are considered. The candidate's sex simply and exclusively disqualifies her for the job. The same would hold true if an employer believed that people of Italian ancestry lacked leadership ability. Every candidate with an Italian surname would be disquali-

■ **EXHIBIT 2-7**

DISPARATE TREATMENT PROOFS

Prima Facie **Case:**

- Complaining party is a member of a protected class.
- Complaining party was qualified for the job in question.
- Complaining party was rejected.
- The position remained open to others with equal or fewer qualifications than the complaining party.

Respondent's Rebuttal:

- The respondent's actions are based on legitimate nondiscriminatory reasons.
- The respondent's actions are based on a *bona fide* occupational qualification.

Complaining Party's Rebuttal:

- The respondent's legitimate nondiscriminatory reasons are a pretext (a reason given to hide the respondent's real reason for the employment action).

fied strictly because of, and for no other reason than, national origin. The discrimination in either case is intentional and based on personal prejudices rather than on the individual candidate's ability to do the job in question.

When federal courts hear complaints of disparate treatment, they investigate the allegation in a systematic manner following a set of legal proofs. The burden of these proofs shifts from the complaining party to the respondent and back again as they are satisfied. The **respondent** is the party against whom the complaint is made.[45] Exhibit 2-7 summarizes these proofs.

THE PRIMA FACIE CASE. The complaining party has the initial burden of proving that a Title VII violation may have occurred. The legal terminology for this is called establishing a *prima facie* case. The phrase, *prima facie,* literally means first face or first appearance. In its legal sense, it means there is enough evidence to establish that Title VII has been violated unless the respondent can refute, or disprove, this evidence.[46]

To establish the *prima facie* case under disparate treatment theory, the complaining party must first demonstrate that he or she is a member of a protected class. If the individual cannot demonstrate that he or she is a member of a protected class, Title VII is not applicable. Remember that under Title VII, it is unlawful to treat employees differently because of race, color, religion, sex, or national origin.

To illustrate this point, let's assume that an employer has just interviewed a job applicant for a position in the secretarial pool. The applicant is wearing a gay liberation button, and the interviewer informs the applicant that he will not be hired because the company's management does not hire homosexuals. The applicant is outraged and claims that this action violates Title VII, but does it? Is the applicant entitled to protection under Title VII? Is homosexuality (also known as sexual preference) a class protected under Title VII? Is sex? Is sexual preference the same as *sex*? Federal courts have held that *sex* is a biological condition that does not encompass sexual orientation.[47] In essence, the applicant in this example would not be able to pursue the rejection any further under Title VII (though in some states, he could be protected under state law) because he is not a member of a protected class.

On the other hand, if the applicant was a male and was not hired because the company did not hire *men* for positions in its secretarial pool, Title VII would apply. In this scenario, the applicant was not hired because of his *sex* (a biological condition), a class of individuals protected by Title VII. Because he was denied employment because of his *sex*, Title VII would be the appropriate law to apply.

Meeting Qualifications. The next stage of establishing a *prima facie* case involves demonstrating that the candidate applied for the position in question, met the qualifications for the position, and was rejected. In the first part, a person who did not apply for a position could hardly claim discrimination, since he or she had suffered no injury from the employer. Invariably, disparate treatment cases arise from rejection for employment, layoffs, denial of promotions, disciplinary actions, etc. Consequently, the candidate had to be aware of his or her eligibility for some job outcome. In the event of layoffs or terminations, an employee would be aware of possible job loss. The Title VII claim would arise from this job loss if someone with fewer qualifications was retained. There is no unlawful discrimination if the individual denied employment was not qualified for the job, or if the individual who was laid off was less qualified than those who were retained. The major exception to this is *bona fide* seniority systems.[48]

The matter that involves a significant amount of time is the issue of the applicant's qualifications. Again, is the complaining party truly qualified for the specific job in question? If the person lacks the qualifications for the job, the *prima facie* case is not made and the complaint will be dismissed. Always bear in mind that Title VII *does not* guarantee a job to every person regardless of qualifications.[49] Even under a permissible affirmative action program, the applicant receiving preferential treatment must at least meet minimum job qualifications.[50] Simply stated, there is nothing in Title VII that requires an employer to hire or retain an unqualified employee.

Mixed Motive Decisions. Very closely related to disparate treatment is the issue of *mixed motive* employment decisions. Since the enactment of the Civil Rights Act of 1991, it is unlawful to even consider an employee's or applicant's protected class status when making an employment decision, *even if the decision would have been exactly the same in the absence of the protected class consideration.* Therefore, if a decision maker considered a candidate's race as well as his education, job-related work experience, and objective performance, the entire decision process violates Title VII. To demonstrate this, let's assume that an African American salesperson has applied for a promotion to district sales manager. The promotion decision is made by a three-member board. While reviewing the candidate's promotion packets, one board member remarks that she is concerned that some of the corporate customers may not respond well to an African American district sales manager. This is a consideration of the candidate's protected class status (race) and, of and by itself, violates Title VII.

If the applicant can demonstrate that his race was the motivating factor in *not* receiving the promotion, he would be eligible for a remedy under Title VII for unlawful discrimination. If consideration of his race caused him not to be promoted, and the position was filled by someone with equal or fewer qualifications, his complaint would be one of simple disparate treatment.

However, now assume the job was given to a candidate who was *more* qualified than the complaining party (provided that the employer can objectively prove this). But suppose word leaked out to the African American applicant that a board member had expressed concern that his race would affect his performance, a consideration that clearly violates Title VII. As a result, the African American applicant files a complaint with the EEOC. If, during the subsequent investigation, the company produces evidence that shows the other applicant's education, experience, and performance were clearly superior to that of the African American applicant, then the decision would appear to have included both legitimate (education, experience, and performance) and illegitimate (race) considerations.

Interestingly, Title VII is not violated when the complaining party is denied the employment benefit (i.e., hiring, promotion, assignment, etc.) and it is given instead to an applicant in the same protected class with equal or fewer qualifications. As an example, assume that Allison O'Reilly, a female engineering graduate, applied for the following position:

> Industrial Engineer Needed. Candidates should have a minimum of four years experience in light manufacturing. A B.S. degree in Industrial or Mechanical Engineering is essential.

O'Reilly received her degree in industrial engineering from Massachusetts Institute of Technology (MIT) in 1995 and has spent the past six years working for an electronic parts manufacturer in Sioux City, Iowa. She is very disappointed when she discovers the job was given to Dee Dee Burt, a female sales representative with a degree in marketing and no manufacturing experience. O'Reilly decides to file a sex discrimination complaint.

If we were to apply the proofs for disparate treatment to the situation with O'Reilly, our analysis would reveal the following:

1. O'Reilly is a member of a protected class based on her sex.

2. O'Reilly was qualified for the position and applied for it.

3. O'Reilly was rejected.

4. The position remained open and was filled by someone with fewer qualifications; in fact, it was filled by someone who was unqualified.

However, O'Reilly has no Title VII claim. Why? Because the "someone" who was less qualified (Burt) is also a member of O'Reilly's protected class. O'Reilly can hardly claim that the employer discriminated against her because of her sex, if the employer hired another woman instead. Obviously, the decision was not based on the applicant's qualifications, but neither was it based on sex. Title VII does not protect applicants from bad decisions, only decisions based on the applicant's protected class.[51]

The reason all of this is important is tied to the remedies awarded by the court. If race was the sole motivating factor, the African American applicant is entitled to all of the remedies authorized for disparate treatment. If race had been considered, but the employer can produce convincing evidence that the outcome would have been the same (the objectively more qualified candidate was promoted) in the absence of racial consideration, then the employer's liability is limited to:

- Injunctive and declaratory relief.
- Attorneys' fees.
- Court costs.[52]

In short, the employer is still declared to have violated Title VII. The employer will be ordered not to consider race in future promotion decisions, and, at the discretion of the court, it may have to reimburse the African American applicant for his attorneys' fees and court costs. It will not, however, have to promote the African American applicant, pay him back pay, or pay him punitive or compensatory damages.

RESPONDENT'S REBUTTAL. When a complaining party has successfully carried the burden of proof, the burden shifts to the respondent, who has two avenues to pursue. The organization can justify its employment decision as based on a *bona fide* **occupational qualification (BFOQ),** or it may contend that the decision is based on legitimate nondiscriminatory reasons. As will be seen, it is far more difficult to establish a BFOQ than a legitimate nondiscriminatory reason.

BFOQs. BFOQs are extremely rare and very limited in their application. Under Title VII, they are further limited only to the protected classes of sex, religion, and national origin (see Exhibit 2-8). The federal courts have long declared that there is no BFOQ for race.[53] Note that in this chapter's opening scenario, the board of education would not be permitted to defend its layoff decision as a BFOQ, because race can never be used as a BFOQ. In other categories, a BFOQ essentially allows an employer to use protected class status as a qualification for the job in question. The use of BFOQs in employment decisions is specifically authorized by Section 703(e) of the Civil Rights Act of 1964:

It shall not be an unlawful employment practice for an employer to hire and employ employees . . . on the basis of religion, sex, or national origin in those certain instances where religion, sex, or national origin is a bona fide occupational qualification reasonably necessary to the normal operation of that particular business or enterprise.[54]

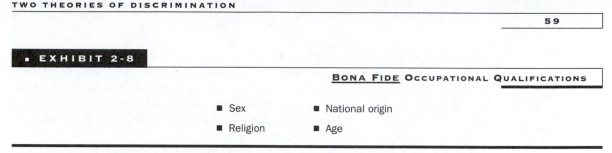

■ **EXHIBIT 2-8**

<u>BONA FIDE</u> OCCUPATIONAL QUALIFICATIONS

■ Sex   ■ National origin

■ Religion   ■ Age

SOURCE: 42 U.S.C. 2000e-2(e)(1); 29 C.F.R. § 1625.6.

BFOQs on the basis of age are also permitted under the Age Discrimination in Employment Act.[55]

This means that there may be specific instances when an employer can, for example, hire only females for a particular job. Or there may be circumstances in which members of a particular religion would be considered for a job, and members of other religions could legally be excluded. This is not nearly as large a loophole as it seems to be.

In the case of *Diaz v Pan American Airways*, a federal appeals court interpreted the BFOQ being "reasonably necessary to the normal operation of a particular employer" to mean that the BFOQ must be at the very essence of the business.[56] In other words, the very essence of the business is threatened by not hiring members of one specific class. In *Diaz*, a male filed an EEOC complaint alleging sex discrimination on the grounds that Pan American Airlines would only hire female applicants for the position of flight attendant (at that time they were still called stewardesses). The complaining party noted that the principal function of the airline was to safely transport passengers from one airport to another. Any function not directly tied to passenger safety while in flight is not part of the essence of the business. Even if passengers preferred female attendants, so long as men can perform safely and efficiently the duties of a flight attendant, the men should not be excluded.[57]

In determining whether or not a BFOQ based on sex, religion, or national origin can be used, two criteria should be considered. First, the essence of the business operation would be undermined by not hiring members of one protected class. Second, there is a factual basis for believing that all, or substantially all, members of the protected class in question cannot perform the principal duties of the job. In *Dothard v Rawlinson*, the Supreme Court stated that sex discrimination is only valid when the essence of the business operation would be undermined if the practice was eliminated.[58]

In one case, a psychiatric hospital specializing in treating sexually abused adolescents was permitted to discriminate on the basis of sex in making shift assignments because some of the patients responded better to female staff than to male staff.[59] Similarly, a county jail was able to use a BFOQ defense in assigning a female jailer to the 12 A.M. to 8 A.M. shift because of a regulation requiring a female jailer be present at all times when female prisoners are incarcerated.[60]

For another example of a situation under which a BFOQ would be upheld, consider a meat packing plant that excludes all non-Jews from its Kosher foods processing unit. Under a religious BFOQ, it is permissible because foods that are marketed as Kosher must meet strict preparation standards, and the preparation is further tied to a religious ritual that must be performed by a member of the Jewish faith. Therefore, no non-Jew may even assist in the preparation of meat marketed "Kosher." Other common instances in which BFOQs are permitted are situations requiring female models or male actors.

BFOQs have also been permitted by the courts on the grounds of safety to others. Such was the case in *Dothard v Rawlinson*,[61] where a female applicant sued the State of Alabama because she was denied a position as a guard in male maximum security facility. The Supreme Court ruled that discriminating on the basis of sex was a BFOQ because "the likelihood that inmates would assault a woman because she was a woman would pose a real threat not only to the victim of the assault but also to the basic control of the penitentiary and protection of its inmates and other security personnel."[62]

However, the courts have been consistent in excluding customer preferences from the determination of "essence of the business."[63] If, for example, customers prefer female flight attendants to male ones, this preference would not establish a BFOQ based on sex. In a similar vein, coworkers' preferences have also been excluded as a legitimate criterion for determining BFOQs.[64] Because BFOQs are so narrowly applied, they are rarely used to justify employer decisions challenged under disparate treatment theory. By far the most commonly used disparate treatment defense is legitimate nondiscriminatory reasons.

Legitimate Nondiscriminatory Reasons. Offering a **legitimate nondiscriminatory reason** means the employer contends that the decision to hire, fire, promote, or lay off any employee was based on sound business rationale and not the individual's protected class status. In the absence of evidence that the employer's actions were the result of purely business motives, it will be assumed that the employer acted with discriminatory intent.[65] Because disparate treatment is intentional discrimination, the employer must establish that there was no intention to discriminate. The employer does so by proving the employment decision was based on sound business rationale. Some examples of legitimate nondiscriminatory reasons are found in Exhibit 2-9.

Examining the opening scenario again, the board of education deprived itself of the legitimate nondiscriminatory reason defense because it openly stated its employment decision was exclusively based on race. One teacher was laid off because of her race; the other was retained because of her race. No legitimate nondiscriminatory reason was considered in making the layoff decision. As a result, Title VII was clearly violated by the board's unlawful consideration of the employee's race.[66]

To illustrate this point, consider the case involving an African American employee who was temporarily promoted to a senior operator's position but was later terminated by the employer. The employee alleges racial discrimination. In its rebuttal, the employer states that the termination of the employee was based on a violation of company policy and poor job performance while assuming the

■ **EXHIBIT 2-9**

LEGITIMATE NONDISCRIMINATORY DEFENSES USED TO JUSTIFY
PROMOTIONS, RAISES, LAYOFFS, AND TERMINATIONS

Bona Fide Seniority Systems

To be defensible, the seniority system must be consistently applied to all affected employees, and it was not adopted for discriminatory purposes.

Merit

To be defensible, the merit must be based on objective performance, not subjective criteria.

Quality of Production

To be defensible, the quality must be based on clearly defined, measurable, and disseminated standards.

Quantity of Production

To be defensible, the quantity must be based on clearly defined, measurable, and disseminated standards.

Job-Related Experience

To be defensible, the experience should enhance job performance.

Job-Related Training

To be defensible, the training should be applicable to the incumbent's current job or a future job.

Job-Related Education

To be defensible, the education should be applicable to the incumbent's current job or a future job.

SOURCE: U.S. Equal Employment Opportunity Commission (1995). *Theories of Discrimination: Intentional and Unintentional Discrimination*. Washington, DC: Government Printing Office, pp. A22-A24.

responsibilities of senior operator.[67] The company claimed that two instances of violating work policies and the complaining party's poor performance were legitimate nondiscriminatory reasons for terminating the complaining party. The reason for the employment decision was not the complaining party's race but rather his workplace behavior. To add credence to this point, the employer was able to produce three written reprimands bringing the complaining party's performance deficiencies to his attention.

Same Actor Defense. A rather recent and emerging employer defense in disparate treatment cases is the so-called "same actor defense." Though not accepted in all federal circuits, it has gained acceptance in at least the Fourth, Sixth, Seventh, and Eighth Circuits. The same actor defense is predicated on the inference that there can be no discriminating intent when the manager who fired the employee was the same person (same actor) who hired the employee. The logic is as follows: If the manager who fired the employee truly wished to discriminate against that individual, then the manager would not have hired the individual in the first place.[68]

Thus far, the same actor defense has been applied to discrimination on the basis of sex,[69] race,[70] and age.[71] Yet same actor defenses might be susceptible to challenges on several grounds. In the case of older employees, organizational culture may have changed and become less tolerant of older employees.[72] Additionally, it could be argued that the decision maker hired the protected group member unwillingly due to legal obligations (i.e., to fulfill affirmative action goals).[73]

COMPLAINING PARTY'S REBUTTAL. If the respondent has successfully rebutted the *prima facie* case, the complaining party is afforded one more opportunity to demonstrate that intentional discrimination has occurred. The complaining party can still win the case if he or she can prove that the employer's legitimate nondiscriminatory reason is merely a pretext.[74] *Pretext* means the employer has tried to hide its unlawful discrimination by fabricating an apparently legitimate justification for its actions. There are several means by which a complaining party can demonstrate pretext.[75] For example, in an employee termination case, the employer insists that the action was legitimate based on written reprimands given to the employee. After all, what could be a more nondiscriminatory reason for firing an employee than misconduct? Now suppose that the complaining party could prove that the reprimands were constructed after the fact. That is, the documents were fabricated to make the employer's action appear legitimate, but they had never been administered to the complaining party at all.[76]

An employer's legitimate nondiscriminatory reason is pretextual if it is knowingly false. A less delicate way of putting this is that the employer is caught in a lie. The complaining party may be able to establish a pretext by effectively demonstrating that similarly situated employees of a different class were treated differently than the complaining party. For example, the employer contends that the complaining party was not hired for a position in question because she did not have a college degree, yet three of the last four male candidates hired for the job did not have a college degree either.

Pretext may be shown further by evidence of employer bias. This may come from overheard conversations that a particular manager has openly stated that he does not believe that women can be good managers.[77]

Though usually associated with disparate impact litigation, statistical evidence may be used in establishing pretext. The complaining party may be able to produce workplace statistics that show that the employer's alleged nondiscriminatory criteria have not been applied equally to all employees. Statistical evidence also may be used to indicate that an employer has an established pattern of treating other members of the complaining party's protected class unfairly.

It is very important for managers to note that statistical evidence can be a double-edged sword in disparate impact cases. If workplace statistics can be used to imply a pattern of discrimination by the complaining party, they also can be used by the employer to imply that the organization's motives are nondiscriminatory. Though statistics showing a racially balanced workforce (or even employment of a disproportionately high percentage of protected class employees) are insufficient to conclusively show that an employer's actions are not discriminatory, courts may take the organization's workforce composition into consideration.[78]

The complaining party would likely win the case if it can be shown that employees of other races who had just as many reprimands (or more) were not terminated. In short, the complaining party would have to show that he or she was treated differently than similarly situated employees of other races.[79] It is, therefore, important for employers to ensure that disciplinary actions are administered consistently throughout the organization.

If there was evidence that the employer had a record or history of racially discriminatory practices, the complaining party could make an argument that this most recent instance was racially motivated. The evidence of employer bias, in some instances, could indicate that the articulated legitimate nondiscriminatory reasons are pretextual. This would be especially true under circumstances in which a concurrent EEO investigation of another practice (i.e., hiring practices) was found to be intentional discrimination.

REMEDIES UNDER DISPARATE TREATMENT

A *remedy*, in a legal sense, is the means by which a court prevents the violation of a legal right, or compensates for the violation of that right.[80] In a trial, if it has been determined that an employer has in fact failed to comply with Title VII, the court may impose a penalty on the employer for violating the complaining party's rights. As mentioned previously, the federal district courts are responsible for framing remedies for Title VII violations, and the Act provides them with a broad range of remedies (see Exhibit 2-10) depending on the magnitude of the offense and the nature of the employer's conduct.

At a minimum, the complaining party that wins a case may expect injunctive relief. **Injunctive relief** merely means that the court will order the employer to cease and desist unlawful practices. The court is ordering the employer to

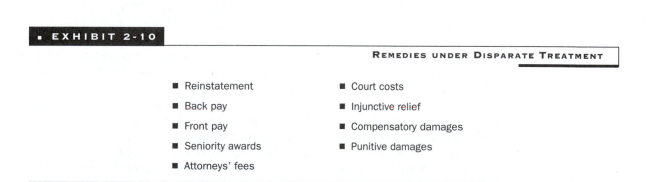

■ **EXHIBIT 2-10**

REMEDIES UNDER DISPARATE TREATMENT

- Reinstatement
- Back pay
- Front pay
- Seniority awards
- Attorneys' fees
- Court costs
- Injunctive relief
- Compensatory damages
- Punitive damages

immediately stop violating Title VII. Any future discrimination on the part of the employer would not only be another Title VII violation but also becomes contempt of court.

The court may further order the employer to *reinstate* the complaining party. In cases of employees who were wrongfully fired, this means that they will get their jobs back. An employee who was unlawfully denied a promotion could now be promoted. An applicant who was denied employment because of discrimination could now be hired.

Reinstatement is not necessarily immediate. Sometimes the complaining party must wait for a vacancy to become available before he or she is reinstated. Trials can take a long time from initiation to conclusion. Employment law violations are rarely resolved in less than two years; often, it takes longer. Additionally, employers are not required to fire existing employees to create vacancies for aggrieved employees.

Assume that a less qualified applicant was hired and has done an exceptional job for the company as a programmer/analyst. Should that employee now be fired because his employer, not the employee, discriminated against the complaining party? A court is unlikely to require the company to fire the new hire, or any other employee for that matter, in order to create a job for the complaining party. The complaining party may have to wait until a new programmer/analyst position is created or an existing one becomes vacant.

This does not necessarily mean that after winning the case the complaining party will be left out in the cold for an unspecified period of time. District courts may also award back pay or front pay. A *back pay* award would mean that the complaining party is entitled to wages (plus interest) that accrue from the time the discrimination first occurs. To demonstrate how this award is imposed, assume a complaining party was wrongfully terminated on January 1, 2001, and immediately files a charge on January 2, 2001. Assume the employee is extremely lucky and the case is tried and concluded by August 29, 2001. Further assume the court's remedies were reinstatement and back pay. Because there is a current vacancy, the employer reinstates the complaining party on September 1, 2001. The complaining party would also be entitled to eight months of back pay, plus interest, to compensate him or her for the period January 1, 2001, to September 1, 2001, the period during which the complaining party was wrongfully unemployed.

Front pay would be used under circumstances in which the complaining party is ordered to be reinstated, but no position is currently vacant. The complaining party is awarded pay and benefits until she is reinstated.[81] This means that the complaining party would be compensated from the date that the company initially discriminated against him or her through the time he or she is finally officially employed by the company. Paying wages and benefits to an individual who is not actually working creates a tremendous incentive to get that individual in the company's workforce to get some return from the pay.

In certain cases, one party may be required to pay the attorneys' fees for the other.[82] Title VII permits a federal court, at its discretion, to award the prevailing party reasonable attorneys' and experts' fees.[83] In practice, employers are far more likely to be required to pay these fees when the complaining party prevails than when the opposite occurs.

Some courts have ordered complaining parties to pay for their employer's attorneys' fees and court costs when the complaining party's allegations were proven false and knowingly groundless.[84] In short, employees who make false claims about discrimination by employers are susceptible to the same penalties as employers who make false claims of not discriminating against employees. At least for attorneys' fees and court costs, either party may be held liable if they are caught lying or openly trying to circumvent justice.

COMPENSATORY AND PUNITIVE DAMAGES. In instances where the employer's conduct has been particularly irresponsible, the court may award compensatory or punitive damages. The legal standard the complaining party must establish is that the employer engaged in its discriminatory practices "with malice or with reckless indifference to the federally protected rights of [the complaining party]."[85] To achieve this, the complaining party must show that the employer was aware of the obligation not to discriminate against the complaining party and engaged in the discriminating action anyway. Since disparate treatment is, by definition, intentional discrimination (knowingly discriminating against any employee or applicant because of the individual's race, color, religion, sex, or national origin), there is an inherent risk of incurring compensatory or punitive damages. It should be further noted that compensatory and punitive damages are restricted to cases involving disparate treatment. Compensatory and punitive damages *cannot* be awarded in cases involving disparate impact.[86] Furthermore, even in instances of *disparate treatment,* compensatory and punitive damages cannot be awarded if the employer is a government agency or political subdivision.

Compensatory damages are those imposed by a court to "compensate" the complaining party for monetary and nonmonetary harm suffered as a result of the discrimination.[87] Suppose that, as a result of a wrongful termination, an employee not only loses his paycheck, but his house (which is sold at a loss) and his car. Among the damages that the court can award are money to compensate the complaining party for these losses. An attempt will be made to make the complaining party "whole" (this is legalese for returning the employee to the condition in which he or she was before the harm occurred). Usually, the employer will be required to compensate the employee for any lost principal on property. In certain instances, monetary awards may be imposed for nonmonetary harm like emotional distress. The underlying premise is that the monetary award is imposed to compensate the victim of the employer's unlawful actions.

Punitive damages may also be awarded to the complaining party, but these remedies are not intended to compensate the complaining party for any harm the complaining party suffered. As the name implies, **punitive damages** are imposed to punish. Punitive damages are imposed as a painful reminder to an employer of the consequences of blatantly violating Title VII. The rationale behind imposing punitive damages under Title VII is to discourage employers from knowingly violating the Act in the future.

■ EXHIBIT 2-11

MAXIMUM AWARDS FOR COMPENSATORY AND PUNITIVE DAMAGES

Size of Employer's Workforce	Maximum Combined Compensatory and Punitive Damages per Complaining Party
15–200	$50,000
201–300	$100,000
301–500	$200,000
> 500	$300,000

SOURCE: 29 U.S.C. § 1981a.

Whenever compensatory or punitive damages are imposed, they are limited by a ceiling established in the Civil Rights Act of 1991. The ceilings (maximum amount that can be imposed) are based on the number of workers an employer employs in four predetermined ranges (see Exhibit 2-11). These ceilings are the maximum monetary awards that federal judges may impose for compensatory *and* punitive damages for *each* aggrieved party.

To demonstrate how this works, assume that a company which employs sixty-three workers has been found to have intentionally violated Title VII by terminating two employees because of their national origin. Based on the evidence, the judge has decided that the employer's actions violated Title VII and were callous enough to justify compensatory and punitive damages. The judge may award any amount up to $50,000 in damages to each of the two employees. The judge also has the discretion to award different amounts to each party (i.e., $50,000 to one worker and $25,000 to the other). The maximum penalty that the employer could face is $100,000 if the judge determined that both employees could be entitled individually to the maximum penalty. If the employer had one hundred sixty-three employees, then the highest potential penalty would be $200,000 because each aggrieved employee could be awarded individually the $100,000 maximum by the court.

Sometimes newspaper stories report multimillion dollar compensatory or punitive damages awarded by juries. For example, an Iowa jury awarded a female employee of United Parcel Service (UPS) $500,000 in compensatory damages and $80.7 million in punitive damages.[88] Such awards are often misleading if the charge, as it was in this case, was exclusively a Title VII violation. The maximum amount that can be awarded by a court for such a violation is $300,000.[89] It is a peculiarity of the system that when a jury is requested to hear a Title VII case, the court is required not to inform the jury of the limitations of the compensatory and punitive damages.[90] Because of this oddity, juries may award substantial damage awards which the judges must then reduce to the maximum limits shown in Exhibit 2-11.

. EXHIBIT 2-12

SOME OF THE ORGANIZATIONS AUTHORIZED TO SPONSOR TESTERS

- Fair Employment Council of Greater Washington, Inc.
- National Association for the Advancement of Colored People
- The Urban Institute

THE LEGAL STANDING OF TESTERS

Testers are individuals who apply for positions of employment for the sole purpose of determining whether a "tested" employer is engaging in discriminatory hiring practices. If offered the position in question, the tester has no intention of accepting it.

Testers are normally paired; usually a protected group tester is paired with a control tester. The testers provide information on their individual employment applications that would make them equally qualified. There may even be several sets of testers used against a given employer to reduce the defense of an individual fluke, oversight, or personality conflict.[91] Conventionally, the protected group tester will apply for a position first and, if rejected, will be followed by the control applicant. If that applicant is treated differently during the interview, the organization that sponsored the testers may file suit.

The EEOC has accepted charges filed by testers since November 20, 1990.[92] More recently, the EEOC has concluded that tester evidence tends to show a pattern or practice of discrimination and can establish Title VII violations. However, since testers do not intend to take the jobs for which they are applying, they *are not* entitled to reinstatement and back pay.[93] They are, however, entitled to injunctive relief. That is to say, the court will order the employer who discriminated against the tester to cease the discriminatory practice.

Interestingly, the civil rights organizations that send out employment testers may be eligible for compensatory damages. To qualify for this remedy, the organization must be able to show that it diverted resources from other programs to sponsor the testers. In *Fair Employment Council v Molovinsky*, the Fair Employment Council of Greater Washington received $79,000 in compensatory and punitive damages under such circumstances.[94] Organizations that sponsor testers are listed in Exhibit 2-12.

HR PROFESSIONALS AND DISPARATE TREATMENT

To reduce the risk of disparate treatment claims against employers, HR professionals have a great deal of preparation ahead of them. It is imperative that a complete and thorough job analysis has been conducted on every position in the organization. Job analysis is a time-consuming and often boring task to perform. However, no single HR function is as critical as job analysis when it comes to justifying and defending a firm's hiring, promotion, and discharge practices.[95]

From proper job analysis, HR professionals should be able to develop three important bases for making future employment decisions: job descriptions, job specifications, and performance standards.

Job descriptions are the tasks, duties, and responsibilities of the job in question. Job analysis will identify those tasks and duties that are the essence of the job and those that are peripheral to it. These distinctions will be particularly important if the HR professional has to establish a BFOQ, determine job relatedness under disparate impact analysis, or assess qualifications under the Americans with Disabilities Act.

Job specifications are the knowledge, skills, and abilities that an employee or applicant must possess in order to adequately perform the job in question. Most often, job specifications are expressed in advertisements for job vacancies. They often address such issues as education, experience, skills certification, and demonstrated proficiency. Sound job analysis should ensure that job specifications match the job descriptions. After all, it would make no more sense to require a forklift operator to have a B.S. in Transportation Management than to expect a candidate with a GED to be qualified as a programmer/analyst. Improperly formulated job specifications expose the employer to challenges as to which candidate was truly qualified for the job. Though job specifications are very important in disparate analysis because they are used to ascertain the degree of qualification of each candidate, they are absolutely critical for disparate impact analysis. As will be seen in the next chapter, disparate impact analysis concentrates heavily on minimum job qualifications.

Performance standards are the minimum levels of activity and output that a job incumbent must attain if the essential tasks and duties of the job are to be accomplished. Any level of performance that falls below the performance standard simply means that the job is not being done properly. Performance standards establish the basis for any organization's performance appraisal system. Individual employee performance evaluations form the basis for many employment decisions such as promotions, work assignments, layoffs, transfers, discipline, and discharges. If performance standards have been properly constructed, they can be used to challenge employment decisions as being based on legitimate nondiscriminatory rationale. However, arbitrary or inconsistently imposed performance standards offer the employer no protection at all.

After ensuring that job descriptions, job specifications, and performance standards are all based on sound job analysis, the HR professional should then develop policies to ensure that all future employment decisions are predicated on sound business reasons. This not only involves establishing uniform organizational selection procedures but also encompasses making every decision maker aware of the policy or procedure. It does not benefit an organization to have a well-crafted personnel policy if that policy is thrown in a file cabinet or desk drawer and never put into practice. For any company policy to be effective, it must be fully disseminated to all affected personnel. Furthermore, such policies should have the support of upper-level management, and this support should be advertised through the organization.

Finally, after all employment practices have been implemented, HR professionals and managers should continually review these policies. Here, there are two concerns, one internal and the other external. Internally, managers and HR professionals should constantly review all actions and decisions arising from the company policies to ensure that those policies are being followed. Some companies get into trouble, not because they did not have a policy to cover a particular Title VII issue (i.e., sexual harassment), but because they ignored their own policy.[96] Internal monitoring would reduce the likelihood of such occurrences.

The external concerns involve the ever-changing nature of employment discrimination laws. Either through the enactment of new civil rights legislation, or, as more often is the case, through federal court decisions or new EEOC regulations, company policies and practices can become obsolete. It is the responsibility of both managers and HR professionals to become aware of these changes and their impact on company operations. When necessary, new policies must be formulated and old ones updated. Again, disseminating these changes becomes critical if the organization is to avoid unnecessary complaints and disruptions.

SUMMARY

This chapter provides a historical overview of equal employment opportunity. Particular attention is given to the Civil Rights Act of 1964's Title VII. The Civil Rights Act was enacted to ensure that employers and managers did not take any individual's race, color, religion, sex, or national origin into consideration when making an employment decision. Title VII is the foundation for most of the laws and regulations related to equal employment opportunity.

Employees who feel they have been discriminated against in employment or workplace decisions may file a complaint with the EEOC or FEPA. There is an established process for handling such complaints, and it is discussed in the chapter.

There are two basic theories of unlawful discrimination under Title VII: disparate treatment and disparate impact. Disparate treatment results from treating individuals differently because of membership in a protected class. Disparate impact focuses on statistical imbalances in the workforce. Disparate treatment theory is discussed in detail in this chapter, and disparate impact theory will be discussed in Chapter 3.

To reduce the risk of disparate treatment claims, HR professional must conduct a thorough job analysis of every position in the organization. Job descriptions, job specifications, and performance standards are the result of proper job analysis.

The members of the protected classes under Title VII have a reasonable expectation of fair (or equal) treatment in the workplace. Employers are expected to provide a workplace that is free from unlawful discrimination, and the federal government has established sufficient disincentives for not meeting this expectation in the form of injunctions, back pay, reinstatement, attorneys' fees, court costs, compensatory damages, and punitive damages. To avoid these legal pitfalls, it is becoming increasingly important for organizations to understand what employment actions and decisions expose them to these penalties and develop employment policies and practices that eliminate potentially unlawful decisions. It is important that managers fully understand how disparate treatment can occur in the workplace and ensure that only legitimate nondiscriminatory reasons are ever used in justifying any employment decision.

KEY TERMS AND CONCEPTS

bona fide occupational qualification (BFOQ)

compensatory damages

conciliation

dismissal

disparate impact

disparate treatment

fair employment practices agencies (FEPAs)

injunctive relief

Jim Crow laws

job descriptions

job specifications

legitimate nondiscriminatory reason

no cause

notice of right to sue

performance standards

prima facie case

protected class

punitive damages

reasonable cause

remand

respondent

testers

Title VII

vacates

QUESTIONS

1. Why was the Civil Rights Act of 1964 enacted? Who is protected under the Act?

2. What are the protected classes under Title VII of the Civil Rights Act of 1964?

3. Discuss the two theories of unlawful discrimination under Title VII.

4. What are the legal proofs required to establish a *prima facie* case for disparate treatment under Title VII?

5. What must an employer prove to rebut the complaining party's *prima facie* case of disparate treatment?

6. How can a complaining party show that an employer's legitimate nondiscriminatory reasons are pretextual?

7. What are the remedies that a federal court may impose for disparate treatment?

8. What is job analysis, and what results from this process? How are these outcomes used by HR professionals?

CASES

1 A company is hiring a director of computer technology. The advertisement stresses a degree in computer engineering and at least two years experience in computer software development. Mark has a degree in civil engineering and has four years experience with the Texas Department of Transportation. He is immediately rejected from consideration and claims discrimination based on national origin. Assuming the specifications for the position are accurate, is Mark qualified for the job?

Another applicant, Fernando, applies for the same position. He has a computer engineering degree from the University of Missouri and has worked since graduation (one year) as a computer programmer for his wife's small software applications company. Is he qualified?

Finally, there is Jerri Lynn, an African American. She has a degree in computer engineering from Texas A&M University and has worked for the past five years for the software development department of Pathway Computers, a large computer manufacturer on the west coast. Is she qualified?

Assume that Jerri Lynn was not hired, but instead the job was offered to Mark. Is there any indication that Title VII was violated? Did Jerri Lynn meet the qualifications? Was she rejected? Was the position filled by someone with fewer qualifications than Jerri Lynn? Was Mark's degree appropriate for the job? Was his work experience with the department of transportation compatible with the experience requirement?

2 Kelly was hired as a broker by Lone Star Mutual, an established conservative stock brokerage firm located in downtown Dallas. During her job interview, Kelly was a model of conservatism, wearing little makeup and a navy business suit. Her degree in finance from the Darden School at Virginia and prior work experience were rated as excellent. According to the interviewer, Kelly appeared to be the perfect fit for the job. She was given a job offer on the spot. Four working days later, she arrived at work in designer jeans and a tight-fitting velour halter top with a Trans AM logo on it. It was obvious to everyone that she was wearing nothing underneath the halter top. Her supervisor, Greg Rose, told Kelly to go home immediately and change into something "more appropriate." He further informed her that all Lone Star employees were expected to wear appropriate business attire while at work as stated in the employee handbook. Kelly refused Greg's request, claiming this rule restricted her right to equal protection under the laws and feminine self-expression. Based on this refusal, Rose promptly fired Kelly. Kelly immediately filed an EEO complaint claiming sex discrimination. Under what circumstances would Kelly win her case? Under what circumstances would she lose her case?

3 As an Activity Therapist Coordinator, Raymond Rayburn organizes and supervises recreational activities for patients at the Rosey Fink Mental Health Center, a facility operated by the Illinois Department of Human Services (IDHS).

He has worked at the Health Center since 1993, and has been employed by the IDHS since 1980. For many years, Rayburn has organized a luncheon at the Health Center to recognize Black History Month.

Rayburn's long career at the Health Center hit a bump in the road in the spring of 1998. On February 5, Rayburn complained in writing to William Thomas, EEO officer for the IDHS, that he was being discriminated against and harassed. His letter detailed various perceived injustices and reported a lack of coordination between Health Center employees, including Rayburn's direct supervisor Umberto Duenos. The letter uses the word "discrimination" twice, but gives no hint that Rayburn is complaining about racial, gender-based, or any other form of legally prohibited discrimination. Rather, Rayburn seems to be complaining simply that he felt that he was being singled out for unfair treatment as compared with coworkers.

On February 25, planning for the Black History Month luncheon went poorly, and some last minute scrambling was required. On February 26, Rayburn apparently abandoned his assigned work area in order to attend a staff training session for which he had not signed up in advance. And on March 4, a coworker complained that Rayburn had been playing basketball with staff from the Engineering Department while a nude patient he was supposed to be supervising wandered off down a hallway.

Rayburn responded to these alleged infractions by claiming that either he did nothing wrong or he was disciplined more harshly than his white coworkers. He claims that Alvin Bush was responsible for compiling a list of Black History Month diners and failed to do so. Rayburn alleges that Activity Therapist Kathy Bennett abandoned her assigned work area on the very same day, February 26, on which he was accused of doing so. Furthermore, he argues that he attended the staff training session during his lunch break and that he was not required to notify his supervisor when he was taking lunch. Ultimately, Rayburn charges that other activity therapists let down their guards while supervising nude patients. It is undisputed that all of these coworkers are white and that none of them were disciplined.

The Health Center notes in response that while Alvin Bush did indeed fail to provide Rayburn with a list, Rayburn had overall responsibility to organize the Black History luncheon. Rayburn delegated the task of making a list to Bush but never followed up. With regard to Kathy Bennett, the Health Center points out that Rayburn cannot show that Bennett abandoned her work area. Unquestionably, Rayburn attended classes without notifying his supervisor and without arranging for a replacement to cover his assigned work area. And the "nude patient" claim is met with the response that Rayburn was disciplined for failing to keep the patient in view at all times.

Duenos, Rayburn's supervisor, investigated all three incidents and decided to discipline Rayburn. Duenos does not supervise Bush or Bennett, but it is undisputed that he has never suspended anyone other than Rayburn. Accordingly, Rayburn was suspended from April 7 to April 14. Rayburn complained to the

Illinois Department of Human Rights on April 13 and received a notice of right to sue. Rayburn alleges that the suspension constituted intentional racial discrimination and retaliation. Is he correct? If so, why? If not, why not?

SOURCE: *Thompson v John J. Madden Mental Health Ctr.*, 2000 U.S. Dist. *LEXIS* 17719 (E.D. Ill. 2000).

NOTES

1. *Taxman v Board of Education of the Township of Piscataway*, 91F.3d 1547, 1551–52 (3rd Cir. 1996).

2. Hummed, J. R. (1996). *Emancipating Slaves, Enslaving Free Men.* Chicago, IL: Open Court, p. 298.

3. Cox, L. and Cox, J. H. (1973). *Reconstruction, the Negro, and the New South.* Columbia, SC: University of South Carolina Press, pp. 211–248.

4. Foner, E. (1988). *Reconstruction: America's Unfinished Revolution, 1863–1877.* New York: Harper & Row, p. 222.

5. 42 U.S.C. § 1982.

6. *Carter v Gallagher*, 452 F.2d.315 (8th Cir. 1971).

7. *Runyon v McCary*, 427 U.S. 160 (1976).

8. U.S. Constitution, Amendment. XIV, § 1.

9. *Plessy v Ferguson*, 163 U.S. 537 (1898).

10. Ibid. (Harlan dissenting) at 559.

11. 347 U.S. 483 (1954).

12. Executive Order 10309 (1951); Executive Order 10590 (1955); Executive Order 10925 (1961).

13. 42 U.S.C. § 2000e-2(a).

14. 110 Cong. Rec., p. 6423.

15. 427 U.S. 273 (1976).

16. *McDonald v Santa Fe Transportation Co.*, 427 U.S. 273, 283–284 (1976).

17. 42 U.S.C. § 2000e(b).

18. Public Law 102–166 § 117(b).

19. 5 U.S.C. § 7201.

20. 42 U.S.C. § 2000e(f).

21. 42 U.S.C. § 2000e-1(a).

22. 42 U.S.C. § 2000e(f).

23. 42 U.S.C. § 2000e-2(f).

24. 42 U.S.C. § 2000e(1).

25. 29 C.F.R. § 1603.102.

26. U.S. Equal Employment Opportunity Commission (June 10, 1997). Filing a charge. **http://eeoc.gov/facts/howtofil.html**

27. 29 C.F.R. § 1601.13.

28. 42 U.S.C. § 2000e-5.

29. 29 C.F.R. § 1601.19.

30. 29 C.F.R. § 1601.28.

31. 29 C.F.R. § 1601.19(a).

32. 29 C.F.R. § 1603.107.

33. Ibid.

34. 29 C.F.R. § 1601.21.

35. 29 C.F.R. § 1601.20.

36. 29 C.F.R. § 1601.27.

37. Black, H. C. (1990). *Black's Law Dictionary*. St. Paul, MN: West Publishing Co., p. 1099.

38. 42 U.S.C. § 1981a.

39. Black, p. 1548.

40. *Carmon v Lubrizol Corp.*, 17 F.3d 791, 795 (5th Cir. 1994).

41. 28 U.S.C. § 1927.

42. Federal Rule of Appellate Procedure 38.

43. 42 U.S.C. § 1988.

44. *Pacific Dunlop Holdings, Inc. v Barosh*, 22 F.3d 113 (7th Cir. 1994).

45. 42 U.S.C. § 2000e(n).

46. *McDonnell Douglas Corp. v Green*, 411 U.S. 792, 802 (1973).

47. *De Santis v Pacific Telephone & Telegraph*, 608 F.2d 327 (9th Cir. 1979); *Holloway v Arthur Andersen & Co.*, 566 F.2d 659, 662–63 (9th Cir. 1977).

48. *American Tobacco Co. v Patterson*, 456 U. S. 63 (1982); *Pullman-Standard v Swint*, 456 U.S. 273 (1982).

49. *Griggs v Duke Power Co.*, 401 U.S. 424, 430–431 (1971).

50. *Johnson v Transportation Agency of Santa Clara County*, 480 U.S. 616, 638-639 (1987).

51. *Oncale v Sundowner Offshore Services, Inc.*, 523 U.S. 75, 80 (1998).

52. 42 U.S.C. § 2000e-2(b).

53. *Malhorta v Cotter & Co.*, 885 F.2d 1305 (7th Cir. 1989).

54. 42 U.S.C. § 2000e-2(e)(1).

55. 29 C.F.R. § 1625.6.

56. 422 F.2d 385, 388 (5th Cir.1971).

57. *Wilson v Southwest Airlines*, 517 F. Supp. 292 (N.D. Tex. 1981).

58. 433 U.S. 321, 332 (1977).

59. *Healey v Southwood Psychiatric Hospital*, 78 F.3d 128, 132–133 (3rd Cir. 1996).

60. *Reed v County of Casey*, 184 F.3d 597, 599 (6th Cir. 1999).

61. 433 U.S. 321 (1977).

62. Ibid. at 336.

63. *EEOC v Sedita,* 816 F Supp. 1291 (N.D. Ill. 1993).

64. *Vigars v Valley Christian Center,* 805 F. Supp. 802 (N.D. Cal. 1992).

65. *International Brotherhood of Teamsters v U.S.,* 431 U.S. 324 (1977).

66. *Taxman,* 91 F.3d at 1567.

67. *Brown v Stone Container Corp.,* 967 F. Supp. 1297, 1300 (S.D.Ga. 1997).

68. *Buhrmaster v Overnite Transportation Co.,* 61 F.3d 461, 463 (6th Cir. 1995); *Rand v C.F. Industries, Inc.,* 42 F.3d 1139, 1147 (7th Cir. 1994).

69. Ibid.

70. *EEOC v Our Lady of the Resurrection Medical Center,* 77 F.3d 145, 152 (7th Cir.1996).

71. *Proud v Stone,* 945 F.2d 796 (4th Cir. 1991); *Lowe v J.B. Hunt Transportation, Inc.* 963 F.2d 173 (8th Cir. 1992).

72. Mollica, P. (1997). Employment discrimination cases in the seventh circuit. *Employee Rights and Employment Policy Journal,* 1:63–111, n. 249.

73. Northup, J. (1998). The "same actor inference" in employment discrimination: Cheap justice. *Washington Law Review,* 73 (1): 212.

74. *St. Mary's Honor Center v Hicks,* 509 U.S. 502, 509–10 (1993).

75. U.S. Equal Employment Opportunity Commission (May 1995). *Theories of Discrimination: International and Unintentional Discrimination.* Washington, DC: Government Printing Office, p. A-4.

76. *Azar v TGI Friday's Inc.,* 945 F. Supp. 485 (E.D. N.Y. 1996).

77. U.S. EEOC. *Theories of Discrimination,* p. A-5.

78. *Furnco Construction Corp. v Waters,* 438 U.S. 567, 578 (1978).

79. *Lisek v Norfolk and Western Railway Co.,* 918 F. Supp. 1202 (N.D. Ill. 1996).

80. Black, p. 1294.

81. U.S. EEOC. *Theories of Discrimination,* p. A-2.

82. 42 U.S.C. § 1988.

83. 42 U.S.C. § 2000e-5(k).

84. *Kahre-Richardes Family Foundation v Baldwinsville,* 953 F. Supp. 39 (N.D. N.Y. 1997); *Christiansburg Garment Co. v EEOC,* 434 U.S. 412 (1978).

85. 42 U.S.C. § 1981(b).

86. Ibid. at § 1981(a)(1).

87. U.S. EEOC. *Theories of Discrimination,* p. A-5.

88. Jury awards woman $80.7 million in suit against UPS (February 12, 1998).*CNN Interactive.* **http://127.0.01:15841/v1?catid = 14680067&md5 = 6d78095c230438740574133b49121c92**

89. 42 U.S.C. § 1981(b)(3)(D).

90. Ibid. at § 1981(c)(2).

91. EEOC Notice No. 915.062 at 2 (November 20, 1990).

92. Ibid.

93. EEOC Notice No. 915.002 (May 22, 1995).

94. Civil Action No. 91-7202 (Sup. Ct. D.C. Aug. 12, 1993).

95. Gatewood, R. D, and Field, H. S. (1998). *Human Resource Selection (4th ed.)*. Fort Worth, TX: The Dryden Press, p. 249.

96. *Hicks v Gates Rubber Company*, 833 F.2d 1406 (10th Cir. 1987); *Yates v Avco Corporation*, 819 F.2d 630 (6th Cir. 1987); *Zabkowicz v West Bend Company*, 589 F. Suppl. 78 (E. D. Wisc. 1984).

3

DISPARATE IMPACT

LEARNING OBJECTIVES

- [ ] Describe the proofs necessary to establish a *prima facie* case of disparate impact.
- [ ] Discuss challenges to allegations of disparate impact.
- [ ] Conduct applicant flow analysis using the four-fifths criterion.
- [ ] Perform workforce tests of representativeness using stock analysis.
- [ ] Explain the remedies available to complaining parties under disparate impact.
- [ ] Discuss the three methods of validating employment practices.
- [ ] Explain measures that employers may implement to reduce adverse impact.
- [ ] Explain the circumstances under which retaliation may occur.

OPENING SCENARIO

Employees of a large manufacturing company bring suit against their employer as a result of complaints about the employment selection criteria the company calls the Formalized Selection Process (the "FSP"). The FSP was administered to all candidates seeking employment as production technicians at the company's newly created Metropolitan Distribution Center. The complaining parties allege that the FSP discriminated against them on the basis of their gender and age in violation of the Civil Rights Act of 1964.

The FSP was administered to one hundred eighty-nine candidates, including internal candidates (current employees) and outside candidates (persons who never worked for the company before), as a two-phase selection device. The first phase was comprised solely of a written or "cognitive" test that focused on five subjects: (1) mechanical comprehension, (2) practical arithmetic, (3) reading comprehension, (4) forms checking, and (5) coding skills. The candidates who achieved an average-percent-correct score of 55 percent or higher passed the written test and were given the opportunity to proceed to the second *phase which consisted of both a group problem-solving exercise (GPE) and a structured interview. The group problem-solving phase tested the candidates' proficiency in five job skills: (1) work orientation, (2) ability to work with others, (3) making choices and solving problems, (4) oral communication, and (5) relevance of prior training and experience. The evaluators in the GPE phase were experienced supervisors. In order to be considered for a technician position, a candidate was required to successfully complete both the written and GPE phases of the FSP.*

Of the one hundred eighty-nine individuals (forty-four women, one hundred forty-five men; fifty-two persons forty years or older, one hundred thirty-seven persons under forty years) who participated in the FSP, one hundred thirty-one (thirty-one women, one hundred men; twenty-two persons forty years or older, one hundred nine persons under forty years) successfully completed the first phase and were permitted to participate in the second phase. Of the one hundred twenty candidates (twenty-nine women, ninety-one men; twenty persons forty years or older, one hundred persons under forty years) who participated in the second phase, nineteen candidates (three women, sixteen men; one person forty years or older, eighteen persons under forty years) were offered employment as technicians. Notice that not all of the candidates who passed the written phase chose to participate in the GPE phase.

In its rebuttal, the company contended that the differences were not statistically significant. The company had also hired an outside consulting firm specializing in job analysis and selection projects to evaluate the company's current and projected workforce needs and to develop the FSP.[1]

FROM DISPARATE TREATMENT TO DISPARATE IMPACT

From a human resource management (HRM) standpoint, Title VII compliance was relatively simple until 1971. Until that point, human resource (HR) professionals were required to ensure that none of their actions were motivated by a discriminatory intent; disparate treatment was the only actionable Title VII violation (refer to Chapter 2). Provided that the employer could prove the action was based on a legitimate, nondiscriminatory reason (and that this reason was not a pretext), the employer was usually assured of avoiding a Title VII violation.

But the view of what constituted unlawful discrimination radically changed with the advent of disparate impact. Perhaps no single statute or court decision has affected HR selection as much as disparate impact. From this point forward, HR professionals and federal regulatory agencies would become increasingly concerned with numbers. Organizations became preoccupied with achieving the "right numbers" in hiring and promotions. Human resource management entered an era in which planners were increasingly concerned with achieving the appropriate representation of women and ethnic minorities in their workforces.

Not only would the selection rates of various protected classes become paramount but so would knowledge of relevant labor markets and validation requirements. The complexities of the disparate impact theory of discrimination will now be examined.

DISPARATE IMPACT

The second theory of discrimination is **disparate impact** (sometimes called **adverse impact**), and it is responsible for the current preoccupation with proportional representation in the workplace. Unlike disparate treatment, disparate impact can be unintentional. This is a crucial difference. Remember that under disparate treatment analysis, the respondent's rebuttal hinges on proving to a court there was no intention to unlawfully discriminate against the complaining party. The employer's defense concentrates on demonstrating that the complaining party's protected class status had no impact on the final employment decision—there was no intent to discriminate. In disparate impact, it is immaterial whether the employer intended to discriminate or not; only the employment outcomes are important.

Perhaps the best way to explain how disparate impact works is to examine the Supreme Court decision that created this theory of discrimination, *Griggs v Duke Power Company*.[2]

THE GRIGGS CASE

Duke Power Company's Dan River plant was organized into five operating departments: (1) Labor, (2) Coal Handling, (3) Operations, (4) Maintenance, and (5) Laboratory and Testing. The lowest paying jobs were concentrated in the Labor Department. Prior to 1965, Duke Power Company required job applicants to possess at least a high school diploma for entry-level hiring for all departments with one exception, the Labor Department. There was no minimum education requirement for the Labor Department. The Labor Department was also the lowest paying unit in the company. Additionally, a high school diploma or its equivalent was required for transfer from this department to another. This meant that any worker transferring from the company's Labor Department jobs to the higher-paying jobs in the other departments had to have a high school diploma or a GED. Beginning in 1965, the company added an additional requirement: any employee seeking placement outside the Labor Department had to achieve a satisfactory score on two aptitude tests—the Wonderlich Personnel Test and the Bennett Mechanical Comprehension Tests. All applicants, including those requesting transfers, were required to meet these standards. Those who met the standards (high school diploma and passing aptitude test scores) were hired or transferred without regard to race, color, religion, sex, or national origin. As a result, if you were a worker in the Labor Department and wanted to get a better-paying job in Operations, you had to pass the aptitude tests, in addition to possessing a high school diploma, or you were not going anywhere.

On the surface, these new requirements appeared benign. After all, *every* applicant was evaluated against the same standards, and no one was given favorable or unfavorable treatment because of race, color, religion, sex, or national origin. However, the company's African American employees challenged these requirements on the grounds that they excluded a far greater proportion of African American applicants than they did white candidates. In fact, according to the 1960 North Carolina census, the education requirements alone would guarantee an imbalance, because 34 percent of white males had completed high school, compared to only 12 percent of African American males.[3] This problem was further compounded by the fact that, of the whites who were eligible to take the aptitude tests, 58 percent would pass. The African American candidates who were eligible to take the tests (those who had a high school diploma) had a passing rate of only 6 percent. In short, the passing rate of African American applicants was a mere 10 percent of their white counterparts. Due to this disparity, the complaining parties argued the education and testing requirements had the effect of denying job opportunities to African Americans at a far greater rate than it did whites.

Using the disparate treatment theory of discrimination, the employer argued the *same* standard had been applied to *all* applicants; hence no individual was treated differently because of his or her protected class status. Since there was no evidence of intentional discrimination, Title VII could not be violated.

Countering this claim, the African American applicants argued that even though the same standards were administered to all applicants, the standards excluded a disproportionate number of African Americans from favorable consideration because job placement was based solely on whether an applicant met them. Furthermore, not only did the diploma and test requirement exclude far more African Americans from selection, the standards did not have anything to do with the jobs from which the African Americans were being excluded. There was no connection between the diploma and test results and a person's ability to perform the specific jobs in question. Moreover, there was evidence that employees who had not taken the tests (employees who had been hired before the new standards were implemented) had performed satisfactorily in the jobs.[4] The selection requirements did not appear to be connected with successful job performance in several categories in the other departments. The Supreme Court, upon hearing the case, concluded:

> The [Civil Rights] Act proscribes not only discrimination but also practices that are fair in form. The touch-stone is business necessity. If an employment practice which operates to exclude Negroes cannot be shown to be related to job performance, the practice is prohibited.[5]

As a consequence of this ruling, disparate impact, a new actionable form of employment discrimination was created. Employers could now be found in violation of Title VII when an employment practice has the effect of adversely affecting a disproportionate number of protected group members, and that practice cannot be shown to be job related. Title VII was evolving from discrimination against individual applicants and employees to discrimination against groups. In order to reduce confusion, you should note the terms *job related* and *business necessity* are often used synonymously, as are the terms *disparate impact* and *adverse impact*.

ESTABLISHING A PRIMA FACIE CASE

Generally, to establish a *prima facie* case under disparate impact, complaining parties must first identify the specific employment practice that has caused the exclusion of applicants because of their membership in a protected group, and then offer reliable, statistical proof that the practice contributed to the exclusion[6] (see Exhibit 3-1). Since the enactment of the Civil Rights Act of 1991, it is no longer enough for complaining parties to merely identify a statistical disparity; they must link the disparity to the specific practices or procedures claimed to have caused the disparity.

This is precisely what occurred in the *Griggs* case when the test scores caused African Americans to be rejected at a rate that was almost ten times greater than the rejection rate of whites. Furthermore, the diploma requirement excluded nearly three times as many African Americans as whites. As a consequence, both components of the selection process (educational requirements and test scores) would have created a disparate impact. However, where an actionable statistical imbalance begins would not be settled until seven years after the *Griggs* decision, and the most popular method for these determinations would be developed by a regulatory agency and not the courts.

Note that any facially neutral standard or criterion for a selection decision—a standard which is applied equally to all candidates—can have disparate impact if it excludes a disproportionately high number of protected class members from

---

■ **EXHIBIT 3-1**

DISPARATE IMPACT PROOFS

Prima Facie Case:

- A facially neutral employment practice has an adverse impact on a protected class (invariably demonstrated by a manifest statistical imbalance)

Respondent's Rebuttal:

- The challenged employment practice is shown to be a business necessity (it is job related)
- Challenge the complaining party's statistics

Complaining Party's Rebuttal:

- There are other practices that would accomplish the same end but have less adverse impact on the protected class

■ **EXHIBIT 3-2**

POTENTIAL SELECTION CRITERIA THAT CREATE DISPARATE IMPACT

- Height requirements
- Weight requirements
- Tests for physical strength/endurance
- Intelligence tests
- Education requirements
- Arrest records

- Conviction records
- Nature of military service/discharge
- Language proficiency
- Credit checks
- Work experience

SOURCE: Jackson, G. (1993). *Labor and Employment Law Desk Book.* Englewood Cliffs, NJ: Prentice Hall, pp. 284–285.

consideration. This places a burden on decision makers to consider the impact that any job requirement is likely to have on the demographic diversity of the applicant pool. A list of selection criteria known to have disparate impact on certain protected groups is provided in Exhibit 3-2. As will be explained shortly, disparate impact, of and by itself, is not a Title VII violation, provided that the facially neutral selection criteria can be proven essential to performing the job in question.

DETERMINING STATISTICAL IMBALANCES

There is no one way to establish statistical imbalances. Federal courts have accepted a number of different methods that demonstrate employment practices have disparate impact (see Exhibit 3-3). The method most commonly used was first developed by the Equal Employment Opportunity Commission (EEOC) in its 1978 *Uniform Guidelines for Employee Selection.*[7] Under the *Uniform Guidelines,* adverse impact is automatically assumed anytime the selection rate for any race, sex, or ethnic group is less than four-fifths (or 80 percent) of the rate for the group with the highest rate.[8] This standard for disparate impact analysis has become popularly known as the **four-fifths rule.** It is the preferred method of analysis by the EEOC and is characterized by its simplicity.

More sophisticated statistical measures have also been recognized by the courts. An employment practice may be assumed to have violated Title VII if the employment practice has a statistically significant adverse impact on members of a protected group. Adverse impact is statistically significant when the disparity between the expected result and the actual result exceeds two to three standard deviations.[9] Standard deviations are a measurement of the probability that a result is a random deviation from the predicted result. The more standard deviations, the lower the probability the result is due to chance.[10] Additionally, disparate impact has been judged to have occurred when the selection rate for a protected class falls outside of a 95 percent confidence interval.[11]

■ EXHIBIT 3-3

STATISTICAL MEASURES FOR ESTABLISHING DISPARATE IMPACT

- Two or three standard deviations
- 95 percent confidence interval
- Four-fifths rule

APPLYING THE FOUR-FIFTHS RULE

Assume ABC Manufacturing has advertised job openings in its expanding Memphis, Tennessee, plant. There are one hundred twenty-five new positions in entry-level manufacturing in the Production Department and twenty new positions for programmer analysts in the Operations Department. The entry-level manufacturing jobs require each applicant to have at least a two-year degree in industrial arts from a two-year college and to pass a hand-and-eye coordination test. Each programmer/analyst must have a bachelor's degree in Management Information Systems (MIS) or Computer Science and pass a test measuring programming skills using C++. Of the three hundred forty applicants applying for the entry-level positions, forty-eight were African American females, of which eighteen had the required degree. Of the one hundred ten African American males applying for these positions, thirty-seven had two-year degrees. There were one hundred forty-six white males and thirty-six white females who applied for the entry-level manufacturing jobs, of which eighty-one males and thirty-two females had the appropriate degrees. Of the fifty-five African Americans (eighteen females and thirty-seven males) who passed the education requirements, fifty-three (sixteen females and thirty-seven males) passed the hand-and-eye coordination test. All fifty-three were offered employment. Of the one hundred thirteen whites (thirty-two females and eighty-one males) who passed the education requirements, one hundred four (twenty-eight females and seventy-six males) passed the hand-and-eye coordination examination, of which seventy-two (twenty-eight females and forty-four males) were offered jobs at the facility. The question is, has disparate impact occurred?

The Civil Rights Act of 1991 requires that each stage of the selection process be examined separately.[12] In the case of the one hundred twenty-five entry-level manufacturing positions, the process consisted of possessing a two-year degree in industrial arts and passing a hand-and-eye coordination exam. Since this is a two-stage selection process, each stage must be analyzed separately.

In Stage I, all candidates are screened to determine if they possess the specified education requirements; those who do not are rejected automatically. Those who have two-year degrees pass the Stage I and move to Stage II. Only those who pass this stage (the manual dexterity test) will be considered for employment. A finding of disparate impact in only one of the stages will establish a _prima facie_ case. However, not even favorable treatment at the end of the process for the group suffering the disparate impact will mitigate the disparity in one stage of the selection process.

■ EXHIBIT 3-4

APPLICANTS WITH A TWO-YEAR DEGREE IN INDUSTRIAL ARTS

	African Americans		Whites		Total	
	Applied	Passed	Applied	Passed	Applied	Passed
Male	110	37	146	81	**256**	**118**
Female	48	18	36	32	**84**	**50**
Totals	**158**	**55**	**182**	**113**	**340**	**168**

Assessing disparate impact in this manner is known as applicant flow analysis. **Applicant flow analysis** examines the effect of the questioned selection criterion only on the actual candidates who applied for the position. This was the same method used to analyze the *Griggs* case. The premise is simple—the selection rate is calculated for each class of candidates (i.e., whites, African Americans, Hispanics, Asian Americans, females, males, etc.).

This selection rate is a simple calculation. The number of members of a given class who passed the criterion (i.e., had the appropriate education requirements) is divided by the total number of members of that class who applied for the job. The class that has the highest selection rate becomes the benchmark against which all other selection rates are compared.[13] To illustrate this, we can calculate the selection rate for whites for Stage I. Remember that one hundred forty-six white males and thirty-six white females applied for the entry-level positions, for a total of one hundred eighty-two white applicants (this becomes the denominator). Of those one hundred eighty-two qualifying white applicants, one hundred thirteen (eighty-one white males and thirty-two white females) met the minimum education requirements. Consequently, the selection rate for white applicants at Stage I was 62.1 percent (or 113 ÷ 182) (see Exhibit 3-4).

When disparate impact (adverse impact) is investigated on the basis of race, the male and female rates for each racial group are combined. Therefore, of the one hundred fifty-eight total African American applicants (one hundred ten males and forty-eight females), fifty-five (thirty-seven males and eighteen females) had the required education and were allowed to continue in the selection process. The other one hundred three were rejected based on this requirement. To put it another way, the selection rate of African American applicants at Stage I was 34.8 percent (55 ÷ 158). This is where the four-fifths rule will be applied using the following formula:

(Selection Rate of the Protected Class) < .8
(Selection Rate of the Group with the Highest Rate)

This is the standard established by the EEOC as the preferred means of determining disparate impact in most instances.[14]

In this example, we would conclude that disparate impact has occurred if the selection rate of the African American candidates is less than 80 percent of the selection rate of the white applicants, or:

$$0.348 < 0.8 \, (0.621)$$

$$0.348 < 0.497$$

Since the selection rate of the African American applicants (34.8 percent) *is* less than 80 percent of the selection rate of the white candidates (49.7 percent), disparate impact has occurred. Does this mean the company is in violation of Title VII? In other words, does this statistical imbalance alone violate Title VII? Not necessarily, as will be explained shortly. When an employer can prove the criterion that caused the disparate impact is a business necessity, Title VII is not violated.

Next, the second stage of the selection process, the hand-and-eye coordination test, must be evaluated. Again, because we are examining alleged racial discrimination, the male and female scores for both classes (passing versus not passing) are combined (see Exhibit 3-5).

It is important to remember that only those candidates who met the first criterion, the two-year degree, are eligible to move to second-stage consideration and take the hand-and-eye coordination test. This means that only the fifty-five African Americans who had the appropriate education were permitted to take the coordination test. Of these applicants, thirty-seven of the males and sixteen of the females (a total of fifty-three) passed the hand-and-eye coordination test. Of the one hundred thirteen whites who moved to Stage II, seventy-six of the men and twenty-eight of the women (a total of one hundred four) passed the coordination examination. Applying the four-fifths rule to Stage II of the application process, the selection rate for African Americans (96.4 percent, or fifty-three African American applicants who passed divided by fifty-five total Stage II African American applicants) will be compared to the second stage selection rate for white applicants (92 percent, or one hundred four divided by one hundred thirteen). The analysis would appear as follows:

$$0.92 < 0.8 \, (0.964)$$

$$0.92 < 0.771$$

■ EXHIBIT 3-5

APPLICANTS WHO PASSED THE COORDINATION TEST

	African Americans		Whites		Total	
	Tested	Passed	Tested	Passed	Tested	Passed
Male	37	37	81	76	**118**	**113**
Female	18	16	32	28	**50**	**44**
Totals	**55**	**53**	**113**	**104**	**168**	**157**

Note that at this stage the African Americans are the group with the highest selection rate—96.4 percent to the whites' 92 percent. However, since the 92 percent selection of white applicants *is not* less than 80 percent of the selection rate of African American candidates (77.1 percent), there is no adverse impact in the second stage of the company's selection process. This reversing or reversal of comparison groups may appear odd, but the *Uniform Guidelines* clearly states that the comparison is made against the group with the highest selection rate.[15]

Even though there was no adverse impact in Stage II, the complaining parties have established a *prima facie* case because of the adverse impact in the first stage. The most important fact to remember under disparate impact is that the *prima facie* case is established by a statistical imbalance in any stage of the selection process.[16] The second fact to remember is that this disparity, of and by itself, does not establish a Title VII violation. Statistical imbalances by themselves are not unlawful. The adverse impact only violates Title VII if the criterion that caused the imbalance (in this example, the two-year college degree) *cannot* be shown to be job related.

BOTTOM-LINE STATISTICS

Generally, bottom-line statistics cannot be used as a defense for disparate impact. In the past, some employers attempted to avoid litigation by offering the bottom-line statistics as a defense of their selection processes. **Bottom-line statistics** refer to the selection rates of protected class members at the conclusion of the selection process. In other words, bottom-line statistics focus on the final outcome of the selection process. They only compare the proportion of protected group members actually hired or promoted against the selection rate of the group with the highest rate. To illustrate this, think back to the ABC Manufacturing scenario. Assume all fifty-three of the remaining African American applicants (those who passed both Stages I and II) were hired to fill the employer's one hundred twenty-five vacancies. Consequently, fifty-three of the original one hundred fifty-eight African American applicants were eventually given employment (see Exhibit 3-6).

That would leave seventy-two positions to be filled by those white applicants who successfully passed the first and second stages of the selection process, the

■ EXHIBIT 3-6

NUMBER OF APPLICANTS WHO PASSED THE
SECOND SCREENING TEST AND WERE HIRED

	African Americans		Whites		Total	
	Applied	Hired	Applied	Hired	Applied	Hired
Male	110	37	146	44	256	81
Female	48	16	36	28	84	44
Totals	**158**	**53**	**182**	**72**	**340**	**125**

educational requirements and the hand-and-eye coordination test. Assume that, of the seventy-six white males who passed these two stages, forty-four were offered employment. Of the white females who passed this second stage, all twenty-eight were hired. In short, seventy-two of the one hundred eighty-two total white applicants of both sexes were eventually employed by the company.

Based on these bottom-line results, the company could attempt to justify its employment actions on the grounds that when the final outcome of the employment decision process is examined, African American candidates were not hired at a substantially lower rate than whites. The company could argue that the African American candidates were not unfavorably treated because their ultimate selection rate did not fall short under the four-fifths rule. The company might argue that if the final results of the selection process are examined closely, there is no adverse impact for African Americans.

The African American selection rate at the bottom line was 33.5 percent (fifty-three of one hundred fifty-eight African American applicants were hired). Though this rate is lower than the selection rate for whites (39.6 percent, or seventy-two of one hundred eighty-two applicants), it is still within the threshold of the four-fifths rule.

$$0.335 < 0.8 \, (0.396)$$

$$0.335 < 0.317$$

Though the bottom-line statistics in our example do _not_ reveal adverse impact against African Americans, both case law[17] and the Civil Rights Act of 1991[18] are quite clear in severely limiting their use. As part of a multiple stage selection process, bottom-line statistics offer no defense for an employer, although there may be some situations in which a complaining party may use them in establishing the _prima facie_ case.

According to the Civil Rights Act of 1991, a _prima facie_ case of disparate impact is usually established when:

> a complaining party demonstrates that a respondent uses _a particular employment practice_ that causes disparate impact on the basis of race, color, religion, sex, or national origin and the respondent fails to demonstrate that the challenged practice is job related for the position in question and consistent with business necessity.[19]

Essentially, this means that if one stage in a multiple-stage selection process causes adverse impact, a complaint can be made. However, it is the complaining party's responsibility to identify which stage causes the adverse impact. In most instances, the complaining party is no more allowed to use bottom-line statistics to initiate a Title VII action than the respondent is allowed to use the bottom line to defend itself against such actions. Not surprisingly, HR professionals are continually monitoring each phase of their selection processes to ensure that they minimize adverse impact.

When bottom-line statistics are permitted by a court, they may be used only by the complaining party. If the complaining party can demonstrate that an employer's decision-making process is so complicated and its various stages or elements are so intertwined that they cannot be separated for individual analysis, the complaining party is permitted to use bottom-line statistics.[20]

Assume a university uses multifaceted teaching evaluations as part of its annual performance appraisal for assigning promotions and raises to faculty. This evaluation consists of five components:

1. Classroom teaching in degree programs.
2. One-on-one/small group teaching.
3. Teaching in continuing education/distance learning programs.
4. Developing teaching materials/making presentations and publishing related to teaching.
5. Developing courses and curricula.

Further assume a group of female faculty members allege that overall teaching evaluations have a disparate impact on women.

If these five elements of a faculty member's evaluation were incapable of separation in the final decision process (particularly since some could be entirely or partially based on subjective assessment), bottom-line statistics for the outcome of the overall teaching evaluation could be used by the complaining parties.[21] When a decision-making process includes particular, functionally integrated practices that are components of the same criterion (in this case, teaching) or method of administration, functionally integrated practices may be analyzed as a single employment practice.[22]

The message is clear for HR professionals. When designing multifaceted evaluation instruments, the contribution of each individual component to the final decision must be readily identifiable. Once confusion arises as to how the components affected the final decision, the complaining party is afforded the opportunity to resort to bottom-line results.

RESPONDENT'S REBUTTAL

Once the *prima facie* case has been established, the respondent (the employer) assumes the burden of rebutting the allegations of adverse impact. The employer can defend the disparate impact by challenging the complaining party's statistical analysis or data, thus demonstrating that the adverse impact does not exist or demonstrating that the specific selection criterion or employment practice that caused the statistical imbalance is job related or a business necessity.

DEMONSTRATING ADVERSE IMPACT DOES NOT EXIST

The easiest defense for an employer to use (in terms of time, effort, and money) is proving disparate impact does not exist. If there is no adverse impact, there is no Title VII violation. The major advantage to this defense is that the respondent (the employer) would not have to establish the validity of the criterion or practice in question. As you will see, validation can be a very complicated process. The Civil Rights Act of 1991 explicitly makes this point by declaring:

> If the respondent demonstrates that a specific employment practice does not cause the disparate impact, the respondent shall not be required to demonstrate that such practice is required by business necessity.[23]

For example, if in the first stage of ABC Manufacturing's selection process, seventy-nine African Americans (instead of fifty-five) had possessed the requisite two-year degree in industrial arts, would a statistical imbalance have occurred? Yes, it could be argued that an imbalance exists, since the selection rate for African Americans (50 percent, or $79 \div 158$) is less than that of the white applicants (62.1 percent, or $113 \div 182$), but is it sufficiently severe to meet the four-fifths standard?

$$0.50 < 0.8 \ (0.621)$$

$$0.50 < 0.497$$

Since the African American selection rate of 50 percent is not less than 80 percent of the selection rate for whites (49.7 percent), the four-fifths rule was not violated. Consequently, in one sense (a strictly legal one), disparate impact would not exist.

However, in our original example, only fifty-five African American applicants passed the first criterion, and disparate impact appears to exist. This leaves the respondent with only two options: challenge the complaining party's statistics or prove that possessing a two-year degree in industrial arts is job related.

OTHER MEANS OF CHALLENGING STATISTICS

Challenging the complaining party's statistics may take several forms. First, the sample size may be too small and thus the selection or rejection of a single individual would substantially affect proportional outcomes.[24] To demonstrate the impact that a small sample size would have on the statistical or proportional outcomes, assume the number of African American applicants was sixteen instead of the one hundred sixty-eight in the ABC Manufacturing scenario. Also assume that seven of the sixteen possessed the requisite two-year degree. Further assume the numbers for the white applicants were the same—one hundred thirteen of the one hundred eighty-two white candidates held the degree. Based upon an application of the four-fifths rule, the outcome would be as follows:

$$7/16 < 0.8 \ (113/182)$$

$$0.438 < 0.8 \ (0.621)$$

$$0.438 < 0.497$$

By strictly following the four-fifths rule, disparate impact would be concluded. But look what would have happened if only one more African American applicant had possessed the appropriate two-year degree:

$$8/16 < 0.8 \ (113/182)$$

$$0.50 < 0.8 \ (0.621)$$

$$0.50 < 0.497$$

The number of African American applicants was so small that a single individual can make a substantial difference in the statistical outcome. In this case, each individual would affect the selection rate of African Americans by 6.25 percent, compared to 0.6 percent in the original example. The small sample size would either overstate or understate the imbalance. More importantly, the effects of variance in the sample are increasingly likely to be due to random error[25] rather than discrimination.

The general convention is that correlational studies require at least thirty subjects to establish significance. In other words, the outcome would not be statistically significant, and the results would likely occur at random. The general rule in statistical analysis is the larger the sample size, the greater the degree of precision.[26]

EXAMINING RELEVANT LABOR MARKETS

The complaining party's findings may be called into question by pointing out that many of the applicants for the position in question were not qualified applicants. When job relatedness is examined, persons who do not possess *bona fide* job requirements cannot be treated as legitimate candidates.

Suppose a university has posted the position of professor of business management. The job specification for this position states that successful candidates must possess a doctorate in management from an accredited university and must demonstrate research in the field of management. Of the four hundred applicants for the position, eighty-eight are African American, of which twelve are passed through the first stage (doctorate in management). Of the three hundred twelve white applicants, one hundred sixty-eight are passed through stage one screening. Simple four-fifths analysis, without considering relevant qualifications, would conclude the following:

$$12/88 < 0.8 \ (168/312)$$

$$0.136 < 0.8 \ (0.538)$$

$$0.136 < 0.43$$

One would conclude disparate impact. However, is someone with a doctoral degree in elementary education, sociology, or history qualified to teach undergraduate and graduate level courses in management? Very persuasive arguments can be made that they would not be qualified. To be an effective instructor of a college-level management course, the instructor would be expected to have a doctoral degree in that field. Hence, even though disparity exists, it exists due to job-related reasons. The individuals who do not possess the qualifications for the job (a degree in the appropriate field) are not viable candidates.

COUNTERVAILING STATISTICAL EVIDENCE

Finally, the respondent may attempt to challenge the complaining party's statistics by offering counter evidence. This can often be accomplished by analyzing the complaining party's data with either more sophisticated or more representative statistical methods. Stock analysis, or measures of representativeness (as opposed to the applicant flow analysis used in previous examples), is one such means of countering the complaining party's allegations of statistical imbalance in applicant flow. **Stock analysis** provides statistics on the composition of the employer's workforce and how that workforce compares to its relevant labor market. In order to be accurate, stock analysis begins with properly identifying the relevant labor market for the job in question. This is an extremely critical point. Too often, stock analysis is based on general population statistics and includes (or overrepresents) the portion of a protected class who actually possesses requisite job qualifications. If this has occurred, then the stock analysis is easily challenged as not truly reflecting the relevant labor market.

STOCK ANALYSIS. In the ABC Manufacturing example, the employer may have identified the relevant labor market for entry-level machine operators as all individuals with the appropriate education within a one-hour commute of the plant. Based upon data obtained from the Bureau of Labor Statistics, the employer estimates that this relevant labor market is comprised of 116,000 individuals: 13,950 African Americans, 10,000 Hispanics, 2,500 of Asian ancestry, and 89,550 non-Hispanic whites. Using these figures, the employer is able to develop proportional estimates of the relevant labor market. In this case, it is 77.2 percent white, 12 percent African American, 8.6 percent Hispanic, and 2.2 percent Asian.

The employer can now determine the proportion of its internal workforce that is African American and compare that to the proportion of African Americans in the relevant labor market. This proportional comparison is also known as a measure of representativeness and is accomplished using the following formula:

(Proportion of Protected Class in Employer's Internal Workforce)
< (Proportion of Protected Class in Relevant Labor Market)

Assume the employer audits the workforce and discovers that of 5,400 current employees, 1,050 are African American (19.4 percent). Applying stock analysis, the employer would offer the following statistics:

$$\frac{1,050}{5,400} < \frac{13,950}{116,000}$$

$$0.194 < 0.12$$

The argument would be that, despite the adverse impact shown by applicant flow analysis, African Americans are actually overrepresented in the company's workforce. In fact, the proportion of African Americans in the company's internal workforce is over 60 percent that of their representation in the labor market (19.4 percent to 12 percent, respectively). In certain instances, the EEOC and courts have accepted stock analysis as demonstrating good faith.

JOB RELATEDNESS OR BUSINESS NECESSITY

Assume the initial hiring statistics are true in the ABC Manufacturing example, and only forty African Americans possessed the two-year degree and passed Stage I. The burden of proof would now shift to the company to demonstrate that the requirement for entry-level manufacturing personnel to hold a two-year degree in industrial arts is a business necessity or that the complaining party's statistical data is flawed. In order for any employment practice to be established as a business necessity, it must be validated as job related. The common source for guidance on validation is the *Uniform Guidelines*.[27] The premise behind **job relatedness** or **business necessity** as a defense is that even though the requirement causes adverse impact, it is absolutely essential to performing the job in question. Therefore, good job analysis is critical.

Though job analysis is an essential part of virtually all HR practices, is it more crucial in establishing the job relatedness of a selection criterion? **Job analysis** is the systematic gathering of information about a job in an organization. Such information should describe the activities, results, equipment, material, individuals, and working conditions that characterize the job in question.[28] Ideally, this information can then be used to develop the three outcomes of job analysis: job descriptions, job specifications, and job performance standards.

Job descriptions describe what activities the job entails. This means identifying the essential tasks, duties, and responsibilities associated with the job in question. Assuming a proper job analysis was used, review the job description for a computer operator in Exhibit 3-7.

Job specifications provide the knowledge, skills, and abilities that a job incumbent must possess in order to properly perform the essential tasks, duties, and responsibilities contained in the job description. Note that in the job description of the computer operator, the duties primarily consist of data entry and following precise instructions given by a computer programmer. In order to accomplish these tasks, the computer operator does not have to possess many specialized skills. Not surprisingly, the job specifications for this position require only a high school education and some basic keyboard skills. In contrast, a computer programmer, whose job requires a broader range of more complex tasks, duties, and responsibilities, requires more knowledge, skills, and abilities to perform them adequately.

Job performance standards identify the minimum acceptable level of employee behavior or output expected of an entry-level employee. Should the employee's work performance fall below this level, the essential job functions are not being performed. Unfortunately, most job analysis focuses only on the job description and job specification components of the position in question and fails to clearly describe minimum performance expectations. Performance standards define the levels of performance expected of an employee in each major activity for which that employee is held accountable.[29] Since meeting these standards is the basis for many HR practices (i.e., retention, raises, promotions, etc.), it is critical that they be tied to job analysis in order to establish their job relatedness.

▪ EXHIBIT 3-7

JOB DESCRIPTION

Job Title: Computer Operator

I. GENERAL SUMMARY OF RESPONSIBILITIES

Computer operator oversees the operation of computer hardware systems, ensuring that these machines are used as efficiently as possible. Works with networks of personal computers. Computer operator must anticipate problems and take preventive action as well as solve problems that occur during operations.

II. SPECIFIC DUTIES AND RESPONSIBILITIES

1. Controls the console of computer workstation while entering data in packaged or developed software. (60%)
2. Works from operating instructions prepared by programmers, users, or operations managers to set controls on the computer and on peripheral devices required to run a particular job. (15%)
3. Operates separate peripheral equipment. (5%)
4. Prepares printouts or other output for distribution to computer users. (5%)
5. Loads the equipment with disks and paper as needed. (5%)
6. While the computer is running, monitors the control console and responds to operating and computer messages. (5%)
7. Maintains log books listing each job that is run and events such as machine malfunctions. (5%)

III. JOB SPECIFICATIONS

1. Education, high school graduate or equivalent.
2. Experience with IBM compatible personal computer data entry.
3. Knowledge and skill in using Excel spread sheets.
4. Knowledge in operating laser jet printers.
5. Ability to take instructions and pay attention to detail in data entry and maintaining log books.

SOURCE: U.S. Department of Labor (1997). *Dictionary of Occupational Titles.* Washington, DC: Government Printing Office.

DETERMINING ESSENTIAL AND NONESSENTIAL FUNCTIONS. In order to determine if an individual with a disability is qualified, the HR professional must do a little job analysis. The particular job in question must be examined to determine the *essential functions* of the job. Remember that most job descriptions include many nonessential functions in the list of tasks, duties, and responsibilities. It is

JOB DESCRIPTION FOR A SECRETARY/RECEPTIONIST

JOB DESCRIPTION

Job Title: Secretary/Receptionist

Department: Administrative Services

Position of Immediate Supervisor: Director of Administrative Services

I. GENERAL SUMMARY OF RESPONSIBILITIES

Types, edits, and distributes various correspondence to clients and internal staff. Transmits and proofs various essential status reports for day-to-day operations.

II. SPECIFIC DUTIES AND RESPONSIBILITIES

1. Types daily correspondence and reports. (40%)
2. Proofs and prints out final copies for distribution. (5%)
3. Receives handwritten copies and places them in priority files. (2%)
4. Types special projects, such as proposals, quotations, systems analysis, and customer and client surveys. (5%)
5. Transmits documents through the use of electronic mail. (2%)
6. Opens and distributes mail. (15%)
7. Receives and places priority on rush requests and special projects. (2%)
8. Answers telephone. (20%)
9. Takes messages and routes them to appropriate party. (5%)
10. Maintains log of long-distance calls. (2%)
11. Stocks the secretarial supply room. (2%)
12. Maintains the reception area in a neat, clean, and professional manner, to include watering office plants.
13. Performs other duties as directed.

III. JOB SPECIFICATIONS

1. High school diploma or GED, 1–2 years of college helpful.
2. Knowledge of Corel WordPerfect and Corel Quattro Pro.
3. Must have a good eye for neatness and quality type documents.
4. Must lift 25-pound containers to a shelf of 72".
5. Ability to work well with others in developing proposals and projects.
6. Pleasant telephone voice and demonstrate courtesy on the telephone.

SOURCE: U.S. Department of Labor (1997). *Dictionary of Occupational Titles.* Washington, DC: Government Printing Office.

the HR professional's task to eliminate the nonessential functions associated with a specific job, leaving only the essential duties.

To illustrate how this is done, review the job description in Exhibit 3-8. Assume that it is accurate and has been validated. Be aware that this is a fairly simple job; more complex job descriptions will require more analysis. The job of secretary/receptionist will at least demonstrate the process.

What are the secretary/receptionist's essential job functions? Assuming that the job description is correct in terms of the estimated time the employee devotes to the primary duties, what activity consumes most of the employee's time? Note that many job descriptions do not provide this information. When they do not, the HR professional must collect that information. In this example, 40 percent of the secretary/receptionist's time is devoted to word processing, therefore this is an essential job function. Answering the telephone occupies another 20 percent of the employee's time and could be judged essential. Opening and distributing mail also demands a sufficient amount of time (15 percent). If any of these three tasks are not adequately performed by the secretary/receptionist, the primary reasons for creating this position have not been accomplished.

What about some of the other functions? They all occur infrequently or account for a very small percentage of the employee's job activities. Note the requirement to maintain the copy paper inventory, and the requirement to restock this inventory. This would require the secretary/receptionist to be able to lift twenty-five pounds (the weight of a box of copy paper) at least to the highest shelf in the storage room. If the highest shelf is seventy-two inches above the ground, the employee must be physically able to lift twenty-five pounds seventy-two inches.

Also among the lesser duties, the secretary/receptionist is responsible for watering the plants in the company reception area, and the secretary/receptionist is responsible for ensuring the reception area is maintained in a neat, clean, and professional manner. This implies some general household duties. The HR professional would have to clarify just what these household duties include.

VALIDATION STUDIES.   For many students, and many HR professionals for that matter, few things are as mundane and boring as validation. It can be an arduous, time-consuming task. Although validation may be an underappreciated task, nothing is more critical to any organization's disparate impact defense than a properly conducted validation. Without validating a challenged employment practice (whether it is a hiring criterion like a professional certification, or promotion criteria like good performance evaluations), an employer will lack the documentation necessary to prove a questioned employment practice is job related. The use of any selection device (even though it appears neutral at face value) that has a disparate impact on members of protected classes and that has not been properly validated by the employer constitutes a discriminatory act.[30]

The EEOC recognizes three general types of validation studies: (1) criterion-related validity, (2) content validity, and (3) construct validity.[31] Though criterion-related validation is the preferred method, not all jobs lend themselves to such studies. A brief discussion of each follows.

Criterion-Related Validation. **Criterion-related validity** is demonstrated by empirical data proving a selection procedure is predictive of the important elements of the job in question. If an ability test is administered to individuals applying for the job of programmer/analyst, and if the test scores are significantly correlated with successful performance of the key elements of the job, then the test has criterion-related validity. In short, test scores have criterion-related validity if they are an accurate predictor of job performance.

To illustrate this point, recall ABC Manufacturing's second type of open position—programmer/analyst. Job analysis previously indicated that the primary functions of the job include working on multiple projects in a team programming environment involving object-oriented programming, HTML, Unix Shell Scripting, VBScript, and JavaScript.

As part of the selection process, all applicants are required to take a written examination to assess each individual's knowledge of the C++ programming language. Any candidate who fails to attain a score of 60 percent on the written examination is removed from further consideration for employment. If the written examination causes disparate impact among women but can be validated as an accurate predictor of job success as a programmer, the employer will be able to establish a job relatedness/business necessity defense. The employer may do this in two ways. First, high scores on written tests evaluating C++ programming knowledge are correlated with satisfactory work performance on those actual work assignments requiring C++ programming. Second, low scores (particularly those below 60 percent) on written tests evaluating C++ programming knowledge are correlated with poor or unacceptable job performance.

In establishing a relationship between the predictor of performance (in this case the test) and the actual performance, concurrent validation and predictive validation are the two methods available to HR professionals. Under **concurrent validation,** the correlation coefficients between test and performance are determined by administering the test to *current* employees and correlating the test scores to their individual performance evaluations. This allows for the performance data and test scores to be collected and analyzed "concurrently." This points to a major advantage of concurrent validation—it can be done quickly. Because it can be done in a timely manner, it is also less expensive for the company.

However, the results of the concurrent validation may be somewhat biased because the sample (the current employees who take the test) overrepresents successful workers. It can be assumed that poor-performing employees are removed from the workforce over time, leaving mostly competent employees. Since primarily good performers take the test, there is no way to determine if poor performers would have scored equally well on the test. Therefore, it can be argued that if poor performers could score just as well as good performers, then the test *is not* an accurate predictor of job performance. If the test then has a disparate impact on a protected class but does not accurately predict job performance, the employer has no business-necessity defense for the disparate impact and will likely be found in violation of Title VII. Fortunately, studies have demonstrated that there are no significant differences in the validity estimates of those using concurrent validation and those using predictive validation.[32]

Predictive validation is another means of establishing criterion-related validity. When **predictive validation** is used, the test is given to applicants rather than current employees. The results are then archived for future use. After an appropriate passage of time (usually the end of the probationary period or the conclusion of a performance evaluation cycle), performance data on each new employee is gathered. Correlations between test scores and actual performance are then determined and analyzed.

If it can be statistically demonstrated that there is a moderate to strong relationship between the test and job performance, the test will be job related. Predictive validity, because it tests both good and poor performers, is the preferred validation method of the EEOC.[33]

Content Validity. **Content validity** involves having the applicant perform a "fair sample" of work to be performed.[34] In other words, the applicant is required to perform a task or duty from the actual job for which he or she is applying. For example, requiring a secretary to type a letter on a personal computer using a specific word processing package would be a selection criterion with content validity. Physical tests for firefighters such as dragging one hundred-pound dummies seventy feet in a self-contained breathing apparatus have been ruled to have content validity.[35] The important factor in content validation is that the employment test in question must be based on thorough job analysis to ensure the skills and abilities being tested are truly necessary for successful job performance.[36]

Content validation tends to be more appropriate for selection criteria, especially those of a physical nature, that measure the abilities and skills that are prerequisites for entry-level job performance.[37] However, it is the employer's responsibility to prove the selection criterion itself is an important part of the job.[38] If the validation measures only duties and tasks that are peripheral to the job in question, there is no content validity.

Assume an entrance examination has been developed for firefighters that measures their cooking skills. It could be argued that since meals must be prepared and eaten at the station during shifts, this is an important skill. Poor cooks are not conducive to good morale. However, is this an essential job function for a firefighter? Would job analysis show that cooking was among the critical responsibilities of the position? Imagine how ineffective a selection process for firefighters would be if it consisted only of a pen and paper examination on basic fire safety and a cooking exercise. Doubtless, the cooking exercise could accurately rate the candidate's culinary skills, but because it ignores more essential job functions, it would be a poor predictor of successful firefighting ability. However, carrying heavy firefighting equipment up and down ladders or the ability to evacuate unconscious people from burning buildings would be critical. The guidance is relatively simple—the abilities being tested by content validation must be essential to the successful performance of the job and not be marginal activities.

Content validation provides no insulation against disparate impact if the knowledge, skills, or abilities measured by the test can be acquired quickly or after a brief orientation period.[39] For example, an employer in a sheet metal plant is hiring machine operators and requires candidates to operate a metal punch as part of the selection process. This requirement has adverse impact on Asian Americans. The employer may argue this "test" encompassed virtually all of the essential job functions of the position of machine operator. In this instance, the employer may be correct. However, to anyone who has never operated a metal punch, turning it on and then operating the machine seems to be a daunting request. Yet, after a short training session (perhaps no more than thirty to sixty minutes), the task is readily achievable.

In evaluating the sufficiency of an employer's content validation, the courts usually rely on the following standards:

■ Criteria are based on job analysis.

■ The personnel who developed the criteria used reasonable competence in constructing the test itself.

■ The content of the selection criteria must be related to the job in question.

■ The evaluation of candidates against the selection criteria must identify those candidates who are better able to perform the job.[40]

Construct Validity. Of the three validation methods, **construct validity** is probably the most complicated because it involves evaluating abstract characteristics (i.e., decisiveness, innovation, sound judgment, etc.) that are important for successful job performance. Unfortunately, those constructs are often hard to measure.

Construct validity is really two validation studies. First, the employer must prove the construct is essential for the successful performance of the job in question (i.e., decisiveness is essential to the position of branch manager). Next, the employer must prove the construct can be accurately measured. This means extensive job analysis must be conducted to identify critical work behaviors.[41] Ultimately, the employer is responsible for providing proof that the selection procedures measure the degree to which candidates possess the identifiable construct determined important for successful job performance.[42]

Assume an employer has demonstrated that "decisiveness" is a very important characteristic for a branch manager. However, the personality assessment test that the employer uses to evaluate "decisiveness" in candidates for the position is a poor predictor of that construct. Though the behavioral trait, "decisiveness," is critical to job performance, the personality test does not accurately identify the trait in applicants. Consequently, the selection process lacks construct validity.

On the other hand, if the personality assessment test could accurately identify the level of decisiveness possessed by a candidate, but the construct was not essential for the job's performance, the selection process would again lack construct validity. Imagine the level of "decisiveness" required by a bank teller to perform the essential functions of the job compared to a branch manager. As always, the importance of thorough job analysis cannot be overstated.

OTHER METHODS OF ESTABLISHING JOB RELATEDNESS. Validation is not just limited to statistical validation methods. There are situations and circumstances under which criterion-related, content, and construct validation would not be practical. As the Supreme Court noted in *Teamsters v United States,*

> [s]tatistics are . . . competent in proving employment discrimination. We caution only that statistics are not irrefutable; they come in infinite variety and, like any other kind of evidence, they may be rebutted. In short, their usefulness depends on all the surrounding facts and circumstances.[43]

One of these surrounding facts is that the safety of coworkers, customers, or other parties can be shown to be an essential function of the job.[44] In one instance, applicants for positions with a transit authority filed an EEOC complaint alleging the transit authority's policy of not hiring applicants who received methadone treatments had a disparate impact on African Americans and Hispanics (Methadone is a drug given to persons undergoing rehabilitation for narcotics addiction.) The complaining parties contended the transit authority's policy had a disparate impact because 81 percent of the applicants it affected were African Americans or Hispanics.[45] In fact, at the time, 62 to 65 percent of all methadone-maintained persons in New York City were African Americans or Hispanics.[46] Despite the obvious impact this policy had on the two protected classes (excluding more African Americans and Hispanics from eligibility than any other ethnic group), the safety concerns for the passengers using the transit authority's services easily established the job relatedness/business necessity of this requirement.

In the case of *Spurlock v United Airlines,*[47] the question arose as to whether work experience can be job related in the absence of a statistical validation study. In this case, any applicant for flight officer on a United Airlines crew had to have a minimum of five hundred hours of flight time, a college degree, a commercial pilot's license, and an instrument rating. The college degree was considered necessary to substantiate an applicant's ability to understand and retain information during training. The five hundred hours of flight experience were important for successful completion of the airline's flight training program and reducing training costs.[48] Applicants without the five hundred hours took longer to train and had a lower passing rate than applicants who possessed the previous flight experience.

Under similar circumstances in *Washington v Davis,* the Supreme Court concluded that a verbal skills test that predicted applicant success in training was job related, despite its disproportionate affect on African Americans.[49] Though the test had not been validated for job performance, it had been correlated with police academy training scores. The verbal skills test was an accurate predictor of an applicant's ability to successfully complete training.

Some jobs, by their nature, do not lend themselves to easily quantified, objective standards that form the basis for statistical validation. For example, most middle- and upper-level management positions are more likely to be evaluated on subjective and discretionary criteria (i.e., decisiveness, creativity, sound judgment, motivational abilities, etc.). Even though such traits cannot be measured by standardized tests, they are, nonetheless, critical to the performance of the job in question.[50] When establishing the job relatedness of any subjective employment criterion, the employer is required to provide evidence of its "manifest relationship to the employment in question." To establish this manifest relationship, the employer would have to prove an employee who could not exercise sound judgment would be unable to successfully perform the job .[51]

COMPLAINING PARTY'S REBUTTAL

Even if the employer is able to establish the job relatedness or business necessity of the employment practice creating the statistical imbalance, the complaining party is afforded one last opportunity to challenge that practice. The complaining party can offer evidence that there are other practices that would accomplish the same objective as the challenged practice, but would have less disparate impact on the protected class. Accordingly:

> If [complaining parties], having established a *prima facie* case, come forward with alternatives to [respondents'] hiring practices that reduce the racially disparate impact of practices currently being used, and [respondents] refuse to adopt these alternatives, such a refusal would belie a claim by [respondents] that their incumbent practices are being employed for nondiscriminatory reasons.[52]

Employers could be directed to adopt another selection criterion or test that would have less disparate impact. However, this "criterion" would have to accomplish the same end as the rejected criterion. This is more easily said than done by the complaining party.

For HR professionals, this means that current selection processes need to be validated. Those that create disparate impact should be more closely reviewed and analyzed for possible replacement by a less exclusive process. It may be unrealistic to assume that all practices can be replaced, but some can. The effort to do so would not only reduce the likelihood of losing a case in court but also could increase the pool of qualified applicants available to the organization.

PERFORMANCE APPRAISALS AND EMPLOYMENT DISCRIMINATION

Since the discussion of disparate impact and disparate treatment is complete, perhaps it would be a good time to look at an employment practice likely to get an employer in trouble with both. Performance appraisals are at the very heart of HRM. Besides being a valuable tool (when they are properly conducted) for employee feedback, many organizations use performance appraisals to provide information needed to make important employment decisions. Ask a manager who should get the largest pay raise, and most will respond that it should go to the best worker. But who is the best worker? Usually (sometimes hopefully) it is the worker with the best performance evaluation/appraisal. Not surprisingly, individual employee performance appraisals are a major factor in determining pay raises, promotions, bonuses, transfers, retentions, layoffs, and terminations.[53] And, when they are done properly, they are an invaluable management tool. Unfortunately, when they are not done properly, they can become a potential Title VII complaint or an embarrassment during an equal employment opportunity (EEO) investigation or trial.

From a strictly legal perspective, performance appraisals are treated as "tests."[54] Just as with any other "test," a performance appraisal must be validated. A performance appraisal is useless to an employer if it cannot be shown to accurately measure the essential functions of the job it alleges to evaluate.

In some instances, an organization's own formal performance evaluations are used against it in court as evidence of unlawful discrimination. Evaluations which are highly subjective and reflect only the rater's opinion about an employee's abilities, rather than an objective assessment of actual work performance, may also include the rater's conscious or unconscious prejudices.[55] Performance appraisals known as graphic rating scales (see Exhibit 3-9) may be particularly susceptible to a high degree of subjectivity. Evaluation criteria such as attitude are especially nebulous and may have little to do with successful job accomplishment.

RETALIATION

Whether a complaining party files a disparate impact or a disparate treatment claim against an employer, Title VII protects that employee from any retaliatory action taken by the employer.[56] Specifically, it is an unlawful employment practice for an employer to discriminate against an employee for "making charges, testifying, assisting, or participating in enforcement proceedings."[57] This is essentially a whistleblower's clause. **Whistleblower** refers to an employee who reports his or her employer's violation of some statute or regulation. The whistleblower's clause is intended to protect the employee's statutory right to report Title VII violations. It also protects witnesses from discriminatory employment actions and encourages them to come forward with their testimony. The antiretaliation provisions also create a disincentive for employers to attempt to impede EEOC investigations by threatening or coercing employees not to file *bona fide* charges. Furthermore, such provisions are intended to dissuade employers from pressuring employees not to provide critical evidence to investigators.

For HR professionals, this means special attention should be directed toward training management and supervisory personnel in avoiding the perception that management is intimidating complaining parties (see Exhibit 3-10). As

■ EXHIBIT 3-9

GRAPHIC RATING SCALE

Name	Employee Number	Date of Hire	
Department Name		Job Title	
Salary Grade	Time in Present Years Months Position	Date of Review	Date of Prior Review

Performance Appraisal Statement and Comments: This form provides a suggested format in which to comment on the employee's performance against job requirements. Please consider all statements carefully. You should check one of the suggested comments on the scale and write your own statement or status of the incumbent's performance within the "Remarks" section. This enables you to provide an overall rating on each factor as well as to comment on specific characteristics of the position of the individual evaluated.

Factors	Evaluations	Remarks
Job Knowledge Consider knowledge of own job and department's function; the understanding of principles, methods, or processes used.	□ 5. Exceptional understanding of all phases of the job. □ 4. Full knowledge of all job duties; exceptional understanding of some phases of the job. □ 3. Full knowledge of the job. □ 2. More knowledge is needed for fully effective performance. Knowledge is adequately improving. □ 1. Lacks adequate comprehension of job; adequate improvement is not observed.	
Technical Skills Consider the degree of proficiency and strengths or weaknesses in such technical skills as clerical, secretarial, technician, or paraprofessional.	□ 5. Exceptionally proficient in all technical skills. □ 4. Fully competent in technical skills; exceptionally proficient in some technical skills. □ 3. Fully competent in technical skills. □ 2. More skills are needed for fully effective performance. Skills are adequately improving. □ 1. Lacks adequate job skills; adequate improvement is not observed.	

SOURCE: Hills, F. S., Bergmann, T. J., and Scarpello, V. G. (1994). *Compensation Decision Making*. Fort Worth, TX: The Dryden Press, p. 364.

further precaution, the employer and its management representatives must take special care not to treat complaining parties or witnesses any differently once a charge is filed. This does not mean the organization should not attempt to conduct its own investigation. Instead, it means the organization should not initiate any adverse action against the complaining party for filing the charge. This also includes any disciplinary actions that could be construed as retribution for the employee's filing. It is not always enough to have acted properly and legally; it is also important to *appear* to have acted properly and legally. If disciplinary action is contemplated against the complaining party for a legitimate work-related reason, it may be better to postpone it until after the EEOC has concluded its investigation. Whether an organization has decided to postpone disciplinary actions or not, the reason for the action should be documented to preclude any connection to unlawful retaliation.

In its simplest form, **retaliation** occurs when an employer (or its management representatives) takes adverse action against an employee for filing, or threatening to file, an EEO complaint (see Exhibit 3-11). Retaliation is a serious problem and has been increasing steadily. By 2000, retaliation accounted for 27.1 percent of all discrimination charges filed with the EEOC.[58] That was an approximate increase of 124 percent in the actual number of charges since 1990, when retaliation was only 12.1 percent of total charges.[59]

■ **EXHIBIT 3-10**

EXAMPLES OF UNLAWFUL RETALIATION

- Denying an employee the right to participate in the EEO process. This includes threatening to take adverse action against an employee who:
  * Files an EEO complaint
  * Provides testimony or evidence in an EEO hearing

- Harassment and intimidation

- Denial of employment benefits

- Discharge

- Discipline

- Demotion

- Reassignment

- Unjustified performance evaluations

- Acceleration of disciplinary action

- Undeserved negative references for former employees

- Unwarranted contesting of unemployment compensation claim

SOURCE: U.S. Equal Employment Opportunity Commission (1995). *Theories of Discrimination*. Washington, DC: Government Printing Office, p. A-20.

■ **EXHIBIT 3-11**

THE THREE ELEMENTS OF A RETALIATION CLAIM

■ Protected activity
  * Opposition to unlawful discrimination
  * Participation in the EEOC complaint process

■ Adverse action

■ A casual connection between the protected activity and its adverse action

An often misunderstood facet of retaliation is that it is not limited strictly to the victims of real or perceived discriminatory workplace actions. Third parties are also protected. Retaliation protection covers employees who oppose what they reasonably believe was unlawful discrimination and are then punished for their opposition.[60]

Suppose a male employee, Brian, was aware that his supervisor, Dave, had stated no woman would ever be promoted to shop foreman in the plant. When Brian recommends one of his subordinates, Anne, to fill one of two vacant shop foreman positions, he is told by Dave that Anne is not qualified. Believing that Dave's aversion to female shop supervisors, rather than individual qualifications, had more to do with Anne's rejection, Brian encouraged Anne to take the matter to Dave's boss, Bob. Upon hearing that Brian has encouraged a subordinate to make an EEO complaint against him, Dave decided it was time that Brian be "taught a lesson." Dave assigned Brian to less desirable projects. The following month when annual employee performance evaluations were given, Brian received a marginal evaluation and was not recommended for a raise (previously all of Brian's performance evaluations were well above average, and he always received merit raises).

Even though Brian was not the initial object of unlawful discrimination (that was Anne), he was punished because of his opposition to that unlawful discrimination. As a result of Brian's advice that Anne complain to Bob, Dave's superior, Brian was retaliated against by being denied a pay raise and given a poor performance appraisal. In order to make Dave's conduct toward Brian actionable under Title VII, Brian must make the connection between his retaliatory treatment and the assistance he provided Anne in making her complaint.

Another important characteristic of retaliation complaints HR professionals should remember is that third parties do not have to be members of the protected class against whom the initial discrimination was directed.[61] In our previous example, Dave's discrimination was directed against women; however, Brian, a male, was retaliated against because of his objection to discrimination against women. Similarly, whites who openly oppose unlawful discrimination against African Americans, or Protestants who oppose unlawful discrimination against Jews, are protected against retaliation.[62]

General guidance for HR professionals would be to train all management personnel on the potential pitfalls of taking any action that could be perceived as retaliatory against any employee who has made an EEO complaint, assisted another employee in making an EEO complaint, or provided testimony in an EEO investigation. This includes verbally threatening to take retaliatory action. HR professionals should also ensure that documentation is provided (and maintained) for all adverse personnel actions, especially disciplinary actions, discharges, rehabilitative transfers, and poor performance appraisals. This documentation could be used later to establish that such undesirable employment actions are based on legitimate business reasons and not on unlawful retaliation.[63]

It is always important to remember that any action taken against an individual for voicing opposition to an employer's discriminatory practices would establish a claim of retaliation (see Exhibit 3-12).[64] Hence, if an employee refuses to obey an order which he or she believes would violate Title VII and is punished for disobedience, this could be retaliation.[65] Additionally, it would be retaliatory discrimination if an employer denied an employee's transfer request to a more desirable position (provided the complaining party was qualified) because the employee had previously filed an EEOC complaint.[66] Whatever the nature of the adverse action that occurred, it is a Title VII violation if it can be linked to a protected activity (filing a claim, providing testimony for another employee who filed a claim, objecting to an employer's discriminatory actions, or refusing to engage in discriminatory action).

It would be unrealistic to assume all claims of retaliation are meritorious. Either through malice or ignorance, some employees may allege retaliation when none has occurred. When this happens, the employer's defense is to demonstrate that the adverse actions were based on legitimate retaliatory reasons. For example, in *Pereira v Schlage Electronics*, the complaining party alleged she was terminated by her employer because she had made several complaints alleging sexual harassment by her coworkers.[67] The employer stated she was fired because of an inability to get along with her coworkers, stealing coworkers' tools, and misappropriating

■ **EXHIBIT 3-12**

EMPLOYEE ACTIVITIES PROTECTED FROM RETALIATION

- Filing a charge or complaint alleging discrimination

- Threatening to file a charge or complaint alleging discrimination

- Assisting another employee to file a charge or complaint alleging discrimination

- Complaining about discrimination

- Organizing or participating in a group which has among its objectives opposing unlawful employment discrimination

- Refusing to obey a workplace order because of a "good faith" belief that it is lawfully discriminatory

SOURCE: U.S. Equal Employment Opportunity Commission (1995). *Theories of Discrimination*. Washington, DC: Government Printing Office, p. A-19.

other employees' work.[68] Because the complaining party could not demonstrate the employer's nonretaliatory reasons for terminating her were false (pretextual), the federal district court denied her retaliation claim. As in so many other EEO-related areas, the necessity for maintaining records to document the nondiscriminatory reasons for disciplinary action is evident.

In the vein of "an ounce of prevention is worth a pound of cure," avoiding retaliation complaints can best be advanced by first ensuring all management personnel are aware that it is one of the fastest-growing EEO complaints. Perhaps the most effective training would focus on explaining to supervisory and management personnel their EEO obligations, the necessity for having clearly established discipline and discharge policies, and the need for documentation to support all adverse personnel actions. It is hoped that by exposing the legal consequences posed by retaliation for the organization, supervisors will be more conscious of their own behavior and actions when dealing with employees who have filed or are threatening to file an EEO action. This does not mean workplace discipline and order must grind to a halt—it means the rationale for such discipline should be obvious and, above all, documented.

FRIVOLOUS COMPLAINTS

In some instances when the complaint is knowingly false or malicious, the complaining party may be disciplined. Assume, based on our previous example, Dave had never uttered the statement that no women would be promoted in his area of operation, and Brian had conspired with Anne to fabricate the charge against Dave. Brian's actions are not motivated by a good faith opposition to unlawful discrimination; they are instead predicated on some ulterior reason. This is very important for HR professionals. If the company punishes Brian for encouraging Anne to make a false complaint, it does not violate Title VII.[69] However, it is absolutely critical that the company proves it is reacting against a *false* complaint and not a Title VII complaint.

If, at the time, the company had no reason to believe Anne's complaint was false and took action against Brian, Title VII was violated. The burden is then on the company to demonstrate that the complaint was later determined to be malicious and false, and that its subsequent actions were initiated against Brian for encouraging *a false* EEO complaint and not merely encouraging *an* EEO complaint.[70]

A FINAL LOOK AT DISPARATE IMPACT

Using actual applicant flow analysis and the four-fifths rule, the opening scenario where employees have brought suit against their company's formalized selection process (FSP) can now be analyzed for disparate impact. First, the information should be arranged in a schedule for easy analysis (see Exhibit 3-13).

■ EXHIBIT 3-13

OUTCOMES OF OPENING SCENARIO SELECTION

FSP Phase	Tested	Passed	Percentage Passed
Male	145	100	69.0
Female	44	31	70.5
Over 40	52	22	42.3
Under 40	137	109	79.6
GPE Phase	Participated	Hired	Percentage Passed
Male	91	16	17.6
Female	29	3	10.3
Over 40	20	1	.05
Under 40	100	18	18.0

Note that each component of the selection process is evaluated individually. Hence, the selection rates in the written phase must be analyzed separately from those in the GPE phase. Because the two phases in this selection process are easily identifiable, the complaining party would have to demonstrate which component (phase) caused the disparate impact and could not rely on bottom-line statistics.[71]

Initially, there would appear to be disparate impact in the written component for those employees over forty years old.

$$0.423 < 0.8 \ (0.796)$$

$$0.423 < .637$$

Additionally, in the final phase group problem-solving exercise (GPE), the actual offers of employment appear to create disparate impact for both protected groups, women and applicants over forty. For women, the four-fifths analysis reveals:

$$0.103 < 0.8 \ (0.176)$$

$$0.103 < 0.141$$

As for the older applicants, four-fifths analysis would initially indicate an even greater imbalance in the selection process.

$$0.05 < 0.8 \ (0.18)$$

$$0.05 < 0.144$$

Having read the chapter, do you find these statistics to be compelling enough to establish a Title VII violation? In the findings of the actual court case from which this scenario was drawn, a federal district court judge drew the following conclusions:

> [The] plaintiffs have not put forth reliable statistical proof that either procedure [the GPE and the FSP] had a statistically significant adverse impact on minorities or women plaintiffs, as a matter of law, and have failed to establish a *prima facie* case of disparate impact discrimination on the basis of race or gender. [The] defendant is entitled to summary judgment as a matter of law. Although the statistical analysis reveals that the written test [GPE] had a statistically significant adverse impact on persons forty or older, the [FSP] was properly validated and job-related. Plaintiffs failed to show that the [FSP] was not job-related or that a viable alternative exists which would not have an adverse impact on the plaintiff class. Because plaintiffs failed to carry their burden of proof, as relates to the disparate impact age discrimination claim, summary judgment will be entered in favor of [the employer].[72]

SUMMARY

This chapter focuses on disparate impact theory of discrimination under Title VII of the Civil Rights Act of 1964. Disparate impact, sometimes called adverse impact, is the theory responsible for the current preoccupation with proportional representation in the workplace. Unlike disparate treatment, disparate impact may be unintentional. The *Griggs v Duke Power Company* ruling created this theory.

If HR professionals are to reduce their employers' exposure to charges of disparate impact, it is essential that job analysis be performed on all existing and anticipated positions in the organization. Once the essential job functions of each position have been identified, all subsequent employment practices directed toward a candidate for that position or current job incumbent must be validated based upon those essential functions. As tasks and duties are added or removed from a position, the job descriptions, job specifications, and performance standards must likewise be updated. This means job analysis and validation must be ongoing processes. It also means all employment practices require continual monitoring and updating.

The importance for HR professionals to maintain records and documentation of the validation of each employment practice cannot be overstated. This means reviewing performance appraisals to ensure they accurately measure essential job functions and do not overemphasize nonjob-related behaviors. It also means documentation must be maintained to prove adverse employment actions (i.e., discharge, demotion, and denial of promotions and pay raises) are based on the employee's work-related behavior and actions. It is always important to remember that once disparate impact occurs, the employer has the burden of showing the reason for the imbalance (whether it is a performance appraisal, test score, physical requirement, or educational requirement) is job related.

If the documentation is not available, the practice causing the disparity cannot be explained as a business necessity. If the organization cannot prove a business necessity causes a statistical imbalance, the organization will be judged to have violated Title VII.

This also creates an incentive for HR professionals to make use of both flow and stock analysis to identify potential EEO complaints. Once a particular practice has been identified as having a disparate impact on a protected group, the HR professional can then attempt to determine if its cause is a lawful, job-related reason or a questionable one (indefensible in court). Any and all questionable practices should be discontinued. Additionally, any practice that causes disparate impact, even when validated, should be further analyzed in order to determine if it could be replaced by another practice which would accomplish the same end but have less disparate impact.

KEY TERMS AND CONCEPTS

adverse impact
applicant flow analysis
bottom-line statistics
business necessity
concurrent validation
construct validity
content validity
criterion-related validity
disparate impact
four-fifths rule

job analysis
job descriptions
job performance standards
job relatedness
job specifications
predictive validation
retaliation
stock analysis
whistleblower

QUESTIONS

1. Distinguish between disparate impact and disparate treatment. How does the burden of proof differ?

2. What is the four-fifths (80 percent) rule? How is it used?

3. What is meant by the term "relevant labor market" and how is it used in EEO investigations?

4. What are the three recognized methods of conducting a validity study and how do they differ from one another?

5. What are the employer's rebuttals in disparate impact cases?

6. Differentiate between flow analysis and stock analysis.

7. Respond to this comment: "The only way to avoid an equal employment suit today is to hire by the numbers." Is this ethical? Is this legal?

CASES

—■—

1 The following table shows the passing rates of various candidate groups in an employer's promotion selection process:

Candidate Group	Number Applying	Number Receiving Passing Score	Passing Rate (%)
African Americans	48	26	54.17
Hispanics	4	3	75.00
Indians	3	2	66.67
Whites	259	206	79.54
Unidentified	15	9	60.00
Totals	**329**	**246**	**74.77**

Forty-six persons were promoted to permanent supervisory positions, eleven of whom were African American and thirty-five of whom were white. The overall result of the selection process was that, of the forty-eight identified African American candidates who participated in the selection process, 22.9 percent were promoted and of the two hundred fifty-nine identified white candidates, 13.5 percent were promoted. Has disparate impact occurred? Why or why not? Are the final promotion results sufficient to be a defense to the respondents' suit? Why or why not?

2 SEPTA is a regional mass transit authority that operates principally in Philadelphia, Pennsylvania. In 1989, in response to a perceived need to upgrade the quality of its transit police force, SEPTA initiated an extensive program designed to improve the department. As part of this program, SEPTA dedicated its transit officers primarily to patrolling the subways and limited their responsibilities to serve as guards at other SEPTA property. In addition, SEPTA increased the number of its officers from ninety-six to two hundred and introduced a "zone concept" for the areas they patrol. SEPTA also began to consider methods by which it might upgrade the physical fitness level of its police officers.

In 1991, SEPTA hired Dr. Paul Davis, an expert exercise physiologist who has extensive experience in designing physical fitness employment tests for various law enforcement agencies, to develop an appropriate physical fitness test for its police officers. Dr. Davis initially met with SEPTA officials in order to ascertain SEPTA's objectives. Dr. Davis determined that SEPTA was interested in enhancing the level of fitness, physical vigor, and general productivity of its police force. Once Dr. Davis had determined SEPTA's objectives, he went on a ride-along with SEPTA transit police, and over the course of two days and approximately twenty hours, he rode the SEPTA trains in order to obtain a perspective on the expectations of SEPTA transit officers.

Dr. Davis next conducted a study with twenty experienced SEPTA officers, designating "subject matter experts" (SMEs) in an effort to determine what physical abilities are required to perform the job of SEPTA transit officer. From the responses Dr. Davis received in this study, he determined that running, jogging, and walking were important SEPTA transit officer tasks and that SEPTA officers were expected to jog almost on a daily basis.

Dr. Davis then asked the SMEs to determine what level of physical exertion was necessary to perform these tasks. The SMEs estimated that it was reasonable to expect them to run one mile in full gear in 11.78 minutes. Dr. Davis rejected this estimate as too low based upon his determination that any individual could meet this requirement. Ultimately, Dr. Davis recommended a 1.5-mile run within twelve minutes. Dr. Davis explained that completion of this run would require that an officer possess an aerobic capacity of 42.5 mL/kg/min, the aerobic capacity that Dr. Davis determined would be necessary to perform the job of SEPTA transit officer.

Dr. Davis recommended that SEPTA use the 1.5-mile run as an applicant screening test. He understood that SEPTA officers would not be required to run 1.5 miles within twelve minutes in the course of their duties, but he nevertheless recommended this test as an accurate measure of the aerobic capacity necessary to perform the job of SEPTA transit police officer. Based upon Dr. Davis' recommendation, SEPTA adopted a physical fitness screening test for its applicants which included a 1.5-mile run within twelve minutes. Beginning in 1991, the 1.5-mile run was administered as the first component of the physical fitness test; if an applicant failed to run 1.5 miles in twelve minutes, the applicant would be disqualified from employment as a SEPTA transit officer.

It is undisputed that for the years 1991, 1993, and 1996, an average of only twelve percent of women applicants passed SEPTA's 1.5-mile run in comparison to the almost 60 percent of male applicants who passed. For the years 1993 and 1996, the time period in question in this litigation, the pass rate for women was 6.7 percent compared to a 55.6 percent pass rate for men. In addition, research studies confirm that a cutoff of twelve minutes on a 1.5-mile run will have a disparately adverse impact on women. SEPTA concedes that its 1.5-mile run has a disparate impact on women. Does the SEPTA standard create disparate impact for female applicants? Why or why not? Does the SEPTA standard create disparate impact for African American applicants? Why or why not? Does the SEPTA standard violate Title VII? Why or why not?

SOURCE: *Lanning v SEPTA*, 181 F.3d 478 (3rd Cir. 1999).

Notes

1. This scenario was drawn from the factual background in *Jones v Pepsi-Cola Metro. Bottling Co.*, 871 F. Supp. 305 (E.D. Mich. 1994).

2. 401 U.S. 424 (1971).

3. 401 U.S. at 430 n. 6.

4. Ibid. at 431–432.

5. Ibid. at 431.

6. *Wards Cove Packing Co. v Antonio*, 490 U.S. 642, 657 (1989).

7. 29 C.F.R. § 1607 (1997).

8. 29 C.F.R. § 1607.4D.

9. *Hazelwood School District v U.S.*, 433 U.S. 299, 309, n. 14 (1977).

10. *Ottaviani v State University of New York*, 875 F.2d 365, 370–71 (2d Cir. 1980).

11. *Castaneda v Partida*, 430 U.S. 482 (1976); *EEOC v Sears, Roebuck & Co.*, 839 F.2d 302 (7th Cir. 1988); *Payne v Travenol Laboratories*, 673 F.2d 798 (5th Cir.), cert. denied, 459 U.S. 1038 (1982).

12. 42 U.S.C. § 2000e-2(K)(1)(B)(i).

13. 29 C.F.R. § 1607.4D.

14. Ibid.

15. 29 C.F.R. §1607.4D.

16. 42 U.S.C. § 2000e-2(k)(1)(A).

17. *Connecticut v Teal*, 457 U.S. 440, 452.

18. 42 U.S.C. §2000e-2(k)(1)(B)(i).

19. Ibid. at § 2000e-2(k)(1)(A)(i).

20. 42 U.S.C. § 2000e-2(k)(1)(B).

21. CCH Business Law Editors (1991). *Civil Rights Act of 1991: Law and Explanation*. Chicago, IL: Commerce Clearing House, Inc., pp. 21–22.

22. Ibid., *citing interpretive memorandum*, 137 Cong. Rec. § 15276, October 25, 1991.

23. 42 U.S.C. § 2000e-2(k)(1)(B)(ii).

24. 29 C.F.R. § 1607.3D

25. Gay, L. R. and Diehl, P. L. (1992). *Research Methods for Business and Management*. New York: Macmillan Publishing Company, pp. 140–141.

26. Hamburg, M. (1977). *Statistical Analysis for Decision Making (2d ed.)*. New York: Harcourt Brace, p. 249.

27. 29 C.F.R. § 1607.14.

28. Gatewood, R. D. and Feild, H. S. (1998). *Human Resource Selection (4th ed.)*. Fort Worth, TX: The Dryden Press.

29. Bergmann, T. J. and Scarpello, V. G. (1998). *Compensation Decision Making (4th ed.)*. Fort Worth, TX: Harcourt College Publishers, p. 408.

30. *Firefighters Institute for Racial Equality v City of St. Louis*, 588 F.2d 235 (8th Cir.) *cert. denied* 443 U.S. 904 (1978).

31. 29 C.F.R. § 1607.5B.

32. Gatewood, R. D. and Feild, H. S. (1998). *Human Resource Selection (4th ed.)*. Fort Worth, TX: The Dryden Press, p. 166.

33. 29 C.F.R. § 1607.7.

34. 29 C.F.R. § 1607.5.

35. *Zamlen v City of Cleveland*, 906 F.2d 209 (6th Cir. 1990).

36. *Guardians Assn. of Police Depts. v Civil Service Commission of New York*, 633 F.2d 232, 242 (2d Cir. 1980).

37. *Zamlen*, 906 F.2d at 218.; *U.S. v City of Wichita Falls*, 704 F.Supp. 709, 714 (N.D. Tex. 1988).

38. *Legault v aRusso*, 842 F.Supp. 1479 (D. N.H. 1994).

39. 21 C.F.R. § 1607.5(F).

40. *Guardians Assn.*, 630 F.2d 79.

41. 29 C.F.R. § 1607.14D.

42. 29 C.F.R. § 1607.16E.

43. 431 U.S. 324, 339–340 (1977).

44. *New York City Transit Authority v Beazer*, 440 U.S. 568, 587 (1979).

45. Ibid. at 578.

46. Ibid.

47. 475 F.2d 216 (10th Cir. 1972).

48. Ibid. at 218–219.

49. 426 U.S. 229, 252 (1976).

50. *Watson v Fort Worth Bank & Trust*, 487 U.S. 977, 991 (1988).

51. Ibid. at 999.

52. *Watson v Fort Worth Bank & Trust*, 487 U.S. at 998 (O'Connor, J.) (1988).

53. Arvey, R. D. and Faley, R. H. (1988). *Fairness in Selecting Employees (2d ed.)*. Reading, MA: Addison-Wesley Publishing Co.

54. *Albemarle Paper Co. v Moody*, 422 U.S. 405 (1975).

55. *Robinson v Union Carbide Corporation*, 538 F.2d 652, 662 (5th Cir. 1976).

56. 42 U.S.C. § 2000e-3(a).

57. Ibid.

58. U.S. EEOC. *Charge Statistics FY1992 through FY2000*, **www.eeoc.gov/stats/charges.html**

59. U.S. Equal Employment Opportunity Commission (1990). *Annual Reports for Fiscal Year 1990*, p. 17; The U.S. Equal Employment Opportunity Commission (January 12, 2000). *Charge Statistics FY1992 Through FY2000*. **www.eeoc.gov/stats/charges.html**

60. U.S. Equal Employment Opportunity Commission. (1995). *Theories of Discrimination*. Washington DC: Government Printing Office, p. A-19

61. Ibid.

62. Ibid. at p. A-20.

63. *Byrd v Ronayne*, 61 F.3d 1026 (1st Cir. 1995); *Raney v Vinson Guard Service, Inc.*, 120 F.3d 1192 (11th Cir. 1997).

64. *EEOC Compliance Manual* § 8–1 (1998).

65. *Moyo v Gomez*, 40 F.3d 982 (9th Cir. 1994), *cert. denied* 513 U.S. 1081 (1995).

66. *McClam v City of Norfolk Police Dept.*, 877 F. Supp. 277, 282 (E.D. Va. 1995).

67. 932 F.Supp. 1095 (N.D. Cal. 1995).

68. Ibid. at 1100.

69. *Monteiro v Poole Silver Co.*, 615 F.2d 4, 8 (1st Cir. 1980); *Bartulica v Paculdo*, 411 F.Supp. 392, 396–7 (W.D. MO 1976).

70. *Collins v Mallinckrodt Chemical*, 959 F.Supp. 1123 (E.D. Mo. 1996).

71. *Wards Cove*, 490 U.S. at 657.

72. *Jones v Pepsi-Cola Metro. Bottling Co.*, 871 F. Supp. 305 (E.D. Mich. 1994).

4

SEX DISCRIMINATION

☐ Identify the different forms of sex discrimination.

☐ Identify employment practices that can potentially create sex discrimination.

☐ Understand the circumstances under which mixed motive sex discrimination can occur.

☐ Understand when sex is a *bona fide* occupational qualification (BFOQ).

☐ Describe the legal proofs necessary to establish sexual harassment.

☐ Describe in-house investigations for sexual harassment.

☐ Describe sexual harassment policies.

OPENING SCENARIO

Two individuals are applying for the position of production supervisor. Glenda McKay has a degree in production and operations management (POM) and three years experience working as a shift supervisor for a national manufacturer of appliances. Brian Ruddell has an associate's degree from Lafayette County VoTech in automotive mechanics and was a shop foreman at Robinson Brothers' Alternator Repair Shop. Dave Nichols, the plant superintendent making the hiring decision, is hesitant about hiring a woman for the position. Dave feels the job requires a tough, no-nonsense management style. Dave also believes women are passive leaders at best. Although Glenda's education and prior work record are impressive, Dave decides to hire Brian.

SEX DISCRIMINATION

Sex discrimination, discrimination based on an individual's sex, is the second largest source of Title VII violations after race discrimination. In 2000, discrimination on the basis of sex accounted for almost 31.5 percent of all charges handled by the Equal Employment Opportunity Commission (EEOC).[1] Because women are entering the workforce in increasing numbers, and because the vast majority of sex discrimination complaints are filed by females, special attention should be given to employment practices that can potentially discriminate on the basis of sex.

As an actionable Title VII claim, discrimination on the basis of sex can result from disparate treatment (discussed in Chapter 2) and from disparate impact (discussed in Chapter 3). Over time, other variations of sex discrimination have evolved (see Exhibit 4-1). This chapter examines each of these variations and devotes particular attention to examining the fastest-growing Title VII complaint—sexual harassment.

OVERT SEX DISCRIMINATION

The opening scenario provides an example of overt sex discrimination that is clearly disparate treatment. It is easily analyzed by applying the model provided by *McDonnell-Douglas Corp. v Green* and explained in Chapter 2. To establish a *prima facie* case, Glenda must first show that she is a protected class under Title VII. "Sex" is one of the protected classes; therefore, this is easily established—she is female.

The term *sex* under Title VII refers to a biological condition and not an activity or preference. Hence, treating individuals differently because they are male (or female) is an unlawful employment practice. However, as will be discussed later in this chapter, treating an individual differently based on the individual's sexual preference (some prefer the term sexual orientation) would not be covered under Title VII. Why? Because sexual orientation is not a protected class under Title VII. Only discrimination on the basis of race, color, religion, sex, and national origin is prohibited under Title VII. Discrimination on any other basis *is not* within the confines of this Act. Therefore, the very first requirement for anyone making a complaint is to show Title VII pertains to their class (race, color, religion, sex, or national origin).

■ **EXHIBIT 4-1**

FORMS OF SEX DISCRIMINATION

Overt (disparate treatment)	Sex-plus
Disparate impact on the basis of sex	Pregnancy
Sex stereotyping	Pay differentials
Mixed motives	Sexual harassment

Next, Glenda must prove she applied for the position of production supervisor, which she did; she was qualified for the position, which she was; and she was rejected, which also occurred. The only thing left is to demonstrate the position was eventually given to a male candidate who had equal or fewer qualifications. On the surface, it does appear that Glenda meets the advertised job specifications, and Brian does not. Brian appears to lack both the required education and industry work experience, and yet he was hired. Based on this information, there is reasonable cause to believe Glenda was not selected because of her sex.

Having established the *prima facie* case, the burden now shifts to Dave to offer a legitimate nondiscriminatory reason for hiring Brian instead of Glenda. Should Dave fail to provide a plausible reason why he felt Brian was better qualified for the position than Glenda, Glenda will have won her case. It is unlikely that Dave's theory—women are passive leaders—has the scientific foundations to establish a *bona fide* occupational qualification (BFOQ), least of all a legitimate nondiscriminatory reason.

Overt sex discrimination is not merely limited to hiring decisions, as it was in the opening scenario. It can occur in any employment decision. As with any disparate treatment situation, sex discrimination can result from decisions regarding layoffs, work assignments, or disciplinary actions. It is also important to point out that sex discrimination is not a one-way street; it applies to males as well as females. Federal courts have long held that Title VII's prohibition of discrimination "because of . . . sex" protects men as well as women.[2]

Suppose that in a revised scenario Brian has the degree in POM and the three years of appropriate work experience, while Glenda has the associate's degree and has only worked as a shop foreman. Dave decides to hire Glenda because he feels women have more nurturing leadership styles. From the decision-making standpoint, has anything really changed? This time, Brian was qualified; Glenda was not. What was the reason Brian was rejected? His sex. Why did Dave offer Glenda the position? Her sex. Using the *McDonnell-Douglas Corp. v Green* criterion, do you think Brian could now establish a *prima facie* case for discrimination on the basis of sex?

EMPLOYEE DISCIPLINE. Another employment practice that can result in sex discrimination, and one closely watched by employees, is employee discipline. If, for example, an employer imposes stiffer penalties on male employees who are late for work than it does on tardy female employees, the employer is violating Title VII. Similarly, favoring male employees over equally qualified female employees for training, development programs, or career enhancing work assignments also would result in unlawful sex discrimination.

Employers must be careful to ensure their policies do not subject employees to different conditions of employment that seem to be based on sex—this invariably means *all* employment policies. For example, it is perfectly legal for employers to utilize dress codes, provided the codes are imposed on both male and female employees.[3] Businesses have the right to create policies that project the proper business image. Consequently, dress codes can be a legitimate nondiscriminatory reason provided they are applied equally to all employees. However, if such policies require female employees to dress conservatively, but men are permitted to dress casually (or *vice versa*), sex discrimination has occurred. The simple standard to follow on such policies is to hold male and female employees to the same neutral standards of dress and appearance.[4] It is important to remember the underlying requirement of Title VII is to hold all employees to the same standards, not different ones. Human resource (HR) professionals must review existing policies to ensure they do indeed treat employees equally.

SEX AS A **BFOQ.** In sex discrimination cases alleging disparate treatment, an employer is afforded the traditional defenses of nondiscriminatory reasons and *bona fide* occupational qualifications (BFOQ). Sex is one of the three protected classes in which BFOQ defenses are permitted (the other two are religion and national origin). However, HR professionals are reminded that sex cannot be used to disqualify a party unless it can be clearly demonstrated that all, or substantially all, members of the sex in question cannot perform the essential functions of the job. Examples of instances in which male sex has been a BFOQ include an actor,[5] a guard in a male maximum security prison,[6] a security guard in a job requiring searches of male employees,[7] a janitor in a men's bathhouse,[8] and an attendant in a men's restroom.[9] Some examples of instances where female sex was ruled a BFOQ include an actress,[10] a salesperson in a lingerie department,[11] and custodian in a women's dormitory[12]

As with other BFOQs, these applications are very rare and narrowly defined. The opportunity to establish sex as a BFOQ is usually very remote. In most instances, HR professionals will need to ensure employment decisions are predicated on a legitimate nondiscriminatory rationale.

DISPARATE IMPACT ON THE BASIS OF SEX

There is little need to reiterate the discussion of disparate impact covered in Chapter 3 other than to note employment imbalances on the basis of sex *can* establish a Title VII complaint. Because of the potential for statistical disparities and the higher burden of proof placed on employers under disparate impact, HR professionals have long been encouraged to avoid certain questions on employment applications and during employment interviews (see Exhibit 4-2). Even the EEOC encourages employers to avoid questions about marital status as well as information about an applicant's spouse. Again, the concern for employers is not so much that they will use the information to intentionally discriminate, but it creates the impression that the information *may* be used to discriminate (see mixed motive and sex-plus discrimination). For this same reason, HR professionals are encouraged to refrain from asking for the ages and number of dependent children. In fact, sensitivity on this matter has become so critical that even asking for information about emergency contacts is no longer recommended.

The best guidance offered regarding preemployment applications is to remember applications and interviews have been declared "tests" by both the *Uniform Guidelines* and numerous court decisions.[13] Like any test, the questions asked on

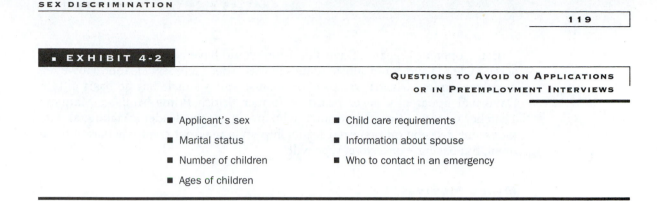

■ **EXHIBIT 4-2**

QUESTIONS TO AVOID ON APPLICATIONS OR IN PREEMPLOYMENT INTERVIEWS

- Applicant's sex
- Marital status
- Number of children
- Ages of children

- Child care requirements
- Information about spouse
- Who to contact in an emergency

applications and during interviews should be job related. In fact, the EEOC warns employers that "any preemployment inquiry in connection with prospective employment which expressed directly or indirectly any litigation, specification, or discrimination as to sex shall be unlawful unless based on a *bona fide* occupational qualification."[14] In the case of preemployment questions, the operative word is "indirectly." Words that could indicate an applicant's sex could also be construed as indirectly indicating sex-based discrimination. This would place an employer in a disadvantageous position if discrimination charges were filed and there was a statistical imbalance of female employees.

SEX STEREOTYPING

The opening scenario is a straightforward example of sex stereotyping. Under **sex stereotyping,** the decision maker holds some generalized belief about behaviors or characteristics attributed to a particular gender. These conceptions (more often misconceptions) then influence subsequent employment decisions.[15] Sex stereotyping results in actionable discrimination because it violates Title VII's basic requirement that gender must be irrelevant to employment decisions. The effect of stereotyping on the employment decision in the opening scenario is easily demonstrated by a syllogism:

Major Premise: All women are passive leaders.

Minor Premise: Glenda is a woman.

Conclusion: Glenda is a passive leader.

Because of Dave's preconceived opinion that women are passive leaders, Glenda will not be selected for a leadership position *because of her sex*. Since sex stereotyping is likely to influence employment decisions and because it is contrary to Congress's intent to establish gender-neutral employment practices, it is unlawful.[16]

For HR professionals, this means extreme care should be taken to ensure no candidate for hiring, promotion, or discharge is discussed in sex-based terms during evaluation. This could be accomplished through clear policy statements and training. However, it must be monitored and supported by upper-level management.

In the opening scenario, Dave's decision would have been lawful if he had observed Glenda and could substantiate she was indeed a passive leader. However, merely assuming Glenda was passive because she is female has no basis in fact. Dave had apparently never heard of former British Prime Minister Margaret Thatcher or any of the other women who are aggressive leaders. Making an employment decision on preferred leadership style may not create disparate treatment, but basing it on a stereotype will.

MIXED MOTIVES

Sex stereotyping may lead to another variation of employment discrimination—mixed motives. As mentioned in Chapter 2, **mixed motives** occur when the employment decision is affected by at least two motives: a legitimate (job related) reason and an illegitimate reason (i.e., sex stereotyping).[17]

To illustrate how mixed motives involving sex discrimination occur, let's assume a decision maker is overheard saying he would prefer to place a man in a particular middle-management position. Assume one of the applicants is a woman, and she was not selected for the position. The decision maker's remarks are relayed to the female applicant who then files a complaint with the EEOC.

In the ensuing investigation, the employer argues that more than one reason determined the final promotion decision. Although the manager's remark indicated he was biased toward a male candidate, there is also evidence that the female applicant's job performance was mediocre and clearly inferior to that of the other candidates. The employer contends that, based on her job performance, it would not have promoted the female candidate anyway. This was precisely the case in the Supreme Court's 1989 decision, *Price Waterhouse v Hopkins*.[18]

In this landmark Supreme Court case, a female senior manager was evaluated for partnership in a national accounting firm. During her evaluation for the promotion, several evaluators (partners in the firm) expressed negative reservations about her personality because Hopkins was a woman.[19] According to the findings of fact, she was known to be very aggressive, often to the point of abrasiveness. Several evaluators thought this was inconsistent with what they believed was proper behavior for a woman (this was sex stereotyping). Some of the comments made included: she was "macho," "overcompensated for being a woman," and needed to take "a course in charm school," as well as objections about "a lady using foul language."[20] One evaluator went as far as to advise that she needed to "walk more femininely, talk more femininely, dress more femininely, wear makeup, have her hair styled, and wear jewelry."[21] All of these comments were sufficient to establish sex stereotyping, and had the decision been based *only* on the comments, the case would have been simple disparate treatment.

However, as is often the case, employment decisions are based on many factors. In *Price Waterhouse v Hopkins*, the employer also claimed the eventual decision not to grant a partnership to Hopkins was predicated on legitimate business reasons. As in any disparate treatment situation, the employer's defense against the complaining party's *prima facie* case is that the employment practice is based on "legitimate nondiscriminatory reasons."[22] The respondent contended the decision not to promote Hopkins was based on her poor interpersonal skills—she was unduly harsh with her staff and was difficult to work with.[23] The problem the court must resolve is: Did the employer engaged in an unlawful practice when it impermissibly considered sex in making an employment decision, but would have arrived at the same conclusion had it used only legitimate nondiscriminatory criteria? Today, the answer to the question is always "yes." This determination is preordained based on language contained in the Civil Rights Act of 1991. According to that statute,

> an unlawful employment practice is established when the complaining party demonstrates that race, color, religion, sex, or national origin was a motivating factor for *any* employment practice, even though other factors also motivated the practice.[24]

This is very clear language. It means *all* mixed motive employment decisions automatically violate Title VII.

Before continuing, one point must be clarified regarding mixed motives. Students often get confused about the difference between mixed motive and constructive discharge. Hopefully, this confusion can be alleviated. In a true mixed motive situation, the decision maker considered at least one legitimate criterion and one unlawful one. Let's say an employer had considered an employee's industrial sales experience (a legitimate reason) *and* the customer's preference for male sales representatives (an unlawful criterion) when deciding who would be hired. This would be a case of mixed motive, as both criteria were evaluated in making the decision. In contrast, **constructive discharge** occurs when job conditions have become so unpleasant that a reasonable person would have felt compelled to resign.

REMEDIES FOR MIXED MOTIVES. There is an interesting paradox in mixed motive sex discrimination (see Exhibit 4-3). The moment the employer or its agent considers an applicant's sex, Title VII is violated, and an unlawful practice is committed. However, there is less here than meets the eye. Even though the employment decision itself is flawed and unlawful, the employer may avoid damage awards under Title VII if it can be proven the employer would have taken the same action in the absence of the discriminatory factor.[25]

Assume an employer can show that, given an employee's work record, it still would have denied him or her a promotion even though it had considered the employee's national origin. Technically, when the employer considered a prohibited subject (an applicant's origin) in making the decision, Title VII was violated. However, because the same decision would have been made in the absence of considering the applicant's national origin, the employer will not be required to reinstate, hire, promote, provide back pay, pay compensatory damages, or pay punitive damages to the affected applicant. The only remedies a court could impose under such circumstances would be declaratory or injunctive relief (see Chapter 1) and, perhaps, attorneys' fees and court costs.[26] Also, the employee is

■ **EXHIBIT 4-3**

REMEDIES AVAILABLE UNDER MIXED MOTIVES

Remedies, if it can be shown that the same employment decision would have been reached in the absence of the discriminatory rationale:

■ Declaratory or injunctive relief
■ Attorneys' fees
■ Court costs

Remedies, if it can be shown that the employment decision was made on the basis of the discriminatory rationale:

■ Injunctive relief
■ Reinstatement
■ Promotion
■ Front pay

■ Back pay
■ Attorneys' fees
■ Punitive and compensatory damages

still afforded the opportunity to demonstrate the employer's legitimate nondiscriminatory rationale is a pretext. As in any disparate treatment case, should the employee prove to the court that the employer's preferred reasons are pretextual, the employer becomes liable to a wide range of damages and awards. However, if the employer can demonstrate it would have drawn the same conclusion *in the absence of the discriminatory motive,* the employer will not be liable for reinstatement, back pay, or damages.[27] The only remedies the complaining party would be entitled to under such circumstances are injunctive relief (the employer will be ordered to cease consideration of sex in all future decisions) and, possibly, attorneys' fees.[28]

HR professionals should understand that if the employer fails to convince the court the same result would have occurred without the discriminatory motive, then the employer is liable for the full remedies for sex discrimination. Since mixed motive is analyzed as a disparate treatment case, the employer is exposed to a broader range of liabilities. Consequently, the employer may not only be liable for the traditional Title VII remedies (injunctive relief, reinstatement, promotion, front pay, back pay, and/or attorneys' fees), but it may also be liable for punitive and compensatory damages.

SEX-PLUS DISCRIMINATION

Employers may have practices that, on the surface, appear facially neutral but may not be impartially enforced. **Sex-plus discrimination** occurs when members of one sex who possess a specific characteristic or condition are treated differently from members of the opposite sex who have the same characteristic. Perhaps the best way to demonstrate how sex-plus discrimination operates in practice is to examine the findings from the landmark Supreme Court decision on the issue, *Phillips v Martin Marietta Corp.*[29]

The complaining party alleged a violation of Title VII of the Civil Rights Act of 1964 because of her sex. In the ensuing trial, the federal district court judge granted summary judgment for the respondent based on the following information:

- The employer informed the complaining party that it was not accepting job applications from women with preschool-age children.

- As of the time of the motion for summary judgment, the employer employed men with preschool-age children.

- At the time the complaining party applied, 70–75 percent of the applicants for the position she sought were women and 75–80 percent of those hired for the position in question—assembly trainee—were women; hence no question of bias against women as such was presented.[30]

In short, the respondent's defense was that there was no discrimination against women because more women than men were hired for the positions.

On appeal, the Supreme Court took particular note of the fact that during the period in question, men with preschool-age children were hired by the respondent. It is important to remember Section 703(a) of the Civil Rights Act of 1964 requires that persons of like qualifications be given employment opportunities irrespective of their sex. Title VII was obviously violated in this instance because men were hired with a peculiar condition (preschool-age children), and women with the same condition were not. In essence, the respondent did not discriminate against all women, just those with preschool-age children. The Supreme Court concluded an employment procedure which permitted one hiring policy for women and another for men was clearly discrimination on the basis of sex.

For HR professionals, this means all selection policies should be audited to ensure they are free from bias. Any written or *de facto* employment practice that excludes women with a particular characteristic but ignores the same characteristic in men (marital status, children, etc.) is a Title VII violation.

PREGNANCY DISCRIMINATION

The Pregnancy Discrimination Act of 1978 amended Title VII to include discrimination on the basis of pregnancy, child birth, or related medical conditions.[31] The intent of this statute is to ensure pregnancy is treated like any other medical-related condition in the workplace.[32] For example, denying disability benefits to a pregnant employee who is on maternity leave while providing those same benefits to male employees for other medical reasons would violate Title VII.[33]

The ironclad rule of the Pregnancy Discrimination Act is that Title VII views pregnancy as a medical condition; to treat it differently from any other medical condition that causes a temporary absence from the place of employment would be a violation. Therefore, if an employer has a medical leave policy permitting an employee to draw up to thirty days paid leave due to injury or illness, a female employee going through child birth is entitled to the same thirty days of paid leave (do not confuse voluntary paid medical leave with the involuntary unpaid leave mandated by the Family and Medical Leave Act—discussed in Chapter 9). Additionally, the employer must also hold a job open for a pregnancy-related absence for the same amount of time that jobs are held open for employees on sick or disability leaves. If injured employees are allowed seven months to return to work, then so are female employees after child birth. Similarly, an employer is required to treat a pregnant employee as it would any medically disabled employee with regard to performing the essential tasks and responsibilities of the job. If a temporarily disabled employee is given modified tasks or temporary job assignments, then a pregnant employee is entitled to the same treatment. If the employer makes no such accommodations for other employees, it is not required to make special ones for a pregnant employee.[34]

Additionally, an employer cannot refuse to hire a female applicant because of her pregnancy-related condition so long as she is able to perform the major functions of the job for which she is applying. Neither can an employer terminate a female employee for becoming pregnant. Pregnant female employees must be permitted to work at all times during their pregnancies so long as they are able to perform their jobs.[35] If, on the other hand, an individual is unable to perform the major functions necessary for the job, the employer does not have to provide an alternative job *unless* the employer has provided other employees who temporarily could not perform their work with alternative jobs. Again, the pregnant employee is entitled to all the benefits the employer has elected to provide employees for other medical contingencies. This does not mean the employer is required by law to provide pregnant workers with more or special benefits,[36] but neither is the employer permitted to provide less.

Prima facie proofs for unlawful pregnancy discrimination are only slightly different than other disparate treatment cases. In order to establish a *prima facie* case of pregnancy discrimination, the complaining party must show:

1. That she was pregnant.
2. That she was qualified for the job.
3. That she was subjected to an adverse employment decision.
4. That there was a connection between her pregnancy and the adverse employment decision.[37]

There is an interesting twist to pregnancy discrimination in regard to pregnancy medical benefits. In the case of *Newport News Shipbuilding and Dry Dock Co. v EEOC*,[38] the Supreme Court ruled married male employees were entitled to the same medical benefits for pregnancy as married female employees. The company's medical insurance plan provided for hospitalization benefits for pregnancy-related conditions for its female employees, but it provided *fewer* pregnancy benefits for the spouses of male employees. The male employees complained they were given different medical benefits than their female counterparts, and the reason for this difference was based on sex. The Supreme Court agreed. Employers are now required to provide the same level of pregnancy-related health benefits for the spouses of male employees that they do for their female employees.

■ EXHIBIT 4-4

PREGNANCY DISCRIMINATION COVERAGE

Condition Covered	Conditions Exempted from Coverage
■ Disability benefits*	■ Elective abortions
■ Sick leave*	■ Sick leave*
■ Health insurance*	■ Health insurance*
■ Leave of absence*	■ Temporary work assignments*
■ Abortion (when the life of the mother would be endangered)	■ Job restructuring
■ Medical complications arising from abortion	
*When provided for other disabilities/ medical conditions.	*When not provided for other disabilities/ medical conditions.

SOURCE: *Turic v Holland Hospitality*, 85 F.3d 1211 (6th Cir. 1996); 29 C.F.R. § 1604, Appendix; 42 U.S.C. § 2000 e(k).

One final warning. Because Title VII prohibits discrimination on the basis of sex, pregnancy-related benefits cannot be limited to only married female employees. These benefits must be provided to all female employees, regardless of the employee's marital status. Consequently, employers may not deny pregnancy-related medical benefits to employees who have out-of-wedlock births.[39] Those pregnancy-related accommodations covered, and those exempted, by the Pregnancy Discrimination Act are listed in Exhibit 4-4.

PAY DIFFERENTIALS

The statute making it unlawful to differentiate pay on the basis of sex for individuals in the workplace is the Equal Pay Act of 1963. Though this Act is actually an amendment to the Fair Labor Standards Act of 1938, the prohibition on discrimination in compensation on the basis of sex is enforced by the EEOC. The antidiscrimination provision clearly states:

No employer having employees subject to any provisions of this section shall discriminate, within any establishment in which such employees are employed, between employees on the basis of sex by paying wages to employees in such establishment at a rate less than the rate at which he pays wages to employees of the opposite sex in such establishment for equal work on jobs the performance of which requires equal skill, effort, and responsibility, and which are performed under similar working conditions, except where such payment is made pursuant to (i) a seniority system; (ii) a merit system; (iii) a system which measures earnings by quantity or quality of production; or (iv) a differential based on any other factor other than sex.[40]

In short, the Equal Pay Act protects men and women who perform substantially equal work in the same establishment from sex-based wage discrimination. In order to establish an Equal Pay Act claim, the complaining party must first demonstrate he or she received unequal pay for "equal work on jobs the performance of which required equal skill, effort, and responsibility, and which are performed under similar working conditions."[41] However, pay differentials are permitted on grounds other than sex.

In its most blatant form, pay discrimination would occur if two employees, one male and one female, occupy the same position, have the same essential job functions, have held their position for the same number of years, and have equal performance evaluations but are paid different salaries. As long as the jobs require equal skill, effort, and responsibility and are performed under similar working conditions, the rate of pay must be equal for our two individuals.

It would be an Equal Pay Act violation if a real estate agency provided one commission schedule for residential property for its female associates and another schedule for its male associates. It does not matter which sex was placed at a disadvantage if the sales were performed under similar working conditions. Only if the employer can demonstrate the individuals differed in job performance, seniority, or some other work-related dimension will pay differentials be permitted.[42]

Another potential complaint arising from the Equal Pay Act is that it may be violated when employers replace existing job incumbents with members of the opposite sex. For example, where an employee of one sex is assigned to a given position to replace an employee of the opposite sex but then is compensated at a lower rate of pay than the employee who was replaced, a *prima facie* violation of the Equal Pay Act occurs. The employer's only rebuttal to this *prima facie* case is to demonstrate that the wage differential is justified under one or more of the statute's four affirmative defenses. Thus, the difference between the replacement employee's and departing employee's pay is based on either seniority, merit, quantity or quality of production, or some other factor other than sex. Hence, a female senior machinist can be compensated at a higher hourly rate than a male junior machinist because the higher pay is a function of the employee's seniority and not the employee's sex. Similarly, a male technical writer whose work has fewer errors than a female counterpart may receive higher pay based on the accuracy, or quality, of his work and *vice versa*.

DIFFERENTIATING BENEFITS BASED ON SEX.   Differences in benefits because of sex are similar to pay differentials because of sex. However, differences in benefits violate Title VII rather than the Equal Pay Act. Benefit differentials fall neatly into Title VII's proscription on discrimination ". . . against any individual with respect to his compensation, terms, conditions, or privileges of employment, because of such individual's race, color, religion, sex, or national origin. . . ."[43] As always, any employment decision in which consideration is given to an employee's sex risks violating Title VII.

In the landmark case covering differing benefits, *City of Los Angeles Department of Water & Power v Manhart*,[44] an employer, noting that women have a greater life expectancy than men, modified its retirement plan to provide women with smaller pensions. The rationale was that such programs cost more for women, as a class, because of their greater life expectancy. Reminding the employer that Title VII protects individuals and not classes, the Supreme Court held that maintaining different benefits based on an individual's sex did indeed constitute unlawful discrimination. After all, not *all* women live longer than men, and it is still technologically impossible to determine just how long any individual will live. Remember, Title VII prohibits discrimination against any *individual* on the basis of that *individual's* race, color, religion, *sex*, or national origin.[45]

This standard of judicial review has also been applied when women are required to make higher contributions to an employer's deferred compensation program using sex-based actuarial tables.[46] In short, the Supreme Court has eliminated the use of sex-based actuarial tables in calculating pension contributions or retirement annuities. It does not matter that, as a group, women live longer than men; employers cannot require individual women to pay more for their benefits than individual men.

SEXUAL HARASSMENT

Perhaps *the* EEO complaint of the 1990s was sexual harassment. Since its inception in 1976,[47] no complaint under Title VII has been so misunderstood. Neither has any Title VII violation experienced such a meteoric growth rate. By fiscal year 2000 sexual harassment complaints had come to represent more than 26.5 percent of all Title VII actions investigated by the EEOC (see Exhibit 4-5).[48]

■ EXHIBIT 4-5

SEXUAL HARASSMENT CHARGES INVESTIGATED BY THE EEOC, 1990–2000

Year	Charges	Year	Charges
1990	3,217	1996	15,342
1991	6,883	1997	15,889
1992	10,532	1998	15,618
1993	11,908	1999	15,222
1994	14,420	2000	15,588
1995	15,549		

SOURCE: U.S. Equal Employment Opportunity Commission (January 18, 2001). *Sexual Harassment Charges EEOC & FEPAs Combined: FY 1992-FY 2000.* **http://www.eeoc.gov/stats/harass.html**

■ **EXHIBIT 4-6**

<u>GUIDELINES ON DISCRIMINATION BECAUSE OF SEX AS DEFINED BY THE **EEOC**</u>

Harassment on the basis of sex is a violation of Section 703 of Title VII. Unwelcome sexual advances, requests for sexual favors, and other verbal or physical conduct of a sexual nature constitute sexual harassment when:

1. Submission to such conduct is made either explicitly or implicitly a term or condition of employment.
2. Submission to or rejection of such conduct by an individual is used as the basis for employment decisions affecting such individual.
3. Such conduct has the purpose or effect of unreasonably interfering with an individual's work performance or creating an intimidating, hostile, or offensive working environment.

SOURCE: 29 C.F.R. § 1604.11(a).

Actionable sexual harassment is a violation of Title VII of the Civil Rights Act of 1964. According to the Equal Employment Opportunity Commission's *Guidelines on Sex Discrimination*,[49] **sexual harassment** is defined as unwelcome sexual advances, requests for sexual favors, and other verbal or physical conduct when such actions result in one of three consequences. First, sexual harassment becomes actionable when submission to these sexual advances is made explicitly or implicitly a condition of the victim's employment. Second, actionable sexual harassment exists when submission to or rejection of such requests by the employee becomes the basis for future employment decisions affecting that individual. The third form of unwelcomed conduct that would establish a Title VII violation results when such conduct has the purpose or effect of unreasonably interfering with the employee's work performance or creating "an intimidating, hostile, or offensive working environment."[50]

Because the first two conditions involve the withholding or granting of tangible employment benefits in exchange for sexual favors, harassment of this nature is referred to as *quid pro quo* **sexual harassment.** The third consequence constitutes a slightly different sexual harassment claim, that of "hostile environment" sexual harassment. It is important to distinguish between these two general classifications because the legal proofs required to substantiate each differ (see Exhibits 4-7 and 4-8).

QUID PRO QUO SEXUAL HARASSMENT

A party filing a complaint of *quid pro quo* sexual harassment must be able to substantiate the following:

1. The alleged victim belongs to a class or group protected under Title VII. That is to say, the object of the alleged harassment was either male or female.

2. The alleged victim was subjected to unwelcome sexual harassment. The alleged victim did nothing, by word or deed, to encourage the harassing

behavior. Neither did the alleged victim do anything to indicate the behavior was acceptable to her [or him]. If the alleged victim truly and voluntarily participated in the behavior, it could hardly have been "unwelcome."[51]

3. Because sexual harassment is a form of sex discrimination, the sexual harassment in question must be shown to have been based on the alleged victim's sex. The alleged victim must prove the conduct at issue was not merely tinged with offensive sexual connotations but actually constituted discrimination because of sex.[52] The critical issue here is whether the members of one sex are exposed to disadvantageous conditions of employment (in this case unwelcomed behavior of a sexual nature) to which members of the other sex are not exposed.

4. Submission or rejection of these advances is made explicitly or implicitly a condition of the victim's employment. If the alleged victim complains about the unwelcomed behavior, he or she may not be promoted, not recommended for a raise, be denied a desired work assignment, or be discharged. On the other hand, if the employee tolerates or concedes to the unwelcomed behavior, he or she is rewarded with some tangible workplace benefit, or at a minimum is permitted to keep his or her job.

However, the complaining party has the burden of proving there is a connection between the alleged harasser's conduct and the loss of employment benefits as was the case in *Anderson v University Health Center*.[53] The complaining party alleged certain remarks by a supervisor constituted sexual harassment. The complaining party failed to establish any connection between these alleged remarks and her termination. The supervisor in question was not her immediate superior nor the one who made the decision to terminate her. The complaining party also failed to offer evidence to create an issue of fact that her discharge was due to her rejection of any sexual advances. The evidence provided by the employer established a legitimate nondiscriminatory reason for the complaining party's termination. The federal district court concluded there was no evidence to prove the complaining party's job was dependent upon her response to any alleged sexual advances.[54]

From the HR professional's standpoint, *quid pro quo* sexual harassment is the simpler to monitor of the two forms of sexual harassment because only a relatively select group of employees can be perpetrators. It is key to this form of sexual harassment that tangible employment benefits must be involved. Consequently, only those employees who can offer or withdraw these benefits can initiate this action. In other words, the pool of potential harassers is limited to supervisory personnel and other members of management. Policies and training programs focused on this relatively small class of employees would be the most likely deterrent.

The most ominous feature of this form of harassment is the fact that the EEOC's *Guidelines on Sex Discrimination* explicitly state the employer is responsible for the acts of its supervisory personnel in *quid pro quo* situations "regardless of whether the employer knew or should have known of their occurrence."[55]

■ **EXHIBIT 4-7**

PROOFS FOR QUID PRO QUO SEXUAL HARASSMENT

- The complaining party is a member of a protected class.

- The conduct of a sexual nature was *unwelcomed*. The complaining party did not encourage it by word or deed.

- But for the complaining party's sex, he or she would not have been subjected to the unwelcomed conduct.

- The complaining party's acceptance or rejection of the unwelcomed conduct would affect tangible job benefits.

- *Respondeat superior.* When the employer knew, or should have known, of the harassment and failed to take appropriate action.

Despite this Draconian pronouncement, the employer may yet avoid even this automatically imposed liability, provided that it can meet the requirements of the affirmative defense discussed in the liability section of this chapter. Potential employer liability provides an incentive for the organization to act swiftly against the alleged harassing supervisor once an allegation of sexual harassment is made. This concern for strict liability has been reinforced by two recent Supreme Court decisions, *Burlington Industries v Ellerth*[56] and *Faragher v City of Boca Raton*.[57]

Interestingly, nothing in the *Guidelines on Sex Discrimination* requires the employer to follow due process for the accused sexual harasser. This does not, however, relieve the HR professional of the moral obligation to conduct a thorough investigation and ensure due process to *all* parties.

HOSTILE ENVIRONMENT SEXUAL HARASSMENT

Because of its peculiar characteristics, the elements, or legal proofs, necessary to substantiate a claim of hostile environment sexual harassment differ slightly from those of *quid pro quo* sexual harassment. In fact, the first three proofs for hostile environment sexual harassment are identical to those for *quid pro quo* sexual harassment:

1. The employee making the complaint must belong to a protected class.
2. The conduct or behavior the employee was subjected to was *unwelcomed*.
3. Except for the individual's sex, he or she would not have been subjected to the alleged harassment.

The fourth element, which deals with the severity or pervasiveness of the conduct, is the point upon which most of these cases fail or prevail:[58] the alleged harassment was severe or pervasive enough to alter the terms or conditions of employment and create an abusive work environment.[59] If the complaining party cannot demonstrate the harasser's conduct was not serious enough[60] or of sufficient frequency[61] to have affected the complaining party's psychological well-being and work performance, then there is, legally, no sexual harassment.[62] In

hostile environment sexual harassment claims, the unwelcomed behavior of a sexual nature must be sufficiently severe or pervasive as to alter the victim's conditions of employment,[63] or the harassment must be of a sufficient severity or frequency to create an abusive work environment. This standard is not achieved by merely showing the conduct in question offended the victim, but by demonstrating the alleged harassment affected the *terms, conditions, or privileges* of the victim's employment.[64] Examples of sufficiently severe or abusive work environments would be those that:

- Affect the psychological well-being of the victim.[65]
- Detract from the employee's job performance.[66]
- Create an abusive work environment.[67]
- Result in a constructive discharge.[68]
- Keep the employee from advancing her [his] career.[69]

What is most disturbing about hostile environment claims is that the pool of potential harassers is virtually limitless. Unlike *quid pro quo* sexual harassment in which harassers are restricted more or less to the ranks of the organization's management, almost anyone is a potential harasser under hostile environment. For example, a hostile work environment could conceivably be created by a supervisor, coworker, customer, vendor, or visitor to the employer's place of business. The HR professional's concern is that, regardless of who is engaging in the sexual harassment, it still remains the employer's responsibility to eliminate it. The courts and the EEOC hold the employer responsible for maintaining a harassment-free work environment.[70]

The employer can be held liable for hostile environment sexual harassment if it fails to remedy or prevent a hostile work environment of which it was aware or should have been aware.[71] Once the employer is made aware of the alleged sexual harassment, the *Guidelines on Sex Discrimination* recommends "immediate and appropriate corrective action"[72] be taken. When imposing corrective action, it is important to understand that employers must ensure the remedies initiated are

. EXHIBIT 4-8

PROOFS FOR HOSTILE ENVIRONMENT SEXUAL HARASSMENT

- The complaining party is a member of a protected class.
- The conduct of a sexual nature was *unwelcomed.* The complaining party did not encourage it by word or deed.
- But for the complaining party's sex, he or she would not have been subjected to the unwelcomed conduct.
- The unwelcomed conduct was so severe or pervasive as to create an intimidating and adverse work environment.
- *Respondeat superior.* When the employer knew, or should have known, of the harassment and failed to take appropriate action.

"reasonably calculated to end the harassment"[73] and should be "assessed proportionately to the seriousness of the offense."[74] Employers are held to an even higher standard when the hostile environment was created by a member of the organization's management.

Employers who have acted expeditiously and have imposed what the courts consider appropriate action have successfully avoided liability. On the other hand, employers who have merely "slapped the wrist" of the harasser have been held liable.[75] Again, an incentive is created to insulate one's self by imposing swift punishment and sanctions on the party accused of harassment.

EMPLOYER LIABILITY FOR SEXUAL HARASSMENT

Since the perpetrator is often a supervisor who relies on actual or apparent authority to extort sexual considerations from victims, *quid pro quo* claims usually result in an automatic application of employer liability for sexual harassment.[76]

DIRECT VERSUS INDIRECT LIABILITY. To appreciate the impact that indirect liability would have on employers, it is necessary to understand the conditions under which an employer is directly liable for the hostile work environment created by its agents (usually management and supervisory personnel). Under the concept of **direct liability,** an employer is liable for the hostile environment sexual harassment of its agent, only if the employer knew, or should have known, that the harassment was occurring and failed to take immediate and appropriate corrective action.[77] In essence, the employer is held responsible for failing to make a reasonable effort to prevent the harassment from recurring.

Vicarious liability, on the other hand, is so broad and inclusive in its nature that it is sometime referred to as *strict liability*. Under the concept of **vicarious liability,** an employer can be found liable for the wrongful actions of its agent regardless of whether or not the employer knew, or should have known, of the agent's sexual harassment. An employer may be indirectly responsible for the sexual harassment of one of its supervisory personnel when the following conditions are met:[78]

1. *The unlawful harassment occurred within the scope of the supervisor's employment.* Essentially, the supervisor was instructed or required, as part of his job, to create a sexually hostile environment. For example, a supervisor is told by his immediate superior to make things so uncomfortable in the workplace that the newly hired female employee will quit. In the majority of instances, a supervisor's harassing conduct has been judged to be outside the scope of his employment.[79] In hostile environment, the supervisor is acting outside of his [or her] authority to hire, fire, discipline, or promote.

2. *The supervisory personnel, though acting outside the scope of their employment, were aided in accomplishing the harassment by the existence of the agency relationship.* This means that the supervisor uses the position and the authority specifically delegated to that position to pressure the employee to

. **EXHIBIT 4-9**

LIABILITY FOR ACTIONABLE SEXUAL HARASSMENT

Alleged Harasser	Quid Pro Quo	Hostile Environment
Supervisor	Vicarious (strict) liability	Vicarious (strict) liability with affirmative defense
Coworkers, customers, and vendors	Not applicable	Direct liability

SOURCE: Robinson, R. K., Frink, D. D., Reithel, B. J., and Franklin, G. M. (1998). Vicarious liability for hostile environment sexual harassment: Examining the implications of the *Ellerth* and *Fargaher* decisions. *Labor Law Journal* 49 (8): 1240.

submit to the harassment.[80] For example, the supervisor can threaten the employee with termination, no raises, or no promotion if she [or he] refuses his advances.

For employers, this means any sexual harassment involving supervisory personnel places them in an extremely difficult position. Even if appropriate action is taken after notification of the harassment, the employer could still be responsible for compensatory and punitive damages since the employer is responsible for the actions of its representatives, even when it was unaware of those actions.

The Affirmative Defense. In circumstances in which a supervisor has indeed created a hostile work environment, the employer can escape liability if two criteria have been satisfied: the employer exercised reasonable care to prevent and promptly correct any sexually harassing behavior and the complaining party unreasonably failed to take advantage of any preventive or corrective opportunities provided by the employer or to otherwise avoid harm.[81]

In order to demonstrate the employer exercised *reasonable care* to prevent sexual harassment, it is essential that the employer has a clear sexual harassment policy and has disseminated it to *all* employees. In *Ellerth*, the Supreme Court provided guidance on this matter.

> While proof that an employer had promulgated an antiharassment policy with complaint procedures is not necessary in every instance as a matter of law, the need for a stated policy suitable to employment circumstances may appropriately be addressed in any case when litigating the first element of the defense.

As a matter of practicality, firms without sexual harassment policies will find themselves hard pressed to sustain the first criterion. Employers should further note that at a minimum, these policies should contain the following:[82]

- A statement that sexual harassment will not be tolerated.
- A definition of sexual harassment.
- Examples of conduct and behavior that could constitute sexual harassment, including both *quid pro quo* and hostile environment forms.

- A choice of channels for reporting sexual harassment, including how to report harassment during nonwork hours. This provides the employee an option if one of the company officials in the complaint procedure is the alleged harasser or has close ties to the harasser.
- Information on how the organization will handle the complaint to include conducting a thorough investigation and maintaining confidentiality.
- A statement that the organization will take appropriate corrective action to remedy any violation of the policy.
- A statement that the organization will take appropriate disciplinary action against any party making a fraudulent claim of sexual harassment.

Still, no policy by itself will insulate an employer. All members of the organization must be aware of the policy's complaint procedures; to be effective, it must be disseminated. It would perhaps be advisable to create and maintain some documentation that each employee was familiarized with the policy and how (and where) to file a complaint. A document attesting to this fact would go a long way in establishing that the employer was earnest in preventing sexual harassment and that the employees had been made fully aware of internal means of resolving misconduct.

Because these new standards of liability only affect supervisory personnel, it is recommended that these personnel be trained in their obligations under company policies regarding sexual harassment. As in documenting that rank-and-file employees were made aware of antiharassment policies, a record of supervisory training should be maintained as well. Again, this would provide evidence that the employer was exercising *reasonable care* in preventing sexual harassment.

The second criterion, the complaining party *unreasonably failed* to avail herself [or himself] of the company's preventive or corrective policies, appears to address the issue of employer notification. Unfortunately, determining what is *unreasonable failure* to use the company's antiharassment complaint procedure is not clearly defined in either case. The problem with federal courts is that terms like "reasonable" and "unreasonable" are sufficiently flexible to allow for broad interpretation in subsequent litigation. A company would hope that by providing evidence of a viable complaint/notification procedure, and proving the alleged victim was aware of the means to report the harassment, the court would recognize that failure to utilize this mechanism was done strictly at the victim's own volition. This would be particularly true if the employer's policy made provisions for filing a complaint without exposing the victim to undue risk and had a clearly delineated mechanism for investigating and resolving such complaints. Any failure on the part of the victim to use these procedures would go a long way toward satisfying the second criterion. The Supreme Court has, in effect, placed a greater burden on the complaining party to notify the employer of alleged sexual harassment when the employer has provided a viable antiharassment mechanism.

As a final word on the affirmative defense, the reader must understand that it applies exclusively to hostile environment sexual harassment attributed to

■ EXHIBIT 4-10

WHO COMMITS SEXUAL HARASSMENT IN THE WORKPLACE?

Position of the Alleged Offender	Percentage
Coworker/Group of coworkers	67
Manager/Immediate supervisor	47
Visitor/Business contact	11

SOURCE: Percentages collected in a 1986 Bureau of National Affairs survey. Because respondents could choose more than one response, cumulative percentages total more than 100 percent Bureau of National Affairs (1987). *Sexual Harassment: Employer Policies and Problems.* Washington, DC: BNA.

supervisors.[83] The affirmative defense cannot be applied in *quid pro quo* sexual harassment. In instances where supervisory personnel threatened the employee with loss [or gain] of tangible job benefits, no affirmative defense is permitted to extenuate the employer's liability.

Who Is a Supervisor?   Since employers are exposed to a stricter level of liability when a participant in sexual harassment is a supervisor, it is important to understand just which employees qualify as supervisors. Titles are never a sufficient indicator of management status; this is determined by duties, responsibilities, and authority. Based on new EEOC guidelines, if an individual meets one of three criteria, that person is considered a supervisor (see Exhibit 4-11).[84] First, an individual is considered a supervisor if he or she possesses the authority to take or recommend tangible employment actions affecting the employee (i.e., raises, retention, termination, promotion, etc.).[85] Additionally, an individual who has the authority to direct an employee's daily work assignments is considered a supervisor by the EEOC. This second criterion is particularly broad because the "supervisor" need not have the authority to recommend employment actions and satisfies this requirement when given only temporary authority to direct work.[86] Finally, an individual is a supervisor—for liability purposes—if that individual is regarded by the employee filing the complaint as having actual authority over the employee, *even when no such authority (permanently or temporarily) has been granted.*[87]

The issue of who is a supervisor poses a significant threat to organizations, one where HR professionals must take an active role. If the employer is to be insulated from vicarious liability, it is absolutely critical that all supervisory personnel be trained on their responsibilities to maintain a harassment-free work environment. Because of the broad nature of the EEOC's definitions of "supervisor," HR professionals must ensure that all potential "supervisors" (under the EEOC's definition) are included in this training. Often, employees with titles like "team leader" are not viewed as *bona fide* management personnel by their organizations, but they could be treated as such by the EEOC.

EEOC GUIDANCE AS TO WHO IS A SUPERVISOR

- Has authority to initiate employment actions.
- Has authority to recommend employment actions.
- Has permanent authority to direct an employee's work activities.
- Has temporary authority to direct an employee's work activities.
- Is reasonably believed by the employee to have actual authority over the employee.

SAME SEX SEXUAL HARASSMENT

On March 4, 1998, the Supreme Court of the United States unanimously ruled in *Oncale v Sundowner Offshore Services, Inc.* that Title VII's prohibition on hostile environment sexual harassment can be violated when the harasser and the harassed are of the same sex.[88] Despite the great deal of attention this decision received from the popular media, its impact on current workplace practices may be less than initially believed.

SEXUAL ORIENTATION.   In regard to sexual orientation, there is currently no Title VII recognition or protection. Contrary to popular misconceptions, nothing in the language of Title VII implies that sexual orientation (preference) is among the list of protected classes. In fact, federal court rulings have explicitly excluded Title VII protection for homosexuals,[89] effeminacy,[90] and transsexuals.[91] Even in the previously discussed *Oncale* decision, the Supreme Court ruled that while workers are protected from unwelcomed conduct of a homosexual nature, homosexuals are not protected under Title VII from harassment specifically directed toward homosexual conduct.

To illustrate this point, it would be a Title VII violation if a homosexual female manager demanded sexual favors from a homosexual female subordinate. This would satisfy the requirement to demonstrate the homosexual female employee was treated differently because of her sex. The male subordinates could not have been the objects of the homosexual female supervisor because she would not have been attracted to males. Consequently, the homosexual female worker's sex is what made her the object of the supervisor's unwelcomed advances.

However, if the same homosexual female employee was being verbally and physically harassed by her supervisor or coworkers because of her homosexuality, this would *not be actionable under Title VII.* Title VII protects workers against discrimination based on sex (gender), not sexual preference. However, several states and municipalities have enacted statutes or ordinances that prohibit harassment of homosexuals and transsexuals. Hence, overt discrimination on the basis of sexual preference could be litigated under these laws.

SUMMARY

This chapter introduces sex discrimination, the second largest source of Title VII violations after race discrimination. Discrimination based on sex can result from overt sex discrimination (disparate treatment), disparate impact, sex stereotyping, mixed motives, sex-plus, pregnancy, pay differentials, and sexual harassment.

Particular attention is devoted to the fastest-growing Title VII complaint, sexual harassment. Sexual harassment is defined as unwelcome sexual advances, requests for sexual favors, and other verbal and physical conduct of a sexual nature. Actionable sexual harassment occurs in two forms: *quid pro quo* sexual harassment and hostile environment sexual harassment. *Quid pro quo* sexual harassment involves the withholding or granting of tangible employment benefits in exchange for sexual favors. From an HR professional's standpoint, this is the simpler of the two to monitor because only a relatively select group of employees can be perpetrators. Hostile environment sexual harassment involves alleged harassment that is severe or pervasive enough to alter the terms or conditions of employment and create an abusive environment. What is most disturbing about hostile environment sexual harassment is that the pool of potential harassers is limitless.

KEY TERMS AND CONCEPTS

constructive discharge
direct liability
hostile environment sexual harassment
mixed motives
quid pro quo sexual harassment

sex discrimination
sex-plus discrimination
sex stereotyping
sexual harassment
vicarious liability

QUESTIONS

1. Identify and briefly describe the eight forms of sex discrimination actionable under Title VII.
2. How does mixed-motive sex discrimination differ from constructive discharge issues? Give an example of each.
3. How do the remedies for mixed motives differ from the remedies for other Title VII violations?
4. Differentiate *quid pro quo* sexual harassment from hostile environment sexual harassment. Is the employer's liability for the harassment affected by the organizational position of the alleged harasser? If so, how?
5. What should be included in an employer's sexual harassment policy?
6. How does Title VII treat discrimination on the basis of sexual orientation?

CASES

—■—

Instructions: Read the following findings of fact from actual federal sexual harassment cases. Using the burdens of proof necessary to establish a prima facie *case, determine if actionable sexual harassment has occurred. Next, determine which form of sexual harassment occurred:* quid pro quo, *hostile environment, or both. If you concluded there is actionable sexual harassment, what corrective action would you recommend?*

1 A female federal government employee filed a complaint against her male supervisor for creating a hostile work environment. The charges against the supervisor were based upon four separate sexually offensive incidents that occurred over a three-year period. Three of these incidents directly involved the complaining party, and the fourth involved a comment made about a female visitor who came to the office.

Specifically, the charges involved another female employee overhearing the supervisor remarking the complaining party was the "Dolly Parton of the office" in a conversation with two visitors to the facility. On one occasion, during a private telephone conversation initiated by the complaining party, the supervisor speculated on the frequency of her sexual relations after her recent divorce. Then, the supervisor touched the complaining party's hair once and commented on how luxurious it felt. Finally, the supervisor was overheard making a joke to a male employee about a female nonemployee who had entered the office wearing very tight shorts.

During this three-year period, the complaining party never gave any indication that her supervisor ever requested sexual favors of her or any other female employee. Based on the supervisor's aforementioned comments and actions, the complaining party filed a formal complaint of sexual harassment with her agency.

SOURCE: *Downes v FAA*, 775 F.2d 288 (Fed. Cir. 1985).

2 The complaining party was employed as a revenue agent for a government agency in San Mateo, California, and stated she was sexually harassed by a male supervisor. The complaining party was initially assigned a work station twenty feet in front of his desk. One day, she accepted the supervisor's invitation to join him for lunch. At this time, there was no indication of sexual harassment.

Shortly afterward, the supervisor began hanging around the complaining party's desk. On several occasions, he asked her to go out with him. She declined. Not wanting to have further social contact with him, the complaining party began avoiding the office during lunchtime. Shortly thereafter, the supervisor handed the complaining party a note which read: "I cried over you last night and I'm totally drained today. I have never been in such constant turmoil! Thank you for talking with me. I could not stand to feel your hatred for another day."

The complaining party became frightened and left the room. The supervisor followed her into the hallway and asked her to talk to him. She left the building. The note was shown to her department head who felt it was sexual harassment. However, the complaining party requested that she be allowed to handle the situation herself. She asked a male coworker to tell her supervisor to leave her alone.

The next day, the supervisor called in sick, and the complaining party left for training in St. Louis before he returned. While in St. Louis, she received a single-spaced, three-page letter from her supervisor similar in content to the first note.

The complaining party telephoned her department head, reporting she was frightened and upset. She then requested that either she or the supervisor be transferred, because she did not feel comfortable working in the same office with him. Consequently, the department head told her supervisor he was not to contact her again, and then he was transferred to San Francisco. The supervisor immediately filed a grievance through his union which resulted in his being allowed to transfer back to San Mateo one month later with a promise not to bother the complaining party. The complaining party responded by filing a formal sexual harassment complaint.

SOURCE: *Ellison v Brady*, 924 F.2d 872 (9th Cir. 1991).

3 May Gilbert began working for Amalgamated Baking Company (ABC) in May 1996, as a sales supervisor at its Vernon, California, facility. In May 1997, ABC promoted her to food sales account manager and in May or June 1998 promoted her again to conduct training for southern California distributors. Ken Weinzimmer, ABC's senior vice president for sales and marketing, and/or Dwight Carnahan, ABC's president, approved each promotion.

ABC offered Gilbert a job in Texas. She accepted the offer and in January 1999, with Carnahan's approval, began working as the first sales supervisor at ABC's Fort Worth, Texas, facility. ABC did not then have distributors, routes, or trucks in the Dallas/Fort Worth area. No employees reported to Gilbert. In February 1999, Gilbert hired her husband to work under her supervision as a distributor.

ABC promoted Gilbert in January 2000 to the position of district sales manager for the Dallas/Fort Worth area; she received a pay raise as well. Carnahan and Gilbert's supervisor, John Davis, approved the promotion and raise. Gilbert then supervised up to eighteen distributors, of whom up to ten operated out of ABC's Dallas facility. Although ABC eventually gave her a 4 percent raise in September 2000, she received lower compensation than did male district sales managers in other areas, and ABC did not give her access to a cellular telephone. Gilbert complained about this treatment, implying she was being treated differently because she was a woman.

In April 2001, several distributors whom Gilbert supervised complained she was treating them unfairly by favoring her husband in assigning the best routes, providing him advance knowledge of sales contests and other activities, and giving him other considerations. The distributors also complained of her poor supervision. They asserted Gilbert was one reason for the high distributor turnover in the market. A few days later, the distributors advised Carnahan of additional complaints of favoritism they asserted Gilbert had shown to her husband. Carnahan referred these complaints to Weinzimmer.

Carnahan and Weinzimmer then met with the distributors, took their grievances seriously because they viewed them as ABC customers, concluded that the distributors' complaints were valid, and followed up by meeting with Gilbert.

Carnahan discussed with Gilbert the possibility of transferring her to Houston and also offered her a distributorship, both of which she refused. Carnahan then terminated Gilbert's employment.

Gilbert alleges ABC fired her as an act of retaliation for her previous complaints about sex discrimination in pay and not being given a cellular phone.

SOURCE: *Vickers v International Baking Company*, 2000 U.S. Dist. LEXIS 17995 (N.D. Tex. 2000).

NOTES

1. U.S. Equal Employment Opportunity Commission (January 18, 2001). *Charge Statistics FY 1992 Through FY 2000.* **http://www.eeoc.gov/stats/charges.html**

2. *Newport News Shipbuilding & Dry Dock Co. v EEOC,* 462 U.S. 669, 682 (1983); *Oncale v. Sundowner Offshore Services,* 523 U.S. 75 (1998).

3. *Bellissimo v Westinghouse Electric Corp.,* 764 F.2d 175 (3rd Cir. 1985).

4. *Willingham v Macon Telegraphy Publishing Co.,* 507 F.2d 1084 (5th Cir. 1975).

5. Ibid.

6. *Dothard v Rawlinson,* 433 U.S. 321 (1977).

7. *Sutton v National Distillers Products Co.,* 445 F.Supp. 1319 (D.C. Ohio 1978).

8. *Brooks v ACF Industries,* 537 F.Supp. 1112 (S.D. W.Va. 1982).

9. *Wigginess, Inc. v Frutchman,* 482 F.Supp. 681 (S.D. N.Y. 1979).

10. 29 C.F.R. § 1604.2(a)(2).

11. Ibid.

12. *Hernandez v University of St. Thomas,* 793 F.Supp. 214 (D. Minn. 1992).

13. 29 C.F.R. § 1607.2 (B); *Cook v Billington,* 59 FEP Cases 1010 (D.C. D.C. 1992); *Garland v USAir, Inc.,* 767 F.Supp. 715 (W.D. Pa. 1991). 366.

14. 29 C.F.R. § 1604.2(a)(2).

15. *Los Angeles Dept. of Water and Power v Manhart,* 435 U.S. 702, 707 (1978).

16. *Price Waterhouse v Hopkins,* 490 U.S. 228, 239–240 (1989).

17. *Miller v CIGNA Corp.,* 47 F.3d 586 (3rd Cir. 1995).

18. 490 U.S. 228 (1989).

19. 490 U.S. at 235.

20. Ibid.

21. Ibid.

22. *McDonnell-Douglas Corporation v Green,* 411 U.S. 792, 802 (1973); *Texas Dept. of Community Affairs v Burdine,* 450 U.S. 248, 252 (1981).

23. *Hopkins v Price Waterhouse,* 618 F.Supp 1109, 1113 (D.C. D.C. 1985).

24. 42 U.S.C. § 2000e-2(m).

25. 42 U.S.C. § 2000e-5(g)(2)(B).

26. 42 U.S.C. § 2000e-5(g)(2)(B)(I).

27. 42 U.S.C. § 2000e-5(g)(2)(B).

28. Ibid.

29. 400 U.S. 542 (1971).

30. Ibid.

31. 42 U.S.C. § 2000e(K).

32. Ibid.

33. *Stansell v Sherwin-Williams Co.*, 404 F.Supp 696 (N.D. Ga. 1975).

34. 29 C.F.R. § 1604, Appendix.

35. Ibid. at APP. 8.

36. *Geier v Medtronic, Inc.*, 99 F.3d 238, 242 (7th Cir. 1996); *Lang v The Star Herald*, F.3d 1308, 1312 (8th Cir. 1997).

37. *Boyd v Harding Academy of Memphis, Inc.*, 88F.3d 410, 413 (6th Cir. 1996).

38. 462 U.S. 669 (1983).

39. U.S. Equal Employment Opportunity Commission (January, 1997). *Facts About Pregnancy Discrimination.* **www.eeoc.gov/facts/preg**

40. 29 U.S.C. § 206(d).

41. *Corning Glass Works v Brennan*, 417 U.S. 188, 195 (1974).

42. *Tomka v The Seiler Corp.*, 66 F. 3rd 1295,1310 (2nd Cir. 1995); *Varner v Illinois State University*, 226 F.3d 927, 929 (7th Cir. 2000).

43. 42 U.S.C. § 2000e-2(a)(1).

44. 42 U.S. 702 (1978).

45. 42 U.S.C. § 2000e-2(a)(1).

46. *Arizona Governing Committee v Norris*, 463 U.S. 1073 (1983).

47. *Williams v Saxbe*, 413 F.Supp. 654 (D.C. D.C. 1976); *rev in part and vacated in part, sub. nom.*, *Williams v Bell*, F.2d 1240 (D.C. Cir. 1978).

48. U.S. Equal Employment Opportunity Commission (January 12, 2000). *Sexual Harassment Charges EEOC & FEPAs Combined: FY 1992–FY 2000.*

49. 29 C.F.R. § 1604.11.

50. 29 C.F.R. § 1604.11(a).

51. *Meritor Savings Banks, FSB v Vinson*, 477 U.S. 57, 68 (1986).

52. *Oncale v Sundowner Offshore Services, Inc.*, 523 U.S. 75, 81 (1998).

53. 623 F.Supp. 795 (W.D. Pa. 1985).

54. 623 F.Supp. at 798.

55. 29 C.F.R. § 1604.11(d).

56. 118 S.Ct. 2275 (1998).

57. 118 S.Ct. 2275 (1998).

58. *Fisher v San Pedro Peninsula Hospital*, 262 Cal. Rptr. 842 (1989).

59. *Meritor*, 477 U.S. at 67 (1986).

60. *Rabidue v Osceola Refining Co.*, 805 F.2d 611 (6th Cir. 1986).

61. *Christoforou v Ryder Truck Rental, Inc.*, 668 F.Supp. 294 (S.D. N.Y. 1987).

62. *Vasconcelos v Meese*, 907 F.2d 111 (9th Cir. 1990).

63. *Jones v Flagship International*, 793 F.2d 714 (5th Cir. 1986); *cert. denied* 479 U.S. 1065 (1987).

64. *Doe by Doe v City of Belleville, Il.*, 119 F.3d 563, 576 (7th Cir. 1997).

65. *Phillips v Smalley Maintenance Service*, 711 F.2d 1524, 1529 (11th Cir. 1983).

66. *Meritor*, 477 U.S. at 63.

67. *Jones v Flagship International*, 793 F.2d 714, 719–20 (5th Cir. 1986).

68. *Young v Southwestern Savings and Loan Assoc.*, 509 F.2d 140, 144 (5th Cir. 1975).

69. *Harris v Forklift Systems, Inc.*, 510 U.S. 17, 20 (1993).

70. *Meritor*, 477 U.S. at 65; 29 C.F.R. § 1604.11.

71. *EEOC v Hacienda Hotel*, 881 F.2d 1504 (9th Cir. 1989).

72. 29 C.F.R. § 1604.11(d).

73. *Katz v Dole*, 709 F.2d 251, 256 (4th Cir. 1983).

74. *Dornhecker v Malibu Grand Prix Corp.*, 828 F.2d 307 (5th Cir. 1987).

75. *Katz*, 709 F.2d at 256.

76. *Davis v Sioux City*, 115 F.3d 1365, 1367 (8th Cir. 1997); *Nichols v Frank*, 42F.3d 503, 513 (9th Cir. 1994); *Bouton v BMW of North America, Inc.*, 29 F.3d 103, 106 (3rd Cir. 1994); and *Kaufman v Allied Signal*, 970 F.2d 178, 185 (6th Cir. 1992).

77. *Katz v Dole*, 709 F.2d 251 (1983); *Barrett v Omaha National Bank*, 726 F. 2d 424 (8th Cir. 1984).

78. *Faragher v City of Boca Raton*, 11 F.3d 1530, 1536 (11th Cir. 1997).

79. *Steele v Offshore Shipping, Inc.*, 867 F.2d 1311, 1311–12 (11th Cir. 1989).

80. *Sparks v Pilot Freight Carriers, Inc.*, 830 F.2d 1554, 1559–60 (11th Cir. 1989).

81. *Burlington Industries v Ellerth*, 524 U.S. 742, 745; *Faragher v City of Boca Raton*, 524 U.S. 775, 780 (1998).

82. Robinson, R. K., Franklin, G. M., and Fink, R. L. (1993); Sexual harassment at work: Issues and answers for health care administrator. *Hospital and Health Services Administration* 38 (2): 175.

83. *Burlington Industries*, 524 U.S. at 745.

84. Bland, T. S. (1999, September). EEOC issues guidance in effort to clarify harassment rulings. *HR News*, 18 (9): 7, 15.

85. Ibid. at 15.

86. Ibid.

87. Ibid.

88. 523 U.S. 75 (1998).

89. *Polly v Houston Lighting & Power Co.*, 825 F.Supp. 135 (S.D. Tex. 1993); Ulane, 742 F.2d 1081, 1087; *DeSantis v Pacific Telephone & Telegraph Co.*, 608 F.2d 327, 329–330 (9th Cir. 1979).

90. *Smith v Liberty Mutual Insurance, Co.*, 569 F.2d 325, 327 (5th Cir. 1978).

91. *Sommens v Budget Marketing Inc.*, 667 F.2d 748,750 (8th Cir. 1982); *Holloway v Arthur Anderson & Co.*, 566 F.2d 659, 662 (9th Cir. 1977); *Voles v Ralph K. Davies Medical Center*, 403 F.Supp. 456,457 (N.D. Cal. 1975); *aff'd mem.* 570 F.2d 354 (9th Cir. 1978).

OTHER PROTECTED CLASSES

LEARNING OBJECTIVES

- ☐ Identify employment practices that violate Title VII on the basis of religion and national origin.
- ☐ Explain what an employer's duty is to reasonably accommodate an employee's religious beliefs.
- ☐ Identify employment practices that potentially discriminate on the basis of national origin.
- ☐ Identify the conditions under which English-only work rules are permissible.
- ☐ Explain the criteria for establishing actionable age discrimination.
- ☐ Understand who is protected and what constitutes a "disability" under the Vocational Rehabilitation Act of 1973 and Americans with Disabilities Act of 1990.
- ☐ Discuss employers' responsibilities to provide reasonable accommodation to applicants or employees with disabilities.
- ☐ Understand privacy and confidentiality requirements imposed on medical information.

OPENING SCENARIO[1]

A *woman who is 5'2" tall and weighs three hundred twenty pounds applies for the position of "institutional attendant for the mentally retarded (IA-MR)" at the state Mental Health Retardation Hospital (MHRH). During a preemployment physical examination, a MHRH nurse notes that the applicant was morbidly obese, but found no limitations to her ability to perform as an IA-MR. Medically, a person is considered morbidly obese when that individual weighs more than twice his or her optimal weight, or is in excess of one hundred pounds over his or her optimal weight. Based upon this information, the director of the MHRH rejected the applicant because he felt that applicant's obesity might* *hamper her ability to evacuate patients in the event of an emergency, placed her at a greater risk of developing serious ailments, and her obesity could increase the likelihood of the applicant filing a workers' compensation claim.*[2]

The applicant filed a complaint that the MHRH had discriminated against her in violation of the Americans with Disabilities Act (ADA). In her complaint, she argued that she had applied for the position of IA-MR. She further contended that she should be protected under the ADA because she had been perceived as being disabled by her prospective employer. The employer had excluded her from consideration for employment solely because of her perceived disability, being obese. Furthermore, she contended that she was qualified for the position despite her perceived disability based on her two previous tenures in that same position and her previous work record while performing in those positions. The applicant had, in fact, worked in this position on two previous occasions, once for two years and another for four. A review of her personnel files revealed a spotless work record.

The employer contended that the applicant did not have a disability as defined under the ADA, since she was merely overweight.

―――――――――― ■ ――――――――――

INTRODUCTION

This chapter examines the remaining classes receiving protection under Title VII (religion and national origin) as well as those protected under the Age Discrimination in Employment Act (age) and the Americans with Disabilities Act (disabilities). Because the Vocational Rehabilitation Act of 1973, which applies to holders of federal contracts and subcontracts, contains virtually the same language and requirements as the Americans with Disabilities Act, these two statutes will be discussed together. For consistency, the two remaining protected classes under Title VII will be addressed first, bringing our examination of the Civil Rights Act of 1964 to a close.

RELIGION AS A PROTECTED CLASS

Compared to the other protected classes, Title VII complaints based upon religious discrimination are quite rare. In fact, it was not until 1996 that charges of religious discrimination exceeded 2 percent of the total charges handled by the Equal Employment Opportunity Commission (EEOC).[3] However, religious discrimination charges have risen steadily since 1992, when they accounted for only 2.5 percent of all Title VII charges. In actual number they have increased from 1,388 in 1992 to 1,939 in 2000, a 39.7 percent increase.[4] They still, however, account for the smallest number of Title VII complaints by a protected class. However, as the American workforce becomes increasingly diverse a growing number of religious beliefs will appear in the workplace. In addition to Judeo-Christian religions, employers may expect to find employees who are Muslims, Hindus, and Buddhists (just to name a few). Consequently, religious accommodation will become more complex, and complaints may be expected to rise.

RELIGIOUS EXEMPTIONS

Perhaps one of the reasons that religious discrimination charges occur so infrequently is because the religious exemption under the Civil Rights Act of 1964 permits preferential treatment to *bona fide* religious organizations. Often referred to as the Section 702 exemption because of its location in the original Act, the **religious exemption** states that the prohibition on religious discrimination:

> . . . shall not apply . . . to a religious corporation, association, educational institution, or society with respect to the employment of individuals of a particular religion to perform work connected with the carrying on by such corporation, association, educational institution, or society of its activities."[5]

In essence, this means religious organizations are permitted to make hiring and discharge decisions based on an applicant's or employee's religious affiliation. To be eligible for this exemption, the religious corporation, association, education institution, or society activities must show some connection between the position and the religion. If this connection is clearly visible, preferential hiring is permitted and, if not, preferential hiring is prohibited (see Exhibit 5-1).

To illustrate this point, let's examine the case of *Killinger v Samford University*.[6] In this case, a faculty member was hired to teach courses in religion in the School of Divinity at a Baptist university. After hiring, the faculty member was removed from the Divinity School and relegated to teaching undergraduate classes. The faculty member contended that he was being discriminated against (prohibited from teaching in the Divinity School) because his religious philosophy was incompatible with the fundamentalist theology advanced by the leadership of the Divinity School. The university contended that, as a religious institution, it was

---

■ EXHIBIT 5-1

RELIGIOUS EXEMPTED ENTITIES UNDER SECTION 702

- Religious corporations (i.e., Presbyterian Church in America, Southern Baptist Convention, Roman Catholic Church, etc.)

- Religious associations (i.e., National Council of Reformed Churches, etc.)

- Religious educational institutions (i.e., University of Notre Dame, Emory University, etc.)

- Religious societies (i.e., Knights of Columbus, Reformed University Fellowship, etc.)

covered by Title VII's religious exemption. The Eleventh Circuit agreed with the university by concluding:

> The Section 702 exemption's purpose and words easily encompass Plaintiff's case; the exemption allows religious institutions to employ only persons whose beliefs are consistent with the employer's when the work is connected with carrying out the institution's activities.[7]

Clearly, religious education is at the core of a religious university, especially in its Divinity School. As a Baptist university, Samford was permitted to lawfully discriminate in favor of Baptists when making teaching assignments. The principal criteria for eligibility for a Section 702 exemption is that the organization must clearly be a religious corporation, association, education institution, or society, and it must exhibit some ministerial function. To establish this, the religious institution's primary duties must consist of teaching, spreading the faith, church governance, supervision of religious order, and participation in religious ritual or worship (see Exhibit 5-2).[8] It is equally important to show that the institution in question is owned in whole or in substantial part by a particular religion. Moreover, if it can be shown that a particular institution is not owned, supported, or managed by a religious entity, no exemption will be permitted.[9] In short, the organization in question would be viewed by the courts as secular, not religious. Even if the organization in question is owned by a religious institution, it may not necessarily be eligible for the religious exemption. Any organization which claims to be religious but lacks any religious content will be considered a secular organization and not entitled to the Section 702 exemption.[10]

It is important to note that the Section 702 exemption only permits religious institutions to discriminate on the basis of religion, not gender or race.[11] However, the Title VII ban on sex discrimination does not apply in cases where a particular religion has theological prohibitions for ordaining women as ministers, priests, or positions of church leadership. For example, it is a basic tenet of faith that only men can be ordained as priests in the Roman Catholic Church. Therefore, Title VII cannot be used to require the Catholic Church to ordain women on the grounds of sex discrimination in employment. However, in all other positions, discrimination based on sex would be prohibited.

■ EXHIBIT 5-2

CRITERIA FOR ESTABLISHING A SECTION 702 EXEMPTION

- Teaching
- Spreading the faith
- Church governance

- Supervision of religious order
- Participation in religious ritual
- Worship

SOURCE: *Little v Wuerl*, 929 F.2d 944, 947–48 (3d Cir. 1991).

RELIGIOUS DISCRIMINATION

Notwithstanding Section 702's religious exemption which, as we have seen, permits differential treatment of members of religious faiths, Section 703 makes it unlawful for secular organizations to otherwise discriminate on the basis of religion. Here, disparate treatment and disparate impact (discussed in Chapters 2 and 3) are applicable. If an employer who is not a religious organization subjects an employee to poor treatment in the workplace because the employer, or its agent, dislikes the employee's religious beliefs, the employer has violated Title VII.[12] As in any disparate treatment situation, the complaining party establishes a *prima facie* case by proving the employer treated him or her differently from other employees because of the individual's religious beliefs.[13] Unless an applicant's religion can be shown to be a *bona fide* occupational qualification (BFOQ), a secular employer may not discriminate on the basis of religion.[14]

RELIGIOUS ACCOMMODATION

Merely ensuring an employee's religious beliefs have not affected employment decisions is not enough to avoid charges of religious discrimination. Employers may find themselves in violation of Title VII when they fail to make "reasonable accommodation" for an employee's religious practices.[15] That is correct. Employers must refrain from considering an individual's religious beliefs in making decisions, and they must make accommodations for those beliefs after employment. The additional requirement to provide such accommodation comes from Section 701 of the Civil Rights Act of 1964. This is not to be confused with Section 703, which prevents discrimination on the basis of religion. Specifically, Section 701 states:

> . . . [t]he term "religion" includes all aspects of religious observance and practice, as well as belief, unless an employer demonstrates that he is unable to reasonably accommodate to an employee's or prospective employee's religious observance or practice without undue hardship on the conduct of the employer's business.[16]

Under this concept of **religious accommodation,** an individual establishes a *prima facie* case of religious discrimination by demonstrating that: (1) the individual has a *bona fide* belief that compliance with an employment requirement would be contrary to his religious beliefs or practice, (2) the individual informed the employer of the conflict, and (3) the individual was disciplined or discharged for failing to comply with the conflicting employment requirement (see Exhibit 5-3).[17]

Assume that Dave Leroy, a senior machinist, has recently had a religious experience and become a deacon in the First Baptist Church. Due to his recent faith and position in the church, Dave announces that he will no longer be able to work on Sundays. This would be in keeping with his religious obligation to keep the covenant and keep the Sabbath holy.[18] In June, the plant superintendent informs all employees that they will have to work seven-day shifts for the next two weeks in order to meet a client's deadline. Leroy informs the plant superintendent that

ESTABLISHING A _PRIMA FACIE_ CASE FOR RELIGIOUS ACCOMMODATION

■ The individual has a _bona fide_ belief that compliance with an employment requirement would be contrary to his or her religious beliefs or practice.

■ The individual informed the employer of the conflict.

■ The individual was disciplined or discharged for failing to comply with the conflicting employment requirement.

SOURCE: _Wilson v U.S. West Communications_, 58 F.3d 1337, 1340 (8th Cir. 1995).

working on Sunday conflicts with his religious beliefs. The superintendent tells Leroy that if he is not at his workstation on Sunday, he will be fired. When Leroy fails to show up for work that Sunday, his employment is terminated. This series of events would be sufficient to establish Leroy's Title VII claim.

In its rebuttal, the employer must show that it met its obligation to "reasonably" accommodate the employee's religious beliefs and practices, or that the accommodation would impose an undue hardship on the employer.[19] By proving the employee's desired accommodation would impose an undue hardship, the accommodation becomes "unreasonable."

In practice, the employer's obligation to accommodate an employee's religious beliefs is not as burdensome as accommodating an employee's disability (discussed later in this chapter). The employer must show the costs incurred in making the accommodation. The employer cannot automatically claim that the accommodation causes undue hardship because it would merely increase administrative or marginal costs. Accommodation costs must be weighed against the employer's size, total operating costs, and the number of employees requiring accommodation.[20] This is an easy standard to achieve because the employer is required to make reasonable efforts to accommodate an employee's religious beliefs.[21] However, this does not guarantee employees any accommodation or the accommodation of their choice.[22]

There are some circumstances under which accommodations are more likely to be judged as unduly burdensome. Normally, any accommodation becomes an undue hardship if it results in changing a _bona fide_ seniority system. This occurs when, in order to accommodate the employee's religious practices, the employer must deny another employee a shift preference guaranteed by the company's seniority system.

Common methods of achieving religious accommodation include arranging for a voluntary swap of work schedules among employees, instituting flexible scheduling to allow employees to make up time lost to religious observances, or requiring employees to arrive or depart early to meet religious observances. If swaps or flexible schedule patterns cannot accommodate the employee, a transfer to a comparable job within the company may be in order. In some instances it may be that such accommodation could actually benefit an employer. Assume a delivery company offers seven-day-a-week delivery service. Some Jewish and other employees who may have religious objections to working on their Sabbaths would have little concern about working on Sundays, the Christian Sabbath. Seventh Day Adventists, Worldwide Church of God members, and Jehovah's Witnesses also hold religious tenets against working on Saturdays. Again, because their Sabbath is a day other than Sunday, they could be scheduled to work for Christian employees on that day. Granted, this may make scheduling a little more difficult, but it can solve an accommodation dilemma. In this regard, having a religiously diverse workforce might be used to some employers' advantage.

Interestingly, even accommodations involving work schedules can quickly cross the line into undue hardship. Returning to the scenario above involving Dave Leroy, Leroy's employer could prove that accommodating his absence for religious observance would require hiring another machinist; recall that *all* employees were required to work two seven-day weeks, so this would preclude shift changes. The employer could probably establish that accommodating Leroy would cause an undue hardship, since it would involve the expense of hiring an additional employee, either permanently or temporarily.

To illustrate how employer size and the number of employees requiring accommodation affect "undue burden," let's assume an employer has 100 employees and that 20 percent are Orthodox Jews. In March, all of the Jewish employees request to take their vacation time to observe Passover. The employer could make a convincing argument that accommodating 20 percent of the workforce to observe Passover would leave it terribly understaffed and could constitute an undue hardship. On the other hand, assume only one employee is an Orthodox Jew. Accommodating a single employee is unlikely to have the same impact and would not create an undue hardship.[23]

RELIGIOUS ACCOMMODATION AND UNION DUES

One final issue under religious accommodation is the payment of union dues. This issue not only affects unions but may also involve employers who are responsible under their collective bargaining agreements to deduct union dues from the payroll. If an employee's religious faith prohibits joining or paying dues to any organization outside of the church, can they still be required to pay the equivalent of dues to the union that represents them in the bargaining unit?

This situation occurred in *Tooley v Martin Marietta Corp.*[24] Martin Marietta Corporation and the United Steelworkers of America had negotiated a collective bargaining agreement containing a union shop provision. Under such an arrangement, the company was obligated to discharge any employee who failed to join the union and pay union dues. Three of the employees who were Seventh Day Adventists refused to join the union. They contended that their religion prohibited them from becoming members of or paying a service fee to a union. In an attempt to achieve a compromise, the three workers offered to contribute an amount equivalent to union dues to a mutually agreed upon charity. The union refused and held the employer to the union shop clause in the collective bargaining agreement. Therefore, the three employees would have to join the union and pay dues or the employer would have to terminate their employment. If the employer failed to do so, the employer would be in violation of the collective bargaining agreement, and it would be an unfair labor practice under the National Labor Relations Act.[25]

The affected employees argued that both the union and the company were required under Title VII to make reasonable accommodation for their religious beliefs,[26] unless it caused an undue hardship. The Steelworkers responded that it did create an undue hardship and was, therefore, not a reasonable accommodation. This argument focused on the contention that substituting a charitable contribution in lieu of dues created an undue hardship on the union by denying it funds necessary for the union's operations. The union further argued that the charity accommodation was unreasonable because it was contrary to the National Labor Relations Act's authorization of union shop agreements.

The court concluded that Title VII was applicable in this case and that both the union and the company were obligated to make a reasonable accommodation. The court also found that substituting a contribution to a mutually agreed upon charity was not an undue hardship. Thus, the court enjoined the union and the company from discharging the plaintiffs for failing to pay union dues so long as they make equivalent contributions to the mutually acceptable charity.

NATIONAL ORIGIN AS A PROTECTED CLASS

National origin (sometimes called ethnicity) is the last protected class under Title VII to be discussed. Like the preceding protected classes (race, color, sex, and religion), employers cannot consider a candidate's national origin when making *any* employment decision. In a similar vein, employees are protected against any consideration of their ethnicity that could result in disparate treatment, harassment, or mixed motives. Furthermore, disparate impact on the basis of national origin is actionable under Title VII, just as it is for sex and race.

Because members of many ethnic groups often display nationality-specific characteristics (i.e., particular religious affiliations, speech patterns, languages, surnames, etc.), Title VII can be violated when a connection is made between unfavorable treatment in the workplace and such ethnic characteristics (see Exhibit 5-4). For example, a parishioner from St. Basil's Greek Orthodox Church might be assumed to be of Greek ancestry by an employer who happens to be predisposed against Greeks. Conversely, an applicant with the name Mustapha Kamal may be assumed to be of Turkish descent by a potential employer who dislikes Turks and consequently treats Mustapha differently than other candidates with non-Turkish surnames. Whether the employee is actually of Turkish descent is immaterial. If he is *assumed* by the employer to be Turkish and is treated differently because of

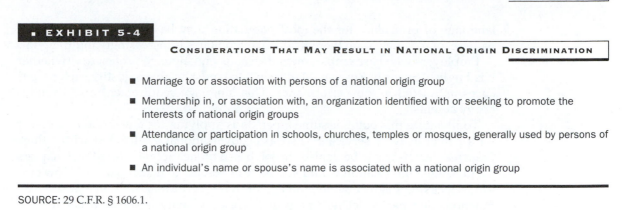

■ EXHIBIT 5-4

CONSIDERATIONS THAT MAY RESULT IN NATIONAL ORIGIN DISCRIMINATION

- Marriage to or association with persons of a national origin group

- Membership in, or association with, an organization identified with or seeking to promote the interests of national origin groups

- Attendance or participation in schools, churches, temples or mosques, generally used by persons of a national origin group

- An individual's name or spouse's name is associated with a national origin group

SOURCE: 29 C.F.R. § 1606.1.

this assumption, Title VII is violated.[27] In addition, a potential violation may result when an employee is a member of an organization associated with specific ethnic groups and, therefore, is assumed to be a member of such ethnic groups. For example, a member of the Ancient Order of Hibernians might be assumed to be of Irish ancestry, just as a member of La Raza might be assumed to be a Chicano.

An interesting point to note about national origin discrimination is that it is not limited to the actual members of the ethnic group against whom discrimination is directed. If an employer punishes nonethnic employees for associating or fraternizing with members of an ethnic group whom the employer finds distasteful, Title VII has been violated. If an employee is subjected to adverse employment outcomes because he or she is married to a member of an ethnic group the employer finds offensive, Title VII is again violated on the basis of national origin. To illustrate, assume a white, non-Hispanic male employee has a wife who is of Cuban ancestry. Also, assume the employer disapproves of mixed marriages between "Anglos" and Hispanics. As a result of this attitude, the employee is continually passed over for promotion and receives no merit pay raises. The white male employee is being discriminated against on the basis of his wife's nationality. The husband can initiate a complaint of unlawful discrimination under Title VII on the basis of national origin.[28] As the United States's ethnic diversity continues to grow and so-called mixed marriages increase, human resource (HR) managers must be aware of the possibility of claims of adverse employment actions. If an employee does not receive a merit pay raise, the employer should have appropriate documentation (i.e., performance appraisals, counseling statements, etc.) to demonstrate that he or she did not deserve the raise.

LANGUAGE

A potential problem related to ethnicity is language proficiency. A substantial proportion of the workforce's projected growth is from immigration.[29] Many newly-arrived legal immigrants to the United States have limited language proficiency. In some parts of the nation, languages other than English are spoken. The language of preference for the local population may be Spanish, Russian, Vietnamese, or a combination thereof—the United States is increasingly multilingual.

Employers who base employment decisions on language proficiency (whether it is English, Spanish, Russian, Mandarin, etc.) must be able to justify such preferences as related to job performance. This language requirement also includes heavy accents.

To illustrate this point, assume a person is applying for a position as a driver for a parcel delivery service. She speaks conversational English but with a thick French accent. Can she be denied the job based on her accent? Recalling Chapters 2 and 3, what information would you have to possess to make that call? How critical is speaking English without an accent to the performance of the essential job functions of a parcel delivery person? If your job analysis shows it has little, if any, impact on job performance, then rejecting the applicant based on her accent could be unlawful discrimination based on national origin.

Now assume the position for which the heavily accented candidate has applied is that of an air traffic controller. Based on job analysis that may indicate that clearly enunciated communications between the air traffic controller and aircraft pilots are an essential component of the job, can the employer now disqualify the applicant because of her accent? If the employer can demonstrate that her accent is so heavy it affects comprehension, then it is denying her employment based on a job-related reason rather than her nationality.

ENGLISH-ONLY WORK RULES. **English-only work rules** require employees to speak English in certain work situations as a condition of employment. This creates a problem for employers because the *EEOC Guidelines on Discrimination Because of National Origin* currently declare that employer policies prohibiting employees from speaking their primary language at *all* times may create an "atmosphere of inferiority, isolation, and intimidation *which could result in a discriminatory working environment.*"[30] Consequently, any language policy that creates a complete bar to speaking languages other than English is likely to be interpreted by the EEOC as a potential Title VII violation and, therefore, is subject to strict scrutiny.

However, this policy creates a paradox. On one hand, the EEOC has created disincentives to encourage employers not to adopt English-only policies (except where business necessity can be demonstrated). On the other hand, the EEOC expects employers to maintain a working environment free from harassment on the basis of race,[31] sex,[32] and national origin.[33] This is where the employer's dilemma arises—an employer may implement an English-only rule in response to racial or sexual harassment complaints. Will the federal government conclude the employer is merely meeting its obligation to maintain a harassment-free workplace? Or will it conclude the employer is discriminating against non-English speakers on the basis of nationality?

The apparent solution to this dilemma was offered in the Ninth Circuit case, *Garcia v Spun Steak Company*.[34] Spun Steak Company, a California poultry and meat processor, implemented an English-only rule for the expressed purpose of promoting racial harmony in the workplace. The company's policy was initiated in response to complaints that some Hispanic workers were using their bilingual capabilities to make "derogatory, racist" comments about an African American coworker in Spanish. As a repercussion of perceived racial harassment, the employer imposed a new policy that only English would be spoken in the company during work periods. It is important to note that this policy was not an all-inclusive prohibition; Spanish could still be spoken during lunch breaks and on the employees' own time. However, no language other than English could be spoken in work areas during work times.

The Spanish-speaking employees then argued the language policy was discriminatory because it denied them a privilege enjoyed by English-only speakers (the ability to talk in the language with which they felt most comfortable) and it created an atmosphere of inferiority and intimidation.[35] The Ninth Circuit observed that Title VII is not intended to protect employees from policies that "merely inconvenience" them; rather it exists to protect them only against practices that have a *significant* impact.[36] Because the employees in this case were bilingual, the Ninth Circuit concluded that the English-only rule did not preclude conversation on the job, merely Spanish conversation while engaged in normal work activities. All employees could still converse in English.

The policy was a business necessity—it was in place in order to prevent certain employees from using their fluency in a language other than English to intimidate monolingual coworkers who were members of other ethnic groups. Thus, the Ninth Circuit concluded that the policy did not violate Title VII.

When language restrictions are necessary in the workplace, it becomes incumbent upon the HR administrator to guarantee the following general guidelines are observed (see Exhibit 5-5). First, and foremost, is there any alternative to resolving the problem without resorting to limiting the use of a given language?[37] If not, then the HR professional *must* ensure the English-only policy is justified by "business necessity."[38] This rationale must therefore be documented and the policy should be implemented with the expectation that it will be challenged by the offended employees. If it cannot be readily and reasonably justified, you should not have an English-only policy.

Care must also be taken to ensure the policy does not create a universal prohibition throughout the place of employment. Rather, the English-only provisions

---

■ EXHIBIT 5-5

GUIDELINES FOR ENGLISH-ONLY RULES

- ■ Must be justified
- ■ Cannot create a universal prohibition
- ■ Must describe consequences for noncompliance
- ■ Must be communicated to all employees

SOURCE: *Garcia v Spun Steak Company*, 13 F.3d 296 (9th Cir. 1993).

should be limited to those activities and during those times mandated by the previously established business necessity.[39] Invariably, this means limiting the language restrictions to work-related communications and work settings. Requiring employees to speak only English in conversations in nonwork areas during nonwork times should be avoided. Finally, before any English-only policy is enforced, it is absolutely imperative that the employer first makes the affected employees aware of the policy and the consequences for not obeying it. In its *Guidelines on Discrimination Because of National Origin*, the EEOC asserts that any employer's failure to notify its employees of the consequences of violating the English-only requirement would result in the Commission concluding "the employer's application of the [English-only] rule as evidence of discrimination" if it then took disciplinary action.[40] As always, documentation of both the business justification for the policy and the specific notification process is highly recommended.

IMMIGRATION REFORM AND CONTROL ACT

One final issue closely related to national origin discrimination comes from the Immigration Reform and Control Act of 1986 (IRCA). This statute was enacted for the purpose of curbing illegal immigration into the United States. IRCA makes it unlawful for an employer to knowingly hire, recruit, or refer undocumented workers (a.k.a. illegal aliens). Additionally, employers are required to verify all employees hired after November 6, 1986, are legally authorized to work in the United States, which would include American citizens, resident aliens, and aliens with the expressed permission of the attorney general to work in the United States.[41] Employers are required to show proof of this verification by having every employee hired after November 6, 1986, complete an INS Form I-9 and provide documentation establishing the applicant's identity and authorization to work (see Exhibit 5-6). The most common documents used to establish employment authorization and applicant identity are a social security card *and* a state driver's license. In order to clearly demonstrate the employer verified the applicant's identity, photocopies of the two sources of documentation should be filed with the INS Form I-9. Failure to maintain IRCA's documentation can subject the employer to civil fines ranging from a minimum of $100 per each individual worker without an INS Form I-9 to a maximum of $1,000 per individual worker.[42]

In addition to prohibiting the hiring of illegal aliens, IRCA also prohibits discrimination in hiring and discharge based on national origin (as does Title VII) and on citizenship status.[43] These antidiscrimination provisions are intended to prevent employers from attempting to comply with the Act's work authorization requirements by discriminating against foreign-looking or foreign-sounding job applicants. Of particular concern for smaller organizations is that IRCA's antidiscrimination provisions apply to smaller employers than those covered by EEOC-enforceable laws. IRCA's national origin discrimination provisions also apply to employers with between four and fourteen employees (those employers who would not be covered by Title VII).[44] IRCA's citizenship discrimination provisions

> ■ **EXHIBIT 5-6**
>
> **VERIFICATION REQUIREMENTS UNDER THE IMMIGRATION REFORM AND CONTROL ACT**

Documents Establishing Both Employment Authorization and Identity	Documents Establishing Only Employment Authorization	Documents Establishing Only Identity
U.S. passport	Social Security card	State driver's license
Certificate of U.S. citizenship	U.S. birth certificate	State identification for those under age 16
Certificate of naturalization	Other documentation authorizing employment in the U.S. approved by the attorney general	
Resident alien card (if the card contains a photograph of the individual)		
Foreign passport with the authorization of the attorney general to work in the U.S.		

SOURCE: 8 U.S.C. 1324a(b)(1)(B).

effectively extend protection against discrimination based on national origin to all workplaces with at least four employees.

Because lawmakers were concerned that the verification process and penalties for hiring undocumented workers might cause employers to be reluctant to hire applicants of Hispanic origin, IRCA contains provisions making an unfair immigration-related employment practice for:

> a person or other entity to discriminate against any individual (other than an unauthorized alien) with respect to the hiring, or recruitment or referral for a fee, of the individual employment or the discharging of the individual from employment—(a) because of such individual's national origin, or (b) in the case of a citizen or intending citizen (as defined in paragraph [3]) because of such individual's citizenship status.[45]

As a further concern, Title VII may be violated during the verification process if individuals of one national origin group (e.g., Hispanics) are subjected to greater scrutiny than individuals from other groups. For example, an applicant with a Hispanic surname is given a thorough background investigation while a candidate with a western European surname only has her driver's license and social security card photocopied. This would be a Title VII violation because the individual with the Hispanic surname was subjected to different treatment (a more rigorous application process) because of his national origin.

In complying with IRCA's verification requirements, it is important to treat all employees the same. If thorough background checks are initiated, they must be initiated on *all* applicants, not just those of one particular national origin. It should be noted that IRCA does permit employers to give preference in hiring and recruiting of U.S. citizens over foreign nationals if the two individuals are *equally qualified.*[46]

PROTECTION BASED ON AGE

The Age Discrimination in Employment Act (ADEA), like the Equal Pay Act, is not an amendment to the Civil Rights Act of 1964, but an amendment to the Fair Labor Standards Act of 1938.[47] This is an important distinction because the remedies for ADEA violations are not the same as those afforded under Title VII.

The next thing that managers need to know about the ADEA is that it has resulted in one of the fastest-growing equal employment complaints. This is due in large part to the fact that the baby boom generation is aging and constitutes a significant portion of the workforce. By 1999, age discrimination claims accounted for 18.3 percent of all charges handled by the EEOC.[48]

Additionally, there are variations as to which employers are required to comply with the ADEA's antidiscrimination provisions. Under the ADEA, the term "employer" means a person engaged in an industry affecting commerce who has twenty or more employees for each working day in each of twenty or more calendar weeks in the current or preceding calendar year.[49] Compare this to Title VII's application to employers with *fifteen or more* employees.[50]

The ADEA of 1967 makes it unlawful to: ". . . fail or refuse to hire or to discharge any individual or otherwise discriminate against any individual with respect to his compensation, terms, conditions, or privileges of employment, because of such individual's age." Further, it is unlawful for an employer to even segregate or classify employees on the basis of age.[51] However, the prohibitions on age discrimination are limited to individuals who are at least forty years of age.[52] Initially, this protection on the basis of age covered only individuals who were between forty and sixty-five years old.[53] The upper limit was extended to seventy years old by a 1978 amendment.[54] As of a 1986 amendment, ADEA discrimination on the basis of age encompasses all employees and applicants who are over forty; there is no upper age limit.[55]

The ADEA's ban on age discrimination means that should an employer refuse to hire an applicant for a job based solely on the premise that the employer thinks the individual is too old for the job, that employer violates the ADEA. If an employee is not promoted because the employer feels that she is too old to perform the work at the next level, the ADEA is violated. If, during a downsizing, an employer decides to lay off all employees over fifty years old, the ADEA is violated. Like Title VII, the ADEA mandates that employment decisions must be based on factors other than the employee's age.

The ADEA is not automatically violated every time an over-forty employee is not promoted or is terminated. If the employment decision is based on legitimate

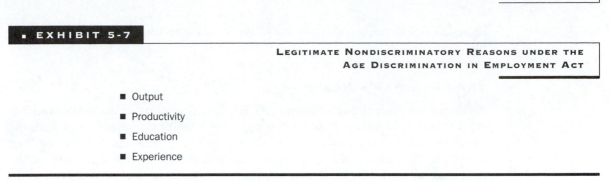

■ EXHIBIT 5-7

LEGITIMATE NONDISCRIMINATORY REASONS UNDER THE
AGE DISCRIMINATION IN EMPLOYMENT ACT

- Output
- Productivity
- Education
- Experience

reasons other than age, no unlawful discrimination has occurred (see Exhibit 5-7). However, if the employee's age *was* a consideration in the employment decision, the whole process is tainted. Since the ADEA requires employers to evaluate employees on their merits, not their age,[56] the employer could be facing a mixed motive case at best.

ESTABLISHING A PRIMA FACIE CASE OF AGE DISCRIMINATION

To establish a *prima facie* case of unlawful discrimination under the ADEA, it must be proven that:

1. The complaining party was in an age group protected by the ADEA.
2. He or she was discharged or demoted [or refused employment].
3. At the time of the discharge or demotion, the complaining party was performing his or her job at a level that met his or her employer's legitimate expectations.
5. Following the complaining party's discharge, he or she was replaced by someone of comparable qualifications who is significantly younger.[57]

The fourth proof, replacement by someone who is "significantly younger," is a relatively recent innovation. Prior to 1996, it was assumed the ADEA would be violated only when the over-forty employee (the protected class under the ADEA) was replaced by someone under forty years old. However, with the Supreme Court's decision in *O'Connor v Consolidated Coin Caterers, Corp.*,[58] the ADEA may be violated if an older employee is replaced by an over-forty employee who is significantly younger. In the O'Connor case, a fifty-six year old employee with twelve years of service in the company was discharged and replaced with a forty year old employee. The employer contended that since the forty year old employee was also a member of the same protected class (forty years old and older) the ADEA was not violated. The Supreme Court concluded, however, that "[t]he fact that one person in the protected class has lost out to another person in the protected class is thus irrelevant, so long as he has lost out because of his age."[59] The purpose of the ADEA is quite clear; an employee's (or applicant's) age cannot be used in making any employment decision.

THE EMPLOYER'S REBUTTAL

An employer confronting an alleged ADEA violation must demonstrate convincingly that the employment decision is based on a legitimate reason, which means the employer has the burden of convincing the court that its decision was *not* based on the individual's age. If the contested matter involves promotion, the employer must demonstrate that the younger candidate was more qualified. In all cases, there must be a clear connection between the decision criteria and the job in question. This becomes particularly troublesome for the employer because the ADEA permits jury trials for all violations.[60] Remember, under Title VII, trials by a jury are also allowed, but only when a complaining party seeks compensatory or punitive damages.[61] Under the ADEA, jury trials may be requested for *any* violation.

For the HR staff, this means guaranteeing education requirements, performance expectations, seniority requirements, and other skill and knowledge requirements have been clearly identified for the position in question. It is equally important to communicate these position requirements to all potential applicants before the selection process even begins. All position announcements should clearly and concisely state all of the required qualifications a successful candidate must possess. This precaution is intended to reduce unrealistic expectations among potential applicants who do not possess the necessary requirements. As always, position requirements and qualifications must be directly related to successful job performance. Consequently, it is imperative that proper job analysis has been conducted on the job in question and the criteria have been validated (see Chapter 3). As with other Equal Employment Opportunity (EEO) matters, the presence of nonessential job requirements unnecessarily exposes an employer to litigation and undermines the organization's rebuttal in court.

In instances where the employer can prove the position was given to the more qualified candidate, the ADEA is not violated. This is a legitimate nondiscriminatory reason because the individual's qualifications determined the employment outcome, not the individual's age.

AGE AS A BONA FIDE OCCUPATIONAL QUALIFICATION. Some *bona fide* occupational qualifications (BFOQs) permit employers to use age as a disqualifier, but as with most BFOQs, they are very rare. In *Western Airlines v Criswell*,[62] the Supreme Court examined an employment practice that imposed a mandatory retirement age of sixty on all flight crew members (pilots, copilots, and flight engineers). The airline's argument for the mandatory retirement was that after the age of sixty, medical research indicated that physical and mental capabilities are prone to "sudden or subtle incapacitation."[63] To strengthen its arguments, the airline cited Federal Aviation Administration regulations that prohibited any individual who had reached the age of sixty from serving as a pilot or copilot on any commercial flight. The airline adopted this policy and merely added flight engineers. The employer contended that its mandatory retirement of flight crews was a BFOQ reasonably necessary to the safe operation of the airline. Remember, as with all BFOQs, it must be proven that the age-biased BFOQ is "reasonably necessary" for normal business operation, and that the "reasonable necessity" is narrowly defined.[64]

The complaining parties provided evidence that the process of psychological and physiological deterioration caused by aging varies greatly with each individual.[65] Not surprisingly, there is evidence that shows that some older workers can perform at levels equal to or even better than younger coworkers. The complaining parties argued mandatory retirement ignores individual differences. The airline, they further argued, should determine mandatory retirements on a case-by-case basis rather than on an arbitrary age ceiling. After all, the ADEA compels employers to evaluate their employees who are forty years or older on their merits and not their age.[66] The flight engineers and several pilots who wanted to become flight engineers also pointed out that in emergency situations, the flight engineer's duties are less critical to passenger safety than the pilot's. The complaining parties then argued that Western Airlines's BFOQ defense for flight engineers was insufficient to justify its legitimate concern for passenger safety.[67]

In its ruling, the Supreme Court concluded the BFOQ exception was meant to be an *extremely* narrow exception to any general prohibition of age discrimination under the ADEA.[68] In essence, the airline had failed to show that all, or substantially all, of flight engineers over sixty were unable to safely perform their duties. The mandatory retirement age for flight engineers (not pilots or copilots) violated the ADEA.

THE COMPLAINING PARTY'S REBUTTAL

If the employer offers a seemingly legitimate BFOQ, the complaining party may still win the case, provided that he or she can prove the employer's legitimate business reasons are a pretext. If the HR staff has done its job properly, this likelihood is greatly reduced. Again, good job analysis and documentation are critical.

REMEDIES FOR ADEA VIOLATIONS

The ADEA is not an amendment to the Civil Rights Act of 1964; therefore the ADEA remedies available to a complaining party who proves age discrimination are limited to reinstatement, back pay, front pay, promotion, and/or attorneys' fees.[69] In the event that willful age discrimination has occurred, the ADEA provides for liquidated damages as well.[70]

PROTECTION BASED ON A DISABILITY

The first law to provide federal protection for applicants and workers with disabilities was the Vocational Rehabilitation Act of 1973 (VRA).[71] This is a fairly narrow statute in that it applies only to those employers who: (1) hold a federal contract or subcontract in excess of $2,500, (2) are a depository of federal funds, and (3) receive federal grants or aid assistance.[72] Employers who did not meet these conditions had no obligations concerning employees with disabilities until the Americans with Disabilities Act of 1990 (ADA) was enacted. The VRA provided the foundation from which the ADA would arise.

When first enacted, the definition for a *qualified handicapped person* under the VRA[73] was the same as a *qualified individual with a disability* under the ADA.[74] Additionally, the definitions for *reasonable accommodation, undue hardship, physical or mental impairment, major life activities*, and *handicap/disability* in the two acts are virtually identical. To know the provisions of one of these statutes is to understand the provisions of the other. To alleviate this redundancy, The Vocational Rehabilitation Act Amendment of 1992[75] changed the term *handicapped person* to *individual with a disability* and the term *handicapped* to *disability*. Now, the two laws are almost indistinguishable, and because of these marked similarities, our discussion will focus on the ADA. The major difference between the two acts is that the VRA requires employers who hold federal contracts or subcontracts in excess of $10,000 to take affirmative action in hiring qualified individuals with a disability.[76] Beyond this affirmative action requirement, both the VRA and the ADA are identical in their employment discrimination provisions.

AMERICANS WITH DISABILITIES ACT

The ADA was passed by Congress and signed into law by President George Bush on July 26, 1990. The major objectives of the law are to prevent employment discrimination against a qualified individual on the basis of a real or perceived disability (Title I), prohibit discrimination against individuals with disabilities in public transportation (Title II), and provide for public accommodation and access for persons with a disability (Title III). It is Title I's prohibition against discrimination in the terms and conditions of employment because of an individual's disability that is of particular concern to us. Perhaps the most important thing to remember is that Title I protects only *qualified individuals* with a disability from employment discrimination. It does not protect unqualified individuals with a disability any more than the other EEO laws protect unqualified individuals. It is therefore critical for HR professionals to understand when an individual is qualified and when he or she is not. When examining this issue, the HR professional must understand who is required to comply with the Act, who is disabled, and who is qualified.

COVERED ENTITIES. The ADA applies to all private-sector employers with fifteen or more employees. It applies to all employment agencies regardless of whether they are public or private. Labor unions with fifteen or more members must comply with the ADA, as well as all state and local governments. Even joint labor-management committees on apprenticeship are required to follow the provisions of the ADA's Title I. You may have already noticed that the same employers who are covered under Title VII of the Civil Rights Act of 1964 must also comply with Title I of the ADA.

Under the ADA, no covered entity shall discriminate against a qualified individual with a disability because of such individual's disability in regard to job application procedures; the hiring, advancement, or discharge of employees; employee compensation; job training; and other terms, conditions, and privileges of employment.[77]

Although the ADA is very similar to Title VII and the ADEA, there is one significant difference. Under Title VII, the protected classes are fairly easy to identify. Gender is easy to establish; the complaining party is either male or female. Race and ethnicity also can be readily established. Age under the ADEA, likewise, can easily be verified through a number of legal documents (i.e., birth certificates, medical records, etc.). All of these classifications possess an "all or nothing" nature. You are either female or you are not. You are either Hispanic or you are not. You are either over forty years of age or you are not. Disability, however, occurs in degrees. An individual may fall anywhere on the scale from marginally disabled to completely disabled. The extent to which an individual is disabled often determines whether or not he or she is *qualified* to perform a particular job in question and the length which employers must go to accommodate the individual. The ADA adds further confusion through its definition of *disability*.

DISABILITY.   When assessing any ADA claim, the HR professional has two questions to answer: is the applicant disabled and is the individual qualified? From the ADA's inception, some critics have contended that it casts an overly broad net on this matter.[78] Under the ADA (and VRA), the term **disability** means: A physical or mental impairment that substantially limits one or more of the major life activities of an individual, a record of such impairment, or regarding an individual as having such an impairment. This means that those who currently are disabled are protected under the ADA. Additionally, those who were disabled but have since recovered or have been rehabilitated are covered. Surprisingly, applicants or employees who are not now, nor have they ever been, afflicted with a mental or physical disability covered under the ADA may still be protected if the employer *thought* they had a disability and discriminated against them because of the imagined disability. As strange as this may sound, an employer can violate the ADA by erroneously assuming a nondisabled individual is disabled.

This situation occurred in the opening scenario. The director of the MHRH rejected the applicant because he *assumed* she could not perform some of the essential job functions (i.e., patient evacuation). It was merely his *perception* that she would not be able to evacuate her patients in a timely manner and that she was a workers' compensation risk. He could offer no basis in fact for this presumption.

An employer runs the risk of triggering an ADA claim any time an employment decision is based on an individual's perceived disability. In one case, an employer refused to hire an applicant for the position of electrician because a drug test indicated his blood sugar was high, and the employer assumed he was diabetic. The employer's action was based on the assumption that the applicant had

DISABILITY AS DEFINED UNDER THE AMERICANS WITH DISABILITIES ACT

- A physical or mental impairment limiting a major life function
- A record of such impairment
- Is regarded as having an impairment

an impairment that would substantially restrict his ability to perform the essential functions of the job. However, this was a false assumption, and the applicant, who was not disabled as defined under the ADA, was able to perform all essential functions of an electrician. Because the applicant was perceived to be disabled and the decision not to hire him was based on that perceived disability, the employer violated the ADA.[79]

The meaning of *disability* under the ADA entails having a physical or mental impairment that substantially limits one or more of the *major life activities*. Unless we know what these major life activities are, this definition is not going to be very helpful. The EEOC, the agency responsible for enforcing the ADA, defines **major life activities** as caring for one's self, performing manual tasks, walking, seeing, hearing, speaking, breathing, learning, and working.[80] As for *physical impairment*, this can be any physiological condition, disfigurement, or loss of one of eleven body systems (see Exhibit 5-9).

In a recent Supreme Court decision, the Court ruled that individuals with impairments corrected by medical or other measures to normal, functional abilities are not "disabled" under the ADA.[81] Such is the case of individuals who have their eyesight corrected by glasses[82] or persons with high blood pressure that is controlled with medication.[83] In either case, the physical impairment, once corrected, no longer substantially affects the individual's major life function, and

BODY SYSTEMS WHICH CONSTITUTE PHYSICAL IMPAIRMENT
UNDER THE AMERICANS WITH DISABILITIES ACT

Neurological	Digestive
Special sense organs	Genito-urinary
Respiratory	Hemic and lymphatic
Speech organs	Skin
Cardiovascular	Endocrine
Reproductive	

SOURCE: 29 C.F.R. § 1630.2(h).

hence, it is not a disability. Although the individuals are impaired, they are not sufficiently impaired to be disabled as defined by the ADA.

Mental impairment encompasses any mental or psychological disorder that results in mental retardation, organic brain syndrome, emotional illness, mental illness, or specific learning disabilities. These are very broad areas and encompass an extremely wide range of conditions.

QUALIFIED INDIVIDUAL WITH A DISABILITY.   If you have at least a general idea of what qualifies as a disability, then it is easier to determine that any person who has a physical or mental impairment based on these criteria would be an "individual with a disability." In employment situations, the ADA does not protect "individuals with a disability." It only protects "*qualified* individuals with a disability."[84] The next step is to ascertain when a candidate with a disability is qualified.

A **qualified individual with a disability** is one who can perform the essential functions of the job in question with reasonable accommodation; therefore the principal concern is whether or not an individual with a disability can perform the essential functions of a particular job with or without reasonable accommodation.[85]

The essential functions, according to the EEOC, can be ascertained by examining three criteria.[86] First, the function is essential if the position in question exists for the purpose of performing that function. For example, driving a truck is the purpose of the job position of long-distance truck driver. Therefore, this is the essential component of that job. The next issue deals with the number of other employees available to perform the function or among whom the performance of the function can be distributed. If a task associated with the job can be assigned to another employee without disrupting the primary purpose for the job in question, that task would not be essential. Suppose one of the duties for a long-distance truck driver included changing the motor oil every three thousand miles. Since this task could easily be assigned to company maintenance personnel, it would not be an essential function. However, driving the truck safely from destination to destination could not be assigned to another employee—it would be an essential function. The final factor considered by the EEOC involves the degree or skill required to perform the function. Returning to our previous example, changing oil requires little skill and expertise compared to actually driving, maneuvering, and backing a tractor trailer. The more skill required to perform a task, the more difficult it is to assign to an employee in a different job category. Additionally, requisite expertise makes the task more essential to the job in question.

All of this means basic job analysis for each position in an organization is absolutely critical. It further means that job analysis, and the resulting job descriptions and job specifications, must be continually monitored and reviewed to ensure they provide *current* and *accurate* information about each specific job. If the essential tasks, duties, and responsibilities associated with any given job are flawed, it is unlikely that reasonable accommodation can be ascertained.

Having clearly established what the essential functions of the job are, the HR professional can then concentrate on the individual's qualifications. If the candidate can presently perform the essential functions without any assistance from the employer, that candidate is a qualified individual with a disability. To deny such an individual employment based on the individual's physical disability (when he or she has previously proven the essential job tasks can be performed) would be an obvious violation of Title I of the ADA.

Had the director of the MHRH in the opening scenario tested the applicant's ability to evacuate patients (an essential job function), there may have been a different outcome. She could have been tested by participating in a fire drill involving real patients. If the applicant could not adequately evacuate her patients within a prescribed time frame (determined by job analysis and local fire codes), she would be unqualified for the position in question. Since the ADA protects only qualified individuals with a disability (either real or perceived), the applicant would not have cause to file under the ADA.

Interestingly, not all candidates can demonstrate work performance so clearly. Some candidates may require reasonable accommodation.

REASONABLE ACCOMMODATION.   **Reasonable accommodation** refers to modifications that would permit the individual with a disability to perform the essential functions of the job in question, provided these modifications do not create an undue hardship for the employer. The first thing a manager or HR professional should do when any individual requests reasonable accommodation under the ADA is to clarify the individual's degree of impairment. The actual physical or mental impairment must "substantially limit" a major life activity. If the impairment is corrected by medication or other measures, the individual making the accommodation request does not have an impairment that "substantially limits" a major life activity and would not be protected under the ADA.[87] For example, a diabetic who can function perfectly normally so long as she is under medication would not have a disability under the ADA. So long as she monitors her blood-sugar levels and takes her insulin shots, the diabetic can operate as well as someone without diabetes.[88] While under medication, her major life activities are not "substantially limited."

On the other hand, an employee who was confined to a wheelchair, even though he is capable of mobility, would not be capable of the same mobility of a nonimpaired person. He would meet the ADA's requirement for "disability" because he would be "substantially limited" in his ability to walk. The diabetic's corrective measures (medication) overcame her limitations to perform daily activities; hence, she would not have met the ADA's definition of being "disabled."[89] In the case of the paraplegic, he was still limited in his ability to go about his daily activities despite his corrective measure, the wheelchair. His mobility was improved by the wheelchair, but it was still short of that of a nonparaplegic.

Managers and HR professionals must always remember that assessment of whether or not an individual is disabled under the ADA must be done on an individualized basis.[90] Also, remember that the final determination of whether an individual has a disability is not necessarily based on a diagnosis of the individual's impairment, but if the impairment is corrected, does it still substantially limit a major life activity?[91]

Once determining an applicant or employee is disabled under the ADA, the decision maker may now move to the next question: Can the individual perform the essential job functions with or without reasonable accommodation? Again, if the individual can perform the essential job functions without any accommodation, he or she is qualified. If not, what is the appropriate reasonable accommodation that would permit performance of these functions?

In determining reasonable accommodation, the employer may ask the individual for reasonable documentation about the disability and functional limitations. But employers should be careful. The ADA prohibits the employer from requesting medical information which is not pertinent to the accommodation.[92] This usually precludes employers from requesting complete medical records on the individual in question because such records would include a good deal of information not related to the accommodation.[93] The EEOC recommends that when requesting medical information, employers should specify what types of information they need regarding the disability and the functional limitations it imposes. Remember, once this information is obtained, the employer is responsible for keeping it confidential.

Making accommodation under the ADA is far more complex and complicated than religious accommodation under Title VII. The EEOC has developed three categories of "reasonable accommodation" under the ADA. Under the EEOC's guidance, when attempting to accommodate an applicant or employee, an employer should consider modifying the job application process, modifying the work environment, or modifying the benefits and privileges of employment.[94]

Modifying the Job Application Process. Modifying the job application process entails avoiding anything in the selection process that could be construed as discriminating against applicants because of disability. First and foremost, an employer cannot ask an applicant if he or she is disabled. In fact, the EEOC contends that an employer may not even ask an applicant if he or she needs reasonable accommodation before a conditional job offer is made.[95] The only exception to this is under circumstances in which the applicant's disability is apparently obvious, or the applicant has voluntarily disclosed information about his or her disability. In most instances, the employer is permitted to inquire if reasonable accommodation is necessary only after an offer of employment has been made.

Employers may also be required to modify tests or testing methods to accommodate applicants. A deaf applicant may require a sign language interpreter for an interview. An applicant with attention deficit disorder may require someone to read a written examination.

If the accommodation requested by the applicant causes the employer an *undue hardship*, the applicant would not be a *qualified individual with a disability*. The accommodation would not be reasonable, and the employer would not be compelled to hire the applicant. For example, a paraplegic applies for the position of truck driver at a small delivery company. But technology is not available that would permit the applicant to perform the essential functions of the job. Therefore the accommodation needed would indeed cause undue hardship.

Modifying the Work Environment. In the second category of accommodation, physical modifications to the work environment, a number of actions may be taken. First, the employer's existing workplace can be made more accessible. This includes reconfiguring work areas to make them wheelchair accessible. Physical modifications may require manuals and work procedures to be provided in Braille. Making other physical modifications to work areas may be as simple as lowering a worktable so it can be reached by an employee in a wheelchair. But it could also be as elaborate as acquiring a state-of-the-art TTY keyboard telephone system to allow a deaf and mute employee to make and receive telephone calls.[96]

Another work environment accommodation is *job restructuring*. This involves identifying the essential job functions (see Chapter 3) and eliminating or reassigning nonessential job functions that the disabled employee cannot perform. A paraplegic secretary confined to a wheelchair has the job description in Exhibit 5-10. Only 2 percent of her job involves stocking printer paper in the supply room. Although the door is sufficiently wide to allow her easy entry and exit from the supply room, boxes of copy paper weigh twenty-five pounds each and must be stored on shelves that are as high as six feet from the floor. The employer could lower the shelves (and double the size of the storage area), or this one aspect of the job could be assigned to another employee. Since the stocking duties are a marginal portion of the secretary's duties, assigning these tasks to another employee would be the more reasonable action to take.

Often, permitting an employee to work in a *flexible or part-time schedule* would be sufficient accommodation. This is particularly effective for those employees who have become disabled since hiring.

Suppose an employee requests that her workday be reduced to six hours per day to allow her to attend physical therapy sessions in the afternoon. Usually, the employer would be required to adjust the employee's schedule, if it does not significantly disrupt the employer's operations (cause undue hardship).

Modifying the Benefits and Privileges of Employment. When job restructuring, workplace modification, and flexible scheduling will not accommodate the employee with a disability, the employer may want to consider reassignment. It is important to note the employer is not required to create a position for the employee. The employer is only required to consider reassignment to a vacant position for which the employee is qualified. In addition, the employer is not required to promote the employee to a higher position. Under most circumstances, the employee must be reassigned to a vacant job which is equivalent in terms of pay, status, benefits, and other relevant factors as the job the employee is leaving.[97]

The final accommodation available to employers is use of accrued paid leave and/or unpaid leave. Situations that could require leave as an accommodation include medical therapy, recuperation time, training for prosthetic devices, repair time for wheelchair accessible vans, training for sign language, acquiring a guard dog, or avoiding temporary workplace conditions that adversely affect the

▪ EXHIBIT 5-10

JOB DESCRIPTION FOR A WORD PROCESSING SECRETARY

JOB DESCRIPTION

Job Title: Word Processing Secretary

Department: Administrative Services

Position of Immediate Supervisor: Director of Administrative Services

I. GENERAL SUMMARY OF RESPONSIBILITIES

Types, edits, and distributes various correspondence to clients and internal staff. Transmits and proofs various essential status reports for day-to-day operations.

II. SPECIFIC DUTIES AND RESPONSIBILITIES

1. Types daily correspondence and reports. (50%)
2. Proofs and prints out final copies for distribution. (10%)
3. Receives handwritten copies and places them in priority files. (2%)
4. Types special projects, such as proposals, quotations, system analysis, and customer and client surveys. (20%)
5. Transmits documents through the use of electronic mail. (10%)
6. Logs updates, volume, and turnaround time records of completed work. (2%)
7. Receives and places priority on rush requests and special projects. (2%)
8. Serves as a backup for the receptionist. (2%)
9. Stocks the secretarial supply cabinet. (2%)
10. Performs other duties as directed.

III. JOB SPECIFICATIONS

1. High school diploma or GED, 1–2 years of college helpful.
2. Knowledge of Microsoft Word, Corel WordPerfect, Microsoft Excel, and Corel Quattro Pro.
3. Must have a good eye for neatness and quality type documents.
4. Must lift 25-pound containers to a shelf of 72″.
5. Ability to work well with others in developing proposals and projects.

SOURCE: Modified from Burack, E. H. and Mathys, N .J. (1987). *Human Resource Planning: A Pragmatic Approach to Manpower Staffing and Development* (2d ed.). Lake Forest, IL: Brace-Park Publishing.

disability.[98] Normally, the employer will allow the employee to exhaust any accrued paid leave and then permit a certain amount of unpaid leave.

Suppose an employee is scheduled to receive a new prosthetic leg. The installation, therapy, and training on the artificial limb is projected to take two weeks (ten workdays). The employee has accrued four days of paid leave. The employer could reasonably expect to permit the employee to use the four days of paid leave and then six days of unpaid leave.

The use of employee leave has become complicated with the enactment of the Family and Medical Leave Act (FMLA) of 1993 which mandates that covered employees are entitled to twelve weeks of unpaid leave and are allowed to return to their job in the event of specified emergency situations (the FMLA is addressed in greater detail in Chapter 9). Employers now must decide which law is more applicable to a given situation, the ADA or the FMLA. There may be some instances in which both could apply.

Undue Hardship.   Any accommodation demanded of the employer is reasonable only as long as it does not create an undue hardship on the employer. Unfortunately for managers and HR professionals, this is determined too often on a case-by-case basis.[99]

In determining **undue hardship**, the ADA requires that four factors be considered (see Exhibit 5-11).[100] First, what is the overall cost of the accommodation compared to the overall financial resources of the facility, number of persons employed by the facility, and its projected effect on the operating expenses of the facility? Second, the overall financial resources, number of employees, and number and location of all the facilities owned by the employer are considered in regard to the cost of the accommodation. Third, the accommodation must be considered in light of the type of operation in which the employer is engaged. This includes considering the organizational structure, the functions of the workforce, the geographic separateness of facilities, and the degree of administrative or fiscal interdependence between the facility and other operations of the employer. Fourth, the impact that the accommodation will have on the operation of the facility in question must be considered. All of these considerations are extremely broad and

■ **EXHIBIT 5-11**

**CONSIDERATIONS FOR UNDUE HARDSHIP UNDER
THE AMERICANS WITH DISABILITIES ACT**

- Cost of the accommodation
- Size (number of employees)
- Number and type of facilities
- Composition and structure of workforce
- Essential job functions

make developing viable HR policies difficult. Finally, provided proper job analysis was performed on the job in question, the employer is *not* required to change the *essential job functions*.

To illustrate the impact of these considerations, let's assume that an employee of a small grocery store has been diagnosed with non-Hodgkin's lymphoma. The grocery store currently assigns four clerks and one assistant manager per shift; three of the clerks restock the shelves. The employer has determined that there are just enough clerks per shift to efficiently serve its customers, keep shelves restocked, maintain cleanliness, and reduce shoplifting. In order to receive chemotherapy and adjust to its debilitating effects, the employee requests three weeks leave, a reduced work schedule, and fewer duties. The employer insists that accommodation will require hiring another employee and redistributing work responsibilities on the shift during which the disabled employee works.

Based on the small size, lack of fiscal resources, functions of the workforce, and impact on daily operations at the grocery store, the requested accommodations may be judged to create an undue hardship. However, the same circumstances in a large regional chain of grocery stores may not create an undue hardship and, therefore, would be a reasonable accommodation.

CONFIDENTIALITY OF MEDICAL INFORMATION

The ADA has greatly restricted the use of preemployment medical examinations and inquiries. It has also created a very fine line between permissible inquiries and prohibited ones during interviews. For example, it is unlawful to ask applicants if they have a disability or to inquire into the nature or severity of any perceivable disability.[101] However, it is permissible to ask applicants to perform job-related functions. At the same time, preemployment medical examinations are unlawful, but, under certain circumstances, an employer may require an applicant to take a medical examination *after* a job offer is made and *before* the applicant begins working.[102] One of the certain circumstances previously mentioned is that *all* new hires, regardless of disability, are required to take a post-hiring medical examination.

The other restriction is that once the medical information has been collected, the employer is responsible for keeping it confidential. Often, this responsibility is delegated to the HR department, which in most organizations is responsible for maintaining employee medical records. In the case of employee medical records, the key words have now become "extremely limited access." The only circumstances under which these files can be accessed by anyone are clearly detailed by the ADA and limited to only three circumstances.[103] First, management personnel may be informed of medical conditions requiring work restrictions or other reasonable accommodations. Second, company first aid and safety personnel may be informed if the employee's disability might require emergency treatment. Finally, the medical records may be made available to government officials investigating ADA compliance. Other than those instances, the medical records should be kept safeguarded. Most disclosures of employee medical records are likely to result in ADA violations.

■ EXHIBIT 5-12

PREEMPLOYMENT MEDICAL INQUIRIES

In Making Preemployment Inquiries, Employers May Not Ask Candidates about the Following:	In Making Preemployment Inquiries, Employers May Ask Candidates If:
The existence of a disability	They can perform the essential functions of the job in question
The nature of a disability	
The severity of a disability	

SOURCE: 29 C.F.R. §§ 1630.13 & 1630.14.

DRUG REHABILITATION, TESTING, AND THE ADA

The term "qualified individual with a disability" also includes any individual who is participating in a supervised drug rehabilitation program and no longer using illegal drugs, has completed a supervised drug rehabilitation program and is no longer using illegal drugs, or is erroneously regarded as engaging in using illegal drugs and is no longer engaging in such use.[104] Note that in each instance the phrase "is no longer engaging in the use of illegal drugs" is essential to remaining a qualified individual with a disability. The ADA does not protect current substance abusers. In fact, the Act specifically authorizes covered employers to prohibit the use of drugs and alcohol in the workplace, requires that employees not be under the influence of drugs and/or alcohol during work hours, and holds drug and alcohol users to the same employment and performance standards as other employees.[105]

The ADA clearly states that employers have the right to require their employees to conform to the requirements established under the Drug-Free Workplace Act.[106] Although the ADA has placed severe restrictions on the use of medical examinations by employers, "tests to determine the illegal use of drugs shall not be considered a medical examination."[107] This permits employers to conduct preemployment drug screening and drug testing following an employment offer.

SUMMARY

This chapter identifies unlawful employment practices that result from discrimination on the basis of religion, national origin, age, and disability. Discrimination in employment based on religion and national origin is prohibited under Title VII of the Civil Rights Act of 1964. Applicants and employees are protected from discrimination based on age under the Age Discrimination in Employment Act. The Vocational Rehabilitation Act of 1973 and the Americans with Disabilities Act of 1990 protect applicants and employees from discrimination based on a disability.

Once again, knowledge of an employer's compliance responsibilities must be translated into policies and practices to preclude potential litigation. In the case of English-only rules, managers must walk the fine line between meeting the organization's business-related needs while avoiding discrimination based on national origin.

The ADA presents even more concerns for managers and HR professionals, especially in the area of job analysis. As noted, determination as to whether an applicant is qualified hinges on assessing two important factors: What is the extent of the applicant's disability and, in light of the disability, can the applicant perform the essential functions of the job with or without reasonable accommodation? To make these determinations and assess the degree of accommodation, the essential job functions must be identified and understood. The ADA has further increased the HR professional's responsibility for maintaining the confidentiality of personnel records, particularly medical records.

Because many of these policies will eventually result in written policy statements or in employee handbooks, employers are placed in an awkward predicament. Compliance with these federal statutes and regulations requires dissemination to employees. However, formal dissemination often requires documentation, and this documentation takes the form of employee handbooks. As will be explained in the next chapter, handbooks and written policies may create implied or explicit employment contracts.

KEY TERMS AND CONCEPTS

disability
English-only work rules
major life activities
qualified individual with a disability

reasonable accommodation
religious accommodation
religious exemption
undue hardship

QUESTIONS

1. What organizations are afforded religious exemptions under Section 702 of the Civil Rights Act of 1964?
2. What three types of employers can engage in preferential treatment on the basis of religion?
3. To avoid a Title VII violation, English-only work rules must satisfy what four criteria?
4. Under what conditions can sex be a *bona fide* occupational qualification (BFOQ)? Provide an example.
5. What three things does Title I of the Americans with Disabilities Act of 1990 prohibit?
6. What is "reasonable accommodation" under both the Vocational Rehabilitation Act of 1973 and the Americans with Disabilities Act of 1990?
7. How is "undue hardship" determined under both the Vocational Rehabilitation Act of 1973 and the Americans with Disabilities Act of 1990?

CASES

1 The class members in a recent court action worked as operators for Primo Operator Services, Inc. The recruitment and hiring of the operators was based or conditioned on their bilingual ability, and in particular, their ability to speak Spanish, because of a need for the employer's business to service Spanish-speaking customers when connecting long-distance telephone calls. The ability to speak Spanish was viewed by the employer as an asset in conducting its business. In fact, class members were tested at or about the time of hire to verify their ability to speak and understand Spanish.

Primo then enacted a "Speak-English-Only" policy prohibiting the speaking of Spanish on the company premises. The policy was posted on the door at the entrance of the "DNSI" building in which Primo was located. This sign specifically warned about the employer's language policy. The same sign also conspicuously coupled the policy with a warning about weapons, implying a combined concern about the conduct of those persons who speak a language other than English, Hispanic employees in this case, and setting the scene for stigmatization of those to whom the policy was directed. Specifically, the sign read:

> Absolutely No Guns, Knives, or Weapons of any kind are allowed on these Premises at any time! English is the official language of Primo Operator Services, Inc. All conversations on these premises are to be in English. Other languages may be spoken to customers who cannot speak English.

This policy prohibited the speaking of Spanish at all times, including during free moments operators had between calls, during lunch, in the employee break room, when making personal telephone calls, and before and after work if inside the building. Under the employer's policy, the only time it was acceptable to speak Spanish was when assisting a Spanish-speaking customer. Confined to the close quarters of a small work area in which, before the hiring of non-Hispanic operators starting in mid-January 1996, everyone spoke Spanish, the employees of Primo were required to refrain from speaking in Spanish to their coworkers at all times. Working shoulder to shoulder, workers experiencing free time between calls, including those persons working on the night shift, were required to speak to their Hispanic colleagues in English or face discipline or dismissal. Lunchroom conversations, even between a Hispanic husband and wife, could not include Spanish words or phrases. The employer stipulated and thereby admits that it went as far as to plan installation of a public telephone outside of the building so that Hispanic employees would have to go outside to make personal phone calls during which they might speak Spanish.

On January 16, 1996, the employer required the class members to sign a memo detailing the employer's English-only policy as a prerequisite to continued employment. Class members testified and former Vice President Bill Robinson admitted that it was understood that if the employees did not agree to the prohibitions imposed by the policy, their employment would be terminated. Six employees who refused to sign the memo were immediately terminated. Does Primo's English-only policy violate Title VII? Why or why not? What standards must any English-only policy meet in order to avoid a Title VII violation?

SOURCE: *EEOC v Premier Operator Services*, 113 C. Supp.2d 1066 (N.D. Tex. 2000).

2 Gerardo Morales is suing his former employer, Vitell, Stocks & Company, for religious discrimination under Title VII and the Michigan Elliott-Larsen Civil Rights Act. Morales alleges in his complaint that Vitell discriminated against him because of his Native American religion and his national origin by allegedly requiring that he cut his hair.

Morales was employed as a salesperson in Ann Arbor, Michigan's Briarwood Mall Vitell store from October 1994 until February 1996. He worked on the selling floor in the Vitell "Brand Central" home electronics department. When he was hired in the Fall of 1994, Morales was given a copy of the "Vitell Associate Handbook," which stipulated:

> PROFESSIONAL APPEARANCE
> All associates represent Vitell to our customers and are expected to be well groomed and neatly dressed in professional, businesslike clothing. Because fashion is constantly changing for both men and women, hard and fast rules for dress are difficult to establish.
> The unit or store manager generally decides what makes an appropriate businesslike appearance. Your manager, supervisor, or personnel representative will discuss with you the importance of wearing the right kind of clothing and will explain the appropriate clothing for the job you perform.

Consistent with corporate policy, the Ann Arbor store also issued a dress code which Morales received when he started working. The dress code stated:

> It is the policy of this company that all associates, as representatives of Vitell to your customers, be expected to dress in appropriate business attire and adhere to commonly accepted standards of grooming and dress which represent a professional and businesslike image at all times.
> The Unit Manager and members of the Store Staff will make the final determination on what is appropriate attire. Any questions on what attire is acceptable should be directed to the Unit Manager or the Store Staff.
> The following are guidelines for proper dress for our associates:
> MEN
> Beards and contemporary hair styles are acceptable, but should be maintained in a neat, trimmed manner.

When Morales was hired by Vitell in the Fall of 1994, his hair was collar-length, and therefore, according to Vitell, in compliance with store policy.

Morales' supervisor for the first year of employment was Henry Riordin. Riordin was the first manager to confront him about his hair in late summer 1995 when Morales had his hair in a short ponytail. Riordin did not discipline or direct Morales to do anything about his hair, but rather merely advised him that Walter Galt, the general store manager, did not approve of male salespersons wearing their hair in ponytails. Morales did not tell Riordin that wearing his hair long or in a ponytail was part of his Native American religion. Shortly after Riordin had this conversation with Morales, Riordin was replaced by Alan Cochet.

Cochet discussed Morales' hair with him in October of 1995 upon the direction of the general store manager, Walter Galt. On October 25, 1995, Cochet gave Morales a memo stating that his ponytail and hair length were not in compliance with Vitell personal appearance policies, and that he had until November 1 to bring himself within compliance with the policies. It was in connection with Cochet's memo that Vitell was informed that Morales objected to Vitell's hair length policy on religious grounds. On October 30, 1995, Morales' attorney, Elizabeth Benett, wrote Galt:

> [Morales] is of Native American descent, and he practices traditional Native American religion. Traditionally, growing the hair long has sacred significance in Native American religion. A policy which unequivocally prohibits male employees to have long hair discriminates against men who practice traditional Native American religion.

Upon learning that Morales' religious beliefs precluded him from cutting his hair, Galt, Cochet, and Dagney Taggert, Vitell's human resources director, met with Morales in the first week of November of 1995 in an attempt to accommodate his religious beliefs, and asked him to tuck his hair into the collar of his shirt or jacket. Morales testified that he could not comply with the proposed accommodation at that time because his hair was not long enough to tuck into his collar.

In light of his protestation that his hair was not long enough to tuck into his collar, Morales was told that he could wear his hair out in a ponytail for approximately two months, until it grew long enough to tuck into his collar. Vitell managers all testified that Morales agreed to this accommodation in November of 1995. Morales, however, testified in his deposition that he agreed only that he would wear his hair in a ponytail for two months, and then, at that time, he would decide whether he would tuck it into his collar. Morales never stated in November of 1995 anything to suggest that tucking his hair into his collar would violate his religious beliefs.

On February 6, 1996, two and one half months later, Galt reiterated the terms of the accommodation agreement and asked Morales to tuck his hair into his collar. Morales flatly refused to even attempt to tuck his hair in.

Morales further testified that even if his employer had told him that he had to tuck his hair into his collar for safety reasons, such as if he had a job working around machinery, whether or not he would decide to comply with the employer's directive would depend on "whether or not [he] wanted that job enough to make those accommodations." At his deposition, Morales, whose hair is now nearly waist-length, took the position that tucking his hair into his collar, no less than cutting his hair, would violate his religious convictions. He actually testified that any demand made upon him would violate his religious beliefs.

It is undisputed, however, that during the course of his employment Morales never told his employer that tucking his hair into his collar would violate his religious beliefs.

Despite Morales' refusal to attempt to comply with Vitell's proposed accommodation, Vitell did not immediately terminate his employment. Rather, he was urged by his supervisor to go home and reconsider his position. Cochet testified that he kept Morales on the schedule for a period of time in the hope that he would return. Morales eventually chose not to comply with Vitell's proposed accommodation and thereby terminated his employment. At no time did Morales offer any alternatives, but instead demanded that he be allowed to work and wear his hair any way he wanted.

Soon after he terminated his employment, Morales obtained a job at Health Foods Market in Ann Arbor and has sustained little or no economic damages. On April 4, 1996, Morales filed a charge of religious discrimination with the Michigan Department of Civil Rights and the EEOC, alleging that his "religious beliefs which stem from [his] Native American ancestry do not allow [him] to cut his hair short." He charged that Vitell discharged him because he refused to cut his hair. Has Morales established actionable discrimination on the basis of religion? Why or why not? Has Morales established actionable discrimination on the basis of national origin? Why or why not? What must Vitell do to demonstrate that his efforts at accommodation were reasonable?

SOURCE: *Vargas v Sears, Roebuck & Co.,* 1998 U.S. Dist. LEXIS 21148 (E.D. Mich. 2000).

NOTES

1. This scenario is based on the findings of fact in *Cook v Rhode Island,* 10 F.3d 17 (1st Cir. 1993).

2. Ibid. at 34, n. 13.

3. U.S. Equal Employment Opportunity Commission (January 18, 2001). *Charge Statistics From the U.S. Equal Employment Opportunity Commission FY 1992 through FY 2000.* **http://www.eeoc.gov/stts/charges.html**

4. Ibid.

5. 42 U.S.C. § 2000e-1(a).

6. 113 F.3d 196 (11th Cir. 1997).

7. Ibid. at 200.

8. *Little v Wuerl,* 929 F.2d 944, 947–8 (3d Cir. 1991).

9. *EEOC v Kamehameha School,* 990 F.2d 458 (9th Cir. 1993).

10. *Fike v United Methodist Children's Home of Virginia, Inc.,* 547 F.Supp. 286 (E.D. Vir. 1982).

11. *EEOC v Mississippi College,* 626 F.2d 477 (5th Cir. 1980).

12. *Shapolia v Los Alamos National Laboratory,* 773 F.Supp. 304, 305 (D. N.M. 1991); *aff'd without comment,* 13 F.3d 406 (10th Cir. 1993).

13. *Breech v Alabama Power Company,* 962 F.Supp. 1447, 1456 (S.D. Ala. 1997).

14. *Kern v Dynalectron Corp.,* 577 F.Supp. 1196 (N.D. Tex. 1983).

15. 29 C.F.R. § 1605.

16. 42 U.S.C. § 2000e (j).

17. *Wilson v U.S. West Communications*, 58 F.3d 1337,1340 (8th Cir. 1995); *Beadle v City of Tampa*, 42 F.3d 633, 636 n.4 (11th Cir. 1995); *Bhatia v Chevron U.S.A., Inc.*, 734 F.2d 1382,1383 (9th Cir. 1984).

18. Exodus 20:8.

19. *Chalmer v Tulon Company of Richmond*, 101 F.3d 1012, 1019 (4th Cir. 1996).

20. U.S. Equal Employment Opportunity Commission (May 1995). *Theories of Discrimination: Intentional and Unintentional Discrimination.* Washington, DC: Government Printing Office, p. A-14.

21. *EEOC v BJ Services Co.*, 921 F.Supp. 1509 (N.D. Tex. 1995).

22. *Lee v ABF Freight System, Inc.*, 22 F.3d 1019 (10th Cir. 1994).

23. U.S. Equal Employment Opportunity Commission (January 15, 1997). *Facts About Religious Discrimination.* **http://www.eeoc.gov/facts/fs-relig.html**

24. 648 F.2d 1239 (9th Cir. 1981).

25. 29 C.F.R. § 158(a)(5).

26. 42 U.S.C. § 2000e (j).

27. 29 CFR § 1606.

28. 29 CFR § 1606.1.

29. Bowman, C. (1997). BLS projections to 2006—a summary. *Monthly Labor Review,* 120 (11): 3–5.

30. 29 C.F.R. § 1606.7(a).

31. 29 C.F.R. § 1606.7(a) at § 1603.

32. 29 C.F.R. § 1606.7(a) at § 1604.11.

33. 29 C.F.R. § 1606.7(a) at § 1606.8(a)

34. 998 F.2d 1480 (9th Cir. 1993).

35. Ibid.

36. Ibid. at 1488.

37. Piatt, B. (1993). *Language on the Job: Balancing Business Needs and Employee Rights.* Albuquerque, NM: University of New Mexico Press.

38. 29 C.F.R. § 1606.7(b)

39. Ibid.

40. Ibid.

41. 8 U.S.C. § 1324a(b).

42. 8 U.S.C. § 1324a(e)(5).

43. 8 U.S.C. § 1324a.

44. 8 U.S.C. § 1324(a)(2)(B).

45. 8 U.S.C. § 1324b(a).

46. 8 U.S.C. § 1324(a)(4).

47. Pub. L. 90–202, 81 Stat. 602 (Dec. 15, 1967).

48. U.S. Equal Employment Opportunity Commission (January 18, 2001). *Enforcement Statistics and Litigation.* **http://www.eeoc.gov/stats/charges.html**

49. 29 U.S.C. § 630.

50. 42 U.S.C. § 2000e (b).

51. 29 U.S.C. § 621.

52. 29 U.S.C. § 623.

53. Pub. L. 90–202, § 2, (1967).

54. Pub. L. 95–256, § 3a (1978)

55. Pub. L. 99–592, § 2(c)(1) (1986).

56. *Western Air Lines, Inc. v Criswell*, 472 U.S. 400, 422 (1985).

57. *O'Connor v Consolidated Coin Caterers Corp.*, 517 U.S. 308 (1996).

58. 517 U.S. 308.

59. Ibid. at 312.

60. 29 U.S.C. § 626(c)(2).

61. 42 U.S.C. § 1981a(c).

62. 472 U.S. 400 (1985).

63. Ibid. at 404.

64. *Dothard v Rawlinson*, 433 U.S. 321, 334 (1977).

65. *Criswell* at 409.

66. Ibid. at 422.

67. Ibid. at 408.

68. Ibid. at 412.

69. *Cancellier v Federated Department Stores*, 672 F. 2d 1312 (9th Cir.), *cert, denied* 459 U.S. 859 (1982).

70. *Skalka v Fernald Environmental Restoration Management Corp.*, 178 F.3d 414 (6th Cir. 1999).

71. 29 U.S.C. § 791 *et. seq.*

72. Ibid. at § 794.

73. Pub. L. 93–112, §. 7 (1973).

74. 42 U.S.C. § 12 111(8) (1998).

75. Pub. L. 102–569, 106 Stat. 4346 (Oct. 29, 1992).

76. 29 U.S.C. §. 793.

77. 42 U.S.C. § 12 112(a).

78. Becker, G. S. (September 14, 1992). How the disabilities act will cripple business. *Business Week:* 14.

79. *EEOC v Chrysler Corp.*, 917 F.Supp. 1164 (E.D. Mich. 1996).

80. 29 C.F.R. § 1630.2(I)(1997).

81. *Sutton v United Airlines Inc.*, 527 U.S. 471 (1999).

82. Ibid.

83. *Murphy v United Parcel Service, Inc.*, 527 U.S. 516, 520 (1999).

84. 42 U.S.C. § 12112.

85. Ibid. at § 12111(8).

86. U.S. Equal Employment Opportunity Commission (1991). *The Americans with Disabilities Act: Your Responsibilities as an Employer*. Washington, DC: Government Printing Office, pp. 3–4.

87. *Sutton v United Air Lines*, Inc., 527 U.S. 471, 474.

88. Ibid. at *23.

89. Ibid.

90. Ibid. at *22.

91. *Bragdon v Abbott*, 524 U.S. 624 (1998).

92. U.S. Equal Employment Opportunity Commission (March 2, 1999). *Enforcement Guidance: Reasonable Accommodation and Undue Hardship under the Americans with Disabilities Act.* **www.eeoc.gov/docs/accommodation.html**

93. Ibid.

94. Ibid.

95. Ibid.

96. *Davis v Frank*, 711 F. Supp. 447 (N.D. Ill. 1989).

97. 29 C.F.R. part 1630, appendix 1630.2(o) (1997).

98. U.S. Employment Standards Administration (2001). *Compliance Guide to the Family and Medical Leave Act.* **http://www.dol.gov/dol/esa/public/regs/compliance/whd/1421.htm**

99. *Stone v City of Mount Vernon*, 118 F. 3d 92, 101 (2d Cir. 1996).

100. 42 U.S.C. § 12111(10)(B).

101. 42 U.S.C. § 12112(d)(2)(A).

102. 42 U.S.C. § 12112(d)(2)(B).

103. 42 U.S.C. § 12112(d)(3)(B).

104. 42 U.S.C. § § 12114(a) & (b).

105. 42 U.S.C. § 12114(c).

106. Ibid. at 12114 (c)(3).

107. Ibid. at 12114(d).

AFFIRMATIVE ACTION

6

LEARNING OBJECTIVES

- ☐ Recognize the difference between affirmative action and equal employment opportunity.
- ☐ Describe the difference between involuntary and voluntary affirmative action programs.
- ☐ Understand the arguments for preserving or eliminating affirmative action.
- ☐ Identify the conditions under which affirmative action is permissible under Title VII.
- ☐ Identify the conditions under which public sector employers may engage in affirmative action.
- ☐ Describe the major components of an affirmative action plan.
- ☐ Develop a permissible affirmative action plan.
- ☐ Identify employment practices that could create reverse discrimination complaints.

OPENING SCENARIO

A *small private college is trying to fill the position vacancy for its director of equal opportunity and regulatory compliance. A search committee has been formed, and during its first meeting, the following position announcement has been presented for committee approval:*

POSITION: Director of Equal Opportunity and Regulatory Compliance

QUALIFICATIONS: Bachelor's degree from an accredited institution required; graduate degree preferred. Demonstrated supervisory skills, ability to work in positive relationships and to communicate with all segments of the university community, experience with computer-based applications, and ability to interpret and manage data used in preparation of reports submitted to federal and state regulatory agencies required for effective performance of the job.

RESPONSIBILITIES: Administer the Office of Equal Opportunity and Regulatory Compliance; prepare university's affirmative action plan and related compliance reports to federal and state regulatory agencies; conduct educational training sessions for university community on issues pertaining to equal opportunity and affirmative action; prepare and maintain statistical information for regulatory reports; supervise support staff and student workers; investigate complaints of equal opportunity violations; maintain affirmative action job classification files and ensure the files are in compliance with federal and state regulations; serve as university's Sections 503/504, ADA, and Title IX Coordinator; prepare university responses to EEOC, OCR, and OFCCP charges; and perform related duties as required. Reporting line for the Director of Equal Opportunity and Regulatory Compliance is to the Provost of the university.

APPLICATION PROCEDURE: Submit letter of application which addresses the advertised qualifications, comprehensive resume, and names, addresses, and telephone numbers of three current references.

One of the committee members, Charles Silvey, expressed concern that the job responsibilities and qualifications did not seem to be consistent with one another. It appeared to Charles that anyone with a bachelor's degree in any field could apply for the job. Should not the candidate at least have training in human resource management or business management?

Elizabeth Day responded that the field was immaterial, since the candidate could easily learn on the job. Besides, requiring a professional degree could result in more minority candidates being excluded from the applicant pool. However, Elizabeth did have a problem with the minimum requirement being only a bachelor's degree. After all, she contended, the faculty had little respect for anyone who did not possess a doctorate. Elizabeth then recommended that the candidate should have a terminal degree (a doctorate).

William Eaton next suggested that whatever criteria were chosen, they must be framed to ensure that either a minority or female candidate is chosen for the position. After all, he contended, white males lack the empathy to understand affirmative action issues. The committee then began discussing the merits of these proposals.

THE HISTORY OF AFFIRMATIVE ACTION

No topic in employee relations has generated as much controversy and emotion as affirmative action. When one looks at the preferential treatment component of affirmative action programs, one is immediately confronted with a practice that has not only polarized American society but has the potential of disrupting the workplace as well. Not surprisingly, no other employment practice is more misunderstood or abused as affirmative action.

On July 2, 1965, the Civil Rights Act of 1964 provisions mandating color-blind employment practices became effective.[1] Within one hundred fourteen days, President Lyndon Johnson signed Executive Order 11246. Executive Order 11246 provided the motivation for race-conscious recruiting and hiring under affirmative action.[2]

The term "affirmative action" can be traced to the earlier Executive Order 10925. In this order, President John F. Kennedy urged federal contractors to take "affirmative action" to ensure individuals, during employment, were treated without regard to their race, color, religion, sex, or national origin.[3] However, under Executive Order 11246, each contractor or subcontractor was required to file a compliance report with the contracting federal agency or secretary of labor. It was this requirement to monitor applicants and selection outcomes that led to race-conscious employment practices.

These compliance reports required contractors to provide information on practices, policies, programs, and *employment statistics.* Over time, these requirements would evolve into more elaborate reporting formats such as the EEO-1 through EEO-6 reports and the very sophisticated formalized affirmative action programs delineated in *Revised Order No. 4.*[4] ***Revised Order No. 4*** contains the Office of Federal Contract Compliance Programs' (OFCCP) guidance for constructing programs that would meet their standards of review.

In theory, affirmative action was intended to "level the playing field," or allow groups that had previously been discriminated against to catch up with those who faced no such barriers. Proponents of affirmative action still make this argument. Opponents often argue there have already been over three decades of such programs. Many proponents insist there can be no equality of opportunity until affirmative action has leveled the field.

Affirmative action plans eventually received limited statutory recognition with the enactment of the Vocational Rehabilitation Act of 1973. This statute requires certain federal contractors and grant recipients to take affirmative action in employing *qualified handicapped individuals.* One year later, the Vietnam Era Veteran's Readjustment Assistance Act of 1974 contained language requiring specified federal aid recipients and contractors to provide similar affirmative action in employing Vietnam-era veterans.

By 1978, affirmative action programs were becoming common enough in both the public and private sectors that the Equal Employment Opportunity Commission (EEOC) issued its *Uniform Guidelines on Employee Selection Procedures.* These guidelines contained provisions covering affirmative action obligations and encouraged the adoption of voluntary affirmative action programs.[5] The EEOC maintains that affirmative action is a legitimate means to achieve equal employment opportunity and is not only permitted but encouraged.[6]

In practice, affirmative action focuses employers' attention on the racial, ethnic, and gender composition of their internal workforces compared with the relevant external labor market. Employers then must determine whether given protected groups are represented in proportion to their percentage of the relevant labor market. Under specific circumstances, employers are permitted to make race-, ethnic-, or gender-conscious decisions to achieve (but not maintain) proportional representation. Both federal courts and regulatory agencies have established guidelines where protected classes may receive preferential treatment under an affirmative action plan and not violate Title VII or the Equal Protection Clause of the Fourteenth Amendment. However, failure to comply with these guidelines will expose organizations to reverse discrimination.

THE NATURE OF AFFIRMATIVE ACTION

Affirmative action has many different meanings and can be applied to at least four general employment practices. First, affirmative action can be the intentional recruitment of applicants or the utilization of training programs to impart necessary job skills for current employees who are members of underutilized protected groups.[7] An **underutilized protected group** is a protected group under Title VII that is underrepresented in the workforce in proportion to the relevant external market. Second, affirmative action can be the implementation of measures to eliminate any prejudices that managers and supervisors have toward underutilized protected groups in the employer's workforce.[8] Third, affirmative action can imply the identification of existing employment practices which work to foster and promote underutilization of a particular protected group and the removal of such practices.[9] Fourth, affirmative action can involve the preferential hiring and promoting of protected group members in order to remedy underutilization.[10] Because of the potential legal liability for employers, the remainder of this chapter will examine the preferential component of affirmative action and its consequences for employers. Any further reference to "affirmative action" will mean the preferential treatment element.

The preferential treatment of protected group members often is initiated by an employer (or a court) to correct some past discrimination in the selection, promotion, or employment of women and minorities. This is particularly true when it can be proven the underutilization of the protected group is a present effect of the employer's past discriminatory practices. The preferential treatment form of affirmative action is also the component that has led many critics to assert that such actions constitute reverse discrimination. It is the least popular form of affirmative action and is responsible for much of the opposition to such programs. In fact, public opinion polls conducted during the past twenty-five years reveal that between 70 to 80 percent of the respondents oppose granting preferential treatment to individuals based on racial or ethnic classifications[11] (see Exhibit 6-1).

Most Americans do not seem to be opposed to the more benign forms of affirmative action, the three forms other than preferential treatment. Polls show majority support for special training or education programs for underrepresented protected group members to enhance their qualifications for better jobs or college entrance.[12] However, once in competition for a position or benefit (such as promotions or choice assignments), most survey respondents indicate the benefit should ultimately go to the *most qualified* applicant, regardless of the group to

■ EXHIBIT 6-1

PUBLIC OPINION SURVEYS ON AFFIRMATIVE ACTION SHOWING
AMERICANS NOT FAVORING* PREFERENTIAL TREATMENT

Demographic Category	Year of Survey				
	1977	1980	1984	1989	1995†
All Categories	89	90	90	90	87
Ethnicity:					
Non-Whites	70	71	73	86	83
Whites	91	93	92	93	89
Gender:					
Men	88	89	89	90	87
Women	90	91	91	90	87
Political Party:					
Democrats	89	86	87	83	81
Republicans	93	94	95	95	92

*Percentages of respondents not identifying with the former viewpoint in the question, "Some people say that, to make up for past discrimination, women and minority groups should be given preferential treatment in getting jobs and places in colleges. Others say that their ability, as determined in test scores, should be the main consideration. Which point of view comes closer to how you feel on the subject?"

†Phrasing of question was somewhat different for survey taken in 1995.

SOURCES: Statistics for the years 1977, 1980, 1984, and 1989 were drawn from G. Gallup, Jr., *The Gallup Poll*, for the respective year of the survey: (1977): 1057–1060; (1980): 106–107; (1984): 141–143; and (1989): 231. The statistics for 1995 were drawn from the CNN, *USA Today*, and Gallup Organization surveys of February 24–26, 1995 and March 17–19, 1995.

which the applicant belongs.[13] By the late 1990s, public dislike of preferences culminated in increased organized support for the elimination of the fourth form of affirmative action through such measures as the California Civil Rights Initiative (a.k.a., Proposition 209),[14] Washington State Civil Rights Act (a.k.a., I-200),[15] and an increase in reverse discrimination litigation.

ARGUMENTS SUPPORTING AFFIRMATIVE ACTION

Both proponents and opponents of preferential treatment offer powerful arguments for retaining or eliminating such programs[16] (see Exhibit 6-2). As the United States enters the new millennium, this debate is likely to intensify. The following is a brief overview of the principal arguments offered by *both* sides of the debate.

CORRECTING PAST WRONGS. Many advocates of preferential treatment view it as a means of providing reparations for groups that have been discriminated against historically—ethnic minorities and women. From this retributive perspective, preferential treatment is a means to repay groups for historical discrimination. An argument popularly offered is that African Americans do so poorly in the workplace in terms of income and education due to "three hundred years of slavery." Thus, since they have been historically victimized, society owes them the opportunity to catch up. Although this view is widely held by the proponents of affirmative action, it has not been accepted by the courts. Practitioners are warned that the Supreme Court has held that *societal discrimination* does not come under the domain of either Title VII[17] or the Equal Protection Clause.[18] As the Supreme Court noted in the 1989 *Croson* decision, if courts permitted preferences based on the harm that various minorities suffer at the hands of general society, personal opportunity and achievement would be lost in a mosaic of shifting preferences based inherently on unmeasurable claims of past wrongs.[19] This bluntly means employers cannot use *societal discrimination* to justify their preferential programs.

However, the courts have long held that employers *are* responsible for the present effects of any discrimination in which they engaged.[20] Consequently, any injury caused by the employer's actions must be remedied or corrected. Affirmative action has been accepted as one of those remedies. Therefore, employers are justified (if not compelled) to correct their own discriminatory actions but precluded from correcting society's past discrimination.

ACHIEVING ECONOMIC AND OCCUPATIONAL EQUITY. Due to centuries of oppression, many proponents of affirmative action contend that some ethnic groups are ill prepared to take full advantage of equal opportunities. One analogy often used is that these groups got to the starting line after the race had begun. Under this perspective, affirmative action is seen as a temporary device designed to make "the race" fair. Without this help, ethnic minorities would be doomed to being left behind, never being able to quite catch up to the income levels of those groups that got a head start. Under this line of reasoning, preferential treatment becomes the means of correcting these societal inequities and ensures ethnic minorities can achieve the American dream.

BREAKING DOWN STEREOTYPES. Affirmative action, it is theorized, is also necessary in order to break down stereotypes about women and ethnic minorities. By ensuring they are appropriately represented at all levels of the organization, other employees will, in theory, learn to respect and appreciate female and minority employees. The basic benefit of this inclusion is that superiors, peers, and subordinates alike will see, through daily contact, that women and ethnic minorities are as technically competent as any other employees. By achieving a balanced workforce, other employees may see that the negative attitudes they held against these groups were unfounded. Through education, contact, and example, all employees of an organization will develop a new respect and understanding for the preferred classes.

ROLE MODELS. Affirmative action is necessary in order to provide role models for successive generations. By observing members of their own ethnic groups as successful business leaders, physicians, attorneys, and other professionals,

■ **EXHIBIT 6-2**

THE AFFIRMATIVE ACTION DEBATE

Arguments For	Arguments Against
Correcting past wrongs	Fighting discrimination with discrimination
Achieving economic and occupational equity	Group rights v individual rights
Breaking down stereotypes	Reinforcing stereotypes
Role models	Punishing the innocent

children from these groups will be encouraged to succeed as well. As more members from these groups succeed, even more will be encouraged to try. In the long run, this process would eventually eliminate the economic and educational inequities that currently exist along ethnic lines. Proponents contend these anticipated results will take decades to achieve, but by maintaining affirmative action programs, they will eventually be attained. The underlying belief is that in the absence of discrimination, all occupations will be representative of the ethnic composition of the population.[21] However, the Supreme Court ruled in *Wygant v Jackson Board of Education* that role models cannot be used to justify preferences.[22]

ARGUMENTS AGAINST AFFIRMATIVE ACTION

Opponents have long contended that the use of preferential programs clearly violates Title VII's prohibition of basing *any* employment decision on *any* individual's race, color, religion, sex, or national origin. Although the stated goal of affirmative action is the elimination of race and gender inequity in employment practices, preferential treatment attempts to accomplish this goal by practicing race and gender consciousness.[23] This contradiction—creating a racially neutral society through the use of race-conscious actions and decisions—is at the very heart of the current affirmative action debate.

The situation creates an interesting paradox. On one hand, employers are required by the Civil Rights Act of 1964 to make racially neutral decisions. On the other hand, affirmative action requires them to make racially conscious decisions. However, the federal courts have been reluctant to satisfactorily resolve this dilemma. Beyond expressing concern that "[r]acial and ethnic distinctions of any sort are inherently suspect and thus call for the most exacting judicial examination,"[24] the judiciary has resorted to constructing complicated rules and procedures to perpetuate the distinctions.

FIGHTING DISCRIMINATION WITH DISCRIMINATION. One of the most common arguments against these programs asks the question, how can Americans move to a color-blind society by encouraging race-conscious programs like affirmative action? In other words, can you eradicate discrimination with discrimination?

In practice, it is argued, preferential treatment actually creates racial barriers rather than removing them. When a white male who has never discriminated against anyone loses out to an individual of an ethnic minority, and that individual has never been discriminated against, hostility will result.[25]

GROUP RIGHTS VERSUS INDIVIDUAL RIGHTS. Affirmative action shifts the premise of equal opportunity from individual rights to group rights. Title VII was intended to protect any *individual* from discrimination because of "such *individual's* race, color, religion, sex, or national origin."[26] Affirmative action, instead of focusing on individual outcomes, concentrates on group outcomes. How a *group* is proportionately represented in a workplace supercedes *individual* interests.

REINFORCING STEREOTYPES. Opponents of affirmative action have long contended that when minimally qualified preferred group members are selected for hiring or promotion over more qualified nonpreferred group candidates, notions of inferiority and hostility will naturally follow.[27] The conclusion is often drawn that had it not been for an applicant's ethnicity or gender, he or she would not possess the qualifications to *fairly* compete for the job. Opponents offer the adage that when affirmative action talks, merit walks. Proponents of affirmative action too frequently conclude that if employment outcomes were truly left to merit, there would be very few preferred group members in the organization at all, and that protected groups cannot compete in a workplace based on equal opportunity.

PUNISHING THE INNOCENT. If affirmative action is a device designed to repay one group for the evils of past discrimination, who pays whom? There exists a very real fear that persons who have not actually been discriminated against will be advanced at the expense of persons who have neither practiced nor benefited from discrimination.[28] The argument is as follows: Suppose the granddaughter of a man who benefited from the preferential promotion of whites in the late 1950s is applying for a promotion in a major marketing firm today. Is it fair for her to bear the burden of her grandfather's benefiting from discrimination by now being passed over for promotion in favor of the less qualified grandson of an African American man who was discriminated against in the 1950s?

Regardless of your personal feelings about affirmative action, the cold hard fact of the matter is that it is a legal practice common to many businesses and organizations. In its legal form, it does not please many proponents who believe it does not go far enough. Nor does it please opponents who believe it should not exist at all. The outcome of this highly political debate is better left to the ballot box. As a human resource manager, your primary obligation to your employer is to guarantee compliance with the laws and regulations that cover affirmative action. Your task will be to walk the very fine line between permissible affirmative action and reverse discrimination.

INVOLUNTARY VERSUS VOLUNTARY AFFIRMATIVE ACTION

The two broad categories of affirmative action programs are involuntary affirmative action and voluntary affirmative action (see Exhibit 6-3). The significant difference between the two is that **involuntary affirmative action** is a remedy imposed by a court when an employer has been found in violation of Title VII or the Equal Protection Clause. For example, a state agency may have engaged in blatant and continuous racial discrimination in its hiring practices. The court may then order preferential hiring of qualified applicants of the race against whom the agency had discriminated. The action, provided it is narrowly tailored to do so, is intended to correct the present effects (the underrepresentation of members of the race against which unlawful discrimination had occurred) of the past discriminatory hiring practices.

Voluntary affirmative action is applied to all other programs *not* imposed by a court, including consent agreements, programs developed for eligibility in certain federal programs, and programs created by an employer for the expressed purpose of eliminating the effects of past discriminatory policies and practices.

On some occasions, an employer may be required to establish an **affirmative action plan (AAP)** as the result of a court order. Under such circumstances, the court is compelling an employer to engage in affirmative action, particularly in its preferential treatment aspect, to remedy some past discriminatory practices. Involuntary affirmative action has been recognized as a remedial tool to alleviate discriminatory employment practices since 1965, when the Supreme Court ruled in *U.S. v Louisiana* that "[a] district court not merely has the power but the *duty* to render a decree which will, so far as possible, eliminate the discriminatory effects of the past, as well as bar like discrimination in the future."[29] This perspective was reinforced in the 1987 case, *U.S. v Paradise,* where the Supreme Court ruled that court-imposed race-conscious relief is justified so long as the nonprotected group candidates are qualified.[30]

The authority to require involuntary affirmative action is drawn from Title VII of the Civil Rights Act of 1964. Title VII empowered federal courts to impose

■ **EXHIBIT 6-3**

TYPES OF AFFIRMATIVE ACTION

Involuntary

■ Court imposed

Voluntary

■ Consent arrangements

■ Eligibility for federal contracts or grants

■ Voluntarily initiated programs

affirmative action where the employer is engaging in unlawful employment practices, either intentionally *or* unintentionally. Specifically, Section 706(g) of Title VII empowers the court to "[e]njoin the respondent from engaging in unlawful employment practices, and order such affirmative action as may be appropriate, which may include, but is not limited to, reinstatement of hiring of employees, with or without back pay or any other equitable remedy as the court deems appropriate."[31] Based on the interpretation of this clause, federal courts have ordered AAPs to rectify racial and gender imbalances that are present in an employer's workforce as a result of prior discriminatory practices.

VOLUNTARY AFFIRMATIVE ACTION PLANS

There are three types of voluntary affirmative action plans: consent arrangements, eligibility requirements, and voluntarily initiated plans.

CONSENT ARRANGEMENTS. Closely associated with involuntary AAPs are consent arrangements. Under a consent decree, the employer and the complaining party(ies) enter into an agreement creating an AAP *prior to* a judgment (an involuntary remedy) being rendered by the court. In these instances, the employer has been found guilty of some discriminatory employment practice. Rather than depending on the court to impose an AAP of its design, the employer opts for a solution that would be mutually acceptable to all involved parties. Once the parties to the suit have agreed to a formal plan, it is presented to the court for approval. Barring any obvious flaw in the plan developed by the employer and the aggrieved party(ies), the court will approve the implementation of the consent decree.

To illustrate this practice, suppose an employer was found to have discriminated against female employees in its promotion practices and a court-ordered remedy was pending. The employer instead chooses to meet with the affected female employees and develop an AAP acceptable to them. Such an arrangement may be more realistic than one fashioned by a federal judge unfamiliar with the employer's business. It could also improve relations with the aggrieved employees by demonstrating the employer is sincere in its desire to make amends for its previous actions.

Let's assume the solution mutually agreed to was to set aside 50 percent of all promotions for *qualified* women. The employer may be agreeable to this, and likewise, the female employees may find it acceptable. However, one group of employees—males—might see this arrangement as detrimental to their interests. If the plan was implemented as stated, men could feasibly see 50 percent of their advancement opportunities disappear during the life of the AAP. Since it is a well-held principle in American jurisprudence that individuals cannot be held to a contract to which they are not a party,[32] the Civil Rights Act of 1991 now provides a degree of protection to third parties of consent decrees. If a group of employees will be adversely affected by the consent arrangement, they should be notified of its contents and given the opportunity to have their arguments heard.

Thus, the Civil Rights Act of 1991 requires that all parties affected by a consent agreement must be notified of the actual terms of the agreement and afforded the opportunity to present objections to provisions that would adversely affect their interests.[33] Failure to include a representative for the other applicants or employees affected by the consent agreement could expose the company to legal challenges in the future.

Because the AAP is developed outside of the courtroom and submitted to the court for approval before the court provides one of its own, such plans are treated as voluntary programs. Even though they are court approved, these AAPs are subject to the same scrutiny as any other voluntary plan when reverse discrimination is alleged.[34]

The Civil Rights Act of 1991 imposes limitations on challenges to such AAPs to preclude third parties from initiating an indefinite number of litigations. The law contains language that strengthens the finality of consent decrees. The Act modifies accepted contract theory by declaring "an employment practice that implements and is within a consent judgment or order that resolves a claim of employment discrimination under the United States Constitution or federal civil rights laws may not be challenged under the circumstances described in subparagraph (B)."[35] Among the circumstances mentioned in the Act that limit challenges to consent decrees are those persons who, prior to the entry of the decree, had notice of the pending arrangement and had a *reasonable opportunity* to voice their objections to its contents. If "a reasonable opportunity to present objections to such judgment" was provided to affected parties, no party may challenge the judgment at a later date.[36] Having been notified of the decree's contents and given the opportunity to express their dissent, should the affected parties not take advantage of this opportunity, they may not raise the issue at a later date. Additionally, current or future employees may not challenge a decree later if their interests or views were reasonably represented by another party, or parties, who challenged the judgment prior to its entry. In essence, if any employee or group of employees with similar interests to the aggrieved party either presented or *had the opportunity to present objections to the initial decree,* then the aggrieved party is prevented from raising the issue at a future date.

From the employer's standpoint, the Civil Rights Act of 1991 provides a good degree of insulation against future reverse discrimination suits, *if* the employer takes precautions to include all affected parties in the initial negotiations. Since the Act bars all after-the-decree challenges by adversely affected parties, provided that they were given sufficient notification of the consent agreement and given an opportunity to intervene before it was adopted, employers need only ensure these accommodations are made.[37] The concept is quite simple. If the employees are provided the opportunity to voice their concerns initially, they may not raise them at a later date.

ELIGIBILITY FOR FEDERAL AID OR CONTRACTS. The next form of voluntary affirmative action involves establishing eligibility for federal contracts. It is "voluntary" to the extent the employer has the choice of establishing an AAP or being disqualified from federal contract consideration. Therefore, any organization wishing to do business with the federal government must adopt such programs and assume affirmative action obligations.[38]

Employers and entities affected by this form of voluntary affirmative action include:

1. Prime contractors and subcontractors with fifty or more employees and a federal contract of $50,000 or more.
2. Organizations with government bills of lading which total $50,000 or more.
3. Depositories for federal funds in any amount.
4. Firms that serve as issuing or paying agents for United States savings bonds.[39]

Any employer meeting these conditions must develop a written affirmative action compliance program for each of its establishments or have its contracts or deposits removed. If you receive government money, you must comply with the government's regulations.

The classes of employees entitled to preferential selection under federally mandated AAPs are more extensive than those under Title VII. Certain federal statutes require affirmative action be taken for qualified individuals with a disability[40] and Vietnam Era veterans,[41] in addition to women and ethnic minorities. Thus, the list of classes that utilization analysis applies to includes race, sex, national origin, disability, and veteran status. Remember, the need to establish a formal AAP with goals and timetables is dependent upon the size of the government contract or subcontract the employer holds.

VOLUNTARILY INITIATED PROGRAMS. In addition to those employers who "voluntarily" initiate AAPs in order to maintain federal contracts, some employers may be motivated to adopt affirmative action as a result of social or ethical responsibility. The employer may also be acting out of a desire to create corporate legitimacy or may be attempting to avoid potential unlawful discrimination charges. Regardless of employer motives, care should be taken to ensure the voluntary AAP criteria are met. Courts will expect such plans to be based on some "manifest imbalance" in the employer's workforce—an imbalance which is best supported by good utilization analysis. Always remember that in order to be permissible under Title VII, a voluntary plan must be remedial in nature.[42]

Although the EEOC contends it does not require employers to follow mandatory methods and formats, the agency does state that an acceptable AAP should contain three elements: a reasonable self-analysis, a reasonable basis for concluding affirmative action is appropriate, and reasonable action.[43] However, the EEOC also encourages employers to follow the more exacting guidelines presented by the Office of Federal Contract Compliance Programs' (OFCCP) *Revised Order No. 4.*[44] The reasonable self-analysis could be accomplished through the utilization analysis described in *Revised Order No. 4.*

PERMISSIBLE AFFIRMATIVE ACTION UNDER TITLE VII

Recall from Chapter 2 that Title VII prohibits discrimination in employment against *any individual* on the basis of that *individual's* race, color, religion, sex, or national origin. It applies to:

- Private employers with fifteen or more employees.
- Labor unions with fifteen or more members.
- Public and private employment agencies.
- Educational institutions (public and private).
- State and local governments.

Even the Congress of the United States is covered, although the rest of the federal government is not. Therefore, these employers and organizations must construct any AAP very carefully to avoid a Title VII violation.

How can you develop a racially or ethnically conscious preferential AAP that *does not* violate Title VII's prohibitions against treating individuals differently because of race, color, religion, sex, or national origin[45] or even classifying them in that manner?[46] Critics of affirmative action have long argued that Section 703(j) of Title VII makes it unlawful. This subsection states:

> Nothing contained in this subchapter shall be interpreted to require any employer, employment agency, labor organization, or joint labor-management committee subject to this subchapter to grant preferential treatment to any individual or group because of race, color, religion, sex, or national origin of such individual or group on account of an imbalance which may exist with respect to the percentage of persons of any race, color, religion, sex, or national origin . . . in the available workforce in any community, state, section or other area.[47]

Although this language appears fairly straightforward, in *Steelworkers v Weber*, the Supreme Court interpreted this passage to actually *permit* preferential treatment. In the opinion for the court, Justice William Brennan wrote that had Congress truly intended to prohibit all race-conscious affirmative action, it would have substituted the word *permit* for *require* in the first clause of Section 703(j).[48] Because the clause did *not* read, "[n]othing contained in this subchapter shall be interpreted to *permit* any employer . . . ,"voluntary preferential programs could be permitted. Whether or not you agree with the court's ruling in this matter, it is now the law of the land and the precedent for subsequent cases. Therefore, affirmative action does not, of and by itself, violate Title VII.

In overcoming the hurdle of Section 703(j), the Supreme Court had to impose restrictions on AAPs to avoid undoing Title VII entirely. For any preferential program to be permissible under Title VII, four criteria must be satisfied. The plan: (1) must be *justified* by mirroring the purposes of Title VII, (2) must not *unnecessarily trammel the interests* of employees belonging to nonpreferred groups, (3) must not create an *absolute bar* to the advancement of employees belonging to

■ EXHIBIT 6-4

STANDARDS AFFIRMATIVE ACTION MUST MEET
TO BE PERMISSIBLE UNDER TITLE VII

■ The plan must be *justified*.

■ The plan must not *unnecessarily trammel the interests* of employees belonging to nonpreferred groups.

■ The plan must not create an *absolute bar*.

■ The plan must be a *temporary measure*.

SOURCE: *Steelworkers v Weber*, 443 U.S. 193, 208 (1979).

nonpreferred groups, and (4) must be a *temporary measure* designed to attain, but not maintain a racial balance.[49]

In a purely legal sense, if any one of these conditions is not satisfied, then the AAP is unlawful, and reverse discrimination has occurred. Because these criteria are so important to the development of programs permissible under Title VII, each criterion will be examined in more detail.

JUSTIFICATION OF AFFIRMATIVE ACTION

The first condition is that any affirmative action pursued by an employer must be *justified*. Under voluntary programs, affirmative action is a remedial action. Thus, the preferential treatment is pursued for the purpose of eliminating any traces of previous discrimination. The easiest means of satisfying this requirement is to produce documentation that the organization had, at one time, implemented policies that specifically denied or limited the employment opportunities available to members of specific protected classes. For example, a company may have excluded African Americans from outside sales jobs, or a fire department may have denied women access to firefighter positions. Any evidence of policies or practices that segregated certain jobs by race, color, religion, sex, or national origin would provide the foundation for justifying a program.

Interestingly, mere historical knowledge that an employer had discriminatory policies is insufficient, by itself, to justify preferential treatment. The employer must show there is still some remaining effect from these past policies, which is often demonstrated by a gross statistical imbalance in the employer's internal workforce.[50] The underlying rationale is that because of the employer's past discriminatory hiring or promoting practices, individuals were denied access to positions due to their race, color, religion, sex, or national origin. As a consequence of years of engaging in such practices, the members of the affected protected classes became **underrepresented** (or what we call "underutilized" when referring to AAPs) in the workplace. Federal courts have accepted underrepresentation (statistical imbalance) as an indication of the present effects of previous discrimination.[51]

From a practical standpoint, the absence of underrepresentation jeopardizes the employer's contention that preferential affirmative action is necessary (justified). It is, therefore, imperative that before *any* organization embarks on an AAP, it must first conduct *utilization analysis* to assess whether underrepresentation exists. The absence of this justification removes the permissibility of any AAP under Title VII and exposes the employer to reverse discrimination litigation.[52]

UNNECESSARILY TRAMMELING INTERESTS

If the program is justified, the AAP must determine whether it **unnecessarily trammels** the interests of individuals who are not members of the "preferred group." *Trammel* means to confine or hinder—and in this case, it means the AAP cannot unnecessarily restrict the rights of individuals who are members of non-preferred groups.

As mentioned in Chapter 2, more than 67 percent of the workforce is afforded some statutory protection under federal EEO laws; therefore, these individuals are members of protected classes. The problem with affirmative action is that not *all* members of protected classes are entitled to preferential treatment. As ethnic diversity continues to increase in the United States, more and more of the parties filing reverse discrimination complaints are themselves members of protected classes. In such instances, they are not the protected class receiving preferential treatment under the AAP in question because their ethnic group was not "underrepresented" in their workplace. For instance, a Hispanic student filed suit against a university's race-based scholarship program that favored only African Americans.[53] Likewise, a female applicant who was denied admission to a professional school filed a reverse discrimination suit against race-based admissions programs.[54] Therefore, in order to distinguish between those groups designated to benefit from affirmative action and those not designated, the terms preferred group and nonpreferred group will be used.

The term **preferred group** includes all employees or applicants entitled to preferential treatment under an AAP, while the term **nonpreferred group** includes all employees or applicants *not* entitled to preferential treatment under an AAP, including those who are members of protected classes. For example, if an AAP permits preferential hiring of African Americans and Hispanics, all other ethnic classifications would be placed in the single category of *nonpreferred group*. Not only would whites be in this category, but so would Asian Americans, Puerto Ricans, Cubans, American Indians, and so on.

To avoid unnecessarily trammeling the interests of nonpreferred employees, employers must walk a very fine line. The major problem imposed by this standard lies in the word *"unnecessarily."* As stated explicitly in the Supreme Court's decision in *Weber*, "[a]t the same time, the plan does not unnecessarily trammel the interests of the white employees."[55] This has been widely interpreted to imply that there are circumstances under which it may be *necessary* to trammel the rights of nonpreferred groups. Or, in the words of Chief Justice Warren Berger, "[W]hen effectuating a limited and properly tailored remedy to cure the effects of prior discrimination, such a 'sharing of the burden' by innocent parties is not impermissible."[56]

In other words, the interests of employees from nonpreferred groups can be restricted, but only within very narrow limitations and only in order to eliminate a manifest imbalance. Just what those limitations are is hard to determine and could vary on a case-by-case basis. However, some employment actions are readily recognized as unnecessarily trammeling nonpreferred employee interests. For example, terminating or demoting an individual who is a member of a nonpreferred group in order to create a vacancy for an applicant of a preferred group would violate this standard.[57] In some instances, federal courts have determined that the rights of nonpreferred employees have been unnecessarily trammeled when their promotion and advancement opportunities have been unduly restricted by affirmative action.[58] Unfortunately for employers, the line between what would constitute necessary and unnecessary trammeling is not always easily discerned.

ABSOLUTE BARS

Determining whether a given program creates an absolute bar is much easier. An affirmative action program creates an **absolute bar** when it excludes from consideration for any position *all* parties who *are not* members of the preferred group. By setting aside specific positions to be filled only by individuals who belong to specific ethnic or racial groups, the plan creates an inflexible quota. Although federal courts have long permitted employers to consider race and ethnicity under formal AAPs, they have not permitted such consideration to be the *sole* decision criterion.[59] When an applicant's race, sex, or ethnicity becomes the *only* factor in determining eligibility for a position, Title VII is violated.[60]

In an attempt to meet affirmative action goals, employers, or their well-meaning HR managers, unintentionally create absolute bars in recruiting and selecting practices. Take for example the affirmative action officer who once told a department head that she would not approve any more employment recommendations from his department unless the candidate was either African American or female. In essence, *all* male non-African American candidates were barred from consideration for any position in that department based solely on their sex and race, which needlessly exposes the employer to reverse discrimination. Even under affirmative action goals, if a *qualified* member of the *preferred* group cannot be found, the position must be offered to the most qualified *nonpreferred* group member. The position need not remain vacant until filled by a member of the preferred group. If the position remains unfilled, an unacceptable absolute bar is maintained.

AFFIRMATIVE ACTION MUST BE TEMPORARY

The courts further acknowledge that permitting preferential treatment under affirmative action to continue in perpetuity would undermine the purpose of Title VII. Instead of eliminating racially conscious hiring, the program would instead institutionalize it. To avoid this, all AAPs must demonstrate that they are temporary measures. Recall that affirmative action, in theory, was intended to be a remedial device to "even the playing field," or, in legalese, "to eliminate the present effects of past discrimination."[61] Once the affirmative action goals are attained, the program should be terminated. As a consequence, any plan that continues to operate after achieving its goals does so in violation of Title VII.

In practice, however, some "temporary" plans have operated for over thirty-five years. It is not uncommon for preferential hiring to become so ingrained in an organization's selection criteria that it becomes the standard operating procedure. Even the EEOC, the agency that oversees many AAPs and even publishes guidelines for such programs,[62] was successfully sued for reverse discrimination because its own plan had become a permanent fixture. The EEOC continued operating its preferential hiring and promotions for members of preferred groups long after statistical imbalances were eliminated. By continuing hiring practices that favored ethnic minorities and women when no statistical disparity existed between the numbers of these employees in the EEOC's internal workforce and the external labor force, Title VII was violated.[63] The EEOC's own case illustrates how easy it is for an organization to overemphasize the importance of preferential selection and lose sight of the stated goal of such programs (making the transition from affirmative action to equal employment opportunity). The advice for employers is simple: Once you have eliminated the statistical imbalance, document it, and cease all affirmative action.

PERMISSIBLE AFFIRMATIVE ACTION IN THE PUBLIC SECTOR

Public sector employers (i.e., governments, public schools, public universities, public hospitals, law enforcement, fire departments, etc.) not only have to avoid violating Title VII when they implement affirmative action initiatives but are also constrained by the Fourteenth Amendment's Equal Protection Clause. The **Equal Protection Clause** specifically states that: "No State shall make or enforce any law which shall abridge the privileges or immunities of citizens of the United States; nor shall any State deprive any person of life, liberty, or property without due process of law, or deny to any person within its jurisdiction the equal protection of the laws." Therefore, state and local governments are forbidden from treating individuals differently because of some characteristic which they cannot change, like race or ethnicity. The Equal Protection Clause renders race and ethnicity irrelevant in governmental decision making.[64]

As with Title VII, federal courts have been confronted with the dilemma of remedying the effects of past discrimination through preferential treatment programs while, at the same time, maintaining equal treatment. Again, there is no satisfactory solution, and the courts have concluded that there are some instances in which the necessity to address past state-imposed discrimination may place a burden on innocent third parties. It is not our intent or purpose to discuss either the morality or efficacy of this course of action, only to present its consequences for public sector employers. Racial or ethnic preferences have increasingly been seen as facially suspect when initiated by a government agency.[65] Compared to

THREE GENERAL COMPONENTS OF A
FORMAL AFFIRMATIVE ACTION PLAN

- Utilization analysis
- Goals and timetables
- Action plan

their private sector counterparts, government employers are held to a higher standard of judicial review.[66]

DEVELOPING AN AFFIRMATIVE ACTION PLAN

A formal AAP is comprised of utilization analysis, goals and timetables, and an action plan. The utilization analysis determines the degree to which any protected class is underutilized in the workplace. An underutilized group would then become the preferred group under the plan for preferential hiring or selection. Once the extent of the underutilization is known, the employer will establish specific and measurable goals for eliminating the imbalance and a timetable in which to achieve the goals. Finally, the action plan identifies the steps and actions to be implemented by the employer to accomplish the stated goals.

UTILIZATION ANALYSIS

The purpose of **utilization analysis** is to determine the extent to which ethnic minorities and/or women are being "underutilized" by the organization in question. "Underutilization" is defined as having fewer ethnic minorities or women in a particular job group than would reasonably be expected by their availability.[67] A "job group" means one or more jobs that have similar content, wage rates, and opportunities. For example, a metal press operator, a sheet metal cutter, and an assembler all working on a small assembly line under similar working conditions and for similar wages could be covered by the same job group. On the surface, utilization appears to be very similar to stock analysis as discussed in Chapter 3. Its calculations are in fact essentially the same, but the factors considered when determining the relevant minority population make it far more cumbersome.

- In December 2000 the OFCCP replaced the eight-factor analysis used to determine the availability of minorities and women with a more simplified two-factor analysis.[68] This change now requires that contractors use the following two factors when determining availability of underutilized groups:

    1. The percentage of minorities or women with requisite skills in the reasonable recruitment area. The reasonable recruitment area is defined

    as the geographical area from which the contractor usually seeks or reasonably could seek workers to fill the positions in question.

  2. The percentage of minorities or women among those promotable, transferable, and trainable within the contractor's organization. Trainable refers to those employees within the contractor's organization who could, with appropriate training which the contractor is reasonably able to provide, become promotable or transferable during the AAP year.[69]

The new rule defines the contractor's "reasonable recruitment area" as "the geographic area from which the contractor usually seeks or reasonably could seek workers to fill the positions in question."[70] This is not a very specific definition, and no doubt it will be subject to broad interpretation. Also under the rule, the term "trainable" refers to those workers currently employed by the contractor who "could, with appropriate training which the contractor is reasonably able to provide, become promotable or transferable during the AAP year."[71] Again, the definition is sufficiently broad to be open to a wide range of interpretations. Ultimately, it is likely that the OFCCP itself will make the determination as to what the contractor is "reasonably able to provide."

Not only must the employer identify those members of the underutilized group that currently possess the requisite skills, knowledge, and ability for the job group in question, it must also estimate those that have the potential to acquire those requisite skills.

As with any analysis of representativeness, utilization analysis is absolutely dependent upon accurate job analysis and validated selection criteria. Flawed job descriptions and job specifications will improperly specify the requisite skills, knowledge, and abilities that a job incumbent must possess. As a consequence, the affirmative action goals predicated on utilization analysis will be bogus.

The 1989 case of *City of Richmond v J. A. Croson Co.* demonstrates how public organizations may be vulnerable to litigation when they initiate an AAP without first conducting adequate utilization analysis. The City of Richmond, through its Minority Business Utilization Plan, issued the requirement that primary contractors of construction projects had to subcontract *at least* 30 percent of the dollar amount of every municipal contract to minority businesses.[72] Under this plan, the City of Richmond defined a "minority business" to be a business from anywhere in the country with at least 51 percent of that business being owned and controlled by African American, Spanish-speaking, Oriental, Indian, Eskimo, or Aleut citizens. The Supreme Court affirmed the Fourth Circuit Court of Appeals' judgment that the 30 percent figure was chosen arbitrarily and was not tied to the number of minority subcontractors in Richmond or to any other relevant number.[73] In fact, if the City of Richmond had conducted proper utilization analysis, it would have discovered that only 4.7 percent of the contractor firms in the United States are owned by minorities, and the actual percentage of minority contractors in Richmond is somewhat less. The City of Richmond failed to identify the relevant labor market—those members of ethnic minorities with the requisite qualifications to be subcontractors—and then determine whether contract awards indicated that they were being underutilized.

In the absence of utilization analysis, proving a "manifest imbalance" in awarding contracts existed (as a result of past discrimination), the Supreme Court concluded that the City of Richmond had established an affirmative action goal with no basis in fact. In short, the City of Richmond had not established a compelling government interest to justify its preferential treatment of minority subcontractors. This led the Court to rule that Richmond had discriminated against the white plaintiff because of race, an action which is prohibited under the Equal Protection Clause.

To further illustrate the importance of accurately specifying relevant labor markets, let's assume a particular university is conducting utilization analysis to develop its AAP. The affirmative action officer has decided to examine the utilization of minorities and women for faculty teaching positions within the College of Business and has come up with the faculty distribution found in Exhibit 6-6.

By converting the current staffing table to a percentage of the College's faculty, the results in Exhibit 6-7 are available for comparison with national statistics.

The university's position announcement states:

Assistant Professor. State University seeks a full-time, tenure-track assistant professor of management to begin fall semester, 2002. Responsibilities include: teaching (6–9 credit hours per semester, including occasional distance education classes), advising (at the graduate and undergraduate levels), research (resulting in scholarly publications), and service to the profession and university. Qualifications include: (1) graduate course work and teaching experience in one of the following fields: (a) international business/international management, or (b) strategic management; (2) a record of refereed, scholarly publications; and (3) an earned doctorate in management. Experience in distance education is desirable. Preference will be given to candidates who excel in the above areas. To apply, please submit a letter of application, curriculum vitae, three letters of recommendation, and copies of undergraduate and graduate transcripts to Professor Carol Smith, Chair, Search Committee, College of Business, State University. Review of applications will begin October 20, 2001, and continue until the position is filled. AA/EEO.

■ EXHIBIT 6-6

DISTRIBUTION OF BUSINESS/MANAGEMENT FACULTY BY PROTECTED CLASS

	White (Not of Hispanic Origin)	African American (Not of Hispanic Origin)	Hispanic	Asian or Pacific Islander	American Indian or Alaska Native	Total Male and Female
Male	21	0	1	2	0	**24**
Female	6	1	1	0	0	**8**
Totals	**27**	**1**	**2**	**2**	**0**	**32**

■ EXHIBIT 6-7

PERCENTAGE OF BUSINESS FACULTY BY PROTECTED CLASS

	White (Not of Hispanic Origin)	African American (Not of Hispanic Origin)	Hispanic	Asian or Pacific Islander	American Indian or Alaska Native	Total Male and Female
Male	65.6%	0%	3.1%	6.3%	0%	**75.0%**
Female	18.8	3.1	3.1	0	0	**25.0**
Totals	**84.4**	**3.1**	**6.3**	**6.3**	**0**	**100.0**

In performing its utilization analysis, the College of Business decided to compare its faculty to the population of all full-time college and university faculty in the United States. After all, the College of Business concluded, the university has to conduct nationwide searches to fill faculty positions. Therefore, national statistics are appropriate for making its workforce comparisons. Based on figures from the United States Department of Education, the national proportion of full-time faculty members with teaching duties is shown in Exhibit 6-8.

As a result, the affirmative action officer declares African Americans and women are underrepresented in the College of Business. Internally, 3.1 percent of

■ EXHIBIT 6-8

PERCENTAGE OF FULL-TIME FACULTY
(WITH AND WITHOUT DOCTORATES) 1995

EEO Classification	Total Numbers	Percentage
Male	360,150	65.4%
Female	190,672	34.6
Totals	**550,822**	**100.0**
White (not of Hispanic origin)	468,518	85.1
African American (not of Hispanic origin)	26,835	4.9
Hispanic	12,942	2.3
Asian or Pacific Islander	27,572	4.9
American Indian or Alaska Native	2,156	0.4
Non-resident aliens	10,853	2.0
Race unknown	1,946	0.4
Totals	**550,822**	**100.0**

SOURCE: U.S. Department of Education, Faculty and Instructional Staff, http://chronicle.com/weekly/almanac/1999/facts/6folks.htm

the college's faculty are African American, while the education statistics selected for comparison indicate that 4.9 percent of all full-time faculty are African American. Using the same statistics, one would expect 34.6 percent of the faculty to be female when in fact only 25 percent of the faculty positions in the College of Business are held by women. The next step would be to develop action plans and timetables to eliminate the underutilization (the statistical imbalance).

Unfortunately, the utilization analysis is terribly flawed. The figures upon which the affirmative action officer based the conclusions do not reflect the skills necessary to be an effective *management* professor. The figures used to make the comparison between the proportion of minorities and women in the College of Business faculty and the national labor market included terminal degrees in *all* fields, everything from agriculture to zoology. However, to be an effective professor of international management, one must have at least a degree in *management* or *international business*. An applicant with a doctorate (Ed.D.) in education leadership will not perform well teaching international management nor in publishing in that field. Hence, the appropriate comparisons must be with applicants who possess terminal degrees in business. Those percentages are provided in Exhibit 6-9.

After reviewing these figures, underutilization still exists, but it is with Asian Americans, and here, only slightly. African Americans and women, as classes, are actually overrepresented.

If the university had created a plan based on the all-inclusive figures rather than the specialized needs of the business faculty, the college could have seen its AAP successfully challenged in court. The university did not accurately define *how many* persons were truly qualified to fill the business faculty positions.

■ **EXHIBIT 6-9**

FACULTY DEMOGRAPHIC COMPOSITION OF AACSB SCHOOLS FOR 1998

EEO Classification	Number in Sample (N=441)	Percentage of Total
Male	17,472	78.1%
Female	4,895	21.9
Totals	**22,367**	**100.0**
White (not of Hispanic origin)	18,258	81.6
African American (not of Hispanic origin)	697	3.1
Hispanic	330	1.5
Asian or Pacific Islander	1,519	6.8
American Indian or Alaska Native	59	0.3
Non-U.S. citizens	1,504	6.7
Totals	**22,367**	**100.0**

SOURCE: AACSB—The International Association of Management Education (1999). Faculty Demographic Composition of AACSB Schools. *School Fact Form.* http://www.aacsb.edu/Publications/Newsline/view.asp?year=1999&file=spdemand_t4.html

Hence, the affirmative action goals based on *all* degrees would have resulted in preferential treatment being extended to women and African Americans when *no statistical imbalance existed*. This would expose the employer to a reverse discrimination complaint being brought under Title VII.[74] Since the university was a public institution (a state university), this could have resulted in an Equal Protection Clause complaint as well.[75]

As shown in this illustration, too often, AAPs are initiated without proper consideration of the skills a job incumbent truly needs. Failing to consider the relevant labor market for applicants is a frequent problem. Thus, it is critical to be mindful of these issues before embarking on any preferential treatment program. If utilization analysis is not properly conducted, all actions that follow are superfluous, and they may expose the organization to Title VII litigation.

GOALS AND TIMETABLES

Assuming the utilization analysis was properly conducted, the next step in developing an AAP is to create goals and timetables. In the event of substantial disparities in the utilization of specific groups, it is unreasonable to expect an immediate resolution. In such instances, the organization must eliminate the imbalances incrementally over time. In some cases, underrepresented groups may not be underutilized in lower-skilled entry positions, but they are absent in management and supervisory ranks. In order to generate a sufficient number of qualified minority applicants for the supervisory positions, it may be necessary to allow such individuals time to gain supervisor-related experience. After all, someone who does not fully understand the process can hardly be expected to supervise workers performing it. Additional time may be warranted for supervisory education and training programs as well.

If the employer is recruiting from an area that is a significant distance from its facility, the recruiting process will take longer to complete. When jobs require specific and technical skills, recruiting may be even more complicated.

Suppose a company is trying to fill an industrial engineering position. It is likely that the employer would have to recruit nationally. Compare this to recruiting for day laborers where the recruiting effort would not go too far beyond an hour's commute of the plant. It is reasonable to expect most nationwide recruiting drives to last six to twelve months, while local recruiting efforts last only a few days or weeks.

Because of the difficulty in locating underrepresented group members with requisite skills, it is also possible that affirmative action goals will *not* be attained. Provided the employer has shown a good faith effort to attain them, the OFCCP and the EEOC are unlikely to take adverse action against the employer. Failure to attain goals may be traced to unrealistic goals based on faulty utilization analysis. In such instances, a new, proper analysis should be conducted and the goals adjusted accordingly. Overly ambitious timetables may often be the culprit. If so, an employer should seriously reexamine the underlying assumptions for identifying minority and female applicant goals and then modify the timetable to reflect the more realistic expectations.

ACTION PLANS

The **action plan** is the nuts and bolts of an AAP. These are, as the name implies, action-oriented programs designed to eliminate problems *and* attain previously established goals and objectives.[76] Some techniques suggested by the OFCCP to increase the flow of minority and female applicants are:[77]

- Recruit through organizations that serve as advocates for minority and female rights such as the Urban League, National Organization for Women, welfare rights organizations, and state employment services.
- Include minorities and females in the company's Personnel Relations Staff.
- Actively participate in "job fairs," particularly those held in areas with large minority populations.
- Establish internship and cooperative programs with historically black universities and women's colleges.
- Provide "after school" and work-study jobs for minority youths.
- Provide "summer jobs" for the underprivileged.
- Put pictures of minority and female workers in recruiting brochures.
- Advertise position vacancies in minority news media.
- Brief current minority and female employees of current and future job openings.
- Establish active recruiting programs at secondary schools, vocational-technical schools, and junior colleges with predominantly minority or female enrollments.

One critical point to remember when implementing any AAP is to never select an *unqualified* candidate to fill a position. Note that there is a fine line between *permissible* affirmative action and *unlawful* discrimination. Hiring an unqualified individual crosses that line.

ADDITIONAL REPORTING REQUIREMENTS

In addition to performing utilization analysis, federal contractors and subcontractors (and other entities that come under E.O. 11246) must submit an annual EO Survey to the OFCCP. The EO Survey requires the employer to provide most of the information that is already contained in the EEO-1 Report mentioned in Chapter 1 and then some. The employer must not only furnish the ethnic and gender composition of his or her current workforce in the nine job categories, but must also provide the same information regarding applicants, hires, promotions, and terminations during the previous affirmative action program year (see Exhibit 6-10). Unlike the EEO-1 Report, the EO Survey further requires the employer to break down Hispanic employees and applicants into three distinct categories: Hispanic or Latino (all races), Hispanic or Latino (white race only), and Hispanic or Latino (all other races).

(Text continues on page 219)

U.S. Department of Labor
Office of Federal Contract Compliance Programs
Equal Opportunity Survey
of Federal Contractor Establishments

INTRODUCTION:

The U.S. Department of Labor, Office of Federal Contract Compliance Programs (OFCCP) is conducting this Equal Opportunity Survey (EO Survey) to obtain employment information from federal contractor establishments. We suggest that your EEO/Human Resource Director or Affirmative Action Officer be responsible for completing and/or coordinating the completion of this EO Survey.

WHO MUST COMPLETE THE EO SURVEY

You must complete and return this Survey if **both** of the following statements are true:

...............Your company or corporation is
a federal contractor or subcontractor;
...............Your company or corporation has 50 or more employees;

....and any one of the following statements is true

...............Your company or corporation has a federal
contract or subcontract of $50,000 or more.
...............Your company or corporation is a financial institution
that is an issuing agent for U.S. Savings Bonds and Notes.
...............Your company or corporation serves as a
depository of government funds in any amount.
...............Your company or corporation has government bills of lading which
in any 12-month period total or will likely total $50,000 or more.
...............Your company or corporation has an open-ended or indefinite quantity of
federal contracts or subcontracts (such as a procurement order
or standing invoices) that will total $50,000 or more.

Note: Your facility may or may not be the same location where your company or corporation is performing work under the federal contract or subcontract, but your facility is still considered a federal contractor or subcontractor establishment. For example, Company X has a federal contract or subcontract and has two facilities, A and B. Facility A is performing work under the federal contract or subcontract, Facility B is not. **Both Facility A and B of Company X are federal contractor establishments.**

Note: Your facility is considered a federal subcontractor establishment if it is a subcontractor to a federal contractor and is performing work related to that contract. For example, Company X is performing work under a federal contract. Company Y and Company Z are subcontractors of Company X. Company Y is performing work related to Company X's federal contract. Company Z is not performing work related to Company X's federal contract or any other federal contract or subcontract. **Company X and Company Y are federal subcontractor establishments; Company Z is not a federal subcontractor establishment.**

If your establishment should not complete this EO Survey, please (1) check here ☐ , (2) explain in the space provided below why your establishment should not complete this EO Survey, and (3) sign and date the certification on the next page and return the EO Survey in the envelope provided to the address shown at right.

_____

_____

continued

CONTINUED

INSTRUCTIONS:

This survey has three Parts – A, B, and C. Part A is self-explanatory. Please read all instructions for parts B and C before you begin. If you have any questions, or if you need assistance in completing the EO Survey, you may call our EO Survey Help Desk at 1-800-397-6443 for technical assistance or 1-800-397-6251 for policy assistance.

HOW TO SUBMIT THE EO SURVEY:

A pre-addressed business reply envelope is included for your convenience. Please return the entire completed and signed survey, including these instructions, **within 45 days of the date of receipt** to:

EO Survey Office
Office of Federal Contract Compliance Programs
U.S. Department of Labor
141 Canal Street
Nashua, NH 03064-2879

DID YOU KNOW YOU CAN SUBMIT
THE EO SURVEY *ELECTRONICALLY* ON THE WEB?

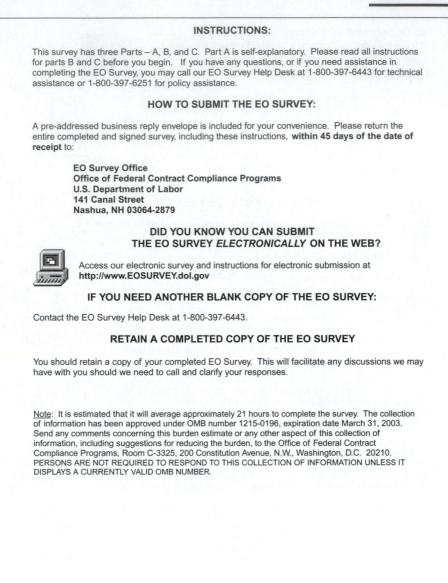

Access our electronic survey and instructions for electronic submission at
http://www.EOSURVEY.dol.gov

IF YOU NEED ANOTHER BLANK COPY OF THE EO SURVEY:

Contact the EO Survey Help Desk at 1-800-397-6443.

RETAIN A COMPLETED COPY OF THE EO SURVEY

You should retain a copy of your completed EO Survey. This will facilitate any discussions we may have with you should we need to call and clarify your responses.

Note: It is estimated that it will average approximately 21 hours to complete the survey. The collection of information has been approved under OMB number 1215-0196, expiration date March 31, 2003. Send any comments concerning this burden estimate or any other aspect of this collection of information, including suggestions for reducing the burden, to the Office of Federal Contract Compliance Programs, Room C-3325, 200 Constitution Avenue, N.W., Washington, D.C. 20210. PERSONS ARE NOT REQUIRED TO RESPOND TO THIS COLLECTION OF INFORMATION UNLESS IT DISPLAYS A CURRENTLY VALID OMB NUMBER.

U.S. Department of Labor
Office of Federal Contract Compliance Programs
Equal Opportunity Survey
of Federal Contractor Establishments

PART A – GENERAL INFORMATION

1. **Your establishment's Employer Identification Number**
    (IRS 9-digit tax number): |__|__|__|__|__|__|__|__|__|

2. **Information regarding a current Federal contract or subcontract for**
    your corporation of at least $50,000 (*You may report any current*
    Federal contract or subcontract of at least $50,000).

    If You are a Federal Contractor:

    a. **Name of Federal contracting agency:**
        _____

    b. **Contract number:**
        #_____

    If You are a Federal Subcontractor:

    c. **Name of Prime contractor:**
        _____

    d. **Contract number:**
        #_____

3. **Expiration date of your establishment's current Affirmative Action**
    Program(s) addressing:

    a. **Race, color, religion, sex, national origin**
        (please enter date in MM/DD/YY format):   ___/___/___

        If you do not know the expiration plan, check this box ------------☐

        If your establishment does not have this document,
        check this box --☐

    b. **Individuals with disabilities**
        (please enter date in MM/DD/YY format):   ___/___/___

        If you do not know the expiration date, check this box ------------☐

        If your establishment does not have this document,
        check this box --☐

continued

CONTINUED

c. Vietnam Era, special disabled, and other protected veterans
(please enter date in MM/DD/YY format): ___/___/___

If you do not know the expiration date, check this box ------------□

If your establishment does not have this document,
check this box ---□

4. Did your establishment list any employment openings with the local
office of your state employment service and/or America's Job Bank
during the period January 1 through December 31 of the most recently
concluded calendar year, or during the 12-month period covered by
your most recently concluded Affirmative Action Program (AAP) year,
if it does not coincide with the calendar year?

No employment openings were listed------------------------------□

No employment openings were listed,
but all employment openings were either
positions filled from within, executive
and top management positions, or positions
for 3 days employment or less --------------------------------□

Yes, employment openings were listed---------------------------□

If yes, how many employment openings were listed?-----[_____]

5. If your address or other identifying information on the mailing label
was incorrect, please provide the corrected information below:

Establishment:_____

Street Address or P.O. Box:_____

_____

City, State, Zip Code:_____

EEO-1 Number for this establishment:_____

Note: For complete guidance, refer to Executive Order 11246, as amended
and its implementing regulations at 41 CFR Parts 60-1 through 60-50;
Section 503 of the Rehabilitation Act of 1973, as amended and its
implementing regulations at 41 CFR Part 60-741; and 38 U.S.C. 4212, the
Vietnam Era Veterans' Readjustment Assistance Act of 1974 (VEVRAA),
as amended and its implementing regulations at 41 CFR Part 60-250.

CONTINUED

Time Frame: (check one):
☐ - The following personnel activity covers the most recently concluded calendar year
☐ - The following personnel activity covers the most recently concluded Affirmative Action Program year, which is not January 1 through December 31

	American Indian or Alaska Native	Asian	Black or African American	Native Hawaiian or Other Pacific Islander	White	Hispanic or Latino (all races)	Hispanic or Latino (White race only)	Hispanic or Latino (all other races)	Race unknown
OFFICIALS AND MANAGERS									
Male									
Female									
PROFESSIONALS									
Male									
Female									
TECHNICIANS									
Male									
Female									
SALES WORKERS									
Male									
Female									
OFFICE AND CLERICAL									
Male									
Female									
CRAFT WORKERS									
Male									
Female									
OPERATIVES									
Male									
Female									
LABORERS									
Male									
Female									
SERVICE WORKERS									
Male									
Female									

continued

CONTINUED

SPECIAL TERMS YOU NEED TO KNOW TO COMPLETE THE SURVEY:

Certifying Officer – An employee of your company or corporation working at this establishment that has the authority to certify the accuracy of EEO-1 Reports, Affirmative Action Programs, etc. (example: Human Resources Manager, Plant Manager, EEO Officer). The Certifying Officer should sign this EO Survey on the line indicated at right.

Federal Contracting Agency - Any department or agency in the executive branch of Government, including any wholly owned Government corporation, which enters into contracts.

Employer Identification Number - The 9-digit number which each corporation, partnership, or sole proprietorship has been assigned based on its application (Form SS-4) to Internal Revenue Service for an identification number.

Applicant – The concept of an applicant is that of a person who has indicated an interest in being considered for hiring, promotion, or other employment opportunity. This interest might be expressed by completing an application form, or might be expressed orally, depending upon the employer's practice.

Employees - For the purposes of this EO Survey, the term "employees" applies only to your "full time" employees, as the term "full time" is defined by your company. Do not report personnel activity or compensation data on "part time" employees, as the term "part time" is defined by your company.

Promotion - Any personnel action resulting in movement to a position (1) with higher pay or greater rank, or (2) requiring greater skill or responsibility, or (3) with the opportunity to attain increased pay, rank, skill, or responsibility.

Termination - Any separation, voluntary or involuntary, of an employee from your active or inactive payroll. A termination is a complete break in employment status.

Annual Monetary Compensation – An employee's base rate (wage or salary), plus other earnings such as cost-of-living allowance, hazard pay, or other increment paid to all employees regardless of tenure on the job, extrapolated and expressed in terms of a full year.

Tenure – Length of service; the length of time an employee has been employed by your company or corporation.

INSTRUCTIONS FOR PART B:

WHO TO REPORT ON: Part B information should include applicant, hiring, promotion, termination, and incumbency data for <u>"full time" employees only</u>; however the term "full time" is defined by your company.

TIME FRAME FOR REPORTING: Part B information should report on personnel activity covering your choice of one of the following two time frames:

(1) The period January 1 through December 31 of the most recently concluded calendar year, or

(2) The 12-month period covered by your most recently concluded Affirmative Action Program (AAP) year, if it does not coincide with the calendar year (for example, April 1 through March 31).

<u>Regardless of which of the above time frames you wish to use,
all Part B information must cover the same time frame.</u>

Based on your choice of time frames, please report Applicants, Hires, Promotions, and Terminations for January 1 through December 31 of the most recently concluded calendar year, or for the 12-month period covered by your most recently concluded AAP year. Please report "Employees" as of December 31 of the most recently concluded calendar year, or the last day of the most recently concluded AAP year.

EEO-1 CATEGORY: For each personnel activity identified, fill in the total number for the action indicated, by gender, race, and ethnicity and EEO-1 category. The EEO-1 categories are : **(1) Officials & Managers; (2) Professionals; (3) Technicians; (4) Sales Workers; (5) Office & Clerical; (6) Craft Workers; (7) Operatives; (8) Laborers; (9) Service Workers**. All incumbents listed on the **"Full Time Employees At End Of Year (Calendar or AAP)"** page in Part B of this EO Survey **must be accounted for and reported on in Part C.**

WHAT TO REPORT - PERSONNEL ACTIVITY

Applicants - Please indicate the number of applicants for "full time" positions by gender, race, and ethnicity, sorted by EEO-1 category, for the period of January 1 through December 31 of the most recently concluded calendar year, or for the 12-month period covered by your most recently concluded AAP year.

Hires - Please indicate the number of hires for "full time" positions by gender, race, and ethnicity, sorted by EEO-1 category, for the period of January 1 through December 31 of the most recently concluded calendar year, or for the 12-month period covered by your most recently concluded AAP year. Do not include non-competitive transfers from other facilities of your company or establishment.

Promotions - Please indicate the number of promotions of "full time" employees by gender, race, and ethnicity, sorted by EEO-1 category, for the period of January 1 through December 31 of the most recently concluded calendar year, or for the 12-month period covered by your most recently concluded AAP year. Report the number of promotions within the EEO-1 category where it occurred; however, in instances where there are promotions from one EEO-1 category to another EEO-1 category, report those promotions in the EEO-1 category the individual was promoted into. For example, a person who is promoted from a junior engineer to a senior engineer would be counted as a promotion within the "Professional" EEO-1 category. A person promoted from a senior engineer to a manager would be counted as a promotion into the "Officials and Managers" EEO-1 category.

Terminations - Please indicate the number of terminations of "full time" employees by gender, race, and ethnicity, sorted by your choice of either EEO-1 category, for the period of January 1 through December 31 of the most recently concluded calendar year, or for the 12-month period covered by your most recently concluded AAP year. Include voluntary and involuntary terminations.

Employees at end of Calendar/AAP Year - Please indicate the number of incumbent "full time" employees by gender, race, and ethnicity, sorted by EEO-1 category, as of December 31 of the most recently concluded calendar year, or the last day of the most recently concluded AAP year.

continued

CONTINUED

ABOUT RACE/ETHNIC IDENTIFICATION FOR PART B - You may acquire race/ethnic information necessary for this survey either by visual observation of the work force, or from employment records. If you maintain records, we recommend that you keep them separately from the employee's basic personnel file or other records available to those responsible for personnel decisions. Since OFCCP permits visual observations, the fact that race/ethnic identifications are not present on employment records is not an excuse for omitting the data we request.

Note: The following reflects OMB guidelines regarding the recording and reporting of Hispanic or Latino ethnicity separately from the recording and reporting of racial data, and the establishment of "Native Hawaiian or Other Pacific Islander" as a separate racial category. If you have not yet adjusted your record keeping systems to reflect these changes, see the box at the bottom of this page.

Complete Part B using the following categories. Although persons may identify with more than one racial category, for this EO Survey count each person only once:

<u>American Indian or Alaskan Native</u> – A person having origins in any of the original peoples of North America and South America (including Central America), and who maintains tribal affiliation or community attachment.

<u>Asian</u> – A person having origins in any of the original peoples of the Far East, Southeast Asia, or the Indian subcontinent including, for example, Cambodia, China, India, Japan, Korea, Malaysia, Pakistan, the Philippine Islands, Thailand, and Vietnam.

<u>Black or African American</u> – A person having origins in any of the Black racial groups of Africa. Terms such as "Haitian" or "Negro" can be used in addition to "Black or African American."

<u>Native Hawaiian or Other Pacific Islander</u> – A person having origins in any of the original peoples of Hawaii, Guam, Samoa, or other Pacific Islands.

<u>White</u> – A person having origins in any of the original peoples of Europe, North Africa, or the Middle East.

<u>Hispanic or Latino (All races)</u> – A person of Mexican, Puerto Rican, Cuban, Central or South American, or other Spanish culture or origin, regardless of race.

> <u>Hispanic or Latino (White race only)</u> – A person of Mexican, Puerto Rican, Cuban, Central or South American, or other Spanish culture or origin, and of the White race.

> <u>Hispanic or Latino (all other races)</u> – A person of Mexican, Puerto Rican, Cuban, Central or South American, or other Spanish culture or origin, and of any race other than White.

<u>Race missing or unknown</u> - Applies to **Applicants only**, where a resume or application that is screened is received without any racial or ethnic identification and no further contact is made with the applicant.

■ EXHIBIT 6-10

For Time Frame as Specified on Page 5 in Part B of this EO Survey

	American Indian or Alaska Native	Asian	Black or African American	Native Hawaiian or Other Pacific Islander	White	Hispanic or Latino (all races)	Hispanic or Latino (White race only)	Hispanic or Latino (all other races)	Race unknown
OFFICIALS AND MANAGERS Male									
Female									
PROFESSIONALS Male									
Female									
TECHNICIANS Male									
Female									
SALES WORKERS Male									
Female									
OFFICE AND CLERICAL Male									
Female									
CRAFT WORKERS Male									
Female									
OPERATIVES Male									
Female									
LABORERS Male									
Female									
SERVICE WORKERS Male									
Female									

continued

For Time Frame as Specified on Page 5 in Part B of this EO Survey

	American Indian or Alaska Native	Asian	Black or African American	Native Hawaiian or Other Pacific Islander	White	Hispanic or Latino (all races)	Hispanic or Latino (White race only)	Hispanic or Latino (all other races)	Race unknown
OFFICIALS AND MANAGERS									
Male									
Female									
PROFESSIONALS									
Male									
Female									
TECHNICIANS									
Male									
Female									
SALES WORKERS									
Male									
Female									
OFFICE AND CLERICAL									
Male									
Female									
CRAFT WORKERS									
Male									
Female									
OPERATIVES									
Male									
Female									
LABORERS									
Male									
Female									
SERVICE WORKERS									
Male									
Female									

For Time Frame as Specified on Page 5 in Part B of this EO Survey

	American Indian or Alaska Native	Asian	Black or African American	Native Hawaiian or Other Pacific Islander	White	Hispanic or Latino (all races)	Hispanic or Latino (White race only)	Hispanic or Latino (all other races)	Race unknown
OFFICIALS AND MANAGERS									
Male									
Female									
PROFESSIONALS									
Male									
Female									
TECHNICIANS									
Male									
Female									
SALES WORKERS									
Male									
Female									
OFFICE AND CLERICAL									
Male									
Female									
CRAFT WORKERS									
Male									
Female									
OPERATIVES									
Male									
Female									
LABORERS									
Male									
Female									
SERVICE WORKERS									
Male									
Female									

continued

For Time Frame as Specified on Page 5 in Part B of this EO Survey

	American Indian or Alaska Native	Asian	Black or African American	Native Hawaiian or Other Pacific Islander	White	Hispanic or Latino (all races)	Hispanic or Latino (White race only)	Hispanic or Latino (all other races)	Race unknown
OFFICIALS AND MANAGERS									
Male									
Female									
PROFESSIONALS									
Male									
Female									
TECHNICIANS									
Male									
Female									
SALES WORKERS									
Male									
Female									
OFFICE AND CLERICAL									
Male									
Female									
CRAFT WORKERS									
Male									
Female									
OPERATIVES									
Male									
Female									
LABORERS									
Male									
Female									
SERVICE WORKERS									
Male									
Female									

INSTRUCTIONS FOR PART C:

WHO TO REPORT ON: In order for your EO Survey to be considered a valid submission Part C <u>must</u> contain annual monetary compensation and tenure data for all employees listed as **"Full Time Employees At End Of Year (Calendar or AAP)"** on Page 9 in Part B of this EO Survey, and it <u>must not</u> include monetary compensation and tenure data for anyone else.

TIME FRAME FOR REPORTING: The time frame is December 31 of the most recently concluded calendar year, or the last day of the most recently concluded AAP year, whichever you chose for reporting on Page 9, Part B of this EO Survey.

MINORITY/NON-MINORITY: Employees are to be grouped and reported in four groups: **minority female, non-minority female, minority male, and non-minority male employees**. For the purposes of this EO Survey, a "non-minority" is defined as someone of the White race who is not of Hispanic (or Latino) ethnicity. A "minority" is defined as all races other than White or someone of the White race who is of Hispanic (or Latino) ethnicity, or someone who has reported more than one race.

EEO-1 CATEGORY: Employees are also to be sorted by EEO-1 category. The EEO-1 categories are: **<u>(1) Officials & Managers; (2) Professionals; (3) Technicians; (4) Sales Workers; (5) Office & Clerical; (6) Craft Workers; (7) Operatives; (8) Laborers; (9) Service Workers</u>**.

In order for your EO Survey to be considered a valid submission all end-of-year incumbents listed on the "Full Time Employees At End Of Year (Calendar or AAP)" page in Part B of this EO Survey must be accounted for and reported on in Part C.

WHAT TO REPORT - ANNUAL MONETARY COMPENSATION: For the purposes of this EO Survey, annual monetary compensation is defined as an employee's base rate (wage or salary), plus other earnings such as cost-of-living allowance, hazard pay, or other increment paid to all employees regardless of tenure on the job. Annual monetary compensation should not include the value of benefits, overtime, or one-time payments such as relocation expenses. Annual monetary compensation should be expressed in terms of an annual amount.

Report total annual monetary compensation information for all employees reported in the **"Full Time Employees at end of Calendar/AAP Year"** columns in Part B of

continued

this EO Survey. While all annual monetary compensation figures should be expressed in terms of a full year, please note that this figure *may not reflect an employee's actual earnings for a year.* For those employees who have worked less than a full year (e.g., those employees hired within the last year), please project (extrapolate) their hourly or weekly rate to compute an annual rate.

WHAT TO REPORT - TENURE: For the purposes of this EO Survey, tenure is defined as the length of time an employee has been with your company.

For each relevant EEO-1 category please indicate:

Total Annual Monetary Compensation for All _____ Employees - Please indicate the annual monetary compensation earned by "full time" minority females, non-minority females, minority males, and non-minority males within each EEO-1 category. **Include only those employees listed in the "Full Time Employees at end of Calendar/AAP Year" page in Part B of this EO Survey.**

Lowest Annual Monetary Compensation of any Single _____ Employee - From the figures used to compute the Total Annual Monetary Compensation above, please indicate the lowest single annual monetary compensation among "full time" minority females, non-minority females, minority males, and non-minority males within each EEO-1 category. **Include only those employees listed in the "Full Time Employees at end of Calendar/AAP Year" page in Part B of this EO Survey.**

Highest Annual Monetary Compensation of any Single _____ Employee - From the figures used to compute the Total Annual Monetary Compensation above, please indicate the highest single annual monetary compensation among "full time" incumbent minority females, non-minority females, minority males, and non-minority males within each EEO-1 category. **Include only those employees listed in the "Full Time Employees at end of Calendar/AAP Year" page in Part B of this EO Survey.**

Average Tenure of _____ Employees with Firm - Please indicate the average length of time, in years and months, that "full time" incumbent **minority females, non-minority females, minority males, and non-minority males** within each EEO-1 category. **Include only those employees listed in the "Full Time Employees at end of calendar/AAP Year" page in Part B of this EO Survey.**

PART C -- COMPENSATION DATA BY EEO-1 CATEGORY

Annual Monetary Compensation and Tenure Data by EEO-1 Category for
Employees listed in "FULL TIME EMPLOYEES AT END OF YEAR (CALENDAR OR AAP)" on Page 9 in Part B of this EO Survey

Check one:
☐ - The following compensation data covers full time employees as of the end of the most recently concluded calendar year
☐ - The following compensation data covers full time employees as of the most recently concluded Affirmative Action Program year, which is not January 1 through December 31

	MINORITY FEMALES				NON-MINORITY FEMALES			
	Total Annual Monetary Compensation for All Minority Female Employees	Lowest Annual Monetary Compensation of any Single Minority Female Employee	Highest Annual Monetary Compensation of any Single Minority Female Employee	Average Tenure of Minority Female Employees with Firm — YEARS / MONTHS	Total Annual Monetary Compensation for All Non-Minority Female Employees	Lowest Annual Monetary Compensation of any Single Non-Minority Female Employee	Highest Annual Monetary Compensation of any Single Non-Minority Female Employee	Average Tenure of Non-Minority Female Employees with Firm — YEARS / MONTHS
OFFICIALS AND MANAGERS								
PROFESSIONALS								
TECHNICIANS								
SALES WORKERS								
OFFICE AND CLERICAL								
CRAFT WORKERS								
OPERATIVES								
LABORERS								
SERVICE WORKERS								

continued

■ EXHIBIT 6-10

PART C -- COMPENSATION DATA BY EEO-1 CATEGORY

Annual Monetary Compensation and Tenure Data by EEO-1 Category for
Employees listed in "FULL TIME EMPLOYEES AT END OF YEAR (CALENDAR OR AAP)" on Page 9 in Part B of this EO Survey

	MINORITY MALES					NON-MINORITY MALES				
	Total Annual Monetary Compensation for All Minority Male Employees	Lowest Annual Monetary Compensation of any Single Minority Male Employee	Highest Annual Monetary Compensation of any Single Minority Male Employee	Average Tenure of Minority Male Employees with Firm — YEARS	MONTHS	Total Annual Monetary Compensation for All Non-Minority Male Employees	Lowest Annual Monetary Compensation of any Single Non-Minority Male Employee	Highest Annual Monetary Compensation of any Single Non-Minority Male Employee	Average Tenure of Non-Minority Male Employees with Firm — YEARS	MONTHS
OFFICIALS AND MANAGERS										
PROFESSIONALS										
TECHNICIANS										
SALES WORKERS										
OFFICE AND CLERICAL										
CRAFT WORKERS										
OPERATIVES										
LABORERS										
SERVICE WORKERS										

REVERSE DISCRIMINATION UNDER THE EQUAL PROTECTION CLAUSE

Under the Equal Protection Clause, "No State shall make or enforce any law which shall abridge the privileges or immunities of citizens of the United States; nor shall any State deprive any person of life, liberty, or property, without due process of law; *nor deny to any person within its jurisdiction the equal protection of the laws.*"[78] From its inception, the Fourteenth Amendment's Equal Protection Clause clearly forbade states and their respective subunits from creating any law, regulation, or policy that treated a citizen differently because of race.

Beginning in 1971, the Supreme Court embarked on a series of decisions that interpreted the Fourteenth Amendment in a manner that would allow the Equal Protection Clause to permit limited preferential treatment under specific circumstances—rejecting the notion that Congress must *always* act in a "color-blind fashion."[79]

First, only state and local governments and their agencies can violate the Equal Protection Clause. Private sector employers are not covered under the Fourteenth Amendment. Because the concept that making distinctions among citizens based on their ancestry is contradictory in a society that claims equality under the laws, the courts have been willing to permit government-initiated affirmative action only under extreme circumstances. In recent years, federal courts have become even stricter in their analysis of those circumstances.

Under the principle of *strict scrutiny*, any preferences pursued by a state or local government must pass a two-part test (see Exhibit 6-11). The landmark case establishing this two-part test is *Wygant v Jackson Board of Education.*[80] *Wygant* establishes the standard by which AAPs are permissible under the Equal Protection Clause in the same manner that *Weber* sets the standard under Title VII. Remember, state and local governments must pass *both* of these standards if they are to operate *any* program that grants *preferential employment practices.*

▪ EXHIBIT 6-11

THE TWO-PART TEST UNDER STRICT SCRUTINY

1. The Preferential Treatment Serves a *Compelling Government Interest.*

- The need to eliminate the present effects of past discrimination
- Must be remedial in nature

2. The Preferences are *Narrowly Tailored* to Achieve the Compelling Government Interest.

- The efficacy of alternative race-neutral policies
- The planned duration of the policy
- The relationship between the numerical goal and the relevant population or relevant workforce
- The flexibility of the policy
- The burden that the program places on third parties

SOURCES: *Wygant v Jackson Board of Education*, 476 U.S. 267, 274 (1986); *Regents of University of California v Bakke*, 438 U.S. 265, 307 (1978); *City of Richmond v J. A. Croson Co.*, 488 U.S. 469, 486 (1989).

The first part of this test is to establish that there exists a *compelling government interest* to be served by the affirmative action.[81] If this criterion is satisfied, then the courts will examine the AAP to ascertain if it is *narrowly tailored* enough to accomplish the compelling government interest. Just as under Title VII, the program must be justified. The state or local government must have a strong basis in evidence that its classification of citizens along racial, ethnic, or gender lines is absolutely necessary. For governments and their agencies, this is an even more difficult burden because the expressed purpose of the Equal Protection Clause of the Fourteenth Amendment is to prohibit government decision making from using such irrelevant factors as a person's race.[82]

COMPELLING GOVERNMENT INTERESTS

Essentially, the only government interest that is sufficiently compelling to justify preferential treatment of one group of citizens over another is the need to eliminate the present effects of past discrimination.[83] In establishing this justification, the state or local government has two issues to prove. First, it must clearly identify present effects that can be traced to some previously discriminatory practices. Next, it must show that it actually implemented the discriminatory policy or practice. As in Title VII, statistical imbalances in given job groups are used as evidence of the present effects. However, imbalances, in and of themselves, are not sufficient to justify the preferential treatment. There must be a direct link between the previous discriminatory practices and the current imbalance.

Additionally, courts are becoming more rigorous in requiring governments to clearly demonstrate this connection. Mere knowledge that a government or one of its agencies engaged in *de jure* discrimination is no longer sufficient to establish a compelling government interest in several circuits.[84] *De jure* discrimination refers to discriminatory practices that were enacted into law or published as written regulations or policies.

DIVERSITY JUSTIFICATIONS FOR AFFIRMATIVE ACTION. "Diversity," like "affirmative action," has become a much used, but ill-defined term.[85] It encompasses a wide array of employment ideas ranging from being aware of the demographic changes in the labor market to achieving and maintaining an internal workforce that proportionally reflects the "diversity" of the surrounding population.[86] The last definition of diversity, proportional representation, is being subjected to increased scrutiny by federal courts and is the focal point here. Although diversity consultants stress that diversity is more than affirmative action,[87] if achieving a diversity goal involves giving preferences to applicants based on their race, ethnicity, or sex, the courts will treat the diversity initiative as affirmative action. This is consistent with over four decades of employment law. Federal courts have long viewed any employment practice that openly encourages (or even implies) differential treatment of employees based upon their ethnic, racial, or gender characteristics as a potential violation of Title VII or the Equal Protection Clause.

This is a very real concern as many organizations have adopted diversity as an organizational goal. In some cases, organizations have implemented employment practices to consciously increase the representation of individuals of different gender, ethnic, and cultural backgrounds within their organizations.[88] What is more, the acceptance of proportional representation is becoming increasingly institutionalized as an accepted business practice. The Society for Human Resource Management (SHRM) and the American Society for Training and Development (ASTD), two business-based professional associations, have given formal recognition to diversity programs. In fact, SHRM not only certifies diversity consultants, it also produces a diversity newsletter, *Mosaics*, which it has published since 1995. More convincing evidence of diversity's widespread acceptance can be inferred from the fact that most business management and human resource management textbooks now contain chapters or sections devoted to managing diversity.[89] It is important to note that the legality of a goal to achieve diversity is not the question here, but the means of attaining it is.

One very significant aspect of diversity goals differentiates them from affirmative action goals. Specifically, diversity goals are permanent whereas affirmative action goals are temporary. However, when challenged, diversity programs are challenged as affirmative action and reviewed under the same standards. This means any diversity program which is predicated on proportional representation is potentially a violation of Title VII of the Civil Rights Act of 1964 and/or the Equal Protection Clause.

Since the 1990s federal circuit courts have held any race- or ethnic-based preferential treatment to ever increasingly rigorous standards of judicial scrutiny. In at least five instances, public sector employers who either directly, or indirectly, attempted to advance the argument that achieving diversity was a compelling government interest for their preferences lost. In three instances, federal circuit courts explicitly declared that diversity does not establish a compelling interest that would justify preferences.[90] In one case, a circuit court indirectly overturned diversity justifications by holding that decisions predicated on retaining minorities strictly because of underrepresentation would not withstand a constitutional challenge.[91] The most interesting case, *Taxman v Board of Education of Piscataway*,[92] not only held that a goal of maintaining racial diversity could violate the Equal Protection Clause, but it could also violate Title VII. In this decision, the Court of Appeals for the Third Circuit was emphatic that it could not accept the premise that a "nonremedial diversity goal is a permissible basis for affirmative action under Title VII."[93] The goal of maintaining a racially diverse workforce, in the absence of any remedial justification, would unnecessarily trammel the interests of employees who were members of nonpreferred racial groups, and it would equally fail to be a temporary measure by maintaining a racial balance.[94]

NARROWLY TAILORED PROGRAMS

Once the government agency or department has justified its use of affirmative action through the demonstration that the program serves a compelling government interest, the program must then clear the second hurdle: It is **narrowly tailored** to achieve its ends. In other words, was the preferential treatment designed in such a way as to minimize the harm to innocent third parties? There appears to be an emerging consensus that in determining whether a plan is sufficiently narrowly tailored, the courts should consider five key factors:[95]

- The efficacy of alternative race-neutral policies.
- The planned duration of the policy.
- The relationship between the numerical goal and the percentage of preferred group members in the relevant population or relevant workforce.
- The flexibility of the policy, including waivers if the goal cannot be met.
- The burden that the program places on innocent third parties.

ALTERNATIVE RACE-NEUTRAL POLICIES. By the mid-1990s, federal courts began to require governments to demonstrate they have considered and exhausted race-neutral alternatives before being allowed to resort to racial preferences.[96] Unless the government can demonstrate an individual suffered direct harm from the agency's practices, neutral alternatives must have been examined first. For example, assume a municipal fire department refused to consider three female applicants for the position of firefighter. Two years later, the department decides to make amends for its past discriminatory policies by implementing a new AAP. Because the three female applicants, provided they were at least minimally qualified for the position, suffered actual injury from the previous policy, the department could engage in preferential hiring. As identified victims of, in this case, gender-based discrimination, the three women would be entitled to remedial affirmative action. This action would correct the effect of the discrimination they had suffered.

But what about situations in which there are no identified victims of discrimination? What occurs when there is underrepresentation of a protected group that had historically been discriminated against? Under this situation, the department must demonstrate it considered gender-neutral alternatives, but none of these alternatives would have adequately eliminated the statistical imbalances caused by the past discrimination. An example of a race-neutral alternative would be replacing a selection criterion (such as written test) with another that would have less disparate impact on the group in question (actual performance of a task). Remember that whatever selection criterion is substituted, it must still be validated. Regardless of its justification for initiating any preferential program, the initiators must be prepared to show that explicit racial or gender preferences were pursued as a "last resort" option.[97]

DURATION OF THE PROGRAM. Just like their private sector counterparts, AAPs initiated by public sector organizations are expected to be *temporary* measures. Any use of racial or gender preferences by a government or its subdivisions must be limited to ensure they do not outlast their need. They need not take on a life of their own.[98] As under Title VII, public sector affirmative action should cease once the goals of the plan have been attained. Public sector programs can no more be used to maintain a balanced workforce than private sector ones.[99]

GOALS AND RELEVANT LABOR MARKETS. Another striking similarity between factors affecting narrowly tailored programs and the Equal Protection Clause and programs permissible under Title VII is the necessity to develop goals based on the relevant labor market. Once again, any affirmative action goal must be based upon the proportion of underrepresented group members who possess the requisite skills, knowledge, and abilities to perform the job in question. Hence, the appropriate percentage to determine underutilization of Hispanic teaching staff in a given school district is not the population of Hispanics in that school district. The appropriate percentage for comparison is Hispanic composition of the qualified public school teacher population in the relevant labor market.[100]

THE FLEXIBILITY OF THE PROGRAM. This standard of scrutiny in the public sector bears a good deal of similarity to the absolute bar provisions under *Weber*. In the event that there are not enough of the preferred group applicants possessing the minimum requirements for the benefit in question (i.e., promotion, hiring, etc.), the positions may be filled with qualified applicants of nonpreferred groups.

Assume a law enforcement agency is operating an AAP with a goal stating that 25 percent of all promotions to sergeant should go to African Americans. To be eligible for promotion, *all* candidates must pass the civil service test, have a minimum of four years experience as a patrolman, and have at least satisfactory ratings on annual performance evaluations during the three years prior to applying for promotion. Also, assume these criteria have been properly validated. This year there are eight vacancies for sergeant. Under ideal circumstances, this means that possibly two promotions could be assigned to African American applicants who meet or exceed the minimum qualifications. However, through no fault of the department, only one African American candidate met the prerequisites for eligibility. The employer would create an inflexible quota if it promoted an *un*qualified African American candidate or *did not* fill the vacancy when qualified candidates from nonpreferred groups were available.

The appropriate course of action would be to promote the qualified African American candidate to one position and fill the remaining seven positions with the most qualified candidates from other ethnic backgrounds. Employers get into trouble with their AAP when they operate under the assumption that minority set-asides are reserved *exclusively* for minority candidates. There must be no absolute exclusions; to do so creates hard and fast racial quotas.

IMPACT ON THIRD PARTIES. The final factor to consider when determining whether or not a plan is sufficiently narrowly tailored is the burden that it places on innocent third parties. In practice, this appears to be very similar to avoiding trammeling the interests of nonpreferred group members. Consequently, laying off or firing individuals to create opportunities for applicants from preferred groups would naturally impose too heavy a burden.[101]

The problem confronting public sector employers is just *where* is the line drawn between a preferential goal that imposes an unacceptable burden on third parties. Remember that federal courts have "permitted" innocent persons to shoulder the burden of redressing grievances not of their making.[102]

REVERSE DISCRIMINATION AND FEDERALLY MANDATED AFFIRMATIVE ACTION

Until 1995, the federal government enjoyed a far more lenient judicial review of its AAPs than either private sector organizations or state and local governments. Federally mandated programs only had to meet standards of "intermediate scrutiny" (as opposed to strict scrutiny). Although the exact legal differences between *intermediate* and *strict* scrutiny are tedious, intermediate scrutiny would permit the federal government to engage in preferential treatment as long as the government could prove the program met some legitimate government end. For example, if the federal government concluded that increased minority representation in the broadcast industry was necessary for the sake of achieving sufficient diversity, such a goal would be considered an "important government objective."[103] Just as with state governments, strict scrutiny places a more onerous burden on federal government agencies to establish the necessity of imposing preferential practices. And, just as with the Fourteenth Amendment, **strict scrutiny** under the Fifth Amendment requires the public employer to first establish that any preferences serve a "compelling government interest" and, second, that the preferences are "narrowly tailored" to achieve that interest. Under strict scrutiny, increasing minority representation would not establish a "compelling government interest," and the preferential treatment would not be allowed.

Today, intermediate scrutiny is no longer available to the federal government. Since June 12, 1995, federal programs are now evaluated under the same level of strict scrutiny under which state and local programs are examined. The standards discussed in the previous section now apply to the federal government.

In *Adarand Constructors v Pena*,[104] the Supreme Court, in a 5–4 decision, ruled that there is an implied Equal Protection Clause in the Fifth Amendment. In this ruling, the Supreme Court held that the two-part test of the *Wygant v Jackson Board of Education* (the standard for testing state and local preferential programs) would be applied to federal programs mandating race-based preferences. Hence, all federal classifications must now serve a compelling government interest and must be narrowly tailored to achieve that interest.[105]

AVOIDING REVERSE DISCRIMINATION

Developing and implementing AAPs is increasingly placing employers between a rock and a hard place. On one hand, failure to have a plan places the employer in jeopardy of losing eligibility for government contracts. The employer is further deprived of a legal means by which it can hire-by-the-numbers to reduce its exposure to disparate impact claims. On the other hand, race- and gender-based preferences are being increasingly challenged as reverse discrimination. Consequently, the employer must walk a legal tightrope between disparate impact litigation and reverse discrimination.

With reverse discrimination on the rise, an interesting phenomenon has occurred. In the past, it was thought the complaining parties in such suits were restricted to being white males. As American society has become more ethnically diverse, more reverse discrimination suits are being initiated by the so-called protected groups. Technically, preferential treatment is extended only to members of the protected group or groups that are underrepresented. This, of course, means members of protected groups that are *not* underrepresented are not entitled to preferential treatment. Hence, these nonpreferred group members are initiating suits when they feel they are being denied employment opportunities and benefits.

In California, the number of employment lawsuits pitting members of one ethnic group against those of another is on the rise. Furthermore, this trend can be expected to increase as American demographics continue to diversify. The following practices invariably result in reverse discrimination and, therefore, should be avoided:

- Barring all nonpreferred group members from consideration for the position or benefit in question. This could occur by refusing to hire, or to approve the hiring of, any individual except from the preferred group.
- Selecting *un*qualified members of the preferred group.
- Establishing inflexible quotas or setting aside a specific percentage of positions for reserved members of the preferred group.
- Not establishing affirmative action goals on the relevant labor market for the job in question. Too often, this occurs when goals are predicated on national or regional ethnic proportions of the population rather than the proportion of ethnic minorities possessing the requisite job skills.
- Terminating, laying off, or demoting members of nonpreferred groups to ensure employment opportunities for members of the preferred groups.

PRACTICAL APPLICATION

Let's return to the opening scenario. It should be apparent that position announcements must reflect the minimum knowledge, skills, and ability the applicant must possess in order to perform the essential tasks, duties, and responsibilities of the job. The first thing the committee should have done was to ensure proper job analysis had been conducted. This would not only provide the essential tasks, duties, and responsibilities that the Director of Equal Opportunity and Regulatory Compliance had to perform but also the skills, knowledge, and abilities the director must possess in order to perform the job.

Assume the responsibilities in the position announcement are accurate. A great deal of the job involves submitting reports to regulatory agencies, investigating alleged violations of numerous laws, developing AAPs, and ensuring university practices do not violate federal and state civil rights laws. If the candidate is not familiar with these laws and regulations, he or she will not be able to perform the job adequately. If the candidate is not knowledgeable of *Revised Order No. 4,* he or she can hardly be expected to develop a legally permissible AAP.

In light of this, do you believe someone with a bachelor's degree in social work or elementary education would have the proper training and knowledge of the governing laws to be an effective Director of Equal Opportunity and Regulatory Compliance? Do you believe a candidate with a Ph.D. in oriental philosophy would be any better qualified? Does Charles Silvey's suggestion that the candidate possess at least a bachelor's degree in HRM or business management seem reasonable? The committee may even wish to go further and require experience in related positions.

Does Elizabeth Day's recommendation that the candidate have a doctorate have any merit? Focusing on the job's tasks, duties, and responsibilities, would not having a doctorate prevent a candidate from fulfilling the job functions?

Finally, is William Eaton's insistence that the committee select either a female or member of an ethnic minority a valid argument? Why or why not?

SUMMARY

This chapter provides a detailed look at affirmative action. No topic in employee relations has generated as much controversy as affirmative action, and no other employment practice is more misunderstood or abused. Simply stated, affirmative action was intended to ensure individuals are treated without regard to their race, color, religion, sex, or national origin during employment.

There are two types of affirmative action programs: voluntary and involuntary. The preferential nature of affirmative action programs runs the risk of violating either Title VII or the Equal Protection Clause, if they are not properly constructed or implemented. Such programs are permissible under Title VII only if they are justified, do not unnecessarily restrict the rights of other employees, do not create an absolute bar, and are temporary in duration.

For public sector employers, it is essential to comply with Title VII, but it is also necessary not to violate the Equal Protection Clause of the Fourteenth Amendment. To have a permissible affirmative action program under the Equal Protection Clause, government employers must ensure the programs serve a *compelling government interest* and are *narrowly tailored* to achieve that interest.

To guarantee affirmative action programs do not violate either Title VII or the Fourteenth Amendment, HR professionals should properly construct the plans. No affirmative action program can be initiated until utilization analysis has been conducted, and utilization analysis cannot begin until proper job analysis has been performed on all positions in the organization. Only after proper utilization analysis has been completed can affirmative action goals and timetables be developed. Finally, existing affirmative action programs must be periodically reviewed to ensure they are current and to preclude potential reverse discrimination challenges.

KEY TERMS AND CONCEPTS

absolute bar
action plan
affirmative action plan (AAP)
Equal Protection Clause
involuntary affirmative action
narrowly tailored
nonpreferred group
preferred group

Revised Order No. 4
strict scrutiny
underrepresented
underutilized protected group
unnecessarily trammels
utilization analysis
voluntary affirmative action

QUESTIONS

1. What is affirmative action? How is affirmative action distinguished from equal employment opportunity?

2. What are some arguments supporting affirmative action? What are some arguments against affirmative action?

3. Distinguish between involuntary and voluntary affirmative action.

4. What are the three components of an affirmative action plan under the OFCCP's *Revised Order No. 4*? Which is the most important?

5. What are the four circumstances under which affirmative action can be implemented?

6. How does the two-part test determine if an affirmative action program is permissible under the Equal Protection Clause? Which Supreme Court decision imposed these requirements on state and local governments? Which Supreme Court decision imposed these requirements on the federal government?

7. You have been asked by your employer to review the current affirmative action program. What is the very first thing that you will either do or ensure has been done before reviewing the plan? In developing your plan, what three basic components must that plan contain? Provide four conditions that your plan must meet in order to be "permissible". Hint: *Steelworkers v Weber*, 433 U.S. 193, 208 (1979).

CASE

■

I n 1974, the U. S. Department of Justice brought a civil rights action against the City of Memphis, Tennessee, in which it alleged that the city had engaged in race and gender discrimination in the hiring and promotion of city employees. To settle this lawsuit, the city and the U. S. entered into a consent decree that was approved by the U. S. District Court for the Western District of Tennessee in November of 1974. In the decree, Memphis denied that it had unlawfully discriminated but admitted that certain aspects of its past practices may have given rise to an inference that it had engaged in unlawful discrimination. The decree stated that its purpose was "to insure that blacks and women are not placed at a disadvantage by the hiring, promotion, and transfer policies of the city, and that any disadvantage to blacks and women which may have resulted from past discrimination is remedied so that equal employment opportunities will be provided to all." Moreover, the decree provided:

> In determining whether this purpose has been achieved, an appropriate standard of comparison is the proportion of blacks and women in the Shelby County civilian labor force. The City, therefore, agrees to undertake as its long-term goal in this decree, subject to the availability of qualified applicants, the goal of achieving throughout the work force proportions of black and female employees in each job classification, approximating their respective proportions in the civilian labor force.

The decree further stated that Memphis could apply for dissolution of the decree at any time after five years subsequent to the date of its entry.

The city was sued again when in August of 1975 the Afro-American Police Association filed in the same district court an action in which it alleged that the promotion practices of the Memphis Police Department were racially discriminatory. To settle this action, the parties entered into a consent decree that was approved by the district court in March of 1979. In the stipulation of facts that was submitted along with the decree, the city denied that it had "intentionally engaged in unlawful employment discrimination with respect to the employment of blacks on the Memphis Police Department in the period since March 24, 1972," but admitted that "historically blacks have been excluded from or limited in hiring or promotional opportunities within its police department." The decree declared that its purpose was "to prohibit unlawful discrimination in the promotional practices of the Memphis Police Department, and to eliminate any effects of prior discrimination." The decree thus provided that "to the extent that qualified black applicants are available . . . the percentage of promotions awarded to blacks at each rank shall constitute at least the percentage which blacks constitute in the next rank below."

In 1981, the City of Memphis and the U. S. entered into an "amended consent decree," in which they agreed that "certain provisions of the 1974 decree have served their purpose, and the goals of that decree should be updated to meet present circumstances." The 1981 decree "substituted for the 1974 decree" and was approved by the district court. The 1981 decree reaffirmed the 1974 decree's long-term goal of remedying any disadvantage to blacks that may have resulted from past discrimination, and retained, subject to the availability of qualified applicants, "the goal of achieving in the Divisions, and where applicable, the job categories and classifications specified in this decree, proportions of black and female employees approximating their respective proportions in the relevant Shelby County civilian labor force." The 1981 decree also provided that promotional vacancies within the uniformed rank structure of the Police ... Division shall be filled in accordance respectively with the terms of the consent order entered on March 20, 1979, in *Afro-American Police Ass'n v City of Memphis*.. ... The 1981 decree stated that it was not "intended to require the City to hire unnecessary or unqualified personnel, or to hire, transfer, or promote a less qualified person in preference to a better qualified person." The 1981 decree further provided that the city could move for its dissolution at any time after March 1, 1984, but the city has yet to do so.

The litigation now in question, referred to as the Aiken litigation, concerns Memphis Police Department promotions to the rank of sergeant during the years 1988 and 1989. The promotion process for all of these positions consists of four components: (1) a written examination, (2) an evaluation of the employee's performance record, (3) seniority points, and (4) an oral interview. After completing this process, each candidate for promotion is assigned a numerical score and placed in rank order.

In 1988, the Memphis Police Department made seventy-five promotions to the rank of sergeant, for which two hundred ten officers competed. After the promotion candidates were placed in rank order, it was discovered that, while 32.4 percent of the officers in the rank below sergeant (which is patrol officer) were black, only 9.3 percent, or seven, of the top seventy-five candidates were black. To meet the consent decree's goal of proportionate black promotions, the city promoted not only the seven blacks among the seventy-five top-ranked candidates, but also nineteen other blacks who were ranked below the seventy-fifth position.

Similarly, in 1989, the Memphis Police Department made ninety-four promotions to the rank of sergeant, for which one hundred seventy-seven officers competed. Since only 16 percent, or fifteen, of the ninety-four top-ranked candidates were black, the city promoted in addition to these fifteen candidates, eighteen other black candidates who were ranked below the ninety-fourth position.

The Aiken plaintiffs are white officers in the Memphis Police Department who were denied promotions to sergeant in 1988 and/or 1989, despite having been ranked higher than most of the black candidates who were promoted to sergeant. The Aiken plaintiffs sued the City of Memphis, and both the Memphis Mayor and Director of Police Services in their official and personal capacities. Under which statutes may the complaining parties file? What must the complaining parties prove if they are to establish a viable reverse discrimination claim? Do you feel that the current program is permissible? Why or why not?

SOURCE: *Ashton v City of Memphis*, 49 F.Supp.2d 1051 (W.D. Tenn. 1999).

NOTES

1. Pub. L. 88-352, Title VII, § 716(b), July 2, 1964, 78 Stat. 266.

2. Exec. Order 11246, 30 Fed. Reg. 12319 (1965), *reprinted as amended in* 42 U.S.C. § 2000e (1996).

3. Exec. Order 10925, 3 C.F.R. 448 (1959–1963).

4. 41 C.F.R. § 60-2.1(a) (1996).

5. 29 C.F.R. § 1607.13 (1996).

6. 29 C.F.R. § 1608.1 (1996).

7. 29 C.F.R. §§ 1608.2(1) & (2).

8. 41 C.F.R. § 60-2.21.

9. 41 C.F.R. § 60-2.23(e).

10. 29 C.F.R. § 1608.4(c).

11. Gallup, G. Jr. *The Gallup Poll* [for the following years] (1997): 1057–1060; (1980): 106–107; (1984): 141–143; (1989): 231; Johnson, K. (March 24, 1995). "Affirmative action: Four groups' views." *USA Today*, p. 1.

12. Johnson, K. and Stone, A. (March 24, 1995). "Affirmative action: Four groups' views." *USA Today*, p. 1.

13. CNN, USA Today, Gallup Organization (1995). *Attitudes Toward Affirmative Action: A Nationwide Survey*, February 24–26 and March 17–19, 1995.

14. Cal. Const. Art 1 § 31 (a).

15. Rev Code Wash. (ARCW) § 49.60.400 (1999).

16. Bergmann, B. R. (1996). *In Defense of Affirmative Action*. New York: Basic Books; Eastland, T. (1996). *Ending Affirmative Action: The Case for Colorblind Justice*. New York: Basic Books; Roth, B. M. (1994). *Prescription for Failure: Race Relations in the Age of Social Science*. New Brunswick, NJ: Transaction Publishers; Nieli, R. (ed.) (1991). *Racial Preference and Racial Justice: The New Affirmative Action Controversy*. Washington, DC: Ethics and Public Policy Center.; Rosenfeld, M. (1991). *Affirmative Action and Justice*. New Haven, CN: Yale University Press; Thomas, R. R. (1991). *Beyond Race and Gender: Unleashing the Power of Your Total Workforce*. New York: AMACOM Press; Steele, S. (1990). *The Content of Our Character: A New Vision of Race in America*. New York: St. Martin's Press.

17. *Taxman v Board of Education of Piscataway*, 91 F.3d 1547, 1560 (3rd Cir. 1996).

18. *Wygant v Jackson Board of Education*, 476 U.S. 267, 274 (1986); *Regents of University of California v Bakke*, 438 U.S. 265, 310 (1978).

19. *City of Richmond v J. A. Croson Co.*, 488 U.S. 469, 505–506 (1989).

20. *Croson*, 488 U.S. at 493.

21. *Teamsters v U.S.*, 431 U.S. 324, 340 n. 20 (1977).

22. *Wygant*, 476 U.S. at 276.

23. Belz, H. (1991). *Equality Transformed: A Quarter-Century of Affirmative Action*. New Brunswick, NJ: Transaction Publishers.

24. *Bakke*, 438 U.S. at 291.

25. Bork, R. H. (1996). *Slouching Towards Gomorrah*. New York: Regan Books, p. 242.

26. 42 U.S.C. § 2000e-2(a)(1).

27. *Croson*, 488 U.S. at 493.

28. *Billish v City of Chicago*, 989 F.2d 890, 897 (7th Cir. 1993).

29. 380 U.S. 145 (1965).

30. 480 U.S. 149, 183 (1987).

31. 42 U.S.C. § 2000e-5(g)(1)(1996).

32. See *Martin v Wilks*, 490 U.S. 755 (1989).

33. 42 U.S.C. § 2000e-2(n)(1) (1996).

34. *Wilks*, 490 U.S. at 765.n.6.

35. Pub. L. No. 102–166, § 108.

36. Ibid.

37. Robinson, R. K., Allen, B. M., Terpstra, D. E., and Nasif, E. G. (1992). "Equal employment opportunity requirements for employers: A closer view of the Civil Rights Act of 1991." *Labor Law Journal*, 43, (11): 725–734.

38. *United States v Mississippi Power and Light Company*, 638 F.2d 899 (5th Cir. 1981).

39. 41 C.F.R. § 60-2.1(a)(1996).

40. Rehabilitation Act of 1973, 29 U.S.C. § 794

41. Vietnam Era Veteran's Readjustment Act, 38 U.S.C. § 2021.

42. *Cunico v Pueblo School Dist. No. 60*, 917 F.2d 431, 437 (10th Cir. 1990) (*citing, inter alia, United Steelworkers v Weber*, 443 U.S. 193 (1979)); *Wygant v Jackson Board of Education*, 476 U.S. 267 (1986).

43. 29 C.F.R. § 1608.4 (1996).

44. 29 C.F.R. § 1608.4(a) (1996).

45. 42 U.S.C. § 2000e-2(a)(1).

46. 42 U.S.C. § 2000e-2(a)(2).

47. 42 U.S.C. § 2000e-2(j) (1996).

48. 443 U.S. 193, 205 (1979).

49. *Steelworkers v Weber*, 443, U.S. 193, 208.

50. *Johnson v Transportation Agency, Santa Clara County*, 480 U.S. 616, 632 (1987).

51. *Cunico v Pueblo School District No. 60*, 917 F.2d 431 (10th Cir. 1990); *Bennett v Alexander* (In re Birmingham Reverse Discrimination Employment Litigation), 20 F.3d 1525, 1539 (11th Cir. 1994).

52. *Taxman*, 91 F.3d at 1560.

53. *Podberesky v Kirwan*, 38 F.3d 147 (4th Cir. 1994).

54. *Hopwood v State of Texas*, 78 F.3d 932 (5th Cir. 1996).

55. *Weber*, 443 U.S.at 208.

56. *Fullilove v Klutznick*, 448 U.S. 448, 484 (1980).

57. *Teamsters*, 431 U.S. at 371–379; *Firefighters Local Union No. 1784 v Stotts*, 467 U.S. 561, 579 (1984).

58. *Bennett*, 20 F.3d at 1542; *San Francisco Police Officers Association v San Francisco*, 812 F.2d 1125, 1132 (9th Cir. 1987).

59. *Bennett,* 20 F.3d at 1541.

60. Ibid.

61. *Johnson,* 480 U.S. at 620.

62. Affirmative Action Appropriate under Title VII of the Civil Rights Act of 1964, As Amended, 29 C.F.R. § 1608 (1999).

63. *Jurgens v Thomas,* 29 FEWP Cases 1561, 1581 (N.D. Tex. 1982).

64. *Shaw v Reno,* 509 U.S. 630 (1993); *Palmore v Sidoti,* 466 U.S. 429, 432 (1984); *Bakke,* 438 U.S. at 307.

65. *Bakke,* 438 U.S. at 291.

66. *Adarand Constructors, Inc. v Pena,* 515 U.S. 200 (1995).

67. 41 C.F.R. § 60-2.11(b).

68. 165 Fed. Reg. 68031 (November 13, 2000).

69. 41 C.F.R. § 60-2.14(c).

70. Ibid.

71. Ibid.

72. *Croson,* 488 U.S. at 477.

73. Ibid. at 480–481.

74. *Hazelwood School District v United States,* 433 U.S. 299, 308 (1977).

75. *Wygant,* 433 U.S. at 274; *Croson,* 488 U.S. at 492.

76. 41 C.F.R. § 60-2.13(f).

77. Ibid. at § 60-2.24(e).

78. U.S. CONST. amend. XIV, § 1.

79. *Swan v Charlotte-Mecklenburg Board of Education,* 402 U.S. 1, 18–21 (1971); *McDaniel v Barresi,* 402 U.S. 39, 41 (1971); *Franks v Bowman Transportation, Co.,* 424 U.S. 747 (1976); *Bakke,* 438 U.S. at 299.

80. 476 U.S. 267 (1986).

81. *Palmore v Sidoti,* 466 U.S. 429, 432 (1984).

82. *Croson,* 488 U.S. at 495; see also, *Loving v Virginia* 388 U.S. 1, 11 (1967); *Hirabayashi v United States,* 320 U.S. 81, 100 (1943).

83. *Bakke,* 438 U.S. at 307; *Wygant,* at 274; *Croson,* at 486.

84. *Hopwood v State of Texas,* F.3d 953 (5th Cir. 1996); *Podberesky v Kirwan* 38 F.3d 147, 154 (4th Cir. 1994); *Middleton v City of Flint,* 92 F.3d 396, 409 (6th Cir. 1996).

85. Robinson, R. K., Franklin, G. M. and Terpstra, D. E. (1994). "Diversity in the '90s." *HR Focus,* 71 (1): 9.

86. Arredondo, P. (1996). *Successful Diversity Management Initiatives: A Blue Print for Planning and Implementation.* Thousand Oaks, CA: Sage Publications, p. 15.

87. Loden, M. (1996). *Implementing Diversity.* Chicago, IL: Irwin; Thomas, R. R. (1991). *Beyond Race and Gender: Unleashing the Power of Your Total Workforce.* New York: AMA; Loden, M. and Rosener, J. B. (1991). *Workplace America! Managing Employee Diversity as a Vital Resource.* Homewood, IL: Business One Irwin.

88. Lynch, F. (1997). *The Diversity Machine*. New York: The Free Press, p. 177.

89. Daft, R. L. (1997). *Management (4th ed.)*. Fort Worth, TX: The Dryden Press; Cascio, W. F. (1995). *Managing Human Resources (4th ed.)*. New York: McGraw-Hill; Noe, R., Hollenbeck, J., Gerhart, B., and Wright, P. (1997). *Human Resource (2d ed.)*. New York: McGraw-Hill; Gomez-Mejia, L., Balkin, D., and Cardy, D. L. (1995). *Managing Human Resources*. Englewood Cliffs, NJ: Prentice-Hall.

90. *Hunter v The Regents of the University of California*, 190 F.3d 1061, 1074 (9th Cir. 1999); *Wessmann v Gittens*, 160 F.3d 790, 800 (1st Cir. 1998) (the concept of "diversity" implemented by BLS does not justify a race-based classification); *Lutheran Church-Missouri Synod v FCC*, 141 F.3d 344, 354 (D.C. Cir. 1998); *Hopwood v State of Texas*, 78 F.3d 932, 944–945 (5th Cir. 1996).

91. *Cunico*, 917 F.2d at 439.

92. 91 F.3d 1547.

93. Ibid. at 1561.

94. Ibid.

95. *U.S. v Paradise*, 480 U.S. 149, 171 (1987) (plurality opinion).

96. *Podberesky*, 38 F.3d at 160–161, *Bennett*, 20 F.3d at 1545–1546.

97. *Alexander v Estepp*, 95 F.3d 312, 315 (4th Cir. 1996).

98. *Hayes v North State Law Enforcement Officers Association*, 10 F.3d 207, 216 (4th Cir. 1993).

99. *Johnson*, 480 U.S. at 639–40.

100. *Hazelwood School District v U.S.*, 433 U.S. 299, 308 (1977).

101. *Peightal v Metropolitan Dade County*, 26 F.3d 1545, 1561 (11th Cir. 1994).

102. *Bakke*, 438 U.S. at 298.

103. *Metro Broadcasting, Inc. v F.C.C.*, 467 U.S. 547, 600 (1990).

104. 515 U.S. 200 (1995).

105. Ibid. at 240–241.

REGULATION OF EMPLOYEE RELATIONS

7

EMPLOYMENT-AT-WILL, EMPLOYEE HANDBOOKS, AND EMPLOYEE PRIVACY ISSUES

LEARNING OBJECTIVES

- ☐ Understand the situations that erode an employer's ability to exercise employment-at-will.
- ☐ Explain the advantages and disadvantages of having an employee handbook.
- ☐ Explain how an employee handbook can create an implied contract.
- ☐ Identify those circumstances in which an employer may violate an employee's privacy interests.
- ☐ Describe how absolute privilege and qualified privilege may reduce an employer's exposure to litigation.
- ☐ Explain the circumstances under which an employer might lawfully monitor employee e-mail.
- ☐ Distinguish between negligent hiring and negligent retention and understand the implications of each.

OPENING SCENARIO[1]

The following letter was sent to a job applicant by the senior vice president of marketing for D. L. Nichols & Sons, Inc.:

Dear Mr. Frink:

The purpose of this letter is to confirm D. L. Nichols & Sons' offer of employment. It is our hope that you will take advantage of this offer.

We are offering you employment as our Sales Director for Southeastern Operations with a salary of $100,000 per year. Your work responsibilities will be throughout the twelve states of our Southeastern Region, but your office will be located in our corporate headquarters in Atlanta. We realize that this will necessitate you and your family to move to Atlanta; however, D. L. Nichols & Sons will reimburse you for all moving and relocation expenses.

Should you accept our offer, your employment will begin immediately. You and your family will be afforded free accommodations in our corporate condominium for up to one year. The corporate condominium is conveniently located within walking distance from our headquarters complex.

Upon hiring, you will immediately become eligible for full insurance coverage and the other benefits and executive prerequisites we discussed during our last interview. To refresh your memory, I have taken the liberty of enclosing all the relevant benefit brochures.

Please give serious consideration to this offer and let me know of your decision no later than 4 P.M. (EST) next Friday, the 25th. We are confident that you are well qualified for this position and are relying on you to raise sales in our Southeastern Region to $25 million within a year's time.

Sincerely,
Gregory Rose
Sr. Vice President, Marketing

Mr. Frink accepted D. L. Nichols & Sons' job offer and began his employment in May. However, after several heated discussions with Mr. Rose over the allocation of promotion and advertising budgets, Mr. Frink was fired in September. When Mr. Frink protested his termination, Mr. Rose reminded him that he never signed a written employment contract with the corporation. Mr. Rose stated, "Since there was no formal contract and Georgia is an employment-at-will state, D. L. Nichols & Sons has the legal right to terminate your employment at any time and without notice. The company is exercising its employment-at-will rights, and there is nothing that you can do about it. Have a nice day."

EMPLOYMENT-AT-WILL

Employment-at-will is actually an old common law concept based on the premise that if the employee can terminate his or her employment relationship with an employer anytime he or she sees fit, and for any reason, the employer is entitled to do the same. Say, for example, that you have taken a job (while working your way through college) at a local fast-food restaurant. After working there one week, you conclude that it is interfering too much with your studies and you decide to quit. Can the employer force you to keep working against your will? In the absence of a written employment contract, the answer is "no." In fact, you are not even legally required to give two weeks notice, though this is usually the customary and ethical thing to do.

The employment-at-will doctrine holds that if you, the employee, have the freedom to quit at your own volition, then the employer has an equal right to fire you at his or her own volition. Or, put another way, under employment-at-will doctrine an employer may terminate an employee for a good reason, a bad reason, or no reason at all.[2] Again, this concept merely mirrors the employee's right to voluntarily quit for a good reason, bad reason, or no reason at all.

The vast majority of employee terminations are done for good reasons (i.e., poor performance, violating work rules, excessive absences, theft, etc.). In fact, a good manager would never terminate a subordinate for any reason other than a good reason. If this is so, then why are employers so concerned with protecting their employment-at-will rights? The answer is simple: documentation. If an employer does not enjoy employment-at-will, then each termination must be for just cause, which then places the burden on the employer to prove the firing was justified—this requires additional documentation. For example, the employer must provide tangible evidence that the employee is being terminated for a behavioral problem (i.e., insubordination, fighting, theft, threats, harassment, etc.), performance deficiencies (i.e., inability to perform essential job functions, violation of policies or rules, etc.), or a financial exigency (i.e., plant closings, reductions in force, reengineering, etc.). If such documentation can be produced (and is factual), the discharge is likely to be judged as for a "just cause." In the absence of such documentation, the termination will be suspect.

Naturally, the previously mentioned rationales are all good reasons not to keep an employee on the payroll; however, in the absence of employment-at-will, an employer may be required to substantiate them. Loss of employment-at-will status, therefore, increases the administrative and record keeping duties of the human resource (HR) department. As a practical matter, there are many factors that already erode employment-at-will doctrine (see Exhibit 7-1).

■ **EXHIBIT 7-1**

SITUATIONS THAT ERODE EMPLOYMENT-AT-WILL

- Contracts (explicit and implied)
- Just cause statutes
- Equal employment opportunity laws

- Whistleblower clauses
- Public policy
- Good faith and fair dealing

CONTRACTUAL RELATIONSHIPS

Two situations can arise creating a contractual obligation for terminating an employee for only just cause reasons. There may be an explicit contract that creates such a guarantee, or the guarantee may be derived from an implicit contract. Employees and employers are aware of explicit contracts, having agreed to the terms and conditions of employment and having expressed them in a written manner. Implied contracts, however, may occur unbeknownst to the employer. As we shall see shortly, implied contracts often occur because of a verbal or written statement made by the employer that the employee interpreted as a guarantee of continued employment. The employer may not have intended to make such a guarantee, but some state courts have ruled that such statements do prevent employee discharges except for just cause.

EXPLICIT CONTRACTS.   There is no employment-at-will when an explicit contract exists. An **explicit contract** is a written document (in most instances) that exists between the two parties (the employer and the employee) establishing the terms of employment. Usually, a period of employment is specified, as well as other terms and conditions of that employment. To terminate an employee who is formally contracted to perform specific work for a specific period of time for either a bad reason or no reason at all would be a breach of the contract. This also applies to employees covered under collective bargaining agreements negotiated by a labor union, which are in effect labor contracts. Consequently, all contractual employees may only be terminated for just cause.

As a primer for business law courses, you should know that a contract consists of two important parts: mutual assent and a consideration.[3] *Mutual assent* is founded upon the offer (sometimes called "promise") and acceptance.[4] The offer is communicated by one party (in our case, the employer) to the other (the employee). Essentially, the employer must communicate an offer to the employee to perform in a particular manner in exchange for the employee agreeing to reciprocate by acting as requested. In a business setting, a seller advertises or communicates that he or she is willing to perform in a particular manner by providing a product or service to a buyer (the second party), provided that the buyer agrees to act as requested (i.e., pay the asking price for the product or service initially offered). It is important to note that no offer becomes effective until it has been communicated to the second party.[5] In an employment situation, the employer invariably communicates an offer to pay a particular salary for a specified period of time if the employee agrees to perform as requested (i.e., perform specific work activities).

In either case, mutual assent does not occur until the second party accepts the offer by willingly agreeing to be bound by the terms of the offer. Acceptance occurs when the buyer pays the requested purchasing price for a good or service, thus obligating the first party to provide that good or service. In the instance of employment contracts, acceptance occurs when the employee signs the written contract, obligating the employer to pay the agreed-upon salary for the agreed-upon period. The employee also obligates himself or herself to perform the agreed-upon work activities for the agreed-upon period.

Still, we do not have a binding contract until the offer and acceptance have been validated by consideration. *Consideration* is defined as a bargained-for exchange and is based on the premise that one promise (i.e., providing a product or service) is consideration for another promise (i.e., receiving the payment). Consideration is the price paid for the offer or promise. There is no contract when the second party refuses to pay the first party's asking price. Neither is there a contract if the seller refuses to provide the product when the buyer offers to buy only at a lower price. Or in an employment situation, no contract exists if the employee refuses to work for the employer's initial salary offer, or the employer refuses to meet the employee's counteroffer.

During contract negotiations in employment, an employee may refuse to sign a contract because he or she feels that either the salary is too low or the period of obligated employment is too long. Conversely, the employer may feel that the employee's wage demands are too high or the contract duration is too short. In either instance, there is no contract because there is no agreed-to or bargained-for exchange.

There are two other elements that must be present for a contract to be legally enforceable. First, no contract is legally enforceable if it requires either party to perform an unlawful act. The so-called contracts in Mafia genre films for "hit men" to execute various and sundry people are not contracts in the true legal sense. In a more serious view, an employment contract with a certified public accountant requiring him or her to create knowingly false financial records is not an enforceable contract. Any contract, employment or otherwise, must be legally consistent with existing law and sound public policy.[6]

Second, the parties to the contract must be legally competent, which means all parties must be legally capable of entering into a contract. In most cases, the parties must be adults (check individual state statutes to determine the legal age of adulthood, also called "age of majority"). Minors enjoy the legal right to avoid contracts. Insanity or impaired mental state may also be used as a means to void a contract. Even circumstances involving a temporarily impaired mental state (i.e., intoxication) can be used as a defense in breach-of-contract litigation.

Breach of contract is the real concern in contractual employment relationships. Once a contract becomes legally enforceable, the party that fails to provide the previously discussed consideration is legally liable for breaching the contract. Not only is an employer liable for breaching the contract for terminating an employee for any reason other than just cause, the employee breaches the contract if he or she attempts to sever the employment relationship before the contract expires.

IMPLIED CONTRACTS. Not all contracts are explicit; some may be implied. An **implied contract** results when a contract can be inferred by the actions or conduct of the parties rather than stated in an expressed offer and acceptance. This is also called an implied-in-fact contract. Three conditions will establish an implied-in-fact contract: A party furnished some service or property; that party had an expectation to be compensated for the service or property furnished, and the other party knew, or should have known, that compensation was expected; and the other party had an opportunity to decline the service or property, and did not.[7] In employment environments, implied contracts are often alleged to hold that some assurance was made by the employer that the employee would enjoy continued employment so long as he or she did a good job. These implied contracts often arise when an employee can prove he or she received some assurance of employment for a specific period of time. In essence, the employee offers good job performance with the expectation, based on the employer's oral statements or written policies, that such performance will be compensated by continued employment and job security.

In some states, courts have required that the employer make clearly expressed promises of termination for cause, not vague assurances, before an implied contract can be established.[8] Such assurances of permanent employment may be verbal or in writing, but they must be expressed by the employer. Yet in other states, no expressed assurance is required.[9] Unfortunately, a broad spectrum of interpretation exists among the various state jurisdictions as to what constitutes an actionable assurance of job security.

In most employment situations, implied contracts can arise when an employee receives written or oral assurances (other than in a formal contract) about job security or continued employment. These assurances can take many forms. For example, some state courts have held that an oral statement to the effect that an employee will be employed by the company as long as he or she continues to perform the job satisfactorily is an implied contract.[10] In other states, there must be an unequivocal guarantee of continued employment in writing.[11] For example, a handbook with the following statement would be necessary to establish this unequivocal guarantee:

> The employees of XYZ Company are guaranteed continued employment provided that they obey the work rules contained herein.

In the absence of such language, the relationship is assumed to be at-will.

Our opening scenario is an example of a statement (this one was in writing) that established an implied contract. Note that Mr. Rose's letter to Mr. Frink contained three references to a definite one-year period of time. The salary was for one year, the free condominium was available for "up to one year," and the sales performance expectations were for "within a year's time." This would appear to promise Mr. Frink employment for a specific period of time—one year.

Additionally, any written personnel policies or guidelines that imply employment guarantees may constitute an implied contract.[12] Perhaps the most widely accepted means (at least from a state court standpoint) of establishing implied employment contracts are employee handbooks. In the landmark case, *Toussaint v Blue Cross and Blue Shield*, the complaining party successfully argued that he was wrongfully discharged because his employer had not terminated him in accordance with the progressive discipline procedures promised in the employee handbook.[13] Employee handbooks will be examined in greater detail later in this chapter, but they do present a perplexing dilemma for employers. In most state jurisdictions, employee handbooks often establish implied contracts, thus eroding the employer's employment-at-will rights. However, failure to have written policies and procedures to ensure fair and consistent handling of HR decisions may unnecessarily expose the employer to litigation under state and federal employment laws. This is especially true for laws and regulations regarding federal sexual harassment (Chapter 4) and harassment based on national origin (Chapter 5).[14] Herein is the dilemma confronting HR professionals: Failure to state the policies in a handbook may expose the employer to litigation under a myriad of equal employment laws, while having a handbook may expose the employer to litigation for wrongful discharge under breach of an implied contract.

The solution is for HR professionals to properly develop and implement employee handbooks. An employer must guarantee the employee handbook is properly worded, and, once it is developed and implemented, must follow its procedures. This situation means more work from HR professionals and line managers; they must enforce these provisions and policies. This will, in the long run, offset the liability and remedies that could result from Title VII and state tort lawsuits.

JUST CAUSE STATUTES

Only one state, Montana, has passed a just cause discharge statute. Under a **just cause** law, employers are limited to discharging employees only for broadly and statutorily defined reasons. Just cause reasons for terminating an employee usually include misconduct, poor performance, or reductions in an employer's workforce due to financial reasons. Failure to follow such legislative guidance results in a wrongful discharge under which the employee may seek legal redress. As previously mentioned, the problem for employers is that they are required to substantiate that the termination was indeed for just cause reasons.

Many states, although not enacting just cause statutes, have passed laws that prohibit the termination of employees for several specific reasons (see Appendix 7-A at the end of this chapter). For example, eighteen states have passed legislation that forbids employers from discharging any employee who refuses to take a polygraph test or based on the results of a polygraph test. These restrictions are in addition to those imposed by the Federal Employee Polygraph Protection Act discussed in Chapter 8.

Additionally, fifteen states have their own state labor laws (in addition to the National Labor Relations Act) protecting employees who engage in organizing activities (see Appendix 7-A). There are also forty-five states with state equal employment opportunity laws that can be more inclusive (in terms of classes of workers they protect) than federal laws. Furthermore, thirty-two states provide varying degrees of protection from termination for employees who are performing duties in the National Guard or the Army, Navy, Air Force, or Marine Corps Reserves. Also, numerous states provide statutory recognition for other employee activities that would be considered public policy issues (e.g., jury duty, reporting unlawful activities, political activities, etc.). Connecticut even guarantees employees First Amendment rights in the workplace. This means, at least in Connecticut, an employer may not terminate an employee for stating his or her opinion on a matter of public concern.

EQUAL EMPLOYMENT OPPORTUNITY AND OTHER EMPLOYMENT LAWS

Employment-at-will is stopped in its tracks by the equal employment opportunity statutes at federal, state, and local levels. Although employment-at-will permits an employer to fire employees for bad reasons, unlawful discrimination is not one of them. Any employer automatically loses its employment-at-will status when it impermissibly uses race, color, religion, sex, national origin, or qualified individuals with disabilities in its termination decisions (see Chapters 2–6).

WHISTLEBLOWER CLAUSES

Another statutory limitation on terminating employees arises from whistleblower clauses. Employment-at-will cannot be used as a justification for termination when the employee has reported the employer's violation of any law that contains a whistleblower clause. You will recall that **whistleblower clauses** protect employees from employer retaliation for reporting violations of the specific law in question. Most federal statutes (i.e., the National Labor Relations Act, Occupational Safety and Health Act, Fair Labor Standards Act, Civil Rights Act of 1964, etc.)[15] contain these clauses. Usually, if the employee is terminated for "blowing the whistle," he or she is at least entitled to reinstatement, back pay, and attorneys' fees under federal laws.[16]

Finally, many state laws make it unlawful to retaliate against employees who file workers' compensation complaints, report unsafe working conditions under state workplace safety laws, or report violations of state minimum wage laws (see Appendix 7-A).

It is essential for managers and HR professionals to know that any action taken against a whistleblower must be consistent with the treatment initiated against other employees under similar situations. If, for example, a whistleblower has been discharged for excessive tardiness, while other employees with the same record remain on the payroll, a wrongful discharge could be easily deduced. Most agencies that enforce federal statutes are very sensitive to constructive discharges and are more likely to initially believe an employee who alleges that he or she is being retaliated against. This does not imply whistleblowing employees cannot be disciplined for breaking work rules, only that they cannot be singled out for harsher punishment than other employees. Managers and HR professionals, because of the likelihood that retaliation will be alleged, have the additional burden of providing the necessary documentation to prove discipline was justified. This means not only proving the whistleblower violated a rule or policy *but also* that he or she was not treated differently from other violators. Showing consistency with previous disciplinary actions is extremely important.

PUBLIC POLICY

A termination violates **public policy** when an employee is discharged for refusing to violate a law or ordinance, fired for refusing to avoid a civic duty or obligation (i.e., jury duty or when summoned as a witness), or terminated for engaging in a legal right (see Exhibit 7-2). Take, for example, the case of *Peterman v International Brotherhood of Teamsters*,[17] in which an employee was fired for refusing to submit false and untrue statements to a California legislative committee. The employee lost his job for refusing to commit perjury. The employee was forced to choose between breaking the law and securing his continued employment. Demanding an employee lie under oath or refuse to provide testimony clearly requires the employee to violate a legal obligation and, therefore, is an unequivocal public policy violation.

Public policy can also be violated when an employer retaliates against an employee for enjoying a legal right or entitlement. For example, even in the absence of a whistleblower clause, discharging an employee for filing a workers' compensation claim resulting from a work-related injury would be in violation of public policy.[18] Further, discharging an employee for even threatening or indicating that he or she will file for workers' compensation violates public policy.[19]

Not surprisingly, there may be instances when an employee makes a false allegation against an employer. When allegations of public policy violations arise, the employer's only defense is to offer a job-related reason (a just cause reason) to explain the employee's termination. Legitimate business reasons that could substantiate just cause terminations include poor job performance, low quality of work (it is advisable to show that the employee received repeated warnings), tardiness, or increased absenteeism (in the event of workers' compensation claims, the employer must ensure these absences are not injury related).

It is the HR professional's duty to maintain specific documentation that substantiates the employer's legitimate business reason for terminating the employee in question. However, managers must supply this proper documentation to HR professionals. More than just good record keeping (although that is important too), documentation entails having good disciplinary policies in effect and ensuring management personnel are aware of their responsibilities under these policies and are trained in the implementation and recording of disciplinary actions.

▪ EXHIBIT 7-2

PUBLIC POLICY ISSUES

- Engaging in a legal right
- Engaging in a legal duty
- Refusing to perform an illegal act

Good Faith and Fair Dealing

Some states (approximately thirteen of them) permit an employee to bring suit when an employer's termination is intended to either intentionally cause the employee injury or to deprive the employee of some benefit or compensation to which he or she is entitled.[20] In essence, the employer has behaved in an outrageous or patently unfair manner toward an employee. Perhaps the most often cited case used to demonstrate wrongful discharge under good faith and fair dealing is *Fortune v National Cash Register Co.*[21] In this case, a salesman who had made $5,000,000 in sales for his employer was terminated to avoid paying him over $92,000 in sales commissions that the sales earned him.[22] In a jurisdiction recognizing good faith and fair dealing, any attempt to deprive an employee of an earned wage or benefit would be a violation.[23]

EMPLOYEE HANDBOOKS

Employee handbooks often present a double-edged sword for employers. On one side, they provide a valuable means for disseminating important work-related information and policies to employees. On the other hand, an employee handbook may be viewed as an implied contract by many courts, thus eroding an employer's employment-at-will prerogatives. This may create a "you can't live with them and you can't live without them" situation. In truth, it is far more likely that employers "can't live without them" because properly constructed employee handbooks provide far more benefits than costs (see Exhibit 7-3).

One important benefit of a handbook is that it provides proof of antiharassment policies. (This issue has already been addressed in detail in Chapter 4.) What better means of demonstrating an employer's good faith effort to maintain a harassment-free workplace than to have the antiharassment policy statement (and reporting procedures) prominently displayed in the organization's employee handbook. The federal courts' increased emphasis on employers' policies and procedures in establishing an affirmative defense makes publication of such policies crucial. In the absence of proof that an employer has a policy and the employee was aware of the policy, there is no affirmative defense.[24]

Practical Guidance on Language

There are other considerations when developing an employee handbook. Because of the concern over potential litigation, there is a tendency for the HR professionals who write the handbooks to use overly legalistic terminology. This usually results in handbooks that are written well above the reading comprehension levels of the employees for whom the handbooks are intended. The cardinal rule to remember when writing an employee handbook is: If the employees cannot read and understand the contents, it is a waste of time and paper. A good employee handbook is readable and conveys the employer's policies and behavioral

SAMPLE LISTING OF POLICIES INCLUDED IN EMPLOYEE HANDBOOKS

- Welcoming statement
- Purpose of the handbook
- Disclaimers (to maintain employment-at-will status)
- Definitions of terms
- Antiharassment policy
- Dress code
- Attendance/tardiness policy
- Disciplinary policies
  * Progressive discipline
  * Offenses resulting in immediate discharge
  * Penalties/disciplinary outcomes
- Behavioral expectations
  * Prohibited workplace conduct
- Workplace safety policies
- Limitations on outside employment
- Dating policies
- Nepotism/employment of family members policy
- Telephone use policy
- Employee surveillance/monitoring policy
- E-mail/Internet access policy
- Substance abuse policy
- Disclosure of confidential information policy
- Restrictions or solicitation on company property policy
- Explanation of employee benefits
  * Health insurance
  * Dental insurance
  * Other insurance
  * Employee discounts
  * Educational reimbursements
  * Credit unions
  * Paid sick leave
  * Family and Medical Leave Act issues
  * Jury duty leave
  * Military service leave
- Wage/salary policies
- Travel reimbursement policy
- Open door policy

expectations to the employees. Several authorities on employee handbooks suggest that initial drafts of the handbook should be tested on a sample of employees before it is published and disseminated.[25] The ultimate purpose of any employee handbook or organizational policy is communication. If the employer's message is not effectively communicated, then one can hardly expect compliance.

Some employers operate in multilingual work environments. Such employers should be aware that this may necessitate multilingual handbooks and written policies. For example, an employer may have a number of workers whose verbal

English skills are marginal and whose written English skills are even more limited. However, their oral and written Spanish skills may be good. As a result, it would make sense for the employer to provide a Spanish version of the employee handbook for these employees.

In other work environments there may be a problem with employees' written language skills in general. According to the National Institute for Literacy, approximately 20 percent of the United States workforce reads at or below the fifth-grade level.[26] An employer with a workforce that reads at this level may have to consider additional methods for communicating company policies. One means of assuring this is to conduct classes on the handbook's contents during new employee orientations. Providing training sessions when new policies are implemented is another method. Because of the importance of documenting each employee's awareness of the material, it becomes necessary to maintain records of these training sessions or classes. In some instances employers may even administer examinations at the conclusion of such classes to verify that employees are aware of company policies.

REDUCING IMPLIED CONTRACT EXPOSURE

When writing an employee handbook, employers should make every effort to reduce their implied contract exposure. There are several ways to do this, but keep in mind that the legalities of these suggestions vary significantly from state to state.

First, review handbooks and organizational policies for any phrases such as "permanent employee," "probationary employee," or "regular employee."[27] Such language could be construed to mean the employer is giving up employment-at-will rights at the conclusion of the probationary period. Further, it could be inferred that at the end of the probationary period, the employee moves to a "just cause" status as a "permanent employee."

As demonstrated in the opening scenario, any written statements should be void of references of employment for specified periods of time, which is especially true for handbooks. If an employer explicitly stipulates employment for a definite time period, the employee can only be terminated for just cause.[28]

Second, the handbook should contain a written statement that the handbook or policy is not a guarantee of job security or permanent employment. However, in some states these disclaimers are not recognized, and virtually all handbooks constitute implied contracts.[29] Most states will allow employers to preserve their employment-at-will rights provided that the disclaimer is not contradicted or compromised by some other provision contained elsewhere in the handbook. Suppose an employer has inserted the following disclaimer at the beginning of the employee handbook:

> This handbook is not, nor is it intended to be, a contract of employment. All employees are employed at will. No agent of this company has the authority to alter this relationship, and no employee should interpret any remarks by such agents as a guarantee of continued employment. The management of XYZ Company reserves the right to terminate your employment at any time.

Now assume that in the employee discipline portion of the employee handbook, the following policy is provided:

Employees who have completed one or more years of service with XYZ Company are expected to give two weeks notice of their intention to terminate their employment. The company reserves the right to terminate without notice any employee, probationary or permanent, for the following reasons:

1. Fighting.
2. Furnishing confidential information to unauthorized persons.
3. Reporting to work under the influence of drugs or alcohol.
4. Illegal possession of alcohol or drugs on company property.
5. Falsifying any employment records.
6. Possession of firearms or other weapons on company property.
7. Willful damage of company property.
8. Insubordination.

For other offenses, to include unsatisfactory performance, excessive absenteeism, or tardiness, no permanent employee will be terminated without first being afforded the progressive disciplinary procedures afforded in Section IV (Disciplinary Procedures) of this handbook.

The confusion should be apparent. The employer, in the disclaimer, states that the company is reserving the employment-at-will prerogative. However, in the employee discharge policy, the employer appears to tell employees that they will be terminated only for "just cause." In instances when employers make statements in writing that employees will only be terminated for just cause, some courts have held that the employee can then only be discharged for just cause, even though the employee had no guarantee of employment for a definitive period.[30]

The lesson for managers and HR professionals is quite simple. Employers should audit employee handbooks and remove any language that contradicts employment-at-will disclaimers. In the event of contradictions, courts are more likely to interpret the implied contract's terms in favor of the employee.

ENSURING DUE PROCESS

Due process refers to an employee's right to fair and consistent treatment in regard to terms and conditions of employment.[31] Simply stated, due process is the employee's guarantee against arbitrary and capricious treatment in the workplace.

Public sector (or government) employees enjoy far stronger due process protection than their private sector counterparts. Public sector employees have a significant amount of workplace protection because of there unique position as citizen-employees. The Fifth and Fourteenth Amendments, guaranteeing due process and protecting citizens from arbitrary actions by the government, carry over into public sector work environments. In its employee relations, the government must walk a fine line between its rights as an employer and its employees' rights as citizens.

In the private workplace, due process is not quite the same as due process of law and is, in most instances, not a statutory right—particularly in an employment-at-will environment. This does not imply private sector workplaces are without due process protection. Providing for due process (even in the absence of a legal requirement to do so) is the ethical approach to follow. It is simply the right thing to do. Furthermore, it is a sound management practice that benefits the organization by creating positive employee–employer relations.

At times, private sector employers may find themselves obligated to provide for due process through collective bargaining agreements, explicit contacts, or implicit contracts. Since most employee handbooks cover such matters as disciplinary actions and terminations, it is not surprising that they often provide procedures to make such determinations. Once these procedures have been committed to in writing, the employer is expected to follow them.

One of the ways employers can ensure they are providing for adequate due process is through proper in-house investigations. A properly conducted in-house investigation not only helps employers document that steps were taken to find the facts surrounding work rule violations, it further ensures any discipline taken by the employer was justified and fairly imposed. When offering employees due process, it is important to note that you are actually promising them two forms of due process: substantive and procedural.

Substantive versus Procedural Due Process

Substantive due process focuses on the purpose or the reason of employment practices that ensures an employee has not been arbitrarily disciplined or terminated.[32] Substantive due process assures the employee that no disciplinary action is taken against him or her unless there is clear and convincing evidence that the employee committed a disciplinary offense.

Another element of substantive due process is ensuring the disciplinary action imposed on the offender was appropriate for the offense committed. This is often referred to as "distributive justice."[33] Simply stated, "Does the punishment fit the crime?" If the employer's disciplinary actions are judged by the employees to be too harsh (or too lenient in some cases), the employer will have failed to provide adequate substantive due process. For example, a policy which calls for immediate termination the first time an employee returns late from a break might appear arbitrary to many employees.

A final element of substantive due process involves the consistent application of an organization's disciplinary policies to all employees. That is to say, disciplinary actions are imposed equally on all offenders. A good gauge to follow is provided by Douglas McGregor's well-known Hot Stove Principles.

DOUGLAS MCGREGOR'S HOT STOVE PRINCIPLES

- Like a hot stove which burns immediately, disciplinary actions should be administered quickly.

- Like a hot stove which gives a warning, so too should discipline.

- Like a hot stove which consistently burns everyone who touches it, discipline should be applied to all employees who violate the rule.

- Like a hot stove which burns everyone in the same manner, regardless of who they are, discipline must be impartially imposed.

SOURCE: McGregor, D. (1967). "Hot stove rules of discipline." In Straus, G. and Sayles, (eds.) *Personnel: The Human Problems of Management*. Englewood Cliffs, NJ: Prentice Hall.

According to McGregor, discipline operates like a hot stove in four basic ways (see Exhibit 7-4). First, discipline should be immediate. It should be administered as soon after the offense is committed as is practical, which does not mean managers should rush to judge. Rather, as soon as the investigation results confirm a disciplinary offense occurred, the disciplinary consequences should be imposed. This strengthens the cause-and-effect relationship between the offense and the disciplinary action.

Second, like a hot stove, the organization's disciplinary policies should give a warning. As one gets closer to a hot stove, the warmer or hotter it becomes. Similarly, the closer an individual gets to violating a work rule or company policy, the more averse attention that employee draws. No disciplinary action should come as a surprise. The employee should be told of the rule and informed that he or she is violating or close to violating the rule. As the employee comes closer to a violation, the warnings should become stronger.

Third, discipline is consistent. Like the hot stove that burns anyone and everyone who touches it, disciplinary actions should be imposed on every employee who violates the policy. It does not matter who the employee is; whether he or she has a good or poor work record, the individual is held accountable for the action.

Finally, discipline is impartial. Disciplinary actions are based on the magnitude of the offense, just like the severity of the burn increases the longer you touch the hot stove. This is really the distributive justice concept all over again. An employee who commits a major offense (i.e., theft of company property) should be subjected to greater punishment than an employee who commits a lesser offense (i.e., tardiness as a first offense).

Procedural due process refers to the fairness of the procedure used by the organization in determining whether its work rules or policies have been violated. Procedural due process focuses on such factors as notifying the accused party of the allegations against him or her. It also includes affording the accused a hearing with an opportunity to respond to the allegations and present witnesses and evidence to support his or her position before an impartial party or parties. Thus, procedural due process is provided when any accused party is permitted to respond to charges in an impartial forum.

In-house investigations will provide procedural due process if they are pursued from a fact-finding standpoint. Any internal process that is pursued strictly from the perspective of "building a case" against one party or the other provides neither substantive or procedural justice and may open an employer to further litigation.

CONDUCTING IN-HOUSE INVESTIGATIONS AND HEARINGS

Whether confronted with establishing a just cause discharge or a complaint of unlawful discrimination, it is absolutely essential that HR professionals have policies and procedures in place to investigate such allegations. No organization should take an adverse action against any employee before it has gathered sufficient information to substantiate that such action is necessary. In short, an employee should not be held accountable for a work rule violation until you have enough information to indicate that he or she did indeed violate the rule. Employers and their representatives often get themselves into trouble when they react before finding enough facts or hearing the accused employee's side of the story (see Exhibit 7-5).

Take, for example, an incident that involved a hospital administrator who was charged with sexual harassment by three of his female subordinates. The hospital's sexual harassment policy had been disseminated to its employees. The policy contained a process for filing complaints as well as an alternative process in the event that a direct supervisor was involved in the alleged harassment. The hospital was also aware of the potential liability it faced in the event of *quid pro quo* sexual harassment (see Chapter 4). Realizing the administrator had placed the hospital in jeopardy by engaging in the sexual harassment of three female subordinates, the administrator was confronted by his superiors. Immediately after

---

■ EXHIBIT 7-5

ERRORS TO AVOID IN INVESTIGATIONS

- Excessive delays in starting the investigation
- Inadequate feedback to the parties during the investigation process
- Inappropriate disclosure of confidential information
- Lack of thoroughness in the investigation
- Failure to complete the investigation

SOURCE: Cole, E. K. and Hustoles, T. P. (1997). *How to Conduct a Sexual Harassment Investigation.* Washington, DC: National Association of College and University Attorneys.

being informed of the charges made against him, the administrator was fired. The hospital believed it had taken immediate and prompt corrective action that would then guarantee the harassment would not recur. However, in its rush to judgment, the hospital failed to verify that any sexual harassment had actually occurred. The administrator was terminated merely on the unsubstantiated accusation that he had harassed the three women. No investigation had been launched by the hospital, nor had the administrator been afforded any opportunity to defend himself against the allegations.

Fortunately for the administrator, he was a contractual employee and could not be fired except for just cause. In the absence of an investigation, this was difficult for the hospital to establish. During the protracted litigation that ensued (breach of contract), two of the women eventually came forward with a confession that their sexual harassment complaint had been a fabrication. It seems the administrator was a very demanding boss. The women thought that if they made a sexual harassment complaint against him, the administrator would back off from the demanding management style. They had never intended for him to lose his job, only for him to stop supervising them so closely. Things, however, had quickly gotten out of hand. In the end, the hospital paid a sizable damage award for breaching the contract and defaming the administrator's good name—all because it acted without first investigating.

What follows is a general description of a generic investigation. Think of it as the bare-bones essentials that any investigation should possess. Remember, the more complicated the allegations, the greater the amount of detail that must be examined in the investigation. Still, the process of fact finding is essentially the same.

Whether for sexual harassment or for willful destruction of company property, appropriate organizational responses follow the same general process:

1. A complaint or allegation is received.

2. An investigation is conducted.

3. Appropriate corrective action is implemented.

4. Management monitors affected employees to ensure that desired results occur.

RECEIVING A COMPLAINT. The first thing HR professionals must remember about any complaint or reported violation is that it may not be truthful or factual. It goes without saying that the complaint should be documented. It is also imperative that whoever is assigned the task of investigating the allegation approaches this task in an impartial manner. If the investigation is not conducted in an impartial manner, it will not be a proper investigation and may be subject to later legal challenges.

It is important to keep the complaint and the proceedings as confidential *as possible*. We say *as possible* because, in the event of litigation or intervention by a government agency (i.e., EEOC, OFCCP, NLRB, etc.), the employer may be compelled to disclose all materials to the government. This fact should be conveyed to the parties involved in the investigation. However, barring a subpoena from a court or agency, it is advisable to avoid disclosure because of potential defamation allegations.

It is important to let both parties know that the organization cannot guarantee the matter under investigation can be kept confidential permanently. To promise absolute confidentiality may actually expose the employer to litigation. However, making the parties aware that no permanent offer of confidentiality exists may reduce the employer's exposure to potential breach of contract litigation by eliminating the employee's argument that he or she justifiably relied on defendant's alleged promise of permanent confidentiality in cooperating in the investigation.[34]

THE INVESTIGATION.   Investigations are exercises in fact finding. Generally, investigations should be structured to answer questions that will establish either that an organizational policy or work rule was violated or that it was not. Some of the typical questions which should be asked are listed in Exhibit 7-6.

In the event of an incident in which witnesses were present, written statements regarding what they saw should be collected as soon as possible. Witnesses should put their observations in their own words. Avoid having supervisors or any other company representative "coach" the witnesses on their responses. This could be construed as the organization trying to coerce the witnesses into fabricating testimony to support the company's interests. HR professionals must go to great lengths to ensure that facts (not just collaborating evidence) are gathered and that the investigation always appears to be systematic and fair.

TAKING APPROPRIATE CORRECTIVE ACTION.   In the event that the facts indicate a violation has indeed occurred, the next step is to determine the appropriate corrective action that must be taken. When an organization takes any corrective action including disciplinary action, the punishment should always fit the violation (see Exhibit 7-7).

■ EXHIBIT 7-6

QUESTIONS TO ASK IN AN INVESTIGATION

- What happened?
- When did it happen?
- What did you do or observe?
- What is the background of the incident?
- What documentation or physical evidence is present?
- Who else witnessed the incident?
- What were their observations?

FINDINGS FROM INVESTIGATION

- Is the alleged perpetrator innocent or guilty?

- If innocent, what should be done to maintain or restore his or her credibility?

- If guilty, how serious was the infraction of organizational rules?

- What other policies were violated?

- Was the violation intentional or unintentional?

- Was the violator aware of the organizational policy or work rule?

- Was the violator cooperative in the investigation?

- Were there other violators?

- What corrective action is appropriate?

- What corrective action has the organization imposed for similar violations in the past?

SOURCES: Bureau of National Affairs (1987). *Sexual Harassment: Employer Policies and Problems.* Washington, DC: Bureau of National Affairs, Inc.; Hubbartt, W. S. (1993). *Personnel Policy Handbook: How to Develop a Manual That Works.* New York: McGraw-Hill.

PRIVACY CONCERNS

Privacy expectations of employees in both the public and private sectors have increased with the expansion of employee rights in the workplace. State statutes as well as court decisions have created an incentive (some might say a disincentive) for employers to examine their policies and procedures for securing personnel files. There are many misconceptions about the rights of employees to privacy in the workplace. The degree to which employees are afforded privacy protection hinges on whether the employee works for a public or private sector employer.

In regard to workplace privacy, there are really two major areas of concern. The first potential legal pitfall involves the disclosure of information about an employee to other parties. The other issue involves information gathering or surveillance of the employee.

When employees bring privacy-related legal action against their employers, it is often for invasion of privacy. Employees' right to privacy in the private sector workplace is governed by state tort law. A "tort" is merely a wrong or injury that is actionable in court. There are four torts that cover an individual's right to privacy: unreasonable intrusion upon the seclusion of another, publicity that unreasonably places another in a false light before the community, unreasonable publicity given to another's private life, and misappropriation of another's name or likeness.[35] Most employer surveillance and monitoring activities are likely to be challenged on the grounds that such activities are an unreasonable intrusion into the employee's private affairs. Employer disclosure of employee information or records is either litigated as an unreasonable publication of the employee's private life or placing the employee in a false light in the community.

PUBLIC AND PRIVATE SECTOR EMPLOYEES AND DISCLOSURE

Most Americans are aware that, as citizens of the United States, they are endowed with certain rights to privacy that are protected by the Constitution.[36] However, many individuals do not understand that these constitutional protections are limited only to intrusion into their privacy by governments (federal, state, or local).[37] Although some states (most notably Michigan and California) have enacted laws specifically protecting individual privacy rights in the private sector, the majority have not.[38] On the whole, there are very few statutory prohibitions on nongovernmental employers that cover invasion of privacy other than the state tort laws previously mentioned.

Employees in the public sector enjoy far greater privacy protection than their private sector counterparts because their employers are governmental entities.[39] Since the privacy statutes do not differentiate between intrusion from the government as an information seeker or as an employer, the result is that the personnel records of government employees are entitled to far greater protection from public access. For example, a government employee, as a citizen, has certain rights to privacy protection from the government, who is also his employer. In the private sector, there are far fewer prohibitions on public disclosure of personnel documents. State tort statutes may, however, provide some recourse and protection against disclosure of certain private sector personnel records.

DISCLOSURE OF PERSONNEL RECORDS. Disclosure of information about employees is a major privacy concern for HR professionals. Although few laws regulate private sector employers' personnel records (the notable exception is the ADA's requirement to keep employee medical information confidential), tort action under slander and libel create a substantial incentive to safeguard employee information. Both terms relate to injury to the employee that results from public disclosure of information about that employee. If the information is disclosed orally, it may be slander; if in writing, it is potentially libelous. To be either one, the comments must challenge the employee's reputation in the community.

INVASION OF PRIVACY AND DEFAMATION

By disclosing an employee's performance appraisal results, a company may run afoul of the common law torts of invasion of privacy and defamation. These state tort laws would also apply to private organizations not explicitly covered by state privacy legislation.

Invasion of privacy and defamation claims address the manner and scope of disclosing highly personal matters such as an employee's qualifications and performance.[40] **Defamation** is distinguished from privacy in that defamation focuses on injury to the employee's reputation, while privacy torts are tied to the resulting emotional injury. Defamation laws may vary in their specific provisions from state to state, but they all possess some generic elements.[41] In defamation, the aggrieved party must demonstrate that:

1. *A statement was made concerning the individual.* In the case of performance information, these statements could involve whether the employee adequately performed assigned tasks, failed to follow instructions, missed deadlines, etc.

2. *The statement was presented as fact and is substantially false.* This may be very susceptible to the reliability and validity of the performance appraisal instrument. If the instrument is flawed, a strong argument could be made that its inferences about an employee's work performance are false. This would be particularly true if an instrument purporting to measure performance was overly subjective or measured nonwork related behaviors.

3. *The statement impugned the employee's character or abilities and caused actual injury to his or her reputation.* This element is particularly worrisome to HR professionals as any poor evaluation of an employee that is publicized would undoubtedly have disastrous effects on his or her reputation at that organization, or even within the industry, as in the case of higher-level employees.

4. *In order to be actionable, the defamatory statement must be "published."*

Making statements about the employee in question in public is an example.

EMPLOYER DEFENSES AGAINST DEFAMATION

When confronted with a defamation charge, the employer would have three general defenses on which to rely. The first defense would be to demonstrate that the statement was true. The truth is proof against defamation.[42] In cases involving the disclosure of performance information, a validated performance appraisal (see Chapter 3) becomes indispensable. The statement made by the organization would not be "substantially false," and the complaining party would be unable to establish defamation if the performance appraisal is valid and substantiated.

Failing to establish this, the employer may resort to two other defenses based on either an *absolute privilege* or *qualified privilege* regarding the dissemination of any employee information. The term "privilege" in a legal context refers to an organization's exemption from liability for speaking or publishing defamatory words concerning an individual.

Qualified privilege (also called conditional privilege) may also be asserted as a defamation defense in an employment context. In the instance of **qualified privilege,** immunity is based on the fact that the statement was made in the performance of some judicial, social, or personal duty.[43] Under this doctrine, the employer would have to demonstrate that the published communication (e.g., teaching evaluation scores for a university instructor) was made in good faith between the concerned parties with a common interest in the subject matter addressed.[44] Unlike absolute privilege, qualified privilege may be lost or exceeded.[45] To illustrate this point, the employer could attempt to justify its disclosure of an instructor's teaching evaluations as relevant to students' matriculation by ensuring that students can select the more effective instructors. This is assuming, of course, that the teaching evaluations accurately measure teaching effectiveness and course knowledge. However, even if this is substantiated to the satisfaction of a court, the employer could still lose its qualified privilege based on "abuse" through excessive publication of the defamatory information. Abuse of privilege can occur when the information in question is accessible to parties to whom the privilege does not apply, in this case, nonstudents.[46] An illustrative example of how this could occur may be an instance where a faculty member is applying for a position at another institution and the published teaching evaluations fall into the hands of the prospective employer. This would be a particular problem if the faculty member's recent scores were much lower than usually received (perhaps due to a new preparation, unfamiliar subject material, etc.) and considered by the prospective employer to reflect the instructor's overall ability.

Privilege is said to be absolute when the employer is protected from liability regardless of the motive for publishing information about the individual in question and regardless of the truth or falsity of the information. **Absolute privilege** in regard to disclosing personnel information, to include performance evaluation scores, could be attained merely by having the individual faculty member's written permission to do so.[47] This would provide the best and surest insulation against future litigation, but it must be clearly understood that such consent cannot be obtained under duress.

SEARCH AND SEIZURE

Perhaps no privacy issue is as misunderstood as searches in the workplace. Searches not only include such matters as physical searches of desks, lockers, vehicles, and other items on the employer's premises but employee surveillance, telephone monitoring, and computer monitoring as well. Private sector employers enjoy far greater latitude in conducting searches and surveillance of their workplaces than government employers. As one court noted, requiring an employer to obtain a warrant whenever the employer wishes to enter an employee's office, desk, or file cabinets for a work-related purpose would seriously disrupt the routine conduct of business and would be unreasonable.[48]

This does not mean employers enjoy unrestrained liberty to monitor or search their employees with impunity. There are limitations imposed by state laws regulating invasion of privacy.

PHYSICAL SEARCHES. Employers generally have access to company-owned property when searching for work-related materials. In one case, *O'Bryan v KTIV Television*, a federal district court held that an employee failed to establish a common law invasion of privacy claim as a result of a search of his desk.[49] The court ruled that searching an employee's desk did not establish a common law invasion of privacy claim under state law. In this particular situation, it was concluded that the employee did not have a reasonable expectation of privacy in the contents of his desk since it was not locked and contained work-related information needed by coworkers.[50]

This, however, is not the case when searches are conducted for the purpose of acquiring nonwork-related information. The method by which an employer carries out any inquiry into an employee's private concerns may constitute an intrusion upon the employee's right to privacy. If that inquiry fails to give due regard to the employee's privacy or reveals personal matters unrelated to the workplace, the employer may be sued under state tort laws. Several courts have ruled that searching an employee's work space may constitute a tortuous invasion of privacy, if the search is conducted in such a way as to reveal information unrelated to the workplace.[51] A tortuous invasion of privacy is merely one which creates an injury to the employee that is actionable under state law. For example, an employer is not authorized to open mail addressed to a person at the workplace that appears to be personal.[52] Mail addressed to an employee from company clients, suppliers, or vendors may be assumed to contain work-related material, but mail from the employee's mother or mail marked "personal" or "confidential" is far more likely to contain nonwork-related information.[53]

VIDEO SURVEILLANCE AND MONITORING. There is increasing concern about employee monitoring in the workplace. Employers may even be justified in monitoring employees' activities off the job. This type of surveillance most frequently occurs when an employer is investigating workers' compensation claims. In some instances, when the employer has reason to suspect that the injury is not legitimate, a private investigator may be hired to acquire evidence to prove the employee's claim is fraudulent. In *Saldana v Kelsey-Hayes Co.*, the Michigan Supreme Court concluded that an employer's legitimate business interest in investigating an employee's claim of work-related injury outweighed the employee's privacy interest in not being monitored in his home.[54]

Employers may use video surveillance in the workplace for a number of legitimate purposes (e.g., security, employee safety, performance monitoring.). However, employers should avoid placing surveillance cameras in locations where employees may have strong privacy expectations. Unless there is an overriding business concern, it is suggested that cameras not be installed in employee lounges or restrooms. Connecticut expressly forbids the use of electronic surveillance devices (voice as well as video devices) in employee restrooms, lounges, and locker rooms.[55]

TELEPHONE MONITORING. Because some jurisdictions have held that the improper interception of employees' phone calls may constitute a tortuous invasion of privacy,[56] monitoring company telephones must be done very carefully. The employer must have a legitimate business reason for monitoring its employees' telephone conversations.[57] For example, an employer who monitors telephone calls in an effort to ensure quality control would be doing so to achieve a work-related purpose. An employer's asserted interest in recording phone calls "must be balanced against the degree of intrusion resulting from the employer's methods to obtain the information."[58] If the nature of the employee's job entails using the telephone to transact company business, and the quality of the employee's communications affects those transactions, the employer may monitor the job-related conversations. In this case, the employer's need to know how well the employee is communicating with customers outweighs the employee's expectation of privacy.

The second consideration involves employee awareness that calls are being monitored. Not only must the monitoring activities be considered reasonable, the employees must know the employer is monitoring incoming and outgoing calls.[59] If employees are aware that calls on the company phone are subject to monitoring by the employer, they can hardly claim later that they enjoyed an expectation of privacy. The point, quite simply, is if you are going to monitor company telephones, make certain you let your employees know.

Assume a computer manufacturer has several employees who operate the company's "help line." Customers who are having difficulty installing computers or having trouble operating software can call the "help line" for technical assistance. The employer expects "help line" employees to communicate solutions to the customers effectively and understandably. This is particularly important because most customers are not technocrats and have trouble understanding instructions with technical terminology. Additionally, the employer knows customers become easily frustrated when assistance is delayed as a result of busy telephone lines. Consequently, the employer has a policy of no personal telephone calls during work hours on the "help line" telephones. A separate line is available for employees to make personal calls during breaks or to receive emergency calls. Additionally, during new employee orientation and in the employee handbook, the employer has informed all employees that in order to make service quality control checks, the employer will monitor "help line" calls. The employer has also informed workers of the penalties which may be incurred for using "help line" telephones for personal calls. By taking these actions, the employer has removed the employee's expectation of privacy on the "help line" telephones.

MONITORING E-MAIL.   Generally speaking, there is no reasonable expectation of privacy in e-mail communications made on an employer's equipment. In the case, *Smyth v The Pillsbury Co.,* one federal district court even held that an employee had no expectation of privacy for e-mail messages sent to his supervisor over a companywide e-mail system, even though the employer had previously promised the plaintiff that the e-mail messages would not be intercepted by management.[60]

DRUG TESTING

Drug testing is invariably an issue of search and seizure (discussed in the previous section). However, the increased use of drug testing in today's workplace requires a separate and distinct discussion.

Since the Fourth Amendment protects citizens against unreasonable search and seizure, many employees are under the false assumption that employers may not conduct drug testing without employee consent. The error is one of confusing public sector constitutional limitations with private sector employment. The constitutional prohibition only applies to "unreasonable" searches conducted by the government.[61] Even government employers can conduct drug testing provided they can show that such searches are "reasonable."[62]

The Drug-Free Workplace Act provides a great deal of insulation for employers by requiring holders of government contracts, or subcontracts, as well as recipients of federal grant and aid money to maintain a drug-free workplace.[63] But even private sector employers may initiate drug testing programs provided they are uniformly applied to all employees. Private sector employers may require drug testing as part of their preemployment screening procedures as long as *all* applicants are tested.[64] Employers may also require random drug testing and alcohol testing throughout an individual's employment, again, provided that *all* employees are subject to the random testing.[65] Additionally, drug testing may be implemented in circumstances where the employer has a reasonable basis for suspecting that an employee is under the influence of drugs during work hours and when an employer has a legitimate business interest in having the work performed by employees who are not impaired by drugs or alcohol use.[66] As an example, a school bus driver who shows up for work intoxicated or under the influence of cocaine would pose a far more serious threat to an employer's legitimate business interest than a stock boy similarly incapacitated.

Perhaps the simplest means to eliminate privacy issues arising from drug testing is to get employees to consent to drug testing and waive related statutory rights.[67] In addition, informing employees that they may be subject to unannounced random drug and alcohol testing may serve as a deterrent to substance abuse. Not only are such warnings ethical, they may have a practical effect.

One final word of caution about drug testing in the workplace. Since the results of the actual drug test can ultimately result in an employee's work record being blackened, or even terminating the employee for just cause, it is critical that the test itself be accurate. HR professionals should ensure the testing is conducted by a licensed and approved laboratory. It is also recommended that first time offenders be enrolled in employee assistance programs (EAPs).

NEGLIGENT HIRING, RETENTION, AND MISREPRESENTATION

Negligent hiring has become a significant source of employment litigation. This is a tort arising from state law and varies to some degree from state to state.[68] In general, **negligent hiring** becomes actionable when an employer fails to exercise ordinary care in hiring or retaining an employee and that employee creates a foreseeable risk of harm to a third party.[69] For example, assume an employer hires a programmer analyst who is known to have been terminated from her previous place of employment for threatening a coworker with physical violence. Shortly after employing the programmer analyst, she physically assaults an auditor from the accounting department following an argument over a program's output. The employer could be held liable for the injuries sustained by the auditor if the following can be established: The employer knew or reasonably should have known of the employee in question's tendency toward violence (or even incompetence), the employee in question committed a tortuous act against the third party, and the employer owes a duty of care to third parties within the zone of foreseeable risks created by the employment relationship.[70] In this example, the employer knew the new programmer analyst had a record of violent behavior. The programmer analyst assaulted and injured a coworker, a third party. The employer owes its employees a safe work environment and jeopardized that safety interest by knowingly hiring a volatile programmer analyst. Therefore, the company has committed negligent hiring.

Negligent retention, sometimes called **negligent supervision,** is very similar to negligent hiring, except the knowledge that an employee presents a danger to coworkers or other third parties (through violent behavior or incompetence) is based on the employee's demonstrated performance. To illustrate this slight distinction, consider the scenario concerning negligent hiring. In that scenario, the employer hired a programmer with a known tendency toward violence. Expanding the scenario to include the following situation will provide a good example of negligent retention. Since beginning employment, the programmer analyst has been repeatedly counseled about her violent outbursts when contradicted by coworkers. She has, on at least four occasions, verbally assaulted and physically threatened coworkers, as demonstrated by formal complaints made against her. Despite the employer's knowledge of the programmer analyst's ongoing violent behavior, she has not been terminated, or even disciplined, for her actions. When the programmer analyst finally physically assaults a coworker, the employer may be held liable for the coworker's injuries. Although aware of the programmer analyst's violent behavior, the employer failed to make reasonable efforts to prevent injury to others.[71]

Not only may employers be held liable for injuries to third parties caused by current employees, they may be held liable for injuries caused by former employees. Under **negligent misrepresentation,** an employer may be responsible for acts of workplace violence or incompetence at the employee's *new* place of employment. This is only an issue when the former employer provides a positive recommendation or evaluation of the former employee's performance and knowingly omitted incidents of workplace violence,[72] inability to perform critical work tasks, or sexual harassment.

In order to establish an employer's negligent misrepresentation, the complaining party must demonstrate that the former employer provided false information to the new employer, the new employer relied on that false information in making an employment decision, and the new employer was exposed to liability for injuries to a third party because of the reliance on false information.[73]

The lesson for HR professionals is simple. To prevent negligent hiring, thorough background investigations should be conducted, and applicants with potential liability problems should be screened. To avoid negligent retention charges, employees who pose a threat to the safety and health of others, even with training and counseling, and those who cannot perform their duties should be removed from the workplace. Finally, when giving reference information to potential employers on former employees, employers should provide only factual information in order to avoid negligent misrepresentation. There is no law that requires an employer to provide a recommendation, good or bad, for a former employee. However, if a recommendation is provided, it must be honest.

Summary

This chapter deals with employment-at-will, employee handbooks, and employee privacy issues. Employment-at-will is based on the notion that if the employee can terminate the employment relationship at any time, the employer is free to do the same. It should be clear that when it comes to an employer's employment-at-will rights, there is less there than meets the eye. In reality, there appear to be very few situations under which an employer may actually terminate employees for bad reasons or no reasons at all, and the erosion of employment-at-will has placed an ever-increasing burden on employers to demonstrate that terminations are for good reasons.

Although employee handbooks have contributed to the erosion of employment-at-will terminations, they provide far more benefit as a means for justifying legitimate employer actions. It is important that employee handbooks be thorough. However, they should be easy to read and to be understood by all of a company's employees.

Whatever employment practices or policies an employer creates and enforces, they must be perceived as justified and fair by the employees if they are to be effective. This means ensuring employees are aware of the policies, the rationale behind the policies, and the consequences for violating the policies. A burden is therefore placed on all managers to not only be familiar with the employer's workplace rules but also to make efforts to ensure that the rules are fairly enforced. And, as a final word of caution, employers should never take disciplinary action unless there is evidence (as the result of a proper investigation) that the individual employee did indeed commit the disciplinary offense. Thus, it is a good idea to provide due process to all employees. Due process is the employee's guarantee against arbitrary and capricious treatment. Unfortunately, only public sector employees enjoy significant due process protection in the workplace.

Private sector employers enjoy far greater latitude than their public sector counterparts when it comes to privacy in the workplace. However, managers must ensure that monitoring and surveillance activities do not cross the line into tortuous invasion of privacy. This means being aware of any limitations placed on the employer by state law or municipal ordinance. However, common sense needs to be applied. Job-related surveillance (monitoring security, safety, or productivity) is one matter; monitoring restrooms when there is no job-related justification is another. Abusive monitoring and surveillance is likely to result in public opinion calling for regulation and government intervention. Perhaps the best course to follow if you are going to monitor your employees is to ensure that they are aware that they are being monitored and are given the reasons for the surveillance.

Employers may also be held liable for negligent hiring, negligent retention, or negligent misrepresentation. It is imperative that employers protect themselves from negligent hiring claims through the preemployment screening process, negligent retention actions by acting swiftly to terminate employees who cause a threat to coworkers and other third parties, and negligent misrepresentation situations by providing only factual information on past employees when it is requested.

KEY TERMS AND CONCEPTS

absolute privilege	negligent misrepresentation
defamation	negligent retention
due process	negligent supervision
employment-at-will	procedural due process
explicit contract	public policy
implied contract	qualified privilege
just cause	substantive due process
negligent hiring	whistleblower clauses

QUESTIONS

1. Under the employment-at-will doctrine, an employee may be terminated for what three reasons (*Payne v Western and Atlantic Railroad Co.*)?

2. What are four limitations to the employment-at-will doctrine? Provide an example of each.

3. Why would some HR professionals call employee handbooks a double-edged sword? Why would an employer need to have an employee handbook?

4. What is due process? Distinguish between substantive and procedural due process.

5. When conducting an in-house investigation, what are the primary concerns of the investigator?

6. What are the main privacy concerns of American employees? Discuss each.

7. Distinguish between negligent hiring, negligent retention, and negligent misrepresentation.

CASES

1 Dave Nichols was employed as a sales representative by B. J. Reithel, Inc., a telemarketing company. Nichols's immediate supervisor was Greg Rose, and Rose's supervisor was Victoria Bush. Reithel, Inc. was under contract with Consolidated Telephone to solicit advertising for its telephone directories from present and prospective advertisers. All such solicitation was done by telephone, and Nichols was hired and trained to make these calls.

Reithel, Inc. has an established policy, of which all employees are informed, that monitoring solicitation calls is part of its regular training program. The monitored calls are reviewed with employees to improve sales techniques. This monitoring is accomplished through a standard extension telephone, located in the supervisor's office, which shares lines with the telephones in the employees' offices. Employees are permitted to make personal calls on company telephones, and they are told that personal calls will not be monitored except to the extent necessary to determine whether a particular call is of a personal or business nature.

In April or May 2001, during his lunch break, Nichols received a call in his office from a friend. At or near the beginning of the call (there are conflicting indications), the friend asked Nichols about an employment interview Nichols had with another company (Banjoville Sales Company, a competitor of Reithel, Inc.) the evening before. Nichols responded that the interview had gone well and expressed a strong interest in taking the Banjoville Sales job.

Unknown to Nichols, Rose was monitoring the call from his office and heard the discussion of the interview. After hearing the conversation (how much is unclear), Rose told Bush about it. Later that afternoon, Nichols was called into Bush's office and was told that the company did not want him to leave. Nichols responded by asking whether he was being fired. Upon discovering that his supervisor's questions were prompted by Rose's interception of his call, Nichols became upset and tempers flared. The upshot was that Bush did fire Nichols the next day. However, Nichols complained to Bush's supervisor and was reinstated with apologies from Bush and Rose. Within a week, Nichols left Reithel, Inc. to work for Banjoville Sales. Two weeks later, Nichols filed suit against Reithel, Inc., claiming that monitoring his personal phone call was an invasion of his privacy. Will Nichols prevail in his lawsuit? Why or why not? Under what circumstances may a private sector employer monitor the phone conversations of its employees?

SOURCE: *Watkins v L. M. Berry & Company*, 704 F.2d 577 (11th Cir. 1983).

2 On October 1, 1995, Mark Walker was hired by CTE to be its general sales manager. At the time Walker became CTE's general sales manager, Frances Wieble was the local sales manager. Walker had previously been employed at Talbert, Inc. as an account executive. He eventually became Talbert's general sales manager before taking the position with CTE. In the fall of 1997, CTE was purchased by Galt, Inc.

In November of 1997, Alfred G. Blythe became vice president and general manager for CTE. Prior to that time he had worked at Talbert in Mobile, Alabama. While at Talbert, Blythe had worked with Walker. At some unidentified point after Blythe became CTE's general manager, he mentioned to Walker that Galt had paid $21,000,000 for CTE. Blythe further expressed his opinion that he thought Galt had paid too much for the company, and that as a result, costs would have to be cut and revenues increased.

Late in 1999, Walker's title and duties were changed, and he was given the title of CTE's national sales manager. CTE, at that time, no longer had a general sales manager. In the fall of 2000, Blythe approached Wieble about conducting a review of CTE's sales department and making recommendations for its improvement. Prior to that time, Wieble had been critical of Walker's performance as CTE's general sales manager. Wieble recommended that she be made CTE's general sales manager and that Jennifer Edmonds be promoted to CTE's local sales manager. She further recommended that Walker be given the position of CTE's local and regional sales account executive.

On November 9, 2000, Walker was demoted to this position. An account executive is responsible for both servicing CTE's existing clients and recruiting new clientele. At the same time, Wieble was promoted to CTE's general sales manager and assumed the duties formerly performed by Walker as national sales manager. Edmonds was promoted to CTE's local sales manager. Both Wieble and Edmonds are females. Wieble was thirty-three years old at the time of her promotion to general sales manager.

As a result of his demotion to an account executive, Walker was given a desk and credenza in the "bull pen" with the other account executives. The bull pen is an office area with ten to fifteen cubicles in the center. In November of 2000, an unknown person or persons went through Walker's desk and credenza and removed from them certain CTE sales information. Neither the desk nor the credenza were locked, and the only items removed were property belonging to CTE.

Walker was aware that CTE employees were permitted to enter his office in his absence to retrieve work-related documents. But when he learned of the search of his desk and credenza, he confronted Edmonds about it. Edmonds, Wieble, and Blythe denied any knowledge about the search. It is unknown who conducted the search of Walker's desk.

On May 7, 2001, as a result of his demotion, Walker filed charges of discrimination with the state Human Rights Commission alleging unlawful search and seizure of his workplace and invasion of his privacy. Does Walker have a case? If so, upon what grounds? If not, why not? Under what circumstances may an employer search an employee's office space?

SOURCE: *O'Bryan v KTIV Television*, 868 F. Supp. 1146 (N.D. Ia. 1994).

Notes

1. Scenario was developed from the facts in *Rosen v Gulf Shores, Inc.*, 610 So.2d 366 (Miss. 1992).

2. *Payne v Western & Atlantic Railroad Co.*, 81 Tenn. 507, 518 (1884).

3. Cross, F. B. and Miller R. L. (1995). *West's Legal Environment of Business (2d ed.)*. St. Paul, MN: West Publishing Company.

4. Corley, R. N. and Shedd, P. J. (1990). *Fundamentals of Business Law (5th ed.)*. Englewood Cliffs, NJ: Prentice Hall.

5. Ibid.

6. Ibid.

7. Cross and Miller, pp. 181–5.

8. *Foley v Interactive Data Corp.*, 765 P.2d 373, 385 (Cal. 1988); *Ryan v Upchurch*, 474 F.Supp. 211, 213 (S.D. Ind. 1979).

9. *Toussaint v Blue Cross and Blue Shield*, 408 Mich. 579 (Mich. 1980).

10. *Ebling v Masco Corp.*, 292 N.W. 2d 880 (Mich. 1980).

11. *Dubard v Biloxi H. M. A., Inc.*, 1999 Miss. App. LEXIS 468 (October 19, 1999).

12. *Toussaint*, at 610.

13. Ibid. at 614.

14. 29 C.F.R. § 1604.11 App. A and 29 C.F.R. § 1606 App. A.

15. 29 U.S.C. § 1001 *et. seq.*; 29 U.S.C. § 651 *et. seq.*; 29 U.S.C. § 201 *et.seq.*; 42 U.S.C. § 2000e *et. seq.*

16. 42 U.S.C. § 2000e-5.

17. 29 Cal. Rptr. 399 (1963).

18. *Boyd v Winton Hills Medical & Health Center, Inc.*, 711 N.E. 2d 1014 (Ohio 1999).

19. *Abels v Renfro Corp.*, 436 S.E. 2d 822, 826 (N.C. 1993).

20. Bureau of National Affairs (1991). *Employment Guide*. Washington, DC: Bureau of National Affairs, pp. 10:87–88.

21. 364 N.E. 2d 1251 (Mass. 1977).

22. Ibid. at 1254.

23. *Firgeleski v Hubbell, Inc.*, 1999 Conn. Super. Lexis 397; *Raffaele v Ryder Dedicated Logistics, Inc.*, 931 F. Supp. 76 (D. Mass. 1996); *Gupta v New Britain General Hospital*, 687 A.2d 111 (Conn. 1996).

24. *Faragher v City of Boca Raton*, 524 U.S. 775, 804 (1998); *Burlington Industries v Ellerth*, 524 U.S. 742, 764 (1998); *Kolstad v American Dental Association*, 527 U.S. 526 (1999).

25. Hubbartt, W. S. (1993). *Personnel Policy Handbook: How to Develop a Manual That Works*. New York: McGraw-Hill, Inc.; Luna, J. (August 30, 1995). Case studies. *CCH Ideas and Trends*. Chicago, IL: Commerce Clearing House, Inc.

26. National Institute for Literacy (2000). *Fast Facts on Literacy*. **http://www.nitl.gov/newworld/fastfact.htm**

27. *Fox v T-H Continental, Ltd.*, 78 F.3d 409 (8th Cir. 1996).

28. *Ridenhour v IBM Corp.*, 512 S.E. 2d 774 (N.C. App. 1999).

29. *Leikvold v Valley View Community Hosp.*, 688 P.2d 170, 174 (Ariz. 1984).

30. *Goodyear Tire and Rubber Company v Portilla*, 879 S.W.2d 47, 52 (Tex. 1994).

31. Abraham, Y. T. and Flippo, E. B. (1991). *Managing a Changing Workforce.* Chicago, IL: Commerce Clearing House, Inc.

32. Holley, W. H. and Jennings, K. M. (1994). *The Labor Relations Process (5th ed.).* Fort Worth, TX: The Dryden Press.

33. McGregor, D. (1967). "Hot stove rules of discipline." In Strauss, G. & Sayles, L. (eds.). *Personnel: The Human Problems of Management.* Englewood Cliffs, NJ: Prentice Hall.

34. *Lau's Corp. v Haskins*, 405 S.E.2d 474, 476 (Ga. 1991).

35. Restatement (Second) of Torts § 652A.

36. *Griswold v Connecticut*, 381 U.S. 479, 483–484 (1965).

37. Hames, D. S. and Diersen, N. (November 1991). "The common law right to privacy: Another incursion into employers' right to manage their employees?" *Labor Law Journal*, 42 (11):757–765.

38. Harstein, B. A. (Spring 1992). "Rules of the road in dealing with personnel records." *Employee Relations Law Journal*, 17 (4): 673–692.

39. Sovereign, K .L. (1994). *Personnel Law (3rd ed.).* Englewood Cliffs, NJ: Prentice Hall.

40. Sanford, B. W. (1987). *Libel and Privacy: The Prevention and Defense of Litigation.* Clifton, NJ: Prentice Hall Law & Business.

41. O'Brien, D. M. (1979). *Privacy, Law, and Public Policy.* New York: Praeger Publishers.

42. *Brady v Ottaway Newspapers, Inc.*, 445 N.Y.S.2d 786 (N.Y. App. 1981).

43. Black, H. C., Nolan, J. R., and Nolan-Haley, J. M. (1990). *Black's Law Dictionary (6th ed.).* St. Paul, MN: West Publishing Co.

44. *Restatement (Second) of Torts* § 596.

45. Rapp, J. A. (1993). *Education Law.* New York: Matthew Bender & Co.

46. *Abofreka v Alston Tobacco, Co.*, 341 S.E.2d 622 (S.C. 1986).

47. *Restatement (Second) of Torts* § 583.

48. *O'Connor v Ortega*, 480 U.S. 709 (1987).

49. *O'Bryan v KTIV Television*, 868 F. Supp. 1146 (N.D. Iowa 1994), *aff'd in part*, 64 F.3d 1188 (8th Cir. 1995).

50. Ibid. at 1159.

51. *Doe v Kohn, Nast and Graf*, 862 F. Supp. 1310 (E.D. Pa. 1994).

52. *Vernars v Young*, 539 F.2d 966 (3d Cir. 1976).

53. *Borse v Piece Goods Shop, Inc.*, 963 F.2d 611, 621 (3d Cir. 1992).

54. 443 N.W.2d 382, 384 (Mich. Ct. App. 1989).

55. Conn. Gen. Stat. § 31–48b (1999).

56. *Awbrey v Great Atlantic & Pacific Tea Co., Inc.*, 505 F. Supp. 604, 608–10 (N.D. Ga. 1980); *Jackson v Nationwide Credit, Inc.*, 426 S.E.2d 630 (Ga. App. 1992), *cert. denied*, 206 Ga. App. 900 (1993); *Benoit v Roche*, 657 So. 2d 574 (La. App. 1995); *Oliver v Pacific Northwest Bell Telephone Co.*, 632 P.2d 1295, 1298 (Or. App.), *rev denied*, 642 P.2d 310 (Or. 1981); *Walker v Darby*, 911 F.2d 1573 (11th Cir. 1990).

57. *Simmons v Southwestern Bell Tel. Co.*, 452 F. Supp. 392, 394 (W.D. Okla. 1978), *aff'd* 611 F.2d 342 (10th Cir. 1979).

58. *Pulla v Amoco Oil Co.*, 882 F. Supp. 836, 867 (S.D. Iowa 1994), *aff'd in part and rev'd in part on other grounds*, 72 F.3d 648 (8th Cir. 1995).

59. *Ali v Douglas Cable Communications.*, 929 F. Supp. 1362, 1382 (D.C. Kan. 1996).

60. 914 F. Supp. 97 (E.D. Pa. 1996).

61. *Stein v Davidson Hotel Co.*, 945 S.W.2d 714 (Tenn. 1997).

62. *Lyons v Norfolk & Western Railway Co.*, 163 F.3d 466 (7th Cir. 1999).

63. 41 U.S.C. § § 701 & 702.

64. *Pilkington Barnes Hind v Superior Court*, 77 Cal.Rptr.2d 596 (Call. App. 1998).

65. 41 U.S.C. § 701.

66. *Kraslawsky v Upper Deck Co.*, 65 Cal.Rptr.2d 297 (Cal. App. 1997).

67. *Poulos v Pfizer, Inc.*, 711 A.2d 688 (Conn. 1998); *Adams v Kaiser Aluminum*, 685 So.2d 269 (La. App. 1996).

68. Long, A. (1997). "Addressing the cloud over employee references: A survey of recently enacted state legislation." *William and Mary Law Review*, 39: 177–183.

69. *Pennington v Dollar Tree Stores, Inc.*, 104 F.Supp.2d 710, 715 (E.D. Ky. 2000).

70. Befort, G. (1997). "Pre-employment screening and investigation: Navigating between a rock and a hard place." *Hofstra Labor Law Journal*, 14: 365, 376.

71. *Ponticas v K.M.S. Investment*, 331 N.W.2d 907, 915 (Minn. 1983).

72. *Randi W. v Muroc Joint Unified School Dist.*, 929 P.2d 582, 595 (Cal. 1997).

73. Davis, J. (2000). Survey of developments in North Carolina and the Fourth Circuit, 1999: Potential violence to the bottom line—Expanding employer liability for acts of workplace violence. *North Carolina Law Review*, 78: 2067.

STATE WRONGFUL DISCHARGE LAWS

State	Filing Workers' Comp Claim	Filing Wage Claim	Filing Safety Violations or Refusing Unsafe Working Conditions	Summoned as Witness to Official Proceeding	Time Off to Vote	Jury Duty	Workers Political Activities Influencing Votes	Reporting Violations of any Law	Polygraph Tests	Reservist or Veteran Protection	State EEO Law	State Union Activities
Alabama	X		X			X						
Alaska	X		X		X	X			X		X	
Arizona	X		X		X	X				X	X	
Arkansas		X			X	X					X	
California[1]	X		X	X	X	X		X	X	X	X	X
Colorado					X	X					X	X
Connecticut[2]	X					X					X	
Delaware		X				X	X		X	X	X	
Florida	X		X			X				X	X	
Georgia					X					X	X	
Hawaii		X	X	X	X	X			X	X	X	X
Idaho		X					X		X	X	X	X
Illinois		X	X	X	X	X				X	X	
Indiana		X	X		X	X		X		X	X	
Iowa			X		X		X		X	X	X	
Kansas		X		X	X		X				X	
Kentucky		X		X	X	X	X			X	X	
Louisiana		X				X	X	X		X		
Maine		X	X					X		X	X	
Maryland		X	X		X			X				
Massachusetts[3]		X	X			X	X		X	X	X	X
Michigan		X	X			X	X	X	X	X	X	X
Minnesota		X	X	X	X	X		X	X	X	X	X
Mississippi							X			X	X	X

[1] California employers cannot terminate employees for disclosing the amount of their wages.

[2] Connecticut guarantees First Amendment rights in the workplace.

[3] Massachusetts employers cannot fire workers in retail establishments for refusing to work on Sunday.

State	Filing Workers' Comp Claim	Filing Wage Claim	Filing Safety Violations or Refusing Unsafe Working Conditions	Summoned as Witness to Official Proceeding	Time Off to Vote	Jury Duty	Workers Political Activities Involving Votes	Reporting Violations of any Law	Polygraph Tests	Reservist or Veteran Protection	State EEO Law	State Union Activities
Missouri	N/A	X	N/A	N/A	X	N/A	X	N/A	N/A	N/A	X	
Montana[4]	N/A	N/A	N/A	N/A	N/A	X	N/A	N/A	X	X	N/A	N/A
Nebraska			X		X	X	X		X	X	X	
Nevada			X		X		X				X	
New Hampshire		X						X			X	
New Jersey	X	X					X	X	X	X	X	
New Mexico	X	X	X		X	X	X			X	X	
New York[5]	X	X	X	X	X	X	X	X		X	X	
North Carolina	X	X		X		X	X				X	
North Dakota		X				X				X	X	
Ohio[6]	X	X			X	X	X			X	X	
Oklahoma	X				X	X				X	X	
Oregon	X	X	X	X		X	X		X	X	X	X
Pennsylvania	X	X		X		X		X	X		X	X
Rhode Island		X				X	X		X	X	X	X
South Carolina	X	X	X	X		X	X				X	
South Dakota		X			X	X	X			X	X	X
Tennessee			X	X	X	X	X				X	
Texas	X			X	X	X				X	X	
Utah			X	X	X		X			X	X	X
Vermont		X	X			X			X	X	X	X
Virginia	X		X			X				X		
Washington		X	X	X					X	X	X	
West Virginia		X				X	X		X	X	X	X
Wisconsin	X	X		X	X	X	X		X	X	X	X
Wyoming	X	X	X		X	X	X				X	X

[4]Montana has a just cause discharge statute.

[5]New York employers cannot require employees to take psychological stress tests or to be finger printed.

[6]Ohio employers cannot fire an employee because of a court order to withhold child support payments for wages.

Wage, Hour, and Related Statutes

LEARNING OBJECTIVES

- ☐ Describe the basic provisions of the Fair Labor Standards Act.
- ☐ Explain the federal limitations on the use of child labor.
- ☐ Distinguish between exempt and nonexempt employees under the Fair Labor Standards Act.
- ☐ Describe who is required to pay the prevailing wage under the Davis-Bacon, Walsh-Healy, and McNamara-O'Hara Service Contract Acts.
- ☐ Explain the circumstances under which an employer has a legal obligation to inform employees of plant closings or major layoffs.
- ☐ Discuss the conditions under which employers are prohibited from using polygraph testing in employment.

OPENING SCENARIO

Bob DeWright had worked in the blueprinting department at Swartzwelder's Engineering and Architectural Supply for several years. Bob's principal duties involved taking customer orders, producing blueprints to customers' specifications, performing routine maintenance on the machines, and keeping the work area clean. As a blueprint machine operator, Bob worked five days per week from 8 A.M. to 5 P.M. with one hour off for lunch. Bob's rate of pay was $10 per hour.

In December, the owner, Mr. Swartzwelder, informed Bob that in recognition of his hard work and loyalty, he was to be promoted. Effective immediately, Bob was the executive vice president of reprographic services with a monthly salary of $1,900.

Bob quickly discovered that his new duties as executive vice president included taking customer orders, producing blueprints to customers' specifications, performing routine maintenance on the machines, and keeping the work area clean. However, Bob now worked six days per week and usually ten hours per day. Bob realized that if he worked by *his old hourly rate, he would be making roughly $2,800 per month (taking overtime into account) instead of the $1,900 he currently made. Armed with this knowledge, Bob confronted Mr. Swartzwelder and asked to be paid overtime. Mr. Swartzwelder was quick to inform Bob that since he was promoted to management, he was not entitled to overtime payments. Upset by this response, Bob threatened to file a complaint with the Wage and Hour Division (WHD) of the Department of Labor. Shortly thereafter, Mr. Swartzwelder fired Bob for his poor attitude and lack of loyalty. In a moment of anger, Mr. Swartzwelder told Bob, "Go ahead and whine to the Wage people. I know the law and it's on my side in this matter!"*

THE FAIR LABOR STANDARDS ACT

The Fair Labor Standards Act (FLSA) is one of the oldest statutes regulating the private sector workplace. Enacted in 1938 as part of President Franklin Roosevelt's New Deal, the FLSA was intended to lessen the effects of the Great Depression by creating an incentive for businesses to hire more employees. This was to be accomplished by creating a minimum wage, imposing a penalty for working any employee beyond forty hours per week, and placing limitations on the use of child labor (see Exhibit 8-1). The Act's method for encouraging employers to hire more workers was quite simple. For each hour worked in excess of forty during a 168-consecutive-hour work week, the employer would have to pay the employee an additional 50 percent of the base pay rate for overtime. **Overtime** is legally defined as any hours worked in excess of forty during a 168-consecutive

---

■ **EXHIBIT 8-1**

MAJOR PROVISIONS OF THE FAIR LABOR STANDARDS ACT

- ■ Minimum Wage
  - * $5.15 (since September 1, 1997)
  - * 90-calendar day $4.25 youth minimum wage

Overtime
  - * Time and one-half for each hour worked in excess of 40 during a 168-consecutive-hour work week

- ■ Child Labor
  - * 16- and 17-year-old workers prohibited from working hazardous jobs
  - * 14- and 15-year-old workers prohibited from working in hazardous jobs and limited in the number of hours they may work per day and per week

SOURCE: U.S. Employment Standards Administration (1999). *Fair Labor Standards Act Employee/Employer Advisor.* http://www.dol.gov/elaws/flsa.htm

hour work week.[1] Additionally, the FLSA contained provisions entitling workers to receive a minimum hourly wage set by the federal government. In 1938, the first minimum wage was $0.25. As of September 1, 1997, the minimum wage had risen to $5.15.[2]

To demonstrate how the FLSA was intended to increase employment, we will examine its effect on payroll at the time of its enactment in 1938. Assume, on average, an employer with twenty employees has been working them sixty hours per week at an hourly rate of pay of $0.25. Prior to the FLSA, this hourly rate of pay would remain constant regardless of the number of hours worked. So, at the end of the week, the employer would pay the employees $15 (60 hours × $0.25/hour) each, for a total payroll of $300 ($15 weekly wage × 20 employees). Following the enactment of the FLSA, each employee would have to be paid $17.50 each ($0.25 × 40 hours + $.375 × 20 hours of overtime) for a total payroll of $350. Thus, as a result of the FLSA, payroll expenses increased by nearly 17 percent with no change in productivity. An employer could avoid this penalty by simply reducing the amount of overtime worked, but there would not be enough man hours to complete the scheduled work. If the employees were merely given forty hour work weeks, production would be reduced by 33 percent (800 hours compared to the 1,200 hours previously worked). Instead, the easiest method to reduce the amount of overtime would be to increase the size of the workforce—hire more employees. By hiring ten more workers, the employer would be able to accomplish 1,200 man-hours of work for $300 ($10 weekly wage (× 30 employees) as opposed to $350 if twenty employees had to work overtime ($0.25 × 40 hours + $.375 × 20 hours of overtime). This was how the FLSA would work—in theory. However, this simple solution may no longer be applicable in the twenty-first century. One must remember that the 1930s were simpler times, and workers did not have the mandated or voluntary benefits that they have now come to expect (i.e., pensions, health insurance, life insurance, paid vacations, paid sick leave, etc.). The FLSA's incentive to hire more employees is presently diminished because providing benefits to new hires (which usually is 70 percent of base pay)[3] is greater than the overtime penalty (50 percent of the base pay rate).

COVERED EMPLOYERS AND EMPLOYEES

Private sector enterprises with an annual gross volume of sales of $500,000 or more are covered under the FLSA.[4] However, even when the employer is not covered under the FLSA, individual employees may be covered. Such covered employees include those who produce, receive, ship, transport, or load goods that are moving in interstate commerce.[5] Additionally, individual employees may be protected under the Act if their work entails preparing, handling, or transmitting information or documents in interstate trade.[6] Under such broad coverage, it would be difficult to find an employee who is not entitled to protection under the FLSA, and consequently an employer who is not required to comply with its provisions.

MINIMUM WAGE

Currently, the FLSA requires a minimum wage of at least $5.15 per hour. This hourly rate becomes the base by which all wage and hour claims are made. To determine whether an employer is in compliance, the employee's weekly gross pay is divided by the number of hours worked. Considering overtime compensation in the calculations, the hourly rate must equal at least the federal minimum wage. For example, if an employee is covered by the FLSA and the employer is paying a flat salary of $250 per week, regardless of the hours worked, compliance would be based on this $5.15 per hour minimum wage rate.

Suppose our employee worked consistently fifty hours per week. Would the employer be in compliance with the FLSA? The determination would be based on forty hours at $5.15 ($206) and ten hours of overtime at $7.725 ($77.25) for a total of $283.25. Since the employee received only $250 per week, but was entitled to $283.25 per week, the employer is not in compliance. The employer must make up the difference of $33.25 per week.

Human resource (HR) professionals must be aware that when state minimum wage requirements exceed the federal minimum wage, the higher wage must be paid (refer to Exhibit 8-2). For example, in California, the state minimum wage is $6.75 (effective January 1, 2002; until then, the minimum wage in California is $6.25). Consequently, all California employers must pay employees at least $6.75 rather than the $5.15 federal hourly minimum wage. If our employee in the previous example was working in California, the employer would be responsible for compensating the employee at a rate of $371.25 for a fifty-hour work week, forty hours at $6.75, or $270, plus ten hours at $10.125 (1.5 × $6.75), or $101.25.

NONEXEMPT EMPLOYEES.   Having discussed the FLSA's general minimum wage and overtime requirements, it is necessary to identify those employees for whom the FLSA applies and those for whom it does not. When dealing with the FLSA, the two important classifications of employees are *exempt employees* and *nonexempt employees*. A **nonexempt employee** is any employee who is entitled to protection under the FLSA's minimum wage and overtime provisions. Failure to provide minimum wages and overtime payments for nonexempt employees will result in a FLSA violation.

Because the FLSA is an all-encompassing act intended by Congress to cast the broadest coverage possible, it is easier to identify the employee classifications that it does not cover than to list all those that it does cover. Therefore, the FLSA does not list those occupational classifications that are nonexempt; it specifies only the exempt classifications.

EXEMPT EMPLOYEES.   **Exempt employees** are those employees specifically excluded from the FLSA's protection for minimum wage and overtime. The Act specifically excludes some employees on the basis of their employer. Individuals employed by the federal government are excluded, as are individuals employed

STATE MINIMUM WAGES AS OF JANUARY 1, 2001*

States, Etc. with Minimum Wages Higher than Federal Minimum Wage	Basic Minimum Wage Rate
Alaska	$5.65
California	$6.75
Connecticut	$6.70
Delaware	$6.15
District of Columbia	$6.15
Hawaii	$5.25
Massachusetts	$6.75
Oregon	$6.50
Rhode Island	$6.15
Vermont	$5.75
Washington	$6.75

States with Minimum Wages Lower than Federal Minimum Wage*	Basic Minimum Wage Rate
Georgia	$3.25
Kansas	$2.65
New Mexico	$4.25
Ohio	$4.25
Texas	$3.35
Wyoming	$1.60

* Applies to employers not covered under FLSA.

Note: Alabama, Arizona, Florida, Louisiana, Mississippi, South Carolina, and Tennessee do not have state minimum wage laws. All other states have minimum wages that are the same as the federal minimum wage.

SOURCE: U.S. Department of Labor. Minimum Wage Laws in the States. **http://www.dol.gov/dol/esa/public/minwage/america.htm**

by the United States Postal Service.[7] State employees not subject to state civil service laws, public elected officials, or members of an elected official's personal staff are not covered by the FLSA.[8]

Beyond the exemption of certain government employees, the FLSA provides exemptions from minimum wage *and* overtime payments as well as partial exemptions from overtime only. Although a comprehensive list of these exemptions is provided in Exhibits 8-3 and 8-4, our discussion will focus on the five most common exemptions: *bona fide* executives, *bona fide* administrative employees, *bona fide* professionals, outside sales personnel, and computer professionals.

Bona Fide *Executives.* It is important to note that an employee's title is meaningless when establishing *bona fide* executive status or any other exemption category. The determination is based on explicit conditions in the *Code of Federal*

■ EXHIBIT 8-3

EMPLOYEES EXEMPT FROM MINIMUM WAGE AND OVERTIME UNDER THE FLSA

- Administrative personnel
- Babysitters on a casual basis
- *Bona fide* executives
- Commissioned sales employees
- Companions for the elderly
- Computer professionals paid at least $27.63 per hour
- Farm workers
- Federal criminal investigators
- Fishing employees
- Home workers making wreaths
- Newspaper delivery employees
- Newspaper employees of limited circulation newspapers
- Professionals (including academic or administrative personnel and teachers in elementary or secondary schools)
- Salesmen, parts men, and mechanics employed by automobile dealerships
- Seamen on other than American vessels
- Employees of seasonal and recreational establishments
- Switchboard operators

SOURCE: 29 U.S.C. § 213.

Regulations.[9] To be an executive/manager, the individual's primary duties must consist of the management of his or her area of the organization. In fact, the manager cannot spend more than 20 percent of time in nonmanagement activities. In retail or service organizations, managers may not spend more than 40 percent of time in nonmanagement activities. Additionally, the manager must regularly direct the work of two or more employees and have the authority to hire, promote, or fire (or recommend such actions) these employees. The manager must also receive a salary of at least $345 per week.[10]

To demonstrate why these requirements are important when assessing "exempt" employee status, let's return to our opening scenario. If Bob is a *bona fide* executive, as his new title implies, he is not entitled to minimum wage and overtime payments. However, the Wage and Hour Division (WHD) does not rely on titles; it relies on the criteria mentioned previously. In order to determine whether Bob is an exempt employee, the WHD investigator will have to analyze his work duties according to the stated standard. What percentage of Bob's time is spent in nonmanagement activities? Actually, 100 percent; he performs no

■ **EXHIBIT 8-4**

EMPLOYEES EXEMPT FROM OVERTIME UNDER THE FLSA

- Aircraft salespeople
- Airline employe
- Amusement/recreational employees in national parks/forests/ Wildlife Refuge System
- Boat salespeople
- Buyers of agricultural products
- Country elevator workers (rural)
- Domestic employees who live-in
- Farm implement salespeople
- Firefighters working in small (less than 5 firefighters) public fire departments
- Forestry employees of small (less than 9 employees) firms
- Fruit and vegetable transportation employees
- House parents in nonprofit educational institutions
- Livestock auction workers
- Local delivery drivers and drivers' helpers
- Lumber operations employees of small (less than 9 employees) firms
- Motion picture theater employees
- Police officers working in small (less than 5 officers) public police departments
- Radio station employees in small markets
- Railroad employees
- Seamen on American vessels
- Sugar processing employees
- Taxicab drivers
- Television station employees in small markets
- Truck and trailer salespeople

SOURCE: 29 U.S.C. § 213.

management duties. This alone would be sufficient to establish that Bob is not a *bona fide* executive. How many employees does Bob supervise? The answer is none, less than the minimum of two required. Having no employees under his charge would preclude further evaluation on whether Bob had the authority to hire, fire, or promote his subordinates (or at least make such recommendations). Only Bob's salary would be in compliance with the stated requirements. Therefore, based on this analysis and even though his job title is executive vice president of reprographic services, Bob is *not* a *bona fide* executive/manager under the

FLSA. As a direct consequence of this determination, Bob *is not* exempt from the FLSA's minimum wage and overtime requirements. Thus, Mr. Swartzwelder would have to pay the overtime compensation that Bob had accrued.

Bona Fide *Administrative Employees.* The WHD has established standards for determining which employees are legitimately exempted from the FLSA as *bona fide* administrators. To be classified as a *bona fide* administrator, an employee's work must be related to the management policies or general business operations of the employer or the employer's customers. In the case of educational institutions, the employee's duties must be tied to the administration of the educational establishment or institution. Whether in an educational institution or other organization, the "administrator" must customarily and regularly exercise discretion and independent judgment.[11] Similar to *bona fide* executives, *bona fide* administrators cannot spend more than 20 percent of work hours in nonadministrative activities. Administrative personnel in retail or service establishments may not spend more than 40 percent of their time in nonadminstrative activities. Administrative employees must be compensated on a salary or fee basis at a rate of not less than $345 per week.

Bona Fide *Professionals.* The term "employee employed in a *bona fide* profession" applies to any employee whose primary job responsibilities are tied to performing work:

1. Requiring knowledge of an advance type in a field of science or learning customarily acquired by a prolonged course of specialized intellectual instruction and study, as distinguished from a general academic education and from an apprenticeship, and from training in the performance of routine mental, manual, or physical processes.

2. That is original and creative in character in a recognized field of artistic endeavor (as opposed to work which can be produced by a person endowed with general manual or intellectual ability and training), and the result of which depends primarily on the invention, imagination, or talent of the employee.

3. Teaching, tutoring, instructing, or lecturing in the activity of imparting knowledge and who is employed and engaged in this activity as a teacher in the school system or educational establishment or institution by which he is employed.

4. That requires theoretical and practical application of highly-specialized knowledge in computer systems analysis, programming, and software engineering, and who is employed and engaged in these activities as a computer systems analyst, computer programmer, software engineer, or other similarly skilled worker in the computer software field.[12]

Not surprisingly, the work professionals perform requires the consistent exercise of discretion and judgment in its performance. Primary job duties of *bona fide* professionals also tend to be intellectual in nature. A *bona fide* professional under the FSLA cannot devote more than 20 percent of work time to nonprofessional activities (nonintellectual or creative work), and these professionals must be compensated on a salary or fee basis at a rate of not less than $345 per week.

Outside Sales Personnel.   Outside sales personnel are employees who are employed for the purpose of customarily making sales away from the employer's place of employment.[13] As with the other exempted classifications, persons engaged in outside sales cannot spend more than 20 percent of work hours in non-sales activities.[14]

Computer Professionals.   A computer professional is any employee who is employed as a computer systems analyst, computer programmer, software engineer, or other similarly computer-skilled worker.[15] As in the previous categories, the employee's title is not sufficient to establish this. The employee's primary duties must involve the application of systems analysis techniques and procedures including consulting with users to determine hardware, software, or system functional specifications. Additionally, an employee who designs, develops, documents, tests, or modifies computer systems or programs would most likely be a computer professional under the FLSA.[16] A person hired for the simple task of data entry on a computer would not be a computer professional regardless of the title possessed.

In addition to performing the previously mentioned job duties, the employee must be compensated at a rate of at least $27.63 an hour in order to be a *bona fide* computer professional.[17]

OTHER MINIMUM WAGE ISSUES

Although the FLSA is primarily known for establishing the federal minimum wage, it also includes other important minimum wage-related provisions. Most notable are provisions related to youth subminimum wage, full-time student workers subminimum wage, tipped employee minimum wage, and compensatory time.

YOUTH SUBMINIMUM WAGE.   Newly hired employees who are less than twenty years old may be paid a subminimum wage during their first ninety consecutive calendar days of employment. This subminimum wage is established at a rate which is not less than $4.25 an hour. As a safeguard against potential abuse, employers are prohibited from terminating employees at the conclusion of the ninety-day period for the purpose of hiring another subminimum wage employee to keep wages at the $4.25 level. An employer cannot fire an employee who has completed the ninety-day subminimum wage period to avoid paying him or her the standard federal minimum wage ($5.15 per hour).

FULL-TIME STUDENT WORKERS SUBMINIMUM WAGE.   Full-time student workers are another category of workers that can be paid a subminimum wage. A full-time student worker is anyone, regardless of age, who meets the requirements of a full-time student at the institution of higher education that employs him or her.[18] The subminimum wage authorized by the Secretary of Labor for full-time students is an amount not less than 85 percent of the current national minimum wage. Currently, this amount is $4.38 per hour ($5.15 × .85).[19]

In order to obtain authorization to pay the subminimum wage to full-time student workers, the college or university must apply for a certificate with the appropriate regional office of the Wage and Hour Division (WHD) of the Department of Labor. The purpose of the application is to ensure that the institution of higher education is not using student workers for the purpose of reducing full-time employment opportunities for other (nonsubminimum wage) workers.[20] For example, the WHD is unlikely to issue a college a certificate if the purpose of the application is to replace two full-time secretaries with four part-time student workers.

One final, and somewhat peculiar, stipulation is attached to the use of full-time student workers. There are specific restrictions on the amount of time they are authorized to work per week. Odd as it may sound, the WHD has interpreted the FLSA to restrict the employment of full-time students of institutions of higher education to be the same as those for full-time students who are at least fourteen years of age.[21] Therefore, full-time college students are held to the same total weekly worker hours as fourteen- to sixteen-year-olds in the FLSA's child labor provisions. Full-time students will not be permitted to work at subminimum wages for more than eight hours per day nor more than forty hours per week when school is not in session.[22] When school is in session, full-time students are limited to only twenty hours per week at the subminimum wage.[23] The twenty-hours-per-week limitation does not apply on days that are full-day school holidays, although the eight-hour-per-day restriction still applies.[24]

TIPPED EMPLOYEES MINIMUM WAGE. Some employees are treated differently under the FLSA because of the peculiar nature of compensation within their industries, such as tipped employees. Employers, particularly those in the hotel and restaurant industries, who employ tipped employees (e.g., waiters and waitresses) may credit a certain amount of the tips received against the employer's minimum wage obligation when certain conditions are met. The FLSA requires an employer to pay a tipped employee not less than $2.13 an hour in wages.[25] In the event an employee's tips combined with the employer's cash wage of $2.13 an hour does not equal the minimum hourly wage, the employer must make up the difference.[26]

To illustrate this point, assume a waiter works for a restaurant forty hours per week. The employer pays the waiter the $2.13-an-hour wages prescribed by the FLSA, for a total of $85.20. If the employee only makes $100 in tips for the week, the employer must make up the difference between the sum of what the employee actually made in tips plus the employer's $2.13-per-hour contribution ($185.20) and the $206 an hour the waiter would have received had he been paid at the $5.15 minimum hourly rate. In this example, the waiter was actually compensated $185.20 ($100 in tips and $85.20 by the employer). Had he been paid the minimum wage, he would have received $206. Therefore, the employer must make up the difference of $20.80 ($206.00 − $185.20).

COMPENSATORY TIME.   Employees of a public sector (governmental) employer may receive compensatory time. **Compensatory time**, not to be confused with "compensable time," is time off in lieu of overtime compensation. However, this compensatory time off must be calculated at a rate not less than one and one-half hours for each hour of employment for which overtime compensation would have been paid.[27] For example, if a government employee had worked 46 hours in a 168-consecutive-hour work week, that employee would be entitled to 9 hours of compensatory time (6 hours over 40 times 1½).

Private sector employers may also use compensatory time to compensate employees for overtime with one important catch. Whereas public sector employees may accrue compensatory time, private sector employees may not. The compensatory time must be used within the pay period it was accrued. Specifically, public employers may carry compensatory time over from one period to another, but private employers may not. For employees who are private sector employees and are paid on a weekly basis, compensatory time is not a viable option. It would have to be used in the same week in which it was accrued.

COMPENSABLE TIME.   **Compensable time** refers to the difference between situations in which employees are entitled to be paid for their time and when they are not. The FLSA requires nonexempt employees be paid for all hours worked, but what about hours in which the employee is required to be at the place of work although not actually performing work? Employees are not required to be compensated during meal breaks when they are not performing work-related services for their employers,[28] but if they have to remain at their work stations and perform work-related tasks, they must be compensated. For example, a receptionist who eats lunch at her desk while answering the company's telephones is entitled to compensation.

Arriving to Work Early.   When employees are required to report to work prior to the shift period or scheduled work period in order to prepare for the day's activities, that is compensable time. Assume an employer requires employees to be present at the workplace fifteen minutes prior to "clocking in" for the purpose of performing preventive maintenance checks on equipment. Because such activity is an integral part of the job to which the employee is assigned, the employee must be compensated for those fifteen minutes.[29] The employer may even be responsible for work that is not required of the employee but is performed voluntarily. If an employee arrives early and begins performing normal work-related duties before "clocking in," that time is compensable time.[30] For HR professionals, the solution to the dilemma is simple. Either have the employees clock in when performing job-related work, or do not permit them to perform such work until the scheduled time period.

Break and Rest Periods.   There is still considerable debate over whether or not break and rest periods are compensable time. The Wage and Hour Division of the Department of Labor contends that only break periods of twenty minutes or longer are noncompensable.[31] For any period less than twenty minutes, the employee must be paid. The circuit courts are split on this matter. As a matter of convention, most employers pay employees while they are on break or rest periods. Although arguably, employees are serving their own interests while on break and not those of employers. Making such periods technically nonwork times makes them noncompensable.[32]

Training Periods. Mandated or compulsory training is any training in which the employee risks termination if they do not attend. Naturally, all mandatory training periods are compensable time. The employee has no choice in being present. Additionally, time spent in compulsory training can be accrued when calculating overtime. For example, an employer requires employees to attend safety training for one hour after the conclusion of their scheduled eight-hour shifts for the next five days. Assuming the training is initiated at the beginning of each employee's 168-consecutive-hour work week, each employee would be entitled to five hours of overtime (the five eight-hour shifts plus five one-hour training sessions for a total of forty-five compensable hours).

Training in which the employee voluntarily engages is usually not compensable. As an example, as part of an employee's career planning, she is told she must earn an M.B.A. degree in order to advance in the organization. Because the employee enrolls in night courses, she is pursuing additional training for her own interests or personal advancement. Time spent in the M.B.A. program would not be compensable time.

Portal to Portal Time. Under normal circumstances, travel time to and from the place of employment is not compensable.[33] Under the 1947 amendment to the FLSA, the so-called Portal to Portal Act, unless the travel time is specifically related to company business, the employer is not required to pay the employee. To distinguish compensable travel time from noncompensable travel time, assume an employee has a one-hour commute to work each morning and a one-hour commute home each evening. This travel to and from work is noncompensable. Now, assume the employee in question is a nonexempt employee. One morning after arriving at his place of employment, a generator repair business, the employee is dispatched to a customer located one hour away from the employer's office. This time, the travel is work related, and consequently, the one-hour travel time to the customer and the one-hour travel time back to the employer's office are compensable. Any travel on company business is compensable time for nonexempt employees.

CHILD LABOR LIMITATIONS

Another provision of the FLSA places limitations on an employer's use of child labor. Employers may assign employees who are eighteen years or older to any position in the workplace, to work at any time, and in virtually any context (provided the working conditions are in compliance with the Occupational Safety and Health Act; refer to Chapter 10). However, for applicants or employees under age eighteen, the FLSA imposes restrictions on work times and working

■ EXHIBIT 8-5

17 HAZARDOUS JOBS IDENTIFIED BY THE SECRETARY OF LABOR THAT ARE OFF LIMITS TO TEENS YOUNGER THAN 18

- Manufacturing or storing explosives
- Driving a motor vehicle and being an outside helper on a motor vehicle
- Coal mining
- Logging and saw milling
- Power-driven wood-working machines
- Exposure to radioactive substances and to ionizing radiations
- Power-driven hoisting equipment
- Power-driven metal-forming, punching, and shearing machines
- Mining, other than coal mining
- Meat packing or processing (including power-driven meat slicing machines)
- Power-driven bakery machines
- Power-driven paper-products machines
- Manufacturing brick, tile, and related products
- Power-driven circular saws, band saws, and guillotine shears
- Wrecking, demolition, and ship-breaking operations
- Roofing operations
- Excavation operations

SOURCE: 29 C.F.R § 570.33.

conditions. Workers sixteen and seventeen years old may work for unlimited hours but only in nonhazardous jobs.[34] Hazardous jobs are listed in Exhibit 8-5 and cannot be assigned to *any* individual younger than eighteen years of age.[35]

Workers between fourteen and fifteen years of age have further restrictions on both the hours that can be worked and the time of day that such work may occur. These allowable working times are also tied to the school year. Workers in the fourteen- to fifteen-year-old age bracket are permitted to work outside school in nonmanufacturing, nonmining, and nonhazardous jobs within specific hourly and time limits depending upon when schools are in session. For example, on school days, fourteen- and fifteen-year-olds are limited to working no more than three hours per day and may only work during a time frame between 7 A.M. and 7 P.M.[36] Furthermore, the total number of hours that can be worked in a school week is capped at fifteen.[37]

During nonschool days, the fourteen- or fifteen-year-old employees may work up to eight hours per day, and during a nonschool week, they may accrue up to forty total hours.[38] During the period from June 1 to Labor Day, the time frame during which fourteen- and fifteen-year-olds may work is expanded to the period 7 A.M. to 9 P.M.[39] Again, fourteen-and fifteen-year-olds are excluded from hazardous jobs even during the summer months.

RECORD KEEPING

The most important function of the HR department, with regard to the FLSA, is keeping the necessary documentation to substantiate the employer's good faith effort to comply with the Act's provisions. In the event of an investigation by the WHD, the employer is responsible for making payroll records available within seventy-two hours.[40] In the event of such a request, the employer must make all records stipulated in Exhibit 8-6 available for inspection and transcription by the WHD administrator investigating the complaint.[41]

REMEDIES AND PENALTIES

When an employer has failed to pay employees the minimum wage or overtime due under the FLSA, the employer is liable for paying *all affected employees* the amount of unpaid minimum wages or unpaid overtime compensation.[42] Returning to our opening scenario, Bob is due the overtime that Mr. Swartzwelder

■ EXHIBIT 8-6

RECORD KEEPING REQUIREMENTS UNDER THE **FLSA**

- ■ Employee's full name and social security number
- ■ Address, including zip code
- ■ Birth date, if younger than 19
- ■ Sex and occupation
- ■ Time and day of week when employee's work week begins
- ■ Hours worked each day
- ■ Total hours worked each work week
- ■ Basis on which employee's wages are paid (e.g., "$6 an hour," "$220 a week," "piecework")
- ■ Regular hourly pay rate
- ■ Total daily or weekly straight-time earnings
- ■ Total overtime earnings for the work week
- ■ All additions to or deductions from the employee's wages
- ■ Total wages paid each pay period
- ■ Date of payment and the pay period covered by the payment

SOURCE: 29 C.F.R Part 516.

failed to pay him. If Bob worked sixty hours per week for three months at $1,900 per month, Mr. Swartzwelder would have to pay him approximately $2,700. This is the difference between his monthly salary of $1,900 and his projected monthly wage at his old hourly rate ($10 per hour) and overtime rate ($15 per hour for every hour worked in excess of forty during the work week). If Bob had indeed worked sixty hours per week for a twelve-week period (three months) he would have earned a total of $8,400 instead of the $5,700 paid him by Mr. Swartzwelder.

The employer would also be responsible for compensating all employees (even the ones who are no longer current employees) for all unpaid minimum wages or overtime that they were not paid, even though they did not file a complaint. When investigating FSLA complaints, the WHD will examine all of the employer's payroll records, and any employee who was not paid overtime or minimum wage is entitled to the difference. The critical point to remember is that the WHD inspects all payroll records of the employer, not just those of the complaining party.

The FLSA, like most federal legislation, contains a whistleblower clause.[43] Therefore, the employer may not take retaliatory action against an employee who has filed an FSLA complaint. In the event that an employer has taken retaliatory action against an employee, as Bob's employer did, the employee may be entitled to reinstatement, in addition to the payment of wages lost and an additional equal amount as liquidated damages.[44]

In situations in which the employer has been judged to have willfully and knowingly violated the FLSA's minimum wage and overtime provisions, additional penalties may be imposed. In circumstances involving repeated and willful violations, an employer may be assessed a fine of up to $1,000 per violation.[45] Among the factors used by the WHD when determining whether the employer has willfully violated the FLSA are:

1. Good faith efforts to comply with the Act.
2. The employer's explanation for the violations.
3. The employer's previous history of violations.
4. The employer's commitment to future compliance.
5. The interval between violations.
6. The number of employees affected by the violation.
7. Whether there is any pattern to the violations.[46]

MYTHS ABOUT THE FLSA

Although the FLSA provides very real compensation requirements, there are limitations to its coverage that are often misunderstood. And, over the years, many misconceptions have developed, particularly among employees. Beyond the minimum wage, overtime, and child labor limitations previously discussed, the FLSA imposes no other requirements on covered employers. Because there

■ **EXHIBIT 8-7**

■ Vacation, holiday, severance, or sick pay

■ Meal or rest periods, holidays off, or vacations

■ Premium pay for weekend or holiday work

■ Pay raises or fringe benefits

■ A discharge notice, reason for discharge, or immediate payment of final wages to terminated employees

is so much misunderstanding of the requirements mandated by the FLSA, some compensation-related benefits or prohibitions that the Act *does not* require are listed in Exhibit 8-7.

Interestingly, the FLSA does not place any obligation on employers to provide vacation, holiday, severance, or sick pay. These are strictly at the discretion of the employer, unless mandated by state law. Neither does the FLSA contain any provision requiring an employer to furnish employees with meal or rest periods, holidays off, or vacations, whether paid or unpaid. Additionally, employers are not obligated under the FLSA to provide premium pay for weekend, night, or holiday work. No portion of the Act compels employers to offer pay raises or fringe benefits. Finally, the FLSA does not mandate any obligation to provide terminated employees with a discharge notice, reason for discharge, or immediate payment of final wages. Many employees believe they must be paid in full all accrued wages immediately upon discharge. This is not true, unless required under state law or local ordinance. In most instances involving employee termination, final payment may be made at the next normally scheduled pay period.

OTHER FEDERAL COMPENSATION LAWS

Other federal laws require certain employers to provide either specific levels of compensation, dictate particular overtime requirements, or both. However, these statutes apply only to a select group of employers—those who hold federal contracts or subcontracts. As a condition for eligibility for the contract in question, the employer agrees to pay the compensation stipulated under the applicable statute.

DAVIS-BACON ACT OF 1931

The Davis-Bacon Act covers any employer who holds a federal construction contract in excess of $2,000.[47] This would apply to any employer contracted to assist in the construction of public buildings or public works of the United States government or any employer who is subcontracted by a prime contractor performing similar work. It also covers employers who are contracted or subcontracted to provide alterations and/or repairs (including painting and decorating) to existing federal buildings.

The primary requirement under the Davis-Bacon Act is that covered employers must pay their employees the prevailing wage for the geographic area in which the work is being performed. The **prevailing wage** is the minimum wage established for each class of workers as determined by the Secretary of Labor. This prevailing, or minimum, wage is invariably the union scale for the geographic area in question.

WALSH-HEALY ACT OF 1936

Originally entitled the Public Contracts Act, the Walsh-Healy Act applies to contractors and subcontractors who hold federal contracts or subcontracts for the manufacture or furnishing of materials, supplies, articles, and equipment in any amount exceeding $10,000.[48] Like the Davis-Bacon Act, the Walsh-Healy Act requires covered employers to pay employees the prevailing minimum wage as determined by the Secretary of Labor. At one time, this statute even required affected employers to pay overtime for any hours worked in excess of eight in any twenty-four-hour period. However, a 1985 amendment[49] eliminated this requirement.

McNAMARA-O'HARA SERVICE CONTRACT ACT OF 1965

The McNamara-O'Hara Service Contract Act applies to contractors or subcontractors who provide services in excess of $2,500 to the United States government. Like the preceding statutes, the Service Contract Act requires covered employers to pay the prevailing wage for service employees for the geographic area in which the services are provided.[50] As with the previous acts, this prevailing wage is determined by the Secretary of Labor and is usually based on the union scale for service workers in the area where the services are contracted.

Unlike the Davis-Bacon and Walsh-Healy Acts, the Service Contract Act contains two additional requirements. First, this statute contains a provision specifying that the covered employers must provide fringe benefits to service employees comparable to the prevailing benefits for that class of workers in the geographic region. Again, these benefits are usually derived from the benefits typical in the collective bargaining agreements of union services workers in the area. Second, there is a provision that no part of the services covered under the statute will be performed in buildings or surroundings or under working conditions which are unsanitary or hazardous to the health or safety of service employees engaged in furnishing the services.[51]

OTHER STATUTES ENFORCED BY THE WAGE AND HOUR DIVISION

The Wage and Hour Division is the enforcement agency for at least two other statutes that may have an impact on the HR department: the Worker Adjustment and Retraining Notification Act (WARN) and the Employee Polygraph Protection Act (EPPA), both of which were enacted in 1988. WARN imposes notification requirements on employers in the event of plant closings or mass layoffs. The EPPA places restrictions on the use of lie detectors in preemployment screening for certain organizations.

WORKER ADJUSTMENT AND RETRAINING NOTIFICATION ACT OF 1988

The Worker Adjustment and Retraining Notification Act applies to any business enterprise that employs one hundred or more employees, excluding part-time employees, or one hundred or more employees who in the aggregate work at least four thousand hours per week, exclusive of hours of overtime.[52] Covered employers are required to provide a sixty-day written notice to employees in the event of a plant closing or mass layoff. No employees may be laid off until the end of this sixty-day period following the written notice. In addition to this employee notification requirement, the employer must notify the state dislocated worker unit (designated under Title III of the Job Training Partnership Act).[53] A written sixty-day notice must also be given to the chief elected official of the unit of local government to which the employer pays the highest taxes.[54]

For the purpose of WARN, the term **plant closing** means the permanent or temporary shutdown of a single site of employment or one or more facilities or operating units within a single site of employment, provided that the shutdown results in an employment loss of fifty or more employees (excluding part-time employees) at the single site during any thirty-day period.[55]

Assume a company employs two hundred workers at two plants. Due to financial demands, one plant employing seventy workers will be closed permanently. Since the closing involved fifty or more full-time employees, the written sixty-day notification would have to be given. If, on the other hand, the closing plant only employed thirty-five employees, WARN's notification provisions would not apply. Be cautious, as there may be state laws that would impose additional requirements to provide notification. HR professionals are responsible for knowing state laws that relate to plant closings as well.

A **mass layoff** occurs when a reduction in force is not the result of a plant closing but involves at least one-third (33 percent) of the employees (excluding part-time employees), *and* at least fifty employees are laid off for at least a thirty-day period. Under this provision, an employer with one hundred twenty full-time employees that had to lay off one-third of its employees would not be required to provide the sixty-day notification. The employer would be covered under WARN (more than one hundred workers were employed), and at least one-third of the workforce was laid off. But this would require that only forty employees be laid off which is ten short of the fifty established in the Act to meet the definition of *mass layoff.*

There is one more circumstance under which a *mass layoff* would be established. In any instance in which at least five hundred employees (excluding any part-time employees) are laid off, regardless of the percentage of the workforce, a mass layoff is considered to have occurred, and the employer is required to provide a sixty-day notice. Therefore, a plant employing two thousand workers would be required to provide notice if it laid off five hundred employees within a thirty-day period, even though this would result in only a 25 percent reduction in force (a proportion less than the 33 percent specified for smaller employers).

An exception to the sixty-day notification is permitted when the closing or layoff is the result of the relocation or consolidation of part or all of the business. However, prior to the closing or layoff, the employer must offer to transfer the affected employees to a different site of employment within a reasonable commuting distance. Furthermore, such transfers cannot result in more than a six-month break in employment.[56] The employer is not required to give notice when it offers to transfer employees to any other site of employment regardless of distance provided that there is no more than a six-month break in employment and that the employee accepts within thirty days of the offer or by the date of the closing or layoff, whichever is later.[57]

To illustrate this point, assume a plant was to be closed on April 1, 2001, and an employee was given the option to transfer to another plant on March 15, 2001. That employee would have until April 14, 2001, to accept or reject the transfer offer. Regardless of the employee's decision, the employer would not have to give a sixty-day notice of the plant closure.

The sixty-day notification period may also be reduced under circumstances that necessitate a plant closing or mass layoff resulting from business circumstances that were not reasonably foreseeable to afford the sixty-day notification. For example, no notice would be required if the plant closing or mass layoff resulted from a natural disaster such as a flood, earthquake, or drought.[58]

EMPLOYEE POLYGRAPH PROTECTION ACT OF 1988

The WHD is also responsible for enforcing the Employee Polygraph Protection Act. The EPPA prohibits most private employers from using lie-detector tests either for preemployment screening or during the course of employment. Specifically, an employer or prospective employer cannot require, request, suggest, or cause an employee or applicant to take or submit to any lie-detector test.[59] Nor can an employer discharge, discipline, discriminate against, deny employment or promotion, or threaten to take any such action against an employee or applicant for refusing to take a lie-detector test. Neither can such adverse employment action be based on the results of a test, for filing a complaint under the EPPA, or for testifying in any proceeding investigating a violation of the EPPA.[60]

It is important to note the EPPA does not provide an absolute prohibition against polygraph testing. There are some exceptions to the Act's ban on the use of polygraph testing in the workplace. Polygraph tests, but no other types of lie-detector tests, may be permitted under limited circumstances. First, federal, state, and local government employers are exempted from the EPPA. Government employees may be required to take polygraph tests as part of their preemployment screening.[61] Second, employers authorized to manufacture, distribute, or dispense controlled substances (i.e., pharmaceutical companies) may use polygraph testing of employees.[62] Private sector employers who provide security services are permitted to use polygraph testing of employees.[63] Polygraph testing may also be used by private sector employers when they are used as part of an investigation of economic loss or injury.[64] In circumstances involving theft, embezzlement, misappropriation, industrial espionage, or industrial sabotage, an employer would be allowed to use a polygraph test as part of an investigation.

Managers and HR professionals need to be aware that the EPPA does not allow indiscriminate use of polygraphs in investigations. The employer must have a reasonable suspicion that a particular employee was involved in the activity under investigation. Therefore, the employer cannot require all employees to submit to a polygraph test as part of an investigation of property theft. Only those employees for whom there is a reasonable cause to suspect can be tested.

In regard to the EPPA, HR professionals and managers should remember that unless a practice in question meets the specified exemptions, the use of polygraph testing should be avoided. In the event that polygraph testing is necessitated (i.e., as part of an accident investigation), HR professionals and managers should ensure the justification for the testing is appropriately documented. It is also advisable that the organization's employee handbook contain a warning to employees that polygraph testing may be used in certain investigations.

The EPPA empowers the Secretary of Labor to bring injunctive actions in United States district courts to halt polygraph testing that violates the Act. It also provides for civil money penalties up to $10,000 against employers who violate any provision of the Act.[65] Finally, the EPPA requires all employers to post notices summarizing the protections of the Act in their places of employment.

SUMMARY

The Fair Labor Standards Act was enacted in 1938 as part of the New Deal. The Act created the minimum wage (currently $5.15 per hour), established a forty-hour work week with time and one-half to be paid for hours worked in excess of forty during a 168-consecutive-hour work week, and placed limitations on the use of child labor.

The Davis-Bacon, Walsh-Healy, and McNamara-O'Hara Service Contract Acts require government contractors and subcontractors to provide either specific levels of compensation, certain overtime requirements, or both.

The FSLA, Davis-Bacon Act, Walsh-Healy Act, and McNamara-O'Hara Service Contract Act are all regulated in whole or part by the Department of Labor. The

Worker Adjustment and Retraining Notification Act and Employee Polygraph Protection Act are also enforced by the Department of Labor. WARN requires notification requirements by employers in the event of plant closings or mass layoffs. The EPPA restricts the use of polygraph tests in preemployment screening.

It should be apparent that ensuring regulatory compliance with equal employment opportunity laws is not the only concern confronting HR professionals. Compensation laws and regulations also cover a significant portion of HR activities and require the constant attention of HR professionals.

In dealing with many of the compensation laws, the obligation for HR professionals is not merely knowing the provisions of these statutes, but understanding to which employees they apply. The requirements imposed by many of these statutes only apply to specific classes of workers, nonexempt employees. For example, under the FLSA, it is essential to know under what circumstances the employee is entitled to overtime and how to calculate these overtime obligations. But, it is equally important to know which employees are entitled to overtime compensation (nonexempt employees) and which are not (exempt employees).

KEY TERMS AND CONCEPTS

compensable time

compensatory time

exempt employees

mass layoff

nonexempt employee

overtime

plant closing

prevailing wage

QUESTIONS

1. What three general employment practices are regulated under the FLSA of 1938? Describe the specific requirements of each.

2. What are the three age categories under the FLSA regarding child labor? What are the restrictions for each category?

3. Provide examples of five classes of employees who would be *exempt* employees under the FLSA's minimum wage *and* overtime provisions. Why are they *exempt*?

4. What employers are required to pay the prevailing wage under the Davis-Bacon, Walsh-Healy, and McNamara-O'Hara Service Contract Acts?

5. Who is covered under WARN? What are the main provisions?

6. Under what circumstances can an employer use lie detectors in making employment decisions? What employers are not bound by these restrictions?

CASE

—■—

Following a short stint as a waitress, Donde Arnold "tried out" for a position as an exotic dancer at Babe's. Arnold began dancing at Babe's in December of 1993. She started working as a waitress in October of 1993. While a waitress, Arnold was paid at a rate of one-half the minimum wage plus tips. As a dancer, Arnold's sole source of income was the tips, or "dance fees," she extracted from customers for the performance of "stage dances" and "table dances." A "stage dance," as the term implies, is a dance performed on a raised platform for the customers at large. A "table dance" is a dance performed off-stage in a relatively smaller space, such as the space immediately in front of a seated customer, or on a couch or tabletop, for one paying customer. In general, a customer paid a "set fee" of $5 or $10 for a table dance.

The relationship between a dancer and Babe's, a Diamond A club, was structured as a licensing arrangement. The dancer and Diamond A entered into a "License to Use Business Premises," which grants the dancer a nonexclusive license to dance and entertain customers at certain specified nightclubs. In exchange for the license, the dancer pays the club a licensing fee, called "shift pay," of $10 per day shift and $15 per night shift. The dancer retains all tips or "dance fees" that she receives from customers for stage dances and table dances and does not report, or otherwise account for, any of her earnings to the club; the club does not pay the dancer any wages or other form of stipend. Is the dancer an exempt employee under the FLSA? Why or why not? Under what circumstances could the dancer be a nonexempt employee?

SOURCE: *Harrell v Diamond A Entertainment*, 992 F. Supp. 1343 (M.D. Fla. 1997).

Notes

1. 29 U.S.C § 207.

2. 29 U.S.C § 206.

3. Thompson, R. (1996). "Benefit costs shift into reverse." *Nation's Business*, 84 (2): 50.

4. U.S. Department of Labor. *Fact Sheet No. 027: Businesses Under Fair Labor Standards Act (FLSA)*. Washington, DC: Government Printing Office.

5. Ibid.

6. Ibid.

7. 29 U.S.C § 203e(2)(B).

8. 29 U.S.C § 203e(2)(C).

9. 29 C.F.R § 541.1.

10. 29 C.F.R § 541.1(f).

11. 29 C.F.R § 541.2.

12. 29 C.F.R § 541.3.

13. 29 C.F.R § 541.5.

14. 29 C.F.R § 541.5(b).

15. 29 U.S.C § 213(a)(17).

16. 29 U.S.C § § 213(a)(17)(A)&(B).

17. 29 U.S.C § 213(a)(17)(D).

18. 29 C.F.R § 519.12.

19. Ibid. at § 519.15.

20. 29 C.F.R § 519.13.

21. Ibid. at 519.12.

22. 29 C.F.R § 519.16.

23. Ibid.

24. Ibid.

25. U.S. Employment Standards Administration, Wage and Hour Division (2001). *Fact Sheet No. 15: Tipped Employees Under the Fair Labor Standards Act (FLSA)*. **http://www.dol.gov/dol/esa/public/regs/compliance/whd/whdfs15.htm**

26. U.S. Employment Standards Administration, Wage and Hour Division (2001). *Fact Sheet No. 002: Restaurants and Fast Food Establishments Under the Fair Labor Standards Act (FLSA)*. **http://www.dol.gov/dol/esa/public/regs/compliance/whd/whdfs2.htm**

27. 29 U.S.C § 207(o)(1).

28. 29 C.F.R § 553.223(c).

29. *Mitchell v King Packing Co.*, 350 U.S. 260 (1956).

30. Ibid.

31. 29 C.F.R § 785.18.

32. *Owens v IT T Rayonier, Inc.*, 971 F.2d 347 (9th Cir. 1992).

33. 29 U.S.C § § 251–262.

34. 29 U.S.C § 212.

35. 29 U.S.C § 212.

36. 29 C.F.R § 570.35.

37. Ibid.

38. Ibid.

39. Ibid.

40. 29 C.F.R § 516.7.

41. Ibid.

42. 29 U.S.C § 216(b).

43. 29 U.S.C § 215(a)(3).

44. 29 U.S.C § 216(b).

45. 29 C.F.R § 578.3.

46. 29 C.F.R § 578.4.

47. 40 U.S.C § 276a.

48. 41 U.S.C § 35.

49. Pub. L. 99–145, § 1241(b) (November 8, 1985).

50. 41 U.S.C § 351(b).

51. Ibid. at § 351(a)(3).

52. 29 U.S.C § 2101(a)(1).

53. 29 U.S.C § 1651 *et seq.*

54. Ibid. at § 2102(a).

55. Ibid. at § 2101(a)(2).

56. Ibid. at § 2101(b)(2).

57. Ibid.

58. Ibid. at § 2102(b).

59. U.S. Employment Standards Administration, (1999). *Fact Sheet No. 036: Employee Polygraph Protection Act of 1988.* **http://www.dol.gov/dol/esa/public/regs/compliance/whd/whdfs36.html**

60. Ibid.

61. 29 C.F.R § 801.10.

62. Ibid. at § 801.13.

63. Ibid. at § 801.14.

64. Ibid. at § 801.12.

65. Ibid. at § 801.42(a).

EMPLOYEE BENEFITS

LEARNING OBJECTIVES

- ☐ Understand the reasons for the growth of employee benefits.
- ☐ Discuss the evolution of government regulation of employee benefits and the costs associated with such regulation.
- ☐ Describe the two major types of employee benefits and major provisions of federal and state laws dealing with employee benefits.
- ☐ Describe the conditions under which an employee is ineligible for unemployment benefits.
- ☐ Describe the circumstances under which an employee is entitled to unpaid leave under the Family and Medical Leave Act of 1993.
- ☐ Understand an employer's obligations under the Employee Retirement Income Security Act of 1974.

OPENING SCENARIO

Jerri Lynn McClure has been working for Frink & Rose Septic Tank, Inc. for two and one-half years. Frink & Rose employs sixty-two employees in Normal, Oklahoma. In March, Jerri Lynn's husband, Kerry, was severely injured in an automobile accident. As a result, Kerry is immobilized and will require home nursing for two months. Jerri Lynn asks her immediate supervisor, Scott Vitell, if she can possibly have the next two months off to care for her husband. Although sympathetic to her plight, Scott informs Jerri Lynn that if she takes her accrued vacation time and he lets her take her accrued sick leave, the most she can have off is one month. Scott further tells her that right now is peak production time, and the company is trying to build up its finished goods inventory to satisfy the expected surge in demand at the beginning of the construction season. In fact, Scott adds, even if he is able to allow her the one month off to take care of Kerry, he really cannot guarantee her old job will be waiting when she returns to work.

Distraught, Jerri Lynn begins discussing the issue with a coworker, Dave LeRoi. Dave tells her that Scott does not know what he is talking about. He says he has heard about a law called the Family and Medical Leave Act that allows anyone with a sick relative to take up to twelve weeks of paid leave from the employer.

Who is right, Scott or Dave? Actually, as we will soon see, neither is right. Yes, there is a Family and Medical Leave Act, but it does not apply to all sick relatives, and it does not mandate paid leave. Although the Act is somewhat complicated, it will solve several of Jerri Lynn's problems.

HISTORICAL PERSPECTIVE OF EMPLOYEE BENEFITS

The number and types of employee benefits offered by employers have grown over the years to now represent a major component in the total compensation program. By some estimates, employee benefits account for roughly 41 percent of all payroll costs.[1] Employee benefits programs have developed to meet important needs of both the employer and the employee. Employers view benefits as a means to achieve organizational goals and objectives by attracting and retaining qualified employees, improving morale, providing a sense of security for employees, and increasing productivity. Employees, on the other hand, view them as an important part of their compensation packages when considering employment opportunities and making choices.

Around the turn of the twentieth century, very few employers offered benefits, and the few that were offered were designed to attract and retain employees with the required education and skills. By the 1920s, an era of "welfare capitalism" emerged in the United States.[2] Welfare capitalism was a concept by which employers voluntarily and intentionally improved the living conditions of employees through various supplements to direct money pay. These employers offered employees what became known as "fringe benefits" such as paid vacations and holidays, insurance benefits, and pension plans. Some employers were motivated to provide these benefits due to a paternalistic attitude toward employees. Others provided benefit packages as a pragmatic means of keeping employees from organizing unions. Regardless of the rationale for providing the benefit packages, fringe benefits became a fixture in American business organizations.

Although the mix of benefit packages offered varied from employer to employer, all of the early welfare programs involved components that could be systematized and classified. Arnold Tolles identified eight broad groups or classes of early welfare programs, many of which are still in use today:[3]

1. *Recreational plans* included athletic teams, glee clubs, and drama clubs. Many employers provided employees facilities such as club houses, recreation rooms, gymnasiums, bowling alleys, and game rooms to bring employees relief from boredom, provide relaxation, and generate group spirit.

2. *Health and safety plans* provided employer-paid physical examinations, first aid, guards on machines, safety instructions, and medical advice and treatment in cases of accidents and sickness on the job.

3. *Education and information plans* included services such as company-sponsored educational programs, company-financed scholarship funds, the provision of technical libraries for employees, and the sponsorship of a variety of seminars.

4. *Economic security plans* are now one of the most costly types of welfare benefits. These provisions included thrift clubs, credit unions, stock purchase plans, paid vacations, paid sick leave plans, and group life, accident, and health insurance plans.

5. *Convenience plans* for employees included a wide variety of effects, the most elemental of which was adequate toilets and washrooms. Other examples included locker rooms, restrooms, lunchrooms, and lunch wagons.

6. *Personal and family problems plans* consisted of emergency financial assistance to the employee, vocational guidance, and advice on problems of health and family finances.

7. *Community interests programs* included such activities as paying for time not worked while the employee is voting, serving on a jury, appearing as a witness, or conducting union duties. Where the employer's facilities were located in isolated areas, they often provided housing for employees and their families.

8. *Employee representation plans*, endorsed by some larger companies, provided collective representation of employees as an alternative to labor unions. These employee representation plans were initially called "work councils" during the 1920s and were later known as "shop committees." Today, these are known as employee empowerment programs, quality circles, or employee participation programs (see Exhibit 9-1).

■ EXHIBIT 9-1

EMPLOYEE BENEFITS BY TYPE OF BENEFITS (EMPLOYERS' SHARE ONLY)

Type of Benefit	1947	1965	1983	1995
Total employee benefits (as percent of payroll)	16.1	28.1	36.6	40.7
1. Legally required payments	2.6	4.2	9.0	8.9
2. Pension, insurance, and other agreed-upon payments	5.0	9.9	13.6	17.2
3. Paid rest periods, coffee breaks, lunch periods, wash-up time, travel time, etc.	1.6	2.4	2.3	2.2
4. Payments for time not worked	5.6	9.6	9.4	9.7
5. Profit sharing payments and other items	1.3	2.0	2.3	2.7
Total employee benefits (as cents per hour)	22.1	88.8	369.1	715.7
Total employee benefits (as dollars per year per employee)	$450	$1,874	$7,582	$14,678

SOURCE: Adapted from surveys in United States Chamber of Commerce editions of *Employee Benefits*.

OVERVIEW OF THE REGULATION OF EMPLOYEE BENEFITS

Not surprisingly, as soon as employee benefits became widespread, government regulation was not far behind (see Exhibit 9-2 for a complete list of laws regulating benefits). Beginning as early as 1921, the Internal Revenue Code was amended to regulate interest income on profit sharing programs and certain

■ EXHIBIT 9-2

Legislation	Provisions
Revenue Acts of 1921, 1926, and 1928	Exempts interest income on profit sharing plans, bonus plans, and pension trusts from current taxation.
Social Security Act of 1935, as amended	Provides for such benefits as retirement, disability payments, health payments, and survivor income.
Labor-Management Relations Act of 1947	Provides fundamental guidelines for the establishment and operation of pension plans administered jointly by an employer and a labor union in Section 302.
Welfare and Pension Plans Disclosure Act of 1958	Requires plan administrators for collectively bargained plans to provide annual financial reports of plans.
Revenue Act of 1961	Amends Section 403(b) to defer taxes of annuity purchases to employees of public educational institutions.
Welfare and Pension Plans Disclosure Act Amendments of 1962	Shifts responsibility for protection of plan assets to the federal government.
Self-Employed Individual Retirement Act of 1962 (Keogh Act)	Allows self-employed individuals a limited deduction of earnings for their own pension contributions.
Tax Reform Act of 1969	Provides guidelines for implementation and application of employer and union jointly administered pension plans.
Employee Retirement Income Security Act of 1974 (ERISA)	Protects private pension plan benefits for participants and establishes the Pension Benefit Guaranty Corporation (PBGC).
Revenue Act of 1978	Introduces qualified deferred taxation compensation plans in Section 401(k).
Economic Recovery Tax Act of 1981 (ERTA)	Extends IRA eligibility to employees covered by employer pension plans and authorizes qualified, voluntary employee contributions, increases contribution limits for IRA and Keogh Plans, and creates incentive stock options (ISO).
Tax Equity and Fiscal Responsibility Act of 1982 (TEFRA)	Establishes alternative minimum tax provisions, restricts qualified retirement benefits for highly paid employees, restricts top-heavy plans, modifies Keogh plans and Social Security integration rules, and establishes requirements for group term life insurance.
Deficit Reduction Act of 1984 (DEFRA)	Imposes various restrictions on benefit plans in an effort to reduce a budget deficit and makes changes affecting 401(k) plans.
Retirement Equity Act of 1984 (REA)	Amends ERISA pension plan provisions to expand employee benefit rights and protections regarding enrollment, vesting, breaks in service, and survivor provisions.
Consolidated Omnibus Budget Reconciliation Act of 1985 (COBRA)	Requires employers to offer extended group health insurance coverage for up to 36 months to employees and dependents whose coverage would otherwise terminate due to qualifying events.

incentive programs offered by employers. By the time of the Great Depression, the era of socialism had begun, and the first federally mandated employee benefits emerged with the passage of the Social Security Act of 1935.

By the early 1970s, most employers and employees viewed employee benefits as an integral part of the total compensation program, and the majority of employees felt they were entitled to receive them as part of the employment relationship.

MAJOR LEGISLATION GOVERNING EMPLOYMENT BENEFITS

Legislation	Provisions
Tax Reform Act of 1986	Establishes major changes in several benefit plans for vesting schedules, Social Security integration, pension plan standards, and tax penalties as well as controlling discrimination in favor of highly paid employees.
Age Discrimination in Employment Act amendment of 1986 (ADEA)	Prohibits mandatory retirement based upon age for most employees.
Omnibus Budget Reconciliation Act of 1986 (OBRA 1986)	Requires that employers allow accrual and participation in established pension plans for employees who continue working beyond age 64 and for employees who are hired within five years of the plan's normal retirement age.
Omnibus Budget Reconciliation Act of 1987 (OBRA 1987)	Increases and extends the PBGC pension insurance premium provisions for participants employed beyond a pension plan's normal retirement age.
Omnibus Budget Reconciliation Act of 1989 (OBRA 1989)	Expands health care continuation under COBRA (1985) and includes some forms of deferred compensation in determining average compensation and Social Security taxable base.
Omnibus Budget Reconciliation Act of 1990 (OBRA 1990)	Increases the excise tax for pension asset reversions, the taxable base for Medicare payroll tax, and the PBGC premium rates.
Older Workers Benefit Protection Act of 1990 (OWBPA)	Amends the Age Discrimination in Employment Act (ADEA) to be applicable to employee benefit eligibility and participation.
Omnibus Budget Reconciliation Act of 1993 (OBRA 1993)	Reduces compensation limit for 401(k) plans, increases amount of Social Security benefits subject to taxation from 50 percent to 85 percent for individuals earning more than $34,000 and married persons filing jointly earning above $44,000, and enacts a cap on deduction of executive compensation in excess of $1 million not linked to performance.
Family and Medical Leave Act of 1993 (FMLA)	Grants employees up to 12 weeks of unpaid leave for various family and employee reasons including an employee's own illness, serious health conditions of an employee's spouse, children, or parents, and to care for a newborn child or a child placed by adoption or foster care.
Health Insurance Portability and Accountability Act of 1996 (HIPAA)	Prohibits group health insurance plans from establishing eligibility rules based on health status, limits duration and extent of excluding preexisting conditions, requires group health insurance plans to track a person's coverage upon leaving the plan to allow that person to gain access to another plan with reduced or no preexisting conditions restrictions, requires special enrollment periods for persons losing other coverage under qualifying circumstances, extends COBRA provisions, and expands ERISA's disclosure requirements.

Despite the expansion of benefits outside of collective bargaining agreements, there was little federal regulatory control over the management of private voluntary employee benefit programs until the Employee Retirement Income Security Act of 1974 (ERISA) was passed. This statute would be to employee benefits what the Civil Rights Act of 1964 was to equal employment opportunity.

In the 1980s and continuing into the present, federal and state governments have actively increased their roles regulating existing employee benefit programs. Government has also legislated tax reforms in order to provide incentives for private employers to create additional benefits as well as improve existing benefit plans. Benefits administration and management of employee benefits programs have been much more complex due to the extensive tax implications.

MANDATORY AND VOLUNTARY BENEFITS

The benefits provided to employees fall into one of two broad categories: mandatory and voluntary. **Mandatory benefits,** quite simply, are those mandated or required by law. Employers have no choice but to provide the benefits. Examples of mandatory benefits include social security, unemployment compensation, workers' compensation, and family and medical leave.

Voluntary benefits are benefits that are not required by law. Thus, the employer may provide them, but no statute or regulation is violated if such benefits are not provided to employees. In reality, failing to provide certain benefits could be disastrous for an organization's recruitment and retention of qualified employees. After all, voluntary benefits have become so commonplace that employees have come to expect them as a normal part of the compensation package. How many people do you know who would work for an employer who does not provide medical insurance, paid vacation time, and a retirement program? Even though employees may expect these benefits, they are still voluntary benefits that employers are not required by law to provide. However, any employer who does not "voluntarily" offer these benefits will have a difficult time attracting and retaining qualified employees.

Although the majority of the benefits employers offer are voluntary, many (especially pension and health care benefits) are regulated by federal and/or state authorities. In certain cases, where there is no law requiring employers to provide the benefit, once employers elect to provide it, the benefit must be administered according to law.

REGULATION OF MANDATORY BENEFITS

From an employee relations perspective, the most relevant mandatory benefits are unemployment compensation, workers' compensation, and family and medical leave. The regulations related to unemployment compensation and family and medical leave will be discussed next. Because of its relationship to workplace safety and health issues, workers' compensation is addressed in Chapter 10.

UNEMPLOYMENT COMPENSATION

Although unemployment compensation programs are administered by individual states, these programs were established by the Social Security Act of 1935.[4] This New Deal legislation was enacted to provide **unemployment compensation** to offset workers' lost income during periods of involuntary unemployment and to help unemployed workers locate new employment. Because the employer's contribution to the unemployment fund is based on the number of unemployment claims filed against it, there is a very real incentive for the employer to maintain a stable workforce.

Unemployment compensation is actually an unemployment insurance program. Like all insurance programs, the amount of premium an employer pays varies based upon the number of former employees who file unemployment claims.[5] As automobile insurance premiums increase with the number of traffic accidents a policyholder has, so too do unemployment compensation premiums increase with the number of employees who are laid off by an employer. The connection is clear: employers with few layoffs pay low state unemployment taxes; those laying off many employees pay high taxes.

COVERED EMPLOYERS. The Unemployment Tax Act defines an "employer" as any entity who paid wages of $1,500 or more in any quarter in the current or preceding calendar year and employed at least one individual on at least one day during twenty weeks in the current or previous year.[6] This covers virtually all employers nationwide. However, various state laws have exempted specific categories of employers from unemployment eligibility. Because exemptions vary from state to state, readers are cautioned to consult the respective state unemployment commission for specific information on exempted employers.

EMPLOYEE ELIGIBILITY. As a rule, certain classes of employees are not entitled to coverage under state unemployment compensation laws. In all states, railroad workers are not entitled to draw unemployment compensation because railroad workers and their families are covered under separate social insurance legislation, the Railroad Retirement Act of 1935,[7] and not the Social Security Act.

Additionally, all states exclude persons who are self-employed from unemployment compensation. Persons who are employed by their immediate family members (parent, spouse, or child) cannot draw unemployment benefits.[8] Full-time students and the spouses of full-time students who provide employment services for schools, colleges, and universities are not provided unemployment insurance coverage.[9] Finally, persons who are currently drawing pensions, retirement pay, or other annuities are disqualified automatically from collecting unemployment compensation.[10] Although all of these classes of individuals are

■ EXHIBIT 9-3

State	Casual Employees	Commercial Fishing Vessels[1]	Hospital Interns	Insurance Agents[2]	Minor News-paper Carriers	Patients Employed by Hospitals	Real Estate Agents[2]	Undocumented Workers
Alabama		X	X	X			X	
Alaska		X	X	X	X	X	X	X
Arizona	X		X	X	X	X	X	
Arkansas	X	X	X	X	X	X	X	
California	X		X	X	X	X	X	
Colorado	X		X	X	X	X	X	
Connecticut	X		X	X	X	X	X	
Delaware				X		X	X	
Florida	X	X	X	X	X		X	
Georgia	X	X	X	X	X	X	X	
Hawaii	X	X	X	X	X	X		
Idaho		X	X	X	X	X	X	
Illinois		X^2	X	X	X	X	X	
Indiana		X^2	X		X		X	
Iowa		X						
Kansas		X		X			X	
Kentucky		X^2	X	X	X		X	
Louisiana		X^2	X	X	X		X	
Maine		X	X	X	X	X	X	
Maryland		X	X	X		X	X	
Massachusetts		X	X	X	X	X	X	
Michigan				X	X		X	
Minnesota	X		X	X	X	X	X	
Mississippi	X	X^2	X	X	X	X	X	
Missouri				X	X		X	

[1]Commercial fishing vessel employees are excluded except those that work for employers with operating offices in that state.

[2]Insurance and real estate agents that work for commission only are ineligible for unemployment compensation.

SOURCE: Jackson, G. E. (1999 Cumulative Supplement). *Labor and Employment Law Desk Book* (2d ed.). Paramus, NJ: Prentice Hall.

universally denied unemployment benefits, states, individually, have excluded other classes of employees (see Exhibit 9-3).

Even if an employee is not in one of the exempted classes, that employee is not eligible automatically for unemployment compensation upon termination. To receive unemployment compensation, the terminated employee must meet three conditions (see Exhibit 9-4). First, the employee must have been involuntarily terminated. Thus, if the employee voluntarily terminates employment (resigns), he or she may be ineligible to draw unemployment benefits, depending on the state regulations.[11] If the employee has been discharged for either misconduct (i.e.,

REASONS STATES DISQUALIFY INDIVIDUALS FROM RECEIVING UNEMPLOYMENT BENEFITS

State	Casual Employees	Commercial Fishing Vessels[1]	Hospital Interns	Insurance Agents[2]	Minor News-paper Carriers	Patients Employed by Hospitals	Real Estate Agents[2]	Undocumented Workers
Montana				X	X	X	X	
Nebraska			X	X	X	X	X	
Nevada					X	X		
New Hampshire			X	X	X	X	X	
New Jersey				X			X	
New Mexico				X	X	X	X	
New York	X						X	
North Carolina		X	X	X	X	X	X	
North Dakota	X		X	X	X	X	X	
Ohio			X	X	X	X	X	
Oklahoma			X	X	X	X	X	
Oregon	X		X	X	X	X	X	
Pennsylvania	X		X	X	X	X	X	
Rhode Island	X	X		X		X	X	
South Carolina	X	X	X	X	X	X	X	
South Dakota			X	X	X	X	X	
Tennessee		X		X		X	X	
Texas			X	X	X	X	X	
Utah			X	X	X	X	X	
Vermont		X		X			X	
Virginia	X	X		X		X	X	
Washington	X			X	X	X	X	
West Virginia				X		X		
Wisconsin		X	X	X	X	X	X	
Wyoming					X	X	X	

■ EXHIBIT 9-4

REASONS FOR INELIGIBILITY FOR UNEMPLOYMENT COMPENSATION

- Voluntarily terminated without good cause
- Involuntary termination for misconduct
- Failure to seek suitable employment
- Unemployment resulting from labor strike

violating a work rule, insubordination, theft, etc.) or failure to meet minimum performance standards, he or she is disqualified from unemployment compensation eligibility.

Second, the terminated employee must be able and willing to work. This means the terminated employee is entitled to unemployment compensation as long as he or she is unemployed and has not refused suitable work. Unemployment claimants are required to make regular visits to the state unemployment commission for the purpose of locating another job. If the claimant fails to actively seek new employment (i.e., does not check with the employment commission regularly) or refuses to accept a comparable position through the employment commission, unemployment benefits may be terminated.

Third, in order to be eligible for unemployment compensation, the terminated employee must have met the state's minimum income and contribution levels. Before a claimant can draw the state's unemployment benefits, he or she must have first earned a certain base wage amount and worked for a minimum period of time (usually at least three months in the previous year prior to the unemployment claim).

Interestingly, in all states except New York and Rhode Island, an individual is ineligible for unemployment compensation if the unemployment is due to a labor strike or work stoppage.[12]

UNEMPLOYMENT BENEFITS.   If an individual is laid off by a covered employer, that individual is entitled to receive unemployment compensation for up to twenty-six weeks. Keep in mind that during this twenty-six-week period, the claimant must be actively seeking suitable employment. The amount of unemployment compensation the individual may draw per week is established by the individual state. In all states, this amount is based on a percentage of the employee's average weekly pay (usually 50 percent) and a maximum ceiling, whichever amount is smaller.

FAMILY AND MEDICAL LEAVE

Family and medical leave is provided under the Family and Medical Leave Act of 1993 (FMLA). Effective as of August 5, 1993, the FMLA requires that eligible employees receive up to twelve weeks of *unpaid* leave for the birth of a child, adoption of a child, care of an immediate family member (spouse, child, or parent) suffering from a "serious health condition," or recovery from a personal "serious health condition."[13] In determining an employee's entitlement to FMLA's mandatory leave, two questions must be addressed:

■ Is the employer a covered entity (required to comply with the provisions of the Act)?

■ Has the employee in question met the FMLA's eligibility requirement?

COVERED EMPLOYERS. Private sector employers must comply with the FMLA when they employ fifty or more employees for at least twenty work weeks in the current or previous year, including joint employers and successor employers. The term **joint employers** refers to two or more employers who employ the same individual. Think of a situation in which the employee is paid by an employment service (i.e., Kelly or Manpower) and contracted to work for yet a second employer (i.e., Western Corporation or Lockheed Martin).[14] Even though the employee receives his or her pay check and benefits from Manpower, if Lockheed Martin controls and supervises the employee's work activities, Lockheed Martin is a joint employer.

A **successor employer,** as the name implies, is an employer who replaces another employer. If one company was acquired by another company, the acquiring company is the successor employer. If company X acquires company Y, as the successor employer, company X has also acquired company Y's FMLA obligations. In regard to the fifty or more employee criterion, these fifty employees must reside within a seventy-five-mile radius of the place of employment.[15] If these conditions are met, the fifty or more employees and the seventy-five-mile radius, the employer is required to follow the FMLA. If either one is not met, the employer does not have to comply with the Act.

To demonstrate the effect this requirement has, assume an employer operates a business from two locations—one in Flagstaff, Arizona, with one hundred employees, and another in Shreveport, Louisiana, with thirty-five employees. All of the Flagstaff employees live within the seventy-five-mile radius and each person meets the individual twelve month and 1,250 hours of service requirement as well. All of these employees are eligible for FMLA leave.

But what about the company unit in Shreveport? It has only thirty-five employees of which only twenty-eight live within the seventy-five-mile radius. Does the company have to grant them FMLA leave? The answer is yes. A corporation is considered a single employer and cannot separate its divisions and plant locations.[16] If the company consisted only of the Shreveport facility, it would not be covered under the FMLA leave.

One additional feature of the FMLA, and somewhat unusual for a federal statute, is that *all* public sector employers (federal, state, and local) are also covered entities under the Act.[17] Additionally, public and private educational institutions, regardless of size, must provide FMLA leave to their employees.

EMPLOYEE ELIGIBILITY. Determining employee eligibility can become a little more complicated than determining employer coverage. Just because an individual is working for a covered employer does not, of and by itself, mean the particular employee is eligible for FMLA leave. The employee is not automatically eligible if the employer is a covered entity. If the employer *is* covered, then the employee must meet *all three* of the following conditions (see Exhibit 9-5). First, the employee must have worked for the employer for at least twelve months. However, this twelve-month period does not have to be continuous service.[18]

■ **EXHIBIT 9-5**

BASIC ELIGIBILITY PROVISIONS FOR THE **FMLA**

- ■ Employee must have worked for the employer for at least twelve months (can be nonconsecutive).
- ■ Employee must have worked in excess of 1,250 hours to be eligible.

SOURCE: 29 U.S.C. § § 2611 and 2612.

Second, the employee must have worked for at least 1,250 hours during the twelve months preceding the beginning of the FMLA leave.[19] Again, these 1,250 hours do not have to be continuous. The 1,250 hours are equivalent to twenty-four hours worked in each of the fifty-two weeks of the year, more than 104 hours worked in each of the twelve months of the year, or forty hours worked per week for more than thirty-one weeks (more than seven months) of the year.[20] Third, only those employees who work at a facility where at least fifty employees reside within seventy-five miles of that location are eligible employees.[21] For example, if a company employs sixty people in August, but expects that the number of employees will drop to forty in December, the employer must grant FMLA benefits to an otherwise eligible employee who gives notice of the need for leave in August for a period of leave to begin in December.

Are employees who have accrued 1,250 hours but not yet worked for the organization for twelve months entitled to FMLA? No, the requirement expressly states that employees must have worked for the employer for at least twelve months.

CONDITIONS REQUIRING FMLA LEAVE.   Assuming the employer and employee are both covered under the FMLA, what are the circumstances by which an employee may request leave? There are two broad categories of leave: parental leave and leave related to a serious health condition.

Parental Leave under the FMLA.   An employee is entitled to FMLA leave for the birth or adoption of a child.[22] This "parental leave" applies to either parent (fathers as well as mothers). The FMLA also permits leave for foster care. The parental leave provisions are more restrictive than the serious health condition leave permitted under the Act. For example, parental leave cannot be taken intermittently; it must be taken in a single increment. Therefore, the employee cannot take off four weeks now, four more weeks later, and four more weeks further in the future. If the employee takes four weeks of parental leave now, there will be no future parental leave.

The second major difference regarding parental leave is that it *must* be taken within twelve months of the birth or adoption. If the father or mother wishes to take FMLA parental leave twelve months and one day after the child's birth, it is too late. The employee's right to the leave has already expired.[23]

Finally, if both parents work for the same organization, they are collectively limited to only twelve weeks of leave.[24] Both the father and the mother cannot separately request twelve weeks of parental leave (a total of twenty-four weeks leave between the two employees). If they wanted to split the parental leave evenly, then each would be limited to requesting only six weeks. They may choose any combination of leave provided it does not exceed the twelve-week maximum.

Serious Health Condition Leave under the FMLA. Covered employees are entitled to up to twelve weeks unpaid leave to care for themselves or family members in the event of a "serious health condition." Serious health conditions will be discussed in the next section, but for now our discussion will focus on who is a family member according to the FMLA.

Under the Act, employees are entitled to take *unpaid* leave to care for a "spouse, son, daughter, or parent who has a serious health condition."[25] A spouse is a husband or wife recognized as married under state law. This includes common law marriages in those states recognizing such forms of marriage,[26] but it does not include couples that are merely cohabitating. In order to be eligible for spousal leave, there must be a legally recognized relationship.

Sons and daughters include minor children (those under eighteen years of age) and children who have reached their majority (eighteen years or older) but are incapable of caring for themselves due to a physical or mental disability. Sons or daughters may be biological offspring, foster children, adopted children, step children (if legally adopted), or a legal ward.[27] As with spouses, there must be a legally recognized relationship.

An employee may request FMLA leave in order to care for a parent. However, that employee has no FMLA entitlement to care for parents-in-law. For example, a covered employer must permit a female employee to take up to twelve weeks of unpaid leave to care for her mother, but the employer does not have to allow her a single minute of leave to take care of her mother-in-law.

Interestingly, as in parental leave situations, married couples are permitted only a total of twelve weeks leave between them to handle serious health conditions of family members.[28] If the wife, for example, has already exhausted eight weeks leave during the current twelve-month period to care for her ailing father, her husband could only take a maximum of four weeks if his mother needed assistance.

One major difference between serious health condition leave and parental leave is that any FMLA leave used to care for ill family members can be taken intermittently.[29] Where parental leave can be taken only in a single period of time, serious health condition leave can be taken incrementally—a few days now, a few days later.

The employer has the right to require the employee to provide documentation when requesting family leave. Employees seeking FMLA leave for the serious health condition of a family member may be required to verify the relationship of the family member.[30] In addition, the employer may demand verification of the family member's serious health condition.[31]

Regardless of the reason for the FMLA leave, parental leave or serious illness leave, the employee is guaranteed to return to his or her job or a comparable position at the leave's conclusion. In the opening scenario, Jerri Lynn likely would be able to return to her old job at the conclusion of her requested two months' leave.

Employees with Serious Health Conditions. When it comes to establishing serious conditions of either the individual employee or a family member, it is important to understand what criteria the FMLA designates as demonstrating a serious health condition. Such conclusions are not left to either the employer or the employee, but are strictly defined in the Act.

The FMLA defines serious health conditions as "an illness, injury, impairment, or physical or mental condition that involves inpatient care in a hospital, hospice, or residential medical care facility; or continuing treatment by a health care provider."[32] The critical point to make about serious health conditions is that they are *not* minor illnesses or injuries that last only a few days. Maladies like minor food poisoning,[33] ear aches, influenza, colds, or cosmetic treatments (like acne) do not qualify as serious health conditions.[34] Instead, conditions requiring at a minimum an overnight stay in a hospital are more likely to rise to the level of a serious health condition. Other maladies or conditions that would meet this standard of severity would be broken bones, chronic illnesses (such as asthma and diabetes), surgery, medical conditions requiring prolonged episodic treatment (such as chemotherapy or radiation treatment), or any permanent long-term conditions that require monitoring (such as stroke or terminal illness).[35]

Unfortunately, the definition offered in the FMLA is unduly broad. In an attempt to clarify what constitutes a "serious health condition," the Employment Standards Administration developed specific regulations. Under these regulations, a "serious health condition," for the purposes of the FMLA, is established when one or more of the following conditions is met:

1. A period of incapacity (i.e., inability to work, attend school, or perform other regular daily activities due to the serious health condition, treatment therefor, or recovery therefrom) of more than three consecutive calendar days, and any subsequent treatment or period of incapacity relating to the same condition.

2. Any period of incapacity due to pregnancy, or for prenatal care.

3. Any period of incapacity or treatment for such incapacity due to a chronic serious health condition.

4. A period of incapacity which is permanent or long term due to a condition for which treatment may not be effective. Examples include Alzheimer's, a severe stroke, or the terminal stages of a disease.

5. Any period of absence to receive multiple treatments (including any period of recovery therefrom) by a health care provider or that would likely result in a period of incapacity of more than three consecutive calendar days in the absence of medical intervention or treatment, such as cancer

(chemotherapy or radiation), severe arthritis (physical therapy), or kidney disease (dialysis).[36]

Based on these regulations, some federal courts have concluded that for an employee to prove he or she has a serious health condition and is entitled to FMLA leave, two facts must be established.[37] First, the employee must demonstrate that he or she was unable to work for at least three consecutive days. Second, the employee must show that he or she received subsequent treatment in which he or she was either seen at least twice by a health care provider or obtained a regimen of treatment under a health care provider.[38]

Despite the Employment Standards Administration's narrowing of the definition of a serious health condition, there is still room for abuse since conditions such as the common cold, flu, and nonmigraine headaches would meet at least one of the aforementioned two facts.[39] Interestingly, the Society for Human Resource Management's December 1996 *Work and Family Survey* found that approximately 60 percent of responding firms had experienced significant costs due to FMLA implementation and enforcement; most of the cost incurred resulted from hiring temporary employees to cover the FMLA employee's work or assigning the work to coworkers, thus creating overtime costs.[40] Approximately 51 percent of the respondents reported that they had not received any benefits from FMLA compliance.[41]

ADVANCE NOTIFICATION FOR FMLA LEAVE. The FMLA requires that employees give employers at least thirty days' notice when the reason for the leave is "foreseeable." However, the thirty-day requirement does not apply in situations when the serious health condition requiring the leave was sudden. Under such circumstances, the employee is merely required to provide employer notification as soon as possible. This exception makes the thirty-day notification requirement virtually pointless except in instances where scheduled medical treatments are known well in advance. Employees who have advance knowledge of a scheduled medical service or treatment must always provide timely notification. It is important that employers make employees aware of their responsibilities in this area and of the consequences of failing to provide proper notification when the date of the treatment was known.

For example, if on September 15, an employee knows that he is scheduled for in-patient surgery on October 16, he is required by the FMLA to notify the employer of this fact within twenty-four hours. Yet the employee neglected to provide the company with this timely notification and waited until October 1 to request the leave. Provided the employee has no reasonable excuse for this oversight, the employer can delay the leave up to *thirty days after the employee gives notification.*[42] The employee could be required to reschedule the surgery. However, it is recommended that human resource managers avoid using this rule in instances when delaying the treatment could adversely affect the employee's health. It is one thing to make a point, and it is quite another to cause harm.

DETERMINING UNPAID LEAVE. If an employer already offers employees paid leave (i.e., vacation, sick leave, personal leave), the unpaid leave mandated by the FMLA may run consecutively with the paid leave, provided the employer has identified such leave as being taken for a FMLA reason. For example, assume an employer provides employees with two weeks paid sick leave as a benefit. Now assume an employee requests the full twelve weeks under the FMLA for a medical emergency. The employee cannot demand two weeks paid leave in addition to the twelve weeks unpaid leave (a total of fourteen weeks). The FMLA authorizes the employer to require the employee to substitute any of the accrued paid vacation leave, personal leave, or family leave.[43] Using the previous example, the employer may include the two weeks paid sick leave as part of the FMLA required leave, for a total of twelve weeks (two paid and ten unpaid weeks).

In our opening scenario, Jerri Lynn could draw her paid vacation to run concurrently with her FMLA leave. If she had one month's leave accrued, this would guarantee her a stream of income for the first of the two months' FMLA leave requested. However, during the second month, Jerri Lynn would have no income from her employer.

CALCULATING THE TWELVE-MONTH PERIOD UNDER FMLA. The FMLA provides several options when establishing from which date the twelve-month eligibility period is calculated. Employers may select one of four options for determining this twelve-month period:

1. The calendar year.
2. Any fixed twelve-month "leave year" such as a fiscal year.
3. A year required by state law.
4. A year starting on the employee's "anniversary" date.[44]

The twelve-month period is measured forward from the date an employee's first FMLA leave begins, or a "rolling" twelve-month period is measured backward from the date the employee uses FMLA leave.[45]

REGULATION OF VOLUNTARY HEALTH BENEFITS

Although currently there is no federal law requiring private sector employers to provide health care coverage, employers are required to provide continued coverage to former employees under certain circumstances. Typical of most voluntary benefit programs, once an employer implements a group health insurance program for employees, that program is subject to federal regulation. Interestingly, the statutes that regulate health care benefits are actually amendments to the Employee Retirement Income Security Act, an act which is more commonly associated with retirement benefits and is discussed in greater detail at the end of this chapter.

CONSOLIDATED OMNIBUS RECONCILIATION ACT OF 1985, AS AMENDED

The Consolidated Omnibus Reconciliation Act (COBRA) regulates group health insurance programs. Specifically, COBRA directs covered employers to offer continuation of group health care protection to participants and certain dependents for eighteen or thirty-six months, where coverage would otherwise cease upon termination of employment. COBRA further requires employers to continue health insurance coverage to separated employees due to voluntary or involuntary termination of employment at the group insurance rate plus a two percent administrative charge. Additionally, employers must provide the continued coverage when there is a reduction of work. Employers also are required to extend this coverage to the spouse of an employee in the event of the death of the employee or divorce.

COVERED EMPLOYERS AND PLANS.   COBRA covers all employers engaged in interstate trade but exempts certain employers and specific plans. For one, employers with fewer than twenty employees are exempt from COBRA's provisions. In addition, a government health plan or any health plan administered by religious organizations are not covered by the Act.

QUALIFYING EVENTS.   Certain conditions, referred to as **qualifying events** (see Exhibit 9-6), require continued coverage under COBRA if the employee, dependents, or divorced spouse elects to be covered within a sixty-day period from occurrence of the qualifying event. One qualifying event for COBRA eligibility would be a reduction in an employee's work hours to part-time status resulting in no coverage under the existing plan or termination of employment for any reason other than gross misconduct.[46] If an employee loses his or her job because of an economic downturn, the employer must continue coverage, but if the employee is terminated because of documented insubordination, the employer does not have to provide continued coverage.

There are also qualifying events that entitle the dependents of a covered employee to continued health benefit coverage. The spouse and minor children of an employee are entitled to continued coverage in the event of the death of an employee.[47] Additionally, these dependents are entitled to continued coverage in the event of a divorce or legal separation from the employee.[48]

▪ EXHIBIT 9-6

QUALIFYING EVENTS UNDER COBRA

- ▪ Qualifying events for the employee
  - * Reduction in hours to part-time status
  - * Termination for other than gross misconduct
- ▪ Qualifying events for an employee's dependents
  - * Death of the employee
  - * Divorce or legal separation from the employee

SOURCE: 29 U.S.C. § 1163.

DURATION OF CONTINUED COVERAGE.   The period of COBRA coverage varies based on the particular circumstances of the qualifying event. In the event of an employee's termination, the employee is usually entitled to continued group health coverage for eighteen months.[49] If the terminated employee is disabled, the coverage period is extended by an additional eleven months.[50]

If the qualifying event is the employee's death or divorce (including legal separation), the employee's former spouse and dependents are entitled to group health insurance coverage for thirty-six months.[51] The maximum age for a dependent child to be eligible is eighteen.[52] Should a child reach that age within the thirty-six-month period, he or she is no longer covered.

There are other conditions that can shorten the continued coverage period. For example, continued coverage may be terminated if the employer no longer offers group health coverage to employees.[53] To illustrate this, assume an employee is laid off on July 1, 2001, and is not disabled. Under typical circumstances, he or she would be entitled to eighteen months of continued coverage—that employee could expect coverage under COBRA until December 31, 2002. However, if the employer decided to discontinue *all* group health coverage for employees effective April 30, 2002, the laid-off employee's continued health coverage would end on that date as well.

Another justification for terminating continued coverage is the failure of the former employee or the beneficiary to make timely premium payments. The former employee (or his or her dependents in the case of death or divorce) is responsible for making the premium payments for health coverage, not the employer. As with any other insurance policy, should the former employee fail to pay premiums on time, the policy may be canceled.

Finally, the continued health benefits may be terminated if the former employee (or qualified dependent) becomes eligible for Medicare during the continued coverage period.

When a qualifying event occurs, the terminated employee has sixty days from the day coverage would otherwise end to elect continuation of coverage under COBRA. The terminated employee then has up to forty-five days from the date of coverage election to pay the initial premium. The premium for continuation of coverage under COBRA may be as high as 102 percent of the group health insurance rate. For disabled former employees, the premium may be as much as 150 percent of the group rate.[54]

Much like the FLSA in the previous chapter, COBRA's provisions can be subordinate to state laws. State laws mandating health insurance continuation after termination of employment may preempt COBRA when the state law is more strict. If the state law is not as strict as COBRA, the federal law applies.

PAYING FOR THE COVERAGE.   Employers must give the employee (or dependents in the event of death, divorce, or legal separation) notice of the option for continued health care within thirty days of the qualifying event.[55] Most of the legal problems arising from COBRA result from employers failing to either give notice of continuation of medical insurance coverage or doing so in an untimely manner.[56] Once terminated, the employee is still covered under the employer's group health care plan, but he or she must pay the full premium.

For example, assume an employer offers employees a group medical insurance plan in which the employer pays 50 percent of the premium and the employee pays 50 percent. Upon termination, the employee would be responsible for the full 100 percent.[57] In addition, the employee can be assessed up to a 2 percent administrative fee.[58] So, if the employee's contribution was $150 per month for health insurance while employed, it would now be $306 per month upon termination from employment.

THE HEALTH INSURANCE PORTABILITY AND ACCOUNTABILITY ACT OF 1996

In 1996, President Clinton signed into law the Health Insurance Portability and Accountability Act (HIPAA). HIPAA places certain restrictions on the rights of employers and insurers to deny or limit coverage for preexisting conditions. HIPAA also amended COBRA to extend maximum coverage to twenty-nine months for any former employee or beneficiary with qualifying disabilities and amended COBRA's definition of "qualified beneficiary" to include any child born to or placed for adoption with the former employee during the covered period.[59] The regulations under HIPAA allow employees who change jobs or lose jobs to maintain health coverage by requiring later employers to admit them into the group health plan.

HIPAA also imposes requirements on the application of preexisting condition exclusions in group health plans. As defined in HIPAA, a preexisting condition exclusion comprises any limitation or exclusion of benefits because the condition was present before the first day of coverage.[60] The preexisting condition must be disclosed through diagnosis or medical records before the first day of coverage. Group health plans may impose a preexisting condition exclusion only if it is related to a physical or mental condition for which diagnosis was made and care or treatment was recommended or received during a six-month period ending on the enrollment date.[61] The exclusions must be limited to a twelve-month period after the enrollment date or a nineteen-month period in the case of a late enrollment. The period of preexisting condition exclusion must be reduced by the length of any periods of creditable coverage under other group health plans, Medicare, or other similar types of coverage as of the enrollment date. Preexisting condition exclusions do not apply to pregnancy. In certain circumstances, preexisting condition exclusions may not apply to newborns or adopted children.

REGULATION OF VOLUNTARY RETIREMENT BENEFITS

Retirement benefit plans are of two basic types: Defined benefit and defined contribution plans. **Defined benefit plans** are ones in which the employer develops a program that identifies how much a retiring employee will receive each month for the remainder of his or her life. Such plans commonly utilize a benefit formula combining the years of employment with the employer, the employee's age, and the employee's ending salary to compute the amount of the individual's monthly retirement payment.

Defined contribution plans, on the other hand, are based on a prescribed amount invested periodically into an individual account for each employee. Such plans do not have to identify how much is to be placed into the account each year, but they must spell out the process by which it is done. These defined contribution plans are sometimes referred to as individual account plans. Defined contribution plans are exempt from the funding requirements and the plan termination insurance provisions of ERISA. As a consequence, more employers prefer them to defined benefit plans.

EMPLOYEE RETIREMENT INCOME SECURITY ACT OF 1974

Probably the most comprehensive employee benefit regulation statute is the Employee Retirement Income Security Act (ERISA). ERISA does not require employers to offer employee benefit plans; however, once an employer has established a plan, the Act protects the interests of participants and their beneficiaries. Because COBRA and HIPAA are merely amendments to ERISA's provisions governing health care benefits (ERISA's comprehensive nature includes a broad range of employee "welfare benefits"),[62] the remaining discussion will focus only on the Act's pension plan requirements.

ERISA establishes standards of conduct, responsibility, and obligations for fiduciaries of employee benefit plans. It provides for remedies, sanctions, and ready access to the federal courts as well. ERISA is a cumbersome and complicated statute which increases its inherent confusion by dividing enforcement responsibilities between three government agencies: the Pension and Welfare Benefits Administration of the Department of Labor, the Internal Revenue Service of the Department of the Treasury, and the Pension Benefit Guaranty Corporation.

Title I of ERISA was created to protect the interests of employee benefit plan participants and their beneficiaries. First, ERISA requires that sponsors of private employee benefit plans provide participants and beneficiaries with adequate information regarding the plans. This includes a summary plan description[63] and any modifications and changes to the plan.[64] ERISA specifies that the employer must provide each employee with a summary plan description that consists of:

1. The name and type of administration of the plan.
2. The names and addresses of the plan administrator and trustee.
3. The plan's requirements respecting eligibility for participation and benefits.
4. The description of the provisions providing for nonforfeitable pension benefits.
5. Circumstances which may result in disqualification, ineligibility, or denial or loss of benefits.
6. The source of financing of the plan and the identity of organizations through which benefits are provided.

7. The date of the end of the plan year and whether the records of the plan are kept on a calendar, policy, or fiscal-year basis.

8. The procedures to be followed in presenting claims for benefits under the plan, including the office at the Department of Labor through which participants and beneficiaries may seek assistance or information regarding their rights under ERISA.[65]

PROTECTING PARTICIPANTS.   ERISA ensures that plan participants and beneficiaries are protected from discrimination when exercising specific rights in qualified pension plans. In the event that unlawful discrimination occurs, plan participants and beneficiaries may bring a civil action to enforce their rights to their retirement or benefits.

In *Fleming v Ayers,* the Sixth Circuit Court of Appeals upheld the lower court's finding that the plaintiff, Fleming, was discharged in order to avoid paying what were foreseen to be high future medical expenses for her infant child.[66] The court held that the plaintiff was a participant in the defendant's benefit plan and that ERISA prohibits the discharge of "a participant or beneficiary for exercising any right to which he is entitled under the provisions of an employee benefit plan . . . or for the purpose of interfering with the attainment of any right to which such participant may become entitled under the plan. . . ."[67]

Fiduciary Responsibility.   ERISA also imposes stricter accountability on those individuals who have the fiduciary responsibility of managing employee retirement plans. A **fiduciary** is a person who is placed in a position of trust and confidence to exercise a standard of care in the administration or management of an activity.[68] ERISA generally identifies a fiduciary as anyone who exercises discretionary authority or control over a pension plan's management or assets including anyone who provides investment advice to the plan.[69] Fiduciaries who do not follow the principles of conduct outlined in the Act may be held responsible for restoring losses to the plan resulting from their actions.[70] ERISA also gives the pension plan's participants the right to sue for benefits and breaches of fiduciary duty.

Vesting.   The Act provides for minimum standards governing participation, vesting, benefit accrual, and funding of pension plans. **Vesting** means an individual has a nonforfeitable right to pension benefits. ERISA establishes the time frame in which an individual must be employed before becoming eligible to participate in a pension plan and accumulate benefits. The Act provides two methods for becoming vested. One method affords the employer the option of allowing employees to become 100 percent vested after five years of service. For the employee, it means that in the event he or she quits or is terminated before five full years of employment, the employee is not entitled to any pension benefit. The other option permits employers to offer employees partial vesting beginning at the conclusion of the employee's third year of employment and becoming fully vested by the conclusion of the seventh year (see Exhibit 9-7).

BASIC VESTING PROVISIONS UNDER ERISA

7-Year Graduated Vesting Schedule

Years of Vesting Service	Percentage of Accrued Benefit Vested
Less than 3	0%
At least 3, but less than 4	20
At least 4, but less than 5	40
At least 5, but less than 6	60
At least 6, but less than 7	80
At least 7	100

5-Year Vesting Schedule

Years of Vesting Service	Percentage of Accrued Benefit Vested
Less than 5	0
At least 5	100

SOURCE: 29 U.S.C. § 1053(a).

ERISA also establishes detailed funding rules that require plan sponsors to provide adequate funding for pension plans. ERISA requires employers to insure all defined benefit programs through the Pension Benefit Guaranty Corporation, a federally chartered corporation.

RETIREMENT PLANS NOT COVERED BY ERISA. Federal, state, or local government employee plans are not covered by ERISA. Certain church or church association plans are also exempted. Retirement plans that are maintained under state workers' compensation, unemployment compensation, or disability insurance laws are further excluded from coverage under the Act.

Multinational corporations are not required to comply with ERISA for the retirement plans that they have created for foreign nationals at overseas sites. However, the pension plans of United States citizens working for these companies in overseas locations are protected.

SUMMARY OF ERISA'S MAJOR PROVISIONS. ERISA's most significant impact has been in four areas:

1. *Vesting rights.* Vesting is the process by which employees may earn a nonforfeitable right to retirement benefits provided by a plan. Retirement plans can use a participant vesting schedule of either two years, five years, or three to seven years. Vested employees who terminate employment may either have to wait until they reach the plan's early retirement age or normal retirement age before receiving any benefit payments, or they may

be required to take a lump-sum payment if the accumulated vested benefits are $3,500 or less.

2. *Termination insurance.* The Act established the Pension Benefits Guaranty Corporation (PBGC) to administer an insurance fund to which all covered employers with qualified retirement plans must contribute. When a plan terminates leaving unpaid obligations, the PBGC may recover from the employer the cost of paying benefits to vested participants.

3. *Reporting and disclosure requirements.* The Act requires periodic filing of detailed information with both the Department of Labor and the Internal Revenue Service as well as a detailed disclosure to plan participants.

4. *Fiduciary standards.* The Act establishes federal standards of conduct for fiduciaries involved in administering all covered benefit plans. Plan fiduciaries are the individuals who control and manage retirement benefit plans and their assets. The Act requires fiduciaries to act in a prudent manner and make decisions with the benefit of participants in mind. Fiduciaries are personally responsible for breaches of responsibilities. Plan participants are allowed to sue in federal courts to recover losses.

OLDER WORKERS BENEFIT PROTECTION ACT OF 1990

The Older Workers Benefit Protection Act (OWBPA) was enacted to protect older workers from discrimination in benefits based on age. The OWBPA requires employers to provide workers who are over forty years of age with benefits that are equal to those offered to younger employees unless it can be demonstrated that there is a greater cost for providing the benefits to older employees.[71]

The OWBPA also provides a three-week waiting period for older employees who are offered early retirement options. This provision of the Act gives any older employee a period of not less than three weeks from the date that an early retirement offer is made to consider the option before signing any agreement.[72] In addition, the employee can elect to revoke the early retirement agreement within one week of signing the agreement.[73] The OWBPA further requires the employer to advise the employee of his or her right to consult with an attorney prior to signing any agreement.

The Age Discrimination in Employment Act of 1967 (ADEA), which prohibits discrimination based on age, did not address situations under which protected rights or disputed claims could be waived or released. As a result, age discrimination waivers were subject to the same rules as releases of other types of employment discrimination claims. Consequently, there was no statutory, administrative, or court direction for waivers of claims under the ADEA. Most

waivers were simply private agreements between the employer and the former employee, and the parties were free to decide the terms of the waiver.

The OWBPA applies to four different waiver instances: a waiver by an employee who is involuntarily terminated and who has not filed an EEOC charge or lawsuit; a waiver by an employee who is involuntarily terminated pursuant to reductions in force or layoff and who has not filed an age discrimination claim; a waiver in settlement of a disputed claim, either pending EEOC charges or civil actions; and a waiver by an employee who has voluntarily terminated employment pursuant to an incentive program to reduce the workforce. Many of the requirements under the OWBPA are the same in all four instances. Therefore, an employee may not waive any right or claim under the ADEA unless the waiver is knowing and voluntary. The OWBPA, amending the ADEA, asserts that a waiver may not be considered "knowing and voluntary" unless, at a minimum, the following conditions have been satisfied:[74]

1. The waiver is part of an agreement between the employee and the employer that is written in a manner calculated to be understood by such employee, or by the average employee eligible to participate.

2. The waiver specifically refers to rights or claims arising under the ADEA.

3. The employee does not waive rights or claims that may arise after the date the waiver is executed.

4. The employee waives rights or claims only in exchange for consideration in addition to anything of value to which the employee already is entitled.

5. The employee is advised in writing to consult with an attorney prior to executing the agreement.

6. The employee is given a period of at least twenty-one days within which to consider the agreement, or if a waiver is requested in connection with an exit incentive or other employment termination program offered to a group or class of employees, the employee is given a period of at least forty-five days within which to consider the agreement.

7. The agreement provides that for a period of at least seven days following the execution of such agreement, the employee may revoke the agreement, and the agreement shall not become effective or enforceable until the revocation period has expired.

8. If a waiver is requested in connection with an exit incentive or other employment termination program offered to a group or class of employees, an employee is given a period of at least forty-five days to consider the agreement.

In the 1998 case, *Oubre v Entergy*, the United States Supreme Court held that a release signed by the petitioner for receipt of severance pay under an employment termination agreement did not comply with the OWBPA's requirements.[75] Consequently, the terminated employee was permitted to pursue a claim under the ADEA.

INDEPENDENT CONTRACTORS AND EMPLOYEE BENEFITS

Whether an individual is entitled to an employer's benefit package is a function of whether the individual is or is not an "employee" of the employer. There are some individuals who perform work for an employer but are not technically employees. They are instead independent contractors. **Independent contractors,** as their name implies, are independent individuals who contract with employers to perform specific duties, responsibilities, etc. Independent contractors are not employees and are, therefore, not entitled to benefits that are available to employees of a specific employer. Therefore, independent contractors are not entitled to paid vacations, sick leave, paid holidays, insurance coverage, or disability insurance from the employer, even though such benefits may be available to the employer's "employees." Not only are independent contractors not eligible for the employer's voluntary benefits, the employer does not have to provide them with the mandatory benefits (i.e., unemployment compensation, workers' compensation, social security, overtime, etc.). In fact, independent contractors are completely responsible for their own benefits and are even required to withhold their own federal income taxes and FICA taxes (both the employer's and employee's portions).[76]

It is important to note that the distinction between an individual's status as an "employee" or "independent contractor" is not a matter of his or her title but the substance of his or her relationship to the employer.[77] The substance of this relationship is determined through a twenty-factor test developed by the IRS (see Exhibit 9-8). As an example, this twenty-factor test was applied to determine whether certain persons employed by Microsoft Corporation were employees of the company or independent contractors.[78] Microsoft had classified many employees as "freelancers," essentially independent contractors, even though they often participated on the same work teams, performed the same tasks, and worked under the same supervisors as "regular employees." Despite these specific similarities, the freelancers were not entitled to the same benefits enjoyed by the regular employees. In 1989, the IRS had previously applied the twenty-factor test to these "freelancers" and had declared them to be common law employees for tax purposes; Microsoft was now responsible for withholding the freelancers' income taxes, social security taxes, medicare, and unemployment taxes. The U. S. Court of Appeals for the Ninth Circuit took this one step further. Using the same twenty-factor test, the Ninth Circuit now applied it to an employer's obligation to provide voluntary benefits.[79]

■ EXHIBIT 9-8

THE INTERNAL REVENUE SERVICE'S TWENTY-FACTOR CONTROL TEST
TO DETERMINE INDEPENDENT CONTRACTOR STATUS

The Internal Revenue Service, building on the common law test, has set forth a more detailed test for determining whether an individual is an independent contractor for purposes of paying employment tax and withholding. These factors and their applications are as follows:

1. An individual who is required to follow instructions is more likely to be considered an employee.
2. The greater the amount of training needed for the individual to complete an assigned task, the greater the likelihood that the individual will be considered an employee.
3. Where an individual is integrated into the employer's business to a great extent, the individual is more likely to be considered an employee.
4. The fact that an individual personally renders services will weigh in favor of employee status.
5. The fact that the individual hires, fires, and pays assistants, and the employer has no right to do so, indicates independent contractor status.
6. The existence of a continuing relationship is indicative of employee status.
7. The establishment of a set amount of work hours suggests employee status.
8. An individual whose time is substantially devoted to the job is more likely to be considered an employee.
9. The fact that an individual works on the employer's premises suggests employee status.
10. An individual who works according to a sequence set by the employer will more likely be deemed an employee.
11. The fact that an individual submits regular or written reports to the employer will weigh in favor of employee status.
12. An individual who is paid by the project, rather than by the hours, or other period of time, will more likely be considered an independent contractor.
13. An individual who is reimbursed for expenses is more likely an employee.
14. An individual who furnishes the necessary tools and materials for the job is more likely an independent contractor.
15. That an individual makes an investment in the facilities in which he or she works weights in favor of independent contractor status.
16. The fact that an individual's work results in the possible realization of a profit or the risk of a loss suggests independent contractor status.
17. An individual who works for more than one firm at a time is more likely to be an independent contractor.
18. An individual who makes his or her services available to the general public is more likely to be considered an independent contractor.
19. The fact that the employer has the right to discharge the individual suggests an employment relationship (independent contractor relationships are more likely to be contractual).
20. The fact that the individual has the right to terminate the relationship also suggests an employment relationship because independent contractors are usually bound by a contract.

SOURCE: McDermott, N. (November-December 1999). Independent contractors and employees: Do you know one when you see one? *Legal Report.* Alexandria, VA: Society for Human Resource Management, pp. 1–4.

An employer is not required to provide voluntary benefits (i.e., paid holidays, paid vacations, stock options, etc.), but once the employer decides to offer a specific benefit, it must be offered to all eligible employees. The employer cannot arbitrarily declare some individuals to be employees and others to be independent contractors. If an individual is classified as an independent contractor, it must be demonstrated that he or she is truly one.

SUMMARY

This chapter discusses the reasons for the growth of employee benefits, the major legislation governing employee benefits, and the impact of regulation on benefit plans. Employee benefits are either mandatory or voluntary.

From an employee relations viewpoint, the most relevant mandatory benefits are unemployment compensation, workers' compensation, and family medical leave. Unemployment compensation is administered by the individual states, but such programs were established under the Social Security Act of 1935. Family and medical leave is covered under the Family and Medical Leave Act of 1993.

All other benefits are voluntary. The most common of these are health insurance and retirement plans. COBRA does not require employers to provide health benefits, but once an employer chooses to offer such benefits, COBRA's continuation policies for former employees must be followed. Similarly, ERISA does not require employers to provide pension benefits for employees, but once an employer elects to provide a retirement benefit, the Act's fiduciary requirements apply.

Regulations regarding both mandatory and voluntary employee benefits make it essential for benefits administrators to understand their employers' statutory responsibilities. There is more to benefits administration than ensuring that the employer has the appropriate mix of benefits to attract and retain employees. Administrators must also ensure the implementation of the benefits programs does not violate the law.

There are some individuals who perform work for an employer but are not technically employees. They are instead independent contractors, and as their name implies, they are independent individuals who contract with employers to perform specific duties, responsibilities, etc. Independent contractors are not employees and are not entitled to benefits that are available to employees of a specific employer. The IRS has established a twenty-factor test to determine employee versus independent contractor status.

KEY TERMS AND CONCEPTS

defined benefit plans
defined contribution plans
family and medical leave
fiduciary
independent contractors
joint employers
mandatory benefits

qualifying events
successor employer
unemployment compensation
vesting
voluntary benefits
waivers

QUESTIONS

1. Why have employee benefits increased?
2. What are the two types of employee benefits? Provide examples of each.

3. Why was unemployment compensation established? Who is typically entitled to unemployment compensation?

4. What conditions must an employee attain in order to be eligible for mandatory benefits under the FMLA? What are those benefits?

5. What does COBRA regulate? What are the main provisions under COBRA?

6. Why was HIPAA passed?

7. Discuss defined benefit and defined contribution plans.

8. Discuss ERISA's major provisions.

9. How does the OWBPA protect workers?

CASES

1 Leora Nichols is an assistant manager of the Tulsa office of Oklahoma Wholesale Florists (OWF). She began working at OWF in the early 1990s. At that time and during the course of her employment, the company had in place a series of alcohol policies. As shown in the record, the oldest of these policies was set out in the employee handbook received by every employee who joined the company. Nichols acknowledged she received the handbook when she joined the company. In 2000, the company disseminated its "Company Safety Policy, Safety Rules, and Practices," the ninth clause of which stated, "the use of alcohol or illegal drugs on the job or prior to reporting to work is prohibited." While Nichols testified that she did not know whether she had actually read this or the earlier alcohol policy, she admitted that she had received the 2000 policy and signed an acknowledgement that she had received it on March 16, 2000. That acknowledgment stated in relevant part, "I am proud to be employed by Oklahoma Wholesale Florists and will abide by their safety regulations and practices."

At some point in 2000 or earlier, Nichols had been promoted to the position of manager of OWF's Tulsa office. According to her testimony, and that of OWF Vice President David Lynn Gaul, as manager of the office, Nichols was charged with the responsibility of posting the company's alcohol policy on the office's bulletin board. Nichols was demoted from manager to assistant manager in December of 2000.

The company modified its alcohol policy at the end of 2000 or beginning of 2001. On January 9, 2001, Nichols signed another document indicating receipt of the company's drug and alcohol policy. The acknowledgment stated, in relevant part, "I have received a copy of The Oklahoma Wholesale Florists Drug and Alcohol Policy and understand that in order to continue my employment with this company I must abide by the terms of this policy." Again, Nichols said she did not recall whether she had actually read the policy, but admitted signing the acknowledgement.

Nichols' involvement with Oklahoma State Floral Association (OSFA) began prior to her employment with OWF. OSFA held two conventions each year. One of these conventions was a tri-state convention for OSFA members from Nebraska, Kansas, and Oklahoma (NEKANOK). In 2001, without being encouraged or required to do so by OWF, Nichols continued her participation in OSFA and was elected as a committee chairperson for NEKANOK. Part of her duties on this committee required that she assist in the planning of an upcoming NEKANOK convention. It was in this capacity that she chose to meet after work with some colleagues from other florists on July 8, 2001, at the Will Rogers Restaurant to plan the convention's stage decorations.

During the meeting, from 4:30 P.M. to 9:30 P.M., Nichols ate dinner and consumed ten beers, the last of which she drank just before leaving the restaurant. While driving home from the restaurant, along substantially the same path she normally took to get home, Nichols rear-ended another car. As a result of the accident, Nichols sustained injuries to her left shoulder, left elbow, right knee, and right ankle.

At the time of the accident, the police arrested Nichols for driving while intoxicated because of her demeanor and the odor of alcohol on her breath. With her consent, a blood sample was later drawn and submitted to a laboratory for testing. The laboratory results indicated that her blood alcohol content was 0.24, and Nichols pleaded guilty to the offense of driving while intoxicated, which resulted in the temporary loss of her driver's license.

Nichols failed to return to work at OWF after her accident and was terminated. Shortly after she was notified she had been terminated, Nichols filed for unemployment compensation. Do you believe that Nichols is entitled to unemployment compensation? Why or why not?

SOURCE: *Higgins v D.W.F. Wholesale Florists*, 14 S.W.3d 286 (Mo. App. 2000).

2 Frances Atwater began performing services as a computer programmer/analyst for BB&D Bottling beginning in February 1994 until she was terminated in March 2000. Atwater originally heard of the position after answering an advertisement placed by HR Solutions, Inc. Generally, HR Solutions places advertisements seeking individuals to fill certain positions. If HR Solutions determines that an applicant meets the criteria established by BB&D Bottling, the applicant is then interviewed by BB&D Bottling employees who make the ultimate decision as to whether the applicant will be used. In this case, before Atwater commenced work, she met with BB&D Bottling employees, Mildred Mero and Tom Levitiotis. BB&D Bottling provided her with a desk, office space, computer, and other materials needed to perform her work.

Atwater did not meet with a representative from HR Solutions until after she had been working at BB&D Bottling for a few days. Russell Cochet, an HR Solutions representative, met with her and asked her to sign the one and only agreement she ever signed with HR Solutions. Atwater was referred to as an "independent contractor" in the agreement. HR Solutions never promised Atwater that she would be employed by HR Solutions for any period of time or that her services could not be terminated except for cause. Furthermore, Atwater had no agreement, written or oral, with BB&D Bottling regarding her status. Atwater's employment was governed by a series of annual agreements between HR Solutions and BB&D Bottling, known as Master Agreements and Statements of Work (SOWs). The SOWs provided rates of compensation and lengths of employment for Atwater's work at BB&D Bottling.

Regarding payment, Atwater recorded her hours on a weekly basis and submitted them to BB&D Bottling for confirmation. Atwater contends that BB&D Bottling would make payments to HR Solutions, who in turn, remitted payments to her. BB&D Bottling alleges, however, that Atwater was paid directly by HR Solutions, who then invoiced BB&D Bottling for the payment.

Sometime in 1998, Atwater was assigned to the ICS project. ICS is a group of computer programs which run on the AS/400 computer, a mid-sized computer system. According to defendants, the ICS project began in the late 1980s and was originally intended to provide a short-term computerized solution to BB&D Bottling's need to track the whereabouts and status of fountain equipment. Around that same time, BB&D Bottling began development of the Fountain Equipment Tracking System (FET). FET, which is much more complex than ICS, was designed to be the long-term computerized solution to the need to track fountain equipment. Sometime in the early 1990s, BB&D Bottling decided to integrate ICS and FET, which meant that ICS had to be upgraded and converted to a permanent system.

Atwater's duties with ICS included analyzing and programming system enhancements, assisting ICS users in resolving day-to-day problems with the system, and working with the Mid-Range Computer Support group (the MCS group). Atwater also assisted in screening new employees for BB&D Bottling. While working on the ICS project, she was supervised by Bill O' Riley and Robert Harper. O'Riley reported to David Nickles, who reported to Mero, BB&D Bottling's director of application development.

The MCS group consists of computer programmers, operators, and support personnel responsible for maintaining the hardware and operating systems for the various AS/400 computers. The MCS group was managed by Maurice Stokes. Ethan Frink was the manager of the MCS group, reporting to Stokes.

In February 1999, BB&D Bottling's audit department conducted an audit of the AS/400 environment at BB&D Bottling. The audit turned up numerous operational and security deficiencies. MCS was directed to correct these deficiencies in order to secure the AS/400 environment. As a result, MCS took steps to limit the authority that applications support personnel, such as Atwater, had to affect the internal operations of the AS/400s. The MCS group's efforts to secure the AS/400 environment created tension between the MCS group and the ICS group. Atwater alleges that the MCS group's actions were intended to harass and interfere with her performance. She resisted the MCS group's efforts to restrict her HR solutions to the AS/400 system.

On January 28, 2000, Atwater contacted Computer Solutions in Florida, a company which provides contract workers to other companies. Atwater also sent her resume and applied for a job. She informed Computer Solutions that it would be possible for her to relocate in three weeks.

On February 28, 2000, Atwater met with Jennifer Edwards, human resources director of BB&D Bottling, and Jefferson Blythe, BB&D Bottling's senior counsel for labor relations. Atwater's counsel requested the meeting on her behalf. During the meeting, there was a discussion concerning the efforts of Stokes and Frink to sabotage the ICS application. Atwater claims they also discussed how the MCS group was harassing her. There is a dispute regarding whether Atwater asserted that she was a BB&D Bottling employee during this meeting.

Sometime after the meeting, Atwater spoke with O'Riley, the ICS project manager, and told him about the meeting. Whether or not she informed O'Riley of her intention to file a lawsuit against BB&D Bottling generally, it is undisputed that Atwater did not tell O'Riley that she intended to file a lawsuit concerning possible employee benefits. O'Riley immediately informed his supervisor, Nickles, about his conversation with Atwater. At that point, Nickles, who had authority to do so, decided to terminate Atwater.

Soon thereafter, Edwards, Blythe, Cochet, and Nickles met to discuss Atwater. At that meeting, Nickles informed Cochet, the HR Solutions representative, that Atwater's services would no longer be needed. On March 7, 2000, Cochet informed Atwater that her services were no longer needed. Atwater moved to Florida on March 30, 2000, and began working for ComputerPeople.

BB&D Bottling provides its regular employees with benefits which are set forth in a book entitled, *Your World of Benefits Handbook.* Benefits, which are provided to "regular" employees of BB&D Bottling, include: health, dental, dependent life, life insurance, AD&D, business travel accident insurance, dependent care account, flexible spending account, long-term disability, employee retirement plan, employee assistance program, survivors counseling program, severance pay, survivor's benefit program, and a thrift plan.

Is Atwater an employee or an independent contractor? Explain your reasoning. What criteria must be met in order to demonstrate that a party is a *bona fide* independent contractor?

SOURCE: *Wolf v Coca-Cola Co.*, 82 F.Supp. 2d 1366 (N.D. Ga. 1998).

NOTES

1. Bureau of National Affairs (January 1998). Employee benefits cost declined in 1996, survey results. *BNA Bulletin to Management*, p. 29.

2. Tolles, A. (1964). *Origins of Modern Wage Theories*. Engelwood Cliffs, NJ: Prentice Hall, Inc., p. 97.

3. Ibid., pp. 93–97.

4. 42 U.S.C. Chapter 7.

5. 42 U.S.C. § 503.

6. 26 U.S.C. § 3306(a).

7. 45 U.S.C. § Chapter 11.

8. Jackson, G. E. (1999 Cumulative Supplement). *Labor and Employment Law Desk Book (2d ed.).* Paramus, NJ: Prentice Hall.

9. Ibid.

10. Ibid.

11. Ibid.

12. Consolidated Laws of New York, § 591 *et.seq;* Rhode Island General Laws, § 28–44–1 *et seq.*

13. 29 C.F.R. § 825.

14. 29 C.F.R. § 825.106(d).

15. 29 C.F.R. § 825.111.

16. 29 C.F.R. § 825.104(c).

17. 29 C.F.R. § 825.104.

18. 29 C.F.R. § 825.110.

19. 29 C.F.R. § 825.110(c).

20. U.S. Employment Standards Administration (February 2001). "Frequently Asked Questions and Answers." *Family and Medical Leave Act Employee/Employer Advisor.* **http://www.elaws.dol.gov/fmla/wren/faq.htm**

21. 29 C.F.R. § 825.110.

22. 29 U.S.C. § 2612.

23. *Bocalbos v National Western Life Insurance,* 162 F.3d 379 (5th Cir. 1998).

24. 29 C.F.R. § 825.202.

25. 29 U.S.C. § 2612.

26. 29 C.F.R. § 825.113.

27. Ibid.

28. Ibid. at § 825.202.

29. Ibid. at § 825.116.

30. Ibid. at § 825.113.

31. Ibid. at § 825.307.

32. 29 U.S.C. § 2611(11).

33. *Oswalt v Sara Lee Corp.,* 74 F.3d 91 (5th Cir. 1996).

34. 29 C.F.R. § 825.114.

35. U.S. Employment Standards Administration (February 2000). *Fact Sheet No. 28. The Family and Medical Leave Act of 1993.* **http://www.dol.gov/esa/public/regs/compliance/whd/whdfs28.htm**

36. 29 C.F.R. § 825.114(a)(2).

37. *Murray v Red Kap Industries, Inc.,* 124 F.3d 695, 698 (5th Cir. 1997).

38. 29 C.F.R. § 825.114(a)(2)(i)(B).

39. Society for Human Resource Management (July 2000). Legislative Fact Sheets: Family and Medical Leave Act. **http://www.shrm.org/government/factsheets/factfmla00.asp**

40. Ibid.

41. Ibid.

42. 29 C.F.R. § 825.304.

43. 29 U.S.C. § 2612(d)(2)(A).

44. 29 C.F.R. § § 825.110; 825.200; 825.201; 825.202; 825.500; and 825.800.

45. U.S. Employment Standards Administration (2000). Frequently Asked Questions and Answers. *Family and Medical Leave Act Employee/Employer Advisor.*

46. 29 U.S.C. § 1163(2).

47. 29 U.S.C. § 1163(1).

48. 29 U.S.C. § 1163(3).

49. 29 U.S.C. § 1162(2)(A).

50. 29 U.S.C. § 1162(2)(A)(v).

51. 29 U.S.C. § 1162(2)(A)(iii).

52. 29 U.S.C. § 1169(3)(A).

53. 29 U.S.C. § 1162(2).

54. U.S. Department of Labor (1999). *Health Benefits Under the Consolidated Omnibus Reconciliation Act (COBRA).* **http://www.dol.gov/dol/pwba/public/cobra99.pdf**

55. 29 U.S.C. § 1163(2).

56. *Vincent v Wells Fargo Guard Services, Inc.,* 44 F.Supp. 2d 1302 (S.D. Fla. 1999); *Mlsna v Untel Communications, Inc.,* 91 F.3d 876 (7th Cir. 1996); *Switzer v Wal-Mart Stores, Inc.,* 52 F.3d 1294 (5th Cir. 1995).

57. U.S. Pension and Welfare Benefits Administration (July 1999). *Health Benefits Under the Consolidated Omnibus Budget Reconciliation Act (COBRA).* Washington, DC: Government Printing Office, p. 15.

58. Ibid.

59. 29 U.S.C. § 1169.

60. U.S. Pension and Welfare Benefits Administration (June 1999). *Questions and Answers: Recent Changes in Health Care Law.* Washington, DC: Government Printing Office, p. 4.

61. Ibid.

62. 29 U.S.C. § 1002(i).

63. 29 U.S.C. § 1022.

64. 29 U.S.C. § 1024(b).

65. 29 U.S.C. § 1022(b).

66. *Fleming v Ayers & Associates,* 948 F.2d 993 (6th Cir. 1991).

67. Ibid. at 997.

68. Black, H.C. (1990). *Black's Law Dictionary (6th ed.)*. St. Paul, MN: West Publishing Co.

69. 29 C.F.R. § 2584.8477(e)-6.

70. 29 U.S.C. § 1109.

71. 29 U.S.C. § 623.

72. 29 C.F.R. § 1625.22

73. Ibid.

74. 29 U.S.C. § 626(f).

75. *Oubre v Entergy Operations, Inc.*, 522 U.S. 422 (1998).

76. U.S. Department of the Treasury, Internal Revenue Service (2001). Employee or independent contractor? *Employer's Supplement Tax Guide*. Washington, DC: Government Printing Office, pp. 5–7.

77. Ibid. at p. 3.

78. *Vincaino v United States District Court*, 173 F.2d 713 (9th Cir. 1999), *cert denied* 528 U.S. 1105 (2000).

79. Ibid. at 717.

WORKPLACE SAFETY AND HEALTH ISSUES

LEARNING OBJECTIVES

☐ Understand the reasons for government regulation of workplace safety and health.

☐ Discuss the evolution of government regulation of workplace safety and health.

☐ Describe the major provisions of federal and state laws related to workplace safety and health.

☐ Discuss the development of workers' compensation legislation.

☐ Explain the benefits of and problems associated with workers' compensation.

☐ Understand the basic provisions of the Occupational Safety and Health Act of 1970.

☐ Describe the five types of citations issued by the Occupational Safety and Health Administration.

OPENING SCENARIO

Dave Nichols is the new HR manager for Rose and Frink Hotel Management, Inc. (RFHM). On the second day on the job, he is asked by one of the partners, Greg Rose, about a workers' compensation claim filed by a former employee, Scott Douglass.

Douglass was hired as a desk clerk by RFHM at its San Diego location in March 1998. Three to four times a year, Douglass was expected to serve as the manager on duty; this was usually from one week to one month at a time. Generally, a manager on duty looks after the property and employees and handles all the usual daily problems.

Douglass reportedly had no difficulty doing the work until late 1999 when he came under the supervision of a new manager, Gerald McClure. McClure was responsible for two other locations along with Douglass's property. Douglass claimed McClure was often away at the other locations, and he was now being assigned the manager-on-duty *responsibilities more often. During the periods Douglass was in charge, there were often missing reservations, and he was contacted regularly at night regarding problems at the hotel.*

Although Douglass was paid more when he managed, he told McClure it was too much for one person. He stated that he only did the work because he felt responsible, and there was no one else to do it. When other employees quit in early 2000, Douglass filled in to cover their duties and became greatly stressed and symptomatic. He sought medical treatment, never returned to work, and filed for workers' compensation.

During his employment with RFHM, Douglass also had significant personal problems. His deceased father had been an alcoholic. His mother was abusive, and they did not get along. Douglass's brother lost his doctor's license because of drugs and alcohol. His son had been arrested and jailed for various offenses including drugs and spousal abuse and was diagnosed as a schizophrenic. Douglass's daughter had a child out of wedlock, was abused, attempted suicide, and had numerous physical problems.

Douglass himself had a history of troubled marriages. After his first divorce, his wife's parents gained custody of the children who had allegedly been mistreated. His third wife, who had been an alcoholic, died in a boating accident, leading to excessive drinking by Douglass for two years. Douglass's subsequent girlfriend had been in and out of his life due to drug problems. He also had tried drugs, attempted suicide, and filed for bankruptcy.

For evidentiary support of his workers' compensation claim for stress, Douglass obtained medical-legal reports from a psychiatrist, Brian Reithel. Dr. Reithel described Douglass's work stress as beginning with McClure's mismanagement and Douglass's increased workload. In regard to nonindustrial stresses, Dr. Reithel reported much of Douglass's history of family problems, but noted that he had always been able to cope and continue working in the past.

Nichols has been informed by Rose that the company feels that Douglass's workers' compensation claim is unfounded, and the company must do something to keep workers' compensation claims under control. Nichols is asked whether RFHM should contest Douglass's claim with the Workers' Compensation Appeals Board.[1]

HISTORICAL OVERVIEW OF WORKPLACE SAFETY

Prior to the Industrial Revolution, most nonagricultural workers were independent craftsmen. In the event that a craftsman lost work as a result of an occupational accident or illness, he suffered the full economic loss. This was solely the individual's responsibility, as was personal safety while in the workplace. The independent craftsman was expected to assume all personal financial consequences of a workplace injury. If the craftsman did not have sufficient savings to get through the recovery period, he and his family would be destitute.

This predicament continued throughout most of the nineteenth century. As the United States became more industrialized, unsafe and unhealthy working conditions spread. Not surprisingly, the resulting surge of workplace injuries, diseases, and deaths from industrial accidents began to draw society's attention to workplace safety and health.

During this same period, employers continued to operate under the assumption that their employees were completely responsible for occupational accidents and illnesses. As in the past, industrial employees were expected to assume the inherent risks of the job. As had been the case with their independent craftsmen predecessors, when an industrial worker was injured on the job or suffered an illness brought on by prolonged exposure to a harmful work environment, his or her only recourses for compensation were personal savings or through the courts. Deaths and disabling injuries due to occupational accidents were frequent, but relief was rare.

By the latter part of the nineteenth century, a number of mine disasters prompted the American public to pressure governments to regulate industries in order to reduce industrial accidents. One of the earliest attempts to regulate hazardous workplace conditions occurred in the Commonwealth of Massachusetts. Massachusetts passed legislation providing for industrial inspectors. Under this statute, inspectors were given authority to enter factories and could require employers to safeguard employees from dangerous industrial equipment.[2]

A number of states passed laws providing for workers' compensation in the opening years of the twentieth century. **Workers' compensation** laws provided workers with cash benefits for work-related injuries and deaths. Because workers' compensation was established as insurance, the premiums levied on employers increased as the number of claims against employers increased. This created an economic incentive to enhance workplace safety. As a result of employer concern for improving workplace safety and health, work-related accidents and injuries declined steadily from the early 1930s until the late 1950s.[3]

The concept of providing financial relief for workers injured or killed in industrial accidents originated in Europe as early as the 1880s. Switzerland passed a limited no-fault workers' compensation law in 1881, and Germany enacted a similar workers' compensation act in 1884. The German law would become a model for similar laws in the United States.[4] By 1903, most industrialized nations in Western Europe had some form of workers' compensation legislation.[5]

In 1908, the Federal Employees' Compensation Act was enacted in the United States.[6] This Act allowed federal employees injured in certain hazardous jobs to receive limited compensation. In 1916, this legislation was amended to provide coverage to all federal employees.[7] In addition, there are two other federal workers' compensation acts: the Federal Employees' Compensation Act[8] and the Longshore and Harbor Workers' Compensation Act.[9]

On May 3, 1911 Wisconsin became the first state to enact a workers' compensation law (that was not repealed or found to be unconstitutional) for private sector employees.[10] Two other states, Washington and Kansas, had passed permanent workers' compensation laws on March 14, 1911, but they did not become effective until a date later than the Wisconsin law.[11] During the next ten years, forty-three other states would enact similar workers' compensation laws. Currently, there are workers' compensation laws in all fifty states, the District of Columbia, Puerto Rico, and the Virgin Islands.

In the early 1930s, it was estimated that work-related accidents, each year, resulted in as many as twenty thousand employee deaths, eighty thousand employees becoming totally or partially disabled, and more than two million employees losing work time due to injuries.[12] Much of the annual death rate among wage earners during this period was considered to be directly or indirectly due to the nature of workers' employment. The data in Exhibit 10-1 reflects the higher annual death rate for unskilled, semiskilled, and skilled workers than employees in less hazardous occupations from a survey of ten industrialized states conducted in 1930 for a congressional committee.

In the late 1960s, the annual rate of work-related accidents and injuries began to reverse the previous four decades' decline, and there was spreading support for establishing federal standards of occupational safety and health in the workplace. The Occupational Safety and Health Act of 1970 became the first comprehensive federal legislation enacted to apply safety and health standards to practically every employer and employee in the United States. Although federal safety and health standards had been mandated previously in the Walsh-Healey Act of 1936[13] and the Service Contract Act of 1963,[14] these re-

■ EXHIBIT 10-1

ANNUAL DEATH RATE PER 1,000 WORKERS 15–64 YEARS OF AGE IN TEN STATES, 1930

Type of Worker	Tuberculosis	Pneumonia	Accidents	All Causes
Unskilled	1.85	1.36	0.52	14.48
Semiskilled	1.02	0.72	0.34	10.09
Skilled	0.72	0.60	0.34	8.29
Proprietors and managers	0.43	0.52	0.22	7.93
Clerks/Kindreds	0.66	0.51	0.19	7.75
Professionals	0.26	0.39	0.15	6.71
Agricultural	0.47	0.43	0.15	6.23
All Gainfully Employed	0.88	0.69	0.30	9.10

SOURCE: *Hearings Before a Special Committee to Investigate Unemployment and Relief*, U.S. Senate, 75th Congress, Third Session, 1938, vol. 2, p. 1491.

quirements applied only to those employers who held federal construction and service contracts.

The National Safety Council estimates that the work-injury death rate in 1933 was thirty-seven deaths per 100,000 employees.[15] In 1970, the year the Occupational Safety and Health Act was passed, eighteen out of 100,000 employees died from work-related injuries.[16] By 1998, the work-injury death rate had declined to 3.8 deaths per 100,000 employees.[17] The improvements in accident prevention and reduced work-related death rates has been attributed to the combined efforts of industrial management, organized labor, and government.

DEVELOPMENT OF WORKERS' COMPENSATION

It is important to remember that prior to the enactment of workers' compensation statutes, the only recourse for injured workers was to sue their employers for damages under state tort laws. However, injured workers were unlikely to win such suits because of two obstacles to pursuing such litigation. One obstacle arose from the worker's burden of proving negligence on the part of the employer. The second obstacle stemmed from the workers' difficulty in overcoming the three common law defenses (discussed in more detail later) available to employers in negligence suits: assumption of risk, fellow-servant rule, and contributory negligence. As many workers learned, courts held that when workers knew of the risks inherent in the work before accepting employment, they assumed responsibility for their injuries. In many instances, it also could be shown that injuries were in some part the result of the worker's own negligence.[18]

Workers' compensation laws evolved to guarantee benefits would be paid to workers injured on the job and that they would be paid promptly with a minimum of legal formality. This may have been the intention when such laws were originally enacted; however, in most states, claims resolution has become a cumbersome and time-consuming process. Although claims are paid promptly (within one week under most state laws), worker claims are often challenged. Typically, worker claims are contested in quasijudicial workers' compensation appeal board hearings presided over by administrative law judges.

EXCLUSIVITY PRINCIPLE

As part of the fundamental rationale for workers' compensation legislation, an employee injured in the course of employment receives fixed compensation that is described statutorily as the employee's "exclusive remedy" against the employer. This concept is popularly known as the exclusivity principle. Under the **exclusivity principle,** an employee receiving workers' compensation benefits is barred from bringing a common law suit against the employer for a work-related injury. Yet there are several exceptions to this general rule. For example, the exclusivity principle will not apply to cases where injuries are found to be caused by intentional acts of the employer. If an employee can prove an accident arose out of an employer's specific intent to injure the employee, then the employee is not barred from bringing a common law claim.[19] Therefore, if an employer or his or her agent purposely placed an employee in harms way (i.e., told the employee to ignore a safety procedure), the exclusivity principle would no longer apply.

In certain instances, some states permit litigation when it can be shown that an employer was grossly negligent regarding a work-related accident or illness. For example, the conditions causing the accident were so obvious and the resulting injury was so apparent that a reasonable person would have easily anticipated the employee's injury—the employer's failure to eliminate or reduce the hazard was clearly the major factor contributing to the employee's injury.

Even when challenged in court, the employer is still often able to prevail in litigation using any of three previously mentioned defenses (assumption of risk, the fellow-servant rule, and contributory negligence). Even though the employer incurs the additional cost of paying the workers' compensation premiums, this expense is offset by avoiding, or at least reducing, the likelihood of resolving the claim through the courts.

The advantages offered by workers' compensation laws are that in return for assuming liability, not only was the employer's monetary liability fixed to specific statutory amounts, but employees also, by statute, had to forgo any further attempts to recover compensation through common law. In short, when workers' compensation is the employee's exclusive remedy, this relieves the employer of unpredictable, and potentially costly, common law litigation.

EMPLOYEE COMPENSABLE INJURIES AND ILLNESSES

One characteristic of all workers' compensation systems is that the employee is only required to demonstrate that the injury or illness was work related. The employee does not have to show that the employer's actions are responsible for the injury. The basic premise of workers' compensation laws is that the cost of work-related injuries should be assumed by the employer; consequently, providing for such coverage is considered part of the cost of doing business. Workers' compensation quickly evolved into a mandatory benefit program with the expenses associated with the insurance coverage borne by the employer.

WORKERS' COMPENSATION. Workers' compensation is not paid to an individual merely because he or she is injured or ill. The injury or illness must arise from employment; either the injury or illness must be related to work.

Work-Related Injuries. Naturally, an injury sustained while at work is covered. For example, a warehouse employee who is struck and injured by a delivery truck while at work would be entitled to workers' compensation. If the same employee was struck and injured by a delivery truck in front of his home during nonwork time, he would not be eligible for the benefit. Usually, workers' compensation does not apply to injuries sustained during nonwork hours, at a location off the employer's premises, when work duties are not being performed, or while performing activities that are not in the course of employment.[20]

What about employees who engage in work activities off the employer's premises? Any injuries would be covered, provided the employees were engaged in the employer's work, or as some courts have noted, the employer derives substantial direct benefit from the employee's activity.[21] If the activity is not for the employer's benefit, workers' compensation benefits can be denied. Such was the case in *Koger v Greyhound Lines, Inc.*[22] A striking employee was struck by a company bus while he was picketing the employer. The Ohio State Court of Appeals ruled that he was not eligible for workers' compensation because his injury was "not received in the course of, and arising out of, the injured employee's employment."[23]

The same is true for injuries that occur during company outings, company-sponsored events, or company-sponsored sporting events. Injuries to an employee would be covered only if the employee was engaged in the employer's work. Therefore, if attendance at a company party or event is mandatory, any resulting injury is likely to be compensable. On the other hand, if the employee is not required to attend or participate, is not paid to do so, and the event was not sponsored by the employer, the injury is not covered under workers' compensation.[24] Unfortunately, this is not as simple as it sounds.

Assume a company is holding an annual company picnic on company property. Attendance is strictly voluntary. While at the picnic, Craig Billings, an accountant, decides to join a football game. While playing football, Billings fractures his leg. Recall that attendance at the picnic was not mandatory, and the decision to participate in the football game was made by Billings. Therefore, in most states, this would not be a compensable workers' compensation injury.

Now, consider that Faye Gilbert, assistant HR manager, is also at the same company picnic. Gilbert's job at the picnic is to oversee the refreshments and provide enough food and drinks for all employees who attend. While delivering ice, Gilbert slips and breaks her ankle. Although this is the same picnic on company grounds where Billings was injured and not entitled to workers' compensation for his injury, Gilbert is entitled to workers' compensation for her injury. Although the football injury was the result of voluntary participation, Gilbert's injury arose from her employment; she was at the picnic for direct benefit for her employer.[25]

Work-Related Illnesses. As with injuries, illnesses must be shown to arise out of employment—including mental illnesses.[26] Whether for physical or mental illnesses, the employee must establish a causal connection between the disability and the nature of his or her employment. This causal link invariably requires substantial medical evidence to support any claim that occupational exposure to some factor resulted in the illness.[27]

Controlling Workers' Compensation Costs. Workers' compensation costs were approximately $55.2 billion in 1996.[28] The obvious solution to controlling costs is to control the incidents of injury or illness in the workplace. This means creating safety programs and providing employee training to promote safe working behavior. The more emphasis that management places on safety awareness, the more safety conscious employees are likely to become.

When injuries or illnesses do occur, the employer should get a medical assessment as quickly as possible. This information will be essential in determining whether the employee is no longer fit for employment. It can also be used to determine whether the injured employee can be reassigned to less strenuous work. If the employee can continue employment in another position, he or she would not be entitled to disability benefits.

Similarly, the employer should attempt to get a rehabilitation assessment of the injured or ill employee. Again, this could be used to assist in determining the probability of the employee returning to work and/or being reassigned to other work. It is recommended that this assessment be performed within thirty days after the injury if it is to be successful.[29]

Because there is so much abuse in the system—perhaps as much as 10 percent of all workers' compensation claims[30]—employers should investigate all employees who are suspected of submitting false claims and take action against those found to have submitted false claims. Since such employees are engaging in an unlawful activity (fraud), some courts have upheld surveillance of employees off company premises.

EMPLOYER COMMON LAW DEFENSES

The **assumption of risk defense** is based on the philosophy that a person accepts the inherent risks involved in the job, thus absolving the employer of responsibility of injuries or illnesses incurred as a result of the normal risks of a job. The employer must be able to show that the employee was aware of, or should have been aware of, the hazards pertaining to a particular job. Safety briefings and training would provide means of establishing knowledge. Good job analysis and thorough job descriptions of working conditions would be another means of establishing this, provided that the job descriptions were disseminated to the affected employees.

The **fellow-servant rule defense** involves an employer's assertion that injuries or illnesses were derived from the actions, whether accidental or intentional, of another employee. An employee suffering injury or illness from a negligent act of a fellow employee could be remedied by suing the other employee rather than the employer. Properly conducted accident investigations would be a viable method for making such an assertion.

Under the **contributory negligence defense,** an employer claims that the damages for injuries were due, at least in part, to the negligence of the affected employee. Injured workers may not recover awards for damages of which they were primarily responsible. However, if judges or juries determine that responsibility for injuries or illnesses is mutually shared by both the employee and the employer, the liability for damages may be distributed proportionally. Again, well-constructed work rules, proof that the employee was aware of safety procedures, and thorough investigations (documentation) would be helpful in establishing the defense.

WORKERS' COMPENSATION AS INSURANCE

As enacted by each of the fifty states and the territories, workers' compensation laws represent the most prevalent and comprehensive no-fault insurance program in the United States. However, there is no uniform national program. State workers' compensation provisions differ from state to state with regard to procedural aspects, compensation provisions, and jobs covered (see Exhibit 10-2). The state laws also differ in regard to specific types of coverage, insurance funding requirements, and the extent and types of costs and benefits paid. In some states, the insurance company is a single state agency; in others, employers may choose between several private companies. There is even some variance between the states as to what specifically constitutes a work-related, compensable injury.

Despite these and other differences, state workers' compensation laws have several characteristics in common. In all states, only work-related injuries are compensated. Other injuries, illnesses, or preexisting disabilities (unless aggravated by work-related factors) are not covered under workers' compensation. Neither are injuries that are self-inflicted or caused by the employee's willful misconduct.[31] The bottom line is that there must be some casual connection between the employee's injury or illness and work.

All programs provide prompt (compared to litigation) income payments (usually one-half to two-thirds of the affected employee's average pay up to a maximum cap), medical benefits to injured workers, and lump sum survivors' benefits regardless of who is at fault. As mentioned earlier, because these programs are experience rated, they still continue to provide an incentive for employers to develop and maintain safe work programs (a pre-injury objective) and an incentive to get the employee back to work (a post-injury objective).[32] Rehabilitative services provided under workers' compensation reduce overall cases of such programs by returning the employee to work as quickly as possible.

MANDATORY VERSUS VOLUNTARY PARTICIPATION. State workers' compensation laws are either mandatory or voluntary. The vast majority of states have mandatory laws in which *all* employers must carry workers' compensation insurance and comply with the state law by providing specific benefits. Covered employees are afforded no choice, and failure to participate in the program is a violation of the law. Covered employers are typically public and private employers either in certain hazardous industries or in the type of businesses that experience the highest rates of job-related injuries.

State	Type of Law	Availability of State Funds	Private Carrier	Individual Employer	Group of Employers
Alabama	Compulsory	No	Yes	Yes	Yes
Alaska	Compulsory	No	Yes	Yes	No
Arizona	Compulsory	Competitive	Yes	Yes	Yes
Arkansas	Compulsory	No	Yes	Yes	Yes
California	Compulsory	Competitive	Yes	Yes	No
Colorado	Compulsory	Competitive	Yes	Yes	Yes
Connecticut	Compulsory	No	Yes	Yes	Yes
Delaware	Compulsory	No	Yes	Yes	No
Florida	Compulsory	No	Yes	Yes	Yes
Georgia	Compulsory	No	Yes	Yes	Yes
Hawaii	Compulsory	Competitive	Yes	Yes	Yes
Idaho	Compulsory	Competitive	Yes	Yes	No
Illinois	Compulsory	No	Yes	Yes	Yes
Indiana	Compulsory	No	Yes	Yes	No
Iowa	Compulsory	No	Yes	Yes	Yes
Kansas	Compulsory	No	Yes	Yes	Yes
Kentucky	Compulsory	Competitive	Yes	Yes	Yes
Louisiana	Compulsory	Competitive	Yes	Yes	Yes
Maine	Compulsory	Competitive	Yes	Yes	Yes
Maryland	Compulsory	Competitive	Yes	Yes	Yes
Massachusetts	Compulsory	No	Yes	Yes	Yes
Michigan	Compulsory	Competitive	Yes	Yes	Yes
Minnesota	Compulsory	Competitive	Yes	Yes	Yes
Mississippi	Compulsory	No	Yes	Yes	Yes
Missouri	Compulsory	Competitive	Yes	Yes	Yes
Montana	Compulsory	Competitive	Yes	Yes	Yes
Nebraska	Compulsory	No	Yes	Yes	No

[1]New Jersey law provides that workers' compensation coverage may be terminated by either party upon sixty days notice in writing prior to any accident.

[2]Texas law provides for mandatory workers' compensation coverage for certain transportation carriers.

States with voluntary, or elective, workers' compensation laws allow employers to accept or reject insurance coverage at their own volition, but employers choosing not to participate can be sued by workers who are injured or become ill due to a work-related incident. Only three states (New Jersey, Texas, and Wyoming) permit some level of voluntary choice in the workers' compensation insurance participation.[33] However, if employers in these particular states elect to reject insurance coverage, they also waive their rights to use the three common-law defenses mentioned earlier when sued by injured employees. Yes, the partici-

State	Type of Law	Availability of State Funds	Private Carrier	Individual Employer	Group of Employers
Nevada	Compulsory	Exclusive	No	Yes	No
New Hampshire	Compulsory	No	Yes	Yes	Yes
New Jersey[1]	Compulsory	No	Yes	Yes	No
New Mexico	Compulsory	Competitive	Yes	Yes	Yes
New York	Compulsory	Competitive	Yes	Yes	Yes
North Carolina	Compulsory	No	Yes	Yes	Yes
North Dakota	Compulsory	Exclusive	No	No	No
Ohio	Compulsory	Exclusive	No	Yes	No
Oklahoma	Compulsory	Competitive	Yes	Yes	Yes
Oregon	Compulsory	Competitive	Yes	Yes	Yes
Pennsylvania	Compulsory	Competitive	Yes	Yes	Yes
Rhode Island	Compulsory	Competitive	Yes	Yes	Yes
South Carolina	Compulsory	No	Yes	Yes	Yes
South Dakota	Compulsory	No	Yes	Yes	Yes
Tennessee	Compulsory	No	Yes	Yes	Yes
Texas[2]	Elective	Competitive	Yes	Yes	No
Utah	Compulsory	Competitive	Yes	Yes	No
Vermont	Compulsory	No	Yes	Yes	No
Virginia	Compulsory	No	Yes	Yes	Yes
Washington	Compulsory	Exclusive	No	Yes	Yes
West Virginia	Compulsory	Exclusive	No	Yes	No
Wisconsin	Compulsory	No	Yes	Yes	No
Wyoming[3]	Compulsory	Exclusive	No	No	No
Dist. of Col.	Compulsory	No	Yes	Yes	No
Puerto Rico	Compulsory	Exclusive	No	No	No
Virgin Islands	Compulsory	Exclusive	No	No	No

[3]Wyoming law is compulsory for all employees engaged in extra hazardous occupations and elective for all other occupations.

SOURCE: *January 1, 2000 Revision of Table 1 from OWCP*, The Office of Workers' Compensation Programs, Employment Standards Administration. Washington, DC: U.S. Department of Labor.

pation is elective, but it is very risky for any employer to choose not to participate.

State requirements for employers to finance workers' compensation insurance may vary from state to state but usually fall into one of these models. Financing workers' compensation insurance in compliance with state laws may be through paying for a policy with a private insurance company, self-insuring by employers themselves, or paying into a either a monopolistic or a competitive state insurance fund. Most states require employers to pay insurance premiums in advance, although some permit employers to avoid such payments through self-insurance, provided they have proof of financial ability to assume their risks.[34] Some degree of self-insurance is allowed in the workers' compensation laws of forty-eight states.[35]

WORKERS' COMPENSATION BENEFITS.   State workers' compensation laws generally provide payments for lost income while the worker is disabled, payment of medical expenses for work-related injuries or illnesses, lump sum payments or lifetime compensation for disfigurement, benefits for dependent survivors, and rehabilitative assistance (see Exhibit 10-3). State laws ordinarily set minimum and maximum rates for indemnity benefits based on a designated proportion or percentage of an injured employee's weekly wage and the degree of disability. For most states the maximum proportion is based on two-thirds of the state's average weekly wage.

To illustrate how benefits are determined, assume an employee working in Texas has an average weekly pay rate of $900. The employee is injured at work and clearly eligible to draw workers' compensation permanent disability benefits. Texas workers' compensation legislation provides for a weekly payment up to two-thirds of the employee's average weekly pay or $508, whichever amount is smaller.[36] If the worker is eligible for the maximum benefit and two-thirds of $900 (approximately $600 per week) is more than the $508 cap on the benefit, the injured employee will receive the smaller amount, or $508 per week.

Additionally, an employee's weekly benefit is based on the degree to which he or she is disabled. The degree of disability used in determining the weekly benefit amount is based on one of the four following classifications: temporary total disability, permanent total disability, temporary partial disability, or permanent partial disability. Benefits for disability income are generally payable based upon the disabled worker satisfying a waiting period, typically from three to seven days. Each program has a schedule of benefits to determine what percentage of the benefit the disabled employee is eligible to draw.

■ **EXHIBIT 10-3**

BENEFITS PROVIDED UNDER WORKERS' COMPENSATION

- Payment for lost income
- Payment for medical expenses
- Payment for disability (temporary or permanent)
- Dependent survivors' death benefits
- Rehabilitative assistance

Under some state laws, dependent survivors are eligible for lump sum payments in the event that the employee is killed in a work-related incident. In addition, burial allowances are also paid up to a specific maximum amount.

Rehabilitative assistance is generally available to employees disabled as a result of a work-related injury or illness. This particular benefit serves to provide an expedient means to help get disabled employees back to work. All states except Alabama and New Mexico have second-injury funds which serve as an incentive for employers to hire disabled or handicapped employees.[37] The intent of the second-injury fund is to equalize the compensation costs that an employer and the insurance company pays for disabled and nondisabled workers alike. Should the permanently disabled worker incur additional disability due to a work-related accident, the employer's compensation costs are limited to the incremental disability and not the total disability (the preexisting permanent disability plus the newly incurred disability).[38]

CRITICISMS OF WORKERS' COMPENSATION

Workers' compensation laws are considered to generally provide minimal levels of compensation; the emphasis is on *minimum*. Benefits have failed to keep pace with inflation in many cases, and are frequently regarded as inadequate compensation for employees' injuries and disabilities. Increasingly, injured employees are bringing actions in the courts instead of filing claims under workers' compensation statutes, thus undermining the exclusivity principle. In some instances, workers are filing workers' compensation claims *and* filing suits against their employers.

Another problem with workers' compensation is the increase in fraudulent claims. The National Council on Compensation Insurance reports that fraud and abuse of workers' compensation insurance programs have reached a level where more than 10 percent of claim dollars are paid to fraudulent claims.[39] Regretfully, some workers have filed false claims in order to draw permanent or temporary benefits rather than work.

CONTESTING QUESTIONABLE WORKERS' COMPENSATION CLAIMS

Since workers' compensation premiums are experience rated (the more claims against an employer, the higher the premium), employers have a very real incentive to contest or challenge dubious claims. After all, if an employee is truly not eligible for the benefit, it is the employer who will be penalized.

Remember, the injury for which the worker is seeking compensation must be work related. If there is no clear connection between the worker's injury and his or her employment, the worker is not entitled to draw the benefit. For example, an Ohio court held that an employee who was injured when hit by a car while picketing his employer during a strike did not suffer a work-related injury.[40] Injuries arising from off-duty conduct during nonwork hours will usually fail to make the critical connection to employment. The exception to off-duty injuries

■ EXHIBIT 10-4

EMPLOYER CHALLENGES TO WORKERS' COMPENSATION CLAIMS

- Injury or illness is not work related
- Injury or illness is due to preexisting condition
- Injury or illness is due to employee misconduct

- Willfully violating safety rules
- Substance abuse
- Fraud

not qualifying may result from "mandatory" company functions such as banquets, parties, and picnics.[41] In these cases, the injury is usually treated as work related.

In the case of *bona fide* work-related injuries, an employer may challenge the claim on the grounds that it was the result of a preexisting condition. For example, an employee with a medical history of heart problems suffers a heart attack at work while engaging in nonstrenuous activities.[42] Here, there is serious doubt as to whether the employee's work caused or aggravated the health condition. If the preexisting condition does not completely negate the employee's eligibility for workers' compensation, it may mitigate the benefit and permit the employer to utilize the state's second-injury fund.

The key to the opening scenario's outcome hinges on whether the employer can convince the workers' compensation appeals board that Douglass's stress was the result of preexisting conditions. If the employer can provide convincing evidence that the employee's stress is the result of preexisting, nonwork-related factors, Douglass will not be eligible for benefits.

Ultimately, an employer may challenge the workers' compensation claim on the grounds that the injury is the result of misconduct on the part of the employee. This could include fraud (the employee is faking the injury),[43] or it could even include a self-inflicted injury (the employee purposely drops a heavy box on her foot in order to draw the benefit). Employees may also lose eligibility for flagrant violations of work or safety rules, especially those prohibiting substance abuse. In most jurisdictions, employees who are injured while intoxicated are not eligible to draw benefits unless they can show by the preponderance of evidence that their substance abuse did not contribute to the injury (see Exhibit 10-4).[44]

FEDERAL REGULATION OF WORKPLACE SAFETY: THE OCCUPATIONAL SAFETY AND HEALTH ACT OF 1970

The Occupational Safety and Health Act (OSH Act)[45] was passed in 1970 amid much controversy. Proponents contended the government had to take drastic measures to reduce the number of workplace deaths and injuries occurring each year and to lessen workers' exposure to health hazards. The Bureau of Labor Statistics of the United States Department of Labor estimated that, in 1964, slightly more than two million workers were injured in their jobs.[46] Opponents to the OSH Act contended it was an unwarranted intrusion into the workplace.

One peculiar characteristic of the OSH Act is that it created three federal agencies: one to enforce its provisions, one to review these enforcement actions, and one to conduct studies and research for developing standards. These agencies span two executive departments, the Department of Labor and the Department of Health and Human Services.

The primary agency given the responsibility for administering and enforcing the OSH Act is the Occupational Safety and Health Administration (OSHA). This agency was organized as a new division within the Department of Labor. It has the authority, through the Secretary of Labor, to promulgate standards, conduct inspections, and seek enforcement action (fines and/or injunctions) where there has been noncompliance.

The OSH Act also created the National Institute of Occupational Safety and Health (NIOSH), an occupational health research center. Through an unusual twist, this agency is actually organized as part of the Department of Health and Human Services rather than the Department of Labor. NIOSH studies various safety and health problems, conducts research for recommending safety and health standards to be adopted by OSHA, provides technical assistance to OSHA, and conducts training programs.

The third agency provided by the passage of the OSH Act is the Occupational Safety and Health Review Commission (OSHRC), a quasijudicial body, which serves to adjudicate challenged enforcement actions undertaken by OSHA. Like OSHA, the OSHRC is part of the Department of Labor. The OSHRC consists of three members appointed by the President of the United States for staggered six-year terms and is completely independent from OSHA. Penalties for violations based on OSHA recommendations are assessed by OSHRC. As with other federal agencies exercising quasijudicial functions (such as the National Labor Relations Board), OSHRC decisions are appealed directly to the appropriate Federal Circuit Court of Appeals.

OCCUPATIONAL SAFETY AND HEALTH ADMINISTRATION

The Occupational Safety and Health Administration (OSHA) primarily establishes safety standards and conducts workplace inspections. The standards set by OSHA generally require that employers adopt certain practices, means, methods, or processes deemed to be reasonably necessary to protect workers on the job. The Act places an obligation on employers to become familiar with standards applicable to their organizations, to eliminate hazardous conditions to the extent possible, and to comply with the standards. The employees have the responsibility, under the Act, to comply with all rules and regulations that are applicable to their own actions and conduct in the workplace.

Additionally, OSHA requires employers to post notices furnished by the agency in the employers' establishments and keep the notices current.[47] The required notices inform employees of the protections and obligations provided for in the Act as well as provide contact information for assistance and information on specific safety and health standards. Notices are required to be posted in conspicuous places where other organization-related policies and communication to employees are customarily posted. Employers are expected to take reasonable steps to assure the notices are not altered, defaced, or covered by other material. Failure to comply with these posting requirements can result in a $1,000 fine.[48]

OSHA INSPECTIONS AND CITATIONS. In its capacity to conduct inspections and investigations, OSHA is authorized to issue citations and propose fines and penalties for OSH Act violations.[49] Although the OSH Act authorizes unannounced random inspections, most inspections result either from employee complaints[50] or OSHA injury and illness incident reports filed by employers.[51] As a result of such inspections, OSHA inspectors may issue one of five citations for any violation of the OSH Act: imminent danger, serious, other-than-serious, *de minimus*, and willful and repeated.

An **imminent danger violation** occurs when, as the name implies, death or serious physical harm to an employee is imminent (i.e., an open flame in a fireworks factory). The organization must stop the activity immediately, and work may not be resumed until the specified danger has been eliminated or corrected.[52] A **serious violation** is considered where there is substantial probability that death or serious physical harm could result and that the employer knew, or should have known, of the hazard (i.e., a stairway without a guard rail). An **other-than-serious violation** is one involving a situation in which the most serious illness or injury would probably not result in death or serious physical harm (i.e., an extension cord coiled on the floor but not in a pathway). A *de minimus* **violation** arises from a nonserious condition that has "no direct or immediate relationship to safety or health"[53] (i.e., not having partitions between toilets in the restroom). No citations are issued, only a *de minimus* notice.

Finally, there are **willful and repeated violations** that occur when an employer is notified of a violation by a compliance officer and refuses or fails to take corrective action. Essentially, any of the citations mentioned earlier, except *de minimus* violations, can become a willful violation.

The OSH Act prescribes that citations be in writing and explain the particular nature of the alleged violation, including a reference to the provision(s) of the Act, standard, rule, regulation, or order stated to have been violated.[54] The citation will also provide a reasonable time for the abatement of the purported violation. As used by OSHA, the term "abatement" merely means the condition causing the violation has been corrected. The Secretary of Labor, under Section 658(a) of the OSH Act, may decide to issue either a citation or a *de minimus* notice for a certain setting of nonserious violations (i.e., those *de minimus* violations that do not have a direct or immediate impact on employee health or safety).

Employers are required to post a copy of any citation and notice of any proposed penalty in an appropriate location at the facility where the citation occurred.[55] Failure to post the citation could result in a fine not to exceed $7,000.[56] If an employer decides to contest a citation, a notice of such intention to contest must be posted in the same location where the citation is posted.

Challenging OSHA Citations. Should an employer decide to challenge either the citation, the time set for abatement, or the proposed penalty, he or she must do so within fifteen working days from the time the citation and proposed penalty are received.[57] The employer is required to notify the Area Director of the Area OSHA Office in writing. This written notification is called a "Notice of Contest."

If the written Notice of Contest has been filed within the required fifteen working days, the OSHA Area Director forwards the challenged case to the OSHRC, who then assigns the case to an administrative law judge for hearing. Employer representatives and the affected employees have the right to participate in the hearings. The administrative law judge's determination may be submitted for further review by OSHRC upon the request of any party to the case. If the employer is still dissatisfied with the outcome, the OSHRC ruling may be appealed to the appropriate United States Court of Appeals.

An employer may challenge the OSHA citation on a number of grounds. For one, the employer may not be an entity which OSH Act covers. The Act applies to all employers engaging in interstate commerce regardless of size.[58] However, there are specific entities which have been excluded from the OSH Act's definition of "employer." For example, federal (except the United States Postal Service), state, and local governments are specifically exempted from coverage.[59] Businesses operating an Indian reservation are also exempted.[60]

Barring an exemption claim, the employer may challenge the citation on the basis of the OSHA standard itself. In essence, the citation is not being challenged, but the standard upon which it is based is not appropriate. Challenges to OSHA standards will be discussed later in this chapter.

OSHA STANDARDS. The OSH Act gave OSHA broad authority in establishing workplace safety and health standards. The Act provides for the issuance of three categories of standards: interim, permanent, and emergency. **Interim** (or temporary) **standards** are those that the Secretary of Labor was given the power to establish for two years following the effective date of the Act. These were generally taken from preexisting national consensus standards. The two-year authority under Section 29 U.S.C. § 655(a) to promulgate "national consensus standards" as occupational safety and health standards expired on April 29, 1973.

The second type, **permanent standards,** are either newly created or revised from the original interim standards. An advisory committee may be appointed periodically to assist in the issuance of permanent standards. Permanent standards are issued on an as-needed basis or evolve from emergency standards. In either case, permanent standards must follow one process before becoming effective.

Once OSHA has developed a proposed or amended standard, it must publish its recommendation in the *Federal Register*. Upon its publication, the public (particularly employers in the affected industries) is given at least thirty days in which to respond to the recommendation. If any interested party requests a public hearing, OSHA must schedule such a hearing and publicize it to the general population. Within sixty days after the close of the public comment and hearing phase, OSHA is required to publish the new standard and the date it will become effective. The Secretary of Labor has the authority to delay its effective date, for any sufficient cause. In *Industrial Union Dept., AFL-CIO v Hodgson,* a delay of four years for a standard on asbestos dust was considered to be within the scope of the Secretary of Labor's authority.[61]

The third type of standards which may be imposed by the Secretary of Labor are emergency standards.[62] The key to the issuance of an **emergency standard** is the necessity to protect employees from a grave danger. After issuing an emergency temporary standard, the Secretary of Labor must set in motion the procedures for the transition of the emergency standard to a permanent standard, which must occur within six months of the emergency standard's publication.[63] The Secretary may bypass most of the established formalities and create temporary emergency standards when it is believed that workers are in grave danger from exposure to toxic substances or other newly discovered hazards.

In a Fifth Circuit case concerning an emergency standard set for a specific type of pesticide, *Florida Peach Growers Association, Inc. v Department of Labor,* the Court held that death or injury need not occur before an emergency standard is declared, but there must be assurance that a truly serious emergency exists before such a standard is dispensed.[64] All emergency standards are essentially temporary measures because they are effective for only six months. They then either become permanent or expire.

The General Duty Clause. OSHA citations can only be issued for violations of safety standards established under the OSH Act. Because it would be both cumbersome and virtually impossible for OSHA to establish safety standards to cover all situations applicable to all processes in all industries, the general duty clause is also a source for violations. The general duty clause simply requires that "[e]ach employer shall furnish to each of his employees employment and a place of employment which are free from recognized hazards that are causing or likely to cause death or serious physical harm to his employees."[65] This creates a sufficiently broad interpretation to permit its application to any situation not covered by existing OSHA standards.

Although OSHA has promulgated many safety standards, and these standards are notorious for their attention to detail (see Exhibit 10-5), not all unsafe conditions can be foreseen. Thus, the intent of the general duty clause is to make the employer ultimately responsible for those unforeseen or newly created workplace hazards. The general duty clause, in requiring that the workplace be free of "recognized" hazards, concedes that the employer's liability may be limited to those hazards which are detectable. In theory, hazards such as those due to careless acts of an employee of which the employer was unaware are not the responsibility of the employer. An example would include an employee who rashly disregards the safety policies and training of an employer. The burden falls on the employer, however, to show that any employee accident was the result of an employee's negligence and not the employer's negligence. However, the general duty clause also places a great deal of discretion with compliance officers in determining what is and what is not a violation of the OSH Act. Conflict often arises when a compliance officer "recognizes" a hazard which the employer does not. There is a real potential for differences of opinion over what is and what is not a safe situation. Still, according to the OSHA *Field Inspection Reference Manual*, a general duty clause citation will only be issued when there is a serious and recognized hazard in the workplace which can feasibly be abated.[66]

Challenging OSHA Standards. In the event that employers believe OSHA has developed and implemented an unrealistic standard, that standard may be challenged in the United States Court of Appeals during a sixty-day period following issuance of the standard. The Supreme Court, in a case involving standards established for exposure to benzene, affirmed that a standard must address a "significant risk" of material health impairment to be sustained by the courts. In *Industrial Union Department v American Petroleum Institute*,[67] the producers and users of benzene challenged the validity of a one part benzene per million parts of air exposure level standard as being unreasonable. The Supreme Court found that the near zero-tolerance level standard established by OSHA was not reasonable when the Secretary of Labor failed to prove that a standard of ten parts per million did not present a significant risk to health impairment.[68] Consequently, the OSHA standard was successfully challenged and overturned.

When standards are challenged, federal courts have to consider two major questions in deciding their efficacy: Is the standard technologically feasible? and Is the standard economically feasible? Technological feasibility is usually easier to determine than economic feasibility. A Second Circuit Court decision held that OSHA may set standards "which require improvements in existing technologies or which require the development of new technology, and the Secretary of Labor is not limited to issuing standards based on devices already developed."[69] But they must be capable of being developed within the limits of existing technology. This principle, called "technology forcing," has been reaffirmed in other cases. In *United Steelworkers of America v Marshall*,[70] the D.C. Circuit Court held that, in setting standards, OSHA must demonstrate that the protections the standards demand are capable of being put into place by the affected industries. In short, it is unreasonable to hold employers to standards which cannot be technologically achieved. A challenged standard would be considered technologically feasible only if OSHA can demonstrate that "modern technology has at least conceived some industrial strategies or devices which are likely to be capable of meeting . . . [the standard] and which industries are generally capable of adopting."[71]

As for the second question, the Supreme Court defines an economically infeasible standard as one that would make "financial viability generally impossible" for an industry.[72] In *American Textile Manufacturers Institute v Donovan*, the Supreme Court concluded that OSHA must determine "that the industry will maintain long-term profitability and competitiveness when establishing the

■ EXHIBIT 10-5

Standard Number: 1910.25
Standard Title: Portable Wood Ladders
SubPart Number: D
SubPart Title: Walking-Working Surfaces

(a) "Application of Requirements"—This section is intended to prescribe rules and establish minimum requirements for the construction, care, and use of the common types of portable wood ladders, in order to insure safety under normal conditions of usage. Other types of special ladders, fruit picker's ladders, combination step and extension ladders, stockroom step ladders, aisle-way step ladders, shelf ladders, and library ladders are not specifically covered by this section.

(b) "Materials"—

(b)(1) "Requirements applicable to all wood parts."

(b)(1)(i) All wood parts shall be free from sharp edges and splinters; sound and free from accepted visual inspection from shake, wane, compression failures, decay, or other irregularities. Low density wood shall not be used.

(c)"Construction Requirements"—

(c)(1) [Reserved]

(c)(2) "Portable stepladders." Stepladders longer than 20 feet shall not be supplied. Stepladders as hereinafter specified shall be of three types:

Type I—Industrial stepladder, 3 to 20 feet for heavy duty, such as utilities, contractors, and industrial use.
Type II—Commercial stepladder, 3 to 12 feet for medium duty, such as painters, offices, and light industrial use.
Type III—Household stepladder, 3 to 6 feet for light duty, such as light household use.

(c)(2)(i) "General requirements."

(c)(2)(ii)(a) [Reserved]

(c)(2)(ii)(b) A uniform step spacing shall be employed which shall be not more than 12 inches. Steps shall be parallel and level when the ladder is in position for use.

(c)(2)(ii)(c) The minimum width between side rails at the top, inside to inside, shall be not less than 11½ inches. From top to bottom, the side rails shall spread at least 1 inch for each foot of length of stepladder.

(c)(2)(ii)(d) [Reserved]

(c)(2)(ii)(e) [Reserved]

(c)(2)(ii)(f) A metal spreader or locking device of sufficient size and strength to securely hold the front and back sections in open positions shall be a component of each stepladder. The spreader shall have all sharp points covered or removed to protect the user. For Type III ladder, the pail shelf and spreader may be combined in one unit (the so-called shelf-lock ladder).

(c)(3)"Portable rung ladders."

(c)(3)(i) [Reserved]

(c)(3)(ii) "Single ladder."

(c)(3)(ii)(a) Single ladders longer than 30 feet shall not be supplied.

(c)(3)(iii) "Two-section ladder."

(c)(3)(iii)(a) Two-section extension ladders longer than 60 feet shall not be supplied. All ladders of this type shall consist of two sections, one to fit within the side rails of the other, and arranged in such a manner that the upper section can be raised and lowered.

(c)(3)(iv) "Sectional ladder."

(c)(3)(iv)(a) Assembled combinations of sectional ladders longer than lengths specified in this subdivision shall not be used.

(c)(3)(v) "Trestle and extension trestle ladder."

(c)(3)(v)(a) Trestle ladders, or extension sections or base sections of extension trestle ladders longer than 20 feet shall not be supplied.

(c)(4) "Special-purpose ladders."

(c)(4)(i) [Reserved]

(c)(4)(ii) "Painter's stepladder."

(c)(4)(ii)(a) Painter's stepladders longer than 12 feet shall not be supplied.

(c)(4)(iii) "Mason's ladder." A mason's ladder is a special type of single ladder intended for use in heavy construction work.

(c)(4)(iii)(a) Mason's ladders longer than 40 feet shall not be supplied.

(c)(5) "Trolley and side-rolling ladders."

(c)(5)(i) "Length." Trolley ladders and side-rolling ladders longer than 20 feet should not be supplied.

(d) "Care and Use of Ladders"—

(d)(1) "Care." To insure safety and serviceability the following precautions on the care of ladders shall be observed:

(d)(1)(i) Ladders shall be maintained in good condition at all times, the joint between the steps and side rails shall be tight, all hardware and fittings securely attached, and the movable parts shall operate freely without binding or undue play.

(d)(1)(ii) Metal bearings of locks, wheels, pulleys, etc., shall be frequently lubricated.

(d)(1)(iii) Frayed or badly worn rope shall be replaced.

(d)(1)(iv) Safety feet and other auxiliary equipment shall be kept in good condition to insure proper performance.

(d)(1)(v) — (ix) [Reserved]

(d)(1)(x) Ladders shall be inspected frequently and those which have developed defects shall be withdrawn from service for repair or destruction and tagged or marked as "Dangerous, Do Not Use."

(d)(1)(xi) Rungs should be kept free of grease and oil.

(d)(2) "Use." The following safety precautions shall be observed in connection with the use of ladders:

(d)(2)(i) Portable rung and cleat ladders shall, where possible, be used at such a pitch that the horizontal distance from the top support to the foot of the ladder is one-quarter of the working length of the ladder (the length along the ladder between the foot and the top support). The ladder shall be so placed as to prevent slipping, or it shall be lashed, or held in position. Ladders shall not be used in a horizontal position as platforms, runways, or scaffolds;

(d)(2)(ii) Ladders for which dimensions are specified should not be used by more than one man at a time nor with ladder jacks and scaffold planks where use by more than one man is anticipated. In such cases, specially designed ladders with larger dimensions of the parts should be procured;

(d)(2)(iii) Portable ladders shall be so placed that the side rails have a secure footing. The top rest for portable rung and cleat ladders shall be reasonably rigid and shall have ample strength to support the applied load;

(d)(2)(iv) Ladders shall not be placed in front of doors opening toward the ladder unless the door is blocked upon, locked, or guarded;

(d)(2)(v) Ladders shall not be placed on boxes, barrels, or other unstable bases to obtain additional height;

(d)(2)(vi) — (vii) [Reserved]

(d)(2)(viii) Ladders with broken or missing steps, rungs, or cleats, broken side rails, or other faulty equipment shall not be used; improvised repairs shall not be made;

(d)(2)(ix) Short ladders shall not be spliced together to provide long sections;

(d)(2)(x) Ladders made by fastening cleats across a single rail shall not be used;

(d)(2)(xi) Ladders shall not be used as guys, braces, or skids, or for other than their intended purposes;

(d)(2)(xii) Tops of the ordinary types of stepladders shall not be used as steps;

(d)(2)(xiii) On two-section extension ladders the minimum overlap for the two sections in use be as follows:

Size of Ladder (feet)	Overlap (feet)
Up to and including 36	3
Over 36 and up to and including 48	4
Over 48 and up to and including 60	5

continued

■ EXHIBIT 10-5

CONTINUED

(d)(2)(xiv) Portable rung ladders with reinforced rails (see paragraphs (c)(3) (ii)(c) and (iii)(d) this section) shall be used only with the metal reinforcement on the under side;

(d)(2)(xv) No ladder should be used to gain access to a roof unless the top of the ladder shall extend at least 3 feet above the point of support, at eave, gutter, or roofline;

(d)(2)(xvi) [Reserved]

(d)(2)(xvii) Middle and top sections of sectional or window cleaner's ladders should not be used for bottom section unless the user equips them with safety shoes;

(d)(2)(xviii) [Reserved]

(d)(2)(xix) The user should equip all portable rung ladders with nonslip bases when there is a hazard of slipping. Nonslip bases are not intended as a substitute for care in safely placing, lashing, or holding a ladder that is being used upon oily, metal, concrete, or slippery surfaces;

(d)(2)(xx) The bracing on the back legs of step ladders is designed solely for increasing stability and not for climbing.

SOURCE: 29 C.F.R. § 1910.25.

economic feasibility of a standard."[73] This appears to indicate that compliance should not bankrupt the affected employer. However, the employer must provide convincing evidence that compliance with the new standard would indeed threaten the firm's long-term survival. It is always important to remember that most bureaucrats and judges do not have business backgrounds or education.

Requesting Variances from OSHA Standards. An alternative to challenging a standard in the judicial system is requesting a variance. The Secretary of Labor may grant employers an exemption from a standard, under Section 16 of the Act, if it is inappropriate to the employer's particular situation. This is known as a *variance* and is classified as either temporary or permanent.[74] A **temporary variance** may be granted when an employer cannot meet the requirements to comply with a standard by its effective date. In essence, the employer is asking for an extension. The firm cannot be in compliance by the effective date, but it will, eventually, be in compliance. However, to qualify for a temporary variance, the employer must demonstrate that all possible measures are being taken to protect employees and that all steps necessary for compliance are also being taken. Additionally, all employees must be informed by the employer of the variance request. Temporary variances may be granted for the time needed to comply, not to exceed a period of one year. The employer may renew temporary variances up to two times, each of these for a period not to exceed six months.[75]

A **permanent variance** may be granted to an employer who can prove that current conditions or particular methods provide as safe a worksite as those that would exist through compliance with the OSHA standard.[76] The Occupational Safety and Health Agency ordinarily inspects the premises before granting a permanent variance. Again, all employees must be informed of the application for the variance, and of their right to request a hearing on the matter necessitating a variance. Within six months after a permanent variance has been granted, the employees may petition OSHA to modify or revoke the variance.[77] The Secretary of Labor may take similar steps to modify or revoke the variance regardless of employee initiatives.

RECORD KEEPING AND REPORTING REQUIREMENTS

Although all employers engaged in interstate commerce are covered by OSH Act, those who have more than ten employees are required to maintain specific records of job-related injuries and illnesses.[78] Some employers may be selected to be part of a national survey of workplace injuries and illnesses conducted by the Department of Labor's Bureau of Labor Statistics (BLS), in which case the employer will be notified before the end of the year to keep records during the coming year. This is not a voluntary program as any employer selected for the BLS survey *must* maintain the records. Unless an employer has been selected in a particular year to be part of a national survey of workplace injuries and illnesses conducted by the BLS, employers with fewer than ten employees or employers in traditionally low-hazard industries are exempt from maintaining these records.[79] An example of industries that typically are designated as traditionally low hazard include: automobile dealers; apparel and accessory stores; furniture and home furnishing stores; eating and drinking places; finance, insurance, and real estate industries; and service industries such as personal and business services, legal, educational, social, and cultural services and membership organizations.[80]

The OSHA Injury and Illness Log and Summary, OSHA Form 200 (see Exhibit 10-6) and the OSHA Injury and Illness Incident Record, OSHA Form 101 (see Exhibit 10-7) are the two primary recording and reporting forms established by OSHA. Both forms are for the employers' records and are not submitted to OSHA, but they must be available for inspections. The OSHA Form 200 provides a log for recording and reporting injuries and illnesses with a separate line entry for each recordable injury or illness. A recordable injury or illness consists of "work-related deaths, injuries, and illnesses other than minor injuries that require only first aid treatment and which do not involve medical treatment, loss of consciousness, restriction of work or motion, or transfer to another job."[81] There is a summary section of OSHA Form 200 for annual totals of the year's injury and illness experience.

The OSHA Form 101 is a supplementary record to be used as an individual incident record and report form providing more details about each individual recordable injury or illness. This form must be completed and available for reporting purposes within six work days upon experiencing and receiving information of a recordable incident.

An employer with an employee exposed to toxic materials or potentially harmful physical agents in the workplace is required to provide access to exposure and medical records for the employee and the appropriate safety agency.[82] Remember, the Americans with Disabilities Act requires an employer to keep employee records confidential and limit access to them.[83]

(Text continues on page 361)

Log and Summary of Occupational Injuries and Illnesses

NOTE: This form is required by Public Law 91-596 and must be kept in the establishment for 5 years. Failure to maintain and post can result in issuance of citations and assessment of penalties.
(See posting requirements on the other side of form)

RECORDABLE CASES: You are required to record information about every occupational death; every nonfatal occupational illness; and those nonfatal occupational injuries which involve one or more of the following: loss of conciousness, restriction of work or motion, transfer to another job, or medical treatment (other than first aid)
(See definitions on the other side of form)

Case or File Number	Date of Injury or Onset of Illness	Employee's Name	Occupation	Department	Description of Injury or Illness
Enter a nonduplicating number which will facilitate comparisons with supplementary records.	Enter Mo/Day	Enter first name or initial, middle initial, last name	Enter regular job title, not activity employee was performing when injury occurred or at onset of illness. In the absence of a formal title, enter a brief description of the employee's duties.	Enter department in which the employee is regularly employed or a description of normal workplace to which employee is assigned, even though temporarily working in another department at the time of injury or illness.	Enter a brief description of the injury or illness and indicate the part or parts of the body affected. Typical entries for this column might be: Amputation of 1st joint right forefinger; Strain of lower back; Contact dermatitis on both hands; Electrocution - body.
(A)	(B)	(C)	(D)	(E)	(F)
					PREVIOUS PAGE TOTALS =>
					TOTALS (Instructions on other side of form) =>

OSHA No. 200

OSHA INJURY AND ILLNESS LOG AND SUMMARY, OSHA FORM 200

U.S. Department of Labor

For Calendar Year _____ Page: _____ of _____

Form Approved
O.M.B. No. 1218-0176
See OMB Disclosure
Statement on reverse.

Company Name
Establishment Name
Establishment Address

Extent of and Outcome of Injury

Fatalities	Nonfatal Injuries					
Injury Related	Injuries with Lost Workdays					Injuries Without Lost Workdays
Enter Date of death. mm/dd/yy	Enter a Check if injury involves DAYS away from work or restricted work activity or both.	Enter a Check if injury involves DAYS away from work.	Enter number of DAYS away from work	Enter number of DAYS of restricted work activity		Enter a Check if no entry was made in column 1 or 2 but the injury is recordable as defined above.
(1)	(2)	(3)	(4)	(5)		(6)

Type, Extent of, and Outcome of Illness

Type of Illness — CHECK Only One Column for Each Illness (See other side of form for terminations or permanent transfers)

(a) Occupational Skin Disorder or Disease	(b) Dust Disease of the lungs	(c) Respiratory Conditions due to toxic agents	(d) Poisoning (systemic effects of toxic materials)	(e) Disorders due to physical agents	(f) Disorders associated with repeated trauma	(g) All other occupational illnesses
			(7)			

Fatalities	Nonfatal Illnesses				
Illness Related	Illnesses with Lost Workdays				Illnesses without Lost Workdays
Enter DATE of death, mm/dd/yy	Enter a CHECK if Illness involves DAYS away from work, or DAYS of restricted work activity or both.	Enter a CHECK if Illness involves DAYS away from work.	Enter number of DAYS away from work.	Enter number of DAYS of restricted work activity	Enter a CHECK if no entry was made in columns 8 or 9
(8)	(9)	(10)	(11)	(12)	(13)

Certification of Annual Summary Totals by: _____

Title: _____   Date: _____

OSHA 200

POST ONLY THIS PORTION OF THE LAST PAGE NO LATER THAN FEBRUARY 1

355

OMB DISCLOSURE STATEMENT

Public reporting burden for this collection of information is estimated to vary from 4 to 30 (time in minutes) per response with an average of 15 (time in minutes) per response, including the time for reviewing instructions, searching existing data sources, gathering and maintaining the data needed, and completing and reviewing the collection of information. Persons are not required to respond to the collection of information unless it displays a currently valid OMB control number. If you have any comments regarding this estimate or any other aspect of this information collection, including suggestions for reducing this burden, please send them to the OSHA Office of Statistics, Room N-3644, 200 Constitution Avenue, N.W. Washington, D.C. 20210

Instructions for OSHA No. 200

I. Log and Summary of Occupational Injuries and Illnesses

Each employer who is subject to the recordkeeping requirements of the Occupational Safety and Health Act of 1970 must maintain for each establishment, a log of all recordable occupational injuries and illnesses. This form (OSHA No. 200) may be used for that purpose. A substitute for the OSHA No. 200 is acceptable if it is as detailed, easily readable, and understandable as the OSHA No. 200.

Enter each recordable case on the log within six (6) workdays after learning of its occurrence. Although other records must be maintained at the establishment to which they refer, it is possible to prepare and maintain the log at another location, using data processing equipment if desired. If the log is prepared elsewhere, a copy updated to within 45 calendar days must be present at all times in the establishment.

Logs must be maintained and retained for five (5) years following the end of the calendar year to which they relate. Logs must be available (normally at the establishment) for inspection and copying by representatives of the Department of Labor, or the Department of Health and Human Services, or States accorded jurisdiction under the Act. Access to the log is also provided to employees, former employees and their representatives.

II. Changes in Extent of or Outcome of Injury or Illness

If, during the 5-year period the log must be retained, there is a change in an extent and outcome of an injury or illness which affects entries in columns 1, 2, 6, 8, 9, or 13, the first entry should be lined out and a new entry made. For example, if an injured employee at first required only medical treatment but later lost workdays away from work, the check in column 6 should be lined out and checks entered in columns 2 and 3 and the number of lost workdays entered in column 4.

In another example, if an employee with an occupational illness lost wordays, returned to work, and then died of the illness, any entries in columns 9 through 12 would be lined out and the date of death entered in column 8.

The entire entry for an injury or illness should be lined out if later found to be nonrecordable. For example, an injury which is later determined not to be work related, or which was initially thought to involve medical treatement but later was determined to have involved only first aid.

III. Posting Requirements

A copy of the totals and information following the total line of the last page for the year, must be posted at each establishment in the place or places where notices to employees are customarily posted. This copy must be posted no later than February 1 and must remain in place until March 1. Even though there were no injuries or illnessed during the year, zeros must be entered on the totals line, and the form posted.

The person responsible for the annual summary totals shall certify that the totals are true and complete by signing at the bottom of the form.

IV. Instructions for Completing Log and Summary of Occupational injuries and illnesses

Column A - CASE OR FILE NUMBER. Self Expanatory

Column B - DATE OF INJURY OR ONSET OF ILLNESS

For occupational injuries, enter the date of the work accident which resulted in the injury. For occupational illnesses, enter the date of initial diagnosis of illness, or, if absence from work occurred before diagnosis, enter the first day of the absence attributable to the illness which was later diagnosed or recognized.

Columns C through F - Self Explanatory

Columns 1 and 8 - INJURY OR ILLNESS-RELATED DEATHS - Self Explanatory

Columns 2 and 9 - INJURIES OR ILLNESSES WITH LOST WORKDAYS - Self Explanatory

Any injury which involves days away from work, or days of restricted work activitiy, or both, must be recorded since it always involves one or more of the criteria for recordability.

Columns 3 and 10 - INJURIES OR ILLNESSES INVOLVING DAYS AWAY FROM WORK - Self Explanatory

Columns 4 and 11 - LOST WORKDAYS -- DAYS AWAY FROM WORK.
Enter the number of workdays (consecutive or not) on which the employee would have worked but could not because of occupational injury or illness. The number of lost workdays should not include the day of injury or onset of illness or any days on which the employee would not have worked even though able to work. NOTE: For employees not having a regularly scheduled shift, such as certain truck drivers, construction workers, farm labor, casual labor, part-time employees, etc., it may be necessary to estimate the number of lost workdays. Estimates of lost workdays shall be based on prior work history of the employee AND days worked by employees, not ill or injured, working in the department and/or occupation of the ill or injured employee.

Columns 5 and 12 - LOST WORKDAYS -- DAYS OF RESTRICTED WORK ACTIVITY.
Enter the number of workdays (consecutive or not) on which because of injury or illness:
(1) the employee was assigned to another job on a temporary basis, or
(2) the employee worked at a permanent job less than full time, or
(3) the employee worked at a permanently assigned job but could not perform all duties normally connected with it.

The number of lost workdays should not include the day of injury or onset of illness or any days on which the employee would not have worked even though able to work.

Columns 6 and 13 - INJURIES OR ILLNESSES WITHOUT LOST WORKDAYS - Self Explanatory

Columns 7a through 7g - TYPE OF ILLNESS. Enter a check in only *one* column for each illness.
TERMINATION OR PERMANENT TRANSFER - Place an asterisk to the right of the entry in columns 7a through 7g (type of illness) which represented a termination of employment or permanent transfer.

V. Totals
Add number of entries in columns 1 and 8.
Add number of checks in columns 2, 3, 6, 7, 9, 10 and 13.
Add number of days in columns 4, 5, 11 and 12.
Yearly totals for each column (1-13) are required for posting. Running or page totals may be generated at the discretion of the employer.

In an employee's loss of workdays is continuing at the time the totals are summarized, estimate the number of future workdays the employee will lose and add that estimate to the workdays already lost and include this figure in the annual totals. No further entries are to be made with respect to such cases in the next year's log.

VI. Definitions
OCCUPATIONAL INJURY is any injury such as a cut, fracture, sprain, amputation, etc. which results from a work accident or from an exposure involving a single incident in the work environment. NOTE: Conditions resulting from animal bites, such as insect or snake bites or from one-time exposure to chemicals, are considered to be injuries.

OCCUPATIONAL ILLNESS of an employee is any abnormal condition or disorder, other than one resulting from an occupational injury, caused by exposure to environmental factors associated with employment. It includes acute and chronic illnesses or diseases which may be caused by inhalation, absorption, ingestion, or direct contact.

The following listing gives the categories of occupational illnesses and disorders that will be utilized for the purpose of classifying recordable illnesses. For porposes of information, examples of each category are given. These are typical examples, however, and are not to be considered the complete listing of the types of illnesses and disorders that are to be counted under each category.

7a. Occupational Skin Diseases or Disorders. Examples: Contact dermatitis, eczema, or rash caused by primary irritants and sensitizers or poisonous plants; oil acne; chrome ulcers; chemical burns or inflamation, etc.

7b. Dust Diseases of the Lungs (Pneumaconioses). Examples: Silicosis, asbestosis and other asbestos-related diseases, coal worker's pneumaconioses, byssinosis, siderosis, and other pneumaconioses.

7c. Respiratory Conditions Due to Toxic Agents. Examples: Pneumonitis, pharyngitis, rhinitis or acute congestion due to chemicals, dusts, gases, or fumes; farmer's lung; etc.

7d. Poisoning (Systemic Effects of Toxic Materials). Examples: Poisoning by lead, mercury, cadmium, arsenic, or other metals; poisoning by

CONTINUED

carbon monoxide, hydrogen sulfide, or other gases; poisoning by benzol, carbon tetrachloride, or other organic solvents; poisoning by insecticide sprays such as parathion, lead arsenate; poisoning by other chemicals such as formaldehyde, plastics, and resins; etc.

7e. Disorders Due to Physical Agents (Other than Toxic Materials). Examples: Heatstroke, sunstroke, heat exhaustion, and other effects of environmental heat, freezing, frostbite, and effects of exposure to low temperatures; caisson disease; effects of ionizing radiation (isotopes, X-rays, radium); effects of nonionizing radiation (welding flash, ultraviolet rays, microwaves, sunburn); etc.

7f. Disorders Associated with Repeated Trauma. Examples: Noise-induced hearing loss; synovitis, tenosynovitis, and bursitis. Raynaud's phenomena; and other conditions due to repeated motion, vibration, or pressure.

7g. All Other Occupational Illnesses. Examples: Anthrax, brucellosis, infectious hepatitis, malignant and benign tumors, food poisoning, histoplasmosis, coccidioidomycosis, etc.

MEDICAL TREATMENT includes treatment (other than first aid) administered by a physician or by registered professional personnel under the standing orders of a physician. Medical treatment does NOT include first aid treatment (one-time treatment and subsequent observation of minor scratches, cuts, burns, splinters, and so forth, which do not ordinarily require medical care) even though provided by a physician or registered professional personnel.

ESTABLISHMENT: A single physical location where business is conducted or where services or industrial operations are performed (for example: a factory, mill, store, hotel, resturant, movie theater, farm, ranch, bank, sales office, warehouse, or central administrative office). Where distinctly separate activities are performed at a single physicial location, such as construction activities operated from the same physical locations as a lumber yard, each activity shall be treated as a separate establishment.

For firms engaged in activities which may be physically dispersed, such as agriculture; construction; transportation; communications and electric, gas, and sanitary services, records may be maintained at a place to which employees report each day.

Records for personnel who do not primarily report or work at a single establishment, such as traveling salesmen, technicians, engineers, etc., shall be maintained at the location from which they are paid or the base from which personnel operate to carry out their activities.

WORK ENVIRONMENT is comprised of the physical location, equipment, materials processed or used, and the kinds of operations performed in the course of an employee's work, wether on or off the employer's premisis.

EXHIBIT 10-7

OSHA INJURY AND ILLNESS INCIDENT RECORD, OSHA FORM 101

Occupational Safety and Health Administration
Supplementary Record of
Occupational Injuries and Illnesses

U.S. Department of Labor

This form is required by Public Law 91-596 and must be kept in the establishment for 5 years.

Failure to maintain can result in the issuance of citations and assessment of penalties.

Case or File No.

Form Approved
O.M.B. No. 1218-0176
See OMB Disclosure
Statement on reverse.

Employer

1. Name

2. Mail address (No. and street, city or town, State, and zip code)

3. Location, if different from mail address

Injured or Ill Employee

4 Name (First, middle, and last)

Social Security No.

5. Home address (No. and street, city or town, State, and zip code)

6. Age

7. Sex (Check one) Male ☐ Female ☐

8. Occupation (Enter regular job title, not the specific activity he was performing at the time of injury.)

9. Department (Enter name of department or division in which the injured person is regularly employed, even though he may have been temporarily

working in another department at the time of injury.)

The Accident or Exposure to Occupational Illness

If accident or exposure occurred on employer's premises, give address of plant or establishment in which it occurred. Do not indicated department or division within the plant or establishment.

If accident occurred outside employer's premises at an identifiable address, give that address. If it occurred on a public highway or at any other place which cannot be identified by number

and street, please provide place references locating the place of injury as accurately as possible.

10. Place of accident or exposure (No. and street, city or town, State, and zip code)

11. Was place of accident or exposure on employer's premises?   Yes ☐   No ☐

12. What was the employee doing when injured? (Be specific. If he was using tools or equipment or handling material, name them and tell what he was doing with them.)

13. How did the accident occur? (Describe fully the events which resulted in the injury or occupational illness. Tell what happened and how it happened. Name any objects or substances

involved and tell how they were involved. Give full details on all factors which led or contributed to the accident. Use separate sheet for additional space.)

Occupational Injury or Occupational Illness

14. Describe the injury or illness in detail and indicate the part of body affected. (E.g., amputation of right index finger at second joint; fracture of ribs; lead poisoning; dermatitis of left hand, etc.)

15. Name the object or substance which directly injured the employee. (For example, the machine or thing he struck against or which struck him; the vapor or poison he inhaled or swallowed;

the chemical or radiation which irriatated his skin; or in cases of strains, hernias, etc., the thing he was lifting, pulling, etc.)

16. Date of injury or initial diagnosis of occupational illness

17. Did employee die? (Check one) Yes ☐   No ☐

Other

18. Name and address of physician

19. If hospitalized, name and address of hospital

Date of report	Prepared by	Official position

OSHA No. 101 (Feb. 1981)

(See Next Page/Reverse)

■ EXHIBIT 10-7

CONTINUED

SUPPLEMENTARY RECORD OF OCCUPATIONAL INJURIES AND ILLNESSES

To supplement the Log and Summary of Occupational Injuries and Illnesses (OSHA No. 200), each establishment must maintain a record of each recordable occupational injury or illness. Worker's compensation, insurance, or other reports are acceptable as records if they contain all facts listed below or are supplemented to do so. If no suitable report is made for other purposes, this form (OSHA No. 101) may be used or the necessary facts can be listed on a separate plain sheet of paper. These records must also be available in the establishment without delay and at reasonable times for examination by representatives of the Department of Labor and the Department of Health and Human Services, and States accorded jurisdiction under the Act. The records must be maintained for a period of not less than five years following the end of the calendar year to which they relate.

Such records must contain at least the following facts:

1) About the employer - name, mail address, and location if different from mail address.

2) About the injured or ill employee - name, social security number, home address, age, sex, occupation, and department.

3) About the accident or exposure to occupational illness - place of accident or exposure, whether it was on employer's premises, what the employee was doing when injured, and how the accident occurred.

4) About the occupational injury or illness - description of the injury or illness, including part of the body affected, name of the object or substance which directly injured the employee; and date of injury or diagnosis of illness.

5) Other - name and address of physician; if hospitalized, name and address of hospital, date of report; and name and position of person preparing the report.

SEE *DEFINITIONS* ON THE BACK OF OSHA FORM 200.

OMB DISCLOSURE STATMENT

Public reporting burden for this collection of information is estimated to average 20 minutes per response, including the time for reviewing instructions, searching existing data sources, gathering and maintaining the data needed, and completing and reviewing the collection of information. Persons are not required to respond to the collection of information unless it displays a currently valid OMB control number. If you have any comments regarding this estimate or any other aspect of this information collection, including suggestions for reducing this burden, please send them to the OSHA Office of Statistics, Room N3644, 200 Constitution Avenue, NW, Washington, DC 20210

DO NOT SEND THE COMPLETED FORM TO THE OFFICE SHOWN ABOVE

OSHA No. 101 (Feb. 1981)

Additionally, any employee who is exposed to toxic materials or potentially harmful physical agents has a right to access monitoring records kept by the employer, material safety data sheets, and any other exposure records available.

Employees who believe that an OSHA violation has or may imminently occur have certain rights granted under the Act that include: filing a complaint with the appropriate safety and health agency, bringing action in the appropriate district court to order an inspection, taking part in the inspection tour and conference, having the employer post copies of all citations, and inspecting the log of occupational injuries and illnesses.[84]

OSHA INSPECTIONS

The Occupational Safety and Health Act allows an assigned OSHA compliance safety and health officers (CSHOs) to enter, inspect, and investigate an employer's workplace to determine compliance with the standards.[85] The Act requires the CSHOs to conduct inspections during either regular working hours or some other reasonable times. Compliance officers may question any employee, agent, employer, or owner privately during an inspection. All establishments covered by the Act are subject to inspections by OSHA compliance safety and health officers. States with their own occupational safety and health programs may conduct separate workplace inspections using their own qualified state compliance officers.[86]

The OSH Act does provide some rights to employers during a workplace inspection. The OSH Act states that a CSHO must grant an employer the right to accompany a walkaround inspection.[87] This was reinforced in *Chicago Bridge v OSHRC* in which the Seventh Circuit Court of Appeals held that managers and other designated employer representatives may accompany OSHA compliance officers on workplace inspection tours.[88] The Seventh Circuit ruled that by upholding the employer's right to accompany the CSHO, any mere procedural or technical violation noted by the employer would not automatically void a citation. This was a concession to the CSHOs who may have felt that their citations might be overturned on a technicality rather than on merit.

Employers do not have to admit CSHOs on their premises automatically, although such a refusal is hardly recommended. As a government representative, CSHOs are constrained by the Fourth Amendment's restriction on unlawful search and seizure. However, should an employer refuse to permit a compliance officer access to the workplace in order to conduct an inspection, the compliance officer may petition the appropriate district court to issue a search warrant. The 1978 Supreme Court ruling, *Marshall v Barlow's Inc.*, held that the Department of Labor must prove probable cause exists in order to obtain a search warrant.[89] The Court held that the Constitutional protection provided in the Fourth Amendment against unreasonable search of private homes applies to commercial establishments as well. However, any workplace accident or employee complaint would be sufficient to establish probable cause that the OSHA violations are occurring at the employer's place of business.

PENALTIES FOR OSH ACT VIOLATIONS

OSHA may impose penalties for employer violations of the OSH Act. Penalties may be assessed for serious violations, nonserious violations, or willful violations. Penalties are generally based on the gravity of a violation (refer to Exhibit 10-8). An employer who has been cited for a serious violation is assessed a penalty of up to $7,000 for each violation.[90] A penalty for a serious violation may be adjusted downward, based on the employer's good faith, the history of rectifying previous violations, the gravity of the alleged violation, and the size of the business. When an employer willfully violates the Act, that employer may be assessed a penalty of not more than $70,000 but not less than $5,000 for each violation.

If an employer is convicted of a willful violation that has resulted in the death of an employee, the offense is punishable by a court-imposed fine or by imprisonment for up to six months, or both. A fine of up to $250,000 for an individual, or $500,000 for a corporation may be imposed under the Comprehensive Crime Control Act of 1984 for a criminal conviction involving an employee's death.[91]

EMPLOYEES' RIGHTS TO REFUSE TO WORK IN UNSAFE CONDITIONS

The OSH Act protects employees who refuse to work in unsafe conditions under Section 11(c)(1).[92] This provision of the Act further prohibits an employer from discharging, or in any manner discriminating against, any employee because the employee files a complaint or institutes any proceeding under the Act. Just as with the Civil Rights Act of 1964, employers cannot retaliate against an employee for cooperating with investigators or testifying in any proceeding under the OSH Act.

This right to refuse to work in unsafe conditions (not connected with the normal nature of the work) was established in *Whirlpool Corp. v Marshall*. In this deci-

---

■ EXHIBIT 10-8

MAXIMUM PENALTIES UNDER OSHA

Type of Violation	Penalty
Violation of posting requirement	$1,000 for each violation
Failure to correct a violation	$7,000 per day
Willful violation (minimum)	$5,000 for each violation
Willful and repeated violation (maximum)	$10,000 for each violation
Forcibly resisting or interfering with an inspection or investigation	$5,000 and/or imprisonment for not more than 3 years
Forcibly resisting or interfering with an inspection involving a deadly weapon	$10,000 and/or imprisonment for not more than 10 years

SOURCES: 29 U.S.C. § 666(I); 18 U.S.C. § 111.

sion, the Supreme Court held that an employee's refusal to perform an assigned task due to a reasonable fear of death or serious injury is a valid right afforded by Occupational Safety and Health Act.[93] The key word here is *reasonable.* An employee working in an office where the temperature is 50° F because the heating system is not working would be hard pressed to prove that he or she had a reasonable fear of death or serious injury. On the other hand, an employee doing strenuous work on an assembly line where the temperature is 120° F may easily prove a reasonable fear for personal safety or health.

EMPLOYEE PROTECTION AGAINST RETALIATION

Like any of the other statutes previously discussed in this textbook, whistleblowers are protected against retaliation for filing an OSHA complaint. Therefore, any adverse action taken against an employee who requests an OSHA inspection or participates in an accident investigation violates the OSH Act. Managers should ensure that any disciplinary actions, terminations, or transfers of employees who have filed OSHA complaints can be clearly shown not to be connected to the OSHA complaint.[94]

STATE REGULATION OF WORKPLACE SAFETY

Like the Civil Rights Act of 1964, the OSH Act permits individual states to establish and manage their own safety and health programs for the private sector. Under the OSH Act, OSHA may transfer authority to approved states to cover their own occupational safety and health matters. This is very similar in principle to the EEOC's deferring EEO matters to state fair employment practice agencies (FEPAs).

Currently, the OSH Act certifies twenty-three states and two territories that manage their own safety and health programs covering private sector and public sector employees (see Exhibit 10-9).[95] There are two other states operating programs

■ EXHIBIT 10-9

STATES AND TERRITORIES WITH STATE PLANS APPROVED BY OSHA

Alaska	Indiana	Minnesota	Oregon	Vermont
Arizona	Iowa	Nevada	Puerto Rico	Virgin Islands
California	Kentucky	New Mexico	South Carolina	Virginia
Connecticut	Maryland	New York	Tennessee	Washington
Hawaii	Michigan	North Carolina	Utah	Wyoming

Note: The Connecticut and New York plans cover public sector (state & local government) employment only.

SOURCE: *1999 Report from OSHSPA,* The Occupational Safety and Health State Plan Association. Washington, DC: U.S. Department of Labor.

that cover only state and local government employees. In order to receive certification from OSHA, a state must demonstrate that it will conduct inspections to enforce those standards and conduct occupational safety and health training and education programs.

EMERGING ISSUES IN WORKPLACE HEALTH AND SAFETY

Workplace safety and health issues are continually evolving in response to real or perceived threats. Among the safety and health issues that have received increasing attention in the popular media and, consequently, have garnered growing public concern are: Secondhand smoke in the workplace, workplace violence, carpal tunnel syndrome and other musculoskeletal disorders, and work-related stress and emotional disorders.

SECONDHAND SMOKE IN THE WORKPLACE

Most companies in the United States have adopted workplace smoking policies, although they vary from company to company. These policies typically differ in degree of stringency, but they generally serve one primary goal in the workplace: to protect employees from exposure to the chemicals found in environmental tobacco smoke, commonly called "secondhand smoke."

Since the Environmental Protection Agency (EPA) first classified tobacco smoke as a group A carcinogen (similar to asbestos, benzene, and radon), safety officers have become concerned about its connection to workplace illness. One report links secondhand smoke to inducing asthma and increasing the incidence of respiratory infections, and it is also blamed for three thousand lung cancer deaths per year.[96]

In its *Guide to Workplace Smoking Policies,* the EPA recommends that employers build enclosed, ventilated smoking lounges if they allow employees to smoke on the companies' premises. The EPA has strongly endorsed indoor air quality legislation that would require employers to take steps to avoid exposure of their employees to second-hand smoke.[97] Naturally, employers respond to such initiatives by developing internal policies in anticipation of future compliance requirements. Many companies have taken the simplest approach to meeting indoor air quality recommendations by banning all indoor smoking.

Currently, 80 percent of all employees work for companies that have a smoking policy.[98] At least twenty-one states have preempted voluntary employer efforts by enacting laws regulating smoking in private workplaces.[99] Other companies are implementing restrictions on smoking in anticipation of a proposed OSHA standard that would ban smoking in the workplace except in separately ventilated areas (much like the EPA has previously recommended). Remember that under the OSH Act, the "general duty" provision requires employers to provide places of employment "free of recognized hazards that are causing or likely to cause death or serious physical harm to his employee."[100]

Under this broad umbrella, secondhand smoke from cigarettes could easily be covered. Not surprisingly, many employers are opting for smoke-free work environments, rather than contesting the proposed standards and laws.

WORKPLACE VIOLENCE

Media emphasis on shootings in places of employment has highlighted concerns regarding workplace violence. Workplace violence is generally defined as persons committing violent acts against other persons at work or while on duty. A report on workplace violence published by the Department of Justice in 1998 and based on Federal Bureau of Investigation statistics reveals that approximately one thousand employees are murdered each year while performing their work duties.[101] The report also shows that more than two million incidences of workplace violence were reported each year during the survey period between 1992 and 1996.[102] This sounds especially worrisome, particularly in light of the media exposure that such cases attract. However, compare these figures to the 19,650 murders that occur in places other than work each year and the 8,116,240 incidents of violence outside of the workplace.[103] In a workplace of 132,167,000 workers,[104] workplace deaths due to coworker violence are extremely rare, and the workplace is generally safer than the home. Yes, HR professionals and managers need to be concerned about violence in the workplace, but they should not overreact.

While many organizations now have some formal workplace violence policy, a joint survey conducted by the Risk and Insurance Management Society and the American Society of Safety Engineers finds that most have not conducted assessments of the risks for actual workplace violent incidents.[105] Some HR responses to reducing workplace violence include limiting access to facilities, workplace surveillance, employee background checks, and open door policies.

CARPAL TUNNEL SYNDROME AND OTHER MUSCULOSKELETAL DISORDERS

In the 1990s, as more and more personal computers were being utilized in the workplace, a new work-related disorder, carpal tunnel syndrome, emerged. Managers immediately began devoting attention to the health needs of computer operators and users. Since then, scientific and medical literature has concentrated on identifying occupations that subject employees to high biomechanical stress—such as heavy lifting and repetitive motion. All of these conditions are covered under the general term "work-related musculoskeletal disorder" (WMSD). This generalization also includes repetitive stress injuries, also called cumulative trauma disorders, ergonomic injuries, and musculoskeletal disorders, which affect muscles, tendons, ligaments, nerves, bones, cartilage, and blood vessels in the upper and lower extremities, and in the back. Some examples of WMSD include such problems as back injuries, tendonitis, and the previously mentioned carpal tunnel syndrome. There is a cost incentive for reducing WMSD as estimated costs associated with lost days and compensation claims now range from $13 billion to $20 billion annually.[106]

Perhaps the most significant employer response to WMSD is the implementation of effective ergonomics programs. **Ergonomics** is the science of adapting the job to the biomechanical needs of the worker. It is a human engineering process of matching the physical requirements of the job and the physical capacity of the worker. This naturally affects not only job design but the design of the worker's equipment as well.

In some cases, WMSD can be prevented by easy and inexpensive modifications to the workplace. Typical adjustments include adjusting the height of working surfaces, varying tasks for workers, encouraging short rest breaks with physical exercises, and decreasing the number and weight of items workers must lift—job design issues. Furnishing equipment to assist workers with lifting and providing specially designed equipment, such as ergonomically developed computer keyboards, are two simple examples of how employers may reduce risks.

WORK-RELATED STRESS AND EMOTIONAL DISORDERS

Work-related stress is considered a growing problem for workers in today's highly competitive work environment. For a number of reasons (lack of personal autonomy, poor leadership, budgetary constraints, reduced staffing, and so on), many employees have concluded that their jobs do not meet their expectations, and this may cause stress. Some of the factors inherent to jobs that contribute to high levels of work-related stress are workload, control over one's work, extrinsic and intrinsic rewards of work, coworker and supervisor relationships, sense of community in the workplace, perceptions of fairness and equity in the workplace, and compatibility of a person's roles to personal and organizational values.

Stress may be exacerbated as workers become increasingly concerned about achieving and maintaining a balance between family and work obligations. Women, particularly, are torn between workplace and family responsibilities.

HR strategies related to reducing stress involve job design (emphasizing employee control) and developing reward and incentive programs that not only satisfy employee needs but are equitably administered as well. Managerial training programs may be used to ensure that managerial personnel fully understand their leadership roles and the adverse consequences for poor leadership. Clearly communicated expectations and criteria for benefit and incentive eligibility can reduce exaggerated and unrealistic expectations among employees. Flexible work schedules may be developed to accommodate employees' family obligations. Finally, stress management courses can be offered to help employees develop strategies to deal with stress.

SUMMARY

HR professionals and line managers have a very real responsibility for overseeing safety in the workplace. There exist tangible economic incentives to afford workers safe workplaces. An unsafe work environment may cost the employer by increasing workers' compensation program costs and exposing the organization to increased litigation. Conversely, safe work environments may actually reduce expenses.

Workers' compensation laws were among the earliest attempts to address safety and health issues in the workplace. Although workers' compensation laws were originally designed as a system to provide benefits, not necessarily safe worksites, employers who experienced fewer accidents on the job paid lower premiums. Even now, employers who are ambivalent to workers' safety will experience more accidents and incur larger premiums.

The most significant guidance on safety and health from the federal government came with the passage of the Occupational Safety and Health Act in 1970. The OSH Act has extended federal safety and health standards to almost every workplace. The basic goal of the OSH Act was to assure safe and healthy conditions for workers on the job by encouraging employers and employees to reduce workplace hazards, but it has also imposed reporting and record keeping requirements. Employers should endeavor to maintain a safe working environment for employees because it is the right thing to do. However, there is sufficient regulation in this area to compel compliance.

KEY TERMS AND CONCEPTS

assumption of risk defense
contributory negligence defense
de minimus violation
emergency standard
ergonomics
exclusivity principle
fellow-servant rule defense
imminent danger violation

interim standards
other-than-serious violation
permanent standards
permanent variance
serious violation
temporary variance
willful and repeated violations
workers' compensation

QUESTIONS

1. What events led to regulation of safety and health in the workplace?

2. What is workers' compensation?

3. Describe the exclusivity principle of workers' compensation as a legal remedy.

4. Explain the compulsory or elective options regarding employer acceptance under state workers' compensation laws.

5. What are the grounds for challenging an employee's workers' compensation claim?

6. What three federal agencies were established under the OSH Act of 1970? What are the specific functions of each of these three federal agencies?

7. What are the specific requirements for employers under the "general duty clause" of the OSH Act?

8. What are the employees' rights to refuse to work in unsafe work conditions established by the Supreme Court in *Whirlpool Corp. v Marshall*?

CASES

1 Technotics, Inc., a small electronics components manufacturing firm, began operations several months ago. The firm is owned and operated by two young entrepreneurs who know very little about occupational safety and health issues. The company has fifty employees, several of whom operate the heavy equipment needed to package, warehouse, and ship the products.

The firm's owners hired a safety manager, Jim Strong, to develop and administer an industrial safety program. Unfortunately, before Strong could implement a formal safety program, the state occupational safety and health agency compliance officer entered the facility and conducted a tour, unaccompanied by either management or employees. At the end of the compliance officer's tour, Technotics was cited with one serious violation and two other-than-serious violations. The serious violation, a forklift operator not wearing a seat belt, is considered life-threatening, and the employer should have known of the hazard.

The owners want to contest the citations claiming they have made a good faith effort to establish a safety and health program but have not been able to implement such a program. They ask Strong for his suggested course of action. What steps would you recommend if you were the safety manager for this firm? Why?

2 Jeannett Krappels is a former employee of PeoplePower, Inc. Krappels has brought suit against PeoplePower, alleging that PeoplePower terminated her employment in retaliation for filing a workers' compensation claim under the Illinois Worker's Compensation Act.

Krappels was employed by PeoplePower from approximately January of 1999 to July 28, 2000, as a customer service specialist. On January 9, 2000, Krappels suffered a severe work-related injury. The injury prevented her from working at PeoplePower until January 15. On that date, Krappels began to work at home with physician's restrictions on her activities. On January 30, PeoplePower required Krappels to return to working from the office, rather than from home.

After Krappels returned to work, several PeoplePower employees, including her immediate supervisors, became concerned with her repeated absences and poor performance. Several e-mails between Chuck Taylor, who was her supervisor, Bud Busch, who was a regional director, and Mark Walker, who was a regional human resources manager, reflected these concerns. In July of 2000, Krappels apparently began to worry that she might be fired because of her injury and because of the "way she was being treated by PeoplePower after her injury."

In that same month, Monica Lemmon, Krappels' coworker, reported to Taylor and Busch that Krappels had asked her to testify in her workers' compensation case. The parties dispute whether or not Krappels offered to pay Lemmon $1,000 in exchange for her testimony.

On July 28, 2000, Albert Busch, the vice president of human resources at PeoplePower, sent Krappels a letter notifying her that she was terminated. The parties dispute the reason for her termination. PeoplePower claims that Busch's decision to terminate Krappels was based only on information about the alleged bribe Krappels made to Lemmon, while Krappels contends that her termination was in retaliation for her decision to file a worker's compensation claim. Does Krappels have a legitimate workers' compensation claim? What must PeoplePower demonstrate in order to prove they did not retaliate against Krappels?

SOURCE: *Hobbs v Peoplesoft, Inc.*, 2000 U.S. Dist. LEXIS 17087 (N.D. Ill. 2000).

NOTES

1. This scenario is based on the findings of fact in *Sakotas v Workers' Compensation Appeals Board*, 95 Cal. Rptr. 2d 153 (Ca. App. 2000).

2. U.S. Department of Labor (1967). *Growth of Labor Law in the United States*. Washington, DC: Government Printing Office, p. 182.

3. Anton, T. J. (1979). *Occupational Safety and Health Management*. New York: McGraw-Hill Co., pp. 189–190.

4. U.S. Department of Labor, pp. 139–140.

5. Ibid.

6. 35 Stat. 556 (May 30, 1908), codified as amended at 5 U.S.C. § 8101 et seq. in 1916.

7. U.S. Department of Labor, p. 140.

8. 5 U.S.C. § 8101 et seq.

9. 33 U.S.C. § 901 et seq.

10. U.S. Department of Labor, p. 141.

11. Ibid.

12. Lester, R. A. (1949). *Economics of Labor*. New York: The Macmillan Co., pp. 490–491.

13. 41 U.S.C. § 35 et seq.

14. 41 U.S.C. § 351 et seq.

15. National Safety Council (1999). *Injury Facts, 1999 Edition*. Itasca, IL: National Safety Council.

16. Ibid.

17. Ibid.

18. Epstein, R. A. (1982). The historical origins and the economic structure of workers' compensation law. *Georgia Law Review*, 16: 775–779; Anton, pp. 53–56.

19. Ulrich, R. B. (1995). "Survey of Illinois law: Workers' compensation." *Southern Illinois University Law Journal*, 19:999.

20. *Stivinson and Goodyear Tire & Rubber Co.*, 687 N.E.2d 458 (Ohio 1997).

21. *Shade v Ayars & Ayars, Inc.*, 525 N.W.2d 32 (Neb. 1994).

22. 629 N.E.2d 492 (Ohio App. 1993).

23. Ibid.

24. *Dorosz v Green & Seifter*, 708 N.E.2d 162 (N.Y. 1999).

25. *Ludwinski v National Carrier*, 873 S.W.2d 890 (Mo. App. 1994).

26. *Frantz v Campbell County Memorial Hospital*, 932 P.2d 750 (Wyo. 1997).

27. *Rosas v Workers' Compensation Appeals Board*, 20 Cal. Rptr.2d 778 (Cal. App. 1993); *Davis v Dyncorp*, 647 A.2d 446 (Md. App. 1994).

28. Kilgour, J. (January 2000). "A primer on workers' compensation laws and programs." *SHRM White Paper*. Arlington, VA: Society for Human Resource Management.

29. Sovereign, K. (1999). *Personnel Law (4th ed.)*. Upper Saddle River, NJ: Prentice Hall, p. 254.

30. Ibid. at p. 242.

31. *Stivison v Goodyear Tire and Rubber Co.*, 687 N.E.2d 458 (Ohio 1997).

32. Commonwealth of Massachusetts, Department of Industrial Accidents (1999). *Employer's Guide to Workers' Compensation*. Springfield, MA: Department of Industrial Accidents.

33. Office of Workers' Compensation Programs, Employment Standards Administration (January 1999). *State Workers' Compensation Laws*. Washington, DC: U.S. Department of Labor.

34. U.S. Chamber of Commerce (1997). *1997 Analysis of Workers' Compensation Laws*. Washington, DC: U.S. Chamber of Commerce.

35. Office of Workers' Compensation Programs. *State Workers' Compensation Laws*.

36. **http://www.state.tx/dol/wc.htm**

37. U.S. Chamber of Commerce.

38. Alaska Statutes 23.30.205.

39. National Council on Compensation Insurance (1992). *Issues Report 1992, A Summary of Issues Influencing Workers' Compensation*. Boca Raton, FL: National Council on Compensation Insurance.

40. *Koger v Greyhound Lines, Inc.*, 629 N.E.2d 492 (Ohio App. 1993).

41. *Ludwinski v National Courier*, 873 S.W.2d 890 (Mo. App. 1994).

42. *Roberts v Estep*, 845 S.W.2d 544 (Ky. 1993).

43. *Reswelser v Havoil Construction Co.*, 660 So.2d 7 (La. 1995).

44. *Recchi America Inc. v Hall*, 692 So.2d 153 (Fla. 1997).

45. 29 U.S.C. § 651 *et. seq.*

46. U.S. Department of Labor, p. 187.

47. 29 C.F.R. § 1903.2.

48. 29 U.S.S. § 666.

49. 29 U.S.C. § 654(a).

50. 29 U.S.C. § § 2200.70–2200.77.

51. Ibid.

52. Occupational Safety and Health Administration (1993). *Protecting Workers in Imminent Danger*. OSHA Fact Sheet No. OSHA 93–18.

53. 29 U.S.C. § 658(a).

54. 29 C.F.R. § 1903.14(b).

55. 29 U.S.C. § 658(b).

56. 29 U.S.C. § 666(I).

57. 29 C.F.R. § 1903.17.

58. 29 U.S.C. § 652(5).

59. *Donovan v Coeur d'Alene Tribal Farm*, 751 F.2d 1113, 1116 (9th Cir. 1985).

60. 29 C.F.R. § 2200.90.

61. 499 F.2d 467 (D.C. Cir. 1974).

62. 29 U.S.C. § 655(c)(1).

63. 29 U.S.C. § 655(c)(3).

64. 489 F.2d 120, 132 (5th. Cir. 1974).

65. 29 U.S.C. 654(a)(1).

66. U.S. Occupational Safety and Health Administration (2000). *Field Inspection Reference Manual*. Washington, DC: Government Printing Office, § 7C.2.c.1.d.

67. 448 U.S. 607 (1980).

68. Ibid. at 632.

69. *Society of Plastics Industry v OSHA*, 509 F.2d 1301 (2nd Cir. 1975).

70. 647 F.2d 1189 (D.C. Cir. 1980), *cert denied*, 453 U.S. 913 (1981).

71. Ibid. at 1277.

72. *Industrial Union Department v American Petroleum Institute*, 448 U.S. 607 (1980).

73. 452 U.S. 490 (1981).

74. 29 U.S.C. § 655(b)(6)(a).

75. Ibid.

76. 29 U.S.C. § 655(d).

77. Ibid.

78. 29 C.F.R. § 1904 et seq.

79. 29 C.F.R. § 1904.17.

80. 29 C.F.R. § 1904.16.

81. 29 C.F.R. § 1904.12(c).

82. 29 C.F.R. § 1904.12(d).

83. U.S. Equal Employment Opportunity Commission (March 2, 1999). Enforcement Guidance: Reasonable Accommodation Under the Americans with Disabilities Act. **www.access.eeoc.docs/accommodation.html**

84. 29 U.S.C. § 657(f)(1) and (2).

85. 29 U.S.C. § 657(a) and 29 C.F.R. § 1903.7(a).

86. 29 C.F.R. § 1903.7.

87. 29 U.S.C. § 657(e).

88. 535 F.2d 371 (7th Cir. 1976).

89. 436 U.S. 307 (1978).

90. 29 U.S.C. § 666(b).

91. Comprehensive Crime Control Act of 1984, Pub. L. 98–473, Tit. II, 98 Stat. 1976.

92. 29 U.S.C. § 660(c)(1).

93. 445 U.S. 1 (1980).

94. 29 U.S.C. § 653.

95. U.S. Department of Labor (1999). *1999 Report from OSHSPA, The Occupational Safety and Health State Plan Association.* Washington, DC: Government Printing Office.

96. Anonymous (August 1997). "What cigarettes do to American business." *Business and Health,* pp. 10–13.

97. *Respiratory Health Effects of Passive Smoking: Lung Cancer and Other Disorders.* EPA/600/6–90/006F.

98. Ibid.

99. Ibid.

100. 29 U.S.C. § 651, 654(a)

101. Warchol, G. (July 1998). *Workplace Violence, 1992–96.* Washington, DC: Bureau of Justice Statistics, U.S. Department of Justice.

102. Ibid.

103. U.S. Department of Justice (May 2000). *Criminal Victimization in the United States, 1998 Statistical Tables.* Washington, DC: Bureau of Justice Statistics.

104. U.S. Bureau of Labor Statistics (2001). *National Employment: Total Nonfarm Industry.* **http://146.142.4.24/cgi-bin/surveymost**

105. Katz, D.M. (2000). "Study finds lag in violence prevention." *National Underwriter,* 104 (3).

106. National Research Council (1999). "Work-Related Musculoskeletal Disorders: Report, Workshop Summary, and Workshop Papers." Steering Committee for the Workshop on Work-Related Musculoskeletal Injuries: The Research Base. Washington, DC: The National Academy Press.

IV

REGULATION OF LABOR RELATIONS

11

LABOR RELATIONS: HISTORICAL, LEGAL, AND ORGANIZING ISSUES

LEARNING OBJECTIVES

- ☐ Understand the differences between unionized and nonunionized work environments.
- ☐ Distinguish between human resource compliance and labor relations.
- ☐ Provide an overview of the labor relations process.
- ☐ Explain the historical development of unions and labor relations.
- ☐ Discuss the evolution of government regulation of labor-management relations.
- ☐ Describe the major provisions of federal and state laws affecting labor relations.
- ☐ Discuss the primary methods of union organizing.
- ☐ Describe the steps in the union organizing process.

OPENING SCENARIO

The Weinzimmer Company's Peoria, Illinois packing plant recently completed contract negotiations and ratification of a new collective bargaining agreement. The plant was unionized by the United Food and Commercial Workers (UFCW) last July. This is the company's first experience operating under a collective bargaining agreement. Soon after the contract was ratified, problems emerged as managerial personnel began to adjust to working under a labor contract.

On Monday, Neal Mero, one of the production managers, appeared in the plant superintendent's office with a dilemma. During the previous month, the Weinzimmer Company was fortunate enough to be awarded an account to provide Polish sausage to a regional grocery chain. In order to meet the grocery chain's demand, Weinzimmer must work all employees on all shifts eight hours overtime for the next four weeks. Because the organization runs three eight hour shifts per day, five days per week, the overtime must be *performed on Saturdays. Saturday work has been required in the past; however, there was no union or collective bargaining agreement at that time.*

When Ross Fink, the plant superintendent, informs Mero to make arrangements for the Saturday overtime work, Mero tells him that he had begun to do so when Morris Stocks, the shop steward, confronted him. Stocks reported that the collective bargaining agreement gives employees the right to refuse overtime work. Later, when Mero reviewed the contract, Stocks's statements proved accurate. Article III, Section 4, states:

> *Employees shall be notified no less than twenty-four hours in advance of any requirement to work beyond regularly scheduled shifts. In the event that an employee is requested to perform work beyond the shift to which he or she is assigned (see Article XI, Section 2), the employee may refuse said work.*

To further complicate matters, Stocks presented Mero with a letter containing the signatures of twenty-nine employees on the evening shift who were refusing the Saturday overtime work. This was roughly one-third of the evening shift. Mero was also told that shop stewards on the day and graveyard shifts were preparing similar memos.

Furious, Fink tells Mero to inform the shop stewards that there are no state or federal laws that give employees the right to refuse overtime work. According to Fink, "This company has never missed a customer's required deadline, and we won't start now! Any employee who fails to show up for the mandatory overtime will be terminated."

When Mero informs Stocks of Fink's statements, Stocks responds by informing him that the union is filing a grievance on the grounds that Fink is attempting to unilaterally change the collective bargaining agreement that he had previously agreed to follow.

INTRODUCTION

You should recall from Chapter 1 that this textbook examines the impact of federal regulation on two distinct types of work environments—union and nonunion. In 1999, employees who were union members represented less than 13.5 percent of all employees, public and private, in the United States.[1] Although this figure indicates that unionized workplaces have reached the lowest percentage of the workforce since the 1930s, they still present a compliance challenge for human resource (HR) professionals and managers.

The preceding ten chapters addressed HR compliance activities. **HR compliance** is the area of human resource management (HRM) that deals with relationships between managers and employees in regulated, but nonunionized, work environments. Up until this point, you have been introduced to the regulations, statutes, and case law which apply to all employers regardless of whether the employees are represented by labor unions. In this and the final chapter, management and employee relationships in unionized work environments are examined.

Suppose an employer has two hundred full-time employees. It would make absolutely no difference if these employees were represented by a union or not when determining the outcome of a sexual harassment investigation. *All* employers with fifteen or more full-time employees are required to maintain a harassment-free work environment.[2] Whether or not the employees are members of a union bargaining unit has no impact on the Equal Employment Opportunity Commission's (EEOC's) investigation.

Similarly, an employer is required under the Fair Labor Standards Act (FLSA) to pay *any* nonexempt employee one and one-half times his or her hourly rate of pay for every hour worked in excess of forty hours during a 168 consecutive-hour work week.[3] Again, it does not matter whether the employee is a member of a bargaining unit or works in a nonunion workplace, the minimum requirements for overtime under the FLSA must be met.

Simply stated, employers who have **unionized workplaces** (sometimes called **organized workplaces**), those in which a portion of their workers are represented by a labor union, have to meet the same regulatory compliance requirements as any other covered employer. The major difference between union-free and unionized workplaces is that unionized employers have the additional responsibility of complying with collective bargaining agreements and the Labor-Management Relations Act.

OVERVIEW OF LABOR RELATIONS

Labor relations, also known as **industrial relations,** is the functional area of HRM that addresses employment issues arising from unionized workplaces. In such a work environment, HR professionals and managers are not only responsible for ensuring compliance with the federal and state laws that govern all workplaces but must also be especially familiar with federal and state labor laws. In addition to these laws, HR professionals and managers must be knowledgeable of the specific collective bargaining agreement covering their company or facility. For managers, labor relations imposes additional obligations such as negotiating the collective bargaining agreement, recognizing the union's duty to fair representation, resolving grievances, and administering the negotiated agreement. Managers in unionized work environments are confronted with more challenges than their counterparts in union-free environments.

Perhaps the most significant difference in unionized work environments is that the terms, conditions, and rights of employment for specific employees are specified under a contractual arrangement called a **collective bargaining agreement (CBA),** sometimes referred to as a "labor contract." The employees' representatives meet with the employer to negotiate the provisions of the CBA. As a result of this process, many employment practices and employee rights are formalized and guaranteed in the "contract." For example, most CBAs stipulate the wage and benefit packages for all employees in the bargaining unit. The **bargaining unit** includes all employees that the union is certified to represent and who would be covered under the provisions of the CBA. In the CBA, the wages that employees draw are usually based on job assignments and seniority. The CBA also governs such employment practices as due process for disciplinary actions and, in some instances, how work assignments and promotions are conducted.

The CBA places all the employees in the bargaining unit under an explicit contract which the employer is legally obligated to follow. This imposes more employment obligations on the unionized employer than its union-free counterparts face. For instance, assume that during collective bargaining negotiations an employer has agreed to pay double time to any unionized employee required to work on Sunday, regardless of the number of hours the employee worked that week. There are no federal or state laws mandating double time for working on Sunday, or under any other circumstance for that matter. However, because the employer agreed to this level of compensation in the CBA, the employer is now required to satisfy the terms of the CBA. Any failure to do so would violate the CBA. The main rule in collective bargaining is that if you have agreed to do something in your CBA (and it is not illegal), you are committed to honor that agreement for the duration of the CBA.

As in this chapter's opening scenario, CBAs can and do have a substantial impact on how management may use its human resources. After the CBA is **ratified,** approved by the members of the bargaining unit, it becomes the "law" regulating employee and management relations until it expires. The majority of CBAs have a duration of three years, although some have been negotiated with a duration of only one year, while others may be in effect for as long as nine years. If, for example, management had inadvertently agreed in the CBA that employees may refuse to work outside of their regularly scheduled shifts, working overtime would be strictly voluntary until the CBA expired. When management realizes it has agreed to provisions that jeopardize the organization's efficiency, it must either convince the union to agree to renegotiate the overtime provision, which the union has the right to refuse to do, or it will have to wait for the CBA to expire and attempt to remove the provision in the next round of negotiations. The paramount rule of labor relations is to always project the future effects of any provisions before agreeing to them during collective bargaining negotiations.

During the period following ratification of the CBA, disputes invariably will arise over interpretations and applications of the language of the agreement. To minimize the disruptions that such disagreements inevitably cause, most CBAs contain grievance procedures which provide a systematic means for resolving any complaints, commonly called grievances, arising from the CBA to conclude with bringing in outside, neutral, third parties to resolve the disagreement. The contract administration process is addressed in Chapter 12. To understand why collective bargaining entered the American workplace, one must first understand how the labor relations system evolved.

HISTORICAL DEVELOPMENT OF LABOR UNIONS AND LABOR RELATIONS

There have been labor organizations in the United States since before the American Revolution. Yet their period of greatest growth and strength occurred during the 1930s and 1940s. What follows is a brief overview of the evolution of the American labor movement culminating with the development of the national labor code.

UNIONIZED LABOR PRIOR TO 1800

During the colonial period, there were few industries in the thirteen colonies that would eventually become the United States. The colonial economy was predominately based on agriculture. What little manufacturing there was consisted primarily of independent craftsmen operating their own shops. Craftsmen usually learned their trade by serving several years as apprentices to master craftsmen. Shops were relatively small, and workforces comprised a handful of journeymen and apprentices. Most manufactured goods, those mass produced by unskilled workers, were imported from the United Kingdom. Even after independence, the United States still depended heavily on manufactured goods from Europe due to the scarcity of both skilled and unskilled labor in the country.

Trade unions, as we know them today, began in America in the latter part of the eighteenth century. In these times, American production of goods was hampered by a chronic shortage of workers because most unskilled workers, including immigrants, preferred farming their own farms to working for someone else in a town or city.[4] As a result, goods manufactured by skilled workers were forced to compete with cheaper European manufactured goods. The Industrial Revolution in Europe permitted factories to produce goods using work simplification and unskilled labor. This type of production resulted in greater output and much cheaper per unit labor costs. Suddenly craftsmen who might take days to make a single product found the same product manufactured by several dozen unskilled workers (each performing a single step in the manufacturing process) in minutes. Not only was it cheaper to pay an unskilled worker, who willingly worked cheaper because of the marked surplus of unskilled labor available in Europe at the time, but these workers also quickly mastered the simple tasks they were trained to perform. Unskilled workers managed a single, isolated step in the manufacturing process, whereas a skilled craftsman had to know each of hundreds of steps.[5] As a result, more goods were produced in a shorter span of time at vastly lower per-unit costs to the factory owner.

In the United States, owners of the craftsman-based manufacturing were compelled to reduce their per-unit costs in order to compete with the cheaper goods coming from European factories. To accomplish these reductions, owners held down wages, lengthened the typical workday of employees, and sought cheaper sources of labor.[6] In response to these measures, trade societies, the forerunners of craft unions, emerged in the early 1800s to safeguard the status of skilled workers in this changing environment. Their objectives were simple: higher wages, shorter hours, and improved working conditions. Some trade societies introduced the rudimentary principles of collective bargaining.[7] When the shop owners refused to bargain with them or concede to their demands, the trade societies would refuse to work. Since every skilled worker in that trade was a society member, the owner could not hire replacement workers, and his business was effectively shut down. Shop owners responded to these tactics by seeking protection through the courts and were generally successful in charging the trade societies with criminal conspiracy.

UNIONS AS A CRIMINAL CONSPIRACY

In 1806, a Pennsylvania court in *Commonwealth v Pullis*[8] created from English common law what would become known as the **criminal conspiracy doctrine.** In Philadelphia, the cordwainers, skilled craftsmen who made shoes, began to strike against employers who set a lower per-piece rate for shoes being exported to Europe. The employers argued that a lower rate for each pair of shoes was necessary in order to compete with the cheaper shoes manufactured in Europe. From the cordwainers' perspective, this did not really matter because a shoe sold in Europe or a shoe sold in the United States required the same amount of time and effort. Their plan was simple: Stop all production of shoes until the employers agreed to return piece rates to their previous level. Typically, the employers responded to the work stoppages by taking the matter to court.

The court viewed the demand for a wage increase by the Philadelphia cordwainers as tantamount to extortion and ruled it a "criminal conspiracy in restraint of trade" for workers to combine for the purpose of exerting pressure on employers.[9] This ruling made it a criminal activity even to create a union; therefore, unions themselves were unlawful—even being a member of a union was an illegal activity.

Still, unions survived after the ruling. Several new craft unions were even organized. However, these unions were small and geographically decentralized. There was no national labor organization to consolidate labor's power or to speak for the concerns of the working class.

UNIONS ARE NO LONGER A CRIMINAL CONSPIRACY

In 1842, the criminal conspiracy doctrine was finally overturned in a Massachusetts Supreme Court decision, *Commonwealth v Hunt*.[10] The court held that labor unions themselves were no longer criminal conspiracies. However, strikes and boycotts of employers by unions were still viewed as criminal activities. Now, an individual could lawfully be a member of a union but was often prohibited from engaging in certain union activities (i.e., strikes, boycotts, etc.). As a result of the *Hunt* decision, union membership began to expand, and the number of new unions increased.

THE RISE OF NATIONAL LABOR ORGANIZATIONS

At the end of the American Civil War, industrial expansion had dramatically increased the number of Americans who made their livings in manufacturing. Although the United States was still predominately an agrarian economy, manufacturing had made substantial gains. As more of the population turned to industrial occupations, labor unions experienced unprecedented growth. It was not long before unions from one locality began joining with unions in other regions of the country to form national unions.

NATIONAL LABOR UNION.   In 1866, the first federation of national unions, appropriately named the National Labor Union, was formed in Baltimore, Maryland. The National Labor Union's founder and only president was William H. Sylvis of the Molder's Union.[11] During its brief, six-year existence, the National Labor Union supported a number of political agendas which it felt would benefit *all* working Americans. Among its primary goals were the enactment of legislation creating an eight-hour workday and the replacement of the gold standard with paper currency (so-called "greenbacks").

The National Labor Union also supported some openly socialist objectives. By the mid-1850s, socialism had gained considerable support among the European working classes and was popular among many immigrants from Europe who joined the American labor movement. In line with the socialist doctrine of the time period, the National Labor Union called for replacing capitalism by turning the factories over to worker cooperatives. Since 1848, a popular demand among the socialists has been that the workers should control the means of production.[12]

The end came for the National Labor Union when it supported the Greenback Party in the 1872 elections. Following the Greenback Party's humiliating defeat at the polls, the National Labor Union quickly began to disappear.

KNIGHTS OF LABOR.   With the demise of the National Labor Union, union leaders began to realize that a more concerted effort was needed to improve the plight of the working class. In 1869, several unions joined together to form the Noble and Holy Order of Knights of Labor. Like the National Labor Union, the Knights of Labor was primarily concerned with the plight of the working class and called for reforms that would benefit *all* workers. Under the leadership of its founder, Uriah Stephens, and later, in 1878, Terrence Powderly, the Knights pushed for restrictions on child labor, free public education, industrial safety laws, and even graduated incomes. The Knights, like its predecessor, also called for consumer and producer cooperatives to replace capitalism. The high point of the Knight's existence came in 1885 when railroad employees conducted a successful strike against Jay Gould's Wabash Railroad. The strike resulted in better wages and improved working conditions. As a direct result of the Wabash strike, membership in the Knights of Labor rose to more than 702,000.[13]

Unfortunately for the member unions, Terrence Powderly was able to snatch defeat from the jaws of victory. Despite the apparent success of the Wabash strike, Powderly returned to the Knights' practice of avoiding strikes and boy-cotts. The tactic which had accounted for the Knights' spectacular growth was now abandoned. However, the Haymarket Square riot in 1886 had an immediate demoralizing effect on members, who left the organization in droves. Although the Knights of Labor did not fade from existence until the First World War, by the 1890s it was only a shell of its former self and an organization of little importance.

AMERICAN FEDERATION OF LABOR.   As the Knights of Labor began its decline, a new national labor organization, the American Federation of Labor (AFL), emerged. The AFL's founder and president was Samuel Gompers of the Cigar Makers International Union. Interestingly, the nucleus of the AFL was composed of unions that had actually broken away from the Knights of Labor in 1881 to form the Federation of Organized Trades and Labor Unions. Five years later, in 1886, these unions officially became the AFL.

Gompers brought to the labor movement a view of unionism that was markedly different from his predecessors. Whereas the National Labor Union and the Knights of Labor had both focused their efforts on improving the eco-nomic lot of *all* workers, Gompers and the AFL focused their full attention on im-proving the economic lot and self-interest of their members. By operating principally for the benefit of its members, the AFL developed a system that would become known as "business unionism."[14]

Under **business unionism,** the AFL followed four principles of organization that contributed significantly to its ability to survive and prosper. The principles were complete autonomy for member unions, exclusive jurisdiction for member unions, avoidance of any permanent political alliances, and exclusive reliance on collective bargaining negotiations as the primary means of improving the eco-nomic position of organized labor.[15]

The AFL was also an exclusive organization. Unlike the Knights of Labor, that permitted unskilled workers to join its ranks, the AFL was open only to craft unions. Industrial (unskilled) workers were excluded completely. Also, the overtly socialist rhetoric of the National Labor Union and the Knights of Labor was removed. Gompers made no secret of the fact that the AFL was content to co-exist with capitalism, provided that capitalists negotiated higher wages, appro-priate benefits, and shorter work hours with the AFL. Gompers was very careful to ensure the AFL would distance itself from any organization that was con-nected with a socialist agenda. As a result of his efforts, the AFL was perceived as a respectable organization and gained the public acceptance that none of its fore-runners enjoyed.

INDUSTRIAL WORKERS OF THE WORLD.   While the AFL was gaining respectabil-ity as the "aristocrats of labor," many industrial workers turned to more radical labor organizations. The most revolutionary union of the period, if not all of labor history in the United States, was the International Workers of the World (IWW).

The IWW, known as the Wobblies, began as an amalgamation of William "Big Bill" Haywood's Western Federation of Mine Workers and Eugene V. Debs's American Railway Union in 1905. The IWW made no secret that it was ideological, political, and revolutionary. This is hardly surprising since one of its cofounders, Debs, ran for President of the United States as the Socialist Party candidate in 1900, 1904, 1908, 1912, and 1920.[16] The IWW viewed labor relations as a class struggle, and its ultimate goal was to replace the entire capitalist system with socialism.

The IWW had a reputation for violent confrontations, perhaps the most notable of which were the 1912 Lawrence, Massachusetts strike and the 1913 Patterson, New Jersey strike. Needless to say, the IWW never enjoyed public support. During the First World War, the organization was declared subversive. Membership quickly declined during the "Red Scare" following the Bolshevik Revolution in Russia. By the mid 1990s, the IWW had approximately seven hundred active members.[17]

LABOR AS A COMBINATION IN RESTRAINT OF TRADE

Congress passed the Sherman Antitrust Act in 1890 in an attempt to regulate monopolies.[18] Trusts were companies that monopolized industries by driving out competitors, preventing the entry of new ones, and exercising complete control over the prices of products in those industries. The Sherman Act was intended to break up trusts and encourage more competition. Unfortunately for unions, certain federal judges regarded unions as trusts since they had a monopoly power over an employer's source of labor. During a strike conducted by the National Hatters of America against D. E. Loewe & Company's Danbury, Connecticut factory, attorneys for the company derived the idea of challenging the union as an illegal conspiracy in restraint of trade under the Sherman Act. As a result, it was not long before unions were once again declared illegal conspiracies.

By the mid-1910s, unions had gained sufficient political power to prompt Congress to overturn the Danbury Hatter's case with legislation. The Clayton Act of 1914 exempted unions from the antitrust provisions of the Sherman Act. Specifically, Sections 6 and 20 of the Clayton Act exempted certain types of peaceful union activities from the antitrust laws. In Section 20 of the Clayton Act, Congress provided that "no . . . injunction shall prohibit any person or persons, whether singly or in concert, from . . . ceasing to perform any work [or other specified activities]."[19] This was intended to limit the use of court injunctions against striking unions in labor disputes between an employer and employees.

The Clayton Act affirmed the right of unions to strike, boycott, and picket.[20] However, a 1921 Supreme Court decision, *Duplex Co. v Dearing*,[21] weakened the Act, and additional legislation would be required to finally carry out these objectives.[22] Interestingly, as a sign of the growing importance of labor during the First World War, the Department of Labor was created as a part of President Woodrow Wilson's cabinet.

The American Plan

By the end of the First World War, industrial unions enjoyed a period of remarkable growth. The war-time economy had fueled a surge in industrial growth, and industrial unions benefited. However, as America entered the 1920s, industrial unions were confronted by increasingly concerted and well-planned antiunion tactics from employers. To blunt the growth of unions in their respective industries, many employers adopted the so-called "American Plan."[23] This **American Plan** was a combination of tactics designed to prevent unions from organizing their workers. Or, if a union was already in place in the workplace, the tactics were designed to get it out of the company.

During this period, **blacklists,** lists containing the names of union supporters, were shared among employers to prevent union members fired by one employer from being hired by another employer. Employers also made frequent use of industrial spies to infiltrate unions and report on their members, meetings, and plans. In some cases, employers would bribe union officers in **sweetheart arrangements** to work for the good of the company rather than in the interests of the union members.

Employers began to encourage employees to join "sham" or company-dominated unions instead of national unions. A common tactic was the use of yellow-dog contracts as a means of preventing unions. Under a **yellow-dog contract,** employees *would not* be hired unless they signed an agreement not to join a union. Additionally, those who were already employed signed a document promising that they would not participate in union activity. The term *yellow dog* comes from the notion that any union man compelled to sign such a contract would feel like a "yellow dog" for having done so. However, the Supreme Court had previously held that yellow dog contracts were enforceable.[24]

Some employers adopted a tactic known as paternalism. Under **paternalism,** employers owned the houses the employees rented, the stores where employees bought their goods, and in some instances even the banks or credit unions where they banked their money. Employees who supported unions not only stood to lose their paycheck but their homes and credit as well.

In the event of strikes, employers would use a wide range of strike-breaking tactics. Striking employees were often permanently replaced by strikebreakers, replacement employees usually called "scabs" by the union. Companies typically had well-armed company police supported by the infamous Pinkerton Detectives. Physical violence on both sides of the picket line was not uncommon.

During strikes, employers would frequently seek **court injunctions,** orders from a court to cease a specific activity such as a strike. If the union failed to respond to the injunction, its leadership could be held in contempt of court and fined and/or imprisoned. More importantly, since most court injunctions were issued by state courts, local law enforcement agencies could be called in to enforce the injunction.

During the 1920s, there was one particular class of industrial worker that drew the attention of the national government—railway workers. Through a series of strikes, the railway workers had been able to gain nationwide attention by disrupting interstate commerce. In a period before interstate highways and modern aviation, railroads were the major engine of the economy. Stop rail traffic and you stopped the entire economy (industrial and agricultural). Railroad disruptions became so rampant that citizens and businesses alike demanded government intervention.

RAILWAY LABOR ACT OF 1926

In response to the many disruptions in the rail service plaguing the nation, Congress passed the Railway Labor Act in 1926.[25] This Act legitimized the employees' right, in the railroad industry, to organize without interference from management and required railroad employers to bargain collectively with their employees' designated representatives. It further prohibited discrimination against employees in their terms of employment on the basis of union membership.[26] The Act also provided a means for settlement of railway labor disputes through mediation, voluntary arbitration, and fact finding boards.[27] In 1934, the Railway Labor Act was amended to enable air carrier employees to join labor organizations and bargain collectively.[28]

The Railway Labor Act established the National Mediation Board (NMB) and the National Railroad Adjustment Board (NRAB) for dispute resolution in the railroad industry. The NMB is responsible for administering the Railway Labor Act. Among its duties, the NMB is responsible for overseeing the union **representation process,** the means by which a labor union becomes the bargaining representative of the proposed bargaining unit. In this capacity, the NMB determines the appropriateness of the proposed bargaining unit as well as the timeliness of the representation petition.[29] The NMB also oversees the actual representation election. Ultimately, the NMB is responsible for investigating any alleged violations of the Act and mediating during representation elections and contract negotiations. However, grievances arising after the contract is ratified are handled by the NRAB.

THE GREAT DEPRESSION

The Great Depression resulted in the unemployment of almost one-third of the total workforce. The resulting social upheaval and economic devastation was beyond description. Laborers in all skills were in surplus as demand for labor plummeted. These conditions caused wages to fall drastically, and standards of living were reduced to subsistence levels. As the nation struggled with economic collapse, the federal government was pressured to do something to alleviate the plight of the people.

NORRIS-LAGUARDIA ACT OF 1932. In response to growing labor unrest during this period, Congress enacted legislation limiting an employer's ability to obtain an injunction in order to prohibit unions from picketing or participating in strike activities.[30] The Norris-LaGuardia Act declared that "the individual . . . workers . . .

will be free from the interference, restraint, or coercion, of employers ... in self-organization or in other concerted activities for the purpose of collective bargaining or other mutual aid or protection."[31] This language became the source of the provisions later enacted in Section 7 of the National Labor Relations Act. The Norris-La Giardia Act also made the distasteful yellow-dog contracts unenforceable in federal courts.

NATIONAL INDUSTRIAL RECOVERY ACT OF 1933. In yet another response to the economic disruptions created by the Great Depression, Congress enacted the National Industrial Recovery Act of 1933 (NIRA).[32] As part of Franklin D. Roosevelt's New Deal legislation, the NIRA was envisioned as a means of battling high unemployment and low wages.

Section 7(a) of the NIRA guaranteed employees the right to bargain over their wages and other working conditions. Specifically, Section 7(a) provided for the following conditions:

1. Employees shall have the right to organize and bargain collectively through representatives of their own choosing, and shall be free from the interference, restraint, or coercion of employers of labor, or their agents, in the designation of such representatives, or in self-organization or in other concerted activities for the purpose of collective bargaining or other mutual aid or protection.

2. No employee and no one seeking employment shall be required as a condition of employment to join any company union or to refrain from joining, organizing, or assisting a labor organization of his own choosing.[33]

The NIRA, however, was short lived as it was declared unconstitutional in a 1935 U.S. Supreme Court case, *Schechter Poultry Co. v United States.*[34] The Supreme Court held that Congress had exceeded its authority under the Commerce Clause of the Constitution by enacting a statute to regulate the wages and hours of labor employed in the internal commerce of a state.[35] Congress had the power to regulate *interstate* trade, but it had no constitutional authority to regulate *intrastate* trade. Despite the Court's opinion, the NIRA served as the forerunner of the National Labor Relations Act of 1935 not only by permitting self-organization but also creating an administrative board, the National Labor Board, to enforce its provisions.

THE DEVELOPMENT OF THE NATIONAL LABOR CODE

Three federal statutes, encompassing three distinct phases of national labor legislation and enacted twelve years apart, form the basis of current U.S. labor-management relations in the private sector. These three acts comprise the **national labor code.** They include the National Labor Relations Act of 1935 (also known as the Wagner Act), the Labor-Management Relations Act of 1947 (also known as the Taft-Hartley Act), and the Labor-Management Reporting and Disclosure Act of 1959 (also known as the Landrum-Griffin Act).

NATIONAL LABOR RELATIONS (WAGNER) ACT OF 1935

After the U.S. Supreme Court declared the NIRA unconstitutional in 1935, Congress immediately responded by enacting the National Labor Relations Act (NLRA)[36] that same year. The NLRA was designed to promote growth in national income by increasing the purchasing power of workers.[37] The rationale behind the statute was that as worker purchasing power increased, workers would buy more goods, which in turn would stimulate demand for those goods, thereby creating the demand for more labor.

Congress recognized in Section 1 of the NLRA[38] that the Act would provoke conflict between an employer and its employees when bargaining affected the distribution of the proceeds from the business operation. However, since employers held the greater share of bargaining power at the time period of the NLRA's passage, this could be endured in order to achieve the social goal of enhancing the employees' collective strength so they could bargain more effectively for higher wages and better working conditions. This, in theory, would spur economic growth and help end the Great Depression. So strong was the belief that the benefits of collective bargaining would outweigh its costs, President Roosevelt and Congress took measures to ensure the NLRA would not receive the same fate as its predecessor, the NIRA.

The President informed the Supreme Court that Congress was prepared to add more justices to the Court until they achieved a majority necessary to get their laws declared constitutional. Under this threat, the Court yielded to the inevitable and upheld the constitutionality of the National Labor Relations Act.[39]

The NLRA finally established a national policy protecting the right of workers to organize and bargain collectively on issues of wages, hours, and terms and conditions of employment without interference from management. It also defined **unfair labor practices (ULPs),** certain activities that, if practiced by employers, would be considered unlawful under the Act. The Act further imposed a requirement on management to bargain in "good faith" with the employees' representative. It also contained provisions for determining how a union was to be certified as the employees' lawful representative.

THE RIGHT TO ORGANIZE AND STRIKE. The most significant provision of the NLRA is Section 7. It is Section 7 which specifies the rights of employees to engage in union activities. Specifically:

> Employees shall have the right to self-organization, to form, join, or assist labor organizations, to bargain collectively through representatives of their own choosing, and to engage in concerted activities, for the purpose of collective bargaining or other mutual aid or protection.[40]

Specifically, the authorization to " . . . engage in concerted activities, for the purpose of collective bargaining or other mutual aid or protection," conveys the right to strike. However, this right is limited to economic issues and ULPs. Section 13 of the Act reinforces this right to strike by stating that, "except as specifically provided for herein," nothing in the Act should " . . . affect the limitations or qualifications on that right (to strike)."[41] Those exceptions to this right to strike include jurisdictional strikes, recognitional picketing prohibited in Section 8(b)(7), and strikes in violation of a no strike clause in a CBA.[42] Jurisdictional strikes occur when two or more unions are in dispute over the employer's assignment of work to a specific union. Both unions contend that the work should go to their members and not the others. Recognition picketing is picketing that is directed at the employer to get the employer to "recognize" the union as the employees' bargaining representative. Employees may not strike for economic reasons while a CBA containing a no strike/no lockout clause remains in effect.[43]

THE NATIONAL LABOR RELATIONS BOARD. Following the model previously established by the NIRA, the NLRA contained a provision to create an agency, the National Labor Relations Board (NLRB), to administer the Act and to oversee representation elections. The NLRB's major responsibilities are twofold: (1) to determine whether a union is to be the bargaining agent for employees and (2) to adjudicate cases involving ULP charges.

UNFAIR LABOR PRACTICES BY MANAGEMENT. To ensure that workers were not denied their right to organize and bargain collectively, Section 8 of the NLRA established five ULPs by management which are expressly prohibited under the Act. These are summarized in Exhibit 11-1.

Under Section 8(a)(1), an employer and his or her agents are prohibited from interfering with the employees' right to form or join labor organizations. Even assisting employees in forming a labor organization would constitute interfering with the employees' Section 7 rights.[44] Any attempt to restrain or coerce an employee's right to self-organization is a clear violation of the Act. Some examples of employer actions which could constitute such a ULP are spying on unions or their members, threatening to close the facility if the union is certified, or promising pay raises to employees if they will vote against the union.

Management is also prohibited from interfering with the formation or administration of any labor organization or contributing to its financial support under Section 8(a)(2).[45] This is often referred to as *unlawful domination,* and it was intended to eliminate the company unions that were so pervasive under the American Plan.

Under the third ULP, Section 8(a)(3), discrimination with regard to the terms and conditions of employment based on the employee's union membership is prohibited.[46] An employer would violate this section of the NLRA if he or she paid union employees less than nonunion employees. Interestingly, if the employer agreed to pay nonunion employees in the bargaining unit less than union employees in the same jobs, this section would also be violated. In short, employers cannot take an employee's union membership into consideration when making any employment decision.

The fourth ULP, Section 8(a)(4), is often referred to as the whistleblowers' clause. This section makes it a ULP for an employer to take retaliatory action against any employee for filing a ULP or testifying in a NLRB investigation.[47]

■ **EXHIBIT 11-1**

UNFAIR LABOR PRACTICES UNDER THE LABOR-MANAGEMENT RELATIONS ACT

Unfair Labor Practices by Management	Unfair Labor Practices by the Union
Section 8(a)(1): Interference with employees' rights to be represented and to bargain collectively.	**Section 8(b)(1):** Interfering with employees' rights to be represented and to bargain collectively or restraining of employers in selecting their representatives to bargain in their behalf.
Section 8(a)(2): Employer dominance or support of employees' labor organizations.	**Section 8(b)(2):** Causing or attempting to cause employers to discriminate against employees because of their lack of union membership where there is no valid union shop agreement in effect.
Section 8(a)(3): Employment discrimination based upon union activity or affiliation.	
Section 8(a)(4): Retaliation for accusing the employer of an unfair labor practice or for providing testimony in an unfair labor practice proceeding.	**Section 8(b)(3):** Refusal to bargain collectively in good faith with the employer.
Section 8(a)(5): Refusal to bargain collectively in good faith with the union.	**Section 8(b)(4):** Engaging in certain types of secondary strikes or boycotts.
	Section 8(b)(5): Charging excessively large initiation fees.
	Section 8(b)(6): Causing or attempting to cause an employer to pay for services which are not performed or not to be performed (featherbedding).
	Section 8(b)(7): Limitations on recognitional picketing.

SOURCE: 29 U.S.C. § 158.

Finally, Section 8(a)(5) requires the employer to bargain in good faith with the union certified to represent his or her employees.[48] This provision is violated when the employer refuses to negotiate with the union on the mandatory bargaining issues: wages, hours, and conditions of employment.

THE REPRESENTATION PROCESS. Section 9 of the NLRA provides for a means, administered by the NLRB, for employees to select designated employee representatives for the purposes of collective bargaining.[49] Selection of a designated representative is based on a majority showing of the employees in an appropriate bargaining unit for such purposes. The designated representative shall be the exclusive agent for all of the employees in that bargaining unit for the purposes of collective bargaining. The Act provides a petition process for requesting a representation election, hearing, and the election itself.

Organizing Overview. The organizing process actually begins when union organizers become aware of union representation interest. In many cases, disgruntled employees themselves contact the union organizer to express interest in organizing. Because union organizing resources are limited, organizers will investigate such requests before committing themselves. Organizing efforts will not be initiated unless the union feels there is enough interest to win a representation election. In other situations, the union itself may initiate action to represent a group of employees.

If there is enough interest, the union organizer first solicits workers to sign **union authorization cards** indicating interest in having the union become their exclusive bargaining agent. The organizer must attain a sufficient "showing of interest" within the employee group. To pursue a certification, a **showing of interest** must consist of at least 30 percent of the workers of the bargaining unit signing the authorization cards;[50] however, a union will normally not attempt to organize a bargaining unit unless there is at least a 60 percent showing of interest. Because some employees who have signed authorization cards may not vote for the union during the certification/representation election, the union wants a substantial majority of the proposed bargaining unit in their camp before the vote.

A union organizer may send a letter or notice to the employer claiming to represent a majority of its employees and demanding recognition. This notification to the employer may lead to the employer recognizing the union as the exclusive bargaining agent for employees if it is convinced that a majority of the workers have signed cards without duress. In most cases, however, employers refuse to recognize a union, questioning whether the union organizer has a sufficient showing of interest and insisting on an election to answer any representation questions.

A union does not become the exclusive bargaining agent for a group of employees until it is recognized that a majority of the bargaining unit of employees want to be represented. The principle held in Section 9(a) of the NLRA is that a majority representative "shall be the exclusive representative of all the employees in [the bargaining] unit" is the heart of the organizing process.[51] Once the union is certified as the exclusive representative, it has the sole right to represent all eligible employees, whether they are union members or not, in all matters involving wages, hours, and terms of employment with the employer.

Prior to the passage of the NLRA, a union could only gain recognition by persuading an employer to grant such recognition voluntarily.[52] Currently, there are three ways in which a union can become the exclusive bargaining agent for a group of employees: the employer may voluntarily recognize the union, the NLRB may order and supervise a representation election, or the NLRB may issue a directive ordering an employer to bargain.

Voluntary Recognition. If an employer is convinced that a majority of the employees want to be represented by a particular union, the employer may voluntarily recognize the union and commence collective bargaining with its designated representatives. In such cases, the union usually satisfies the employer by showing authorization cards or petitions signed by a majority of the employees in a specific unit.

Nevertheless, a union must follow orderly procedures when obtaining recognition. Section 8(b) of the NLRA[53] establishes a number of ULPs for labor unions.

In this sense, the NLRA prohibits certain union activities used to persuade employers to grant recognition, including making threats, picketing, or threatening picketing without having filed a petition with the NLRB.

Petition to the NLRB. If the employer elects not to voluntarily recognize the union, a petition can be filed with the NLRB for a certification/representation election to determine representation (refer to Exhibit 11-2). Even when the union presents authorization cards or petitions signed by a majority of the employees, the employer may still have doubts as to a sufficient showing of interest. The employer could be concerned that the signatures were collected by improper means.

A refusal of recognition by the employer forces the union to petition the NLRB under Section 9 of the NLRA[54] requesting certification as the exclusive bargaining agent for the employees in the proposed bargaining unit. The union's petition will specify the group or unit of employees it claims to represent. The employer may then challenge the petition by arguing that the unit described is inappropriate for inclusion in a bargaining unit. For example, the union may wish to include clerical workers and production workers in the same unit even though these two classes of workers do not share common skills, compensation, or working conditions. Such disputes over eligibility are typically worked out either by mutual agreement of the parties (an agreement to a consent election) or through a formal hearing. Should the matter go to a hearing, the NLRB will then have to determine what is the appropriate bargaining unit and whether a representation election should be conducted. If the union still enjoys a sufficient showing of interest (30 percent of the proposed bargaining unit) after the appropriate bargaining unit has been resolved, the NLRB may then decide that a **certification/representation election** will be held to determine if a majority of the employees want to be represented by a union.

Within seven days after the election has been ordered, the employer must supply the NLRB with a list of names and addresses of all employees in the appropriate bargaining unit.[55] The list is commonly referred to as an **Excelsior list.** The NLRB will then give the union a copy of the Excelsior list so that both parties have knowledge of the employees who are eligible to vote in the election.

Representation Election Campaign. Once the election date, time, and place have been established, the parties (management, the petitioning union, and any intervener union) continue the election campaign. The union will try to convince the employees that they need to vote for union representation, while the employer will try to dissuade the employees from voting for the union. The parties must campaign within legally established limitations for conduct before an election. This is a period in which ULPs are most likely to occur because both parties are prohibited from using any form of coercion in their campaigns.

When an employer has become aware of a union organizing effort already underway, any changes in wages, hours of work, and other terms and conditions of employment would be very chancy. Changes at this time could constitute a ULP charge under Section 8(a)(1)of the NLRA.[56] In fact, once an election petition is

FORM NLRB-502
(3-96)

UNITED STATES GOVERNMENT
NATIONAL LABOR RELATIONS BOARD
PETITION

FORM EXEMPT UNDER 44 U.S.C. 3512

DO NOT WRITE IN THIS SPACE	
Case No.	Date Filed

INSTRUCTIONS: Submit an original and 4 copies of this Petition to the NLRB Regional Office in the Region in which the employer concerned is located. If more space is required for any one item, attach additional sheets, numbering item accordingly.

The Petitioner alleges that the following circumstances exist and requests that the National Labor Relations Board proceed under its proper authority pursuant to Section 9 of the National Labor Relations Act.

1. **PURPOSE OF THIS PETITION** (*If box RC, RM, or RD is checked and a charge under Section 8(b)(7) of the Act has been filed involving the Employer named herein, the statement following the description of the type of petition shall not be deemed made.*) **(Check One)**

☐ **RC-CERTIFICATION OF REPRESENTATIVE** - A substantial number of employees wish to be represented for purposes of collective bargaining by Petitioner and Petitioner desires to be certified as representative of the employees.

☐ **RM-REPRESENTATION (EMPLOYER PETITION)** - One or more individuals or labor organizations have presented a claim to Petitioner to be recognized as the representative of employees of Petitioner.

☐ **RD-DECERTIFICATION (REMOVAL OF REPRESENTATIVE)** - A substantial number of employees assert that the certified or currently recognized bargaining representative is no longer their representative.

☐ **UD-WITHDRAWAL OF UNION SHOP AUTHORITY (REMOVAL OF OBLIGATION TO PAY DUES)** - Thirty percent (30%) or more of employees in a bargaining unit covered by an agreement between their employer and a labor organization desire that such authority be rescinded.

☐ **UC-UNIT CLARIFICATION** - A labor organization is currently recognized by Employer, but Petitioner seeks clarification of placement of certain employees: (*Check one*) ☐ In unit not previously certified. ☐ In unit previously certified in Case No. _____

☐ **AC-AMENDMENT OF CERTIFICATION** - Petitioner seeks amendment of certification issued in Case No. _____ *Attach statement describing the specific amendment sought.*

2. Name of Employer	Employer Representative to contact	Telephone Number

3. Address(es) of Establishment(s) involved (*Street and number, city, State, ZIP code*)	Telecopier Number (Fax)

4a. Type of Establishment (*Factory, mine, wholesaler, etc.*)	4b. Identify principal product or service

5. Unit involved (*In UC petition, describe present bargaining unit and attached description of proposed clarification.*)		6a. Number of Employees in Unit:
Included		Present
		Proposed (*By UC/AC*)
Excluded		6b. Is this petition supported by 30% or more of the employees in the unit?* ☐ Yes ☐ No *Not applicable in RM, UC, and AC

(*If you have checked box RC in 1 above, check and complete EITHER item 7a or 7b, whichever is applicable.*)

7a. ☐ Request for recognition as Bargaining Representative was made on (*Date*) _____ and Employer declined recognition on or about (*Date*) _____ (*If no reply received, so state.*)

7b. ☐ Petitioner is currently recognized as Bargaining Representative and desires certification under the Act.

8. Name of Recognized or Certified Bargaining Agent (*If none, so state.*)	Affiliation

Address, Telephone No. and Telecopier No. (Fax)	Date of Recognition or Certification

9. Expiration Date of Current Contract. If any (*Month, Day, Year*)	10. If you have checked box UD in 1 above, show here the date of execution of agreement granting union shop (*Month, Day, and Year*)

11a. Is there now a strike or picketing at the Employer's establishment(s) involved? Yes _____ No _____	11b. If so, approximately how many employees are participating?

11c. The Employer has been picketed by or on behalf of (*Insert Name*) _____, a labor organization, of (*Insert Address*) _____ Since (*Month, Day, Year*) _____

12. Organizations or individuals other than Petitioner (*and other than those named in items 8 and 11c*), which have claimed recognition as representatives and other organizations and individuals known to have a representative interest in any employees in unit described in item 5 above. (*If none, so state.*)

Name	Affiliation	Address	Date of Claim
			Telecopier No. (Fax)

13. Full name of party filing petition (If labor organization, give full name, including local name and number)

14a. Address (*street and number, city, state, and ZIP code*)	14b. Telephone No.
	14c. Telecopier No. (Fax)

15. Full name of national or international labor organization of which it is an affiliate or constituent unit (*to be filled in when petition is filed by a labor organization*)

I declare that I have read the above petition and that the statements are true to the best of my knowledge and belief.

Name (*Print*)	Signature	Title (*if any*)
Address (*street and number, city, state, and ZIP code*)		Telephone No.
		Telecopier No. (Fax)

WILLFUL FALSE STATEMENTS ON THIS PETITION CAN BE PUNISHED BY FINE AND IMPRISONMENT (U.S. CODE, TITLE 18, SECTION 1001)

PLEASE REVIEW THE FOLLOWING IMPORTANT INFORMATION BEFORE FILLING OUT A PETITION FORM!

- Please call an Information Officer in the Regional Office nearest you for assistance in filing a petition. The Information Officer will be happy to answer your questions about the petition form or to draft the petition on your behalf.
- Check one of the boxes listed under Question 1 representing the purpose of the petition: RC-a union desires to be certified as the bargaining representative of employees; RM-an employer seeks an election because one or more individuals or unions have sought recognition as the bargaining representative, or based on a reasonable belief supported by objective considerations that the currently recognized union has lost its majority status; RD-employees seek to remove the currently recognized union as the bargaining representative; UD-employees desire an election to restrict the union's right to maintain a union shop clause; UC-a labor organization or an employer seeks clarification of the existing bargaining unit; or AC-a labor organization or an employer seeks an amendment of a certification issued in a prior Board case.
- Under Question 5, please carefully describe the bargaining unit involved in the petition, listing the job classifications included in the unit and the job classifications excluded from the unit.
- After completing the petition form, be sure to sign and date the petition and mail, fax or hand deliver the completed petition form to the appropriate Regional Office.
- The filing of a petition seeking certification or decertification of a union should be accompanied by a sufficient showing of interest to support such a petition—i.e., a showing that 30% or more of the employees in the bargaining unit seek to be represented by the union or seek to decertify the currently recognized union.   If the original showing is not sent to the Region with the filing of the petition, a party must deliver the original showing of interest to the Region within **48 hours** after the filing of the petition, but in no event later than the last day on which a petition may be timely filed.
- Be sure to include telephone and fax numbers of the parties since this will be a significant aid to the processing of the petition.
- Be sure to include the name and address of any other labor organization or individuals known to have a representative interest in any of the employees in the unit described in Question 5 of the petition.
- A petition should be filed with the Regional Office where the bargaining unit exists. If the bargaining unit exists in two or more Regions, it can be filed in any of such Regions. An Information Officer will be happy to assist you in locating the appropriate Regional Office in which to file your petition.

filed by a union, the employer is expected to maintain the *status quo* regarding wages, hours of work, and other terms and conditions of employment until such time that any question of representation has been resolved.

Employees may distribute union organizing materials for the union on company property so long as it is done in nonwork areas (break areas, cafeterias, parking lots, locker rooms, etc.) during nonwork times.[57] Supervisory personnel should be cautioned that disciplining or otherwise retaliating against any employee for supporting the union would be a ULP.[58] This is also a time in which HR managers should be alert for possible constructive discharges of prounion employees. Any employee discipline that is imposed during the campaign is likely to be construed as having an antiunion motive. Therefore, HR managers must ensure work rules are enforced to the same degree as before the campaign and actions requiring discipline are properly investigated and documented.

During the campaign, employers may engage in a number of antiunion activities (see Exhibit 11-3). Employees may be assembled and told that management does not want the union and that it will use all legal means to fight the union. However, under the *Peerless Plywood* **Rule**,[59] all mandatory employee meetings for the purpose of campaigning must cease twenty-four hours prior to the scheduled election.

Secret Ballot Elections. Officials of the NLRB will schedule and supervise the secret ballot election. The ballot will provide two voting options, the name of the

---

■ EXHIBIT 11-3

EMPLOYER ACTIVITIES DURING THE ELECTION CAMPAIGN

- ■ Provide factual antiunion information
  - * Factual information about unions in general
  - * Factual information about the union in question
  - * Factual information about local wages and cost of living
- ■ Announce that you will use all legal means to fight the union
- ■ Send letters to employees
- ■ Use bulletin boards
- ■ Remind employees about dues and strikes
- ■ Remind employees that work rules will still be enforced
- ■ Remind employees that even if they signed an authorization card they do not have to vote "yes" for the union in the secret ballot
- ■ Permit "No Vote" committees (be careful not to violate § 8a(2)).
- ■ Hire consultants
- ■ Train supervisory personnel in labor relations
- ■ Ban union organizers from company property

SOURCE: Leap, T. L. (1995). *Collective Bargaining and Labor Relations (2nd ed.).* Englewood Cliffs, NJ: Prentice Hall, p. 146.

particular union or "no union." The outcome of the representation election is determined by a simple majority of the ballots cast by employees authorized to be in a particular bargaining unit to be represented by a particular union.[60] The petitioning union must receive a simple majority (50 percent plus one additional vote) of the votes cast to win the election, which means that if the union receives an even 50 percent of the votes cast, the petition fails and the employer wins the election.

Suppose a proposed bargaining unit consists of two hundred production employees. Of these two hundred employees, one hundred twenty appear on the day of the certification election to vote. A simple majority of the ballots cast, sixty-one votes, will determine the outcome of the election. It is important to remember that the simple majority is based on the ballots cast (in this case sixty-one) and *not* on a majority of the bargaining unit (one hundred one). If the union wins the majority vote, it will represent all employees of that unit as their bargaining representative for wages, hours, and terms and conditions of employment.

Both parties will be permitted to have an observer to verify eligibility of voters and challenge any votes. The employer observer cannot be a supervisor or a member of management. Neither campaigning nor any form of intimidation will be allowed during the election polling times. If the employer receives a majority of the votes cast, there will be no union certified. In this case, there will be a bar to any further election until at least twelve months have elapsed.

Certification of Exclusive Bargaining Agent.   Should the union receive a majority of the ballots cast during the election, the NLRB will certify the union as the exclusive bargaining agent for the bargaining unit. Management will then be required to bargain in good faith with the union.

National Labor Relations Board Directives.   If the NLRB finds that an employer has committed sufficient ULPs to taint a certification election, it may set aside an election. Having done so, the NLRB could set a second certification election. However, there is the likelihood that the NLRB will conclude that the second is impossible because the employer has committed flagrant ULPs and caused undue harm as a result of the ULPs. The NLRB may order the employer to bargain with the union as the employees' representative if a majority of the bargaining unit employees had previously signed authorization cards. Although employers are expected to conduct aggressive, no-union campaigns, it is imperative to avoid ULPs that could negate the election results.

THE POST-NLRA PERIOD

Within months of the enactment of the NLRA, industrial unions began forming by the hundreds. Many of these unions petitioned the AFL for membership, but the AFL continued to uphold its policy of rejecting unions comprised of unskilled or semiskilled workers. However, not everyone in the AFL agreed with this practice, particularly the president of the United Mine Workers, John L. Lewis. Lewis insisted that it was time for the AFL to abandon its adherence to craft unionism and adopt industrial unionism which entailed organizing industrial workers within the automobile, steel, rubber, textile, and maritime industries.[61] When the AFL refused to change its stance, Lewis and several other unions were expelled from the AFL and formed a competing organization, the Congress of Industrial Organizations (CIO).

The NLRA had clearly swung the balance of power in labor-management relations in favor of labor. However, in some instances, the balance of power may have swung too far. Although the NLRA placed constraints on management's actions in the labor relations process, it placed no such constraints on the union. Understandably, this situation made abuses inevitable. Remember that management could not interfere with the employees' right to organize; however, there was nothing in the NLRA to prevent unions from such interference. Some unions would coerce employees into joining under threats of losing their jobs once the union was voted in or by physical violence.

In those times of inordinate unemployment, some unions (particularly those infiltrated by organized crime) extorted excessive union initiation fees and charged exorbitant dues to members. One either paid the high dues or one did not work. Additionally, closed shops operated freely. In a **closed shop,** a worker had to be a member of the union *before* hiring. Essentially, no applications were accepted from individuals who did not have union cards. In some cases, once the union was certified as the bargaining agent, the union would negotiate a contract that required nonunion employees be terminated, or receive less pay and fewer benefits than union members in the same bargaining unit.

Employees were not the only parties suffering abuse. Employers were taking abuse as well. Management had to bargain in good faith, but the union was not held to this same standard. As a result, some employers were confronted with "take it or leave it" bargaining. This included meeting the union's initial demands or the union would strike against the employer.

Whereas some pre-NLRA employers had been guilty of sweetheart arrangements, some post-NLRA unions were guilty of featherbedding. **Featherbedding** occurs when employees receive compensation for jobs that they are not performing. For example, a union president may be on a company's payroll as a machinist. However, he never shows up for work and receives a full paycheck regardless.

Sometimes employers against whom the union had no argument would suffer due to a phenomenon known as a secondary boycott. A **secondary boycott** is said to occur when a union pickets against an employer who is not directly involved in a labor dispute with that union. For example, a union has a labor dispute resulting in an impasse during CBA negotiations with Employer A. Employer A provides parts for Employer B, who accounts for 55 percent of Employer A's annual sales. The union also represents Employer B's workers. Employer B, who has no dispute with the union, is now picketed by the union in order to put pressure on Employer A to resolve its dispute with the union. In essence, an innocent party (Employer B) is subjected to the financial losses of a boycott in order to increase the financial costs on Employer A, the company against whom the union has a direct dispute.

Perhaps the Second World War and the period immediately following the war turned public opinion against organized labor. Despite a national no-strike pledge by all of the nation's unions,[62] work stoppages did occur (mostly in the mining industry). Naturally, the public viewed these strikes as violations of the no-strike pledge and as unpatriotic during this time of national emergency.[63] Strikes in the coal fields were considered so hazardous to the war effort that the entire industry was taken over by the Department of Interior in 1943.[64] The National War Labor Board was formed to reduce strikes by arbitrating grievances and contract disputes during the war years.

By 1946, wage and price controls established during World War II were lifted, and the nation experienced a surge of strike activity, the most in U.S. history.[65] In that year, there were over 4,985 strikes.[66] Congress determined that it was necessary to amend the NLRA to redress imbalances in the laws affecting labor relations.[67] In 1947, the Labor-Management Relations Act was passed to resolve the inherent flaws in the NLRA and reduce the level of work stoppages.[68]

LABOR-MANAGEMENT RELATIONS (TAFT-HARTLEY) ACT OF 1947

In 1947, amid growing dissension from employers about the increasing strength of labor, a Republican Congress passed the Labor-Management Relations Act (LMRA), also known as the Taft-Hartley Act, over President Truman's veto as an amendment to the NLRA. The LMRA was designed to establish a more balanced playing field for management in the labor relations process. One technical aspect arising from this amendment is that the NLRA is now cited as the LMRA.[69]

Section 7 of the LMRA defined ULPs for unions, established the Federal Mediation and Conciliation Service (FMCS), provided for suits by and against labor unions, and made provision for presidential intervention in strikes that would constitute a national emergency. The overall thrust of this Act was to balance the relative power between labor and management. It also attempted to provide mechanisms through the FMCS and national emergency dispute procedures to reduce the likelihood of a recurrence of the labor strife seen in 1946.[70]

Some of the changes in the LMRA involved clarifying definitions. For example, Section 2 of the NLRA, which provided for definitions of the terms used in the Act, was amended to clarify who was an "employer" and an "employee" for purposes of coverage. Definitions for supervisor, professional employee, and whether a person is acting as an agent of another person were also incorporated.[71] The membership of the NLRB was increased from three to five members by delegating its powers and duties to a quorum of any three members and appointing a general counsel and outlining his or her powers and duties.[72]

The LMRA also expanded employee rights. To protect employees from being coerced or forced into supporting a union, Section 7 was amended by including the following:

> . . . and shall also have the right to refrain from any or all of such activities except to the extent that such right may be affected by an agreement requiring membership in a labor organization as a condition of employment as authorized in section 8(a)(3).[73]

Employees would now have free choice in deciding whether or not they wanted to be represented by a union. Neither management nor a union could interfere with that right.

UNFAIR LABOR PRACTICES BY THE UNION. As Section 8 of the NLRA had imposed restrictions on management in the labor relations process, the union now had similar constraints. Section 8 was now divided into two parts (refer to Exhibit 11-1): ULPs by management (Section 8[a]) and ULPs by the union (Section 8[b]).

Just as management cannot violate an employee's Section 7 rights, Section 8(b)(1) prohibits the union from doing the same. If the union tries to coerce an employee into joining it by threats, signing an authorization card, or voting for it, that union is guilty of a ULP. If a union maintains that any employee who did not support the union will lose his or her job once the union is certified, a ULP has occurred. Threatening nonstriking, nonunion members of the bargaining unit with physical violence or retaliation is also a ULP, as is expelling union members who refuse to engage in unlawful strikes.

An additional clause in Section 8(b)(1) prohibits the union from forcing the employer to choose bargaining agents that the union approves. If the union refuses to bargain with the representatives of management, a ULP has been committed. Management is free to choose its bargaining agents just as the union is free to choose its representatives.

The NLRA prohibited employers from discriminating against employees on the basis of union membership. Under the LMRA, unions are prohibited against discriminating against members of the bargaining unit on the basis of union membership. The so-called "fair representation" provision, Section 8(b)(2), requires the union to treat all members of the bargaining unit equally regardless of whether they are union members or nonunion members. It would be a ULP if the union chooses to negotiate a raise only for the union members in the bargaining unit. Similarly, if the union only processed the grievances of union members of the bargaining unit and not those of nonunion members, Section 8(b)(2) would be violated. It should also be noted that this section makes closed shops unlawful.

The LMRA also made the "take it or leave" bargaining tactics used by some unions a ULP. It required all unions to bargain in good faith. In essence, Section 8(b)(3) merely imposes the same requirement on the union that Section 8(a)(5) imposed on management.

The issue of secondary boycotts was addressed in Section 8(b)(4). This is the most complex of possible ULPs committed by unions and is divided into four subparts.

First, the union cannot force the employer to agree to a hot cargo arrangement in the CBA.[74] A **hot cargo arrangement** permits employees to refuse to handle or ship goods from a nonunion manufacturer. In essence, the employer would not be able to purchase parts or materials from nonunion firms. For example, a truck driver of a neutral employer could refuse to cross a union's picket line and not be disciplined.

Second, the union is prohibited from striking or picketing a third party that is doing business with the primary employer but is not involved in the labor dispute.[75]

Third, a union is prohibited from striking in an effort to force an employer to recognize or bargain with that union when another labor organization has been certified as the representative of the employer's workers.[76] If a union has already been recognized or certified as the bargaining representative, no other union may attempt to usurp that union's authority.

Finally, Section 8(b)(4) prohibits jurisdictional strikes.[77] **Jurisdictional strikes** occur when a particular union attempts to force an employer to assign certain work to employees in its bargaining unit rather than to employees in another labor organization or bargaining unit. Such strikes occur when one union thinks another union is doing "its work." For example, maintenance workers may feel that another bargaining unit, one made up of production workers, has been assigned maintenance work that should be performed by them. The underlying issue is job security.

Section 8(b)(5) outlaws the practice of charging excessive union dues and fees. Featherbedding is prohibited in Section 8(b)(6). Ultimately, recognitional picketing was addressed in the seventh union ULP. **Recognitional picketing** occurs when a union attempts to persuade the employees to recognize it as their official bargaining representative. Recognitional picketing is prohibited where the employer has already lawfully recognized another labor organization.[78] If a union already represents the bargaining unit, another may not try to organize it. Such picketing is also prohibited if a representation election has occurred in the previous twelve months.[79] Neither can representational picketing be permitted if the union has not petitioned the NLRB for certification after a reasonable period of time not to exceed thirty days from the commencement of such picketing.[80] This created the "contract bar" doctrine.

RIGHT-TO-WORK PROVISIONS. Perhaps the most controversial amendments to arise from the LMRA are the right-to-work provisions. Section 14(b) of the NLRA was amended to permit states to pass **right-to-work laws,** laws limiting the level of compulsory union membership (also called "union security") imposed by a CBA. Specifically stated:

> Nothing in this subchapter shall be construed as authorizing the execution or application of agreements requiring membership in a labor organization as a condition of employment in any State or Territory in which such execution or application is prohibited by State or Territorial law.[81]

Twenty-one states have enacted right-to-work laws (see Exhibit 11-4). In order to fully understand the impact of right-to-work laws, it is necessary first to understand the levels of compulsory union membership which *can* be negotiated in a CBA (see Exhibit 11-5).

Compulsory Union Membership in Right-to-Work States. When there is no recognized bargaining agent (essentially no labor union), an **open shop** exists.

■ EXHIBIT 11-4

RIGHT-TO-WORK STATES

Alabama	Nevada
Arizona	North Carolina
Arkansas	North Dakota
Florida	South Carolina
Georgia	South Dakota
Idaho	Tennessee
Iowa	Texas
Kansas	Utah
Louisiana	Virginia
Mississippi	Wyoming
Nebraska	

Once a union is certified or recognized, the union enjoys exclusive bargaining rights status. This is the lowest form of union security. Under an **exclusive bargaining rights** arrangement, employees represented by a union cannot be required to join the union or pay dues as a condition of continued employment (see Exhibit 11-6). However, the CBA negotiated by the union would apply to all the members of the bargaining unit, nonunion as well as union members. This is the union's duty of fair representation and will be discussed in greater detail in the following chapter. Not surprisingly, unions find exclusive bargaining rights repugnant, and they see the nonunion employees as "free riders" on their bargaining effort.

In most right-to-work states, the highest form of permissible compulsory union membership is the agency shop. Under an **agency shop,** membership in the union is still strictly voluntary, but nonunion members of the bargaining unit must pay the union the equivalent of dues (referred to as a "representation fee") to compensate the union for its services as their bargaining agent. So, if union members pay the union $40 per month in dues, nonunion members of the unit will pay the union a monthly fee of $40 as well. Why, you may ask, would any employee pay the equivalent of dues to the union and not join? The answer is simple. If the union conducts a strike vote and goes on strike, only the union members are bound by that vote; nonunion members are not. Union members can be fined and

■ EXHIBIT 11-5

LEVELS OF COMPULSORY UNION MEMBERSHIP

Open Shop	Agency Shop	Modified Union Shop	Closed Shop
Δ	Δ	Δ	Δ
▽	▽	▽	
Exclusive Bargaining Rights	Maintenance of Membership Shop	Union Shop	

■ **EXHIBIT 11-6**

SPECIFICS ON COMPULSORY UNION MEMBERSHIP

	Agency Shop	Maintenance of Membership	Modified Union Shop	Union Shop
Union Membership Requirements	Strictly voluntary.	Partially voluntary. Once an employee joins the union, the employee must remain with the union.	Union members must remain union. All new hires must join union. Employees who were nonunion at ratification may remain nonunion.	All employees in the bargaining unit must join and remain union.
Union Dues	Union members pay dues. Nonunion members pay equivalent of dues.	Union members pay dues. Nonunion members pay equivalent of dues.	Union members pay dues. Nonunion members pay equivalent of dues.	Union members pay dues.
Strike Vote	Union members must honor strike. Nonunion members do not have to honor strike.	Union members must honor strike. Nonunion members do not have to honor strike.	Union members must honor strike. Nonunion members do not have to honor strike.	Union members must honor strike.

disciplined by the union for not honoring the strike vote, but nonunion members cannot. The important distinction in a right-to-work state is that no one may be compelled to be a union member as a condition for continued employment.

Forms of Union Security in Non-Right-to-Work States. In states which are not right-to-work states, forms of compulsory union membership higher than the agency shop can be negotiated in the CBA. For example, the CBA may permit more limited forms of union security such as a maintenance of membership shop. Under a **maintenance of membership shop,** employees are not required to join a union, those who are not union members pay the equivalent of union dues, and any employees who voluntarily join the union must continue their memberships as a condition of employment for the life of the CBA. Simply stated, union membership is voluntary, but once you join the union, you must remain with the union.

However, nonunion employees may file for a rebate for any of this amount which is spent for nonrepresentational purposes, such as political contributions.[82] Effective April 18, 2001, federal contractors are required to display posters at their work locations notifying nonunion employees that they only have to pay the union for costs related to collective bargaining, contract administration, and grievance adjustment.[83]

Another variation of union security is the modified union shop. Under a **modified union shop,** nonunion members at the time of the CBA's ratification may remain nonunion but pay the equivalent of dues, those who are union members at the time must remain union members, and all new hires must join the union in the time frame specified in the CBA.

The highest form of compulsory union membership in states without right-to-work laws is the union shop. If a **union shop** is negotiated, all members of the bargaining unit are required to join the union within the period specified in the CBA, not less than thirty days after employment. To illustrate how a union shop operates, an applicant is hired by an organization that has a union shop provision in its CBA. This union security provision requires all new employees to become union members after a thirty-day probationary period. The employee must do so as a condition of continued employment. Should the new hire fail to join the union after the probationary period, the employee must be willing to join the union and pay dues or the employer is obligated to terminate the employee. If the employer fails to terminate the employee, the employer has violated the provisions of the CBA.

A union shop should not be confused with a closed shop which is unlawful under the LMRA. Recall that a closed shop required the applicant to be a union member *before* hiring.

Religious Exemption to Compulsory Membership. The only exception to compulsory union membership occurs when the new hire has a *bona fide* religious belief against being a member of any organization other than his or her church.[84] The LMRA does not require such individuals to be forced to join a union.[85] However, any employee who is a member of and adheres to established and traditional tenets or teachings of a *bona fide* religion, body, or sect which has historically held conscientious objections to joining or financially supporting labor organizations is still required to pay the equivalent of union dues and initiation fees to a mutually agreed-upon nonreligious, nonlabor charity.[86]

FEDERAL MEDIATION AND CONCILIATION SERVICE AND NATIONAL EMERGENCIES. Title II of the LMRA provides for the Federal Mediation and Conciliation Service (FMCS) to assist in settling unresolved contractual disputes.[87] Title II also provides a means for the President of the United States to intervene during strikes and lockouts determined to be a national emergency by seeking an eighty-day injunction from a federal district court.[88] For a labor dispute to become a national emergency, it must, in the opinion of the President, "imperil the national health or safety."[89] The Attorney General of the United States then must convince the federal judge that the labor dispute constitutes an emergency. A board of inquiry may be convened to investigate and assist in resolving the dispute. Based on the board's finding, the President may have the Attorney General petition a federal district court for an eighty-day injunction.[90] During the eighty-day period, the FMCS will attempt to resolve the dispute between the parties through mediation. If this fails, the NLRB will submit management's final offer to the employees fifteen days prior to expiration of the injunction. The members of the bargaining unit will then accept or reject the offer based on a secret ballot. You might notice the union is completely bypassed in this process. If the bargaining unit votes to accept the final offer, the matter is resolved, and a national emergency is avoided. However, if the bargaining unit rejects the final offer, the President shall make recommendations for appropriate action to Congress.[91]

LABOR-MANAGEMENT REPORTING AND DISCLOSURE (LANDRUM-GRIFFIN) ACT OF 1959

In the period following the enactment of the Labor-Management Relations Act, the number of work stoppages began to decline. Congress then began to focus its attention on internal corruption within the unions.

Labor unions began to draw media attention during the 1950s with regard to racketeering and autocratic methods in their treatment of union members. In fact, in 1954, the Academy Award for Best Motion Picture was awarded to *On the Waterfront,* a movie that portrayed corruption in the longshoreman's union. The following year, the AFL combined with the CIO to create a labor organization with over 15 million members, the AFL-CIO. Also in 1955, approximately one in three American workers belonged to a union.[92] However, public awareness of organized crime in some unions and growing concern that some unions were operating for the benefit of the leadership and not the members was beginning to take its toll. Under increasing public scrutiny and pressure in 1957, the AFL-CIO expelled the International Brotherhood of Teamsters, the Bakery and Confectionery Workers Union, and the Laundry Workers Union, three of its most corrupt unions.

Shortly thereafter, the Eisenhower Administration and the Senate's McClellan Committee, which had investigated union ties with organized crime, recommended that legislation be enacted to protect rank and file union members from corrupt union leaders. In an attempt to make internal union operations more honest and union administration more democratic, the national labor code was again amended with the passage of the Labor-Management Reporting and Disclosure Act (LMRDA),[93] sometimes called the Landrum-Griffin Act, in 1959. The LMRDA primarily regulates the internal affairs of labor unions, although it also places new limits on the power of unions in boycotts and picketing.

The focus of the LMRDA is twofold: to set minimum standards in the conduct of the internal affairs of labor unions and to clarify congressional intent in establishing a national labor policy as stated in the LMRA.[94] The LMRDA was designed to eliminate improper activities, provide standards on financial dealings and business practices of labor organizations, safeguard union election procedures, and close loopholes in earlier legislation protecting employers against secondary boycotts.[95]

The Act established a comprehensive program dealing with three major challenges in labor union operation, disclosure, and democracy reform. The challenges included union membership rights, union officer responsibilities and accountabilities, and security for members in the use of union funds.

UNION MEMBERSHIP RIGHTS. Title I of the LMRDA established a bill of rights for union members.[96] Union members are assured equal rights to participate in union elections, attend union meetings, and vote on union business. Members are also afforded the right to free speech and assembly in and out of union meetings. Dues and initiation fees cannot be increased and assessments cannot be levied without the majority vote of the affected members. In addition, members have a right to sue their labor unions; however, they may be required to exhaust an internal means to remedy the issue before going to the courts. Union members are guaranteed due process in any sanction, disciplinary action, or expulsion. The Act also ensures that union members' existing rights under state or federal law are not limited and that every member is entitled to a copy of any agreement affecting his or her rights as an employee.

Under the provisions of the LMRDA, national or international labor unions must elect their officers at least every five years within a designated manner.[97] Officers at the national or international level must be elected either by a secret ballot of all union members in good standing or through a convention of delegates elected by secret ballot at the local levels. Local labor unions must elect officers at least every three years, allowing all members in good standing to vote by secret ballot. Members in good standing cannot be denied the opportunity to vote or be prevented from becoming a candidate for office. All candidates must be guaranteed equal access to membership roles for campaign purposes. The LMRDA also prohibits labor organizations from using dues or any other union funds collected from members for campaign purposes. The Secretary of Labor may, under certain conditions, conduct a new election if an initial election is found to be in violation of the Act.

UNION OFFICER RESPONSIBILITIES AND ACCOUNTABILITIES. Title II of the LMRDA requires every labor union to have a constitution and bylaws.[98] The labor union is further required to file a copy of its constitution and bylaws with the Secretary of Labor. In addition, an annual financial report must be filed with the Secretary of Labor along with information on financial relationships with union leaders. The union must report any payments made to individuals for the purpose of influencing employees in the exercise of their rights under the national labor laws. The required reports must also be made available to union members, and union members have the right to examine the books, records, and accounts of the labor union upon request.

The LMRDA also requires officers and employees (except clerical and custodial employees) of a labor union to file individual annual reports with the Secretary of Labor listing and describing their family income, stocks and bonds transactions, securities, or any other financial payments (except wages and salaries) made by a firm in which the union represents their employees.[99] Officers and included employees must also report income from, or payments to, a firm that has appreciable dealings with the firms in which the union represents their employees and income from, or payments to, a labor consultant to such a firm.

To preclude collusion, the LMRDA requires employers to file annual reports with the Secretary of Labor detailing and explaining any payments or loans made to labor union officials, payments made to employees for persuasive activities related to labor union activities, payments made for information pertaining to activities in a labor dispute, or agreements made with a labor relations consultant to influence employees in exercising their rights under the Act.[100]

Trusteeships are required to maintain the proper and lawful operation of any of their subordinate labor organizations.[101] National unions are authorized to take over the daily operations of any local union "for the purpose of correcting corruption or financial malpractice, assuring the performance of collective bargaining agreements or other duties of a bargaining representative, restoring democratic procedures, or otherwise carrying out the legitimate objects of such labor organization."[102] Trusteeships of labor unions must file semiannual reports with the Secretary of Labor describing specific information about the subordinate organization, including the financial condition when the trusteeship was assumed over the subordinate union.

SECURITY FOR MEMBERS IN THE USE OF UNION FUNDS.   Title V of the LMRDA imposes fiduciary responsibilities on all union officers, agents, shop stewards, and other union representatives for all money and property of the union.[103] It specifies that anyone who occupies a position of trust in a labor organization must guarantee that all money and property of the union be used for rightful purposes. This title also requires bonding of labor union officers and employees who handle funds or other property belonging to union,[104] prohibits unions from making loans in excess of $2,000 to any officer or employee, and forbids unions or employers from paying the fines of any officer or employee convicted of a willful violation of the LMRDA.[105] Further, Title V prohibits individuals who are members of the Communist Party as well as convicted felons from either holding an office or serving as a consultant with a labor organization.[106]

Ultimately, the LMRDA contains a number of miscellaneous provisions. These include providing the Secretary of Labor investigatory power under the Act,[107] banning extortionate picketing,[108] and forbidding labor unions from punishing or disciplining union members for exercising their rights under the Act.[109]

RELATED LEGISLATION

In addition to the national labor code, there are other statutes that govern labor-management relations in the United States. Three of these laws, the Davis-Bacon Act, the Walsh-Healey Act, and the Worker Adjustment Retraining and Notification Act, were discussed in Chapter 8.

PUBLIC SECTOR UNIONS AND LEGISLATION AFFECTING LABOR RELATIONS

Public sector employees, as a class, are more likely to be unionized than their private sector counterparts. Roughly 37.5 percent of public sector employees are union members compared to only 9.0 percent in the private sector.[110] As union representation of private sector employees has declined, it has actually increased in the public sector.

FEDERAL EXECUTIVE ORDERS

Although some federal agencies, like the Tennessee Valley Authority and the Government Printing Office, were permitted to organize and bargain collectively under the NLRA, the vast majority were not. It was not until the Kennedy Administration that federal employees were permitted to bargain collectively.[111]

Under Executive Order 10988, federal employees were given the right to organize and bargain with their specific agency. However, Executive Order 10988 gave the federal department head to which the agency belonged (e.g., Secretary of Education, Secretary of Housing and Urban Development) the power to determine the bargaining unit and decide the outcome of ULP complaints. Not surprisingly, employees argued that this arrangement placed most of the bargaining power in the hands of the agency.

Many federal employees wanted a system that was similar to the one their private sector counterparts enjoyed. In 1970, employees of the United States Postal Service, were permitted to organize and bargain collectively under the jurisdiction of the NLRB.[112] This arrangement gave postal workers the same labor-management relations as private employees enjoyed under the LMRA, with one major exception. Postal workers, like all federal employees, are *not* permitted to strike. Instead, any labor disputes or impasses in negotiations must be resolved through mediation and arbitration.[113]

CIVIL SERVICE REFORM ACT OF 1978

The most significant labor reform for federal employee labor relations occurred in 1978 with the enactment of the Civil Service Reform Act (CSRA). It was enacted to resolve some of the shortcomings of the previous executive orders.

Like the LMRA, the CSRA provides for ULPs by both the union and the agency (see Exhibit 11-7). Additionally, an independent agency, the Federal Labor Relations Authority (FLRA), operates much like the NLRB in that the FLRA investigates ULP complaints, determines the appropriateness of representation units, conducts representation elections, prescribes criteria and resolves issues relating to determining compelling need for agency rules or regulations governing labor relations, resolves issues relating to the duty to bargain in good faith, and resolves exceptions to arbitrator's awards.[114]

Unlike their private sector counterparts, federal employees covered under the CSRA are not permitted to strike. Instead, labor disputes must be resolved by voluntary mediation conducted by the FMCS, or the matter is submitted to arbitration. Should mediation break down, either party may request that the matter be presented before the Federal Services Impasses Panel (FSIP). FSIP will then conduct hearings, take evidence and testimony, and impose an award. In arbitration, the term "award" is synonymous with a judicial decision. However, FSIP

Unfair Labor Practices by the Agency	Unfair Labor Practices by the Union
(1) to interfere with, restrain, or coerce any employee in the exercise by the employee of any right under this chapter;	(1) to interfere with, restrain, or coerce any employee in the exercise by the employee of any right under this chapter;
(2) to encourage or discourage membership in any labor organization by discrimination in connection with hiring, tenure, promotion, or other conditions of employment;	(2) to cause or attempt to cause an agency to discriminate against any employee in the exercise by the employee of any right under this chapter;
(3) to sponsor, control, or otherwise assist any labor organization, other than to furnish, upon request, customary and routine services and facilities if the services and facilities are also furnished on an impartial basis to other labor organizations having equivalent status;	(3) to coerce, discipline, fine, or attempt to coerce a member of the labor organization as punishment, reprisal, or for the purpose of hindering or impeding the member's work performance or productivity as an employee or the discharge of the member's duties as an employee;
(4) to discipline or otherwise discriminate against an employee because the employee has filed a complaint, affidavit, or petition, or has given any information or testimony under this chapter;	(4) to discriminate against an employee with regard to the terms or conditions of membership in the labor organization on the basis of race, color, creed, national origin, sex, age, preferential or nonpreferential civil service status, political affiliation, marital status, or handicapping condition;
(5) to refuse to consult or negotiate in good faith with a labor organization as required by this chapter;	(5) to refuse to consult or negotiate in good faith with an agency as required by this chapter;
(6) to fail or refuse to cooperate in impasse procedures and impasse decisions as required by this chapter;	(6) to fail or refuse to cooperate in impasse procedures and impasse decisions as required by this chapter;
(7) to enforce any rule or regulation which is in conflict with any applicable collective bargaining agreement if the agreement was in effect before the date the rule or regulation was prescribed; or	(7) (a) to call, or participate in, a strike, work stoppage, or slowdown, or picketing of an agency in a labor-management dispute if such picketing interferes with an agency's operations, or
(8) to otherwise fail or refuse to comply with any provision of this chapter.	(b) to condone any activity described in subparagraph (a) of this paragraph by failing to take action to prevent or stop such activity, or
	(8) to otherwise fail or refuse to comply with any provision of this chapter.

SOURCE: 5 U.S.C. § 7116.

awards are not final and binding as are arbitration awards in the private sector (to be discussed in Chapter 12). FSIP awards may be appealed to the FLRA, which has the authority to overturn the award.

Another difference between the CSRA and the LMRA is that under the CSRA, the union may not bargain for wages. Remember that wages are a mandatory bargaining issue under the LMRA. Wages are a prohibited bargaining issue under the CSRA. Bargaining issues are restricted to conditions of employment.[115] Conditions of employment are further restricted to:

> . . . personnel policies, practices, and matters, whether established by rule, regulation, or otherwise, affecting working conditions, except that such term does not include policies, practices, and matters—
> (A) relating to political activities prohibited under subchapter III of chapter 73 of this title.

(B) relating to the classification of any position.

(C) to the extent such matters are specifically provided for by federal statute.[116]

The agency can refuse to negotiate a particular work rule or personnel policy if it can demonstrate that there is a compelling need for the practice, or changing the practice would have a detrimental effect on the agency's ability to perform its function.[117] If the agency can convince the FLRA that changing the practice in question would adversely affect agency efficiency, the agency would not have a good faith obligation to negotiate that practice.

WHY EMPLOYEES JOIN UNIONS

Studies indicate that there are three general determinants of worker propensity to organize. These are workers' perceptions of their work environment, workers' perceptions of how much influence they may have over their employment conditions, and workers' beliefs about the effects of unions.[118] When employees view their work environment to be poor, feel they have little control or influence over their conditions of employment, and believe a union can help them, they are more likely to be interested in being affiliated with a union.

There are six commonly cited reasons that explain why employees become attracted to unions. These include:

1. Poor supervision
2. Changes that raise concerns of insecurity
3. Poor communication on the part of management
4. Pay rates and benefits that are below industry or area averages
5. Feelings of unfair and unjust treatment
6. Lack of a fair procedure to address grievances[119]

Although these six are the most commonly cited, there are many more reasons that focus on employees not having a voice in decisions that affect their work and not having much, if any, control over their wages, hours of work, and other conditions of employment. In essence, being unionized is often a search for security on the part of those employees who rely heavily upon the employer to provide living wages or salaries.

WHY EMPLOYEES REJECT UNIONS

Just as important as knowing why employees join unions is knowing why they reject them. The two primary reasons why workers reject unions are lack of a compelling reason to join and identification with management.[120] In many cases, employees simply do not see how a labor union can help them do any better than what they can do on their own merits. Sometimes, employees cannot identify with such union philosophical views as "This organization works because we do!"

In other circumstances, a majority of the employees may tend to identify with management and reject a union's attempt to organize them. Some employees hold a perception that they should not be part of a labor union because of their professions, occupations, and status.

SUMMARY

The previous ten chapters addressed HR compliance activities, the area of HRM that deals with relationships between managers and employees in regulated, but nonunionized, work environments. Employers that have unionized workplaces, and those in which a portion of their workers are represented by a labor union, have to meet the same regulatory compliance requirements as any other covered employers. The major difference between nonunionized and unionized workplaces is that unionized employers have the additional responsibility of complying with collective bargaining agreements and the national labor code.

Labor relations is the functional area of HRM that addresses employment issues arising from unionized workplaces. In a unionized work environment, HR professionals and managers are not only responsible for ensuring compliance with the federal and state laws that govern all workplaces, but must also be especially familiar with federal and state labor laws. In addition to these laws, HR professionals and managers must be knowledgeable of the specific collective bargaining agreement covering their company or facility. For managers, labor relations imposes additional obligations such as avoiding unfair labor practices under existing labor laws, negotiating the collective bargaining agreement, recognizing the union's duty to fair representation, resolving grievances, and maintaining contract administration. Managers in unionized work environments are confronted with more challenges than their counterparts in union-free environments.

There have been labor organizations in the United States since before the American Revolution. Yet their period of greatest growth and strength occurred during the latter part of the nineteenth century and early part of the twentieth century. This growth led to the development of the national labor code.

Three federal statutes encompassing three distinct phases of national labor legislation form the basis of current labor-management relations in the private sector. These three acts comprise the national labor code and include the National Labor Relations Act of 1935 (also known as the Wagner Act), the Labor-Management Relations Act of 1947 (also known as the Taft-Hartley Act), and the Labor-Management Reporting and Disclosure Act of 1959 (also known as the Landrum-Griffin Act).

The primary motivation for workers to join a union is to acquire the collective force in bargaining with the employer over subjects such as wages and salaries, hours of work, and other terms and conditions of employment. By being represented by a union, employees often are seeking a united, concerted effort to gain improvements through collective bargaining with the employer.

Unions may become the exclusive bargaining agent for a group of employees by being recognized by a majority of that group of employees and eventually being certified by the NLRB. When a union reaches recognition as the exclusive representative, it has the sole right to represent all eligible employees, whether they are union members or not, in any relations with the employer. Once the union and management have negotiated a CBA, that document imposes yet another compliance obligation for management.

KEY TERMS AND CONCEPTS

agency shop
American Plan
bargaining unit
blacklists
business unionism
certification/representation election
closed shop
collective bargaining agreement (CBA)
court injunctions
criminal conspiracy doctrine
Excelsior list
exclusive bargaining rights
featherbedding
hot cargo arrangement
HR compliance
industrial relations
jurisdictional strikes
labor relations
maintenance of membership shop

modified union shop
national labor code
open shop
organized workplaces
paternalism
Peerless Plywood Rule
ratified
recognitional picketing
representation process
right-to-work laws
secondary boycott
showing of interest
sweetheart arrangements
unfair labor practices (ULPs)
union authorization cards
union shop
unionized workplaces
yellow-dog contract

QUESTIONS

1. Trace the American labor movement from the early1800s to1959. Include the significant labor organizations, labor disputes, and legal issues.

2. Why was the AFL successful when its predecessors were not?

3. What are the three components of the national labor code? What is the purpose of each?

4. What are the five ULPs of management? What are the five ULPs of the union?

5. Explain what is meant by "level of compulsory union membership." Provide seven of these levels. Explain how they differ from one another. What impact did the LMRA have on compulsory union membership?

6. What are the steps of the unionizing process?

7. How are certification election outcomes determined? How is the winner, or loser, determined?

8. What are the significant differences between labor relations established under the LMRA and the CSRA?

9. Why do employees join unions? Why do employees reject unions?

CASES
——■——

1 Some twelve hundred retail sales workers, customer service representatives, and technicians at Clear Voice Wireless have joined the Communications Workers of America (CWA). The union is requesting that Clear Voice Wireless recognize them as the exclusive bargaining agent for the employees after more than 75 percent of the eligible employees signed union authorization cards. According to the CWA, the showing of interest at Clear Voice Wireless was the largest of any employer that they have attempted to organize to date. "Job security concerns in the wake of a recent merger and fair treatment were the chief issues for these workers," said CWA District Vice President Joe Rhodes.

Clear Voice Wireless was formed through a joint venture between two large communication firms. When the CWA organizer, Andy Romero, first visited Clear Voice Wireless, the company dismissed it entirely. Clear Voice Wireless President Nancy Ringer noted that she did not understand why the workers had any interest in unionizing since they are all paid very well, have excellent employee benefit programs, and the company has a strong human resource management department. However, Romero stated, "The employer expects the employees to put the company first, with no questions asked. Yet Clear Voice Wireless maintains a culture that values employee loyalty but not employee involvement." Romero mentioned that the company does not seem to care enough about the employees to give them contemporary benefits such as flexible work hours, telecommuting, job sharing, and compressed work weeks. Because the company has refused to recognize the CWA as its employees' bargaining agent, Romero has threatened to file a ULP with the NLRB.

Is management engaging in a ULP if it refuses to voluntarily recognize the CWA? Why or why not? In view of Clear Voice Wireless' refusal, what can the CWA do?

2 Local 1947 of the United Federation of Postal Clerks and Local 1959 of the National Association of Postal Supervisors are in contract negotiations with the Postmaster of the Northern Mississippi Region. Although each union has a separate CBA, their respective negotiations are going on simultaneously. The two bargaining teams have decided to try to get similar concessions from the Postmaster in their CBAs. Consequently, both have requested a 10 percent pay increase and double overtime for working on federal holidays. The Postmaster has refused to even discuss pay issues with either union. In response, both unions have gone on strike because management has committed a ULP by refusing to bargain in good faith.

Is there any substance to the United Federation of Postal Clerks' claim of a ULP? Why or why not? Is there any substance to the National Association of Postal Supervisors' claim of a ULP? Why or why not? Can the Postmaster take any action against the striking workers? Why or why not?

NOTES

1. U.S. Bureau of Labor Statistics (January 18, 2001). Union Members Summary. **http://stats.bls.gov:80/news.release/union2.nro.htm**

2. 29 C.F.R. § 1604.11.

3. 29 U.S.C. § 207.

4. Primack, M. L. and Willis, J. F. (1980). *An Economic History of the United States.* Menlo Park, CA: The Benjamin Cummings Publishing Company, pp. 40–41.

5. Bloom, G. F. and Northrup, H. R. (1977). *Economics of Labor Relations (8th ed).* Homewood, IL: Richard D. Irwin, Inc., p. 38.

6. Dulles, F. R. (1966). *Labor in America: A History (3rd ed.).* Arlington Heights, IL: AHM Publishing Corp., pp. 10–12.

7. Ibid. at p.28.

8. Philadelphia Mayor's Court, 3 Common and Gilmore 228–233 (1910).

9. Dulles, pp. 26–27.

10. 45 Mass. 111 (Mass. Sup. Ct. 1842).

11. Green, G. and Maroney, J. (1983). *The Labor Story.* Houston, TX: Texas AFL-CIO, p. 9.

12. Marx, K. (1998). *The Communist Manifesto.* New York: Bantam Books, p. 9.

13. Dulles, p. 141.

14. Hoxie, R. F. (1917). *Trade Unionism in the United States.* New York: D. Appleton & Co., p. 274.

15. Megginson, L. C., Franklin, G. M., and Byrd, M. J. (1995). *Human Resource Management.* Houston, TX: Dame Publications, Inc., p. 475.

16. Salvatore, N. (1984). *Eugene V. Debs: Citizen and Socialist.* Champaign, IL: University of Illinois Press, pp. 201–208.

17. "Industrial Workers of the World," Microsoft® Encarta® Online Encyclopedia 2000 **http://encarta.msn.com** © 1997–2000 Microsoft Corporation

18. 15 U.S.C. § 1.

19. 29 U.S.C. § 52.

20. 15 U.S.C. § 17 and 29 U.S.C. § 52.

21. 254 U.S. 443 (1921).

22. Bloom, G. F. and Northrup H. R. (1981). *Economics of Labor Relations (9th ed.).* Homewood, IL: Richard D. Irwin, Inc., p. 677.

23. Green and Maroney, p. 27.

24. *Hitchman Coal Co. v Mitchell,* 245 U.S. 299 (1915).

25. 45 U.S.C. § 151 *et seq.*

26. 45 U.S.C. § 152.

27. Ibid.

28. 45 U.S.C. § 151(a).

29. 45 U.S.C. § 152.

30. 29 U.S.C. § § 101–115.

31. 29 U.S.C. § 102 (emphasis added).

32. 48 Stat. 195 (1933).

33. 48 Stat. 195 § 7 (a) (1933).

34. 295 U.S. 495 (1935).

35. Ibid. at 548.

36. 29 U.S.C. § 151–169.

37. 29 U.S.C. § 151.

38. Ibid.

39. *NLRB v Jones & Laughlin Steel Corp.,* 301 U.S. 1 (1937).

40. 29 U.S.C. § 157.

41. 29 U.S.C. § 163.

42. *Carbon Fuel v United Mine Workers,* 444 U.S. 212 (1979).

43. *Boys Markets, Inc. v Retail Clerks, Local 770,* 398 U.S. 235 (1970).

44. 29 U.S.C. § 158(a)(1).

45. Ibid. § 158 (a)(2).

46. Ibid. § 158 (a)(3).

47. Ibid. § 158 (a)(4).

48. Ibid. § 158 (a)(5).

49. 29 U.S.C. § 159.

50. 29 U.S.C. § 159(a)(1).

51. 29 U.S.C. § 159(a).

52. Beal, E. F. and Wickersham, E. D. (1967). *The Practice of Collective Bargaining (3rd ed.).* Homewood, IL: Richard D. Irwin, Inc., p. 138.

53. 29 U.S.C. § 158(b).

54. 29 U.S.C. § 159(a).

55. *Excelsior Underwear, Inc.,* 156 NLRB 1236 (1962).

56. 29 U.S.C. § 158(a).

57. *Republic Aviation Corp. v NLRB,* 324 U.S. 793 (1945).

58. Ibid. § § 158 (a)(1) and (3).

59. 107 NLRB 106 (1953).

60. 29 U.S.C. § 159(e).

61. Holley, W. H. and Jennings, K. M. (1994). *The Labor Relations Process (5th ed.).* Fort Worth, TX: Harcourt Brace & Co., p. 54.

62. Dulles, pp. 334–344.

63. Holley and Jennings, p. 57.

64. Manchester, W. (1974) *The Glory and the Dream: A Narrative History of America, 1932–1972.* Boston: Little, Brown, p. 403.

65. Ibid. at pp. 440–441.

66. Bloom and Northrup, *Economics of Labor Relations (8th ed.),* p. 216.

67. Manchester, pp. 402–404.

68. Ibid.

69. 29 U.S.C. § 141.

70. Holley and Jennings, p. 81.

71. 29 U.S.C. § 152.

72. 29 U.S.C. § 153.

73. 29 U.S.C. § 157.

74. 29 U.S.C. § 158(b)(4)(A).

75. 29 U.S.C. § 158(b)(4)(B).

76. 29 U.S.C. § 158(b)(4)(C).

77. 29 U.S.C. § 158(b)(4)(D).

78. 29 U.S.C. § 158(b)(7)(A).

79. 29 U.S.C. § 158(b)(7)(B).

80. 29 U.S.C. § 158(b)(7)(C).

81. 29 U.S.C. § 164(b).

82. *Communications Workers of America v Beck*, 487 U.S. 735, 762–3 (1988).

83. 66 Fed. Reg. 19988 (April 18, 2001).

84. *Tooley v Martin Marietta Corp.*, 648 F. 2d 1239 (9th Cir. 1981).

85. 29 U.S.C. § 169.

86. Ibid.

87. 29 U.S.C. § 172.

88. 29 U.S.C. §§ 176–183.

89. 29 U.S.C. § 176.

90. 29 U.S.C. § 178(a).

91. 29 U.S.C. § 180.

92. *The World Almanac of Facts 2000.* Mahwah, NJ: World Almanac Books, p. 154.

93. 29 U.S.C. § 401 *et seq.*

94. Dulles, pp. 387–389.

95. Ibid.

96. 29 U.S.C. §§ 411–415.

97. 29 U.S.C. § 481(a–I).

98. 29 U.S.C. § 431(a–c).

99. 29 U.S.C. § 432(a–c).

100. 29 U.S.C. § 433(a–g).

101. 29 U.S.C. § 461.

102. 29 U.S.C. § 462.

103. 29 U.S.C. § 501.

104. 29 U.S.C. § 502.

105. 29 U.S.C. § 503.

106. 29 U.S.C. § 504.

107. 29 U.S.C. § 601.

108. 29 U.S.C. § 602.

109. 29 U.S.C. § 609.

110. U.S. Bureau of the Census (1999). Union members, by selected characteristics: 1998. *Statistical Abstracts of the United States.* Washington, DC: U.S. Government Printing Office, p. 453.

111. E.O. 10988.

112. 39 U.S.C. § 1209.

113. 39 U.S.C. § 1207.

114. 5 U.S.C. § 7105.

115. 5 U.S.C. § 7102.

116. 5 U.S.C. § 7103(a)(14).

117. 5 U.S.C. § 7117.

118. Kochan, T. (1980). *Collective Bargaining and Industrial Relations.* Homewood, IL: Richard D. Irwin, p. 144.

119. Bloom and Northrup, pp. 39–41; Beal and Wickersham, pp. 56–60.

120. Megginson, Franklin, and Byrd, pp. 505–506.

12

COLLECTIVE BARGAINING
AND CONTRACT ADMINISTRATION

LEARNING OBJECTIVES

☐ Understand the collective bargaining process and the steps involved.

☐ Understand the legal issues related to the collective bargaining process.

☐ Discuss the impasse resolution options in the collective bargaining process.

☐ Explain how the collective bargaining agreement is enforced during the contract administration phase.

☐ Describe the steps in the grievance process.

☐ Describe the union's duty to provide fair representation.

☐ Distinguish between rights arbitration and interest arbitration.

☐ Discuss the steps in the arbitration process.

☐ Explain the circumstances under which a rights arbitration award may be overturned.

☐ Distinguish between union grievance procedures and nonunion grievance procedures.

OPENING SCENARIO

Victoria Bush recently had an altercation with her new supervisor, Scott Vitell. As a consequence, she is being suspended for two weeks without pay for insubordination. Bush has responded to her suspension by filing a grievance. The collective bargaining agreement contract reads as follows:

Section 5.02: The Company agrees that the discharge, or other disciplinary action involving employees, shall be for just cause only, and such action, including the reasonableness of the rule under which the action is taken shall be subject to the grievance and arbitration procedure. Section 5.09: Grievance and Arbitration Procedure—Both parties agree to the desirability of exerting an earnest effort to settle grievances at the earliest possible time. The Union agrees to make a careful investigation of the complaint before processing it under the grievance procedure *and to ascertain whether, in its opinion, the grievance complaint is reasonably justified under this contract and that there are reasonable grounds to believe that the claim is true in fact.*

The company has the written testimony of ten witnesses, eight of whom are blue-collar employees and members of the bargaining unit, that Bush did indeed call Vitell a series of profane words, which culminated with the assurance that she was not going to take any more orders from a [expletive deleted] sissy.

When the shop steward first approached Bush with the opinion that she should just let this one go and not pursue the grievance, Bush threatened to file a compliant with the NLRB that the union had failed to provide her with fair representation. As a result, her union filed the grievance.

THE COLLECTIVE BARGAINING PROCESS

The collective bargaining relationship between a union and an employer begins with the recognition of the union as the exclusive bargaining agent for the employees of the bargaining unit. Essentially, **collective bargaining** is the process by which an employer and the exclusive bargaining agent (i.e., the union) negotiate the terms and conditions of employment.[1] The culmination of these negotiations will be a document, the collective bargaining agreement (CBA), which will stipulate the wages and conditions of employment for all the members of the bargaining unit. Upon **ratification,** approval by the bargaining unit, the CBA will serve as the "law of the shop" for its duration.

There are two major elements of the collective bargaining process that often appeal to workers. First, workers perceive the process as evidence of their collective power to achieve desired objectives by dealing with the employer over such issues as higher wages, better benefits, protection from an employer's unjust behavior, and job security. Second, the representative for the employees is generally experienced and prepared to bargain with management, yet the representative is not under the direct control of the employer. Thus, the workers do not have to participate directly in the process; their representative does this for them.

For the most part, the collective bargaining process involves interaction between a union and its representatives and an employer and its representatives. This relationship can become adversarial and may develop into a considerable power struggle.

LEGISLATION GOVERNING COLLECTIVE BARGAINING

The collective bargaining process in the United States is governed by federal and state statutes, administrative agency regulations, and judicial decisions. As mentioned earlier and discussed previously in Chapter 11, the foremost body of law governing the collective bargaining process is the National Labor Relations Act (NLRA) of 1935. The NLRA guarantees employees the right to bargain collectively by giving unions a statutory right to participate in management's decision-making processes through the negotiation process. As you will recall, the Act further imposes a duty upon employers to bargain in good faith with the union as the employees' exclusive bargaining agent regarding the mandatory issues of wages or salaries, hours of work, and other conditions of employment.[2] It should be noted that management is required to negotiate with the union and not the employees individually. After a union becomes a certified bargaining agent, it is an unfair labor practice (ULP) for management to bypass the union and deal directly with the employees on mandatory issues.[3]

BARGAINING IN GOOD FAITH. One statutory duty imposed on employers by the NLRA is to bargain in good faith with the exclusive bargaining agent of employees.[4] Similarly, the Labor-Management Relations Act (LMRA) of 1947 requires the union to bargain in good faith with the employer.[5] To **bargain in good faith** establishes a doctrine that defines the subjects which must be bargained over exclusively with the certified representative of employees. Such subjects include wages, hours, and terms and conditions of employment.

Because collective bargaining is predicated on the concept that parties will bargain in good faith, it is important to clarify what this concept implies. First, bargaining in good faith does not compel either management or the union to agree to the other's offer or counteroffer. Additionally, neither party is required to forsake their bargaining objectives merely to reach an agreement. As with any negotiation process, the party negotiating from the greater position of strength is the party that will prevail when an accord is eventually achieved. There is nothing in the national labor code that would require either party to ignore its bargaining objectives and accept an unfavorable proposal for the sake of compromise.

If this is the case, then what is the obligation to bargain in good faith? It is probably easier to determine when an employer is *not* bargaining in good faith. For example, a party is not meeting its good faith obligations when he or she *refuses* to negotiate with the other party.[6] A failure to bargain in good faith can result when management rejects all union proposals and fails to make any counterproposals.[7] Federal courts have held that management fails to bargain in good faith when it bypasses the union and seeks to create a contract by taking the mandatory issues directly to the members of the bargaining unit.[8] This particular tactic is named for Lemuel Boulware, the former human resources (HR) director for the General Electric Corporation, who devised it.[9] The NLRB has ruled that since this tactic has the purpose and effect of negating the union's role as the exclusive bargaining representative for the members of the bargaining unit, it is evidence of bad faith bargaining.[10]

The basic rules of good faith bargaining appear to be quite clear and simple. However, many collective bargaining situations stall when one party or the other commits a ULP. The National Labor Relations Board (NLRB), in investigating allegations that a party has failed to bargain in good faith over mandatory subjects, considers the totality of conduct by the parties in making their decisions. This means that the NLRB considers the parties' history of negotiating and other aspects of their conduct in collective bargaining.

MANAGEMENT'S DUTY TO PROVIDE INFORMATION. Yet another circumstance that is likely to result in a failure to bargain in good faith occurs when the union requests CBA-related information and management refuses to provide the requested data.[11] The union is permitted to request information from management on production, general financial status, and human resources, provided that it is relevant to the contract negotiations. For management, it is the NLRB, not they, that decides what is relevant information. For example, management may be arguing for a wage freeze, and the union, to bolster its arguments, may want to argue that the workers are "entitled" to a raise because they have increased productivity. Since the union does not maintain productivity statistics, they would naturally request this information from management. Similarly, the union would not have information on human resource matters like employee turnover, longevity, or percentage of contingent workers. A request to the employer to provide such information would be submitted.

Employers automatically trigger a demand for financial information when they claim that they are unable to pay for a concession.[12] This is predicated on the concept that:

> Good faith bargaining necessarily requires that claims made by either bargainer should be honest claims. This is true about an asserted inability to pay an increase in wages. If such an argument is important enough to present in the give and take of bargaining, it is important enough to require some sort of proof of its accuracy.[13]

For publicly traded employers, requests for basic financial information are not unduly burdensome. In fact, all publicly traded firms are required by the Securities and Exchange Commission (SEC) to provide specific financial records, most notably income statements and balance sheets, as a matter of public record. However, such reports may not contain more specific information like how the employer calculated direct and indirect labor costs.

Privately held companies are under no SEC obligation to publicly disclose financial data and are far less willing to open their books to the union. If an employer does not want its financial records disclosed, then it should refuse to grant the concession based on its *unwillingness* to pay rather than its *inability* to pay.[14] Employers who are unwilling to pay are not required to make disclosure.

NOTIFICATION OF INTENT TO BARGAIN. The bargaining sessions must be mutually arranged by the parties at reasonable times and intervals. Negotiations to reach an agreement may require several bargaining sessions, occasionally extending over several months to a year. The place to hold the bargaining sessions should be a neutral, private location that is mutually set by the parties.

Besides the requirement that the parties must bargain in good faith, the parties are also required to file a formal notification of intent to bargain. The party desiring to open the contract for bargaining must provide a written notice of intent to bargain to the other party at least sixty days prior to terminating or modifying

■ **EXHIBIT 12-1**

- ■ Mandatory
  - * Wages
  - * Hours
  - * Conditions of employment
- ■ Permissive
  - * Contributions to charities
  - * Union logos on products
  - * Strike settlement agreements
  - * Benefits for employees previously retired
- ■ Prohibited
  - * Closed shop
  - * Different benefits for nonunion members in the bargaining unit

any existing CBA.[15] Parties in the health care industry must provide written notice at least ninety days prior to terminating or modifying a labor agreement. The parties must also notify the Federal Mediation and Conciliation Service (FMCS) within thirty days from the notice of intent to bargain. This notice allows the FMCS to monitor the progress of the collective bargaining process and offer to facilitate reaching an agreement, if necessary. When the sixty-day notice of intent to bargain has been served, the terms and conditions of the existing CBA must remain unchanged until the parties have negotiated changes in the agreement.

BARGAINING ISSUES.   The issues involved in the collective bargaining process can be divided into three distinct categories: mandatory, permissive, and prohibited. The U.S. Supreme Court formed this doctrine in *NLRB v Wooster Division of Borg-Warner Corp.* when it differentiated the subjects of collective bargaining that are mandatory, permissive, or prohibited (illegal) (see Exhibit 12-1).[16]

Mandatory bargaining issues are those subjects over which the employer and the union must bargain in good faith. **Permissive bargaining issues,** on the other hand, are those subjects that the employer and the union may discuss, but refusal of a party to bargain over such subjects does not necessarily constitute a ULP. **Prohibited bargaining issues** are those subjects that are unlawful to be included in a CBA. These are subjects that would require either party to violate the NLRA or another law.

STEPS IN COLLECTIVE BARGAINING

Once the bargaining relationship is established between an employer and a union representing a group of employees, the parties must start bargaining in good faith to ultimately reach an agreement. During the collective bargaining process, meaningful collaboration must take place between the parties in order to accomplish an agreement. Once the agreement is reached, the parties must then learn to live with it.

An initial collective bargaining agreement between the parties often imparts different problems than revisions or renewals of existing agreements. In the case of an initial collective bargaining process with a union that has recently organized the workers, the bargaining demands may follow a standard pattern within a particular industry. A national or international union will generally recommend a collective bargaining agreement model similar to their other local unions. The local union committee members bring a number of specific proposals concerning issues such as wage rates and seniority rules that are amassed from the input of local union members.

In the case of collective bargaining with an established union already working under an existing labor agreement, the union's proposals typically center on a number of changes and improvements. The proposals in this situation are generally formed based upon input from the local union members and a review of the major grievance issues that arose during the life of the previous labor agreement. The national or international representative may also bring specific proposed changes and improvements that are of interest to the parent union.

Ordinarily, there are several steps in the collective bargaining process. The discussions in this chapter consider four steps within the collective bargaining process itself: prebargaining, initial bargaining, primary bargaining, and final bargaining.

PREBARGAINING. Prior to commencing collective bargaining for an agreement, whether by a newly organized union or an established union that has been representing a group of employees for quite some time, the parties will spend time analyzing and planning in preparation for negotiations. The representatives of management and the union will identify the issues and the positions of the other party. They will develop proposals, counterproposals, and plans as to how far they will go in conceding their proposals.

Each party, in preparing for bargaining, will normally formulate demands based on what their members want, converge information to support the demands in the form of proposals, and communicate their demands to their constituent groups.

The union commonly gathers information from bargaining unit members to formulate either new demands or extensions of previous demands from past bargaining periods. The union bargaining team will then prioritize the list of demands and inform the membership of their established objectives in the collective bargaining process. On the other hand, it is not uncommon for the employer to wait until the union has presented its proposals, then set its proposals as a defense strategy. Many employers, however, go into the collective bargaining process with some demands formulated based on grievances and labor problems encountered during the term of the labor agreement. Additionally, each party will determine a bottom-line position for their bargaining objectives.

■ EXHIBIT 12-2

TYPICAL ARTICLES OF A COLLECTIVE BARGAINING AGREEMENT

- Scope of the agreement

- Recognition
  * Bargaining unit definition
  * Union security
  * Management rights

- Wages and benefits
  * Rates of pay
  * Employee benefits
  * Premium pay

- Hours of work and overtime provisions

- Grievance and arbitration procedure

- Discipline and discharge

- Seniority

- Voluntary checkoff of union dues

- Miscellaneous provisions

- Term of agreement

Collective bargaining agreements will vary in the number and types of articles or provisions included in the written agreements. Exhibit 12-2 shows some of the typical articles found in CBAs.

Issues.   The NLRA separates bargaining topics into mandatory, permissive, and prohibited issues, as discussed previously. The issues involved in the collective bargaining process are further divided into economic issues and noneconomic issues. Some experienced negotiators maintain that all issues in collective bargaining are economic in nature. Nevertheless, negotiators generally prefer to bargain over the issues that are identified as noneconomic first; when those issues are resolved, bargaining over the economic issues will occur. In many instances, the parties opt to submit the economic issues as a package.

Economic.   The collective term "economic issues" includes wages and many other forms of compensation payments. Wage issues in collective bargaining are traditionally related to the change in the wage rates established for the bargaining unit. The economic package covers many other forms of supplemental payments and benefits. The major types of economic issues that may be considered in collective bargaining are basic wage rates, incentive payments, premium payments, overtime pay, profit sharing, retirement or pension plans, hospital/medical payment plans, life insurance plans, holiday pay, vacation pay, and other types of paid leave.

Noneconomic.   Many issues that are not easily seen as direct economic issues are considered noneconomic or work rule issues. The major noneconomic issues are union security, management rights, subcontracting, hours of work, work assignment, seniority rights, due process rights, grievance and arbitration procedures, working conditions, and job security.

INITIAL BARGAINING.   During the initial session of bargaining, the union and the employer typically agree to establish ground rules for their collective bargaining activities. They often agree to rules regarding communicating with constituent groups and the news media during this initial bargaining phase. Sometimes, the parties will agree to keep information discussed and the status of negotiations within the two bargaining teams until there is an agreement to communicate outside the teams. In many bargaining situations, the parties will also agree that, after the exchange of initial proposals, each party will reserve the right to submit additional proposals.

The parties may agree to defer negotiation of the economic issues until all of the noneconomic issues have been resolved. This accord is most common during the negotiations of an initial agreement or major changes and modifications of an existing agreement, where the bargaining is expected to last a long time.

The union bargaining team will generally submit its proposals first, because the union most likely will want to change the CBA. Parties then may establish some order of the issues discussed in an effort to resolve the easier issues first.

PRIMARY BARGAINING.   During the primary bargaining phase, many proposals are exchanged and discussed. This is the bargaining phase in which the parties make the greatest amount of progress toward a settlement. A great amount of time may be spent clarifying the intent of each proposal submitted by the teams. Proposals are met with counterproposals as the parties make small gains toward settlement. As agreements are made on a particular issue, the parties will generally sign a tentative agreement for that issue and continue negotiations on the unresolved issues.

Caucuses will often be used during this bargaining phase. A caucus provides an opportunity for a party to discuss a proposal or a counterproposal and be assured that all bargaining team members are clear on the party's strategies. Caucuses should be used cautiously, though, since it could appear that one party is not prepared or is stalling the negotiations.

FINAL BARGAINING.   This phase of the bargaining process is often tension filled for the involved parties. Frustration levels may be high for the participants as they are trying to resolve difficult issues. It is not uncommon for discussions to arise from the union bargaining team concerning a possible strike and from the management bargaining team concerning final offers and impasse. Long bargaining sessions in hopes of a settlement on the remaining unresolved issues may bring fatigue to many of the participants. In many circumstances, the bargaining will become more positional than during the primary bargaining phase. When positional bargaining intensifies, the likelihood of a settlement decreases.

REACHING AGREEMENT OR IMPASSE

The NLRA requires the employer and the union to bargain over mandatory issues until an agreement is reached or until an impasse occurs. **Impasse** is defined as the point where the parties have negotiated in good faith and have been unable to come to an agreement. At this point, both parties believe they have moved all that they can. An employer will not be held to have violated the NLRA as long as it continues to bargain in good faith.

IMPASSE RESOLUTION. When a legitimate impasse occurs over a mandatory issue during bargaining, the employer is relieved of the duty to bargain further. The union could call for a strike or some form of picketing activities. The employer could lock out the bargaining unit employees or implement its final best offer made prior to the impasse. However, the employer may find compelling reasons to resolve the impasse to assure labor peace in the workplace. The following discussion explains the options that an employer has when impasse occurs.

Work under Existing Contract. When the parties are close to an agreement and neither side wants a strike or a lockout, the existing contract is extended. If no previous contract existed, the employer could either implement the final best offer made prior to the impasse or maintain *status quo* regarding wages, hours of work, and other conditions of employment.

Strike. If the union is not content with continuing to work without a new labor agreement, they may call for a strike, accompanied by a boycott and picketing. A **strike** is a work stoppage by the union-represented employees for the purpose of coercing management to give in to their demands.

Lockout. Another option available to the employer is to temporarily suspend employment of the bargaining unit employees. This action is referred to as a **lockout.** During a lockout, or even a strike, the employer may continue operating the organization either with supervisors and managers or with temporary or permanent replacements.

Third-Party Options. If the above-mentioned options are not satisfactory for either the employer, the union, or both, they may choose to use a third neutral party in an attempt to resolve the impasse. The four alternatives under this option are fact finding, mediation, arbitration, or mediation-arbitration.

Fact Finding. The **fact finding** process includes a neutral third party assigned to gather the facts and provide clarification of the unresolved issues. The objective of the fact finder is to assess the factual information, produce an organized finding of facts, and provide an explanation of the findings in the prospect of the parties using the information to settle their differences.

Mediation. **Mediation** involves the use of mediators, neutral third parties who facilitate the parties in resolving an impasse. Mediators have no authority to make final binding decisions; they must rely on their skills of persuasion and recommend optional proposals. Mediators are appointed by the FMCS or a state agency established for mediation services. Occasionally, parties will agree to utilize a mediator from a private or community source.

Interest Arbitration. There are two forms of **interest arbitration** available where the neutral third party makes the final and binding decision. One form of interest arbitration involves the neutral third party hearing the bargaining positions of each party and making a decision based on what he or she deems to be appropriate for the labor agreement. The other form of interest arbitration involves the third party hearing or reading the final best proposals of each party, then selecting one of the proposals as a final and binding resolution to the dispute. This form of interest arbitration is typically referred to as **final-offer selection arbitration.**

Mediation-Arbitration. The **mediation-arbitration** process involves the parties using mediation and arbitration. The process involves an initial attempt to find a resolution by mediation. If mediation fails to resolve any remaining issues, the neutral third party plays the role of arbitrator and makes a final binding decision.

LIVING WITH THE AGREEMENT

It is a common misconception that once the CBA has been negotiated all the problems and conflicts in labor relations are over until the next round of negotiations. Nothing could be further from the truth. For the duration of the CBA, continuous, unforseen problems will arise. As a result, the two parties to the CBA, the union and management, now enter the contract administration phase of labor relations.

The CBA becomes the "law of the shop"[17] until the contract expires, and, not surprisingly, the interpretation of this "law" is often questioned. Just as laws passed by Congress are litigated in order to resolve differences in interpretation and implementation, applications of the CBA by management are challenged through grievance procedures. To reduce such conflicts, a mechanism must be established to resolve the inevitable grievances that arise, and this process must be communicated to those affected by it.

If a CBA fails to provide provisions for resolving these conflicts, the only alternatives available to employees are strikes, work slowdowns, or working-to-the-rules. For management, grievances, as with bargaining impasses, offer the potential to resort to a lockout to pressure the union to concede. None of the options operate in the best interests of either the organization or the union members. Therefore, to prevent the use of these more extreme methods of grievance resolution, most CBAs provide for more reasonable conflict resolution methods during the life of the contract. These CBA provisions are called **grievance procedures.** Such provisions specify the step-by-step procedures for resolving any workplace dispute arising from different interpretations of the CBA. In establishing conflict resolution procedures, **contract administration provisions** usually include the assignment of individual responsibilities, establishment of timetables, and even the designation of which grievances can be taken to arbitration. The term **grievance,** in the technical labor relations sense, specifically means any alleged violation of a provision of the CBA. It is important to note that if an issue cannot be tied to a provision of the CBA, then it is technically not a grievance. If there is no grievance, the grievance procedure is not applicable.

To illustrate whether an issue is a grievance, assume a labor union wants its employer to start placing the union's logo on its products. However, the current CBA will be in effect for two more years. The request, by itself, would have been a permissive bargaining issue if negotiations were in progress. Recall that management could refuse to negotiate the issue because it is a "permissive" bargaining issue rather than a "mandatory" bargaining issue. Still, in this example, there is no language in the CBA that addresses the issue. Regardless, the union still wishes to file a grievance. Because this conflict clearly does not involve a CBA provision and there is no violation of the contract, there is no grievance.

In another situation, assume a female medical employee has been suspended for three days without pay under the CBA's progressive discipline policy for a first offense (i.e., reporting late to work). In the CBA, the disciplinary provisions clearly state that first offenders are to receive a written counseling statement. Here, there is a distinguishable difference from what the CBA clearly states, written counseling for first offenses, and the actual action taken, a three-day suspension without pay. Taking this example one step further, the supervisor contends that since the employee was three hours late for work, a written warning is not sufficient; her action demands a stronger sanction. This claim does not change the connection between the disputed action and the CBA. Since the CBA specifies one course of action, and the supervisor has taken another, there is no doubt that the disciplinary action in question would constitute a grievance.

THE GRIEVANCE PROCEDURE

Grievances will result when there is a disagreement over the interpretation and application of a provision of the CBA. Interestingly, such disagreements may occur frequently. Having a grievance procedure provides a means for resolving such disputes without adversely affecting the day-to-day operations of the organization. Whatever that procedure, it results from the negotiation process and may be as complex or as simple as the two parties make it. Hence, grievance resolution can be expected to vary in some degree from CBA to CBA.

SOURCES OF GRIEVANCES

Regardless of the actual process for resolution, nearly all grievances arise from management decisions that adversely affect members of the bargaining unit. Disciplinary actions, particularly terminations,[18] are likely to result in initiating a grievance. Requiring employees to work in unsafe, unhealthy, or otherwise dangerous conditions may cause grievances to be filed.

Sometimes disagreement may occur over which employees are eligible for bonuses, or the actual amount of an incentive to which an employee is entitled.[19] As an example, a company may have a gain sharing program in which the individual employee shares are distributed in July, after end of the previous fiscal year. Is an employee who was hired on April 1, the beginning of the last quarter of the bonus period, entitled to a full share, a partial share (¼), or no share at all? If there is no language in the CBA addressing such a situation, a grievance is likely to occur since there is room for several different interpretations. Other compensation issues that have the potential of becoming grievances are eligibility for pay raises, longevity pay, premium pay, or paid leave.

In some instances, grievances may arise when managers make personnel decisions, such as work assignments,[20] that are overtly contrary to the CBA. Assume a CBA clearly states that the most senior employee is to be offered the opportunity to work overtime and must reject the offer before it can be made to a junior employee. Now, suppose that instead of first asking the most senior employee if he or she would work overtime, a manager arbitrarily assigns the overtime work to the employee thought to be the most productive. This is a situation in which the manager clearly ignored the CBA.

Because many CBAs provide for bumping privileges, grievances may result when senior employees are not permitted to exercise their seniority to "bump" junior employees, particularly for jobs that the senior employees are not qualified to perform. **Bumping rights** are common to many seniority provisions and permit a more senior employee to replace a less senior employee holding a job in the same plant during reductions in the workforce. To illustrate how bumping can work, a senior truck driver who was initially targeted for layoff is permitted to bump a forklift operator with less seniority. If the former truck driver could not adequately operate a forklift, the former forklift operator may file a grievance to get his or her job back. Conversely, if the truck driver is qualified to operate the forklift but was not permitted by management to bump the forklift operator under the CBA, the truck driver could file a grievance.

Yet another common source of grievances is inconsistent application of work rules and policies. First-level supervisors who fail to consistently enforce company policies prompt grievances. Suppose an employee who is five minutes late for work, as a first offense, is sent home without pay. However, another employee who is consistently late to work is never even reprimanded. Such arbitrary or capricious treatment by a supervisor, particularly in the areas of work assignments and discipline, has the potential to be challenged by employees. Very often, grievances are filed when supervisors and managers initiate disciplinary actions without conducting an investigation to determine whether or not the employee had indeed violated a work rule.[21] If it cannot be proven that the employee committed the offense in question, it is difficult to justify the disciplinary action. One reason that employees are drawn to the CBA is that it removes them from an employment-at-will status and places them in a "just cause" arena. It is, therefore, a potential grievance to discipline an employee for just cause without first establishing the just cause.

Not all employee dissatisfaction constitutes a legitimate grievance. It is human nature to complain about the things that displease us. At any given time, there will be some employees who express dissatisfaction with some aspects of their jobs, and many will openly express their discontent. It is not uncommon for employees to complain about management practices, attitudes, behaviors, and decisions. Managers are often accused of playing favorites, not keeping promises, or being too demanding of subordinates. But none of these complaints, of and by themselves, constitute a grievance. There must be some connection between the employment practice and the CBA. Once this connection is established, the formal grievance process may begin.

STEPS IN THE GRIEVANCE PROCEDURE

There is no standard grievance procedure. Some CBAs provide for a three-step procedure; others may contain a six-step process. In some CBAs, the procedure may begin with a verbal grievance being initiated, while others may require a written grievance at every step of the process.

The four-step procedure found in the grievance article in Exhibit 12-3 is the most typical.[22] In this procedure, the grievance process begins when the employee, or his or her shop steward, discusses the grievance with the supervisor. At this step, the grievance is verbal, and if it can be resolved at this level, there is no need to take the matter any further. But if there is no resolution at this juncture, the grievant is permitted to initiate a written appeal within a specified period following notification that the verbal grievance was rejected.

To illustrate how this process operates, let's return to the situation involving the opening scenario. Recall that Victoria Bush has been suspended for two weeks without pay for insubordination. Assume on Wednesday, October 10, Bush and her shop steward confronted her supervisor, Scott Vitell, challenging the action on the grounds that it was not for just cause. According to our procedure, Vitell will have up to two days to respond. On Friday, October 12, he does so. If, at this point, Vitell shows Bush and her shop steward the statements from witnesses and convinces the two that the just cause nature of the discipline was satisfied, the grievance is settled.

■ EXHIBIT 12-3

TYPICAL GRIEVANCE ARTICLE

Step 1: Upon receipt of a properly presented grievance, the supervisor shall provide the grieving employee and shop steward with a reply within two (2) working days. If the reply does not settle the grievance, it may be appealed to Step 2 of the grievance procedure provided such appeal in writing is made within five (5) working days.

Step 2: Grievances properly advanced to Step 2 shall be discussed in a meeting between the personnel manager and/or the personnel manager's designated representative, the aggrieved employee, and the employee's shop steward, and any other persons that the parties mutually agree upon. Such meeting shall be held within three (3) working days. The personnel manager shall give a written reply to the grievance within five (5) working days after the date of the meeting. In the event the reply does not settle the grievance, it may be appealed to Step 3 of the grievance procedure provided a written appeal is made to the operations manager within five (5) days after receipt of the personnel manager's answer.

Step 3: Grievances properly advanced to Step 3 shall be discussed in a meeting between the operations manager and/or the operations manager's designated representative, a grievance committee of no more than three (3) employees, one from each department selected by the union, and the international representative, if requested by either party, plus any other persons that the parties mutually agree upon. Such meeting shall be held within five (5) working days or as soon as possible thereafter. The operations manager shall submit to the local union, with a copy to the international representative, a written answer to the grievance within five (5) working days after the meeting. Should the operations manager's written reply not settle the grievance, it may be appealed to arbitration by the union, provided written notice of the union's intent to arbitrate the grievance is received by the company within ten (10) working days after mailing of the operations manager's Step 3 answer.

Step 4: Only disputes that are a breach or an alleged breach of some express and specific provision of this Agreement shall be subject to arbitration.

SOURCE: Labor Agreement for a Particle Board Plant (1995). Oxford, MS, pp. 3–4.

However, if the employee feels that the matter was not properly investigated or that the witnesses' statements were obtained under duress (i.e., she alleges Vitell pressured the witnesses), the grievance will be pursued and move to the next step. At this next step, the grievance is formalized; that is, the grievance is put in written form. Most companies provide a grievance form for use in these procedures (refer to Exhibit 12-4).

Once the written grievance is filed, there is a time frame established in which the employee's representative must respond in writing to the personnel manager. Once again, these time limits vary from CBA to CBA. In our example, the CBA has established a five-working-day time limit. The grievance is filed on Wednesday, October 17. Assuming Saturday and Sunday are not working days, the personnel manager would have to respond in writing to Bush's grievance no later than Wednesday, October 24. It is very important to be aware of the time limits contained in the grievance procedures. Should the personnel manager fail to respond to Bush's appeal in a timely manner (i.e., respond by Friday, October 26), the grievance could be challenged on procedural grounds. This is of particular

■ EXHIBIT 12-4

TYPICAL FORMAL GRIEVANCE FORM

Name _____ Date _____

Address _____

Department_____ Shift _____

Nature of Grievance: _____

_____

_____

_____

_____

concern if the grievance involves an issue that could eventually go to arbitration. Should management fail to comply with the procedures it agreed to in the CBA, including the time tables, the arbitrator could rule in favor of Bush.[23] However, usually the grievance proceeds to the next step. It should also be noted that any time limits provided for under the CBA's grievance procedures apply to the union as well and could result in the dismissal of the grievance[24] (see Exhibit 12-5).

Continuing with our previous example, and assuming both parties have met their time limits at the second step, the personnel manager has reviewed Bush's formal grievance and has responded in writing that it is the company's conclusion that Bush's grievance is without merit, which means the personnel manager is comfortable with the idea that Bush's discipline was handled in compliance with the CBA and that no violation of the CBA has occurred. If the union disagrees with this conclusion, the grievance may then progress to a third step.

At the third step, the grievance is appealed, again in writing, to a higher level of management, this time to the operations manager. Again, there is a time limit for submitting the appealed grievance (five days following the receipt of the personnel manager's written reply). Assuming the formal grievance was initially unresolved

■ **EXHIBIT 12-5**

<u>TYPICAL GRIEVANCE PROCEDURE</u>

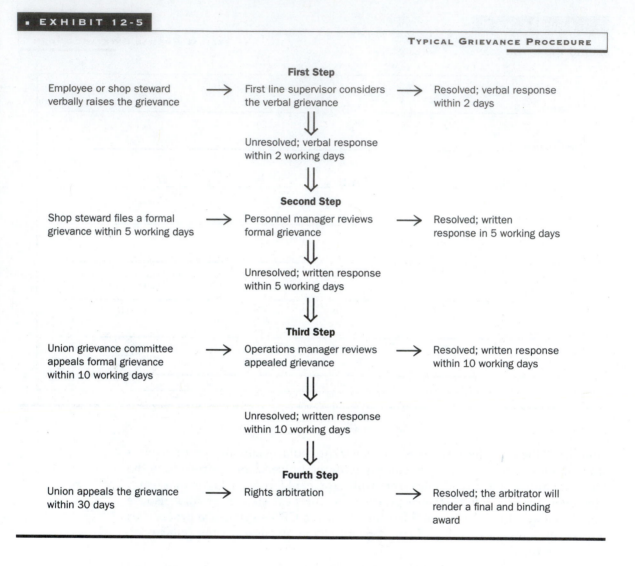

on Wednesday, October 24 and that the company does not work on weekends, Bush would have until Wednesday, October 31 to appeal the grievance.

As at the lower steps, upper-level management would also have a time limit imposed on it to respond to Bush's appeal. In our example, the operations manager has a ten-working-day limit to reply in writing to Bush (technically, the union grievance committee). Consequently, management would have until November 14 to provide its written response.

In our illustration, let's assume the operations manager has reviewed Bush's grievance and, once again, has concluded the company has complied with the

CBA and was fully justified in disciplining Bush for insubordination. If the union grievance committee accepts this conclusion, the grievance is resolved. However, should the union grievance committee conclude that management is still wrong and that the disciplinary action was contrary to the CBA, then the grievance will move to the fourth and final step, rights arbitration, within thirty working days (i.e., take action by December 26). Because the two parties to the CBA cannot resolve the grievance between themselves, the matter will now be turned over to a neutral third party for resolution.

If resolution cannot be achieved within the organization, it goes outside of the organization to rights arbitration, also called grievance arbitration. **Rights arbitration,** often simply called **arbitration,** brings an arbitrator, a neutral third party, in to interpret the terms of the agreement in order to settle the disagreement between management and the union. In rights arbitration, the arbitrator's decision, the **arbitration award,** is normally final and binding on both parties. Before discussing arbitration, however, it is first important to understand the union's duty to fair representation in pursuing employee grievances.

DUTY OF FAIR REPRESENTATION IN GRIEVANCE PROCEDURES

Unions have the **duty of fair representation** imposed on them by the LMRA Specifically:

> It shall be an unfair labor practice for a labor organization or its agent to cause or attempt to cause an employer to discriminate against an employee in violation of subsection (a)(3) or to discriminate against an employee with respect to whom membership in such organization has been denied or terminated on some ground other than his failure to tender periodic dues and the initiation fees uniformly required as a condition of acquiring or retaining membership.[25]

In practice, this requires the union to actively pursue meritorious grievances of *any* member of the bargaining unit. This is especially true under CBAs which have established levels of compulsory union membership at the modified union shop or lower levels. These bargaining units would be comprised of varying percentages of nonunion members. Under the duty of fair representation, the union must just as assiduously pursue the grievance initiated by a nonunion member of the bargaining unit as it would for a union member.[26]

ARBITRATION AND THE ARBITRATION PROCESS

The two general categories of arbitration are interest arbitration and rights arbitration. Interest arbitration, as you should recall, occurs when a neutral party is called in to resolve an impasse between the parties *during* collective bargaining negotiations. As an example, assume management and labor have reached an impasse on an outsourcing clause of the contract during negotiations. The negotiations have come to a complete halt, and the clock is ticking away toward the contract's expiration date. If not resolved, the impasse could result in a strike or lockout. The parties could either resort to mediation or interest arbitration. As discussed earlier in this chapter, under mediation, a neutral party is retained to bring the two parties back to the bargaining table, but his or her recommendations are strictly advisory and not binding. A mediator cannot compel agreement, and should one of the parties remain adamant about their position, the impasse would continue.

Arbitration, unlike mediation, is binding on the parties. In the case of interest arbitration, should the arbitrator hear the arguments of both parties and decide that there will be no outsourcing of any work during the life of the CBA, then both parties are bound by that award. Because of this feature of interest arbitration, it is rarely used in the private sector. Most managers would not be comfortable with the idea that a neutral third party, with little understanding of their industry or company, would have the power to affect their direct and indirect labor costs for the contract duration.

Imagine an impasse occurring over wages. Management's final offer, based on financial forecasts and analysis, has stopped at a 10 percent increase in wages over the next three years or the duration of the contract being negotiated. Further assume the union's last demand was 12 percent, and it will not budge. Now, consider the impact that an interest arbitrator would have on the company if the award favored the union. For this reason, most interest arbitration occurs in the public sector rather than the private sector.

In the private sector, the most common form of arbitration is rights arbitration, which involves a neutral party who is called in to resolve labor disputes arising from a CBA. Under the CBA, the union and management have agreed to submit grievances to an arbitrator for final and binding resolution. In short, rights arbitration occurs *after* collective bargaining negotiations have culminated in a certified CBA.

In the case of rights arbitration, the arbitrator's primary source or guide for making the award is the CBA. If the award is not drawn from the language of the CBA, the award is subject to challenges in court.[27]

DEVELOPMENT OF ARBITRATION: HISTORY AND LEGALITY

Rights arbitration is not a new phenomenon. The 1934 amendment to the Railway Labor Act provided for rights arbitration when it created the National Railroad Adjustment Board (NRAB).[28] The NRAB was given the authority to settle disputes arising out of "grievance or out of the interpretation or application of agreements . . . "[29] However, it would be another twenty-three years before rights arbitration would be universally applied to employers and employees covered under the national labor code.

In 1957, the U. S. Supreme Court granted legal recognition to binding rights arbitration in *Textile Workers Union v Lincoln Mills*.[30] In this decision, the Supreme

THE ARBITRATION PROCESS

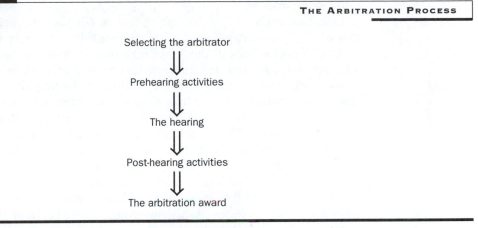

Selecting the arbitrator

⇓

Prehearing activities

⇓

The hearing

⇓

Post-hearing activities

⇓

The arbitration award

Court concluded that agreements between two parties to a CBA to arbitrate grievances were enforceable under federal labor law.[31] Over the years, federal courts would gradually give increasing deference to arbitration awards.

SELECTING THE ARBITRATOR

The arbitration process (see Exhibit 12-6) begins with the selection of the arbitrator who will resolve the grievance. Some CBAs provide for a permanent arbitrator. A **permanent arbitrator** is an individual who is specified under the CBA to hear all grievances arising during the life of the contract. Such arrangements permit for an arbitrator who, over time, has become familiar not only with the CBA, but also the organization's processes and unique characteristics. It is hoped that having an arbitrator who is familiar with the organization and its environment will result in more reasonable and consistent arbitration awards.

Organizations (roughly 95 percent of them) commonly resort to *ad hoc* arbitrators.[32] *Ad hoc* **arbitrators,** as their name implies, are selected on a case-by-case basis, or more accurately, a grievance-by-grievance basis. Each time an unresolved grievance occurs, a new arbitrator is selected. When grievances are few and industry characteristics are not overly complex, *ad hoc* arbitrators tend to be less costly than permanent ones. Additionally, many individuals who serve as *ad hoc* arbitrators often specialize in specific contract areas. For example, one arbitrator may specialize in wage and hour grievances while another may have a preference for grievances arising from discipline and discharge. Such specialization permits arbitrators to develop in-depth knowledge within one area. Whereas permanent arbitrators may be more familiar with the two parties to the arbitration, a specialized *ad hoc* arbitrator may be more familiar with the issue being grieved.

One concern about *ad hoc* arbitrators is whether the arbitrator has a "pro-union" or "pro-management" bias. Although this is rarely the case, the parties are still concerned about the arbitrator's bias. In many instances, the outcome of an arbitrator's awards may indicate that a good number of the awards have favored management. Yet, for another arbitrator, the majority of awards may favor unions. In actuality, the disparity in award outcomes has resulted from the merits of the specific grievances that the arbitrators heard. However, to an outside observer unfamiliar with the arbitration cases, a pro-union or pro-management bias is assumed based on which side, union or management, the majority of the arbitrator's awards favored. This perception may lead to one of the parties vehemently opposing particular arbitrators. Imagine the difficulty this situation would cause if the CBA does not provide a method for resolving disputes arising from arbitrator selection. Management and the union have had to resort to arbitration in the first place because they could not resolve the grievance among themselves. Now, they cannot agree on an arbitrator.

The simplest means of resolving this dilemma is to develop a list of potential arbitrators and permit each party to alternately strike a specified number of names from it. Any remaining names would be acceptable to both parties, or at least less disagreeable. To illustrate, assume the following list of arbitrators is provided:

- Stephanie Crow
- Jon David Dunn
- Neal Mero
- Wendy McKee
- William Schaffer
- Elvis Stevens
- Hamilton Warnock

The union might be permitted to strike three names from the list (say, Dunn, Mero, and McKee). Management would also be permitted to strike three names. Note that even if management struck three different names (i.e., Crow, Schaffer, and Warnock), at least one name would remain (in this case, Stevens). The survivor would then be designated to arbitrate the grievance. If more than one name remained, either one could be selected.

Sources of Arbitrators.   In order to develop a list of arbitrators from which to make a selection, one first must know where to find arbitrators. The best sources for arbitrators' names are: (1) the FMCS,[33] (2) the American Arbitration Association (AAA),[34] and (3) the National Academy of Arbitrators (NAA).[35] Any of these organizations can be contacted for a roster of qualified arbitrators (see Exhibit 12-7).

■ EXHIBIT 12-7

American Arbitration Association
Corporate Headquarters
335 Madison Avenue, Floor 10
New York, NY 10017–4605
(212) 716–5800
http://www.adr.org

Federal Mediation and Conciliation Service
2100 K Street
Washington, DC 20427
(202) 606–8100
http://www.fmcs.gov

National Arbitration Association
403 Lowder Building
College of Business
Auburn University, AL 36849–5260
(334) 844–2817
http://www.naarb.org

PREHEARING ACTIVITIES

Without a doubt, the most important step in the arbitration process is the prehearing activities. Many arbitrations are won or lost based on the effort placed on preparing for the hearing. At this step, management and the union gather all the information necessary to support their arguments during the hearing phase. If the arbitration is based on matters involving employee misconduct, then the facts surrounding the incident, testimony of witnesses, and related evidence must be collected. Should the grievance involve a matter of contract interpretation, then facts surrounding why the contract should be interpreted in a particular manner must be gathered (i.e., notes from the actual bargaining sessions, economic and financial data, evidence of past practices, etc.).

In some instances, a party may decide to prepare prehearing briefs. Prior to the actual hearing, either party may elect to submit a written summary of its arguments to the arbitrator. Such briefs usually contain the relevant facts surrounding the grievance as well as the party's interpretation of applicable provisions from the CBA. The parties may further reinforce their arguments by injecting precedent established in other arbitration awards under similar circumstances. Prehearing briefs attempt to focus the arbitrator's attention on information that the party expects to make its case.

Perhaps the best guidelines for prehearing activities are provided in *Elkouri & Elkouri How Arbitration Works* (by Goggin and Volz). Here, the authors provide a comprehensive checklist for arbitration preparation (see Exhibit 12-8).[36]

AN ARBITRATION PREPARATION CHECKLIST

The nature of the case to be arbitrated should be considered in determining which items of the following "preparation" checklist should be emphasized. Due to the fact that not all items are relevant to every case, there is no significance in the order of the list.

✔ Review the history of the case as developed at the pre-arbitral steps of the grievance procedure.

✔ Study the entire collective agreement to ascertain all clauses bearing directly or indirectly on the dispute. Also, comparison of current provisions with those contained in prior agreements might reveal changes significant to the case.

✔ In order to determine the general authority of the arbitrator, and accordingly the scope of the arbitration, examine the instruments used to initiate the arbitration.

✔ Talk to all persons (even those whom the other party might use as witnesses) who might be able to aid development of a full picture of the case, including different viewpoints. You will thus better understand not only your own case but your opponent's as well; if you can anticipate your opponent's case you can better prepare to rebut it.

✔ Interview each of your own witnesses (1) to determine what they know about the case, (2) to make certain they understand the relation of their testimony to the whole case, and (3) to cross-examine them to check their testimony and to acquaint them with the process of cross-examination. Make a written summary of the expected testimony of each witness; this can be reviewed when the witness testifies to insure that no important points are overlooked. Some parties outline in advance the questions to be asked each witness.

✔ Examine all records and documents that might be relevant to the case. Organize those you expect to use and make copies for use by the arbitrator and the other party at the hearing. If needed documents are in the exclusive possession of the other party, ask that they be made available before or at the hearing.

✔ Visit the physical premises involved in the disputes to better visualize what occurred and what the dispute is about. Also, consider the advisability of asking at the hearing that the arbitrator (accompanied by both parties) also visit the site of the dispute.

✔ Consider the utility of pictorial or statistical exhibits. One exhibit can be more effective than many words, if the matter is suited to the exhibit form of portrayal. However, exhibits that do not "fit" the case, and those that are inaccurate or misleading, are almost certain to be ineffective or to be damaging to their proponent.

✔ Consider what the parties' past practice has been in comparable situations.

✔ Attempt to determine whether there is some "key" point upon which the case might turn. If so, it may be to your advantage to concentrate upon that point.

✔ In "interpretation" cases prepare a written argument to support your view as to the proper interpretation of the disputed language.

✔ In "interest" or "contract writing" cases collect and prepare economic and statistical data to aid evaluation of the dispute.

✔ Research the parties' prior arbitration awards and the published awards of other parties on the subject of the dispute for an indication of how similar issues have been approached in other cases.

✔ Prepare an outline of your case and discuss it with another person in your group. This insures better understanding of the case, and will strengthen it by uncovering matters that need further attention. Then, too, it will tend to underscore policy and strategy considerations that may be very important in the ultimate handling of the case. Use of the outline at the hearing will facilitate an organized and systematic presentation of the case.

SOURCE: Goggin, E. and Volz, M. (eds.) (1997). *Elkouri & Elkouri How Arbitration Works* (5th ed.). Washington, DC: Bureau of National Affairs, pp. 332–334.

THE HEARING

The location of the hearing itself may be provided for in the CBA and, therefore, may be at any place the two parties agree. For the convenience of the parties and the witnesses, locating the hearing on company property is advisable. However, arbitrations can be conducted on so-called neutral ground, such as a hotel conference room.

Who attends the hearing may be a matter of the CBA and the arbitrator's preference. There is nothing to preclude the arbitration from being a public hearing. However, if spectators are likely to be disruptive during the proceedings, public hearings should be avoided. Usually, the hearings are open to management's representatives, the grievant, the grievant's representatives, and witnesses. Either party may have attorneys present as well.

Although arbitration is a quasi-judicial process, the hearing itself is far less formal than a trial, and the rules of evidence are not as stringent as the rules of evidence in a court of law. For instance, circumstantial evidence, evidence that *implies* the truth or falsity of an action, may be given greater weight in an arbitration than in a court of law. The arbitrator is given far more discretion in determining what is relevant evidence than a judge in a trial and may even allow secondhand testimony, often referred to as "hearsay."[37] Rules of evidence that apply to courts do not necessarily apply in arbitration hearings. Unlike juries in trials, arbitrators are qualified to determine the relevance of evidence. Juries usually require instructions from a judge.

The union usually opens the hearing by presenting the grievance in nondiscipline cases, since it is typically the party who claims a contract violation. Management opens the hearing when it involves discipline and disclosure because the employer has the burden of proof to establish that the employee was guilty of the alleged offense. The hearing itself takes on the air of a judicial proceeding and follows a general protocol. The party filing the grievance, the "moving party," opens the hearing by presenting its case that the CBA was violated. The moving party must demonstrate the contract violation through testimony and evidence.[38]

Once the moving party has presented its argument, testimony, and evidence, the other party presents its argument, testimony, and evidence. Each party is permitted to cross-examine the witnesses of the opposite party. Then each party is afforded the opportunity to present rebuttals. Following the rebuttals, each party is permitted to make its closing arguments. By convention, the moving party is the party that closes the hearing. Although either party may raise objections to the other party's evidence, it is the arbitrator's prerogative to finally decide whether it is relevant.

POST-HEARING ACTIVITIES

Following the hearing, the parties may submit post-hearing briefs which will summarize important facts that have surfaced following the hearing and any arguments presented to the arbitrator.

THE ARBITRATION AWARD

Once the arbitrator has reviewed all evidence, testimony, and any post-hearing briefs, he or she will then render an award. The award is a formal, written document which conforms to the following general format:

- A summary of the relevant evidence and arguments presented
- An explanation of the arbitrator's rationale in framing the award
- The remedy, any corrective action which one party or the other must take in order to satisfy the award

However, before the hearing is conducted, there are four criteria that the arbitrator must ensure are satisfied. First, the arbitrator must verify that the issue is an arbitrable issue. Federal courts may intervene and overturn the award if the issue is not arbitrable.[39] Second, the issue must have involved an actual contract violation.[40] This would be necessary to demonstrate that the award is actually drawn from the essence of the CBA. Third, the arbitrator must ensure that the steps of the CBA's grievance procedure were followed. Failure to follow the procedures contractually agreed to by the parties may result in the grievance being dismissed.[41] Fourth, the arbitrator will then ensure the award is predicated on the merits of the facts (i.e., evidence and testimony).

LIMITING FEDERAL COURT INVOLVEMENT IN ARBITRATION

Rights arbitration has turned out to be such an effective and efficient means of grievance resolution that federal courts rarely interfere with the process. The finality of binding arbitration was reinforced to no small degree by a series of three 1960 Supreme Court decisions. Since all three decisions involved the United Steelworkers of America (USWA), they have become known as the *Steelworkers' Trilogy* (see Exhibit 12-9)

The first case of the *Steelworkers'* Trilogy, *Steelworkers v American Manufacturing Company*,[42] limited the role of federal courts in determining the arbitrability of an issue. When an arbitration award is appealed, the federal court is strictly confined to determining whether the CBA permits the issue in question to go to arbitration. The matter of contract interpretation when determining the *merits* of the grievance is the expressed prerogative of the arbitrator, not the courts.

Additionally, a federal court may not intervene and overturn an arbitrator's award based on the court's interpretation of merits of the grievance. This prohibition was established under the second case of the trilogy, *Steelworkers v Warrior & Gulf Navigation Co.*[43] This decision makes the arbitrator, not the court, the party solely responsible for determining the merits of any grievance dispute arising from the CBA. Quite simply, federal courts are excluded from interpreting any grievance on its merit; they may only decide issues of substantive arbitrability.

■ **EXHIBIT 12-9**

Steelworkers v American Manufacturing Co.—Federal courts are limited to determining the arbitrability of an issue.

Steelworkers v Warrior & Gulf Navigation Co.—Federal courts cannot judge a grievance on its merits only its arbitrability. An issue is not arbitrable only if the CBA, with "positive assurance," states it is not.

Steelworkers v Enterprise Wheel & Car Corp.—An arbitration can be overturned by a federal court if:

- there is dishonesty on the part of the arbitrator.
- there is fraud on the part of the parties.
- the award is not drawn from the essence of the CBA.

SOURCES: *Steelworkers v American Manufacturing Co.*, 363 U.S. 564 (1960); *Steelworkers v Warrior & Gulf Navigation Co.*, 363 U.S. 582 (1960); *Steelworkers v Enterprise Wheel & Car Corp.*, 363 U.S. 598 (1960).

In practice, an issue is usually considered to be arbitrable unless there is specific language in the contract stating otherwise. For example, assume a contract contained the following statement: "Shift assignments are completely at the discretion of management and are not subject to grievance procedures or arbitration as outlined in Article VII of this collective bargaining agreement." Such language is sufficiently clear to indicate that any dispute that arises from an employee's assignment to a given shift would not be an arbitrable issue. Should the union file a grievance and then sue the employer to require the employer to take this matter to arbitration, a federal court could rule on the substantive arbitrability of the grievance—most likely against arbitration.

OVERTURNING AN ARBITRATION AWARD. We do not intend to imply that an arbitration award is sacred and totally protected from being overturned. Although in most instances arbitration awards are final and binding, there are some circumstances under which federal courts may intervene and overturn an award. These criteria were established in the third and final case of the *Steelworkers'* Trilogy, *Steelworkers v Enterprise Wheel & Car Corp.*[44]

The arbitration award stands unless there is clear and convincing evidence that it was motivated by unethical or dishonest considerations (i.e., the arbitrator received a bribe from one of the parties). In addition, an award could be overturned if it could be proven that one of the parties to the arbitration presented fraudulent evidence or testimony (i.e., management fabricated false counseling statements and performance appraisals to pretextually discharge an employee).

Finally, an award can be overturned when the arbitrator ignores the specific language of the CBA or otherwise ignores its contractual limitations.[45] Only when it can be shown that the arbitrator fabricated the decision based on personal belief rather than the language of the CBA can the award be reversed by the court. The arbitrator is limited to framing the award within the confines of the CBA. The arbitrator is expressly forbidden to fabricate an award based solely on "personal concept of industrial justice" with no connection to the CBA.[46]

TITLE VII AND OTHER EEO CHALLENGES TO ARBITRATION AWARDS

Federal courts place a great deal of value on the finality of an arbitrator's award. Thus far, you have learned that the award cannot be challenged if it involved a grievance that was arbitrable, there was no dishonesty on the part of the arbitrator, the award was not based on fraudulent evidence submitted by the parties, and the award was drawn from the essence of the contract. However, there are several special exceptions to these challenges.

TITLE VII PREEMPTS TO ARBITRATION AWARDS. In the case, *Alexander v Gardner-Denver Co.*, the Supreme Court ruled that an employee's statutory right to a trial under Title VII is not impeded by a previous submission of a discrimination claim to arbitration under the CBA.[47] In this case, the grievant, Harrell Alexander, filed a grievance claiming that he had been "unjustly discharged."[48] It was further claimed that the discharge was contrary to Article 5, Section 2, of the CBA's antidiscrimination clause which stated that "there shall be no discrimination against any employee on account of race, color, religion, sex, national origin, or ancestry."[49] The arbitrator's award held that Alexander had been discharged for cause.[50]

The grievant had also filed an equal employment opportunity (EEO) complaint with the Colorado Civil Rights Commission and later the Equal Employment Opportunity Commission (EEOC). An investigation by the EEOC determined that there was no reasonable cause to believe that the employer had violated Title VII. However, the complaining party requested and received a right-to-sue letter from the EEOC and pursued the matter in federal district court.[51]

The District Court and later the Court of Appeals for the Tenth Circuit,[52] relying on the precedent established by the *Steelworkers'* Trilogy, held that the arbitration award under the CBA's nondiscrimination clause was final and binding. The Supreme Court viewed the matter differently. It reasoned that Congress, in enacting Title VII, thought it necessary to provide a judicial forum to resolve discriminatory employment claims.[53] The Supreme Court formally declared that the resolution of Title VII claims would be the prerogative of the federal courts and not arbitrators.

OTHER EEO CLAIMS AND ARBITRATION. The Supreme Court has reserved matters arising from the Americans with Disability Act (ADA) claims to be outside the binding nature of arbitration but only when the CBA does not contain a "clear and unmistakable waiver of the covered employee's rights to a judicial forum for federal claims of employment discrimination."[54] Note that although the right to a

■ EXHIBIT 12-10

AMERICAN ARBITRATION ASSOCIATION FEE SCHEDULE AS OF SEPTEMBER 1, 2000

Amount of Claim	Initial Filing Fee	Case Service Fee
Above $0 to $10,000	$500	N/A
Above $10,000 to $75,000		
Above $75,000 to $150,000	$1,250	$750
Above $150,000 to $300,000	$2,750	$1,000
Above $300,000 to $500,000	$4,250	$1,250
Above $500,000 to $1,000,000	$6,000	$2,000
Above $1,000,000 to $7,000,000	$8,500	$2,500
Above $7,000,000 to $10,000,000	$13,000	$3,000
Above $10,000,000	Contact local AAA office	Contact local AAA office
No Amount Stated	$3,250	$750

SOURCE: American Arbitration Association (2000). American Arbitration Association introduces new arbitration fee schedule. http://www.adr.org

federal trial for disability or age discrimination may be specifically waived in lieu of arbitration, Title VII rights to trial are not waivable in a CBA.[55]

In March 2001 the Supreme Court further strengthened the finding of arbitration by expanding its interpretation of the Federal Arbitration Act to include employment contracts.[56] Previously, some circuits had limited the Act's provisions to strictly commercial contracts. By extending coverage to include individual employment contracts, the Court's decision will greatly expand the use of alternative dispute resolution procedures (like arbitration) in nonunion, as well as unionized work environments.

PAYING FOR ARBITRATION

The arbitrator's services are not without cost. In determining the cost of arbitration, one must consider the arbitrator's fees. For example, the AAA's administrative fees are based on the amount of the claim or counterclaim (refer to Exhibit 12-10).

Of course, fees may vary between arbitrators based on experience and expertise. There are also charges for expenses incurred by the arbitrator (i.e., travel, accommodations, meals, etc.). A simple arbitration is likely to cost several thousand dollars. If there are many arbitrations conducted per year, the cost of contract administration can become substantial. Hence the question arises: Who will pay the arbitration costs? The answer: Whoever is designated to do so in the CBA.

Like most matters occurring in labor relations, the ruling document is the CBA, and how arbitration costs are apportioned varies from contract to contract. There are several options:

1. Management pays all expenses
2. The union pays all expenses
3. The union and management split the expenses equally
4. Whoever loses the arbitration is responsible for all expenses

The inherent problem with the first two payment schemes is that it sets up a potential situation for abuse. If one party has been designated to assume the total cost of the arbitration, the other party may be tempted to abuse the arbitration process. If management is responsible for expenses, the union may be inclined to grieve unmeritorious issues. After all, it costs the union nothing to do so. The opposite might occur if the union bore the full cost of arbitration; management might pursue unmeritorious grievances in order to hurt the union financially.

A fifty-fifty split of arbitrator's fees and expenses reduces some of the possible abuses. Under this model, the parties are responsible for their own expenses related to the arbitration. The downside of this formula is that even in meritless cases, the arbitrator's expenses would be halved with the other party. The party with the greater financial resources could, conceivably, threaten arbitration in order to force resolution at a lower level in the grievance procedure.

Ultimately, the scheme of loser-pays-all appears to be the one least likely to encourage abuse. The mechanism for assigning financial responsibility for expenses is very simple; the loser incurs all of the arbitrator's fees and expenses. If a party has a weak grievance, it is better to resolve it in a pre-arbitration step of the grievance. The penalty incurred for pursuing an unmeritorious grievance is to assume full cost for pushing the matter to arbitration when it is without merit. If this was the situation in our opening scenario, Bush's union would be responsible for assuming the cost of taking her grievance to arbitration and then losing.

Special Forms of Arbitration

One method to help contain arbitration costs is expedited arbitration. **Expedited arbitration** involves a single arbitrator hearing several simple grievances in a single session. The written arbitration awards themselves are rendered in abbreviated format. As several grievances are heard and decided together, the cost per grievance is significantly reduced.

In some instances, particularly those involving critical interpretations of contracts, tripartite arbitration may be utilized. In a **tripartite arbitration,** three arbitrators hear the issue. They sit as a tribunal, and the award is based on the majority opinion of the three. Bear in mind that the use of tripartite arbitration is more expensive than the typical single arbitrator model. In tripartite arbitration, the tribunal is frequently composed of one union official, one management official, and a neutral arbitrator. In other cases, it may be comprised of three arbitrators.[57]

The advantage of tripartite arbitration is that in the event of a unanimous decision, that decision is more likely to be accepted by the parties. The disadvantage is that should the parties select highly partisan arbitrators, the neutral arbitrator spends more time mediating between the union and management arbitrators.[58] In addition, awards may be reduced to a compromise among the tribunal members rather than the best judgment of a single arbitrator.

NONUNION GRIEVANCE PROCEDURES

Many nonunion employers have established procedures for handling complaints that are in many ways comparable to formal union grievance procedures. These arrangements are frequently found in the public sector, but more are now being established in the private sector.

Many nonunion grievance procedures permit complaints to go from the immediate supervisor to committees composed of higher-level executives, usually under the responsibility of the HR officer, and to review committees consisting of the top executives or neutral third parties. However, arbitration is not usually provided for in these procedures. The two main purposes of these arrangements are to assure fairness in employee relations and to improve employee attitudes, rather than interpret HRM policies and practices.

SUMMARY

The collective bargaining process is a means by which an employer and a designated union representing a group of employees negotiate the terms and conditions of employment. The objective of the collective bargaining process is to yield a written CBA establishing the set of rules by which labor and management will interact.

The NLRA requires the employer to negotiate in good faith on mandatory subjects of bargaining with an exclusive union representative of its employees. The parties may negotiate on permissive subjects of bargaining, but refusal of a party to bargain over those subjects does not necessarily constitute an unfair labor practice. Prohibited subjects of bargaining are those that are unlawful to be included in a collective bargaining agreement.

The four steps of the collective bargaining process discussed in this chapter are prebargaining, initial bargaining, primary bargaining, and final bargaining. The outcome of such bargaining is either an impasse or an agreement.

An impasse occurs when the parties have negotiated in good faith and have been unable to come to an agreement. The following are alternative methods to pursuing legal means of bargaining impasse resolution: work under an existing contract, strike, lockout, third-party options (fact finding, mediation, arbitration, or mediation-arbitration), and work under no contract.

If agreement is reached and the contract is ratified by the union, the problems are not over. Both sides, the union and management, must live with the contract in the contract administration phase of labor relations. This requires interpreting the contract's meaning and application.

When an employee has a complaint about the interpretation of a provision in the agreement, an effort is made to solve it with the first-line supervisor. If this fails, the formal grievance procedure is used. If the grievance is not settled in the organization, it goes outside to an arbitrator, who makes a binding decision.

What conclusions can be reached about industrial relations? First, some degree of conflict is always present in every union-management relationship. Second, the trend in labor relations has been away from conflict and toward a more accommodating and cooperative relationship. Third, the absence of a union puts a heavier burden on supervisors and managers.

KEY TERMS AND CONCEPTS

ad hoc arbitrators	interest arbitration
arbitration	lockout
arbitration award	mandatory bargaining issues
bargain in good faith	mediation
bumping rights	mediation-arbitration
collective bargaining	permanent arbitrator
contract administration provisions	permissive bargaining issues
duty of fair representation	prohibited bargaining issues
expedited arbitration	ratification
fact finding	rights arbitration
final-offer selection arbitration	*Steelworkers'* Trilogy
grievance	strike
grievance procedures	tripartite arbitration
impasse	

QUESTIONS

1. What is collective bargaining?

2. What are the primary legal requirements for collective bargaining?

3. Identify and describe briefly the basic steps in the collective bargaining process.

4. What is impasse? What are some options during impasse?

5. What occurs in the contract administration phase of labor relations?

6. What is a grievance? What are the steps in a typical grievance procedure?

7. What are the two general types of arbitration? How do they differ?

8. What does duty of fair representation refer to?

9. What are the five steps in the arbitration process? Which is the most important in terms of winning your case?

10. In preparing the arbitration award, what are the four issues that an arbitrator must consider?

11. What are the three Supreme Court decisions in the *Steelworkers'* Trilogy? Discuss each decision's effect on federal courts' authority to overturn an arbitrator's award.

CASES

1 The International Food Workers Union (IFWU) recently organized four hundred workers of the Porter Pet Foods plant located in small community of northeastern Oklahoma. In preparing for negotiation with the representatives of the IFWU, Mary Garcia, the international representative and the Union's organizer, has prepared a model proposal patterned after a number of labor agreements from other IFWU local unions. Garcia is the chief negotiator for the union, assisted by the local union negotiating committee.

During the first bargaining session, Garcia presented the Union's proposals to Joe Woofer, the human resources manager of the plant and the chief negotiator for Porter Pet Foods. Woofer immediately submitted the Company's proposals stating, "This should be considered a complete contract proposal, and it contains everything that we have to offer. We could be here for a very long time beating up on each other, but it is not going to get any better." Garcia replied that she did not consider this action as "good faith bargaining" on the part of the Company. She led the Union's walk out of the meeting, informing Woofer that she would be filing an unfair labor practice charge with the National Labor Relations Board. Is Porter Pet Foods guilty of a ULP? Why or why not?

2 The United Steelworkers of America (USWA) and Kaiser Aluminum Company ended a lockout in September, 2000 with 2,900 USWA members returning to work. The end of the lockout came after the two sides reached a new five-year agreement, ending one of the most bitter labor-management disputes in recent history. The Kaiser Aluminum Company lockout, which started on January 14, 1999, was the longest labor dispute in 1999, accounting for 750,000 idled work days, according to the Bureau of Labor Statistics. The union also said the Kaiser lockout was the longest in the fifty-eight-year history of the United Steelworkers. The lockout was preceded by a three-and-a-half month strike that began on September 30, 1998.

"This has been an epic struggle for our union and the labor and environmental movements in the Americas," said David Foster, Director of USWA District #11 and Chairman of the union's Kaiser Negotiating Committee. "Our members will start receiving special assistance payments from the company immediately, and over the course of the next month, they will return to their jobs. Without the unflagging support of the labor movement throughout the country and especially in the Northwest, and the inspirational support of environmental organizations and activists, this day would not have come."

The NLRB issued a complaint against Kaiser on June 30, 2000, ruling the lockout illegal. As a result of that ruling, Kaiser is facing a potential liability of $337 million in back pay for its locked out employees. "The Kaiser lockout became a social struggle that transcended the narrow parameters of a labor-management dispute. It symbolized the need for Americans of conscience to bridge their differences and focus on building a global movement for economic justice," said USWA's Foster.

During the twenty-two-month labor dispute the USWA launched a multifaceted corporate campaign for economic justice and corporate accountability at Kaiser and its parent, Maxxam Inc. Included among its activities were two shareholder campaigns that sought to elect former U.S. Senators Howard Metzenbaum and Paul Simon and former federal judge Abner Mikva to the Maxxam board of directors.

Explain the impasse resolution approaches used by Kaiser Aluminum. Explain the impasse resolution approaches used by the USWA. What were the major factors leading to the settlement of this dispute between Kaiser Aluminum and the USWA?

3 Bob Wurmzunge has recently become an arbitrator. His first case involves a manufacturing situation in which the grievant, Charlotte Dutton, is alleging that she was assigned to a job which she felt was degrading. Although the contract does not address work assignments, Dutton feels that matters involving human rights and dignity must be resolved through arbitration. Management contends that the management rights clause expressly gives them clear authority to make work assignments. In addition, management contends that there is no provision in the contract that even implies that employees have any inputs in assignments.

Wurmzunge decides that the management rights clause in the contract does not apply in this instance because he agrees with Dutton that individual dignity is an overriding right in the workplace, which he considers the very essence of the NLRA. As a consequence, Wurmzunge decides to overturn Dutton's assignment in the arbitration award.

Dutton's employer is not amused and appeals the arbitration award to the appropriate federal district court. Will the award be overturned? Why or why not? What are the justifications for a federal court overturning any arbitrator's award?

Notes

1. Holley, W. H. and Jennings, K. M. (1994). *The Labor Relations Process (5th ed.).* Forth Worth, TX: The Dryden Press, p. 202.

2. 29 U.S.C. § 158(a)(5).

3. *Golden Eagle Sporting Co. v Brewery Drivers & Helpers, Local Union 133,* 93 F.3d 468, 471 (8th Cir. 1996).

4. 29 U.S.C. § 158(a)(5).

5. 29 U.S.C. § 158(b)(3).

6. *Times Publishing Co.*, 72 NLRB 676 (1947)

7. *Majure v NLRB*, 198 F.2d 735 (5th Cir. 1952).

8. *NLRB v General Electric Co.*, 418 F.2d 736 (2nd Cir. 1969), *cert. denied*, 397 U.S. 965 (1970).

9. Gross, Cullen, and Hanslowe (1968). "Good Faith in Labor Negotiations: Test and Remedies, " *Connecticut Law Review*, 53, p. 1025.

10. *General Electric Co.*, 57 LRRM 1491 (1964).

11. *A.M.F. Bowling Co.*, 314 NLRB 160 (1994).

12. *NLRB v Truitt Manufacturing Co.* 351 U.S. 149, 153 (1956).

13. Ibid. at 152–153.

14. Leap, T. L. (1995). *Collective Bargaining & Labor Relations (2d ed.)*. Englewood Cliffs, NJ: Prentice Hall, pp. 307–308.

15. 29 U.S.C. § 158(d).

16. 356 U.S. 342, 349–350 (1958).

17. Leap, p. 370.

18. *United Food and Commercial Workers v King Soopers, Inc.*, 222 F.3d 1223 (10th Cir. 2000).

19. *Yuasa v International Union of Electrical Workers*, 224 F.3d 316 (4th Cir. 2000).

20. *United Mine Workers v Marrowbone Development Co.*, 232 F.3d 383 (4th Cir. 2000).

21. *Bard Manufacturing Co.*, 91 LA 193 (1988).

22. Holley and Jennings, p. 292.

23. 88 LA 257, 262 (1985).

24. Goggin, E. and Volz, M. (eds.) (1997). *Elkouri & Elkouri How Arbitration Works (5th ed.)*. Washington, DC: Bureau of National Affairs, pp. 276–277.

25. *Ford Motor Co. v Huffman*, 345 U.S. 330 (1953).

26. *Mirand Fuel Co.* 140 NLRB 181 (1962).

27. *Steelworkers v Enterprise Wheel & Car Corp.*, 363 U.S. 593, 597 (1960).

28. 45 U.S.C. § 153.

29. Ibid. at § 157.

30. 353 U.S. 448 (1957).

31. Ibid. at 457.

32. Bureau of National Affairs (1992). *Basic Patterns in Union Contracts*. Washington, DC: Bureau of National Affairs, p. 38.

33. www.fmcs.gov/agency/arbitrat/default.htm

34. www.adr.org

35. www.naarb.org

36. Goggin and Volz, pp. 332–334.

37. Holley and Jennings, p. 331.

38. Zimny, M., Dolson, W., and Barrera, C. (1990). *Labor Arbitration: A Practical Guide for Advocates.* Washington, DC: Bureau of National Affairs, p. 37.

39. *Steelworkers v American Manufacturing Co.,* 363 U.S. 564 (1960).

40. *Steelworkers v Warrior & Gulf Navigation Co.,* 363 U.S. 582 (1960).

41. Stipanowish, S. (1989). Of "procedural arbitrability" the effect of noncompliance with contract claims procedures. *South Carolina Law Review,* 40: 847–881.

42. 363 U.S. 564 (1960).

43. 363 U.S. 582 (1960).

44. 363 U.S. 598 (1960).

45. *United Mine Workers v Marrowbone Development Co.,* 232 F.3d at 388.

46. *Paperworkers v Misco, Inc.,* 484 U.S. 29, 38 (1987).

47. 415 U.S. 36 (1974).

48. Ibid. at 38.

49. Ibid.

50. Ibid. at 42.

51. 346 F. Supp. 1012 (D.C. Colo. 1971).

52. 466 F.2d 1209 (10th Cir. 1972).

53. 413 U.S. at 60.

54. *Wright v University Maritime Service Corp.,* 525 U.S. 70 (1998).

55. 412 U.S. at 51–52.

56. *Circuit City Stores, Inc. v Adams,* 121 S. Ct. 1302 (2001).

57. Carrell, M. and Heavrin, C. (1998). *Labor Relations and Collective Bargaining.* Upper Saddle River, NJ: Prentice Hall, pp. 414–415.

58. Goggin and Volz, pp. 180–181.

absolute bar An exclusion from consideration for any position of all parties who are not members of the preferred group.

absolute privilege A situation where an employer is protected from liability, regardless of the motive, for publishing information about an employee in question and regardless of the truth or untruth of the information.

action plan Action-oriented programs designed to eliminate problems and attain previously established goals and objectives.

actionable discrimination Seeking legal redress for discrimination under a specific statute.

ad hoc **arbitrators** Arbitrators retained on a grievance-by-grievance basis.

adverse impact The theory that is responsible for the current preoccupation with proportional representation in the workplace; see **disparate impact.**

affirmative action plan A formalized program to remedy the present effects of past discrimination or to keep eligibility for federal contracts and grants that is comprised of utilization analysis, goals and timetables, and an action plan.

agency shop A workplace in which union membership is still strictly voluntary, but nonunion members of the bargaining unit must pay the union the equivalent of dues to compensate the union for its services as their bargaining agent.

American Plan A combination of tactics used by employers and designed to prevent unions from organizing their workers or eliminating the workplace of an established union.

applicant flow analysis Assessing disparate impact by examining the effect of the questioned selection criterion on only the actual candidates who applied for the position.

arbitration Process that occurs by bringing in an arbitrator, a neutral third party, to interpret the terms of a collective bargaining agreement in order to settle a disagreement (grievance) between management and the union; also known as **rights arbitration.**

arbitration award The decision of the arbitrator in rights arbitration which is final and binding on both parties.

assumption of risk defense The philosophy that a person accepts the inherent risks involved in a job, thus absolving the employer of responsibility of injuries or illnesses incurred as a result of the normal job risks.

bargain in good faith Concept under the national labor code that imposes a duty upon employers to bargain with the union as the employees' exclusive bargaining agent regarding the mandatory issues of wages or salaries, hours of work, and other conditions of employment.

bargaining unit Includes all employees that the union is authorized to represent and who would be covered under the provisions of the collective bargaining agreement.

blacklists Lists containing the names of union supporters which are shared among employers to prevent union members fired by one employer from being hired by another employer.

bona fide **occupational qualification (BFOQ)** A justification by an organization of its employment decision that allows only persons of a certain sex, religion, or national origin to be considered as qualified for a job.

bottom-line statistics The selection rates of protected class members at the conclusion of the selection process.

bumping rights Rights that permit a more senior employee to replace a less senior employee holding a job in the same plant during reductions in the workforce; bumping rights are common to many seniority provisions in collective bargaining agreements.

business necessity Employment practice that is validated as job related; see **job relatedness.**

business unionism Four principles of organization followed by the American Federation of Labor which contributed significantly to its ability to survive and prosper. These principles included: (1) complete autonomy for member unions; (2) exclusive jurisdiction for member unions; (3) avoidance of any permanent political alliances; and (4) exclusive reliance on collective bargaining negotiations as the primary means of improving the economic position of organized labor.

certification/representation election Election held to determine if a union represents a majority of the employees in the proposed bargaining unit.

closed shop A workplace in which a worker has to be a member of the union before being hired; illegal under the Labor-Management Relations Act.

collective bargaining The process by which an employer and the exclusive bargaining agent (i.e., the union) negotiate the terms and conditions of employment.

collective bargaining agreement (CBA) The terms, conditions, and privileges of employment as specified under a contractual arrangement in unionized work environments.

compensable time Refers to the issue of when employees are entitled to be paid for their time and when they are not; time spent by employees performing work-related tasks is time in which they are due compensation or compensable time.

compensatory damages Damages imposed by a court to compensate a complaining party for monetary and nonmonetary harm suffered as a result of discrimination.

compensatory time Time off granted from a job in lieu of overtime compensation.

conciliation A negotiated settlement with a complaining party.

concurrent validation Determination of the correlation coefficients between test and performance by administering the test to current employees and correlating the test scores to their individual performance evaluations.

congressional intent The court must view the issue in terms of what Congress was trying to accomplish at the time the statute was enacted.

construct validity Method for evaluating abstract characteristics (i.e., decisiveness, innovation, sound judgment, etc.) that are important for successful job performance.

constructive discharge Occurs when job conditions have become so unpleasant that a reasonable person would feel compelled to resign.

content validity Involves having an applicant perform a "fair sample" of work to be performed from the actual job for which he or she is applying.

contract administration provisions Provide for a systematic means for resolving any complaints, commonly called grievances, arising from the collective bargaining agreement to conclude with bringing in outside, neutral third parties to resolve the disagreement; see **grievance procedures.**

contributory negligence defense A situation where an employer claims that the damages for injuries were due, at least in part, to the negligence of the affected employee.

corporate legitimacy The extent to which an organization's objectives, actions, and activities are viewed as being consistent with society's expectations.

court injunctions Orders from a court to cease a specific activity.

criminal conspiracy doctrine Doctrine established by the 1806 ruling by a Pennsylvania court (*Commonwealth v. Pullis*); the doctrine declared that it is a criminal activity to even create a union; therefore, unions themselves were unlawful and even being a member of a union was an illegal activity.

criterion-related validity Demonstrated by empirical data showing that a selection procedure is predictive of the important elements of the job in question.

de minimus **violation** A violation that arises from a nonserious condition that has no direct or immediate relationship to safety or health.

defamation Injury to an employee's reputation by an employer by disclosing highly personal matters, such as details of an employee's qualifications and performance.

defined benefit plans Programs developed by an employer which identify how much a retiring employee will receive each month for the remainder of his or her life.

defined contribution plans Programs based on a prescribed amount invested periodically into an individual account for each employee.

direct liability A situation where an employer is liable for the hostile environment sexual harassment of its employee, only if the employer knew, or must have known, that the harassment was occurring.

disability A physical or mental impairment that substantially limits one or more of the major life activities of an individual, a record of such impairment, or regarding an individual as having such an impairment.

dismissal When the EEOC stops an investigation without any determination being made.

disparate impact A statistical imbalance in a workforce, which is often unintentional and is characterized by imposing the same standards on all people with different outcomes for different groups; see **adverse impact.**

disparate treatment Results from treating individuals in the workplace differently because of their membership in a protected class.

due process An employee's right to fair and consistent treatment in regard to terms and conditions of employment.

duty of fair representation Requires the union to actively pursue meritorious grievances of any member of the bargaining unit.

emergency standard Safety and health standard based on the necessity to protect employees from grave danger.

employment-at-will Old common law concept based on the premise that if an employee can terminate his or her employment relationship with an employer anytime he or she sees fit, and for any reason, the employer is entitled to do the same.

English-only work rules Rules that require employees to speak English in certain work situations as a condition of employment.

Equal Protection Clause The Fourteenth Amendment's clause that states: "No State shall make or enforce any law which shall abridge the privileges or immunities of citizens of the United States; nor shall any State deprive any person of life, liberty, or property without due process of law, or deny to any person within its jurisdiction the equal protection of the laws."

ergonomics The science of adapting a job to the biomechanical needs of a worker by using a human engineering process of matching the physical requirements of the job and the physical capacity of the worker.

Excelsior list A list of names and addresses of all employees in a bargaining unit.

exclusive bargaining rights An arrangement in which employees represented by a union cannot be required to join the union or pay dues as a condition of continued employment.

exclusivity principle The fundamental rationale for workers' compensation legislation in which an employee injured in the course of employment receives fixed compensation that is described statutorily as the employee's "exclusive remedy" against the employer.

exempt employees Employees who are specifically excluded from the Fair Labor Standards Act's protection for minimum wage and overtime.

expedited arbitration A process whereby a single arbitrator hears several simple grievances in a single session.

explicit contract A written document (in most instances) which exists between the two parties (the employer and the employee) establishing the terms of employment.

fact finding The process in which a neutral third party is assigned to gather facts and provide clarification of unresolved issues in a dispute.

fair employment practices agencies (FEPAs) Collectively refers to state antidiscrimination laws and state agencies that work together to investigate racial discrimination.

family and medical leave Provided for by the Family and Medical Leave Act of 1993; requires that eligible employees receive up to twelve weeks of unpaid leave for any of the following reasons: (1) birth of a child; (2) adoption of a child; (3) care of an immediate family member (spouse, child, or parent) suffering from a "serious health condition;" or (4) recovery from a personal "serious health condition."

featherbedding When union officials receive compensation for jobs which they are not performing.

fellow-servant rule defense An employer's assertion that injuries or illnesses were derived from the actions, whether accidental or intentional, of another employee.

fiduciary A person who is placed in a position of trust and confidence to exercise a standard of care in the administration or management of an activity.

final-offer selection arbitration Form of interest arbitration available to the neutral, third party who makes a final and binding decision that involves the third party hearing or reading the final, best proposals of each party, then selecting one of the proposals as a final and binding resolution to the dispute; see **interest arbitration**.

four-fifths rule Standard for disparate impact analysis that assumes that adverse impact (disparate impact) has occurred when the selection rate for any race, sex, or ethnic group is less than four-fifths (or 80 percent) of the rate for the group with the highest selection rate.

grievance In the technical labor relations sense, any alleged violation of a provision of the collective bargaining agreement.

grievance procedures Collective bargaining agreement provisions that specify the step-by-step procedures for resolving any workplace dispute arising from different interpretations of the agreement; see **contract administration provisions.**

hostile environment sexual harassment Unwelcome harassment that is severe or pervasive enough to alter the terms or conditions of employment and that creates an abusive work environment.

hot cargo arrangement Arrangement that permits employees to refuse to process goods from a nonunion manufacturer.

HR compliance The area of human resource management that deals with the relationship between managers and employees in a regulated, but nonunionized, work environment.

imminent danger violation A violation that occurs when death or serious physical harm to an employee is imminent (i.e., an open flame in a fireworks factory); the organization must stop the activity immediately, and work may not be resumed until the specified danger has been eliminated or corrected.

impasse The point at which the parties have negotiated in good faith and have been unable to come to an agreement.

implied contract Can be inferred by the actions or conduct of the parties rather than an openly expressed offer and acceptance.

independent contractors Independent individuals who contract with employers to perform specific duties, responsibilities, etc.; independent contractors are not employees of the companies with which they contract.

industrial relations The part of human resource management that addresses employment issues arising from the unionized workplace, where a union represents the interests of the employees; also known as **labor relations.**

injunctive relief An order by the court for the employer to cease and desist unlawful practices.

interest arbitration The process where a neutral, third party hears the bargaining positions of each party and makes a decision based upon what he or she deems to be included in the labor agreement; see **final-offer selection arbitration.**

interim standards Temporary standards which the Secretary of Labor was given the power to establish for two years following the effective date of the Occupational Safety and Health Act of 1970 and were generally taken from preexisting national consensus standards.

involuntary affirmative action A remedy imposed by a court when an employer has been found in violation of Title VII or the Equal Protection Clause.

Jim Crow laws Laws, named for a character in minstrel shows, that were a means to get around the Civil Rights Acts of 1866, 1870, 1871, and 1875.

job analysis The systematic gathering of information about jobs in an organization.

job descriptions Reports that identify essential tasks, duties, and responsibilities of jobs in question.

job performance standards Standards that identify the minimum acceptable level of employee behavior or output expected of an entry-level employee.

job relatedness A defense that says even though the requirement causes adverse impact, it is absolutely essential to performing the job in question; see **business necessity.**

job specifications The knowledge, skills, and abilities that an employee or applicant must possess in order to adequately perform the essential tasks, duties, and responsibilities contained in job descriptions.

joint employers Refers to two or more employers who employ the same individual.

judicial activism Occurs when judges go beyond their power of merely interpreting the law to actually making law.

judicial restraint The avoidance of judicial activism; essentially the court refrains from law making and restricts its activities to the settlement of legal conflicts.

jurisdictional strikes Occurs when a particular union attempts to force an employer to assign certain work to employees in its bargaining unit rather than to employees in another labor organization or bargaining unit.

just cause Employers are limited to discharging employees only for broadly and statutorily defined reasons such as misconduct, poor performance, or reductions in an employer's workforce due to financial reasons.

labor relations The part of human resource management that addresses employment issues arising from the unionized workplace, where a union represents the interests of the employees; also known as **industrial relations.**

legitimate nondiscriminatory reason An argument made by an employer that the decision to hire, fire, promote, or layoff any employee is based on sound business rationale and not the individual's protected class status.

lockout Occurs when an employer temporarily suspends employment of the bargaining unit employees.

maintenance of membership shop Workplace in which employees are not required to join a union, those who are not union members pay the equivalent of union dues, and any employees who voluntarily join the union must continue their memberships as a condition of employment.

major life activities Defined by the Equal Employment Opportunity Commission as: (1) caring for one's self; (2) performing manual tasks; (3) walking; (4) seeing; (5) hearing; (6) speaking; (7) breathing; (8) learning; and (9) working.

mandatory bargaining issues Subjects over which the employer and the union must bargain in good faith; includes wages, hours, and conditions of employment.

mandatory benefits Benefits mandated or required by law such as social security, unemployment compensation, workers' compensation, and family and medical leave.

mass layoff Under the Worker Adjustment and Retraining Notification Act of 1988, a reduction in force that is not the result of a plant closing but involves at least one-third (33%) of the employees (excluding part-time employees), and at least fifty employees are laid off for at least a thirty-day period.

mediation Involves the use of mediators, neutral third parties, who facilitate the parties in resolving an impasse.

mediation-arbitration A process in which the parties use mediation and arbitration which will involve an initial attempt to find a resolution by mediation; then if mediation fails to resolve any remaining issues, the neutral third party will play the role of an arbitrator and make a final, binding decision.

mixed motives Occurs when an employment decision is affected by at least two motives: (1) a legitimate (job related) reason and (2) an illegitimate reason (i.e., sex stereotyping).

modified union shop A workplace in which nonunion members at the time of the collective bargaining agreement's ratification may remain nonunion but pay the equivalent of dues, those who are union members at the time must remain union members, and all new hires must join the union in the timeframe specified in the CBA.

narrowly tailored Preferential treatment of an affirmative action program designed in such a way as to minimize the harm to innocent third parties.

national labor code Three federal statutes encompassing three distinct phases of national labor legislation, and enacted twelve years apart that form the basis of current U.S. labor-management relations in the private sector including: (1) the National Labor Relations Act of 1935 (also known as the Wagner Act); (2) the Labor-Management Relations Act of 1947 (also known as the Taft-Hartley Act); and (3) the Labor-Management Reporting and Disclosure Act of 1959 (also known as the Landrum-Griffin Act).

negligent hiring When an employer fails to exercise ordinary care in hiring or retaining an employee and that employee creates a foreseeable risk of harm to a third party.

negligent misrepresentation An employer may be responsible for acts of workplace violence or incompetence at the employee's new place of employment if the former employer provides a positive recommendation or evaluation of the former employee's performance that knowingly omitted incidents of workplace violence, inability to perform critical work tasks, or sexual harassment.

negligent retention Retaining an employee with the knowledge that the employee presents a danger to coworkers or other third parties (through violent behavior or even incompetence); also known as **negligent supervision.**

negligent supervision When a supervisor allows an employee to perform a job even though the employee has demonstrated by his or her actions to be a danger to coworkers or other third parties; also known as **negligent retention.**

no cause Occurs when no sufficient evidence is found in an investigation to establish that an unlawful employment practice has occurred.

nonexempt employee Any employee who is entitled to protection under the Fair Labor Standards Act's minimum wage and overtime provisions.

nonpreferred group Includes all employees or applicants *not* entitled to preferential treatment under an affirmative action program, including those who are members of protected classes.

notice of right to sue Notice issued by Equal Employment Opportunity Commission that is requested by the complaining party within ninety days of being formally notified of the agency's no cause determination that allows the complaining party to still bring suit against the employer in federal court.

open shop A company that has no recognized bargaining agent (essentially no labor union) in the workplace.

organized workplaces Workplaces in which a portion of the workers are represented by a labor union; also known as **unionized workplaces**.

other-than-serious violation Safety and health violation involving a situation in which the most serious illness or injury would probably not result in death or serious physical harm.

overtime Legally defined as any hours worked in excess of forty during a one hundred sixty-eight-consecutive hour workweek.

paternalism A situation in which employers owned the houses the employees rented, the stores where employees shopped, and in some instances, even the banks or credit unions the employees used.

Peerless Plywood **Rule** States that all mandatory employee meetings for the purpose of campaigning against the union must cease twenty-four hours prior to the scheduled election.

performance standards The minimum levels of activity and output that an employee must attain if the essential tasks and duties of the job are to be accomplished.

permanent arbitrator An individual who is specified under the collective bargaining agreement to hear all grievances arising during the life of the contract.

permanent standards Safety and health standards that are newly created or revised from original interim standards and are issued on an as-needed basis or evolve from emergency standards.

permanent variance Granted to an employer who can prove that conditions or particular methods provide as safe a worksite as those that would exist through compliance with the Occupational Safety and Health Act standards.

permissive bargaining issues Subjects that the employer and the union may discuss, but refusal of a party to bargain over such subjects does not necessarily constitute an unfair labor practice; includes use of the union logo on products and benefits for previously retired employees.

plant closing Under the Worker Adjustment and Retraining Notification Act of 1988. The permanent or temporary shutdown of a single site of employment or one or more facilities or operating units within a single site of employment, provided that the shutdown results in an employment loss of fifty or more employees (excluding part-time employees) at the single site during any thirty-day period.

precedent Based on the legal principle of *stare decisis*, which means to adhere to decided cases.

predictive validation A means of establishing criterion-related validity by giving a validation test to applicants rather than to current employees.

preferred group Includes all employees or applicants entitled to preferential treatment under an affirmative action plan.

prevailing wage The minimum wage established for each class of workers as determined by the Secretary of Labor.

prima facie case Unlawful discrimination case based on evidence found by an EEOC investigation that concludes there was reasonable cause or sufficient evidence to indicate that a Title VII violation had occurred.

procedural due process Refers to the fairness of the procedure used by an organization in determining whether its work rules or policies have been violated.

prohibited bargaining issues Subjects that are unlawful to be included in a collective bargaining agreement; includes closed shop agreements and providing different benefits for nonunion members in the bargaining unit.

protected classes The original five categories—race, color, religion, sex, or national origin—along with age and disability, against which discrimination is prohibited.

public policy A condition in which an employee cannot be discharged for refusing to violate a law or ordinance, fired for refusing to avoid a civic duty or obligation (i.e., jury duty or when summoned as a witness), or terminated for engaging in a legal right.

punitive damages Damages awarded to a complaining party that are imposed to punish and to be a painful reminder to an employer of the consequences of blatantly violating Title VII.

qualified individual with a disability One who can perform the essential functions of the job in question with reasonable accommodations.

qualified privilege A conditional privilege in which an employer is protected from liability based on the fact that a statement is made in the performance of some judicial, social, or personal duty.

qualifying events Certain conditions that require continued coverage under the Consolidated Omnibus Budget Reconciliation Act.

quid pro quo sexual harassment Harassment that occurs by withholding or granting of tangible employment benefits in exchange for sexual favors.

ratification Approval of a collective bargaining agreement by the bargaining unit.

ratified When a collective bargaining agreement is approved by the members of the bargaining unit.

reasonable accommodation Modifications that would permit an individual with a disability to perform the essential functions of a job, provided that these modifications do not create an undue hardship for the employer.

reasonable cause When the Equal Employment Opportunity Commission's investigation finds enough evidence to believe that an unlawful employment practice has occurred.

recognitional picketing Occurs when a union attempts to persuade the employees to recognize it as their official bargaining representative by picketing.

religious accommodation Employers must refrain from considering an individual's religious beliefs in making decisions, and they must make accommodations for those beliefs after employment.

religious exemption Occurs when religious organizations are permitted to make hiring and discharge decisions based on an applicant's or employee's religious affiliation if they can show some connection between the position and the religion.

remand Process in which the Court of Appeals may vacate part of the decision, instruct the lower court where it erred (improperly interpreted the law), and then return the case to the District Court for reexamination under the Court's of Appeals previous instructions on the point of the law.

representation process The means by which a labor union becomes the bargaining representative of the proposed bargaining unit.

respondent The party against whom a complaint is made.

retaliation Occurs when an employer (or its management representatives) takes adverse action against an employee for filing, or threatening to file, an EEO complaint.

Revised Order No. 4 Contains the guidance of the Office of Federal Contract Compliance Programs for constructing affirmative action programs that would meet their standards of review.

right-to-work laws Laws limiting the level of compulsory union membership.

rights arbitration A process that brings an arbitrator, a neutral third party, in to interpret the terms of a collective bargaining agreement in order to settle the disagreement between management and the union; also known as **arbitration.**

secondary boycott When a union strikes an employer who is not directly involved in a labor dispute with that union.

serious violation Occurs when there is substantial probability that death or serious physical harm could result and that the employer knows, or should have known, of the hazard.

sex discrimination Discrimination based on an individual's sex; the second largest source of Title VII violations after race discrimination.

sex-plus discrimination Occurs when members of one sex who possess a specific characteristic or condition are treated differently from members of the opposite sex who have the same characteristic.

sex stereotyping Generalized belief about behaviors or characteristics attributed to a certain sex.

sexual harassment Unwelcome sexual advances, requests for sexual favors, and other verbal or physical conduct when such actions result in one of three consequences. First, sexual harassment becomes actionable when submission to these sexual advances is made explicitly or implicitly a condition of the victim's employment. Second, actionable sexual harassment exists when submission to or rejection of such requests by the employee becomes the basis for future employment decisions affecting that individual. The third form of unwelcomed conduct that would establish a Title VII violation results when such conduct has the purpose or effect of unreasonably interfering with the employee's work performance or creating "an intimidating, hostile, or offensive working environment."

showing of interest When at least 30 percent of workers in a workplace sign union authorization cards.

statutory law Laws, referred to as statutes, created by legislative bodies and enacted by the federal government.

Steelworkers' **Trilogy** A series of three 1960 Supreme Court decisions involving the United Steelworkers of America that reinforced the finality of binding arbitration.

stock analysis Provides statistics on the composition of the employer's workforce and how that workforce compares to its relevant labor market.

strict scrutiny Under the Fifth Amendment, requires the public employer to first establish that any preferences serve a "compelling government interest" and, second, that the preferences are "narrowly tailored" to achieve that interest.

strike A work stoppage by the union-represented employees for the purpose of coercing management to give in to their demands.

substantive due process Assures an employee that no disciplinary action is taken against him or her unless there is clear and convincing evidence that the employee has committed a disciplinary offense.

successor employer An employer who replaces another employer; if one company was acquired by another company, the acquiring company is the successor employer.

sweetheart arrangements Bribes offered by employers to union officers to work for the good of the company rather than in the interests of the union members.

temporary variance An extension granted when an employer cannot meet the requirements to comply with a safety and health standard by its effective date.

testers Individuals who apply for positions of employment for the sole purpose of determining whether a "tested" employer is engaging in discriminatory hiring practices.

Title VII As part of the Civil Rights Act of 1964, the foundation of most of the laws and regulations that affect equal employment opportunity in the workplace.

tripartite arbitration Occurs when three arbitrators hear an issue.

underrepresented Members of the affected protected classes become underutilized in the workplace because of the employer's past discriminatory hiring or promoting practices.

underutilized protected group A protected group under Title VII that is underrepresented in the workforce in proportion to the relevant external market.

undue hardship Determination made under the Americans with Disabilities Act that requires consideration of four factors: (1) costs; (2) resources; (3) type or operation; and (4) impact of hardship.

unemployment compensation An unemployment insurance program to offset workers' lost income during periods of involuntary unemployment and to help unemployed workers locate new employment.

unfair labor practices (ULPs) Certain activities that, if practiced by employers or unions, would be considered unlawful under the national labor code.

union authorization cards Cards signed by employees indicating their interest in having the union become their exclusive bargaining agent.

union shop When all members of a bargaining unit in a workplace are required to join the union within the period specified in the collective bargaining agreement, usually thirty to sixty days after employment.

unionized workplaces Workplaces in which a portion of the workers are represented by a labor union; also known as **organized workplaces**.

unnecessarily trammels Refers to the fact that an affirmative action program cannot unnecessarily restrict the rights of individuals who are members of nonpreferred groups.

utilization analysis Analysis used to determine the extent to which ethnic minorities and/or women are being "underutilized" by an organization in question.

vacate Reversal of the District Court's decision by the Court of Appeals.

vesting Occurs when an individual has a nonforfeitable right to pension benefits.

vicarious liability An employer can be found liable for the wrongful actions of its agent, regardless of whether or not the employer knew, or should have known, of the agent's sexual harassment.

voluntary affirmative action Affirmative action programs not imposed by a court including: (1) consent agreements; (2) programs developed for eligibility in certain federal programs; and (3) programs created by an employer for the expressed purpose of eliminating the effects of past discriminatory policies and practices.

voluntary benefits Benefits that are not required by law, such as medical insurance, paid vacation time, or retirement programs.

waivers Private agreements between an employer and a former employee waiving the employer of certain obligations.

whistleblower Refers to an employee who reports his or her employer's violation of some statute or regulation.

whistleblower clauses Protect employees from being retaliated against for reporting violations of a specific law in question.

willful and repeated violation Occurs when an employer is notified of a safety and health violation by a compliance officer and refuses or fails to take corrective action.

workers' compensation Laws providing workers with cash benefits for work-related injuries and deaths.

writ of certiorari Applied for when requesting an appeal; if approved, would compel the Court of Appeals to provide records of a case for review by the Supreme Court.

yellow-dog contract A contractual agreement not to join a union that employees have to sign before being hired.

CREDITS

Exhibit 3.2
From *Labor and Employment Law Desk Book,* by Gordon E. Jackson, pp. 284-285. Copyright © 1993. Reprinted by permission of Pearson Education, Inc., Upper Saddle River, NJ.

Exhibit 3.9
From *Compensation Decision Making,* 2nd edition, by Frederick S. Hills, Thomas J. Bergmann and Vida G. Scarpello. Copyright © 1994 by The Dryden Press. Reproduced by permission of the publisher.

Exhibit 7.4
From "Hot Stove Rules of Discipline," by D. McGregor, *Personnel: The Human Problems of Management,* by G. Straus and Sayles. Copyright © 1967. Reprinted by permission of Pearson Education, Inc., Upper Saddle River, NJ.

Exhibit 9.3
From *Labor and Employment Law Desk Book,* 2nd edition, 1999 Cumulative Supplement, by Gordon E. Jackson. Copyright © 1999. Reprinted by permission of Pearson Education, Inc., Upper Saddle River, NJ.

Exhibit 9.8
From "Independent Contractors and Employees: Do You Know One When You See One?" by N. McDermott, *Legal Report,* November-December 1999, pp. 1-4, Published by the Society for Human Resource Management, Alexandria, VA. Reprinted with permission.